Alan Woods with Hugo Chavez

ALAN WOODS was born in Swansea, South Wales, in 1944 into a working-class family with strong Communist traditions. At the age of 16 he joined the Young Socialists and became a Marxist. He studied Russian in Sussex University and later in Sofia (Bulgaria) and the Moscow State University (MGU). He has a wide experience of the international labour movement and has been involved in the Marxist movement in Spain, where he participated in the struggle against the Franco dictatorship, Latin America and Pakistan. He speaks several languages, including Spanish, French, German and Russian.

Alan Woods is the author of many works covering a wide spectrum of issues (politics, economics, history, philosophy, art, music, and science). He is also the political editor of the popular website *In Defence of Marxism* (www.marxist.com) and secretary of the International Marxist Tendency.

Among the books he has written we can highlight *Lenin and Trotsky: What they Really Stood For* and *Reason in Revolt, Marxist Philosophy and Modern Science*, both in conjunction with the late Ted Grant, *Bolshevism: the Road to Revolution*, *Marxism and the United States*, *The History of Philosophy* (online), *Ireland: Republicanism and Revolution*, *The Venezuelan Revolution - A Marxist perspective*, and *What is Marxism?* (jointly with Rob Sewell and Mick Brooks). His books have been translated into several languages, including Spanish, Italian, German, Greek, Turkish, Urdu, Danish, Portuguese, Russian and Bahasa Indonesian.

REFORMISM or REVOLUTION

Marxism and Socialism of the 21st Century

To the workers and peasants of Venezuela,
the real protagonists of the Bolivarian Revolution
and of this book.

REFORMISM or REVOLUTION

Marxism and Socialism of the 21st Century

(Reply to Heinz Dieterich)

Alan Woods

REFORMISM or REVOLUTION
Alan Woods

Published in agreement with Wellred Books, London
for publication and sale only in the Indian Subcontinent
(India, Pakistan, Bangladesh, Nepal, Maldives,
Bhutan & Sri Lanka)

First Published in India, 2009

ISBN 978-93-5002-014-2 (Hb)

Published by
AAKAR BOOKS
28 E Pocket IV, Mayur Vihar Phase I, Delhi-110 091
Phone : 011 2279 5505 Telefax : 011 2279 5641
aakarbooks@gmail.com; www.aakarbooks.com

Printed at
S.N. Printers, Delhi

Contents

Acknowledgements....9

Author's Preface....11

1. Methodology....15
2. Philosophy and science....37
3. Dieterich and historical materialism....77
4. History and economics....107
5. Socialism utopian and scientific....137
6. An outline of Marxist economics....152
7. The economics of Socialism of the 21st Century....187
8. Socialism or Stalinism?....223
9. The future of the Cuban Revolution....269
10. Nationalism or internationalism?....313
11. The state and revolution....331
12. The Venezuelan Revolution....367

Bibliography....411

Acknowledgements

Over the past months I have received a lot of encouragement from many people who were keen to see this book in print. This was a great help to me, since I have more than once regretted having taken the task on in the first place. I hope that the final result will justify the work that so many people have put into it.

I wish to express my thanks to all those who, by their painstaking work, have made the appearance of this book possible. In the first place, my thanks to Mick Brooks for his invaluable help with the section on economics and expert proof-reading, and to Harry Whittacker, Jordi Martorell and Fred Weston, for their proof-reading and valuable suggestions. I must also thank Harry Nielsen, Luke Wilson and Alex Grant for their helpful observations on the chapter on science. In addition, I would like to thank Espe Espigares for her professional layout.

Since we decided to publish the book simultaneously in English and Spanish, I would also like to thank Juana Cobo and Pablo Roldán for the excellent Spanish translation. In addition, a special mention is due to Miguel Fernández, whose considerable literary skills were of great help to me in perfecting and polishing the final text both in Spanish and English.

Above all, my heartfelt thanks to my comrade and companion Ana Muñoz for her invaluable help and encouragement, and for her immense patience in the final proofreading, which was enough to try the patience of a saint!

Author's preface

The publication of the present work requires some explanation. Many friends have asked me why I was taking so much time replying to a man whose books are read by a limited public, mainly in the Latin American universities, and are mostly only available in Spanish. I replied that I had been persuaded by the persistent requests of my friends in Cuba and Venezuela, who, after some years, were fed up of the theoretical pretensions of Heinz Dieterich and wanted me to answer him.

For some years Heinz Dieterich has been waging a noisy campaign, claiming that he has "invented" the idea of Socialism in the 21st Century. This has had some effect on certain circles of the Left in Venezuela and some other countries. As we know, there is an important debate taking place in Venezuela on the nature of socialism, inspired by Hugo Chávez's declarations in favour of socialism.

This is enormously important, not only for Venezuela but for the whole international workers' movement. After the collapse of the Soviet Union, there is a ferment of discussion on the Left on a world scale. The ignominious failure of Stalinism and the unprecedented ideological counteroffensive of the bourgeoisie against socialism have led some to conclude that the "old" ideas of Marxism (scientific socialism) are no longer valid, and that it is necessary to invent something entirely new and original. This is just what Dieterich claims to have done.

During the referendum campaign on constitutional reform in December 2007 the name of Heinz Dieterich suddenly began to acquire greater prominence. He opposed the reform and publicly defended General Baduel, the former Defence Minister who went over to the opposition and campaigned for a "no" vote in the referendum. Later, Dieterich said he supported a "yes" vote "as a lesser evil".

How does it come about that a man who has cultivated the image of a loyal supporter of Chávez and the Bolivarian Revolution should behave in such a way? It came as a shock to many on the Left who had accepted uncritically the audacious claims of Professor Dieterich. But, having carefully read his articles and books for many months, it was not at all surprising to me.

The fact that in a decisive moment Heinz Dieterich took a position that was clearly against the further advance of the Revolution towards socialism is no accident. It is the logical and inescapable conclusion from all his theories and from his peculiar version of "21st Century Socialism" – a kind of "socialism" that is not socialism at all, as wė shall see.

From Anti-Dühring to Anti-Dieterich

In preparing my reply I decided to re-read Engels' famous book *Anti-Dühring*, in which he answers the arguments of a man who, more than a century ago, claimed to have developed a new and original theory of socialism that would render the ideas of Marx (and everybody else) obsolete. I found that the similarity between Dühring and Dieterich to be astonishingly similar, not only in their ideas but even in their way of expressing them.

The first words of its preface are: "The following work is by no means the fruit of any 'inner urge'. On the contrary." Like Engels, I had no wish to write the present book. I agreed reluctantly because I regarded it as an unwelcome distraction from other important work. I thought, rather naively as it turns out, that I could deal with this very quickly. But I was wrong. The more I penetrated into this thick jungle of convoluted prose and even more convoluted ideas, the more it became clear to me that a short reply was impossible. The more I wrote the more I kept thinking of the words of Engels in the Preface to *Anti-Dühring*:

"Nevertheless it was a year before I could make up my mind to neglect other work and get my teeth into this sour apple. It was the kind of apple that, once bitten into, had to be completely devoured; and it was not only very sour, but also very large. The new socialist theory was presented as the ultimate practical fruit of a new philosophical system. It was therefore necessary to examine it in the context of this system, and in doing so to examine the system itself; it was necessary to follow Herr Dühring into that vast territory in which he dealt with all things under the sun and with some others as well." [1]

The writings of Heinz Dieterich are an even bigger and sourer apple than the one old Engels had to bite on. Like Herr Dühring, Heinz Dieterich writes on many subjects and, since he constantly mixes everything up, I was obliged to follow him through all these twists and turns. He seems to be incapable of writing about political economy without dragging in the history of philosophy, or the perspectives for the Bolivian Revolution without speculating on the nature of the universe.

The present book is therefore intended to do two things: to answer the ideas of Heinz Dieterich and also to explain as clearly as possible the classical ideas of Marxism, which in every respect contradict them. I am conscious of the fact that this

1. Engels, *Anti-Dühring*, Preface to 1878 Edition, pp. 9-10, Laurence and Wishart, London 1943.

does not make reading the book very easy. There are some very long quotations – some from comrade Dieterich and others from Marx, Engels, Lenin and Trotsky.

If this book is therefore rather long, the reader must console him or herself with the thought that the universe about which comrade Dieterich strolls with such enviable ease is a lot bigger. We can hope that some day maybe someone will explain to Heinz Dieterich that "brevity is the soul of wit". But until that day arrives, we have no alternative but to answer him point-by-point, page-by-page, galaxy-by-galaxy, and millennium-by-millennium.

In the present book I have attempted to examine the extravagant claims of comrade Dieterich in order to determine to what point they are valid. Is it really true that he has discovered an entirely new and original concept of socialism? If this were true, it would have very serious implications for socialists everywhere. We would have to re-examine all the basic ideas of Marxism and create an entirely new set of ideas and principles.

As the author of this work, I have a duty to make clear to the reader from what standpoint I am approaching this task. I write as a lifelong defender of Marxism. I consider that the ideas of Marx, Engels, Lenin and Trotsky to be as correct and relevant as ever – indeed they are more relevant and necessary now than at any other time. Naturally, if somebody can convince me that they have a body of ideas that is superior to Marxism and makes Marxism obsolete, I am quite prepared to change my opinions.

However, for almost 50 years I have made a careful study not only of all the works of the great Marxist writers of the past but also many of their critics. Having listened to many arguments of people who claimed to provide an alternative, I have yet to hear of anything that could be remotely compared to the depth and richness of Marxism. I have yet to find any body of ideas that comes remotely close to displacing Marxism as a scientific tool for understanding the world in which we live.

The enormous superiority of the method of Marxism can be seen in *The Communist Manifesto*, the founding document of scientific socialism. Written in 1848 by two young revolutionaries, this text is the most modern book one could read today. In fact, it is more relevant today than when it was written. Here we have a perfect description and analysis of the world, not as it was then, but as it is now. How many other books written over 150 years ago can make such a claim? This is a decisive answer to all those who argue that the ideas of Marxism are "old" ideas without relevance to the world we live in!

New ideas?

As to the "new and original" ideas of the 21st Century I will say only this: that to this day, despite all the noise and fuss, among all the vast literary production of the Dieterichs of this world, I have yet to read a single solitary genuinely new idea. What I have found is many old and antiquated notions that have been fished out of the dustbin of history – unscientific and utopian ideas that were long ago answered by Marx, Engels and Lenin, ideas that belong to the prehistory of the workers' movement. These old and tired ideas of pre-Marxian, utopian socialism have been dusted down and presented as 21st Century Socialism. And there are even some simple souls who take this seriously.

All this chattering about "entirely new and original ideas" seems superficially attractive – after all, who would not prefer a nice new car or computer in place of last year's model? But in reality the analogy is false and contradicts our most basic experience. To be new is not necessarily a good thing in all cases, nor is something necessarily bad because it is old. A new car or computer that does not work is worse than an old one that does work. The wheel is a very ancient invention, but it still works rather well after thousands of years. What would we say of a man who demands of us that we abandon the wheel (because it is old) and look for an entirely new kind of wheel – a wheel of the 21st century? What kind of wheel would that be – a square one, perhaps, or a triangular one? Whatever shape it may be, we are convinced that it will not carry us one step further.

For our part, we do not believe there is any need to reinvent socialism, just as we do not need to reinvent the wheel. Of course, it will be necessary to introduce this or that modification, but what is really remarkable is how few adjustments we have to make to the ideas that were worked out by Marx and Engels in the 19th century and developed and enriched by Lenin and Trotsky in the 20th century. We may make this or that change, but in all the fundamentals the basic ideas retain all their vigour and actuality. It is, of course, very good to debate the ideas of socialism and we will participate in this debate with the greatest enthusiasm. What is not so good is that Heinz Dieterich and others claim the right to *a monopoly of the interpretation of 21st Century Socialism*. What is even worse, as we shall see, is that this interpretation of "socialism" turns out to be exactly the same as – *capitalism*.

Heinz Dieterich appears on the international stage as a friend of the Bolivarian Revolution. That is to his credit. The Bolivarian revolution needs all the friends it can get. God knows it has enemies enough! But there are friends and friends. The unfortunate Job in the Bible had cause to regret the consolation offered to him by his friends in his moments of greatest need. And we have no doubt that the revolutionaries of Venezuela will have even greater cause to regret it if they accept as good coin the advice given to them so generously by their friends like Heinz Dieterich. Friendship of this sort reminds us of the old saying:

God preserve us from our friends.
We will sort out our enemies ourselves.

London, 11th May 2008

1. Methodology

In the first decade of the 21st century, humanity stands at the crossroads. On the one hand, the achievements of science, technique and industry point the way forward to a dazzling future of prosperity, social wellbeing and unlimited cultural advance. On the other, the existence of the human race is threatened by the ravishing of the planet in the name of profit. Millions of people live in poverty on the edge of starvation. In one country after another elements of barbarism are appearing. The very future of the planet is threatened by global ecological degradation.

The fall of the Soviet Union was the signal for an unprecedented ideological offensive against the ideas of socialism. The collapse of the bureaucratically controlled planned economies of the East was held up as the definitive proof of the failure of "communism," and, of course, the ideas of Marx. The defenders of capitalism saw the fall of the Soviet Union as proof that their system was the only possible system. They dreamed of a New World Order based on peace and plenty. They imagined that the present temporary boom meant not just a return to the days of their youth but the abolition of all crises. This does not even deserve attention as serious thinking. These are only the pathetic self-delusions of a decrepitude that refuses to look in the mirror.

It did not take long to shatter these illusions. Today, not one stone upon another is left of the dreams of the bourgeoisie. Everywhere we see the awakening of the masses, who are looking for a way out. A new period is opening up. There is a growing questioning of capitalism and an ever-increasing interest in the ideas of socialism and Marxism. In the next period ideas that now are listened to by small groups will be eagerly sought by hundreds of thousands and millions. We see this already in Latin America, where the revolutionary trend has gone further than anywhere else. The Venezuelan Revolution is the final answer to all those cowards and apostates who argued that revolution and socialism were off the agenda.

Lenin was very fond of the Russian proverb "Life teaches". In a revolution people learn fast. That is true of the masses but also of the leaders. Hugo Chávez has undoubtedly learned a lot from his experience of the revolution and he has drawn some important conclusions. It is no accident that Hugo Chávez has opened a debate on the ideas of socialism. The Bolivarian revolution has advanced rapidly and is going beyond the bounds of capitalism and challenging private property. The old society is dying on its feet and the new society is struggling to be born. And what has happened in Venezuela today will happen tomorrow in Britain, in Russia, in China and the USA itself.

The declarations of Hugo Chávez in favour of socialism have sparked off a serious debate in Venezuela, where socialist and Marxist ideas are being enthusiastically discussed in every factory and village, in every market and bus stop. This is not the usual word spinning of intellectual circles in universities. The masses have a serious attitude to ideas because what is involved is not a doctoral thesis but a question of life and death. This means that socialism has come out of the scholar's study and entered the light of day.

From the point of view of Marxism this is a most important development. Marxism is a philosophy that leads to action, and is unthinkable without action. In the words of Marx: "Philosophers have only interpreted the world in different ways: the point, however, is to change it." But not everyone is happy about this. The very next day a veritable army of "left wing" scribes came running to "correct" the President. "Yes, of course, we are in favour of socialism", they say. "But be careful! We want only *Socialism of the 21st Century*"! The great advantage of this is that nobody knows what it means. It is an empty bottle that can be filled with any content one chooses. When we talk about Socialism of the 21st Century, we first have to establish what kind of socialism are we talking about?

What Heinz Dieterich offers us

Heinz Dieterich is a German professor who describes himself as a scientific economist and sociologist. He has been a professor at the Autonomous Metropolitan University in Mexico City (Universidad Autónoma Metropolitana de México) since 1977. And he is one of those academics who are anxious to tell us *what Chávez really means*, as though the President were unable to speak for himself.

Many years ago Heinz wrote books defending Marxism. But now he has rejected all those foolish revolutionary ideas. He claims to have invented something entirely new and original, which he calls "Socialism of the 21st Century" (or the "New Historical Project"). On this and other subjects he has published many books. If the quality of this literary production were as good as the quantity, humanity would have cause to rejoice. So, after considerable hesitation, I was persuaded to examine these new and original theories that promise nothing less than the complete deliverance of humanity in a world of peace and plenty.

By a strange coincidence, if one is to believe what he writes in his books, what Chávez really means coincides exactly with what Dieterich understands by 21st Century Socialism. Since, according to Heinz, this is the only kind of socialism that is either possible or desirable, this is quite logical. And anybody who questions this is destined to be cast into the outer darkness where there is only weeping and wailing and gnashing of teeth. In an interview published in the left wing German newspaper *Junge Welt*, (7/1/06) Dieterich informs us: "I also contributed the idea of a 'socialism of the 21st century,' along with a few other things, in which my modest theoretical contributions can probably help to positively support the process".

This humility greatly impresses us. Heinz's "modest theoretical contributions" can "*probably* help" to "support the process". He has "contributed" the idea of a socialism of the 21st century, that is to say, he, and not Chávez, has invented it ("along with a few other things"). And therefore, *he*, and not Chávez or anyone else, has the god-given right to tell us what it is. We would be very pleased if somebody were able to explain to us in simple language what the future socialist society will look like. We would be even more pleased if they were able to explain how we can overthrow capitalism with the minimum cost and exertion. Heinz Dieterich promises us all this and more. We therefore consider it our duty to follow him through his great voyage of discovery, in the confident hope of finding not just a pot of gold, like the one said to be waiting for us at the end of the rainbow, but the secret of human happiness, justice and equality. This would be marvellous – if only it were true.

Dieterich and Dühring

Revolutionary socialists are accustomed to the furious onslaughts against socialism and communism – not only those of the open defenders of capitalism and imperialism, but also the reformists (both of the right and the left varieties), and also the so-called radical petty bourgeois intelligentsia, some of whom wish to fight against capitalism, but have not the slightest idea of how to do so. These anti-revolutionary reformist tendencies have always been present. They were answered by Marx and Engels in *The Communist Manifesto*, in the section on petty bourgeois socialism.

Later on, Marx and Engels waged a fierce ideological struggle against the *Katheder Sozialisten* in Germany – the "clever" university professors who sought to place themselves at the head of the workers' movement and water down its revolutionary Marxist ideas. Such tendencies have always played a most pernicious role in the workers' movement. Engels wrote an entire book, *Anti-Dühring*, to answer the ideas of Eugen Dühring, a typical example of the *Katheder Sozialisten*.

After such a thorough demolition job one would have thought that the last word had been spoken, but no. The ideas defended by Heinz Dieterich are the latest expression of the same phenomenon represented by Dühring and the *Katheder Sozialisten*, of whom Heinz Dieterich is the lineal descendent. Dühring boasted that he had discovered an entirely new and original brand of socialism that made Marx irrelevant. In the same way Dieterich argues that his "new and original" theory of "21st Century Socialism" supersedes Marxism and everything else that has gone before.

The present craze for new ideas that will allegedly supersede the "old discredited ideas" of Marxism is not at all an accident. The working class does not live in isolation from other classes and can come under the influence of alien classes and ideologies. This is particularly true in periods of reaction, after great historical defeats when the workers fall into temporary inactivity. Then the petty bourgeois elements (who, like the poor, are always with us) come to the fore, elbowing the workers to one side. The workers' voice is drowned out by the chorus of the "clever" people who have lost all will to fight themselves and are anxious to persuade the workers that revolution brings only tears and disappointment.

It is bad enough that we have to constantly answer the lies and distortions of the bourgeoisie. But now a large number of former "Communists" have openly abandoned Marxism and passed over to the side of the bourgeoisie. Some of these openly attack the ideas they fervently defended in the past. Others continue to pay lip service to Marxism but like Bernstein and Kautsky, wish to "revise" it, to introduce some "small modifications" to "bring it up to date. Like any other science Marxism admits modification and change. Marxism must take into account all the changes in the objective situation, or else it would not be a scientific method but a lifeless dogma. But dialectics shows how a sufficient number of small changes can turn a thing into its opposite.

The truth is that the revisionists do not want to bring Marxism up to date but water it down and liquidate its entire revolutionary content. Such people are moving heaven and earth to erect a barrier between the masses and Marxism, alleging that Marxism is out of date and that we need to create a new and entirely novel system of ideas that will, they assure us, be the authentic socialism of the 21st century. But on closer inspection we see that this brand of ideas is neither new nor socialist, but only a rehash of the utopian attempts of the reformists to create capitalism with a human face.

The sole purpose of this noisy chorus is to divert the attention of the youth, cause the maximum confusion and to act as a barrier to prevent the new generation from gaining access to Marxism. It is only the mirror reflection of the campaign of the bourgeoisie against socialism and communism. But it is far more dangerous and damaging than the latter because it is a campaign waged under a false banner. Its proponents are radically opposed to revolution and socialism but they dare not admit this – possibly even to themselves (to what extent they actually believe in the nonsense they write is something that only an expert psychologist can decide). They disguise their reactionary anti-revolutionary and anti-socialist message under a thick layer of left and radical phraseology that makes it all the more difficult for most people to identify.

Far from being new and original, this is the method of the utopians, each of whom invented a particular scheme for the salvation of humanity and was firmly convinced that the only reason why humanity continued to suffer was because it did not yet have access to these schemes. For the utopians, the class struggle did not exist. They addressed themselves to the enlightened bourgeois with appeals to carry out their utopian plans. The revolutionary role of the working class did not enter into their schemes, just as it does not enter into the reformist schemes of comrade Dieterich.

Despite their fantastic ideas, the old utopians were brilliantly original thinkers who made a great contribution to the development of the ideas of socialism. They were writing at the dawn of capitalism, when industry was virtually confined to one country – England – and the proletariat was still in its infancy. It was therefore natural that they should not base themselves on the working class. But Heinz Dieterich has no such excuse. In the first decade of the 21st century, the development of capitalism has created a powerful working class in every country. Today, not a light bulb shines, not a wheel turns, not a telephone rings, without the permission of the working class. To ignore this colossal power, and to try to put the clock back two centuries, discarding the scientific method of Marx in favour of the fantastic schemes and sentimental rhetoric of the utopians – that is an entirely retrograde and reactionary position.

The method of comrade Dieterich has more in common with the rationalism of the 18th century than Marxist dialectics. Rationalism on the eve of the French Revolution was a revolutionary force. But rationalism in the stage of the senile decay of capitalism, when it is directed against dialectical materialism, can only play a negative role. True, Dieterich still pays lip service to Marxism and dialectics. But this is "Marxism" stripped of its revolutionary essence, deprived of its class basis and the scientific dialectical materialist method. In other word, it is not Marxism at all.

Heinz Dieterich, consciously or unconsciously, is providing a theoretical justification for this. Under the false flag of 21st Century Socialism he is conducting a strident campaign against socialism and socialist revolution. He is introducing confusion into the minds of the cadres of the Bolivarian Movement who have not had enough time or opportunity to acquaint themselves at first hand with the ideas of Marxism. Is he conscious of his role? The question cannot be answered and in any case has not the slightest importance. The way to hell has always been paved with good intentions.

Dieterich's method

Dieterich's latest work on the subject is *Hugo Chávez and Socialism of the 21st Century*. This work makes some very ambitious claims. It offers us an entirely new theory of socialism, which will "go beyond the mere criticism of global capitalism and the historical ("*hermeneutic*") interpretations of what Marx and Lenin 'really meant to say'". [2]

He begins with the laudable intention of explaining his objective – since "basic psychology teaches us that if we cannot define the objective, it is not likely that we shall understand if the tendencies of reality favour the results of our efforts, or are going the opposite way." [3] Yes, this is absolutely true. If we set ourselves the objective of travelling west, it may be useful to observe that our feet are not carrying us towards the east. This is one of the results of a profound study of basic psychology, which also teaches us that if we decide to go upwards, we must at all costs avoid the temptation of proceeding downwards. But let us continue with the definition of our objective.

Not so fast, cries comrade Dieterich, who is determined to show us how difficult it is to define our objectives, still less to achieve them. He continues: "Without the orientation of concrete and specific objectives all human praxis is diffuse and tends to become disappointed or lose its way because of the obstacles that appear along the way." [4]

If I do not set myself concrete and specific objectives when I get out of bed in the morning, such as removing my pyjamas and putting on my clothes, washing my face and brushing my teeth, and putting my shoes on both feet, making sure I have tied the laces, I may never succeed in getting out of the front door. *Human praxis* will be *diffuse* and I may tend to become *disappointed* and *lose my way* because of the obstacles that appear along the way of getting out of the house and commencing my daily activities.

If I wish to stay alive it is not a bad idea to remember to keep breathing. Yes, all this is perfectly true, and more or less evident to most men and women, who do not need a university Professor to explain it to them. But this Professor has a genius for *stating the obvious* and this he displays enthusiastically in all his writings. He shows his erudition by using the most complicated words and expressions like *hermeneutics,* plus a wealth of German and Latin words, that we feel we are learning something new and very profound.

"We learn to walk by walking", we are informed (we did not know this before). But we can walk effectively "only if we are oriented by a compass." [5] The compass that we require in order to walk in the right direction is none other than Heinz Dieterich's theories. So, compass in hand, we eagerly set out on a pleasant and instructive walking tour that will take us to many places before we arrive, safe and sound, in the Promised Land of Socialism of the 21st Century.

2. Dieterich, *Hugo Chávez y el socialismo del siglo XXI*, p. xvii.
3. Ibid.
4. Ibid.
5. Ibid.

Comrade Dieterich now describes not only his objective but his *method* as well. The latter "combines the powerful method of scientific reasoning with the objective of *solidarity and peaceful social coexistence*." [6] To begin with, let us observe that this objective could be accepted in principle by any Social Democrat, reformist, parson or bourgeois philanthropist. In the second place, it is neither new nor original. It is typical of the sentimental daydreams and illusions of the utopian and bourgeois socialists whom Marx and Engels answered long ago in *The Communist Manifesto*.

That all men and women should live together in peace and harmony is the fervent wish of virtually everybody in the world; that human beings should live according to the principle of solidarity is at least as old as the New Testament (actually it is considerably older). We should all love one another, and there should be peace, not war. Amen to that! But already in the Old Testament (Jeremiah, 6:14) we have a fitting reply to all the philistine sentimentalists who say *Peace, Peace, when there is no Peace.*

We are invited to conclude that all the wars, terrorism, starvation, exploitation and oppression are all the result of a little misunderstanding. All that is required is to inform the human race that we must all live in peace, harmony and solidarity, and that this can be achieved by following a few simple suggestions that comrade Dieterich has invented, and now offers to the human race in the convenient form of a paperback book of just over 200 pages. In this slim volume, as we have said, Heinz Dieterich writes about everything under the sun and a few things besides. What is the purpose of all this? It is intended to fill the innocent reader with a sense of awe. It reminds us of the words of the 18th century English poet Oliver Goldsmith, who in *The Deserted Village*, describes the ignorant peasants listening astounded to the village schoolmaster:

"In arguing, too, the parson owned his skill,
For, even though vanquished, he could argue still;
While words of learned length and thundering sound
Amazed the gazing rustics ranged around;
And still they gazed, and still the wonder grew,
That one small head could carry all he knew."

It would be nice to know what Comrade Dieterich really means to say. This is not always easy, since he uses a vocabulary unknown to other mortals. Heinz Dieterich's books are so obscure because in them confusion is piled upon confusion. And in order to cover up his confusion he resorts to a mystifying and unintelligible language, which is supposed to create the impression of a depth of thought that passes all understanding.

6. Ibid., p. xvii, my emphasis, AW.

The writings of Marx and Engels are so clear because they have a clear socialist message. Marx and Engels wrote in beautifully simple language because they were writing for the workers and any averagely intelligent worker can understand their writings. This is no accident. A good writer is someone who knows how to make complicated ideas simple, whereas a bad writer only knows how to make simple ideas complicated. Heinz Dieterich may be accused of many things, but nobody could ever accuse him of being a good writer. The reason these books are hard to read is not because they have a profound content but precisely the opposite. Here the complete lack of real content is generously compensated by a wealth of complicated language, obscure vocabulary and a veritable labyrinth of tangled syntax. On this kind of thing old Hegel once remarked: "Just as there is a breadth which is empty, so there is a depth which is empty also".[7] These words say all that needs to be said on this subject.

How Heinz 'interprets' Chávez

Having made a few complimentary references to Chávez, Dieterich has now established himself – and his theories – firmly in the centre of the stage. Heinz loses no time in presenting his first list, which he pulls out of his pocket with the dexterity of a housewife producing a shopping-list at the grocer's. We are informed that human evolution can be reduced to "three complex strategic dimensions". Why three and not thirty-three, we do not know. Why genetics, economics, religion, philosophy, politics, and other dimensions of human evolution should be excluded from comrade Dieterich's complex strategy is a complete mystery. It is an arbitrary assertion, like all the other arbitrary assertions with which this book is replete.

One notices immediately that Heinz is obsessed with initials. We begin with the *NHP (New Historical Project),* as opposed to the old *HP*. Later we shall be introduced to the *CDS* (*Complex Dynamic Systems*), and their cousins, the *HCDS* (*Historical Complex Dynamic Systems*), the *HAS* (*Human Adaptive Systems*), followed by the *RPB* (*Regional Power Blocs*), the *GS (Global State)*, the *NRPC* (*National-Regional Protectionist Capitalism*), the *TNCs* (*Transnational Companies*), the *IPCC* (*Investigation-Production-Commercialization Complexes)* [I particularly like this one!], the *LZ* (*Leadership Zones*), and many, many more.

This method, like the obscure language he habitually uses, serves to confuse the reader to the point that he or she forgets what comrade Dieterich is writing about. At the same time, it attempts to give unintelligible ideas a false appearance of authority and scientific rigor. Suddenly the most hare-brained ideas seem as respectable as *UNICEF*, H_2O or $E=mc^2$. All that is lacking is the *AAA* (Abstract and Abstruse Aberrations) and the *NAI* (Nonsense of Academic Intellectuals). But let us allow comrade Dieterich to continue with his labour of interpretation:

7. G. W. F. Hegel, Preface *The Phenomenology of Mind*, 1807.

"What Comandante Chávez and the marginalized people of humanity seek and what they need is not a new critique (negation) of a bad reality created by Capital, but the viable alternative of a new and more humane civilization, that is to say, an antisystemic and anticapitalist alternative." [8]

At this point comrade Dieterich takes up the position he has aspired to occupy from the beginning: that of the official interpreter of the innermost thoughts of President Chávez. Since, it appears, the President is not able to express his thoughts in a sufficiently clear manner, Heinz kindly offers his services to explain these thoughts to all humanity. It is not clear to us why President Chávez should require an interpreter. But this is of no importance to Heinz, who frequently "interprets" the President's ideas in a manner that directly contradicts them, as we shall see.

Before considering the muddled reformist and Social Democratic meanderings of comrade Dieterich, let us once more admire our friend's beautiful prose. What is meant by "an antisystemic and anti-capitalist alternative"? Insofar as it may be considered to have any meaning it is: *against all systems in general*. But since, at least on the planet earth, we can only replace one system by another (hopefully better) system, Heinz's characterization of his "viable alternative of a new and more humane civilization" leaves one quite mystified. Evidently, it is not Hugo Chávez but Heinz Dieterich who is in urgent need of an interpreter.

If he means by this that socialism (which, as far as we know, is the only viable alternative of a new and more humane civilization) can only be achieved through the revolutionary abolition of the capitalist system, then he should say so. But he prefers to spin an endless web of confusion with ambiguous phrases instead of saying clearly that the only alternative before the human race is socialism or barbarism. The reason for this ambiguity will become clearer as we advance steadily through this mass of words, cutting through the thick and impenetrable prose of comrade Dieterich, compared to which, cutting one's way through the thick and luxurious vegetation of a tropical rain forest, is child's play.

When a squid is attacked it squirts a cloud of ink. Our Heinz squirts enough ink to fill the entire Caribbean several times over. Once we are surrounded with a sufficient quantity of this black stuff, he hopes we will lose our way in the darkness and thus not be able to detect the real content of his argument, which is this: that in the 21st century it is impossible to carry out a socialist revolution and that therefore all sensible men, women and squid, must make their peace with capitalism and private property as best they can.

Exactly how Heinz Dieterich can make such a message compatible with Marxism and socialism we are curious to see. Therefore, we must arm ourselves with patience and make a determined attempt to grasp his meaning, despite all the obstacles he places in our way. After all, a book that promises so much is surely worth making a little effort to read. And in the end, we look forward in eager antic-

8. Heinz Dieterich, *Hugo Chávez y el socialismo del siglo XXI*, p. xix.

ipation to enlightenment as to the nature of this wonderful and original theory of socialism, human society, history, culture, political economy, science and ethics that comrade Dieterich promises us.

Dieterich and the class struggle

"To publish this book with the title *Socialism of the 21st Century*, just over a decade after the fall of the Berlin Wall is therefore not a utopian or nostalgic act. There is no frivolity or utopianism nor any lack of historical memory in its creation. It is the very period of social evolution which determines its appearance." [9] With these portentous words, the author announces the publication of his books. He assures us that in his work there is neither "frivolity" nor "utopianism", but an inevitable product of History. Several thousand years after Moses came down from Mount Sinai with his tablets of stone under his arm, comrade Dieterich presents us with his book, which, he assures us, is destined to play just such a role for the citizens of the 21st century. He promises us a great deal: the reorganization of the world on the lines of peace, justice and participative democracy. In short, he has discovered the magic formula which poor suffering humankind has been waiting for 10,000 years to hear. Let us see how much he delivers.

"Overwhelmed by the daily existential anguish of his precarious reproduction, without any spiritual transcendence beyond the triviality of consumerism, the alienated subject cannot solve his situation within bourgeois society but only in a kind of qualitative different cohabitation [!!], like participative democracy." [10]

As befits a Moses of the 21st Century Socialism, Heinz Dieterich strikes a prophetic pose making use of language that would make even Jean-Paul Sartre shudder. Here we leave the world of politics altogether and enter the pseudo psychoanalytical idealistic delirium of existentialism. In place of the proletarian class struggle, we have the "fear and trembling" of a Kierkegaard, in other words, the anxiety of the petty bourgeois who feels the ground quake under his feet and does not know what to hang onto to keep his balance.

Instead of the historical materialism of Karl Marx we have a senseless regression to the "alienated Subject" of Hegel. Just as in economics, Dieterich tries to drag us back to the antiquated pre-Marxian doctrines of the utopian socialists, so in philosophy he tries to drag us back to the mystified world of Hegelian idealism. The difference is that in the writings of Hegel the obscure idealistic terminology serves to conceal a great profundity and richness of content, whereas in Dieterich's writings, the obscure mode of expression serves to cover up a complete absence of any content whatsoever.

9. Dieterich, *El Socialismo del siglo XXI*, p. 25.
10. Ibid.

In all his writings, there is not an atom of revolutionary class content. It is no coincidence that comrade Dieterich avoids a clear statement of the socialist programme. Instead, he refers to the objectives of "peace, real democracy and social justice". [11] These worthy objectives can be agreed to by the Pope of Rome, the Quakers, and the Royal Society for the Prevention of Cruelty to Animals, the UN Security Council, all vegetarians and little old ladies from respectable families. This will hardly cause the ruling class to lift an eyebrow.

Comrade Dieterich never approaches the class struggle from a Marxist point of view. In the document *Socialism of the 21st Century – questions and answers*, published in www.rebelion.org, he asks: "Why do the classes fight?" And he replies: "The answer is that social classes, for example, workers, toilers (trabajadores), farmers, professional people, small and big employers (empresarios), fight over the social wealth, that is to say, the surplus product or the economic surplus that society generates. Unfortunately, this fight is comparable to a pack of dogs fighting over a prey that is not sufficient for all. The strongest seize the prey and they marginalize or exclude the others."

To speak of the class struggle as a *dogfight* tells us a great deal about the standpoint of the author. It is not the standpoint of Marxism but of a sentimental petty bourgeois that laments the fact that rich and poor cannot live side by side in peace and harmony, instead of fighting each other "like animals". Instead of arriving at an amicable agreement to share the prey, "the strongest seize the prey and they marginalize or exclude the others." The answer is obvious: the strong must share with the weak in the name of social justice: the lion must lie down with the lamb. But we have heard this sermon already!

All this fiddling and fussing merely irritates the reader, who is obliged to wade through pages and pages of abstract waffle, in the vain hope of finding some coherent idea at the end. He informs us that the workers' parties in the past advocated "an historical project constructed around four constituent elements: the non-mercantile economy, based upon use value, real participative democracy, a democratic state and self-determined rational-ethical subject." [12]

Despite what he says, one will look in vain through all the programmes of all the workers' parties of the world to find such profundities, which are absolutely characteristic of Dieterich's version of 21st Century Socialism. Throughout his books and articles he constantly refers to "the majorities" a mysterious term that he never defines and so nobody knows what it actually means. Not only does this term lack any concrete class content. It also defies the laws of formal logic. While it is possible to speak of *minorities* in the plural, there can by definition be only one majority, not two. At best, one can speak of the (exploited) majority of society, as opposed to the minority of exploiters.

11. Ibid., page 24.
12. Ibid.

This example shows us that, in addition to his complete grasp of relativistic cosmology, our Heinz also shows a profound understanding of mathematics. Let us take the example of a circle divided into two segments. The smallest possible "majority" segment (in whole numbers) would be one of 181 degrees. This is segment A-B. Let us add another "majority" segment C-D, which is also 181 degrees. We now have a circle of 362 degrees, which is, at least on the planet earth, a mathematical impossibility. But in Socialism of the 21st Century, as we shall soon see, everything is possible.

Butterflies and caterpillars

With a flourish of the trumpets, comrade Dieterich now announces his aim, which is neither more nor less than: "the creation of a new scientific-ethical-aesthetic theory of postcapitalist social transformation in the 21st century." [13] This is really excellent. We are to get an entirely new and original theory, which will not only be the key that will open all doors in the realm of science, ethics and aesthetics (that is, just about everything), but will also lay the basis for a "postcapitalist society in the XXI Century." This remarkable new theory has been elaborated, "because the new civilization of participative democracy will be qualitatively different from present-day capitalism, in fact, as different as, for example, a butterfly and a caterpillar." [14]

In case anybody does not know the difference between a butterfly and a caterpillar, comrade Dieterich immediately begins to enlighten us on the subject: "Although the butterfly and a caterpillar share the same genome (they are born from the same 'roots'), they evolve towards qualitatively different forms of life." Having revealed this important truth to us, our learned friend then proceeds to explain (in case we did not know) what these qualitatively different forms of life consist of: "While one of them crawls on the ground, the other flies in the air." [15]

The reader is lost in admiration at this new and original insight, which informs us that caterpillars crawl on the ground, while butterflies fly in the air. Such profundity of thought is quite typical of the kind of new and original ideas of the School of Socialism of the 21st Century. And in case you are wondering what this has got to do with the subject under discussion, our friend Heinz immediately puts our mind at rest: "That is to say, from the same origins, totally different forms of life can evolve. And the same is true of capitalism and participative democracy." [16]

As a matter of fact, not only do caterpillars share the same genome as butterflies, but so does Heinz Dieterich and all other living organisms to some extent. However, this does not mean that Heinz can become a butterfly, however hard he may try. Nor is it possible for socialism (or a "participative democracy") to evolve out of a for-

13. Dieterich, *Hugo Chavez y el Socialismo del Siglo XXI*, p.19.
14. Ibid., p. 32.
15. Ibid.
16. Ibid.

mal bourgeois democracy. The analogy is completely incorrect and misleading. As usual in his writings everything is hopelessly mixed up. Like a brightly coloured butterfly flitting from one cabbage to another, without ever landing, our Heinz flits from one idea to another, without ever coming down firmly and clearly on the side of a clearly defined principled position. He takes one or two phrases from Marx, adds a little bit of Keynes, then throws in a random remark from Montesquieu, and then goes back to scraps of Socrates, Plato and Hobbes, before fluttering off in the direction of postmodernism.

In plain language this is called *eclecticism*. Engels, in his polemic with Dühring (the real spiritual ancestor of Dieterich) referred to his writings as a pauper's broth of eclecticism. But compared to Dieterich's books, the writings of Dühring were a goldmine of wisdom. Eclecticism has always been popular in universities, and never more than at the present time. The standards of intellectual life today are even more miserable than it was in the past – at least in the social sciences. Most modern bourgeois philosophy is simply not worth reading. The postmodernist nonsense (which has clearly left its mark on the thinking of Dieterich) reflects the despair of the bourgeois intellectuals in the period of the senile decay of capitalism.

With the greatest reluctance we are compelled to follow this butterfly through all its random fluttering, waiting patiently for a coherent idea to emerge. At last, our patience is rewarded. Finally our butterfly settles on what appears to be a concrete thought: "But if the animal makes a qualitative leap through its biological predetermination, what will generate the new social state in humanity? [sic] The answer is obvious [really?]: the conscious praxis of human beings. Just as the caterpillar develops in its life cycle the objective conditions for the flight of the butterfly, so capitalist society generates the conditions for the flight of human society towards the socialism of the new Era." [17]

It is not always easy to interpret the thoughts of Heinz Dieterich, if only because very often it seems he does not understand them himself. But let us make an attempt to translate this butterfly-talk into intelligible language. What he appears to be trying to say is only this: capitalism is plagued by internal contradictions and thus creates the objective conditions for its own overthrow. Put that way, it is immediately understandable and undoubtedly correct. But is it really new and original? We shall see.

What Dieterich stands for

In an interview by Cristina Marcano in *Rebelión* published on 2 January 2007, with the title *In Venezuela, Conditions for Building Socialism of the 21st Century Have Been Created*, Dieterich was asked if he had invented the concept of "Socialism of the 21st Century". With his customary modesty, he answered: "Yes. I developed it, beginning in 1996. It has been published with its corresponding theory in book

17. Ibid.

form, from 2000 on, in Mexico, Ecuador, Argentina, Central America, Brazil, and Venezuela, and, outside Latin America, in Spain, Germany, the People's Republic of China, Russia, and Turkey. Since 2001, it has been appropriated all over the world. Presidents like Hugo Chávez and Rafael Correa use it constantly, and so do labour movements, farmers, intellectuals, and political parties."

Now, with all due respect to Heinz, there is more than one person in the world who defends socialism, not only as a concept but as a practical proposition and a necessity for the human race. And since, for the last few years, we have all been living in the 21st century, there are more than one or two people who are 21st century socialists. They did not require the help of Heinz Dieterich to invent it. But, with or without our permission, he has invented it anyway. What precisely has he invented? He continues: "Along with the theory of Socialism of the 21st Century, I advanced the theory of Latin American transition that is expressed in key concepts like the Regional Block of Power (Bloque Regional de Poder or BRP), also already in general use in Latin America. However, the concept Regional Block of Popular Power (Bloque Regional de Poder Popular or BRPP) was proposed by a Venezuelan friend, Douglas Pérez, in a business meeting three months ago." [18]

That this "concept" should be discussed at a business meeting is highly appropriate, since, as we shall show, all of Heinz Dieterich's concepts have an exclusively bourgeois character and does not challenge capitalism and big business in any sense, shape or form. When asked to say briefly what this new socialism consists of, he says: "In brief: a socialism in which the majorities have the greatest historically possible degree of decision-making power in the economic, political, cultural, and military institutions that govern their lives." [19]

This is a highly laudable intention. But let us ask what this "greatest historically possible degree of decision-making power" consists of. In a regime of formal bourgeois democracy, the citizen is allowed to participate in the decision-making process by placing a cross on a bit of paper every four or five years. But the real decisions are not made in a bourgeois parliament or cabinet, but in the boards of directors of the big banks and monopolies that exercise a stranglehold over the economic life of the nation. Unless this stranglehold is broken, all talk about decision-making power is just so much empty chatter.

Does the Dieterichian model of "Socialism of the 21st Century" propose measures to break the power of the landlords, bankers and capitalists? No, it does not. When asked what decisive step should President Chávez take, he first tells us emphatically what he should *not* do. *He should not touch private property*: "A. It is not generalized nationalization of private property, because it does not solve the cybernetic problem of the market. It did not do so in the past and it would not do so today. Socialism today is essentially a problem of informatic complexity." [20]

18. Ibid.
19. Ibid.
20. Ibid.

We will return later to the idea that the problem of socialism is "essentially a roblem of informatic complexity" and the "cybernetic problem of the market". For ıe time being, let us simply register the fact that the inventor of Socialism of the 1st Century is *opposed to the nationalization of the property of the oligarchy* (the clusion of the word *generalised* is only a transparent fig leaf to disguise this fact). hus far we have learned what Chávez should *not* do. But what ought he be doing? et us allow Heinz to speak for himself:

"Hence, the *transcendental step* consists in establishing *socialist accounting* alue) next to capitalist accounting (price), in the State, PDVSA-CVG, and coop- atives, in order to construct an economic circuit of production and circulation par- lel to that of the capitalist market economy. The economy of state and social insti- tions can move step by step toward the economy of value and gain ground against e circuit of capitalist reproduction, until it displaces it in the future. Since the ales of valuation by prices, values, and also volumes are commensurable, there e no ruptures in economic exchanges that could cause a political problem to the vernment. In all this, the State and the majorities play an important role, but both e nowadays mainly with the project of the President." [21]

In the first place, is it really true that the state in Venezuela is "mainly" with the esident? Chávez has stated on many occasions that he faces systematic opposition d sabotage from the bureaucracy that occupies key parts of the State. He has ferred to it as a *counter-revolutionary bureaucracy*, and this description is very curate. Moreover, he has said that there is an old bureaucracy that has been left er from the Fourth Republic and also a new bureaucracy – people who wear red irts and call themselves chavistas, but who are in fact a Fifth Column of the count- revolution. Why does comrade Dieterich not mention this? Why does he ignore when this fact is well known, not only to President Chávez but to every worker d peasant in Venezuela? Can he not see what is evident? Either he does not see it, which case he is completely blind, or he does see it but prefers not to mention it, minimise it and to try to hide it. The first variant would indicate extreme stupid- and light-mindedness, and the second would be a crime against the revolution.

Every clear-thinking person knows that the problem of state power is the central oblem of the revolution, and also that this problem has not been solved. The livarian Revolution can never be victorious until it takes a big broom and sweeps all the rubbish, corruption and careerism, all the nests of counter-revolution that ve found refuge in the State and are gnawing at the bowels of the revolution and dermining it from within. This means a ferocious fight against the bureaucracy l the counter-revolution, which will resist by all means at their disposal. That can y be accomplished by the revolutionary mobilization of the masses. The state l never purge itself!

21. Ibid.

All history shows that the forces of the old society will resist change and that this resistance must be overcome by revolutionary means. What does comrade Dieterich say about this? The great revolution proposed by Heinz Dieterich, the *transcendental step* is all a matter of *accountancy*. This is a revolution that we can carry out without removing our carpet slippers. It is the kind of revolution that breaks no windows, offends nobody and that causes problems for nobody. It does not disturb the nervous system or cause peptic ulcers. It can be carried out quietly, at nigh time, so as not to disturb the sleep of respectable citizens. In short, this is the kind of revolution every sane person dreams of. One wonders why it has never been thought of before!

Why does such a revolution not bother anybody? For the simple reason that *it involves no change at all*, for it is merely a *continuation of the status quo*. What we are talking about is a *mixed economy:* the usual ideal of the reformists and Social Democrats. Here, for once, Heinz is unusually frank and unambiguous: "The economy of state and social institutions can move step by step toward the economy of value and gain ground against the circuit of capitalist reproduction, until it displaces it in the future." [22] This is hardly a new idea. It has been put forward by every reformist and revisionist since Bernstein. The idea is that the state sector coexists alongside the private sector and, slowly, gradually, peacefully, the former displaces the latter, until eventually, capitalism disappears without anybody even noticing it.

Every reformist has dreamed of moving step by step toward socialism, of a peaceful social transformation, without clashes, shocks or unpleasantness, just as every vegetarian dreams of a world in which tigers eat lettuce. But such examples in real history are even rarer than vegetarian tigers in real nature. Of course, there is nothing to stop one from developing such "concepts" – just as there is nothing to stop one daydreaming after a heavy lunch. Heinz Dieterich stresses that the transition from capitalism to socialism will be *gradual*. In one sense that is true. It is not possible to jump straight from capitalism to socialism. But before we can take a single step towards socialism it is first necessary to carry out *a decisive break with capitalism*. It is necessary to expropriate the landlords, bankers and capitalists. And that is what he refuses to accept.

Heinz expands upon his idea of a "parallel circuit of the economy of value", that is, in plain language, a mixed economy: "To create this parallel circuit of the economy of value would be relatively easy, because values exist in underlying form in the present capitalist accounting. Values exist in it in such a way that, with the development of corresponding software, it would be very easy to establish this socialist economic circuit next to the capitalist one. Without this passage to the economy of equivalency, it is not possible to have a socialist economy." [23]

22. Dieterich, *En Venezuela se han creado condiciones para construir el Socialismo del Siglo XXI*, in *Rebelión*, 2/1/07.
23. Ibid.

We shall see later that, far from being easy to work out the exact amount of socially necessary labour present in a given commodity, this is a practically impossible task, and in any case something quite unnecessary for a socialist economy, which is the exact opposite of what our Heinz maintains. And in what way the presence of so-called socialist accounting would displace capitalist accounting (prices) only God and Heinz Dieterich know.

What would be the decisive step that President Chávez would have to take to arrive at Socialism of the 21st Century in Venezuela? To this very pertinent question, comrade Dieterich answers: "They are two: 1. to gradually replace the regulating principle of market economy, price, by the regulating principle of socialist economy, value, understood as time inputs (insumos de tiempo) necessary for the creation of a product; and 2. to advance the economic participation of citizens and workers at three levels: 1. at the macroeconomic level (e.g., national budget); 2. at the mesoeconomic level (municipality); and, 3. at the microeconomic level (enterprise)." [24]

We will deal with the economic theories of 21st Century Socialism in a later section. For the time being we merely point out:

1) Heinz Dieterich is opposed to nationalization and in favour of a mixed economy – that is, capitalism,

2) He is opposed to revolution and in favour of gradualism (that is, piecemeal reform)

3) This has nothing to with Marxism or revolutionary socialism but is merely the old reformism warmed up and served as the very latest menu of the day.

Reformism in Latin America

Reformism has a material base. It thrived in countries like Sweden and Britain during the long period of economic upswing that followed the Second World War. This enabled the bourgeoisie to give important concessions to the working class using Keynesian economic policies. The class struggle in Europe was blunted for a period of decades. But this period was cut across by the slump of 1973-74. For the last thirty years reformist governments in Europe have carried out a programme of counter-reforms, cuts and attacks on living standards. We will explain the reasons for this in a later chapter. Suffice it to say that even in the "rich" countries, like the USA and Western Europe, under present conditions, reformism and Keynesianism are in crisis.

Matters are even clearer in Latin America. Here the crisis is too deep, the conditions of the masses too desperate to allow half-measures. The existence of high deficits does not permit the application of the Keynesian recipes that comrade Dieterich regards as the infallible cure for all ailments. As a matter of fact, the attempt

24. Ibid.

to follow such policies in the 1960s and 1970s was precisely the cause of massive deficits and hyperinflation that had catastrophic effects. We will deal with this question later. For now it is sufficient to point out the self-evident fact that the historical weakness of reformism and Social Democracy in Latin America is the result of the extreme weakness of Latin American capitalism and the impossibility of solving any of the pressing problems of the workers and peasants on a capitalist basis.

Recently there have been several attempts to breathe some life into reformism and "the Third Way" in Latin America. This is no accident. The strategists of capitalism have understood the danger of the revolutionary movement in Latin America. They understand the mortal danger posed by the Venezuelan Revolution and they fear (correctly) that it can spread throughout the continent. In the past they would have sent the Marines to intervene. But this is no longer so easy. So they must resort to other means of halting the revolution and divert it into safer channels. Here the reformists of different trends can play a very useful role as a second line of defence for capitalism.

One attempt to boost reformism in Latin America was the International Forum in Porto Alegre, Brazil, which Heinz Dieterich takes as his starting point. This included such heterogeneous groups and movements as the Mexican Zapatistas, the Colombian FARC and ELN, ATTAC, *Le Monde Diplomatique*, the Brazilian PT, Venezuelan Bolivarians and other groups and individuals. Some of these organizations, like the Brazilian PT and the Bolivarian Movement, represent a significant force with a mass base of workers and peasants, while others represent only small circles of intellectuals, and there were a number of individuals representing only themselves.

The World Social Forum did not pose any challenge to capitalism. Its first meetings were financed, amongst others, by the Ford Foundation. Interviewed about the involvement of the Ford Foundation in the WSF, Lisa Jordan, one of the Foundation's officers had this to say (in open Democracy):

"Why did Ford get involved in the WSF in the first place?

"Lisa Jordan: We value global civic dialogue around global problems. We don't necessarily believe solutions lie with any one sector. Government, business and civil society cannot solve problems separately. There must be dialogue between and amongst these three groupings."

When some groups criticised the WSF for not being revolutionary she replied with commendable frankness: "In fairness, the WSF has never said it is a revolutionary grouping. Its stated principles are those of non-violence. Non-violence is fundamental to how it defines itself. There has always been a very strong peace agenda at the forum; last year's forum issued a very beautiful and profound statement in favour of peace."

The Forum was apparently connected by a phone line to another Forum taking place on the other side of the world, the conference of bankers and capitalists in

Davos, Switzerland. This little detail tells us quite a lot about the mentality and political positions of the organizers of the Porto Alegre gathering. Unfortunately, the telephone connection with Davos did not yield any positive result, for the simple reason that the conflict between oppressors and oppressed cannot be resolved by a telephone conversation or any other kind of conversation. It is a question of mutually exclusive interests. The Porto Alegre Forum was made up of such a hotchpotch of different groups and individuals that it proved difficult to agree almost on anything. Dieterich informs us that no sooner had the question of socialism been raised than the trouble started:

"The next day, the Chilean intellectual Ariel Dorfman argued that in 'such an open' Forum it was unacceptable to say that socialism was the only option. 'I believe that we must not enter into *grandiloquent* rhetoric', said Dorfman who stressed that the Porto Alegre Forum was not a forum to 'a return to the past'. 'I cannot say what the viable option is and I believe neither here nor in Davos do we know it', the writer finished, stressing that it is too soon 'to formulate a single programme of action'." [25]

On one thing we can certainly agree with Ariel Dorfman. He has not the slightest idea of the nature of the present world crisis and therefore has absolutely nothing to offer as an alternative. We also tend to agree with his opinion that the rest of the Forum of Porto Alegre was just as much in the dark as Dorfman himself. In the end, Porto Alegre represented a blind alley. It offered no serious programme for changing society. It was necessary to break through the limitations of reformism and place on the agenda the only real alternative: the socialist transformation of society.

Let us remind ourselves that Hugo Chávez, who was present at Porto Alegre, originally had illusions in the "third way" (a phrase invented by Tony Blair) and believed in the possibility of reforming capitalism. His ideal was not originally socialism but "capitalism with a human face". But after the experience of the first years of the Bolivarian Revolution, Chávez drew the conclusion that this was impossible, and that the "third way" was a fraud – in his own words *a farce.* President Chávez, to his great credit, raised the question of socialism, while Dieterich is doing everything in his power to drag the Bolivarian Revolution away from socialist revolution and towards the swamp of bourgeois reformist politics. What did Heinz Dieterich expect from the Porto Alegre Forum? Let us quote his words:

"The big question is therefore how to accumulate the necessary and sufficient power to turn the world upside down? How to transform the majorities into the masters of the global society? The answer is obvious [really?]: through the New Historical Project (NHP) constructed by them. Its content: participative democracy. This is the theme of this book." [26]

25. Dieterich, *Socialismo del Siglo XXI*, p. 29. Emphasis in original.
26. Ibid., p. 28

The aim is not a small one! It is: "to turn the world upside down and transform the majorities into the masters of the global society". And how is this aim to be realized? Obviously, through the New Historical Project (NHP). Now, it stands to reason that if something is *obvious*, only a fool is unable to see it. In the famous tale of Hans Christian Anderson, a swindler persuaded an emperor to wear an invisible suit, which everybody agreed was *obviously* very fine. Eventually a little boy who had not been informed of this pointed out that the emperor was going about stark naked. His observations probably did not please the emperor or his courtiers, but they had the merit of being true. Like the little boy in the story, we are not clever enough to accept things just because we are assured that they are *obvious*. We would like a little more information and, if possible, some proof that these remarkable assurances are, in fact, correct.

Dieterich's mentors

Heinz says: "There are two schools of thought that have advanced this option [which option?] of a new society in their works on Socialism of the 21st Century: the so-called Scottish School [?], in the brilliant works of the computer expert and economist Allin Cottrell, and the so-called Bremen School (West Germany), around the universal genius Alan Peters, the mathematician Carsten Stammer, the Cuban physicist Raimundo Franco and others who share their views." [27]

We have to rely upon Heinz's word for all this, since nowhere does he tell us what precisely the content of these so-called Schools consists of. This is surprising, for if they are really as important as our friend suggests, surely he could have spared a few lines to let us in on the secret? In the event, the secret is well kept. With all due respect to the Bremen and Scottish Schools and their universal geniuses, we prefer another school altogether: the school of revolutionary Marxism. And, Dieterich and friends notwithstanding, we shall continue to defend the ideas of Marx, Engels, Lenin and Trotsky against all the attacks: not only the attacks of the bourgeois enemies of socialism, but also of the reformists who represent a Fifth Column of the bourgeoisie inside the workers' movement.

The kind of reformism represented by European Social Democracy immediately repels radical elements in Latin America. But there are other kinds of reformism with a more radical and "left wing" coloration. Most of these also come from Europe (despite the constant appeals of Heinz Dieterich to the Patria Grande). They emanate from the universities of Germany, France and Italy where aging ex-revolutionaries, repenting the sins of their youth, are busy searching for the Holy Grail of post-capitalist society. Heinz quotes like-minded thinkers. But, although Dieterich finds their writings all very interesting, they are naturally not sufficient to satisfy his demanding mind: "Nevertheless, despite their cognitive richness, they do not pro-

27. Dieterich, *Hugo Chávez y el Socialismo del Siglo XXI*, p. 32

vide a sufficient base to adequately respond to the call of Comandante Chávez. That is to say, reading them is a necessary condition for the construction of a new theory, but it is not enough." [28]

With so many "Schools" all vying for the honour of being the real founders of Socialism of the 21st Century the reader's head begins to spin. We are accustomed to a situation where there are not enough schools and too many pupils. But in the 21st century world of Heinz Dieterich there are far too many Schools and not many pupils. Nonetheless, we are informed that *it is not enough*. All these thinkers and Schools can only resemble John the Baptist and other prophets of old, condemned to play the role of a voice crying in the wilderness, making straight the way of Heinz Dieterich, who is coming, with compass in hand and book under his arm, to announce the Gospel of Socialism of the 21st Century.

We had never heard of the "School of Bremen" or the "School of Scotland" until we opened the books of Heinz Dieterich. It would appear that the former refers to the ideas of Arno Peters (a one-man school, therefore), to which we now turn our attention. University professors have a notorious tendency to form mutual admiration societies, and comrade Dieterich can be no exception to the rule. For our Heinz, Arno Peters is *one of the greatest geniuses*, if not *the* greatest genius, of our epoch. On page 38 of *El Socialismo del Siglo XXI* we read the following: "To the scientist Arno Peters belongs the merit of having discovered the principle of the future socialist economy, setting out from the structural deficiencies of the national market economy."

In our innocence, we always thought that it was Karl Marx who discovered the principles of socialism and explained how it arises from the contradictions of capitalism, that is, the contradiction between the development of the productive forces and the barriers represented by private ownership and the nation state. But now we have been corrected by Heinz Dieterich who informs us that this discovery is the work of none other than his friend Arno Peters. And if Heinz Dieterich says it, it must be true. This brings to mind the old saying: for the mouse no animal is stronger than the cat. But let us see what his universal genius consists of.

Like Heinz, Arno Peters is a dilettante. That is to say, he likes to dabble in as many fields as possible. In this way he will never be bored. Arno started as a filmmaker and according to some, produced films that were not at all bad. But then he got tired of that and decided to do something new. In the time-honoured German tradition he got his doctorate at the University of Berlin, writing his dissertation on political propaganda. But even this was not enough for Arno's restless ambition. He moved on to the study of Synchronoptic World History. In case you do not know it, this is history that focuses on giving all people of the world an equal voice, by making a timeline with each year getting equal space on a page. This was Professor Peters' first great victory in the fight for equality.

28. Ibid.

The culminating achievement in Peters' life was the development of the Peters World Map. This was an entirely new kind of concept, which, at a stroke, established the principle of *Cartographical Equality*. Although critics made unkind comments about his map ("the land masses look like wet, ragged, long winter underwear hung out to dry on the Arctic Circle", one of them wrote), Peters was triumphant. Having established people's *right to equal space on the printed page*, he had now established their right to *equal space on a map* as well.

Peters' achievements as a cartographer have been exaggerated. He claimed to have discovered something new. He didn't. He claimed the new projection did not distort area. It does. Ever since Ptolemy in the second century mapmakers have struggled with the problem of how to draw a round Earth on a flat sheet of paper, knowing there is no perfect solution, since, if the shapes of continents are correct, the sizes will be distorted, and vice versa. For example, if the lower latitudes are accurately depicted, then the Polar Regions will be grossly distorted. As a matter of fact, only a globe can show all geographical relationships in accurate perspective. Therefore, in the best case, the Peters' map presents the map of the world with distortions that are different to the distortions we have become used to. That is the sum total of his epoch-making achievement in the sphere of cartography.

This epoch-making achievement was accomplished in 1974. Since then many atlases have been produced, only a minority of which, alas, pay any attention to the Peters' model. Moreover, despite the proclamation of equality on the map and written page, real equality is even further away than it was in 1974. The real gap between the developed industrial nations and the economies of Africa, Asia and Latin America has grown steadily wider. If the difference were to be expressed as a map, the continents would by now have drifted apart. Alas, the achievement of genuine equality requires measures a little more drastic than the redrawing of maps!

Having put Ptolemy and Copernicus completely in the shade, Arno Peters moved on from cartography to the realm of politics, history and political economy, where he immediately disposed of the likes of Adam Smith, Ricardo, Marx and Engels. For a chap who has no difficulty in changing the shape of the entire terrestrial globe and ushering in the age of cartographical equality, this was really no trouble at all. Arno Peters now revealed to the world the real way to get equality, the key that opens all doors, the Philosopher's Stone of the 21st Century – the Principle of Equivalence.

We shall be dealing with this, and other interesting matters, in a later chapter. But now we must fly, hanging onto the shirt-tails of comrade Dieterich, into the ethereal realms of science and philosophy, where we will no doubt experience new and surprising adventures.

2. Philosophy and science

Crisis of modern philosophy

Polonius: What do you read, my lord?
Hamlet: Words, words, words.
(Shakespeare, *Hamlet*, Act II, Scene ii)

The crisis of the capitalist system is reflected in a crisis of bourgeois values, morality, religion, politics and philosophy. The mood of pessimism that afflicts the bourgeoisie and its ideologues in this period is manifested in the poverty of its thought, the triviality of its art and the emptiness of its spiritual values. It is expressed in the wretched philosophy of post-modernism, which imagines itself to be superior to all previous philosophy, when in reality it is vastly inferior.

In its youth the bourgeoisie was capable of producing great thinkers: Locke, Hobbes, Kant, Hegel, Adam Smith and Ricardo. In the period of its decline, it is only capable of producing intellectual pygmies. They talk of the end of ideology and the end of history in the same breath. They do not believe in progress because the bourgeoisie has long since ceased to be progressive. When they talk of the end of history it is because they have ended in an historical dead-end and can see no way out. When they talk of the end of ideology it is because they are no longer capable of producing one.

The modern bourgeois philosophers imagine they have killed off the old philosophy (or "metaphysics", as they contemptuously call it) but their imagined victory is like that of Grimm's brave little tailor, who "killed seven at one blow." The seven victims of the tailor were, in fact, flies, not men. And our modern philosophers are, to use a German expression, mere *flea-crackers*. Modern bourgeois philosophy amounts to the total dissolution of philosophy, reducing it entirely to semantics (the study of the meaning of words). This endless discussion of the minutiae of meanings resembles nothing so much as the interminable debates of the medieval Schoolmen on such fascinating subjects as whether angels had sex and how many of them could dance on the head of a pin.

This comparison is not as absurd as it may seem. Actually, the Schoolmen were not fools and made certain advances in logic and semantics (as do their modern equivalents). The problem is that in their obsession with form, they forgot the content altogether. As long as the formal rules were obeyed, the content could be as absurd as one liked. The fact that all this fussing and fiddling and playing with words could be given the name of philosophy at all is a proof of how far modern bourgeois thought has declined. Hegel wrote in the *Phenomenology*: "By the little with which the human spirit is satisfied, we can judge the extent of its loss." That would be a fitting epitaph for all the bourgeois philosophy after Hegel.

Modern bourgeois philosophy claims to have solved all the great philosophical problems of the past. How has it accomplished this mighty feat? By analysing words. This victory puts all the battles of the First and Second World Wars, together with Austerlitz, Waterloo and every other battle completely in the shade. But what is language but ideas that are expressed in speech? If we say we can only know language, we are only restating in a different way the old, worn-out notion of subjective idealism that we can only know ideas, or more correctly, I can only know *my* ideas. This is a philosophical blind alley, which, as Lenin explained long ago, can only lead to solipsism, that is, the notion that *only I exist.*

The worker works with tools and the raw materials furnished by nature. With the aid of these material things men have always transformed the world and controlled their environment. And by changing the world around them, men have also changed themselves. They have gradually lifted themselves above the level of animals and become human. It is this ceaseless human activity – this creativity that springs from collective human labour – that has made us what we are. It is the basis of all human progress, culture and knowledge.

The bricklayer works with bricks, the painter with paint, the ironmonger with iron and the carpenter with wood. But the intellectual works only with words. They are what earn him his daily bread, they fill his life and provide him with work and pleasure. They raise him up or dash him down, give him a reputation, or take it away. They act as a magical charm for charms and spells have to be uttered *as words.* They also give him power over other human beings. In the most primitive societies certain words were taboo, just as they are now. The ancient Israelites were not permitted to utter the name of their God. Nowadays we are not allowed to utter the word capitalism but must instead say "the free market economy".

This is itself a product of the development of the productive forces and the material conditions for human social development. Once the means of production develop to a certain level a surplus is produced. The division of labour (already present in early society in an embryonic form) is the basis upon which arises a class of individuals who are freed from the need to work to produce food but can devote themselves to specialized activities. With the further development of the productive power of society comes the further intensification of the social division of labour, expressed in the rise of castes and classes.

Society is divided into rulers and ruled, exploiters and exploited. At this point consciousness acquires an independent life of its own. A gulf opens up between mental and manual labour. The priests and scribes of ancient Egypt became conscious of the material power of ideas and words, which gave them an authority and a power over their fellow men. The division of society into thinkers and doers dates from that time, as Aristotle points out in his *Metaphysics*. From the earliest times those privileged layers who enjoyed a monopoly of culture have held manual labour in contempt.

For the intellectual, the only reality consists of words. For him, it is really the case that "in the beginning was the Word, and the Word was with God and the Word was God." The idea – or more correctly, the prejudice – of the intellectual that imparts to words a supernatural significance, is merely a reflection of the real conditions of existence of the intellectual. In postmodernism narrative is everything, and we can only know the world through the words of individuals. Here language appears not as a phenomenon that connects people with the world and each other but something that separates and isolates. It is a barrier, beyond which we can know nothing.

The intellectual's mystification of words is therefore not new. It has its roots in the division between mental and manual labour. But it has acquired its ultimate expression in modern bourgeois philosophy. That is hardly surprising, given the fact that the gulf between rich and poor, haves and haves-not, "learned" and "ignorant" is greater now than in any other time in history. The masses have been expropriated, not only physically but also morally and culturally. The language of science is completely inaccessible for the great majority of educated citizens, never mind the uneducated ones. And the situation is even worse with philosophy, which has become utterly bogged down in a morass of terminological obscurantism, compared to which the language of the medieval Schoolmen appears a model of clarity. The prose of Professor Dieterich is a perfect specimen of this literary genre.

The need for dialectics

Modern bourgeois philosophy has become arid and stultified. It is remote from reality and shows a complete disregard for the life of ordinary people. So it is no wonder that people in turn treat it with contempt. At no time in history has philosophy seemed so irrelevant as at present. The total bankruptcy of modern bourgeois philosophy can be explained in part from the fact that Hegel carried traditional philosophy to its limits, leaving very little room for the further development of philosophy as philosophy. But the most important reason for the crisis of philosophy is the development of science itself.

For thousands of years humans have tried to make sense of the world in which we live. This constant search after the truth is an essential part of being human. But for the great majority of our history, this attempt to understand the workings of the universe was deprived of the necessary tools. The insufficient development of the productive forces, science and technology meant that the only instrument available to us was the human brain – a truly wonderful instrument, it is true, but quite inadequate for the immensity of the task.

It is only in the two centuries or so since the Industrial Revolution that the development of science has provided us with the necessary tools to place the study of nature on a sound basis. In particular, the spectacular advances of science and technology in the last fifty years have put every other period of human advance in the shade. In such conditions, the old philosophical speculations about the nature of life and the universe appear as naïve and even ridiculous. Surely science has once and for all freed itself from philosophy? To this question Engels answered in the affirmative, but he added that what remained valid in philosophy was formal logic and dialectics. Science still needs a methodology that will permit it to waste the least possible amount of time and make the fewest possible mistakes.

In the philosophical writings of Marx and Engels we do not have a philosophical system, but a series of brilliant insights and pointers, which, if they were developed, would provide a valuable addition to the methodological armoury of science. Unfortunately, such a work has never been seriously undertaken. With all its colossal resources, the Soviet Union did not produce it. The marvellous insights of Marx and Engels on philosophy and science were left in an undeveloped state. Does this mean that dialectics has been totally absent from the development of modern science? Not at all, the latest developments in the theories of chaos and complexity have a clearly dialectical character.

Dialectics teaches us to study things in motion, not statically, in their life, not in their death. Every development is rooted in earlier stages, and in turn is the embryo and starting point of new developments – a never-ending web of relations that reinforce and perpetuate each other. Hegel already developed this idea in his *Logic* and other works. Dialectics teaches us to study things and processes in all their interconnections. This is important as a methodology in areas such as animal morphology. It is not possible to modify one part of the anatomy without producing changes in all the others.

It is impossible to understand history without the dialectical method. This can be seen in the history of science itself. A major advance in the application of the dialectical method to the history of science was the publication in 1962 of T.S. Kuhn's remarkable book *The Structure of Scientific Revolutions*. This demonstrated the inevitability of scientific revolutions and showed the approximate mechanism whereby these occur. "All that exists deserves to perish" holds good not only for living organisms but also for scientific theories, including those which we currently hold to be of absolute validity.

A dynamic view of the world

Dialectics is a method of thinking and interpreting the world of both nature and society. It is a way of looking at the universe, which sets out from the axiom that everything is in a constant state of change and flux. But not only that – dialectics explains that change and motion involve contradiction and can only take place through contradictions. So instead of a smooth, uninterrupted line of progress, we have a line which is interrupted by sudden and explosive periods in which slow, accumulated changes (quantitative change) undergoes a rapid acceleration, in which quantity is transformed into quality. Dialectics is the logic of contradiction.

The fundamental proposition of dialectics is that everything is in a constant process of change, motion and development. Even when it appears to us that nothing is happening, in reality, matter is always changing. Molecules, atoms and subatomic particles are constantly changing place and form, and always on the move. Dialectics is thus an essentially dynamic interpretation of the phenomena and processes that occur at all levels of both organic and inorganic matter. It is, to quote Engels, the most general laws of nature, society and human thought.

When we first contemplate the world around us, we see an immense and amazingly complex series of phenomena, an intricate web of seemingly endless change, cause and effect, action and reaction. The motive force of scientific investigation is the desire to obtain a rational insight into this bewildering labyrinth, to understand it in order to conquer it. We look for laws that can separate the general from the particular, the accidental from the necessary, and enable us to understand the forces that give rise to the phenomena which confront us.

The bourgeois critics of Marxism (and also the revisionists) have concentrated their attacks on dialectics, which constitutes its methodological foundation. A key part of this attack is the assertion that Engels based himself on old-fashioned science, the science of the 19th century, which has been entirely displaced by the discoveries of modern science (relativity theory and quantum physics). This argument, which is repeated by comrade Dieterich as part of his general assault against the basic principles of Marxism, is entirely false. In the first place, Marx and Engels were by no means uncritical of the science of the 19th century, and in many ways were ahead of their times. In the second place, the results of modern science have entirely vindicated the dialectical approach. All this is a book closed with seven seals to our Heinz who shows that his understanding of modern science is just as poor as his understanding of Marxist philosophy.

Comrade Dieterich likes to quote Hegel. He does this, as usual, in order to impress the reader with his colossal erudition. The great German philosopher was a towering genius of thought who made important discoveries and developed dialectics to a new and higher level. But in Hegel dialectics appears in a mystified, idealist form. The Hegelian dialectic was, to quote Engels, the greatest abortion in the history of thought. In order to rescue what was important in Hegel's dialectic, Marx had to strip it of its idealism and place it on a firm materialist basis. Hegel already worked out the laws of dialectics in detail in the first years of the 19th century.

However, it was Marx and Engels who first gave dialectics a scientific, that is to say, materialist basis. "Hegel wrote before Darwin and before Marx," wrote Trotsky. "Thanks to the powerful impulse given to thought by the French Revolution, Hegel anticipated the general movement of science. But because it was only an anticipation, although by a genius, it received from Hegel an idealistic character. Hegel operated with ideological shadows as the ultimate reality. Marx demonstrated that the movement of these ideological shadows reflected nothing but the movement of material bodies." [1]

In the writings of Hegel there are many striking examples of the law of dialectics drawn from history and nature. But Hegel's idealism necessarily gave his dialectics a highly abstract and arbitrary character. In order to make dialectics serve the "Absolute Idea," Hegel was forced to impose a schema upon nature and society, in flat contradiction to the dialectical method itself, which demands that we derive the laws of a given phenomenon from a scrupulously objective study of the subject matter as Marx did in his *Capital*. Thus, far from being a mere regurgitation of Hegel's idealist dialectic arbitrarily foisted on history and society as his critics often assert, Marx's method was precisely the opposite. As he himself explains:

"My dialectic method is not only different from the Hegelian, but is its direct opposite. To Hegel, the life-process of the human brain, i.e. the process of thinking, which, under the name of 'the Idea,' he even transforms into an independent subject, is the demiurgos of the real world, and the real world is only the external, phenomenal form of 'the Idea.' With me, on the contrary, the ideal is nothing else than the material world reflected by the human mind, and translated into forms of thought." [2]

The reader who wishes to study the laws of dialectics and see how they are applied to a wide range of subjects should read Engels' *Anti-Dühring* and *Dialectics of Nature*. In my book *Reason in Revolt. Marxist Philosophy and Modern Science*, which President Chávez has commented on positively on several occasions, I have attempted to show, with examples from modern science, how dialectical materialism has been completely vindicated by the latest discoveries of physics, chemistry, biology, palaeontology, geology and genetics.

The laws of dialectics can be reduced in the main to three:

The law of the transformation of quantity into quality and *vice versa*;

The law of the interpenetration of opposites;

The law of the negation of the negation.

In *The Dialectics of Nature*, Engels writes: "All three are developed by Hegel in his idealist fashion as mere laws of *thought*: the first, in the first part of his *Logic*, in the *Doctrine of Being*; the second fills the whole of the second and by far the most important part of his *Logic*, the *Doctrine of Essence*; finally the third figures as the

1. Trotsky, *In Defence of Marxism*, The ABC of Materialist Dialectics, p. 66.
2. Marx and Engels, *Selected Works*, Vol. 2, 98.

fundamental law for the construction of the whole system. The mistake lies in the fact that these laws are foisted on nature and history as laws of thought, and not deduced from them. This is the source of the whole forced and often outrageous treatment; the universe, willy-nilly, is made out to be arranged in accordance with a system of thought which itself is only the product of a definite stage of evolution of human thought. If we turn the thing round, then everything becomes simple, and the dialectical laws that look so extremely mysterious in idealist philosophy at once become simple and clear as noonday."[3]

In recent years the crisis of bourgeois ideology has been expressed, among other things, by a general drift towards idealism, mysticism and superstition. Thus, philosophy has a great importance for politics, as well as science. In order to expose the reactionary nature of bourgeois ideology, one must have a consistent revolutionary ideology, a revolutionary philosophy. Having briefly expounded the basic ideas of Marxist philosophy, let us now turn to the entirely new and original philosophical views of comrade Dieterich.

The 'philosophy of praxis'

Since comrade Dieterich has invented an entirely new and original socialism, he must also invent an entirely novel philosophy to accompany it. This he calls the *philosophy of praxis*, which is a question of no less than constructing a "New Historic Project (NHP) for the liberation of mankind." We are further informed that "in its rational or cognitive kernel the NHP must resolve three complex strategic dimensions of human evolution: the scientific-critical, the ethical, and the aesthetic." Nobody knows where this New Philosophy of Praxis came from. There is no mention of this in the speech of President Chávez, which comrade Dieterich was supposed to be commenting on. Whatever this so-called New Philosophy of Praxis may or may not mean, we are assured that it "requires the concurrence of *the best forces and intellects of humanity*"[4] – starting, of course, with Heinz Dieterich himself.

Do we need a new philosophy? That would imply that dialectical materialism is no longer valid. Nowhere does comrade Dieterich tell us why this should be the case. All the most recent discoveries of science, from Stephen Jay Gould's Punctuated Equilibria in the field of evolution to the latest advances in chaos theory have confirmed the complete validity of the dialectical method. This is therefore yet another of Dieterich's gratuitous remarks that display precisely a *frivolous and irresponsible* attitude to theory. Despite having invented the entirely new *philosophy of praxis*, Dieterich continues to refer to dialectical materialism. But in all his writing there is not a single atom of materialism – his whole approach is purely idealist in the worst sense of the word. Nor is there even a hint of dialectics – unless we mean the *dialectic of sophism*, that is, *empty playing with words*.

3. Engels, *The Dialectics of Nature*, Moscow 1954, chapter II. Dialectics, p.83.
4. Dieterich, *The World Revolution Advances Through Hugo Chávez*

Once again his claim to be new and original turns out to be not entirely correct. The term "philosophy of praxis" is copied from the celebrated Italian Marxist Antonio Gramsci, who used it only to avoid the attentions of the fascist censor. Later on certain petty bourgeois intellectuals in Europe found the word "praxis" irresistible (because nobody knew what it meant) and began to repeat it like a flock of chattering parrots. Our Heinz is now carrying on in the same noisy tradition. We therefore know what it is *called*, but we do not yet know *what it is*. This is quite consistent with 21st Century Socialism in general. It is neither fish nor fowl, like Mistress Quickly in Shakespeare's *Henry IV*, whose sex is so indeterminate that "a man knows not where to have her."

In fact, he does not adhere to any method in particular but takes bits and pieces from different sources (none of his thought is original) and throws them all together like an apprentice cook making a stew out of yesterday's stale leftovers. His whole approach and method (insofar as we can speak of a method at all amidst all this shapeless meandering) is thoroughly impregnated with the method of modern bourgeois philosophy. This shallow eclecticism is presented to us as something entirely new and original!

We shall show how this so-called philosophy has nothing in common with the revolutionary Marxist philosophy of dialectical materialism. It is neither new nor original but is taken directly from the most superficial and emptiest of all the modern bourgeois philosophical schools, namely postmodernism. At first sight, this seems strange, because on more than one occasion, Dieterich has criticized postmodernism. But, as we know, his motto is: one of sand and one of cement. Here is what Heinz writes about postmodernism:

"In fact, a strange intellectual fashion has gripped much of the global thinking class and the leaders of the 'left', which makes them swing with cheerful frivolity between the positions of a crude 19th century empiricism and the recent fallacies of postmodernism enriched with old quasi-anarchistic formulas and a false pose of agnostic scepticism." On the harmful influence of postmodernism, we are in complete agreement with comrade Dieterich, who, we note, does not include himself as part of the "global thinking class" – whatever that may be. Our Heinz continues his diatribe against postmodernism and all its works: "The second pole of the alleged contradiction, the prescription of not falling into 'grandiose long-term global prophecies', has made us suddenly regress to the ideology of 'metanarratives' and the 'grand narratives' of bourgeois postmodernism which, with its complete lack of substance, does not merit further discursive consideration."[5]

Like the Inquisitors of old, Heinz casts the postmodernists into the flames of eternal damnation, where they will come to a well-deserved end. But to the reader's great consternation, having kicked postmodernism out of the front door, it is read-

5. Dieterich, *Entre topos y gallinas. La bancarrota de la "izquierda" y sus intelectuales.* In *Rebelión*, 28/2/2004.

mitted immediately by the tradesman's entrance. Although he does not even consider them worthy of any discursive consideration, he quietly appropriates the language, method and content of the postmodernists as part and parcel of the philosophy of praxis, as we shall soon see. This method reminds us of the Japanese proverb about a dishonest butcher: "You hang out a sheep's head and sell dog's meat!"

No more ideology?

Since Heinz Dieterich has long ago abandoned the Marxist standpoint, he is influenced by all the latest "trendy" bourgeois ideas – including postmodernism. He has borrowed the idea of the "end of ideology" from post-modernism without even acknowledging it. In his writings he talks about "postcapitalist" society and he clearly regards himself as the leading proponent of "postcommunism" and "postmarxism". However, nobody, except Heinz Dieterich, has the slightest idea of what this consists of. This convinces him that we are *very mediocre people*, since we lack the ability to recognize genius even when it stands revealed before us.

In *La disyuntiva de Cuba: Capitalismo o nuevo socialismo* Dieterich states that ideology in general – that is, all ideology – is a "false consciousness", and attributes this erroneous idea to Marx, who said exactly the opposite. If we accept this idea, we inevitably land up in a reactionary bourgeois position. In its youth, as we have seen, the bourgeoisie had a revolutionary ideology. In England and France it stood for materialism (in England this took the form of empiricism) and subjected the reactionary medieval-feudal ideology to a merciless criticism. But now, in the epoch of its senile decay, the bourgeoisie is incapable of producing great ideas. It is only capable of producing *mediocre thinkers* producing *mediocre ideas*.

Is it true that Marx considered all ideology as "objectively false consciousness"? No, it is not true at all. *Marxism is itself an ideology* and one that represents a consciousness that accurately and truthfully reflects reality. Tendencies in society find their reflection in ideology, including science. Reactionary ideas can be expressed in science, for example, reactionary theories in genetics that attempt to provide a scientific basis for racism. Marx explains that the ruling ideas of every epoch are the ideas of the ruling class. But in every epoch there are also other ideas (including ideologies) that express the aspirations of the revolutionary class that is striving to assert itself. The fact that the bourgeoisie in the first decade of the 21st century has exhausted its progressive role and has become a brake on the development of civilization is precisely expressed in the poverty of bourgeois culture. This, in turn, expresses itself in the complete absence of any school of bourgeois philosophy worthy of the name. Incapable of any great thoughts, the bourgeois comes to the conclusion (perfectly logical from a bourgeois point of view) that *no great thoughts are possible*.

This narrow bourgeois outlook finds its expression in the so-called philosophy of post-modernism, which is merely a tedious repetition in philosophy of the idea of the *end of history*, expressed as the *end of ideology*. All of Heinz Dieterich's books and articles are thoroughly impregnated with the spirit of this bourgeois philosophy. And this is no accident. The petty bourgeois intelligentsia (as long as it does not break with its class standpoint and pass over to that of the working class) tends to reflect the ideas and moods of the bourgeoisie. Academics who live in the rarefied world of the universities give these ideas and moods – which are a distorted expression of the real relations in society – an abstract and "ideological" form (that is, a fantastic form). They then return it to the bourgeoisie, which puts this university "wisdom" to good use, deceiving and disorienting the student youth and erecting a new barrier between the latter and Marxism.

"No more ideology!" is the new slogan of the bourgeois and petty bourgeois intellectuals. "The old ideas are out of date!" (This applies particularly to the "old ideas" of Marxism, of course). "Give us new ideas!" they shout in a deafening chorus. They shout so loud and repeat the same idea so often that they hope nobody will notice that the famous "new ideas" are conspicuous by their absence. We are sternly ordered to pay no attention to the "old ideas" but when we ask for some evidence of the new and startling ideas that will completely transform our lives, we are met with a contemptuous stare. "Don't be so vulgar! We are still looking for the new ideas. And if we never find them it doesn't' matter, since ideology is only *a false consciousness*!"

'False consciousness'

From a Marxist point of view, insofar as it is possible to speak of "false consciousness" it refers, not to ideology in general, but only to a specific type of ideology that exists in the consciousness of exploited groups and classes and serves to justify and perpetuate their exploitation. The best example of false consciousness is religion, a very powerful influence in the lives of men and women, based on a completely alienated and distorted idea of the relation of humankind with nature. Idealist philosophy is also a form of false consciousness (in fact, all forms of idealism eventually lead back to religion).

The ruling class makes use of this kind of ideology to perpetuate its class rule. In order to combat the reactionary ideology of the ruling class, it is necessary to defend an alternative, revolutionary ideology. Marxism, based on dialectical materialism, is precisely such a revolutionary ideology. But even before Marxism there were advanced thinkers who attempted to fight against the reactionary ideas of the ruling class and defended a revolutionary ideology, such as the great materialist philosophers in pre-revolutionary France, who, with their bold revolutionary ideas, prepared the way for the fall of the Bastille.

The great advantage of using the term "false consciousness" is that it can be used as an insult. In university circles one does not use such vulgar terms as "scoundrel" or "imbecile", which sound too plebeian. But one can always describe someone as having a *false consciousness*, which means approximately that they do not know what is in their own best interest– but you do. That is to say, one can call someone an imbecile without abandoning the strict criteria of good taste.

Dieterich wrongly attributes the expression "false consciousness" to Marx, who never used it. Engels used it only once – in 1893, in a private letter to Mehring. He used the term to explain how he and Marx had not given sufficient emphasis in their writing to the role played by thought in determining social action. In 1920 Lukács introduced the notion of false consciousness as a concept in order to explain *why the working class is not revolutionary*. He defined "false consciousness" in contrast to an "imputed consciousness," a juridical term meaning what people themselves would think if they were to have sufficient information and time to reflect, what they "ought to know," so to speak. In his essay *On Class Consciousness* we read:

"It might look as though [...] we were denying consciousness any decisive role in the process of history. It is true that the conscious reflexes of the different stages of economic growth remain historical facts of great importance; it is true that while dialectical materialism is itself the product of this process, it does not deny that men perform their historical deeds themselves and that they do so consciously. But as Engels emphasizes in a letter to Mehring, this consciousness is false. However, the dialectical method does not permit us simply to proclaim the 'falseness' of this consciousness and to persist in an inflexible confrontation of true and false. On the contrary, it requires us to investigate this 'false consciousness' concretely as an aspect of the historical totality and as a stage in the historical process."

At least Lukács used inverted commas whenever he used the term "false consciousness". We had to wait for the arch-revisionist Herbert Marcuse and the other intellectual snobs of the so-called Frankfurt School to revive "false consciousness". How could one explain the stability of capitalism in the early 1960s? Marcuse did not see the pernicious role of the Social Democratic and Stalinist leaderships of the working class. Instead he blamed the European working class for allegedly being "bourgeoisified" and "Americanized" in books like *One-Dimensional Man.*

These profoundly anti-Marxist ideas expressed the intellectual disorientation and pessimism of the petty bourgeois radicals in European universities at the time. They completely wrote off the working class in Europe and instead looked to "other forces" as a vehicle for the revolution, such as the students (i.e. themselves!), the lumpenproletariat and the peasantry of the Third World. They looked with undisguised contempt at the working class in their own country, with whom they had no contact and about whom they had absolutely no understanding.

These pseudo-revolutionaries were completely divorced from reality – then as now. They lived in a dream world inhabited by phantom revolutionary parties composed of three men and a dog. They passed their days at universities talking endlessly about revolution and engaging in endless debates about this or that obscure theory. As Hegel once said: "From nothing, through nothing, to nothing". That is a very apt description of these student radicals of the 1960s who mostly ended up as the worst kind of bourgeois reactionaries and cynics. The falsity of these ideas was completely exposed by the magnificent revolutionary general strike of May 1968 in France. The working class moved to occupy the factories. Although there were fewer than four million workers in unions, ten million occupied the factories all over France.

The ruling class was taken completely off guard. The "strong man" De Gaulle was demoralized. He told the US ambassador: "all is lost and in a few days the Communists will be in power." This should have been the case, but the Stalinist leaders of the French Communist Party betrayed the movement and the possibility was lost. This is not the place to enter into details about the French general strike. Suffice it to say that all the nonsense about "false consciousness" and the supposedly non-revolutionary character of the working class so assiduously repeated by Marcuse and accepted by people like Ernest Mandel and Heinz Dieterich was exploded by the reality. Despite this, forty years later, Heinz Dieterich repeats the same nonsense – and he has the audacity to attribute it to Marx!

Geniuses in short supply

The main problem facing humanity in the first decade of the 21st century, according to Heinz, is, on the one hand, *intellectual mediocrity*, on the other *the chronic shortage of geniuses*. Having paid tribute to Chávez in a few rhetorical phrases, he can do no less than to say a few nice things about the founders of scientific socialism. He generously pats them on the back, but then laments: "Unfortunately there is no Karl Marx or Friedrich Engels in sight who would have the genius to conceive in hardly three months the critical route to postcapitalist society, as they did in *The Communist Manifesto*, in 1847." Who, then, can help us out of our difficulties, even if he takes a little longer than three months to do it? The reader has to think long and hard before arriving at the answer. In the meanwhile, Heinz continues to lament the chronic shortage of geniuses in the 21st century:

"Neither is there an Albert Einstein, who in the same space of time in 1905 established the foundations of the postnewtonian world, with his papers on quantum theory (March) and on the theory of relativity (June)." [6] And he concludes, with a heavy sigh: "Lacking these extraordinary thinkers, who in a time of record management resolved unknown fundamentals of a virtual reality – the anti-system future – which the rest of the scientists had not even posed, we the mortals, have to lay our hands on the World Spirit, Hegel's famous creature. We are not, of course, speaking of theologized or esoteric phantoms, but of the Collective Spirit of Humanity in its empiric concreteness." [7]

6. Dieterich, *Hugo Chávez y el Socialismo del Siglo XXI*, p. 46.
7. Ibid.

From Marx through Einstein, we now return to the worldview of Hegel. The great German philosopher was undoubtedly a genius, whose works contain many brilliant and profound insights into history. But Hegel's worldview also had a weak side, impregnated with idealism and a mystical view of history. Marx said that in Hegel he found the dialectic upside down. He therefore placed it on its feet. How does our Heinz approach Hegel? He takes the old man firmly by the collar and places him back on his idealist head!

The whole approach of Dieterich to all questions is thoroughly "Hegelian" – in the negative sense of the word. Just as in economics and politics he wants to push us back to the antiquated, pre-Marxian ideas of the utopian socialists, so in philosophy he wants to push us back to the swamp of idealism and mystification. It is the *weak idealist side of Hegel*, and not the rational kernel of his thought, that impresses our Heinz. The Hegelian "World Spirit" is precisely an example of his idealism, his mystification of history. It is precisely this Hegelian esoteric phantom that appeals to the Founder of 21st Century Socialism:

"But how do we use the recourse to the World Spirit in practice? How do we 'lay hands on it'? And what is the functional scientific equivalent of the mystical divine communions of the Catholic prayer and the Eucharist, in this mission of evolving the socialist theory of the 21st Century?" At this point we can only exclaim: Hegel help us! Our Heinz did not require three months, but only a split second to pass from Marx to Einstein, from Einstein to Hegel and from Hegel's World Spirit to the Catholics' prayer and the Eucharist! If there is the smallest atom of logic or coherence in this convoluted reasoning, it would take a genius like the Founder of 21st Century Socialism to discover it! He continues his rapid descent into delirium with the following:

"Marx said that humanity only poses tasks which are in a condition to be solved. This affirmation is correct, because 'hidden' in the conscience or pre-conscience which permits the question, we will find the answer." [8]

Whatever Marx said or did not say, it is very doubtful that we will find the answer to any question in the writings of Heinz Dieterich. Our friend imagines that all history is determined, not by objective factors but by Historical Projects that, it would seem, are "hidden in the conscience or pre-conscience". We will examine comrade Dieterich's theory of history later on. But first we must ask a question. We know what conscience is, but what on earth is "pre-conscience"? If it means anything at all, it must mean an embryonic stage of consciousness, like the mental process of a newborn baby. A baby, as we know, is unable to think coherently and can only express itself in *meaningless babble*, which is all we have here.

As we know, Heinz considers himself to be an expert interpreter, the only problem being that his interpretations are usually wrong, and this is no exception. As usual, he does not present Marx's ideas correctly, but gives us a *Dieterichesque*

8. Ibid., pp. 47 and 46.

interpretation. This is what Marx actually wrote in the well-known passage from the *Preface to the Critique of Political Economy*, which comrade Dieterich paraphrases and in the process *misquotes*:

"In the social production of their existence, men inevitably enter into definite relations, which are independent of their will, namely relations of production appropriate to a given stage in the development of their material forces of production. The totality of these relations of production constitutes the economic structure of society, the real foundation, on which arises a legal and political superstructure and to which correspond definite forms of social consciousness. The mode of production of material life conditions the general process of social, political and intellectual life. It is not the consciousness of men that determines their existence, but their social existence that determines their consciousness. At a certain stage of development, the material productive forces of society come into conflict with the existing relations of production or – this merely expresses the same thing in legal terms – with the property relations within the framework of which they have operated hitherto. From forms of development of the productive forces these relations turn into their fetters. Then begins an era of social revolution. The changes in the economic foundation lead sooner or later to the transformation of the whole immense superstructure.

"In studying such transformations it is always necessary to distinguish between the material transformation of the economic conditions of production, which can be determined with the precision of natural science, and the legal, political, religious, artistic or philosophic – in short, ideological forms in which men become conscious of this conflict and fight it out. Just as one does not judge an individual by what he thinks about himself, so one cannot judge such a period of transformation by its consciousness, but, on the contrary, this consciousness must be explained from the contradictions of material life, from the conflict existing between the social forces of production and the relations of production. No social order is ever destroyed before all the productive forces for which it is sufficient have been developed, and new superior relations of production never replace older ones before the material conditions for their existence have matured within the framework of the old society.

"Mankind thus inevitably sets itself only such tasks as it is able to solve, since closer examination will always show that the problem itself arises only when the material conditions for its solution are already present or at least in the course of formation." [9]

Yes, Marx said that humanity "only poses tasks which are in a condition to be solved", (to use comrade Dieterich's paraphrase). But it was not at all because the answer is "hidden" in the conscience or "pre-conscience" (whatever that might be). It is not a question of consciousness at all but of the level of development of the productive forces, which at a certain stage enters into conflict with the existing legal

9. Marx and Engels, *Selected Works*, Vol.1, *Preface to the Critique of Political Economy*, pp. 503-4.

and social conditions ("the framework of the old society"). Here again Dieterich either misunderstands or distorts Marx and makes him say *exactly the opposite* of what he actually did say.

"The mode of production of material life conditions the general process of social, political and intellectual life. It is not the consciousness of men that determines their existence, but their social existence that determines their consciousness." That is perfectly clear and unambiguous, is it not? Yet Heinz Dieterich manages to turn it completely on its head. Instead of making consciousness depend on the development of the productive forces, he makes what is "hidden in consciousness" the basis of all human history. In other words, he turns Marx into a hopeless idealist.

'Mediocrity'

Heinz refers to the mediocrity of the social sciences and of philosophy in the "countries of historical socialism", which, he informs us, "is intimately linked to the present problem of Cuban transition". In fact, he tells us, "it constitutes, together with the cybernetic problem of Party-state, one of their two deeper roots". [10] So here we have it. The fall of the Soviet Union was due to the *mediocrity of its social sciences and philosophy*. Here the idealist method of Heinz Dieterich stands out in all its crudity. Let us gently correct him on this question by administering a slight dose of materialism: *It was not the mediocrity of the social sciences and of philosophy that caused the bureaucratic degeneration of the USSR but the bureaucratic degeneration that caused the mediocrity of the social sciences and of philosophy in the USSR and the other so-called countries of historical socialism.*

A bureaucratic totalitarian regime is mediocre by its very essence. The essential feature of any bureaucratic machine is routine. The official likes to pursue his work without any interruption, without annoying questions and unwelcome scrutiny by the public – that is to say, by people outside the narrow ranks of the Mandarins. The bureaucrat likes rules and regulations, and insists on seeing them observed to the letter. The world of free thought, broad philosophical generalizations or artistic imagination is completely alien to him.

The living spirit of art, literature and science is the freedom to discuss, to experiment, to make mistakes and to learn from them. The stifling of free discussion imposes severe restrictions on the development of science and is the death of all true art. Insofar as art and science made notable advances in the USSR (which they did) this was thanks to the colossal stimulus that the October Revolution and the nationalized planned economy gave to education and culture in general. But these achievements were made in spite of the bureaucracy, not thanks to it. The same thing can be said of the planned economy in general.

10. Dieterich, *The Alternative of Cuba: Capitalism or New Socialism*, April 12, 2006.

This is true of any bureaucracy, even in the most democratic state. But in a state where the bureaucracy has seized power and constitutes itself a ruling caste, these rules become absolute laws. In Stalin's Russia, the bureaucracy controlled everything and demanded absolute obedience to its rule. The Cult of Stalin, the Great Leader and Teacher,' was only an expression of this. The bureaucracy prostrated itself before the Leader, and in turn they expected the masses to prostrate themselves before the State – that is, the Bureaucracy. The caste of usurpers saw any manifestation of free thought as subversive. Toadyism, cronyism and mind-deadening conformism was the rule. The negative effects of such a regime on art and science are self-evident. No part of cultural or intellectual life escaped the attention of the bureaucrats. In the absence of opposition parties or tendencies, they looked for any traces of critical thought in other fields: philosophy, economics, art, literature, even music. Every aspect of cultural life was policed by inquisitorial bloodhounds like Zhdanov.

When comrade Dieterich complains about mediocre thought in the USSR, he should explain the material basis for this. He does not do so. He cannot do so, because he approaches the whole question not as a Marxist materialist but as an idealist of the most superficial sort. Having failed to explain anything about the bureaucratic degeneration of the Soviet Union, our friend then goes on to claim that this same mediocrity exists also in Cuba, and threatens to undermine the Cuban Revolution. The present writer is not sufficiently well acquainted with Cuban social sciences and philosophy to express an informed opinion as to its merits. But all my dealings with Cuban intellectuals have not given me the impression of mediocrity. Quite the opposite, the impression I have is one of a vibrant intellectual life, a thirst for ideas and a willingness to discuss and debate.

It is true that in the past the colossal intellectual potential of the Cuban intellectuals was limited by all kinds of petty bureaucratic restrictions and censorship. A layer of bureaucratic officials made it their business to stifle debate and discussion and to force Cuba into the straitjacket of Stalinism, on the lines of the USSR. But things have changed a lot lately. At the start of 2007, when one of these old Stalinist censors was interviewed on Cuban television there was a spontaneous reaction with protests of hundreds of Cuban writers, artists and intellectuals who, in the presence of the Minister of Culture, demanded that there be no return to the bad old days. No sign of "mediocrity" there! However, Heinz Dieterich assures us that they are decidedly mediocre, and he should know. What is the reason for this sad state of affairs? Comrade Dieterich informs us that: "The reason for this mediocrity it shares with Latin American philosophy: Both are born of the mystification of the historical truth. They are, in Marx's sense, ideology, that is, objectively false consciousness."[11]

Horror of horrors! It is bad enough to be made aware of the lamentable state of the social sciences and philosophy in Cuba, but it seems that the same horrible sit-

11. Dieterich, *La disyuntiva de Cuba: Capitalismo o nuevo socialismo*.

uation exists throughout the length and breadth of the Latin American continent. We are informed that the entire continent is infected with the same mediocrity, which is apparently born of a "mystification of the historical truth" and ideology, or "objectively false consciousness." Latin American philosophy, he says (with only a few exceptions) "is the daughter of the foundation myth of the Creole elite, which is based on three great historic lies: a) the 'discovery' by the Europeans; b) the homo novo produced by the mestizo-culture; c) the evangelising mission of the Catholic Church."[12]

Which Latin American philosophers is Heinz referring to? We do not know and he makes no attempt to enlighten us on the subject. Since he cites no sources, we are obliged to take his word that the entire content of Latin American philosophy (with only a few exceptions, which unfortunately are also not named) is mediocre, "mystification of the historical truth" and ideology, or "objectively false consciousness." *Dixit Dieterich*! Dieterich has spoken, and we must all accept what he says without question, or else stand accused of mediocrity, mystification, or even more disagreeable things. As we now know, this is quite typical of Dieterich's method: make an unsubstantiated statement (the more outrageous the better), then insult anybody that questions it, then pass on to the next unsubstantiated statement. We do not know whether this is mediocre or not, but it is hardly the best example of scientific rigour one could think of.

Is Latin American thought 'mediocre'?

In Latin America, as in any other part of the world, there have always been two ideologies: the ideology of the ruling class and the ideology of the oppressed masses and the men and women who defended their interests and fought against reaction. The continent has produced many revolutionaries and advanced thinkers, not only Marxists but brilliant revolutionary democrats like Martí, Bolívar, Miranda and others. Were all these thinkers mediocre? Did they stand for a false consciousness? This seems to be the opinion of comrade Dieterich. Unfortunately, we are unable to agree with him. Latin America has produced some very brilliant and original thinkers.

We know little of the earliest thought of the continent. But from what has survived the cultural holocaust, we know that the indigenous cultures, particularly the Aztecs, Mayas, Incas and Tupi-Guarani, produced interesting and sophisticated thought systems long before the arrival of Europeans. Indigenous cosmologies contained many subtleties and complexities and many insights into the phenomena of the natural world.

The Inca ruled the largest empire on Earth until their last emperor, Atahualpa, was murdered by Spanish conquistadors in 1533. The Inca civilisation of the Andes was extremely advanced, but it was long thought to have no writing, other than the

12. Ibid.

elaborate knotted strings known as *khipu*. Archaeologists thought them to be the only major Bronze Age civilisation without a written language. The *khipu* was thought to be only a rough system for remembering accounts. However, Professor Gary Urton, an anthropologist at Harvard University, and a specialist in Pre-Columbian studies questions this view. In his book *Signs of the Inka Khipu* Professor Urton argues the Incas invented a written language disguised in the form of a seven-bit binary code to store information more than 500 years before the invention of the computer.

The Mayans, in addition to their beautiful temples, complex hieroglyphic writing, exquisite jewellery, advanced sculptures, fine pottery and sophisticated works of art, made amazing scientific discoveries, which are just as interesting as those in ancient Egypt. These people had an amazing knowledge of the planets and the solar system. Their mathematics had great precision. The Mayan counting system was ahead of that used in Europe. They used zero and they created a vigesimal system (based on 20) separating the digits in groups of five.

The surviving manuscripts show that the Mayans had calculated the movement of Venus around the sun (584 days). They also calculated the earth year to 365.242 days. This was more accurate than the Gregorian calendar in use in Europe at that time. Unfortunately, not many of these brilliant manuscripts survived. The Spanish Bishop, Diego de Landa consigned all the Mayan manuscripts and works of art that he could find to the flames, because he thought that they contained nothing but suspicion and lies of the devil. What little we have left reveals what the world has lost as a result of the cultural vandalism of the Church.

The destructive activities of the Spaniards soon reduced the once proud peoples of Mesoamerica to an abject condition of servitude and despair. Physical slavery was accompanied by demoralization, disease, depression and alcoholism. But the genocide of the Native Americans did not stop at physical extermination. It also involved an attempt to destroy their art, religion and culture. In order to eradicate all traces of the native culture the Spaniards built Christian churches over the remains of their pyramids and cult centres. We can appreciate the perfect execution of Mexican art from before the conquest, but we can only dimly appreciate the idea that lies behind it. These works of art are more than mere representations: they are religious symbols. These impressive stone images of gods contain an idea. The snake, for example, represented rebirth, through the shedding of its skin: as the crops grow and experience rebirth annually, so does the snake.

But here immediately we find a contradiction. The snake's huge jaws are gaping open, ready to swallow anything in its reach. Within is darkness and destruction – the end of all things. This is a representation of the eternal cycle of death and birth. It is a perfect artistic representation of the unity of opposites, portraying the balance of nature. Life cannot exist without death. In fact we begin to die the moment we are born. This contradiction lies at the heart of the art of Mesoamerica. We see a constant recurrence of opposed pairs: life and death, day and night, death is the sun when it sets, etc. In a primitive and mystified form, here we already find the undeveloped elements of dialectical thought. It is a naïve way of expressing the real contradictions that exist at all levels in nature, thought and society. It is the dawn of genuinely human consciousness, striving to understand the workings of the universe. This striving has not yet freed itself from religion. At this early stage, art, science and religion are really different aspects of one and the same thing.

After the conquistadors had enslaved the Aztecs with fire and sword, the hordes of fanatical priests descended upon them like hungry locusts, greedy for captive souls. Not content with robbing the Native Americans of their lands and wealth, they set about destroying their souls. The agony of this remarkable people is conveyed in the poignant verses of an Aztec poet:

"*Smoke rises, the mist is spreading.*
Weep, my friends and know that by their deeds
We have lost our history."

Philosophy and action

The German poet Goethe wrote: *Am Anfang war die Tat* (in the beginning was the deed). One of the peculiarities of philosophical and social thought in Latin America is that from its earliest beginnings it was linked to action. Whereas in Europe philosophy developed in the tranquil atmosphere of the cloister and the university, in Latin America to a great extent it developed in struggle. The contrast between the "man of thought" and the "man of action", so clearly defined in the European tradition, is radically abolished. The sharpness of social contradictions made such a clear distinction all but impossible.

Academic philosophy began in the 16th century when the Catholic Church began to establish schools, monasteries, convents and seminaries in Latin America. As early as the 16th century Latin America produced remarkable and original thinkers. One of them was the Dominican friar Bartolomé de las Casas. Although he was born in Seville, he became famous for his work in the New World. He was both an original thinker, with ideas far in advance of his age, and an early progressive who defended the rights of native and African peoples and their culture. The enlightened ideas of this great man immediately stepped outside the stillness of the cloister and entered the world of society and politics.

It is true that from the 17th century onwards, philosophy and academic thought in general was used to maintain the status quo. Scholasticism was the dominant trend and the main task of official "science" consisted in justifying and protecting the Catholic faith against Protestantism and science. However, even at that time, there were several remarkable philosophical figures, such as Antonio Rubio, whose studies on logic are remarkably advanced for his day. And what do we say about

Juana Inés de la Cruz? Despite all the problems faced by women at that time, she was not only a fine poet but she had a brilliant philosophical mind and may, with justice, be considered one of the earliest feminist thinkers in America.

In the middle of the 18th century the fresh winds blowing from pre-Revolutionary France, where the Enlightenment was in full swing, reinvigorated thought in Latin America. This had an influence inside the Church in Latin America, where ever since De las Casas, there was always a progressive trend, as well as a reactionary one. A generation of Jesuits tried to break with the thought of Aristotle in order to modernize it, but the expulsion of the Jesuits in 1767 cut across this, and set back the development of philosophy in Latin America.

The 19th century was dominated by the "men of action" – the Liberators. The explanation is quite clear. What was on the order of the day was the liberation of the peoples of Latin America and the Caribbean from the yoke of foreign rule. This could only be achieved by revolutionary means – through revolutionary war. Brazil was the only Latin American country whose independence was acquired without war. There were outstanding figures like José de San Martín, José Miguel Carrera, Antonio José de Sucre, Bernardo O'Higgins and José Gervasio Artigas. They were mainly drawn from the ranks of the *criollo* bourgeoisie (local-born people of European ancestry, typically with Spanish or Portuguese ancestors). In every case they were influenced by liberalism and advanced political and philosophical ideas from Europe.

A revolutionary war differs from an ordinary war because it is inseparable from ideas. In order that the oppressed should free themselves from slavery, they must be aroused by a great idea. A revolution without a revolutionary ideology is a contradiction in terms. The Liberators were men of action, not university eunuchs, but they were all inspired by an idea. That idea came directly from the revolutionary ideals of the French Revolution: Liberty, Equality, Fraternity. The Venezuelan revolutionary Francisco de Miranda (1750-1816), regarded as a forerunner of Simón Bolívar, conceived a visionary plan for the liberation and unification of all of Spanish America.

Simón Bolívar, "El Libertador", (the Liberator) was a talented general but also a politician, revolutionary and a visionary man of ideas. Simón Rodríguez, Bolívar's tutor and mentor, was a philosopher and educator. Rodríguez lived in Italy, Germany, Prussia, Poland and Russia. He would later say of this time: "I stayed in Europe for more than twenty years; I worked in an Industrial Chemistry Laboratory [...] attended some secret socialist-oriented meetings [...] studied a little literature; learned languages and directed a Reading and Writing School in a small Russian town".

Conducting revolutionary activity a few decades later, Ezequiel Zamora, the leader of the Federal War (a national peasant uprising in the 1840s and 50s), was well aware of the ideas of utopian socialism, which had been brought to Venezuela by exiles of the 1848 revolutions in Europe. Under the slogan of "Tierra y hombres libres, horror a la oligarquía" (Free land and men, terror to the oligarchy), he led the peasant masses inspired by the ideal of social equality. His vision was one of a world in which 'there will be neither rich nor poor, neither slaves nor masters, neither powerful nor disdained, but just brothers who without bowing their heads will treat each other as equals'. This was a primitive form of socialism, which could not go beyond its limits in the agrarian Venezuela of the mid 19th century. However, Zamora's vision of a peasant revolution continue to inspire today the Venezuelan peasants in their struggle against the oligarchy, the same oligarchy that betrayed Zamora, killed him treacherously and buried his ideals in the Treaty of Coche.

The Cuban Jose Martí was not just a revolutionary fighter but a thinker, writer and poet. In many literary circles he is considered the Father of Modernismo, predating and influencing other poets such as Rubén Darío and Gabriela Mistral. Some of his "Versos sencillos" seem to contain a premonition of his death:

Que no me entierren en lo oscuro
A morir como un traidor
Yo soy bueno y como bueno
Moriré de cara al sol

May they not bury me in darkness
To die like a traitor
I am good, and as a good man
I will die facing the sun

Considering these great Latin American revolutionaries it is impossible to separate their actions from their ideology, which was that of the bourgeois-democratic revolution. Here we have the revolutionary unity of thought and action. It is possible to say that in most cases, their actions were far in advance of their ideas and that the former had more permanent results than the latter. But nobody can say that they were mediocre.

Simon Bolívar and his contemporaries were great revolutionaries and they stood for the most advanced ideology of the period in which they lived: the period of the bourgeois-democratic revolution. But the epoch in which we now live is the epoch of the proletarian revolution – the epoch of socialism. One would look in vain in the writings of the early Liberators for such an ideology, because its time had not yet come. At most one can find some influence of the early socialist utopians, that is to say, socialist ideas in an undeveloped and embryonic form. The ideology of socialism was born after most of the Liberators had passed away. But as soon as it emerged, Marxism found a fertile ground in Latin America because it accurately describes the reality of the continent. From the beginning Marxist philosophy has always had a big influence in Latin America, reflecting the revolutionary aspirations of the masses and the revolutionary youth and intelligentsia.

The Peruvian José Carlos Mariátegui was an original Latin American Marxist thinker internationally respected for his profound grasp of the ideas and philosophy of Marxism. He was the first one to attempt a Marxist analysis of Peruvian society. He mistakenly thought that the Inca Ayllú (the common property of the land in the village) was primitive communism. In reality, above the Ayllú stood a state apparatus similar to the formations of the Asiatic Mode of Production. However, his idea that the Ayllú could serve as a basis for socialism in the countryside, provided that the workers took power in the cities, is strikingly similar to the comments made by Marx to Zasulich regarding the Russian Mir. He was not only a profound thinker, but also a revolutionary man of action, founding the Peruvian Socialist Party (which joined the Communist International), the first trade union federation and the first peasant's federation of Peru.

Other revolutionary thinkers and activists from the same generation (before the Stalinist degeneration of the Latin American Communist Parties) include Julio Antonio Mella (founder of the Cuban Communist Party and defender of the theory of permanent revolution in Latin America), Farabundo Martí (founder of the Central American Communist Party and the Communist Party of El Salvador, shot dead for his part in the revolutionary uprising of 1932 in this country), and Luís Emilio Recabarren (founder of the Chilean Socialist Workers' Party which then joined the Communist International), amongst others.

Last, but by no means least, we have the Cuban revolutionary Fidel Castro and the Argentinean Ernesto "Che" Guevara. Did they make no contribution? Che Guevara, in particular, showed a keen interest in Marxist theory and developed a criticism of the bureaucratic Soviet model while Heinz Dieterich was still a fervent admirer of "really existing socialism". Were these thinkers all "mediocre", as our Heinz suggests? We may disagree with some of their ideas, but on no account would we describe them as mediocre. That is an epithet that some might say could be applied with far greater justification to the writings of Heinz Dieterich himself.

Heinz Dieterich and the universe

Heinz likes to think of himself as a scientist and he frequently provides us with scientific examples and analogies drawn from an impressively wide field: physics, cosmology, biology, genetics, etc. This creates a most favourable impression and immediately reassures us that we are in the presence of a most erudite person. As usual, he uses a most complicated and difficult terminology, which deepens still further our sense of awe and respect. This lowers our guard and nullifies our critical faculties. For who are we to argue with such an Authority?

In one of his books (*Identidad nacional y globalización. La tercera vía. Crisis en las ciencias sociales*), he affirms gravely that it is impossible for anybody to express any opinion on any subject whatsoever unless he has understood that we live in a cylindrical universe. This implacable affirmation eliminates at a single stroke at least 99.9 percent of humanity from the discussion of 21st Century Socialism – or anything else.

Heinz bases himself on a very respectable authority – Albert Einstein and his Theory of Relativity. This brings to mind the following story. Someone once pointed out to the celebrated English scientist Eddington that it was said that there were only three people in the world who understood Einstein, to which he replied: "Really? And who is the other one?" Now we all know that it was Heinz Dieterich, who, it seems, is able to write on everything under the sun – and a few things besides. The intention is to impress the reader with a breadth of knowledge unequalled since Leonardo Da Vinci. But this initial impression is somewhat spoiled by a closer examination, which reveals some less than perfect formulations. This leads us to suspect that our Heinz's acquaintance with physics, mathematics, cosmology and biology is perhaps not always as impressive as he would have us believe. For instance, on page 32 of *El socialismo del siglo XXI* he writes:

"1) The universe has only *two modes of existence:* as substance (matter) and as energy."

Dieterich thinks that matter and energy are two different things. This is wrong. Einstein's theory of special relativity states that *energy and mass are in reality equivalents*. This is a striking confirmation of the fundamental philosophical postulate of dialectical materialism – the inseparable character of matter and energy the idea that motion ("energy") is the mode of existence of matter. Matter and energy are not just "interchangeable", as dollars are interchangeable with euros; they are one and the same substance, which Einstein characterized as "mass-energy". This idea goes far deeper and is more precise than the old mechanical concept whereby, for example, friction is transformed into heat. Here, matter is just a particular form of "frozen" energy, while every other form of energy (including light), has mass associated with it. For this reason, it is quite wrong to say that matter "disappears" when it is changed into energy.

Einstein's discovery of the law of equivalence of mass and energy is expressed in his famous equation $E=mc^2$, which expresses the colossal energies locked up in the atom. This is the source of all the concentrated energy in the universe. The symbol E represents energy (in ergs), m stands for mass (in grams) and c is the speed of light (in centimetres per second). To give a concrete example of what this means, the energy contained in a single gram of matter is equivalent to the energy produced by burning 2,000 tons of petrol.

Heinz's acquaintance with Albert Einstein is clearly not as intimate as he would have us believe. This is confirmed, as we have seen, by his reference to the "cylindrical universe" which, he assures us, is the cornerstone of all human knowledge. In the Bible Jesus informs us that unless we have faith and become as little children we shall never enter the Kingdom of God. And Heinz Dieterich informs us that unless we believe in the Cylindrical Universe we shall never gain admittance to the realm of 21st Century Socialism.

Heinz claims to base himself on Einstein's equations. He assumes that only one kind of universe can be deduced from Einstein's equations. But as a matter of fact, a number of different universes are allowed by Einstein's equations, not one as our Heinz imagines. Einstein's initial idea was that the universe was spatially spherical ("the surface of a 4D hypersphere") and unchanging over time – leading to a cylindrical universe in space-time. However, the solution of Einstein's equations depends on unknowns such as the average density of the universe. All are based on the assumption that the universe is homogeneous and isotropic. Depending on your assumptions (whether there was or was not a Big Bang, and whether there is or is not such a thing as dark matter, etc.) you can get many different answers.

According to Einstein, the real universe can have one of three different types of evolution, depending on its average density and the strength of the universal repulsion that Einstein hypothesized (the cosmological constant). According to this view, it can expand from a point of singularity and contract back to it; it can expand indefinitely from a point; or it can contract from infinite size to a minimum diameter and re-expand. Three different shapes in space are also allowed. The local density of the universe determines the local curvature of space-time. Supposing that the universe is homogeneous and isotropic (which is supposing a lot) it would be theoretically possible to deduce the global geometry of the universe, which could be closed like a sphere, flat like a plane or open, depending on the average density.

However, all this has a highly speculative and theoretical character. Contrary to what Heinz Dieterich thinks, the equations of Einstein on their own tell us nothing about the topology (or the global geometry) of the universe, a question about which there exists no consensus among scientists. Later theorists have come up with different shapes, so there is no one shape that could be said to be the prevailing view. This book is not the place to explain the philosophical attitude of Marxists to the latest theories of cosmology. I have attempted to do this in *Reason in Revolt*. What is clear is that complex questions like the topology of the universe, its past and future, remain highly controversial and have not yet been settled by current cosmology.

But all this is a matter of supreme indifference to our Heinz. He wants a cylindrical universe and he is determined he shall have one. And if anyone dares to disagree with him, he is automatically prohibited from expressing an opinion, not just on the shape of the universe, but on any other subject whatsoever. In Britain there is a Flat Earth Society, composed of harmless eccentrics who are convinced that the earth is flat. We invite Heinz Dieterich to form a Society of Cylindrical Universalists. It is sure to have at least one member.

Is materialism irrelevant?

In another part of his book *Identidad nacional y globalización. La tercera vía. Crisis en las ciencias sociales*, Heinz Dieterich tells us in so many words that the "old philosophy" (though not, of course, his philosophy of praxis) is as dead as the dodo:

"The discussions on idealism and realism or materialism more and more acquire the character of academic extravagances, before the evidences elaborated by science: before the wonderful discovery of the Big Bang about the origin of the macrocosm, made up of visible and invisible matter (dark matter), crossed by gravitation waves (Einstein), with 'stellar, constant times' of expansion (Hubble) and black holes; the microcosmic deciphering of the plans of construction of biological systems, written in the chemical language of four characters (A, T, C, G) of DNA; the logic of the chaotic behaviour of the individual gas molecule that nevertheless coexists perfectly well with the macroscopic laws of perfect gases; the logic of the behaviour of human social systems that resembles the quantum logic of the behaviour of microcosmic phenomena to a great extent; the cylindrical form of the universe and the interaction between space-time-gravitation discovered by Einstein; the visibility of an atom under the electron microscope and the observation by means of techniques of crystallography of an AIDS virus attacking a cell of the human organism; the imagenology [imagenología ?!] of mental processes and the passage of qualitative or conceptual analyses of mental states, like joy, anger, humour, depression, etc.; towards quantitative biochemical analysis (and remedies); the calculation of time by means of clocks that register, the cesium atoms that vibrate 9.2 billion times per second; in short, before the accumulation of that objective knowledge of reality, the insistence of the old discussions of the philosophers only can seem nonsense." [13]

Here Dieterich's break with Marxism is clearly exposed. He considers the "old" discussions on idealism and realism or materialism to be mere "academic extravagances" and even "nonsense". Thus, with a single stroke of the pen, our Heinz imagines he has liquidated over a thousand years of philosophy, and, in passing, *he has also "liquidated" Marxism,* which is based on the philosophy of dialectical materialism, and therefore incompatible with idealism of any kind. In the last analysis the refusal to defend materialism against idealism represents *a surrender to bourgeois ideology*. And there is absolutely no doubt that Heinz Dieterich has gone down that road.

In one of his last major works, *On the Significance of Militant Materialism* (1922) Lenin sharply criticised those who "retreated in quest of fashionable reactionary philosophical doctrines, captivated by the tinsel of the so-called last word in European science, and unable to discern beneath this tinsel some variety of servility to the bourgeoisie, to bourgeois prejudice and bourgeois reaction." [14]

In the same article Lenin writes: "For our attitude towards this phenomenon to be a politically conscious one, it must be realised that no natural science and no materialism can hold its own in the struggle against the onslaught of bourgeois ideas

13. Heinz Dieterich, *Identidad nacional y globalización. La tercera vía. Crisis en las ciencias sociales*; Editorial Nuestro Tiempo; México, 2000; pp 63-64.
14. Lenin, *Collected Works*, vol. 33, p. 228.

and the restoration of the bourgeois world outlook unless it stands on solid philosophical ground. In order to hold his own in this struggle and carry it to a victorious finish, the natural scientist must be a modern materialist, a conscious adherent of the materialism represented by Marx, i.e., he must be a dialectical materialist." [15]

We believe that Lenin was right and comrade Dieterich is wrong on the question of philosophy. It is true that the astonishing advances of science have resolved in practice many of the questions that occupied the minds of philosophers in the past (let us recall that Isaac Newton, the greatest scientist of the 18th century, described himself as a philosopher). The old speculations about the nature of the universe have been largely settled by the results of observation and experiment. Therefore, according to comrade Dieterich, the discussion between materialism and idealism is no longer relevant.

Is this correct? No, it is not correct. It is true that science and technology have developed to an unheard of extent in the last two hundred years. But under capitalism the real potential of science cannot be realised. The advances of science and technology are entirely subordinated to the greed for profit. The interests of the big transnational companies prevail over the needs of humanity and science. Scientists are made to serve the interests of gigantic military machines producing weapons of mass destruction instead of new medicines and technology that would benefit humanity.

In the period of the senile decay of capitalism we are witnessing a resurgence of primitive ideas, superstition, religious fanaticism (fundamentalism), mysticism and obscurantism. These reactionary philosophies have even penetrated the world of science. Geneticists in the USA have used and abused science to justify inequality, racism and gender discrimination. Some physicists have tried to use developments like quantum physics to defend idealistic, mystical and reactionary views.

Faced with such phenomena, should Marxists merely shrug their shoulders and adopt the position of philosophical neutrality that comrade Dieterich advocates? At a time when the ruling class is organizing a ferocious onslaught against Marxism and materialism, and when idealism and mysticism are spreading like a poisonous epidemic, is it legitimate to advocate a philosophical truce, on the grounds that "the discussions on idealism and realism or materialism are academic extravagances"? Isn't this *frivolous and irresponsible* in the extreme?

Science and philosophy

It goes without saying that the advances of science are of paramount importance. But it is by no means the case that science can dispense altogether with philosophy. Hegel pointed out long ago: "It is in fact, the wish for rational insight, not the ambition to amass a mere heap of acquisitions that should be presupposed in every case

15. Ibid., p. 233.

as possessing the mind of the learner in the study of science."[16] Hegel knew what he was talking about. Scientists study facts, but the facts do not select themselves. One must make hypotheses, and it is not a matter of indifference how these hypotheses are arrived at and by what method.

Science cannot separate itself from society, and scientists can be influenced by incorrect political and philosophical ideas. Let us take just one example from the science of palaeontology and the study of human origins. For about a century the study of human origins was completely undermined by the prevailing idealist philosophy. Following the idealist notion that the brain determines everything, it was assumed that our earliest ancestors would necessarily have a big brain. The search for the "missing link" therefore reduced itself to the search for a humanoid fossil that would display this trait.

So convinced were the anthropologists of this that they allowed themselves to be deceived by the so-called Piltdown Man, which was later exposed as a crude forgery, in which the cranium of a human was combined with the jaw bone of an ape. In fact, by basing itself on idealism, science had been following the wrong track for a hundred years. The exact opposite was the case. The brains of the earliest anthropoid apes were the same size as the brain of a chimpanzee. Frederick Engels already predicted this over a hundred years ago in his remarkable work, *The Part Played by Labour in the Transition from Ape to Man*. He explained that the earliest ancestors of man first separated themselves from the other apes by the upright posture, which freed the hands for labour. This was the precondition for the development of humankind. But the real qualitative leap was the production of stone tools. This was responsible for the development of society, language and culture that decisively sets us apart from all other animals. The late Stephen Jay Gould pointed out that if the scientists had paid attention to what Engels had written, they would have saved themselves a hundred years of error.

What was the problem here? It was a philosophical problem: most scientists were following the prevailing notions of philosophical idealism and therefore they formulated an incorrect hypothesis. There have been many similar cases in the history of science, and this still continues to be the case, as we shall see when we come to examine the Big Bang theory. Lenin commented on the relevance of dialectical materialism to science thus: "Modern natural scientists (if they know how to seek, and if we learn to help them) will find in the Hegelian dialectics, materialistically interpreted, a series of answers to the philosophical problems which are being raised by the revolution in natural science and which make the intellectual admirers of bourgeois fashion "stumble" into reaction.

"Unless it sets itself such a task and systematically fulfils it, materialism cannot be militant materialism. It will be not so much the fighter as the fought, to use an expression of Shchedrin's. Without this, eminent natural scientists will as often as

16. Hegel, *Philosophy of History*, III., Philosophic History § 13.

hitherto be helpless in making their philosophical deductions and generalizations. For natural science is progressing so fast and is undergoing such a profound revolutionary upheaval in all spheres that it cannot possibly dispense with philosophical deductions." [17]

It is surprising that of all the marvellous discoveries of modern science he might have cited, Dieterich chooses the one area where there has been the greatest controversy and where the most mystical and idealist speculation predominates. We refer to the so-called Big Bang theory of the origin of the universe. Needless to say, Heinz Dieterich is a firm adherent of this theory:

"With the paradigm of the Big Bang that explains and dates the existence of the universe in the region of 16 billion years [...] with this set of knowledge, the insistence on the priority of the idea in the behaviour of the universe – or as a quality ontologically separated [sic!] from the substance is simply infantile. In scientific terms, God is a placebo, produced by the existential anguish of the human being and in no way different from other forms of autosuggestion and mental projection of homo sapiens. That this placebo has become good business for the theological bureaucracies who live on it or, also, for many philosophers who live on mysticism, does not change the situation at all." [18]

The Big Bang theory is a model that is said to answer many questions about the universe. But we must bear in mind that it remains a hypothesis, and that it certainly does not answer *all* the questions, as Dieterich imagines. Indeed, as time goes on, ever more questions and discrepancies appear. There is plenty of evidence against the Big Bang. The big bang is supposed to produce energy on a vast scale out of nothing. This contradicts one of the best-tested laws of physics: the conservation of energy. To throw away this basic conservation law in order to preserve the Big Bang theory is something that would never be acceptable in any other field of physics. Yet it is uncritically accepted here.

First of all, let us note that it is not correct to refer to "the big bang theory". There have been at least five different theories, each of which has run into trouble. Lemaître, Gamow, Robert Dicke and others, have all tried to rationalize this theory, but it remains an unproven hypothesis that is open to serious objections. Most of the work done to support it is of a purely theoretical character, leaning heavily on mathematical formulae. The empirical evidence in support of the big bang theory remains quite tenuous. The numerous contradictions between the preconceived big bang schema and the observable evidence have been covered up by constantly moving the goal posts in order to preserve the theory.

The big bang theory relies on a growing number of hypothetical entities: things that we have never observed. The theory cannot survive without assuming all kinds of things such as the inflation field, dark matter and dark energy. Without them,

17. Lenin, *Collected Works*, vol. 33, p. 234.

18. Heinz Dieterich, *Identidad nacional. La tercera vía. Crisis en las ciencias sociales*, pp. 64-65.

there would be fatal contradictions between the observations made by astronomers and the predictions of the big bang theory. In no other field of physics would this continual recourse to new hypothetical objects be accepted as a way of bridging the gap between theory and observation. It would, at the least, raise serious questions about the validity of the underlying theory. But Dieterich has no doubts whatsoever and asks no questions.

Despite his fervent admiration for the Big Bang, he cannot even express the theory correctly. According to the latest version of the theory (known as inflation theory), there can be nothing in the universe older than 14 billion years – not 16 billion as our Heinz affirms. But there is evidence that contradicts this proposition. In 1986, Brent Tully of Hawaii University discovered huge agglomerations of galaxies (superclusters) about a billion light years long, three hundred million light years wide and one hundred million light-years thick. In order for such vast objects to form, it would have taken between eighty and a hundred billion years, that is to say four or five times longer than what would be allowed by the big bangers. Since then there have been other results that tend to confirm these observations.

The history of science shows that even such an apparently secure and all-embracing theory as Newtonian classical mechanics, which was universally accepted as the last word by scientists for a very long time, was eventually shown to be incomplete and one-sided. At a certain stage small discrepancies emerge that cannot be explained. These are initially dismissed as trivial or irrelevant, but eventually lead to the overthrow of the established theory and its replacement by a revolutionary new theory, which remains in force until in turn new discrepancies emerge, and so on.

There is no reason at all to suppose that the present situation in cosmology and theoretical physics will be any different. Especially if we bear in mind that the study of the universe involves a tremendous number of unknown factors. We are basing ourselves of necessity on partial observations of the visible universe, and many errors may creep in as a result of lack of information. To some extent this can be made up for by resorting to abstract mathematical models and the results provided by particle physics, etc. But in the last analysis these results must be checked by experiment and observation. They cannot serve as a substitute for the latter.

There have been many theories in the past that were accepted unquestioningly by scientists because they appeared to explain things, but turned out to be false – for example *phlogiston* and *ether*. There is a striking comparison between these theories and the idea of dark matter which has been posited by the supporters of the big bang theory *in order to explain away the fact that there is simply not enough matter in the visible universe to fit in with the theory*. Naturally, our Heinz accepts this idea without question. He refers to "*the wonderful discovery of the Big Bang about the origin of the macrocosm, made up of visible and invisible matter (dark matter)*". Unfortunately for him, after many years of attempting to discover this dark matter, they have failed to do so. The only dark matter that exits is to be found in the brain of Heinz Dieterich, where it serves as the source of thoughts far more obscure than anything known to science or even to science fiction.

Marx, Engels and science

"It was indeed the rejection of Marx and Engels of the application of Newtonian determinism – that is suitable for the description and explanation of mechanical motion, which is the simplest of all changes, but not for explaining a complex dynamic system (SDC) like society, which allowed them to develop a political-scientific perspective *sui generis*, which was the only one possible to obtain their extraordinary striving after a New Historical Project of the majorities of their time." [19]

Marx and Engels warmly welcomed all the advances of science in their day, but they did not adopt the uncritical attitude of Heinz Dieterich. The dominant theories of physics in the 19th century were those of mechanism, and were heavily influenced by the ideas worked out in the 18th century by Sir Isaac Newton. Marx and Engels (following Hegel), were extremely critical of this mechanical approach to the workings of the universe. Unlike our Heinz who takes as good coin the Big Bang and all the other bits and pieces he has taken over from modern science and vulgarised, the founders of scientific socialism were prepared to reject some of the prevalent views of the science of their day, and many years later, they were shown to have been correct.

In the correspondence of Marx and Engels we find frequent criticisms of Newton's mechanistic method. Emphasizing the dynamic nature of modern materialism Engels wrote: "...the motion of matter is not merely crude mechanical motion, mere change of place, it is heat and light, electric and magnetic tension, chemical combination and dissociation, life and, finally, consciousness." Engels sharply criticized the limited nature of Newton's philosophical views, his one-sided over-estimation of the method of induction and his negative attitude to hypotheses, expressed by him in the well-known words "*Hypotheses non fingo*" ("I do not invent hypotheses"). He referred to him as "the inductive ass Newton". [20]

In the preparatory writings on *The Dialectics of Nature* we read the following: "Newtonian attraction and centrifugal force – an example of metaphysical thinking: the problem not solved but *only posed,* and this preached as the solution." And immediately afterwards: "*Newtonian gravitation.* The best that can be said of it is that it does not explain but *pictures* the present state of planetary motion. The motion is given. Ditto the force of attraction of the sun. With these data, how is the motion to be explained? By the parallelogram of forces, by a tangential force which

19. Ibid., pp. 58-59.
20. Engels, *The Dialectics of Nature*, Natural Science and Philosophy, in Marx and Engels, *Collected Works*, Vol. 25, p. 486.

now becomes a necessary postulate that we *must* accept. That is to say, assuming the *eternal character* of the existing state, we need a *first impulse*, God. But neither is the existing planetary state eternal nor is the motion originally compound, but *simple rotation*, and the parallelogram of forces applied here is wrong, because it did not merely make evident the unknown magnitude, the *x*, that had still to be found, that is to say in so far as Newton claimed not merely to put the question but to solve it."[21]

These lines prove conclusively that Marx and Engels did not merely regurgitate the commonly held views of 19th century science, but had a critical and independent standpoint. Long before the revolution in physics brought about in the early years of the 20th century by the discoveries of quantum physics and relativity, they had decisively rejected the prevalent ideas of mechanism from the standpoint of dialectical materialism. In many ways they were in advance of the scientists of their day.

A good example of this is the important field of evolution. Marx and Engels greatly admired the work of Charles Darwin, and Marx even wanted to dedicate *Capital* to the great English scientist. But even with regard to Darwin, they did not adopt an uncritical attitude. In particular they were critical of Darwin's gradualism, which rules out the possibility of leaps in nature. Darwin viewed evolution as a slow, gradual process, uninterrupted by sudden changes. In fact, he regarded nature in the same way that Heinz Dieterich regards society.

The remarkable American scientist Stephen Jay Gould challenged the gradualist theory of Darwin. In the field of palaeontology Stephen Gould's revolutionary theory of punctuated equilibria – now generally accepted as correct – has completely overthrown the old view of evolution as a slow, gradual process, uninterrupted by sudden catastrophes and leaps. Gould was influenced by the ideas of Marxism, and in particular by Engels' masterpiece *The Part Played by Labour in the Transition from Ape to Man*, which he warmly praised. In his book *Ever Since Darwin*, he refers to Engels' essay:

"Indeed, the 19th century produced a brilliant exposé from a source that will no doubt surprise most readers – Frederick Engels. (A bit of reflection should diminish surprise. Engels had a keen interest in the natural sciences and sought to base his general philosophy of dialectical materialism upon a 'positive' foundation. He did not live to complete his 'dialectics of nature', but he included long commentaries on science in such treatises as the *Anti-Dühring*.) In 1876, Engels wrote an essay entitled, *The Part Played by Labour in the Transition from Ape to Man*. It was published posthumously in 1896 and, unfortunately, had no visible impact upon Western science.

"Engels considers three essential features of human evolution: speech, a large brain, and upright posture. He argues that the first step must have been a descent

21. Engels, *The Dialectics of Nature*, Mechanics and Astronomy, in Marx and Engels, *Collected Works*, Vol. 25, p. 551.

from the trees with subsequent evolution to upright posture by our ground-dwelling ancestors. 'These apes when moving on level ground began to drop the habit of using their hands and to adopt a more and more erect gait. This was the decisive step in the transition from ape to man.' Upright posture freed the hand for using tools (labour, in Engels' terminology); increased intelligence and speech came later."

Gould understood the limitations of Western thought when he wrote that a "deeply rooted bias of Western thought predisposes us to look for continuity and gradual change." He pays warm tribute to Engels for anticipating the discoveries that were to transform the face of palaeontology and evolution a century after his death. Engels was able to make this breakthrough because he based himself on the method of dialectics. This is not new but rather old. It is older than Marx and Engels, and older than Hegel. It is as old as Heraclitus – and that is pretty old. Yet it is far more contemporary than the so-called philosophy of praxis that, in practice, turns out to explain nothing and anticipate nothing.

Dieterich versus Marx

Dieterich's now turns his attention to the founders of scientific socialism. In *Identidad nacional y globalización. La tercera via. Crisis en las ciencias sociales* he presents us with a scheme, which, in his habitual scholastic manner, occupies a complete page. It compares the scientific revolution of Einstein, Planck, Heisenberg, and Gell-Mann with respect to Newton to his own "Theoretical Socialism of the 21st Century" with respect to Marx. The only good thing about this is that it represents a clear admission on Dieterich's part that *his theory is quite different from Marxism both in form and in content.* Here at last is something on which we find ourselves in complete agreement with him!

"In the first place, it is necessary to distinguish between limited statements of regional and temporary scope (decimonónicos), and universal statements. In addition to that evaluation in space and time it is necessary to take into account, secondly, that new objective realities exist that either did not exist in the days of Marx and Engels or were relatively unimportant (e.g. ecology), and that, therefore, must be integrated into the New Historical Project of the majorities. Thirdly, the advance of the sciences and their epistemology allows us to determine the correct methodology of the analysis of Marx and Engels, without violating the structural elements of the procedures of the most advanced contemporary science and not from the scientific interpretations of the reality of the 19th century that Marx and Engels had at their disposal. Fourthly, it is necessary to develop a new discourse ('un nuevo discurso'), not only as far as content is concerned, but with respect to its forms. Finally, it will be necessary to integrate the arts, aesthetics, et cetera in the transforming of the New Historical Project of the majorities of the 21st Century." [22]

22. Dieterich, *Identidad nacional y globalización. La tercera via. Crisis en las ciencias sociales,*

Comrade Dieterich believes that Marx and Engels were "striving after a New Historical Project of the majorities of their time." That is to say, they were attempting to do *exactly the same as Heinz Dieterich.* The difference is that their NHP was only fit for "the majorities of their time." but not, of course, for the 21st century. In other words, their ideas are old fashioned, antiquated, and out of date. And in any case, they were only "*striving after* a New Historical Project", whereas our Heinz has *actually found one*. Naturally, the NHP and Socialism of the 21st Century is immeasurably superior to *The Communist Manifesto*, *Capital* and all that old stuff.

The word "decimonónico" in Spanish has two possible meanings: pertaining to the 19th century or *antiquated.* We have no doubt that Heinz Dieterich regards the ideas of Marx and Engels as pertaining to the 19th century *and therefore antiquated.* By contrast, Heinz Dieterich is not antiquated at all, but very modern. He has not only invented an entirely new and original 21st Century Socialism, but also an entirely new and original 21st Century Language. He claims that Marx and Engels also "developed a new discourse" – "discourse" being one of the fashionable words beloved by the postmodernists who have caused such a profound impression on our Heinz. But the "discourse" of Marx and Engels was not new at all: it was good, plain, old-fashioned German that any person of average intelligence could read and understand.

On the other hand, the "new discourse" of the Founder of 21st Century Socialism is so convoluted that nobody can understand it, except Heinz Dieterich himself – and even that is doubtful. It is to be hoped that eventually every citizen of 21st Century Socialism will be happily conversing with each other with this new and universal discourse. They will discuss in depth not just the Economy of Equivalence but Art and Aesthetics and many other interesting matters. Moreover, they will do all this without "violating the structural elements of the procedures of the most advanced contemporary science" and will carefully avoid making any *limited statements of regional and temporary scope.* In short, everything will be for the best in the best of all possible 21st Century worlds.

Science or pedantry?

On page 65 of the same work we read: "Related to this problem of the abolition or trivialization of the great questions of philosophy, this problem of the complexity of the great paradigms of the natural sciences that makes their adequate philosophical interpretation practically impossible for people who do not have a deep and solid formation in the physical-mathematical sciences and, increasingly, of molecular biology. It is obvious that to be able to infer on [sic] the not strictly scientific implications of knowledge such as the cylindrical form of the universe, the concept of space-time, the curvature of space-time by fields of gravitation, et cetera, one has first to dominate the respective scientific disciplines."

Translated into plain language this means: modern science is very complicated and difficult for ordinary people to understand. It is even more difficult to understand when it is expressed in the new language of the 21st Century. What other pearls of wisdom do we have here? We are informed that in order to understand science it helps to have studied it first, which is also true of many other human activities, such as cookery, carpentry, flower arranging and dancing salsa. At the moment we are attempting to study the most difficult subject of all, namely the mental meanderings of Heinz Dieterich. This has already taken us through the curvature of space-time by fields of gravitation to the very edge of the cylindrical universe, and beyond it, where we shall doubtless find the same inscription they wrote on the old maps of the world: "here be Monsters." But we shall bravely tread where no man has gone before. Forward march!

"Only on the base of a solid knowledge of this type is it possible to try to transpose the logics [sic], concepts and interpretative methods used, as it were, in theoretical physics, to other fields of investigation like, for example, the sciences of society. Not to dominate the complex physical-mathematical paradigms and to give, nevertheless, lessons and lectures on its implicit meaning for politics, aesthetics [and] ethics, means simply, to want to take the second step before taking the first; a procedure that can only finish in the quackery of nebulous speech, senseless analogies and a pretence of precision, where the pseudo-knowledge reigns." [23]

Without intending it, comrade Dieterich has here given a very precise characterization of his own work. But let us deal with his central proposition, which is this: that in order to express an idea about society, economics and politics, it is first necessary to have a complete domination of mathematics, physics and molecular biology. Now, we would be the last ones to deny that such knowledge would be extremely useful. The problem, which has just been so emphatically stated by our friend, is that every one of these important spheres of knowledge is highly complex. In order to completely dominate even one of them would involve a lifetime of work and study. To dominate all three would require the kind of genius that only comrade Dieterich claims to possess. As a matter of fact, it would be too much even for him.

The very idea that it is impossible to speak about society and politics unless you have a doctorate in theoretical physics is preposterous nonsense. It is quite typical of the *quackery of nebulous speech, senseless analogies and pretence of precision* that fills every page of comrade Dieterich's books. And his foolish attempt to pose as an expert in all these fields leads us precisely to a place where *pseudo-knowledge reigns*, for real knowledge here is conspicuous by its total absence. Nobody doubts the colossal importance of the discoveries of modern science. But in the first place, it would be foolish to imagine that science has said its last word, for example, on the nature of the universe (our Heinz thinks it has and is making himself comfortable in his corner of the cylindrical universe).

23. Ibid., pp. 65-66.

In any case, it is not at all the case that the same laws are applicable to every case. The laws that govern physics are not necessarily the same as those that govern biology, chemistry or geology. In each case, the laws of different natural phenomena must be derived from a careful empirical investigation of the facts. The dialectical relationships in nature and the different levels of complexity find their reflection in the different branches of science. It is not possible to apply the same scientific theories to the movement of sub-atomic particles and the movement of galaxies. That is why Einstein developed two entirely separate theories, the theory of special relativity, which deals with non-accelerating systems, and that of general relativity, which deals with accelerating systems, including the effects of gravitation on large objects like galaxies.

This is, of course, all the same to our Heinz. But it is decidedly not all the same for scientists. One can know a lot about relativity theory but be ignorant of quantum physics. Atomic interactions and the laws of chemistry determine the laws of biochemistry, but life itself is qualitatively different. Can anybody imagine that it is possible to express the complexity of life in all its manifold forms in terms of chemistry? No, the two are different and that is why they are two entirely separate fields of study. The laws of biochemistry can explain all the processes of human interaction with the environment. And yet human activity and thought are qualitatively different to the biological processes that constitute them. Each individual person is a product of his or her physical and environmental development. Yet the complex interactions of the sum total of individuals, which make up a society are also qualitatively different. In each of these cases the whole is greater than the sum of the parts and obeys different laws.

Is it possible to understand the laws that govern society by studying the individual psychology of every one of its citizens? It is only necessary to state the question to see its completely absurd character. One can be an expert in psychology and understand absolutely nothing about economics, sociology, history and other social sciences. It is not possible to derive the laws of society from the laws of physics, as comrade Dieterich imagines. It is true, of course, that in the last analysis, all human existence and activity are based on the laws of motion of atoms. We are part of a material universe, which is a continuous whole, functioning according to its inherent laws. And yet, when we pass from the movement of atoms to society, we make a series of qualitative leaps, and must operate with different laws at different levels.

Society is ultimately based upon biology and biology is ultimately based upon chemistry and physics, but nobody in their right mind would seek to explain the complex movements in human society in terms of atomic forces. Complex systems such as human societies have emergent properties that cannot be deduced by looking at the simple rules of interaction of the component parts of the system. It is precisely this crude reductionism that has led some to reduce the problem of crime to the laws of genetics, as reactionaries habitually do. Such reductionism is without any scientific basis whatsoever. Whoever attempted such a thing would be rightly considered a fool and a charlatan by a real scientist.

Therefore, when comrade Dieterich informs us gravely that unless we are aware that the universe is a cylinder, we cannot express a useful opinion about society and the class struggle, we can only shrug our shoulders. This is just the kind of empty and pretentious pedantry that we have come to expect from this particular source. On the contrary, we are quite convinced that it is entirely possible to arrive at a scientific understanding of society without entering into the kingdom of the cylindrical universe or studying its laws, although we do not doubt that these will be the obligatory field of study in every primary school once we are living under 21st Century Socialism.

Genetics and socialism

With his characterisitic pedantry, Dieterich spends several pages of his book *Socialism of the 21st Century* talking about science, the Universe, matter and energy, evolution and other deep matters. In no more than six pages, he takes us on a quick tour of the Universe from the atom passing through the cell, human organisms, and the cosmos "among other phenomena". We are driven at breathtaking speed from *bacteria* to the invasion of *Kosovo*. Even the most superficial reading of this material is enough to raise some doubts in our minds concerning Heinz Dieterich's knowledge of science and sociology. By a most peculiar logic, Dieterich argues that one of the main reasons for the collapse of the USSR was *that the human genome had not yet been discovered.* He writes:

"The historical attempts to build fairer societies have been in a sense attempts against common sense. Without knowing scientifically the main building block, the human being, the desire to establish a just society amounted to attempting to build the roof of a building (superstructure), before having the foundations and walls.

"There was not, of course, any another way possible. Faced with ignorance about 'human nature', good intentions, and religious and metaphysical speculations, and, in methodology, the advance through 'trial and error' had to take the place of the firmer basis of a conscious and planned evolution of society. Despite this stick and string way of progressing, limited to the wisdom of empirical experience and just one step ahead of the thinking of a 'savage', the last millennia have seen considerable progress in many aspects of human existence. Today, however, the task can be addressed more efficiently, with more realism and optimism than at any time in the past, because we have begun to systematically understand the two key elements of the human enigma: its genome and its neural system." [24]

What does all this mean? Only this: that for the last two thousand years it was not possible to establish a "more just society" (we imagine he means socialism)

24. Dieterich, *Socialismo del Siglo XXI*; p.67-8.

because the human genome had not yet been discovered. Therefore, all the attempts of Lenin and the Bolsheviks to change society were doomed to fail, since they did not understand "the two key elements of the human enigma: its genome and its neural system." If only they had had the patience to wait another 90 years!

The human genome is indeed enormously important for socialists – but not for the reasons put forward by Heinz Dieterich. The discoveries made by the Human Genome Project have dramatically confirmed the position of Marxism. For decades, a large number of geneticists have argued that our genes determined everything from intelligence to homosexuality and criminality. This was a very good example of how science cannot be separated from politics and class interests, and how the most eminent scientists can be pressed – consciously or not – into the services of reaction. Now, however, the human genome project has completely exploded the myths of racism. There is very little difference between blacks and whites, Chinese and Indians.

Genes undoubtedly play an important role, but they are no more than the raw material out of which human character develops. The main role is played by society and the social interactions between human beings. There is no such thing as a super-historical morality. Morality is socially determined and changes continually throughout history. A recent documentary on the BBC World Service programme, *Science in Action ("A Good Lie")*, dealt with the research of an American anthropologist into lies. Since he also worked with the CIA to help them with interrogation techniques, he can hardly be accused of left-wing bias. His research showed that people are both very bad at lying and terrible at detecting lies. Lying is something humans have to learn. The investigator also did research on isolated Amazonian tribes and found that they do not lie. He postulated that in early cooperative human society that if you lied or cheated you were just shunned by the rest of the clan. As humans are fairly defenceless animals in isolation this was effectively a death sentence. Therefore there is no evolutionary basis for human dishonesty; it is something we learned through class society.

It is the same with such things as individualism, egotism, lack of solidarity, selfishness and indifference to the suffering of others. These are traits that would have been a sure recipe for the extinction of the human race in the Palaeolithic period, but are now considered to be quite "normal" in the inhuman conditions of modern capitalism with its dog-eat-dog mentality. Margaret Thatcher, that supreme embodiment of bourgeois morality, declared: "there is no such thing as society", and held greed and selfishness up as an ideal for people to follow.

Twenty years later the British bourgeois wonder why there is an epidemic of crime, cruelty and senseless murders. They ought not to be surprised: this is only the expression of the rotten morality of bourgeois individualism put into practice on the streets of London. Since morality is only the reflection of social conditions, it is futile to make appeals for men and women to be better than they are. It is futile to expect people to be fair, honest and just in a society that is manifestly unfair, immoral and unjust to the majority. In order to achieve a different morality it is first necessary to change society.

Marxists, of course, accept that genes play a most important role. They provide to some extent the raw material out of which individual humans are developed. But they represent only one side of a very complex equation. The problem arises when certain people attempt to present genes as the sole agent conditioning human development and behaviour, as has been the case for quite some time now. In reality, genes ("nature") and environmental factors ("nurture") interact upon each other, and that in this process, the role of the environment, which has been systematically denied or downplayed by the biological determinists, is absolutely crucial.

The revelations of the human genome project have decisively settled the old "nature-nurture" controversy. The relatively small number of genes in humans rules out the possibility of individual genes controlling and shaping behaviour patterns such as criminality and sexual preference. The most reactionary conclusions have been drawn from these assumptions: for example, that black people and women are genetically conditioned to be less intelligent than white people and men, that rape and murder are somehow natural, because they are genetically determined; that there is no point in spending money on schools and houses for the poor because their poverty is rooted in genetics and therefore cannot be remedied. Above all, they conclude that the existence of inequality is natural and inevitable, and that all attempts to abolish class society are futile, since it is somehow rooted in our genes.

There is therefore no question that this is a very important moment in the history of science. But is there any reason whatsoever to claim that the discovery of the human genome is the secret that will open all doors to human progress, and that, moreover, its discovery makes possible the achievement of socialism? This is just what Heinz Dieterich says. According to him, socialism was not possible before because men and women did not know these things. Presumably this also was one of the causes (if not the cause) for the collapse of "really existing socialism". If only Gorbachov had had access to the human genome, all history would have been different!

Here we once more enter the mystical realm of idealism in its crudest form. It is true that the human genome has created the conditions for a spectacular advance of human progress. It enables science to cure diseases that were hitherto considered incurable. It will mean that within our lifetime the blind will see, the lame will walk, and other feats that were previously the domain of religious miracles, will be able to be achieved on a routine basis by science. In the future, we may even become masters of our own genes and determine, at least to some extent, our biological evolution. This can have important implications for such things as space travel and the survival of the human race in changed conditions, as the planet becomes a less hospitable place to inhabit.

Yes, all that is true. But similar claims could be made for many other important scientific discoveries. Does this mean that we are nearer to socialism – to humankind's leap from the realm of necessity to the realm of freedom? In one sense, it does. The spectacular advances of science and technology create the material basis for a cultural revolution and for the complete mastery of the environment, for tackling the next great frontier facing humanity – the conquest of space. Yes, all that is true *as a potential.* But a bare potential by no means provides us with the anticipated results. The existence of the lottery means that I can become a multi-millionaire. But between a multi-millionaire *in potential* and a multi-millionaire *in reality*, there is a slight difference, a fact that a quick glance at my monthly bank balance makes painfully clear to me.

In the period of senile decay of capitalism, the advances of science and technology do not guarantee the advance of civilization but, on the contrary, threaten its very existence. What ought to mean the increase of human freedom in practice signifies the increase and intensification of slavery. Let us take just one example. The introduction of new machinery serves to increase the productivity of labour. And it is the increase of the productivity of labour that lays the basis for all human progress. One of the main causes for the collapse of the USSR was that, although the Soviet economy achieved spectacular results, and actually overtook the West in the production of such things as steel, cement, coal and electricity in absolute terms, the productivity of labour in the Soviet Union lagged behind the West.

The reason for this difference was not that the human genome had not yet been discovered, or that the USSR did not have sufficient computers. It was because the Stalinist bureaucracy formed a corrupt ruling caste that suffocated the nationalized planned economy and clogged its pores, creating colossal bungling, waste and mismanagement at all levels. In the first five-year plans, the Soviet economy grew far more quickly than the economies of the capitalist West, but in its last two decades the rate of growth slowed and fell behind. In the end, despite the huge advantages of the nationalized planned economy, the bureaucracy could not get better results than the West. This meant that in the long run it was doomed to fail. This is a striking example of the truth of the basic postulate of Marxism that in the last analysis the viability of a given socio-economic system is determined by its ability to develop the productive forces.

Genes change only very slowly. We have the same genes that our ancestors had 10,000 years ago, and even 100,000 years ago. That is to say, the physical and mental potential of humans has not changed substantially all through history. We have exactly the same potential as men and women in the Neolithic period. The question is: why has this potential not been realized? The answer to this question has nothing to do with genetics and everything to do with the level of development of the productive forces.

Hegel once wrote: "When we want to see an oak with all its vigour of trunk, its spreading branches, and mass of foliage, we are not satisfied to be shown an acorn instead".[25] An acorn is not an oak tree, but only an oak tree in potential. Whether or not that potential will be realized depends on many factors: the quality of the soil, the availability of sunlight and water, and whether the acorn will end up inside the belly of a foraging pig. Comrade Dieterich does not even offer us an acorn, but *only the idea of an acorn*; not a real programme for establishing socialism, but *only the New Historical Project*; not the substance but *only the shadow*.

If one plants a real acorn it can, under favourable circumstances, grow into a healthy oak tree. But if one plants only an ideal acorn, it will produce only an ideal oak tree – that is to say, an imaginary oak tree that exists only in somebody's brain. Under the shade of this imaginary oak tree of Socialism of the 21st Century, one can sit for hours, dreaming of a society in which capitalists and workers rejoice together in an economy of equivalence, in which profits have disappeared, where circles have a circumference of 362 degrees, where the universe is a cylinder, where lions lie down with lambs, and pigs can fly.

25. Hegel, *The Phenomenology of Mind* Preface; on scientific knowledge §12.

3. Dieterich and historical materialism

What is historical materialism?

Historical materialism sets out from the premise that the mainspring of historical development is, in the last analysis, the development of the productive forces – that is, humankind's power over nature. From the very earliest period, men and women have had to struggle for survival, to obtain the bare necessities of life: food, clothing and shelter. The most fundamental difference that separates humans from all other animals is the way in which we do this: through the manufacture and utilization of tools. In *Socialism, Utopian and Scientific*, Engels provides us with a brief outline of the basic principles of historical materialism:

"The materialist conception of history starts from the proposition that the production of the means to support human life and, next to production, the exchange of things produced, is the basis of all social structure; that in every society that has appeared in history, the manner in which wealth is distributed and society divided into classes or orders is dependent upon what is produced, how it is produced, and how the products are exchanged. From this point of view, the final causes of all social changes and political revolutions are to be sought, not in men's brains, not in men's better insights into eternal truth and justice, but in changes in the modes of production and exchange."[1]

This is a more developed expression of ideas that were developed much earlier, in *The German Ideology*, where Marx wrote: "The first premise of all human history is, of course, the existence of living human individuals. Thus the first fact to be established is the physical organisation of these individuals and their consequent relation to the rest of nature.[…] Men can be distinguished from animals by consciousness, by religion or anything else you like. They themselves begin to distinguish themselves from animals as soon as they begin to produce their means of subsistence, a

1. Marx and Engels, *Selected Works*, Vol.3, p. 133.

step which is conditioned by their physical organisation. By producing their means of subsistence men are indirectly producing their actual material life."[2]

The viability of any given socio-economic formation depends in the last analysis upon its ability to guarantee these things. This proposition is really so obvious that it does not admit contradiction. Upon this productive activity everything else depends. The mode of production and exchange has changed many times in the course of human history. With each such change there has been a revolution in social relations. Marx's clearest formulation of this is to be found in the 1859 Preface to his book *A contribution to the Critique of Political Economy*. In order that men and women may think and develop their intellect, write poetry or philosophy, invent religions or paint pictures, they must first produce sufficient food, build dwellings and put clothes on their backs and shoes on their feet.

In the famous dialogues of Plato we have the philosopher Socrates sitting all day in the Agora at Athens, stopping passers-by and asking them questions like: "What is the Good"? The question that occurs to us is the following: in order that Socrates should have the possibility of doing this, someone had to feed him, clothe him, put shoes on his feet and a roof over his head; who was that someone? The answer is: the slaves, whose labour produced most of the goods that the Athenians consumed. The basis of Athenian democracy, art, architecture, sculpture and philosophy was the labour of the slaves who lived a life of hard toil, had no rights whatsoever and were not even regarded as human beings.

A mechanical caricature

Very often attempts are made to discredit Marxism by resorting to a caricature of its method of historical analysis. There is nothing easier than erecting a straw man in order to knock it down again. The usual distortion is that Marx and Engels reduced everything to economics. This patent absurdity was answered many times by Marx and Engels, as in the following extract from Engels' letter to Bloch:

"According to the materialist conception of history, the ultimate determining element in history is the production and reproduction of life. More than this neither Marx nor myself have asserted. Hence, if somebody twists this into saying that the economic element is the *only* determining one, he transforms that proposition into a meaningless, abstract and senseless phrase."[3]

Historical materialism has nothing in common with fatalism. Our fates are not predestined, either by the gods or by the development of the productive forces. Men and women are not merely puppets of blind "historical forces". But neither are they entirely free agents, able to shape their destiny irrespective of the existing conditions imposed by the level of economic development, science and technique, which,

2. Marx and Engels, *Selected Works*, Vol.1, p. 20.
3. Engels, Letter to Bloch, September 21st 1890, Marx and Engels, *Selected Works*, Vol.3, p. 487.

in the last analysis, determine whether a socio-economic system is viable or not. In *The Eighteenth Brumaire of Louis Bonaparte*, Marx explains:

"Men make their own history, but they do not make it as they please; they do not make it under self-selected circumstances, but under circumstances existing already, given and transmitted from the past. The tradition of all dead generations weighs like an Alp on the brains of the living [...]." [4]

Later Engels expressed the same idea in a different way: "Men make their own history, whatever its outcome may be, in that each person follows his own consciously desired end, and it is precisely the resultant of these many wills operating in different directions and of their manifold effects upon the outer world that constitutes history." [5]

As opposed to the utopian socialist ideas of the likes of Robert Owen, Saint-Simon and Fourier, Marxism is based upon a scientific vision of socialism. Marxism explains that the key to the development of every society is the development of the productive forces: labour power, industry, agriculture, technique and science. Each new social system – slavery, feudalism and capitalism – has served to take human society forward through its development of the productive forces.

Historical periods

The prolonged period of primitive communism, humankind's earliest phase of development, where classes, private property, and the state did not exist, gave way to class society as soon as people were able to produce a surplus above the needs of everyday survival. At this point, the division of society into classes became an economic feasibility. On the broad scales of history, the emergence of class society was a revolutionary phenomenon, in that it freed a privileged section of the population – a ruling class – from the direct burden of labour, permitting it the necessary time to develop art, science and culture. Class society, despite its ruthless exploitation and inequality, was the road that humankind needed to travel if it was to build up the necessary material prerequisites for a future classless society.

In a certain sense socialist society is a return to primitive communism but on a vastly higher productive level. Before one can envisage a classless society, all the hallmarks of class society, especially inequality and scarcity, would have to be abolished. It would be absurd to talk of the abolition of classes where inequality, scarcity and the struggle for existence prevailed. It would be a contradiction in terms. Socialism can only appear at a certain stage in the evolution of human society, at a certain level of development of the productive forces.

In contrast to the utopian socialists of the early 19th century, who regarded socialism as a moral issue, something which could have been introduced by enlight-

4. Marx and Engels, *Selected Works*, Vol.1, p. 398.

5. Engels, *Ludwig Feuerbach and the end of German classical philosophy*, Marx and Engels, *Selected Works*, Vol.3, chapter IV, p. 366.

ened people at any time in history, Marx and Engels saw it as rooted in the development of society. The precondition for such a classless society is the development of the forces of production by which superabundance becomes feasible. For Marx and Engels, this is the task of the socialist planned economy. For Marxism, the historic mission of capitalism – the highest stage of class society – was to provide the material basis worldwide for socialism and the abolition of classes. Socialism was not simply a good idea, but was the next stage for human society.

It is not feasible for society to jump straight from capitalism to a classless society. The material and cultural inheritance of capitalist society is far too inadequate for that. There is too much scarcity and inequality that cannot be immediately overcome. After the socialist revolution, there must be a transitional period that will prepare the necessary ground for superabundance and a classless society.

Marx called this first stage of the new society "the lowest stage of communism" as opposed to "the highest stage of communism", where the last residue of material inequality would disappear. In that sense, socialism and communism have been contrasted to the "lower" and "higher" stages of the new society. In describing the lower stage of communism Marx writes: "What we are dealing with here is a communist society, not as it has developed on its own foundations, but, on the contrary, just as it emerges from capitalist society; which is thus in every respect, economically, morally and intellectually, still stamped with the birth marks of the old society from whose womb it emerges." [6]

"Between capitalist and communist society," states Marx, "lies the period of the revolutionary transformation of the one into the other. Corresponding to this is also a political transition period in which the state can be nothing but the revolutionary dictatorship of the proletariat." As all the greatest Marxist theoreticians explained, the task of the socialist revolution is to bring the working class to power by smashing the old capitalist state machine. The latter was the repressive organ designed to keep the working class in subjection. Marx explained that this capitalist state, together with its state bureaucracy, cannot serve the interests of the new power. It has to be done away with. However, the new state created by the working class would be different from all previous states in history, a "semi-state" – a state designed in such a way that it was destined to disappear.

However, for Marx – and this is a crucial point – this lower stage of communism from its very beginning would be on a higher level in terms of its economic development than the most developed and advanced capitalism. And why was this so important? Because without a massive development of the productive forces, scarcity would prevail and with it the struggle for existence. As Marx explained, such a state of affairs would pose the danger of degeneration: "*This development of the productive forces is an absolutely necessary practical premise [of communism],*

6. Marx and Engels, *Selected Works*, Vol. 3, *Critique of the Gotha Programme*, p. 17.

because without it want is generalised, and with want the struggle for necessities begins again, and that means that all the old crap must revive." [7]

The New Historical Project

These, in general outline, are the main propositions of the Marxist view of history. What has our Heinz have to say on the subject? With great ceremony comrade Dieterich announces to the *End of Global Capitalism* and the Dawn of *The New Historical Project*:

"We declare that the first life-cycle of modern society is coming to its end. For the past 200 years, from French Revolution (1789) to the present day, *mankind has lived through the two known kinds of evolution*: capitalism and historical socialism.

"Both methods found it impossible to solve the major problems of mankind. These include: poverty, hunger, exploitation, sexism, racism, the destruction of natural resources and the lack of a true democracy. Therefore our time is characterized by the end of the major social projects of the upper class and the historical working class, which have dominated our era. Emerging global society opens up to a new civilization: participative democracy, socialism of the 21st century." [8]

So there we have it! For the last 200 years (at least) the human race has been languishing under the illusion that the only alternatives before it were capitalism or *historical socialism*. The latter, commonly known as Marxism, has failed, as we saw with the collapse of the USSR. Heinz is far too polite to actually say this in so many words, but that is clearly what he thinks. Therefore, it is high time to throw the old ideas of *historical socialism* into the nearest dustbin and embrace the entirely new and original ideas of 21st Century Socialism and the New Historical Project, which have sprung straight from the brain of Heinz Dieterich, as Minerva sprang from the head of Jupiter.

Dieterich begins rather well. After all, it is not very difficult to denounce the evils of capitalism, though it is rather more difficult to say how these evils can be remedied. He produces some useful statistics on inequality:

"Throughout the world products and services of all sorts are urgently needed, but in spite of this, in Western Europe, 35 million people are out of work; on a world scale the figure 820 millions, almost one third of people on productive age. And the global flow of capital, which is increasingly concentrated, does not create new jobs or material values; they are no longer aimed at profits, but only to generating interest. The volume of the flow of capital has increased ten times in the last six years. Now more than a trillion dollars changes hands every day on a world scale – only one percent of this quantity (10 billion a day) for transactions of world trade – 99 percent of monetary transactions are purely speculative." [9]

7. Marx and Engels *Selected Works*, Vol. 1, *The German Ideology*, p. 37, my emphasis.
8. Dieterich, *Socialismo del Siglo XXI*, p.23, my emphasis, AW.
9. Ibid., pages 44-45.

We are further informed that 600 million people have died of hunger since 1945, and that 44 million people in the European Union are living in poverty (14 percent of the population), that in the USA the corresponding figure is 10 percent for whites and 31 percent for blacks; also that the rich in the United States are getting richer every year, and that in the USA the income of the richest 20 percent has increased 62 percent in the last 10 years, while the income of the poorest 20 percent has fallen by 14 percent. All this is very true. The question is: *what is to be done about it*? Introduce socialism, obviously. On this we agree. But the question is then posed: *what kind of socialism*? And here the differences immediately begin to surface. From the very beginning he raises his banner high: the whole problem facing humanity for the last 10,000 years is *unequal exchange*:

"The triumphal march of *exchange value* through history dynamised 7,000 years ago by the change over from barter to trade, to advance later over hecatombs of victims of 'progress' of civilisation, is drawing to a close. In the final stage, 200 years ago, modern capitalism has ceaselessly revolutionised the productive forces and social relations. But it did not stop there. It generated the anthropological correspondence which was required by its mode of production: the human being, functional to its interests as a producer of commodities and realiser of surplus value.

"The most precious gift of humanity, reason, is being stripped of all critical elements, to remain in a purely instrumental state. However criminal and amoral the end might be, instrumental reason is at its service, with the only function of bringing about the means: from the daily theft of the surplus value of the worker to the scientific killing of oppositionists in the subworld of the global village. The ethics of civic coexistence and solidarity have been replaced by the morality of the strongest, which justifies the agony of half the human race, in terms of its 'incapacity' to compete in the modern Roman circus that is the world market." [10]

Dieterich refers to historical transformations as "projects", that is to say, he defines great historical changes in terms of ideology, thus standing history on its head. *This is precisely the opposite of Marx's method of historical materialism.* Historical materialism does not explain the evolution of human society in terms of the ideas in the heads of men and women, but rather explains the evolution of ideas in terms of objective process that take place in the productive forces and property relations that develop independently of human consciousness and volition. This was explained very clearly in a famous passage from one of the defining works of historical materialism, *The Critique of Political Economy*, where Marx explains the relation between the productive forces and the superstructure:

"In the social production which men carry on they enter into definite relations that are indispensable and independent of their will; these relations of production correspond to a definite stage of development of their material powers of production [...] The mode of production in material life determines the general character

10. Ibid., p. 62-3.

of the social, political and spiritual processes of life. *It is not the consciousness of men that determines their existence, but, on the contrary, their social existence (which) determines their consciousness.*" [11]

Later on in the same work Marx writes: "In considering such transformations a distinction should always be made between the material transformation of the economic conditions of production, which can be determined with the precision of natural science, and the legal, political, religious, aesthetic, or philosophic – in short, ideological forms in which men become conscious of this conflict and fight it out." [12]

This is just what Heinz Dieterich does not do. It is entirely false and unscientific to refer to an "historical project" for capitalism, feudalism and slave societies. In every case it was not the ideas, plans and projects of the ruling class that brought about a change in the society, but it was profound changes in society that at a certain stage found a confused and distorted expression in the minds of men and women.

A sentimental view of history

We have seen in the above quotation how Heinz can rant and rage with great effect about the evils of capitalism, how he can weep and complain about the lack of ethics and theft, but *there is not a single atom of scientific analysis in this entire passage.* Instead, we have a mixture of sentimental rhetoric and theoretical confusion. He begins by restating his unscientific view that divides the whole of human history into two periods: before and after the production of exchange value. Since the only socio-economic system that is based on the production of exchange values is capitalism, which, as comrade Dieterich himself points out, has only existed for the last 200 years, this is clearly wrong.

With his talk about "hecatombs of victims of 'progress' of civilisation", comrade Dieterich wishes to arouse the righteous indignation of the reader, and might even succeed in so doing. But it is impossible to arrive at a rational understanding of human history from a purely sentimental and moralistic standpoint. There have certainly been hecatombs of victims of class society for the last 6,000 years and even longer. But are we supposed to deduce from this fact that there has not been progress for the whole of this period? Such a view would be in complete contradiction to Marxism. It is merely a repetition of the view held by Edward Gibbon in the 18th century that history is: "Little more than the register of the crimes, follies and misfortunes of mankind."

Unlike Dieterich, the author of *The Decline and Fall of the Roman Empire* was an excellent writer and a very good historian. However, Gibbon was writing at a time when historical materialism had not yet been developed. He was unaware of

11. Marx, *The Critique of Political Economy*, my emphasis, AW.
12. Marx and Engels, *Selected Works*, Vol.1, *Preface to A Critique of Political Economy*, p. 504.

the real mainsprings of human history, and in particular did not appreciate the role of the economic factor. He was under the influence of the rationalist ideas of the French Enlightenment. It was therefore inevitable that Gibbon should approach history from an idealist and moralistic standpoint. One can still learn a great deal from the writings of Gibbon, but his approach to history was conditioned by the limitations of his time and therefore presents only one side of the picture.

From the fact that Dieterich places the word progress in inverted commas one can only deduce that he does not think that there has been any real progress in the last 6,000 years. Has there not been any advance from the wooden plough and the bronze chariot to computer science and stem cell research? Certain middle class intellectuals would answer this question in the negative. They wax lyrical about the "good old days" when men and women worked on the land every day of the year, engaged in subsistence agriculture and back breaking labour, living on little more than bread and beer, and sleeping in smoky huts without elementary hygiene. Then they return to their comfortable middle class flats, drink their gin and tonic and sleep soundly in air-conditioned bedrooms.

Marxists do not approach history from a sentimental or moralistic point of view. The whole of human history has been a long hard struggle of men and women to rise above an animal condition and become what they always were potentially: free human beings. The prior condition for this is to satisfy all human needs, in order that men and women will cease to be slaves to their own material requirements. This can only be achieved when industry, agriculture, science and technology reach a sufficient level of development to satisfy all our needs. Therefore, the development of the productive forces represents the key to all human progress, culture and civilization. Whoever does not understand this elementary truth will forever be condemned to a philistine approach to history.

Marxism finds in the development of the productive forces, building and producing machinery, factories, universities, schools, roads, railways and the development of science, technique and skills the key to the development of society and to the class struggle for the surplus produced by the labour of the working class. We live in a period when capitalism has shown that it can no longer develop society. That is the fundamental premise of socialist revolution.

Over 2,000 years ago the Greek philosopher Aristotle wrote in his *Metaphysics*: "For philosophy arose only when the necessities and the physical and mental comforts of life had been provided for." [13] Human culture and civilization begins when a surplus is produced sufficient to free at least a section of society from the need to labour. Aristotle also points out that mathematics and astronomy originated in Egypt because the priests did not have to work. However, the development of the productive forces still remained at a relatively low level. The surplus produced by the

13. Aristotle, *Metaphysics*, p. 55. Everyman's Library, 1961.

labour of the peasants was not sufficient to free everybody from what the Bible describes as the curse of work. That is why, throughout history, culture has always been monopolised by a privileged minority. The narrow base of social production did not permit anything else. That is why socialism was materially impossible in the past. It is true that even 2,000 years ago there were people who advocated communist ideas, but since the material basis for socialism was absent, their ideas necessarily had a utopian and fantastic character.

Engels points out that in any society where art, science and government are in the hands of a minority, that minority will use and abuse its position in its own interest. And this must be the situation as long as the development of the productive forces remains on a low level. However, for the last 6,000 years there has been an almost continuous development of the productive forces, although this was achieved by the most brutal means of exploitation and oppression of the majority. It is possible to be indignant about slavery, a monstrous and inhuman system. But it must be recognised that all of our culture, science and civilisation comes from ancient Greece and Rome, and was based on the labour of the slaves. In the same way, capitalism came onto the stage of history dripping blood from every pore. Nevertheless, in pursuit of profit, the capitalists developed the means of production, and therefore unconsciously laid the bases for a new and qualitatively superior stage of human development: socialism.

Heinz Dieterich also rants and rages about the way in which capitalism exploits the workers, who he describes as "the human being, functional to its interests as a producer of commodities and realiser of surplus value". "The most precious gift of humanity, reason, is being stripped of all critical elements, to remain in a purely instrumental state." This is "criminal" and "amoral", he informs us. Moreover, the capitalist is nothing more than a *common thief* who perpetrates a "*daily theft* of the surplus value of the worker". Here comrade Dieterich's moral indignation knows no bounds. But once again, his analysis is defective. His "most precious gift, reason", has been stripped of its critical elements to the extent that *he confuses Marx with Proudhon.*

It was Proudhon, the precursor of anarchism, who stated that "property is theft", an argument that Marx completely rejected. Such a statement may serve a useful purpose as an agitational slogan, but it is entirely empty of scientific content. Marx answered Proudhon at great length in one of his earliest works, *The Poverty of Philosophy*. Either comrade Dieterich has never read this, *or else he considers that along with 99 percent of Marx's work, this has been superseded by the theories of 21st Century Socialism.* But before we consider these remarkable new theories in greater detail, it is necessary briefly to explain the ideas of Marxism that are supposed to have been rendered redundant by the revelatory new theories of Peters and Dieterich.

On 'historical projects'

The conception of history of Dieterich and Peters has nothing in common with the standpoint of historical materialism. In a completely unscientific manner they divide the whole of history into two compartments: the early phase when there was allegedly "exchange of equivalents" (through barter) and the rest of history, commencing about 12,000 years ago, when there was "unequal exchange". We will deal with the economic theories of Dieterich and Peters in the next two chapters.

For the present, we confine ourselves to the following observation: the appropriation of the surplus created by the labouring population has existed for the last 10-12,000 years. But the way in which the surplus has been appropriated, by what class and on the basis of what property relations has changed many times. This is not at all a secondary question as Dieterich and Peters imagine. The laws of motion of capitalism are not the same as those of slave society or feudalism. The discovery of these laws can only be made through a careful scientific analysis of the concrete features of each system.

In *The German Ideology*, Marx outlines four stages of human society and modes of production (excluding the initial stage of primitive tribal communism): the Asiatic mode of production, slavery, feudalism and capitalism. Was the transition from primitive tribal communism to class society brought about by a conscious decision of the chiefs and their war-bands in the Neolithic period? Was there some kind of Stone Age Heinz Dieterich who persuaded our ancestors to cease hunting harmless mammoths and cave-bears and become vegetarians? It is sufficient to pose the question concretely to realize its absurdly idealist and preposterous character.

We are rather inclined to look for a materialist explanation, based upon climatic changes that changed the pattern of migration of the herds of wild animals and caused a scarcity of game, forcing people to rely increasingly on wild crops that they gradually learned to cultivate. The raising of crops compelled them to adopt a settled existence, creating the first permanent settlements, from which arose the first towns and cities. This was the basis of what Gordon Childe has called the Neolithic Revolution – probably the most important revolution in the whole of human history.

Is it possible to argue that slavery was the result of the "historical project" of the Roman ruling class? Not at all, the Roman state was formed as the result of a long series of wars, first with neighbouring Latin tribes and later, more decisively, in the wars with Carthage, a more advanced civilization. The slave economy arose out of the concrete circumstances of the times. These wars, like all other wars of the period, ended in the capture of a vast number of slaves, which swelled the army of slaves working in the mines and big estates on Roman territory.

To cite just one example, when Tiberius Gracchus raided Sardinia, he took as many as 80,000 captives, to be sold in the slave market at Rome, where the expression "as cheap as a Sardinian" became a proverb. This steady flow of cheap slaves played a fundamental role in stimulating the slave economy. Slave labour has a central contradiction: the productivity of an individual slave is very low, for obvious reasons, and can only be profitably employed on a massive scale. Since slaves do not reproduce in sufficient numbers, a constant renewal of slave labour can only be achieved through war or other violent means. From this point on, the wars waged by Rome often assumed the character of large-scale slave hunts. War was a necessary element in the Roman slave economy.

The spread of slave labour not only destroyed the class of free peasants. It also degraded the value of free labour in general, reducing the free proletarians to the same level of misery as the slaves. On the other hand, a new class of Roman capitalists arose purely on the basis of money and the slave economy – the "knights" or *equites* – who tended to elbow aside the old patrician nobility and jostled with them for political power. All these developments created severe class antagonisms within the Roman Republic, leading to the most ferocious class war.

Feudalism

Maybe feudalism was implanted in Europe as a result of the "historical project" of Attila the Hun? No, sad to say, the barbarian tribes that swept across Europe as a result of the collapse of the Roman Empire were not guided by any historical project, unless burning cities, plunder and rape constituted such a project. It is true that by their actions they hastened the disintegration of a socio-economic system that was already in a state of advanced decay. The slave economy had long since exhausted itself, to the extent that the Roman landowners had "freed" their slaves in most cases and converted them into *coloni*, bound to the land. This was the embryo of serfdom and the feudal system that was later perfected by the barbarians who erected an agricultural society on the ruins of the Roman Empire. But none of this came about as a result of a conscious plan.

Is it possible to speak of a project for capitalism in the period of the decline of feudalism in Europe, from the second half of the 14th century? Did the bourgeoisie in the period of its ascent possess a historical project? Well, the Dutch and English bourgeoisie in the 16th and 17th century had what might be described as such a project. What did this project consist of? *It was based on religion and basically raised the prospect of the creation of God's kingdom on earth.* This "project" was highly successful in inspiring the broad masses to fight against the old feudal society and its ideology, which, in the given conditions, assumed a religious disguise. The Roman Catholic Church constituted a powerful bulwark against change and was one of the most important supports of the feudal order. One of the first tasks of the nascent bourgeoisie was therefore to criticize and expose the Church. Luther, Calvin and the other advocates of Protestantism achieved this.

In essence the Reformation represents an ideological struggle between the bourgeoisie and the old feudal order. *But this class content was not at all evident at the time and it is quite wrong to suppose that the bourgeoisie had a conscious plan to seize power and replace feudalism with capitalism.* They really believed that they were fighting for fundamental religious principles, for the immortal souls of men and women, for the right of every individual to worship as they chose without the interference of priests and bishops. We must distinguish carefully between the real class interests that lie behind the great revolutionary battles of the 16th and 17th centuries in Europe and the ideological forms through which these struggles were reflected in the minds of men and women at the time.

What is the central doctrinal difference between Protestantism and Catholicism? It is the difference between salvation through *faith* and salvation through *works*. The Church of Rome taught that even the greatest sinner could get his time in purgatory reduced through the purchase of papal indulgences. This was a highly convenient doctrine, especially for the wealthy feudal lords who, after a lifetime of debauchery, could obtain salvation by leaving his wealth and land to the Church. It was even more convenient for the Church, which greatly enriched itself thereby.

The Catholic religion was rooted firmly in the feudal mode of production, based on landed property and serfdom. The labour of the serfs provided the feudal lords with their wealth and privileges. The landowner had no need to reinvest in new machinery and modern technology for the same reason that the Roman slave owners did not need to invest in labour-saving devices. Like the slaves, the serfs were forced to provide free labour service, working on the lord's land for so many days a year. The only use the landowner had for the wealth extracted from the serfs was in magnificent displays of luxury, jewels, expensive dress and the like. He could also afford a certain amount of generosity, holding feasts and giving alms to the poor. When he died, he could also bequeath large sums to the Church to say prayers for his soul for generations or to dedicate a church or cathedral. It is no accident that the later Middle Ages in Europe is marked by an explosion of church-building on the most lavish scale.

The bourgeoisie in the period of its revolutionary ascent (in contrast to today) despised all outward shows of ostentation, including (and above all) the ostentation of the Church. The Scripture says: "For where two or three are gathered in my name there am I in the midst of them." (Matthew 18:20.) The Greek word *ekklesia*, from which the word ecclesiastic is derived, did not mean a building at all but a *gathering*. Therefore, for the Protestants the construction of huge cathedrals was not just a sinful waste of money, but an act of blasphemy. Just compare the lifestyle and morality of the feudal aristocracy with that of the nascent bourgeoisie in the phase of what Marx calls the Primitive Accumulation. The average bourgeois lived frugally, saving every penny for the purpose of accumulation. The burghers and their families wore simple black clothes. In Calvinist Holland after the victory of the first bourgeois revolution, all displays of luxury were prohibited. This austerity can be clearly seen in the paintings of the period.

To the church's doctrine of salvation by works, the bourgeoisie advanced the slogan of salvation by faith. This meant that anyone who believed in Jesus Christ could expect to be saved. This was much cheaper than the alternative, and far more efficient. My faith does not cost me a penny, whereas charity and other "good works" can make a serious hole in my pocket. The Protestants objected to the clergy, insisting that every Christian could have direct access to God through the Revealed Word – that is, the Bible. This was a very revolutionary idea for its time. It struck a blow against the whole edifice of the Church – and therefore of the entire feudal order.

Since the Bible contains many revolutionary ideas, denunciations of the rich and so on, the Church did not allow ordinary men and women to have direct access to it. Only the priest was allowed to explain its contents to the people, and to erect an insurmountable barrier between the Bible and the people, it was only available in Latin. Those who attempted to translate it into the vernacular were imprisoned or burnt at the stake (William Tyndall who translated the Bible into English was executed in the 16th century). When Martin Luther gave the Bible to the German people in their own language, he lit the fuse that ignited the Reformation and the Peasants War.

The English Revolution

Not satisfied with the (entirely false) assertion that socialism is not possible unless and until everybody accepts his New Historical Project, Dieterich now wants to inflict this wretched idea on all the revolutions of the past. Thus, if we accept that the revolutionary "must possess a plan" for "a new mode of production and a new superstructure" in order to succeed, it follows that Oliver Cromwell must have had just such a finished plan before he took power. In other words, he must have had his own 17th century equivalent of the NHP, and Cromwell, like Jesus Christ, must have been a moderate social reformer – just like Heinz Dieterich.

In 17th century England, the bourgeoisie carried out a revolution that overthrew the king and cut off his head. Kings had been killed many times before, but this was the first occasion when a king was put on trial, sentenced and executed in the name of the people. What was the "project" of Oliver Cromwell? Was it the establishment of capitalism in England? No, this idea never entered the head of this small landowner from East Anglia. He was fighting for the right of all men to worship as they wished, free from the interference of the bishops.

Oliver Cromwell had no plan either for the superstructure or the economy. If he did, he must have kept it very secret, for there is no mention of such a plan anywhere in his voluminous correspondence and speeches. Anybody who has the slightest knowledge of Cromwell will know that his main motivation was of a religious character. We know that the struggle over religion in the 16th and 17th century were merely the outward expression of deeper class conflicts, and that the inner historical significance of these struggles could only be the rise to power of the bourgeoisie and new (capitalist) relations of production. But to attribute to the leaders of these struggles a prior knowledge of this is sheer nonsense.

One can say that objectively, Cromwell was laying the basis for the rule of the bourgeoisie in England. But in order to do this, in order to clear all the feudal-monarchical rubbish out of the way, he was first obliged to sweep aside the cowardly bourgeoisie, dissolve its parliament and base himself on the petty bourgeoisie, the small farmers of East Anglia (of which he was one), and the plebeian and semi-proletarian masses of town and country. He aroused the fighting spirit of the masses, not by producing plans for the superstructure and economy, but by appealing to the Bible, the Saints and the Kingdom of God on Earth. His soldiers did not go into battle singing the praises of the New Historical Project, but with religious hymns.

This evangelistic spirit, which was soon filled with a revolutionary (and even sometimes a communistic) content, was what inspired the masses to fight with tremendous courage and enthusiasm against the Hosts of Beelzebub. But once in power, Cromwell could not go beyond the bounds established by history and the objective limits of the productive forces of the epoch. He was compelled to turn against the Left Wing, suppressing the Levellers by force, and to pursue a policy that favoured the bourgeoisie and the reinforcement of capitalist property relations in England. In the end, Cromwell dismissed parliament and ruled as dictator until his death, when the English bourgeoisie, fearful that the Revolution had gone too far and might pose a threat to property, restored the Stuarts to the throne. Once again, the rule of the bourgeoisie was established, not according to any pre-ordained plan or "project", but as a result of the objective conditions of production and the class relations that arose from them. The end result bore no relation whatsoever to the subjective intentions (the "projects") of Cromwell and his comrades.

Dieterich's blunders

Now it is very good that Heinz is able to write on many different subjects. But from a scientific writer we are entitled to expect a rigorous approach to the subjects he deals with. Otherwise we will not regard him as a scientist but only a pretentious windbag. Let us see whether our Heinz is as knowledgeable as he pretends to be. Since he loves lists, let us now list just a few of his blunders. Among the innumerable subjects on which he writes is the English Revolution of the 17th century. In an article in *Rebelión* entitled *Does a revolutionary situation exist in Latin America?* (18/04/07) we read the following pearls of wisdom: "Cromwell replaces the three dominant institutions of the old regime, the monarchy, the Vatican and the aristocracy, with the parliament, the protestant national church and the developmental (desarrollista) market economy."

In a single sentence we find at least one fundamental error in every line and sometimes more:

Blunder No.1

Oliver Cromwell, placing himself at the head of the revolutionary petty bourgeoisie and semi-proletarian masses, overthrew the monarchy and settled the matter very neatly by separating Charles' head from his body. But it is entirely incorrect to say that the Vatican, that is the Roman Catholic Church, was one of the "three dominant institutions of the old régime". The Vatican had been effectively removed from England before Cromwell was born and played little if any role in the English Revolution. Charles was married to a French woman who was Catholic, but she was obliged to perform her religious rights in private, since the celebration of Roman Catholic rites in England *was prohibited by law*, which is a very strange position for one of the "three dominant institutions of the old régime" to find itself in.

Blunder No.2

Charles the First was not a *Catholic* but a *Protestant,* and in fact was *the head of the "the national protestant church"*, which, according to our friend, was only established by his overthrow. In fact, the national protestant church (the Church of England) was established by Henry the Eighth who broke with Rome in the previous century. Like Henry, Charles the First held the title of *Fidi Defensor* (Defender of the Faith). Which faith did this title refer to? Not Roman Catholicism, but Protestantism (Anglicanism).

Blunder No.3

Although the establishment of the Anglican Church (long before Cromwell or the English Revolution) led to a complete break with the Vatican, which had to work in underground conditions in England (except for the brief reign of Queen Mary) and was obliged to resort to conspiracies and attempts to assassinate the English monarch, the ritual of the Church did not change substantially. The main difference was that the national (Protestant) church recognized the English monarch as its head, not the Pope of Rome. Charles the First, as titular head of the English Protestant Church, appointed the bishops, who held considerable power. Cromwell did not found the established church. He was not even a member of it. He belonged to the more radical Protestant Church of *the Independents – so called precisely because they were independent of the established national church.*

The Puritans, who were divided into a multiplicity of Churches and sects, which were the forerunners of the clubs in the French Revolution and of modern political parties, had many differences, but they were all united on one thing: *total opposition to the established national church*, which they correctly saw as an instrument in the hands of the reactionary monarchy. The appointment of bishops and the obligation to pay money to the established (Protestant) church, as well as its lavish rituals, were anathema to them. *Oliver Cromwell therefore did not establish the national church but abolished it.* This is precisely the opposite of what Dieterich writes. What Cromwell actually established was the freedom of individuals to worship in any way they desired.

Blunder No.4

The struggle between the bourgeoisie and the old regime in England began as a struggle between King and Parliament. But the wealthy merchants who dominated the parliament in London had no desire to abolish the monarchy, and they were constantly attempting to reach a compromise with the king and establish a constitutional monarchy in which the power would be divided between the bourgeoisie and the aristocratic representatives of the old order. Even in the 17th century, the bourgeoisie was playing a counter-revolutionary role in its own revolution. The bourgeoisie in parliament waged war against the king half-heartedly and in the beginning they lost every battle and it looked as if the king would win. Only when Cromwell and other more radical leaders of the revolutionary petty bourgeoisie came to the fore and seized control of the movement did the revolutionary camp begin to win battle after battle.

We see the same phenomenon in the early stages of every revolution. The moderate wing first rises to the top and strives to restrain the masses, keep the revolution within the limits acceptable to the ruling class and arrive at a compromise. This is precisely the position of Heinz Dieterich today. We have no doubt whatever that if our friend had been alive in 17th century England he would have been a supporter, not of Oliver Cromwell, and still less the communist trend represented by the Levellers and Diggers, but of the moderate Presbyterians in parliament who tried to do a deal with the king.

Oliver Cromwell finally *used the revolutionary army to dissolve parliament*, and he ruled as dictator from then until he died. It is therefore simply not true that Cromwell "substituted the monarchy for parliament," as Dieterich asserts. Rather, he substituted both the monarchy and parliament with himself. Only after Cromwell died did the cowardly English bourgeois dare to re-establish the parliament he had abolished and invite the late king's son, Charles Stuart, to return from French exile and rule together with the bourgeoisie. Even that arrangement did not last long. Charles II was succeeded by James, who really was a Catholic and foolishly tried to turn the clock back. The bourgeoisie was forced to drive the Stuarts from the throne and invite the Dutchman, William of Orange, to become the Protestant king of England in a coup d'état that they comically baptised "The Glorious Revolution". That was in 1688, when Cromwell was long dead. This is the real origin of the English constitutional monarchy, a compromise between the monarchy and the bourgeoisie of which the "constitutional expert" Dieterich seems to be completely ignorant.

Blunder No.5

The real reason why Heinz Dieterich drags in Oliver Cromwell by the hair is not exactly a scientific quest for historical truth (there is, as we have seen, not an atom of historical truth in his entire analysis of the English Revolution). The real motive is to smuggle in the unscientific and anti-Marxist notion of the "historical project." Cromwell did not invent the market economy, to which Dieterich refers. It already existed and had existed in England for at least two centuries, in an embryonic form. Undoubtedly, the victory of Cromwell over the forces of feudal-aristocratic reaction gave a powerful impulse to the further development of these capitalist tendencies.

The brilliant military victories of Cromwell and his generals, especially over Holland, established the unquestioned superiority of English sea power. This in turn prepared the way for the rapid development of overseas trade and the conquest of colonies. The victory of the Puritans in the Civil War reinforced capitalist agriculture in England and an enlightened educational policy assisted the development of science and research. But all this was not the result of a preconceived plan by Cromwell or anybody else. It was the logical result of a particular historical concatenation of circumstances.

What conclusions can we draw from the above?

1) *Heinz Dieterich knows nothing about the English Revolution.*

2) *Nevertheless Heinz Dieterich writes about the English Revolution.*

3) *Therefore, it is not necessary to know about something in order to write about it.*

4) *The proof of the above proposition is to be found in all the other writings of Heinz Dieterich.*

The French Revolution

Matters are no better when we go on to examine the French bourgeois Revolution of 1789-93. It is true that the Revolution was prepared by an intense ideological struggle. The finest representatives of the rising French bourgeoisie clashed with the ideas, morality and philosophy of the decadent feudal-absolutist regime. The ideas of the *philosophes* and encyclopaedists, materialists like D'Alembert, Holbach, Diderot, and radical freethinkers like Voltaire and Rousseau represent one of the high points of the history of philosophy. The criticism of existing ideas and values found its reflection in literature, notably in the plays of Beaumarchais. Surely here we can speak of a bourgeois historical project? This question was answered long ago by Engels in *Anti-Dühring*:

"The great men, who in France prepared men's minds for the coming revolution, were themselves extreme revolutionists. They recognized no external authority of any kind whatever. Religion, natural science, society, political institutions – everything was subjected to the most unsparing criticism; everything must justify its existence before the judgment-seat of reason or give up existence. Reason became the sole measure of everything. It was the time when, as Hegel says, the world stood upon its head; first in the sense that the human head, and the principles arrived at by its thought, claimed to be the basis of all human action and association; but by and by, also, in the wider sense that the reality which was in contradiction to these principles had, in fact, to be turned upside down. Every form of society and government then existing, every old traditional notion was flung into the lumber room as irrational; the world had hitherto allowed itself to be led solely by prejudices; everything in the past deserved only pity and contempt. Now, for the first time, appeared the light of day, henceforth superstition, injustice, privilege, oppression, were to be superseded by eternal truth, eternal Right, equality based on nature and the inalienable rights of man.

"*We know today that this kingdom of reason was nothing more than the idealized kingdom of the bourgeoisie; that this eternal Right found its realization in bourgeois justice; that this equality reduced itself to bourgeois equality before the law; that bourgeois property was proclaimed as one of the essential rights of man; and that the government of reason, the Contrat Social of Rousseau, came into being, and only could come into being, as a democratic bourgeois republic. The great thinkers of the 18th century could, no more than their predecessors, go beyond the limits imposed upon them by their epoch.*" [14]

Isn't this quite clear? Engels, the materialist, explains that the "historical project" of the French bourgeoisie was *only an illusion* – just as the ideas of the English bourgeoisie in the 17th century had been an illusion. In fact, every historical period has its illusions – the fantastic ideas that represent the distorted reflection in men's brains of real social relations. Marx and Engels in one of the earliest works of scientific socialism, *The German Ideology*, already explained this:

"Whilst in ordinary life every shopkeeper is very well able to distinguish between what somebody professes to be and what he really is, our historians have not yet won even this trivial insight. They take every epoch at its word and believe that everything it says and imagines about itself.

"This historical method which reigned in Germany, and especially the reason why, must be understood from its connection with the illusion of ideologists in general, e.g. the illusions of the jurist, politicians (of the practical statesmen among them, too), from the dogmatic dreaming and distortions of these fellows; this is explained perfectly easily from their practical position in life, their job, and the division of labour." [15]

14. Frederick Engels, *Anti-Dühring*, Introduction, General, 1877, my emphasis, AW.

15. Karl Marx, *The German Ideology*, Part I: Feuerbach. Opposition of the Materialist and Idealist Outlooks. B) The Illusion of the Epoch.

Over 150 years later, it is clear that some German ideologists have still not managed to free themselves from the idealist outlook that Marx and Engels ridiculed in these lines. All the fine talk about a "historical project" reduces itself to this.

Socialism and capitalism

It is entirely wrong to say that capitalism was brought about as the result of a conscious plan or project of the bourgeois. Unlike socialism, capitalism can and does arise spontaneously out of the development of the productive forces. As a system of production, capitalism does not require the conscious intervention of men and women. The market functions in the same way as an anthill or any other self-organizing community of the animal world, that is to say, blindly and automatically. The fact that this takes place in an anarchic, convulsive and chaotic manner, that it is endlessly wasteful and inefficient and creates the most monstrous human suffering, is irrelevant to this consideration. Capitalism works and has been working – without the need of any human control or planning – for about two hundred years. In order to bring such a system into being, no special insight or understanding is called for. This fact has a bearing on the fundamental difference between the bourgeois and socialist revolution.

Socialism is different from capitalism because, unlike the latter, it requires the conscious control and administration of the productive process by the working class itself. It does not and cannot function without the conscious intervention of men and women. The socialist revolution is qualitatively different to the bourgeois revolution because it can only be brought about by the conscious movement of the working class. Socialism is democratic or it is nothing.

Right from the beginning, in the transitional period between capitalism and socialism, the running of industry, society and the state must be firmly in the hands of the working people. There must be the highest degree of participation of the masses in administration and control. Only in this way is it possible to prevent the rise of bureaucracy and create the material conditions for the movement in the direction of socialism: a higher form of society characterized by the total absence of exploitation, oppression and coercion, and therefore by the gradual extinction and disappearance of that monstrous relic of barbarism, the state.

Here is also another difference. In order to conquer power, the bourgeoisie had to mobilize the masses against the old order. This would have been unthinkable on the basis of the declared aim of establishing the necessary conditions for the rule of Rent, Interest and Profit. Instead, the bourgeoisie put itself forward as the representative of the whole of suffering humanity. In the case of 17th century England it was supposed to be fighting for the establishment of god's kingdom on earth. In 18th century France it advertised itself as the representative of the rule of Reason.

Undoubtedly, many of those who fought under these banners sincerely believed them to be true. Men and women do not fight against all the odds, risking everything, without that special motivation born of a burning conviction of the rightness of their cause. The declared aims in each case turned out to be pure illusion. The real content of the English and French revolutions was bourgeois and, in the given historical epoch, could have been nothing else. And since the capitalist system functions in the manner we have already described, it did not make much difference whether people understood how it worked or not. On this subject, Trotsky wrote:

"It is utterly impossible to seek the causes for the recurrences of capitalist society in the subjective consciousness – in the intentions or plans – of its members. The objective recurrences of capitalism were formulated before science began to think about them seriously. To this day the preponderant majority of men know nothing about the laws that govern capitalist economy. The whole strength of Marx's method was in his approach to economic phenomena, not from the subjective point of view of certain persons, but from the objective point of view of society as a whole, just as an experimental natural scientist approaches a beehive or an ant-hill.

"For economic science the decisive significance is what and how people do, not what they themselves think about their actions. At the base of society is not religion and morality, but nature and labour. Marx's method is materialistic, because it proceeds from existence to consciousness, not the other way around. Marx's method is dialectic, because it regards both nature and society as they evolve, and evolution itself as the constant struggle of conflicting forces." [16]

A project for socialism?

Even so, it is incorrect to speak of *project* for socialism. This implies a scheme or plan for the future socialist society. *That was not the method of Marx and Engels but of the utopian socialists of the beginning of the 19th century – Saint Simon, Fourier, Robert Owen and Weitling.* They all had a historical project – that is, a fully worked out plan for the future socialist society. Marx and Engels did not have such a plan, and this is one of the main criticisms that Dieterich levels against the founders of scientific socialism. This shows that Dieterich is very much in the tradition of 19th century utopian socialism and not at all in the tradition of scientific socialism.

The working out of blueprints for the socialist society of the future formed no part of the materialist method of Marx and Engels, who were quite content to allow future generations to work out the details for themselves. But this does not at all signify that they left no idea about what socialism would look like. On the contrary, Marx and Engels already traced the general lines in works like *The Critique of the Gotha Programme*, *Capital*, *The Civil War in France*, *The Origin of the Family, Private Property and the State,* and other writings. Lenin later developed these ideas in his writings on the state, especially *State and Revolution.*

16. Leon Trotsky, Introduction to *The Living Thoughts of Karl Marx*.

Unlike the utopian socialists, Marx and Engels did not invent schemes ("historical projects") for the future society, but attempted to derive their ideas about socialism from the real historical conditions and the real movement of the working class. There are elements of the future socialist society already present in capitalism, just as the elements of capitalism were already coming into existence in the later stages of feudalism. Workers' power and socialism are not invented by utopians or in the study of university professors or in Internet chat rooms but arise from the class struggle and the concrete historical experience of the proletariat.

Let us give one important example of Marx's materialist method. In his earlier writings, including *The Communist Manifesto*, the question of the state is not really developed, and the question of the concrete forms of a workers' state ("the dictatorship of the proletariat") is not dealt with at all. Marx did not invent a project for an ideal workers' state, but derived his theory of the dictatorship of the proletariat from the actual experience of the workers of Paris in 1871. The Paris Commune was the concrete basis upon which Marx developed his theory of a workers' state in the transition from capitalism to socialism.

In the introduction to the Second German edition, Marx and Engels write that they felt they could not alter the text of *The Manifesto*, partly because it was already an historic document, but also because in general lines, its message had been validated by history. However, one important modification was necessary in the light of the experience of the Paris Commune, "where the proletariat for the first time held political power for two whole months, this programme has in some details been antiquated. One thing especially was proved by the Commune, viz., that the working class cannot simply lay hold of ready-made state machinery, and wield it for its own purposes."

Marx's conception of workers' power (the dictatorship of the proletariat) was not a utopian project but a practical programme for workers' power, for a workers' democracy, which Marx did not suck out of his thumb but derived from the actual historical experience of the French working class. It was not Marx, or any other socialist theoretician, who invented the "dictatorship of the proletariat" but the ordinary working men and women of Paris. This method was what Trotsky had in mind when he wrote:

"Science does not reach its goal in the hermetically sealed study of the scholar, but in flesh-and-blood society. All the interests and passions that rend society asunder, exert their influence on the development of science – especially of political economy, the science of wealth and poverty. The struggle of workers against capitalists forced the theoreticians of the bourgeoisie to turn their backs upon a scientific analysis of the system of exploitation and to busy themselves with a bare description of economic facts, a study of the economic past and, what is immeasurably worse, a downright falsification of things as they are for the purpose of justifying the capitalist regime. The economic doctrine which is nowadays taught in official institutions of learning and preached in the bourgeois press offers no dearth of important factual material, yet it is utterly incapable of encompassing the economic process as a whole and discovering its laws and perspectives, nor has it any desire to do so. Official political economy is dead. Real knowledge of capitalist society can be obtained only through Marx's *Capital*." [17]

Incidentally, the kind of workers' state that Marx had in mind had nothing to do with the monstrous totalitarian and bureaucratic regimes that Dieterich, to his shame, still describes as "really existing socialism". Marx used the term "dictatorship of the proletariat" at a time when the word dictatorship did not yet carry the kind of connotations that it does today, after the nightmare totalitarian regimes of Hitler and Mussolini, Franco and Stalin, Pinochet and Videla. He based his idea on the Roman Republic, when in time of war, special powers were granted to the "dictator" for a period of one year.

The state is always an instrument of domination of one class over another, and a workers' state is no exception to the rule. The purpose of a workers' state is to overcome the resistance of the old ruling class, the former property owners who will never surrender their power, wealth and privileges without a fight. But there is a big difference between a workers' state and all other states that have existed in the past: they were states representing the interests of a small minority over the big majority of society. Therefore, the state was always a bureaucratic monster, absorbing a huge proportion of the wealth created by the working class on standing armies, the police, the judiciary, prisons, secret police, etc. On the contrary, a workers' state will be a state representing the big majority against a small minority. This will give it an entirely different character.

The Paris Commune was, in fact, a model of proletarian democracy: "In a rough sketch of national organization, which the Commune had no time to develop, it states clearly that the Commune was to be the political form of even the smallest country hamlet, and that in the rural districts the standing army was to be replaced by a national militia, with an extremely short term of service. The rural communities of every district were to administer their common affairs by an assembly of delegates in the central town, and these district assemblies were again to send deputies to the National Delegation in Paris, each delegate to be at any time revocable and bound by the *mandat imperatif* (formal instructions) of his constituents. The few but important functions which would still remain for a central government were not to be suppressed, as has been intentionally misstated, but were to be discharged by Communal and thereafter responsible agents." [18]

17. Leon Trotsky, Introduction to *The Living Thoughts of Karl Marx*.
18. Marx and Engels, *Selected Works*, vol.3, *The Civil War in France*, p. 221.

Who invented the soviets?

If Marx and Engels did not invent the idea of a workers' state, neither did Lenin invent the soviets. The creation of the soviets in the course of the 1905 Revolution in Russia is yet another marvellous example of the creative genius of ordinary working people, once they enter the arena of struggle. Nowhere does the idea of soviets feature in the writings of the great Marxist thinkers prior to 1905. They were not foreseen in the pages of *The Communist Manifesto*, and they were not the creation of any political party. *They were the spontaneous creations of the workers in struggle, the product of the initiative and creative genius of the working class.*

In the first place the soviets represented committees of struggle, assemblies of delegates drawn from the factories. In tsarist Russia there was no opportunity for the creation of a mass reformist labour movement with a privileged labour aristocracy and an ossified bureaucracy at its head. There was a vacuum, which was filled by the soviets. These embryonic organs of workers' power began life as *extended strike committees*. The soviets themselves first arose in the heat of the all-Russian October general strike. In the absence of well-established mass trade unions, the striking workers moved to elect delegates who began to come together in improvised strike committees, which were generalized to include all sections of the class.

Here again, we see how the working class, through struggle, establishes the organizational forms that it needs to bring about the socialist transformation of society. Lenin immediately grasped the significance of the soviets, as did Trotsky, who was elected chairman of the most important of them – the St. Petersburg Soviet. The Bolsheviks in St. Petersburg, unlike Lenin, did not understand the soviets. They did not act like Marxists but like formalists and bureaucrats. They turned up at the first meeting of the Soviet and read out a declaration that the Soviet must either join the Party or else dissolve. The astonished delegates just shrugged their shoulders and passed on to the next point on the agenda.

Marxists always base themselves on the real movement of the working class. In Venezuela the movement in the direction of workers' control came from below. It is too early to speak of soviets in Venezuela yet, but the elements of soviets exist in the form of the workers' committees and "cogestión". The reformists and bureaucrats are doing their best to prevent the movement for workers' control from developing. They all have their "projects" of one kind or another (none of which challenges capitalism), but they insist that there are no conditions for workers' control in Venezuela, that the workers are "too backward" (because they do not understand the New Historical Project) and so on and so forth.

It is really a scandal that people who call themselves socialists (and even communists) should complain about the alleged backwardness of the workers and peasants of Venezuela. Throughout the whole revolutionary process, the masses have shown a very high level of revolutionary consciousness and maturity. At every stage they have been the real motor force of the revolution. They have saved it at every critical moment when it was in danger. Yet to this day middle class snobs dare to speak of the "backwardness" of the masses, their allegedly low political level, immaturity, etc.

In reality it is the reformists who lack revolutionary consciousness and are dragging the movement back. Hiding behind fancy language and all kinds of utopian-reformist schemes, plans and "historical projects", their only role is to confuse and disorient the intellectuals and students who take them seriously. But the real movement of the workers and peasants will leave them far behind. Like the workers in the St. Petersburg Soviet, they will simply shrug their shoulders and pass on to the next point on the agenda.

Marxism and religion

The second part of the book *Socialism of the XXI Century* is devoted to the question of Chávez and Christianity and to the history of Christianity. Some Marxists have criticized Chávez for his frequent references to Jesus Christ as the first socialist. Our friend Heinz naturally has something to say on this subject (he has something to say about everything). He even dedicates his first chapter to it. As usual, he wishes to "help" the President by clarifying some of his ideas. And as usual, instead of clarifying, he piles confusion upon confusion.

Hugo Chávez stands at the head of an overwhelmingly Catholic nation, and is himself a believer. He has always distinguished carefully between the reactionary Church hierarchy, the servant of the oligarchy, and the rank and file priests and the millions of workers and peasants who are religious. That is absolutely correct and any Marxist would do the same thing. Despite their religious beliefs, the workers and peasants are revolutionary, just as the first Christians were. In his weekly television programme *Aló Presidente* (27th March 2005) Chávez said:

"I am a socialist of the new era, of the 21st century, and we are saying that the world should revise the Christian-socialist thesis. If Christ lived here, he would be a socialist, and Simon Bolivar would go straight to socialism."

In an interview with *Time* magazine (Sunday, September 24, 2006), he said: "When I was released from prison [in 1994] and began my political life, I naively took as a reference point Tony Blair's proposal for a 'third way' between capitalism and socialism – capitalism with a human face. Not anymore. After seeing the failure of Washington-backed capitalist reforms in Latin America, I no longer think a third way is possible. Capitalism is the way of the devil and exploitation, of the kind of misery and inequality that destroys social values. If you really look at things through the eyes of Jesus Christ – who I think was the first socialist – only socialism can really create a genuine society."

More recently Chávez advised the heads of the Catholic Church to read the works of Marx and Lenin as well as the Bible. We do not know whether they have taken his advice but as dialectical materialists, Marxists do not believe in the existence of either hell or heaven. There is only one world and we must fight to make it fit for men and women to live in. Our aim is to fight for the socialist transformation of society on a national and international scale. We wholeheartedly welcome the participation of every progressive person, no matter what his or her beliefs in the struggle. Therefore, we welcome the opportunity of the dialogue between Marxists and Christians.

It is clear to any thinking person that the capitalist system is a monstrously oppressive and inhuman system that means untold misery, disease, oppression and death for millions of people in the world. It is surely the duty of any humane person to support the fight against such a system. However, in order to fight effectively, it is necessary to work out a serious programme, policy and perspective that can guarantee success. We believe that only Marxism (scientific socialism) provides such a perspective. Marxists invite men and women to fight to transform their lives and to create a genuinely human society, which would permit the human race to lift itself up to its true stature. We believe that humans have only one life, and should dedicate themselves to making this life beautiful and self-fulfilling. We are fighting for a paradise on this Earth, because we do not think there is any other.

In December 2006 I was invited to participate in the Pan-American Conference of Occupied factories, held in the occupied Cipla plant in Joinville, Brazil. On the platform, side by side with class fighters, revolutionary youth and representatives of the landless peasant movement the MST, was a bishop. He gave a very revolutionary speech, supporting the workers' movement and damning the exploiters to the fires of hell.

In Latin America there are many honest priests who live alongside the workers and peasants and who have placed themselves on the class standpoint of the masses, courageously speaking out against exploitation and oppression. It is absolutely correct and necessary for Marxists to extend a hand of friendship to these honest people and where possible to involve them in the revolutionary movement. Without a scrupulous attitude to this question we would never succeed in winning over the masses to socialism.

Christianity began as a revolutionary movement of the poor and oppressed in the period of decline of the Roman Empire. 2000 years ago the early Christians organised a mass movement of the poorest and most downtrodden sections of society. It is not an accident that the Romans accused the Christians of being a movement of slaves and women. The early Christians were communists, as is quite clear from the *Acts of the Apostles*. Christ himself moved among the poor and dispossessed and frequently attacked the rich. It is not an accident that his first act on entering Jerusalem was to drive the moneychangers out of the Temple. He also said that it is easier for a camel to pass through the eye of a needle than a rich man to enter the Kingdom of God. There are many such expressions in the Bible.

The communism of the early Christians is shown by the fact that in their communities all wealth was held in common. Anyone who wished to join had first to give up all his or her worldly goods. Of course, this communism had a somewhat naïve and primitive character. This is no reflection on the men and women of that time, who were very courageous people who were not afraid to sacrifice their lives in the struggle against the monstrous Roman slave state. But the real achievement of communism (that is, a classless society) was impossible at that time because the material conditions for it were absent.

Christianity and communism

Modern archaeological research and particularly the discovery of the Dead Sea Scrolls have confirmed completely the theses of Karl Kautsky in his brilliant book *The Foundations of Christianity.* Kautsky explained a hundred years ago that the early Christians were members of a radical Jewish sect, the Essenes, who espoused communist ideas and practiced a community of goods until the Romans destroyed them. The Church Fathers were outspoken in their denunciations of private property and advocated the sharing out of all wealth.

In the 3rd century John Chrysostom, bishop of Byzantium, advocated communism. But gradually the tops of the church became detached from the masses and increasingly fell under the influence of alien classes. They were inclined to seek a deal with the authorities, especially when the ruling class realised that it was impossible to suppress the new religion by force and that it was necessary to disarm it by incorporating the tops into the state.

Later, when the Christian church was taken over by the state under the emperor Constantine, the original revolutionary and communist message of Christianity was expunged from the historical record and the Scriptures were purged to suit the interests of the Roman state. In a similar way the genuine ideas of Lenin and the Bolshevik Party were twisted and misrepresented by the Stalinist bureaucracy in Russia after the death of Lenin in 1924. The emperor Constantine ordered the bishops to agree on an orthodox version of the Bible and, when they took too long about it, surrounded the building where they were gathered with his soldiers and stopped all food and drink from entering. They soon came to a satisfactory conclusion!

The long and bloody wars against heretical movements in the later Roman Empire were the way in which the genuine heritage of early Christianity was destroyed by fire and sword. Today we only know the opinions of the "heretics" through the writings of the Church – their bitter enemies. It is rather like trying to understand the ideas of Hugo Chávez by reading the documents of the US State Department. But it is clear that sects like the Donatists in North Africa defended communist ideas until they were exterminated by the Roman state with the enthusiastic support of the Church hierarchy.

From this time onwards, the Christian Church became the faithful servant of the state and the ruling class. The bishops, who became rich and powerful, served the interests of the emperors and later the feudal monarchs and landlords. But there was still a problem. Despite the systematic attempts to purge the Bible of all its revolutionary content, many passages still remained that had a clearly subversive character. This problem was solved by the fact that the Bible was in Latin, a language that nobody understood outside a very small number of priests and scholars. The translation of the Bible by a handful of brave men (many of whom paid for it with their lives) played an important role in the revolutionary movements of the later Middle Ages. Those who were rebelling against the feudal system in the period of its decay looked for inspiration in the writings of speeches of John Wycliffe (in England), Jan Huss (in Bohemia) and Martin Luther (in Germany).

The ruling ideas of every epoch are the ideas of the ruling class. But there are always other ideas that contradict the former and reflect the ideas and aspirations of the revolutionary classes in society. In the Middle Ages and even later, the Church had a stranglehold on the intellectual life of society, and therefore any revolutionary movement had first of all to settle accounts with the existing religion. This they did by attacking the Church hierarchy and exposing its corruption, while defending the original revolutionary message of the early Christians. The Religious Wars of the 16th and 17th centuries were really class wars that were fought under the banner of religion. The Hussites of Bohemia and the Anabaptists of Germany expressed communist ideas, as did the Levellers and Diggers during the English Revolution of 1640-49. In every case they took as their starting point the communism of the early Christians and the Bible.

Marx and Engels for the first time gave communism a scientific character. They explained that the real emancipation of the masses depends on the level of development of the productive forces (industry, agriculture, science and technology), which will create the necessary conditions for a general reduction of the working day and access to culture for all, as the only way of transforming the way people think and behave towards each other. The material conditions at the time of early Christianity were not sufficiently advanced to permit such a development, and therefore the communism of the early Christians remained on a primitive level – the level of consumption (the sharing out of food, clothes, etc.) and not real communism which is based on the collective ownership of the means of production.

However, the revolutionary traditions of early Christianity bear absolutely no relation to the present situation. Ever since the 4th century AD, when the Christian movement was hijacked by the state and turned into an instrument of the oppressors, the Christian Church has been on the side of the rich and powerful and against the poor. Today the main churches are extremely wealthy institutions, closely linked to big business. The Vatican owns a big bank and possesses enormous wealth and power, the Church of England is the biggest landowner in Britain, and so on.

Politically, the churches have systematically backed reaction. Catholic priests blessed the armies of Franco in their campaign to crush the Spanish workers and peasants. The Pope backed Hitler and Mussolini. In Brazil the hierarchy of the Church had no difficulty in collaborating with the military dictatorship, although many rank and file priests took the side of the workers.

What does this mean? It means that there are really two churches: one that stands for the interests of the rich and powerful, the church of the landlords and capitalists, and another that identifies with the cause of the poor people, the workers and peasants. It is absolutely necessary to extend a hand of friendship and enter into a dialogue with the latter, while conducting an implacable struggle against the former. Our task is to put an end to the dictatorship of Capital that keeps the human race in a state of slavery. In order to do this it is necessary to struggle against all kinds of obstacles. Throughout history the hierarchies of the established churches have always sided with the rich and powerful. But the ordinary workers and peasants who are also believers wish to change society.

Although from a philosophical point of view Marxism is incompatible with religion, it goes without saying that we are opposed to any idea of prohibiting or repressing religion. We stand for the complete freedom of the individual to hold any religious belief, or none at all. What we do say is that there should be a radical separation between church and state. The churches must not be supported directly or indirectly out of taxation, nor should religion be taught in state schools. If people want religion, they should maintain their churches exclusively through the contributions of the congregation and preach their doctrines in their own time.

Socialism will permit the free development of human beings, without the constraint of material needs. To the degree that men and women are able to take control of their lives and develop themselves as free human beings, we believe that interest in religion – that is, the search for consolation in an afterlife – will decline naturally of itself. Of course, you may disagree with this prediction. Time will tell who is right. In the meantime, disagreements on such matters should not prevent all honest Christians from joining hands with the Marxists in the struggle for a new and better world.

The class struggle finds its expression in the church, and this is particularly true in Latin America. It is reflected in the Theology of Liberation and similar progressive tendencies in the church. Marxists regard this as a most important phenomenon. We regard it as our duty to enter into a friendly discussion with this trend and to encourage the evolution of Christians towards socialism and Marxism.

Was Jesus Christ a reformist?

In the Bible God creates Man after his own image. Now Heinz Dieterich transplants his 21st Century reformism back into history and recreates it after his own image. President Chávez always refers to Jesus as a *revolutionary and a socialist*. What about Heinz Dieterich? He transforms Jesus Christ into *a Social Democratic reformist*. Instead of courageous revolutionaries and communists, the early Christians become respectable *social reformers and liberals*:

"The reference [of Chávez] to Jesus as the first socialist is applicable from the ethical plane of *the reforming praxis* of the Nazarene and the social coexistences (las convivencias sociales) of the first Christian communities, that is to say, from the third and fourth level of human existence (anthropological)." [19]

Heinz's prose, always leaden footed, here begins to drag itself along even more painfully than usual. But never mind. Let us at least make an effort to discover in what direction he is limping. He continues, either oblivious of the reader's perplexity or indifferent to it: "The first communities were called *Ekklesia*, taking over the terminology and the praxis [how Heinz loves this word!] of the popular assemblies of the political system of Athens, which was the first participative democracy in a class society in the West, governed by a combination of electoral and lottery systems (by lots), a participative democracy that, nevertheless, was not universal but elitist because it excluded women, manual workers, slaves and freedmen." [20]

It is not correct to say that the early Christian communities were modelled on the institutions of Athenian slave-owning democracy. Karl Kautsky pointed out a hundred years ago that the early Christian communities derived from the Essene communities, which were rigorously Jewish and shunned all foreign admixtures. The latest investigations into the Essene community in Qumran in Galilee fully confirms this analysis. The Essenes were a revolutionary Jewish sect, which held communist views strikingly similar to the ideas in the *Acts of the Apostles*. Their founder was said to have been tortured and executed by the Romans, who finally destroyed the Qumran community in the 1st century AD. But let Heinz continue:

"This advance of participative democracy in the 'church of the catacombs', which was later lost when it became converted into the imperial church, is repeated in the individual praxis of Jesus. *The ethic of solidarity, respect for others, compassion for the poor, for the excluded, for those who are discriminated against, and the equality of human rights and practical opportunities in life,* which the Nazarene preached and practiced, was, without doubt, a progressive and antisystemic element in the repressive-tribal-male chauvinist environment of Roman-dominated Palestine." [21]

Having shown he does not understand the early Christian church, Heinz now goes on to present Jesus as *a 21st Century reformist* – a kind of *Galilean Tony Blair*. The reverend Tony Blair would readily say *Amen* to all this, and so would all the other hypocrites, liberals and reformists who cover up the oppressive nature of class society with smug expressions such as "*equal rights*" and "*equal opportunities*", "*the ethic of solidarity*", "*compassion for the poor*", "*respect for others*" and simi-

19. Dieterich, *Hugo Chávez y el Socialismo del Siglo XXI*, p. 21.
20. Ibid. p. 22.
21. Ibid., my emphasis, AW.

lar empty moralistic claptrap that serves as a cover for their subservience to the rich and powerful and their cowardly acceptance of the status quo.

Do we all not have *equal rights* to become billionaires by showing personal initiative? Do we not all have *equal opportunities* to "improve ourselves" by working hard? Do the rich not manifest *the ethic of solidarity* when they give money to charity? And do they not show *compassion for the poor* when they weep over the fate of the starving millions in Africa? Maybe they do, but all this does not change the situation in the slightest degree.

The French writer Anatole France effectively exposed this hypocrisy when he wrote: "The law in its majesty makes no distinction between rich and poor; both are forbidden to sleep under the bridges of Paris." Engels pointed out that *all rights presuppose inequality* and are therefore *bourgeois* rights. The early Christians were not fighting for equal rights but for the New Jerusalem in which there would be no rich and poor and no private property. They were viciously persecuted by the Roman State precisely because they were revolutionaries and communists and not social reformers like Heinz Dieterich, who would have not have alarmed the Romans, or anyone else, in the slightest degree.

4. History and economics

Does Marxism deal with economics 'in general'?

Marxism, as we have seen, deals with history concretely, not in the abstract. Historical materialism carefully deals with the different historical stages through which humankind has developed and explains the particular laws that govern different socio-economic formations. The laws governing slave society are not the same as the laws that govern feudalism, and the latter cannot be equated with the law of motion of capitalist society. Each must be examined separately, and the task of historical materialism is not to impose a preconceived theory on history but to derive the laws of motion from a careful study of each particular case. This is clearly explained by Trotsky in his masterly Introduction to *The Living Thoughts of Karl Marx:*

"It was not Marx's aim to discover the 'eternal laws' of economy. He denied the existence of such laws. The history of the development of human society is the history of the succession of various systems of economy, each operating in accordance with its own laws. The transition from one system to another was always determined by the growth of the productive forces, i.e., of technique and the organization of labour. Up to a certain point, social changes are quantitative in character and do not alter the foundations of society, i.e., the prevalent forms of property. But a point is reached when the matured productive forces can no longer contain themselves within the old forms of property; then follows a radical change in the social order, accompanied by shocks. The primitive commune was either superseded or supplemented by slavery; slavery was succeeded by serfdom with its feudal superstructure; the commercial development of cities brought Europe in the 16th century to the capitalist order, which thereupon passed through several stages. In his *Capital*, Marx does not study economy in general, but capitalist economy, which has its own specific laws. Only in passing does he refer to the other economic systems to elucidate the characteristics of capitalism.

"The self-sufficient economy of the primitive peasant family has no need of a 'political economy,' for it is dominated on the one hand by the forces of nature and on the other by the forces of tradition. The self-contained natural economy of the Greeks or the Romans, founded on slave labour, was ruled by the will of the slave-owner, whose 'plan' in turn was directly determined by the laws of nature and routine. The same might also be said about the mediaeval estate with its peasant serfs. In all these instances economic relations were clear and transparent in their primitive crudity. But the case of contemporary society is altogether different. It destroyed the old self-contained connections and the inherited modes of labour. The new economic relations have linked cities and villages, provinces and nations. *Division of labour has encompassed the planet, having shattered tradition and routine, these bonds have not composed themselves to some definite plan, but rather apart from human consciousness and foresight, and it would seem as if behind the very backs of men.* The interdependence of men, groups, classes, nations, which follows from division of labour, is not directed or managed by anyone. People work for each other without knowing each other, without inquiring about one another's needs, in the hope, and even with the assurance, that their relations will somehow regulate themselves. And by and large they do, or rather were wont to." [1]

These lines explain with admirable conciseness and clarity the essence of Marx's method of historical materialism. How does this scientific clarity compare with the method of Dieterich? On page 39 of his book *Socialism of the XXI Century*, he takes us for a brisk run through human history, beginning with the first stone tools approximately 800,000 years ago. He calculates that the division of labour (in the form of division of activities within the family) began about 80,000 years ago. He then jumps to the domestication of animals and the discovery of agriculture, which he dates at approximately 12,000 years ago. He then immediately introduces barter and exchange. All this seems to be taken from Arno Peters, but the lack of quotation marks makes impossible to know where Peters ends and Dieterich begins. But since they share the same confused ideas this is purely a secondary matter.

In a completely unscientific and unhistorical manner, Dieterich divides the whole of human history into two parts: the early phase of primitive tribal communism, which he claims was based on the principle of "equivalents", and all the rest. Without the slightest basis, he lumps together slave society, feudalism and capitalism. All these societies, he claims, were based upon moneymaking ("chrematistics") and "unequal exchange", whereas previously exchange was conducted on an equal basis.

This completely unhistorical view comes from Arno Peters, who succeeds in mixing everything up and getting into a hopeless mess. *It is completely wrong to*

1. Leon Trotsky, Introduction to *The Living Thoughts of Karl Marx*, published as a pamphlet, *Marxism in our Time*, Pathfinder 1970 pp. 8-10, *my emphasis*, AW.

lump together different socio-economic systems with different economic laws of motion, and different ways of extracting surplus value. It is also completely wrong to describe barter, the earliest form of trade, as the *exchange of equivalents.* It is equally false to say that the capitalist market economy is based on unequal exchange. Marx says *precisely the opposite* in the first volume of *Capital.* We will return to this question later.

Dieterich's presentation of the stages of human development is extremely sketchy and superficial. In particular, the origins of trade are presented in a very confused manner. On pages 41-2 of the same book, we are informed that the transition from barter to trade commence about 7,000 years ago, and that more than 5,000 years ago "[...] this new economic order, created by commerce and war, imposed itself in such a large part of the populated world of those times, that we can speak of the beginning of a new epoch of national economy, which slowly replaced the local economy. In this context, we understand by 'nation' a state entity which has grown up historically with its own tradition and hegemonic orientation; we therefore include here all communities which surpass the framework of local self-sufficiency, which have been maintained from the formation of the first city states about 5,000 years ago, in their character and structure, up to the present day.

"This new epoch, the national economy began about 3,000 years before our epoch when in the river valleys of the Nile, Euphrates and Tigris, the Indus and the Huang-Ho a large quantity of people combined to tame the force of the rivers and use their water for their ends.

At this point, according to Dieterich, "trade and the private appropriation of the land lead to the domination of man by man." As a matter of fact, there was no private ownership of land in the early civilizations of Mesopotamia, Egypt, China and the Indus valley. In all these states land was held by the state, which was in the hands of the monarch and the priest caste. In Egypt under the Ottomans the sultan (that is, the state) owned almost all agricultural land. The state taxed the peasants and controlled irrigation by means of compulsory labour (*corvée*). At the base, as was usually the case with the Asiatic mode of production, the clans had control of the land and the state allowed them to carry on subsistence agriculture and did not interfere except to extract taxes and *corvée.* Private ownership of land was only introduced in the 19th century through the reforms of Muhammad Ali, although the old system had already been undermined by the encroachment of private property through mortgages, pawning, etc. However, all this took place in the late eighteenth and nineteenth centuries and not "3,000 years before our epoch".

True private ownership of land begins, not with Egypt, Mesopotamia, China and India 5,000 years ago, but with Greece and Rome at a far later date. Engels explains in *The Origin of the Family, Private Property and the State*, that landed property in ancient Athens was originally held by the gens, but that in the higher stage of barbarism this broke down:

"In the Heroic age the four tribes of the Athenians were still settled in Attica in separate territories; even the twelve phratries composing them seem still to have had distinct seats in the twelve towns of Cecrops. The constitution was that of the heroic age: assembly of the people, council of the people, basileus. As far as written history takes us back, we find the land already divided up and privately owned, which is in accordance with the relatively advanced commodity production and the corresponding trade in commodities developed towards the end of the upper stage of barbarism. In addition to grain, wine and oil were produced; to a continually increasing extent, the sea trade in the Aegean was captured from the Phoenicians, and most of it passed into Athenian hands. Through the sale and purchase of land, and the progressive division of labour between agriculture and handicraft, trade, and shipping, it was inevitable that the members of the different gentes, phratries, and tribes very soon became intermixed, and that into the districts of the phratry and tribe moved inhabitants, who, although fellow countrymen, did not belong to these bodies and were therefore strangers in their own place of domicile. For when times were quiet, each tribe and each phratry administered its own affairs without sending to Athens to consult the council of the people or the basileus. But anyone not a member of the phratry or tribe was, of course, excluded from taking any part in this administration, even though living in the district." [2]

The undermining of the old gentile constitution gave rise to private property of the land, a growing social differentiation and the class struggle, which in the later history of Athens reached a very acute level. This was hardly the case in the older civilizations mentioned by Dieterich, where class differentiations existed but only in an undeveloped form. We find occasional manifestations of class conflict in ancient Egypt (the first recorded strike was a strike of builders working on the pyramids), but nothing remotely similar to the class struggles and political revolutions that shook Greece and Rome.

It is no accident that the development of feudalism and capitalism took place in Europe, and not in Asia, where the ancient mode of production remained until quite recently and held back social and economic development. As a matter of fact, the "Asiatic economy", in which private ownership of land was virtually unknown, was only overthrown by capitalism in the 19th century. In his celebrated articles on India, Marx pointed out that when the English conquered India they could not understand the system of landed property, which was completely different to the capitalist relations that existed in their own country.

In June 1853 Engels wrote to Marx: "The key to the whole East is the absence of private property in Land". And he attributes the difference to climatological factors: "How comes it that the Orientals did not reach to landed property or feudalism? I think the reason lies principally in the climate, combined with the conditions

2. Marx and Engels, *Selected Works*, Vol.3, Engels, *The Origin of the Family, Private Property and the State*, Chapter V. The Rise of the Athenian State, p. 276.

of the soil, especially the great desert stretches which reach from the Sahara right through Arabia, Persia, India and Tartary to the highest Asiatic uplands. Artificial irrigation is here the first condition of cultivation, and this is the concern either of the communes, the Provinces or the Central Government."[3]

This is just another example of Dieterich's impressionism and his unscientific and slipshod presentation of historical stages. We will see many more, as he jumps, without even blinking, 5,000 years to the 20th century completely ignoring all the intervening stages (slave society, feudalism, and the Asiatic mode of production) taking us immediately from the first city states to the present day. For a man capable of hurtling in a couple of pages from bacteria to the invasion of Kosovo, the description of the whole of human history is obviously mere child's play. Heinz Dieterich displays the same rigorous approach in relation to human evolution that he showed to the rest of the universe. With the same cheerful exuberance, Dieterich merely skates over 5,000 years of history. He cheerfully lumps together entirely different socio-economic systems, without the slightest regard to historical accuracy.

This confused method is not an accident. On page 49 of the aforementioned book we read the following: "If we analyse the economy and its history with respect to the totality of the principles which created its base, we find only two archetypes: the equivalent economy, under which humanity has lived for almost 800,000 years from the beginning of its economic history, and the non equivalent economy, which approximately 6,000 years ago began to place the economy on a new base, and which subjected the entire world to its system."

Here, as everywhere else in his book, Dieterich stands reality on its head. The different productive systems that characterise human society from its beginnings in the dawn of history right down to the present day have never been constructed on the basis of principles of any kind. That is an entirely idealist way of approaching human history. *On the contrary, the principles of political economy have in every period been derived from existing productive and social relations*. In the second place, what does Dieterich mean by a "equivalent economy"? He is referring to the exchange of equivalents. In the period to which he refers – the entire period of 800,000 years from the production of the first crude stone implements to the beginnings of class society in the Neolithic period – there was no systematic exchange, either of equivalents or anything else, as we shall see.

Marx on barter

Trade is believed to have taken place throughout much of recorded human history. There is evidence of trade even earlier than 7,000 years ago. Peter Watson dates the history of long-distance commerce from about 150,000 years ago.[4] But such exchange that took place had an accidental character. There was no money and no

3. Engels, Letter to Marx, June 6, 1853, Marx-Engels, *Selected Correspondence*, p. 82.
4. See P. Watson, *Ideas: A History of Thought and Invention from Fire to Freud*, Introduction, 2005.

merchant class, and trade necessarily took the form of barter. In the first volume of *Capital*, Marx deals with barter. It is worth quoting what he has to say on this subject at length:

"The direct barter of products attains the elementary form of the relative expression of value in one respect, but not in another. That form is x Commodity A = y Commodity B. The form of direct barter is x use-value A = y use-value B. The articles A and B in this case are not as yet commodities, but become so only by the act of barter. The first step made by an object of utility towards acquiring exchange-value is when it forms a non-use-value for its owner, and that happens when it forms a superfluous portion of some article required for his immediate wants. Objects in themselves are external to man, and consequently alienable by him. In order that this alienation may be reciprocal, it is only necessary for men, by a tacit understanding, to treat each other as private owners of those alienable objects, and by implication as independent individuals. But such a state of reciprocal independence has no existence in a primitive society based on property in common, whether such a society takes the form of a patriarchal family, an ancient Indian community, or a Peruvian Inca State. The exchange of commodities, therefore, first begins on the boundaries of such communities, at their points of contact with other similar communities, or with members of the latter. So soon, however, as products once become commodities in the external relations of a community, they also, by reaction, become so in its internal intercourse. *The proportions in which they are exchangeable are at first quite a matter of chance. What makes them exchangeable is the mutual desire of their owners to alienate them.* Meantime the need for foreign objects of utility gradually establishes itself. *The constant repetition of exchange makes it a normal social act. In the course of time, therefore, some portion at least of the products of labour must be produced with a special view to exchange. From that moment the distinction becomes firmly established between the utility of an object for the purposes of consumption, and its utility for the purposes of exchange. Its use-value becomes distinguished from its exchange-value. On the other hand, the quantitative proportion in which the articles are exchangeable, becomes dependent on their production itself. Custom stamps them as values with definite magnitudes.*"[5]

In primitive societies the predominant mode of production is either local subsistence agriculture or hunting and gathering. *People do not produce articles for exchange (commodities) but primarily articles for their own consumption (use-values).* Occasionally these products may be exchanged for the produce of other communities. This takes the form of barter, and has a purely accidental character. Only gradually, after a long period, do the goods exchanged acquire through custom a certain accepted value. Marx continues:

5. Marx, *Capital*, vol. 1, Penguin 1976, pp.181-2, my emphasis, AW.

"In the direct barter of products, each commodity is directly a means of exchange to its owner, and to all other persons an equivalent, but that only in so far as it has use-value for them. *At this stage, therefore, the articles exchanged do not acquire a value-form independent of their own use-value, or of the individual needs of the exchangers.* The necessity for a value-form grows with the increasing number and variety of the commodities exchanged. The problem and the means of solution arise simultaneously. Commodity-owners never equate their own commodities to those of others, and exchange them on a large scale, without different kinds of commodities belonging to different owners being exchangeable for, and equated as values to, one and the same special article. Such last-mentioned article, by becoming the equivalent of various other commodities, acquires at once, though within narrow limits, the character of a general social equivalent. This character comes and goes with the momentary social acts that called it into life. In turns and transiently it attaches itself first to this and then to that commodity. But with the development of exchange it fixes itself firmly and exclusively to particular sorts of commodities, and becomes crystallized by assuming the money-form. The particular kind of commodity to which it sticks is at first a matter of accident. Nevertheless there are two circumstances whose influence is decisive. The money-form attaches itself either to the most important articles of exchange from outside, and these in fact are primitive and natural forms in which the exchange-value of home products finds expression; or else it attaches itself to the object of utility that forms, like cattle, the chief portion of indigenous alienable wealth. Nomad races are the first to develop the money-form, because all their worldly goods consist of moveable objects and are therefore directly alienable; and because their mode of life, by continually bringing them into contact with foreign communities, solicits the exchange of products. Man has often made man himself, under the form of slaves, serve as the primitive material of money, but has never used land for that purpose. Such an idea could only spring up in a bourgeois society already well developed. It dates from the last third of the 17th century, and the first attempt to put it in practice on a national scale was made a century afterwards, during the French bourgeois revolution.

"In proportion as exchange bursts its local bonds, and the value of commodities more and more expands into an embodiment of human labour in the abstract, in the same proportion the character of money attaches itself to commodities that are by Nature fitted to perform the social function of a universal equivalent. Those commodities are the precious metals."[6]

The accidental nature of barter means that products were exchange on a more or less haphazard basis. Gradually, through experience and custom, it might be possible to establish a rough calculation concerning the value of different products: so many beaver skins in exchange for so much tobacco, salmon, or maize. Whether or not these relations really reflected an exchange of equivalents it would be difficult

6. Marx, *Capital*, vol. 1, chapter 2, Penguin 1976, pp.182-3, my emphasis, AW.

to say. The point is that at this stage in human development, we are dealing not with the exchange of exchange values but of *use values*. The members of a tribe living inland are greatly attracted by the coloured shells offered to them by people living near the coast, who in turn are attracted by the beaver skins offered by the former. They haggle and eventually arrive at a satisfactory deal. Are they exchanging equivalents? Not at all. What are being exchanged are *use-values*. Value here has an entirely accidental expression. This has nothing in common with exchange under capitalism.

In the passage quoted above Marx expresses himself with the utmost clarity. What are exchanged in barter are use-values. At this stage, therefore, the articles exchanged "do not acquire a value-form independent of their own use-value or of the individual needs of the exchangers". Use-values are articles for use, and therefore their value is confined on the one hand to their physical characteristics, on the other to the fact that another person wishes to possess them. The way in which such things are exchanged has a largely arbitrary character. Only at a late stage, when trading becomes the norm, and money (the "commodity of commodities") emerges, does this situation begin to change. It is possible to speak about a universal exchange of equivalents only under capitalism. This is precisely the opposite of what Dieterich and Peters argue.

Dieterich bases his entire historical analysis on the idea of an era of equivalence (pre-capitalist modes of production), which was followed by unequal exchange (capitalism). Where does he get this from? Certainly not from Marx who explained in great detail in the pages of *Capital* that capitalism is based on commodity production – the production of exchange values – and the *exchange of equivalents*. To fail to understand that exploitation takes place under capitalism through equal exchange and by means of equal exchange shows a fundamental misunderstanding of *Capital*. Unlike capitalism, pre-capitalist modes of production are dominated by the production of *use values*. Exchange is occasional; the ratios of exchange are accidental. Gift giving and ritual donations are more important than hard calculation of self-interest. Yet according to Dieterich and Arno Peters this was *the age of equivalence*. Thus, they stand reality on its head.

In *Capital*, volume I, Marx shows that exchange originated from *communities exchanging with communities*, not *individuals with individuals*. Why would they bother to exchange if they could produce the same goods themselves? But communities involved in different types of economic activity are scarcely likely to know the value of goods they never produce. It is said that the Native American Indians sold Manhattan to the Europeans for a handful of beads. In what way this represented an "exchange of equivalents" nobody knows. As on every other question, so on economics Dieterich and Peters adopt a moralistic and sentimental attitude instead of a scientific approach. They are following not in the footsteps of Marx but of *Proudhon*. In a footnote in the *Grundrisse*, Marx ridicules the theories of Proudhon and exposes their utopian character:

"Proudhon begins by taking his ideal of Justice, of '*justice éternelle*,' from the juridical relations that correspond to the production of commodities: thereby, it may be noted, he proves, to the consolation of all good citizens, that the production of commodities is a form of production as everlasting as justice. Then he turns round and seeks to reform the actual production of commodities, and the actual legal system corresponding thereto, in accordance with this ideal. What opinion should we have of a chemist, who, instead of studying the actual laws of the molecular changes in the composition and decomposition of matter, and on that foundation solving definite problems, claimed to regulate the composition and decomposition of matter by means of the 'eternal ideas,' of 'naturalité' and 'affinité'? Do we really know any more about 'usury,' when we say it contradicts 'justice éternelle,' équité éternelle 'mutualité éternelle,' and other vérités éternelles than the fathers of the church did when they said it was incompatible with 'grâce éternelle,' 'foi éternelle,' and 'la volonté éternelle de Dieu'?" [7]

In another footnote he writes: "From this we may form an estimate of the shrewdness of the petit-bourgeois socialism, which, while perpetuating the production of commodities, aims at abolishing the 'antagonism' between money and commodities, and consequently, since money exists only by virtue of this antagonism, at abolishing money itself. We might just as well try to retain Catholicism without the Pope." [8]

Reading these lines we must ask ourselves: is the Peters-Dieterich approach to the economic history of society closer to Marx or to Proudhon? The answer is fairly obvious. In an interview entitled *In Venezuela the Conditions for building XXI Century Socialism have been established*, published in *Rebelión* (2/1/07) we read:

"Q. Is the economy of socialism of the 21st century, then, a barter economy?

"A. No. That is as erroneous as the pronouncement that nobody knows how to build Socialism of the 21st Century. The problem of economic injustice does not lie in money. It has nothing to do with whether economy is monetized or functions through exchange in kind (by barter). In the exploitative relation between slave and master, once the initial payment is amortized, money does not intervene, and yet it is one of the worst brutalities in history.

"Injustice exists when a product 'A' is exchanged for a product 'B' and their values – the labour time necessary to produce each one of them – are not equal, that is to say, when equivalents are not exchanged. Whether that exchange of unequal values (unequal labour efforts) is monetized – that is to say, whether it is expressed in monetary or natural form – is secondary."

Although in every class society the owners of the means of production expropriate the surplus value created by the exploited classes, the mode of exploitation is

7. Marx, *Capital*, Volume 1, pp.178-9.
8. Ibid. Volume 1, chapter 2, p. 181.

very different in each case and must be analysed concretely. It is necessary to analyse the different forms of exploitation from a scientific point of view, not from the standpoint of abstract morality and sentimentality. Dieterich does not do this. Instead he lumps together slavery, serfdom and wage labour under a general heading of a purely moralistic character ("injustice"). From such a method we can learn precisely nothing about the phenomena under consideration. We have already seen that wage labour in slave-owning society was the exception, not the rule. Whereas the modern working class produces the surplus value that constitutes the base of all wealth, the ancient Roman proletariat was a parasitic class that lived on the labour of the productive class – the slaves. The ancient proletariat and the modern proletariat therefore have very little in common.

When Dieterich quotes an authority in support of his economic theories, whom does he choose? Not Marx, Adam Smith or David Ricardo, not the French Physiocrats, Hobbes or Locke, but Aristotle! This great thinker, the most encyclopaedic mind of antiquity, was probably the first to deal with political economy. The economy of Greece, like that of Rome, was a slave economy. Most of production was based on agriculture (although there was significant development of the ceramics industry in Athens) and was carried out by slave labour.

On pages 50-51 of *El Socialismo del Siglo XXI*, Dieterich refers to Aristotle as the founder of the science of economics (Marx had already pointed this out long ago). Heinz is very impressed by the fact that *Aristotle had a negative attitude towards "chrematistics"*. "Chrematistics" comes from the Greek word for money, and Dieterich uses it as a synonym for the pursuit of wealth or profit. The great philosopher regarded this as an unnatural use of human ability, and a disturbance of the economy. He quotes Aristotle's words:

"It is justifiably criticised because it is not based upon nature, but only exploitation. Together with it is found the business of usury, which is hated for good reason because it obtains its profits from money itself and not from the things for the sale of which money was invented, since the latter was only intended to facilitate exchange, but interest means that this is multiplied by itself. For this reason, this type of gain is the one which is most directed against nature."

Heinz Dieterich gives us other quotations against selfishness. He tries to trace the origin of all our ills to a kind of economic equivalent of Original Sin, and quotes Aristotle approvingly as his first witness for the defence. The conclusion that we are presumably intended to draw from this is that Aristotle was some kind of early socialist – in fact, a precursor of Socialism of the 21st Century. Such a conclusion, however, would be entirely false and unhistorical. Why was Aristotle hostile to moneymaking? *Because the society in which Aristotle lived was not based on trade, exchange or usury, but on slavery. For the Greek aristocracy, whose ideological expression Aristotle was, moneymaking was regarded with contempt. The selfish pursuit of money for its own sake was seen as an abomination.* At a time when the centre of one's universe was the city-state, the highest aim in life was not to make money but *to serve the state.*

Therefore, when Aristotle expressed a negative attitude towards money making, he was merely expressing the psychology of the ruling class of his own period. *The same Aristotle who denounced money making also defended slavery.* We should not blame him for this any more than we should praise him for attacking greed. In both cases he was only expressing the accepted ideas and morality of his age, and even this great thinker was unable to rise above this standpoint. Our Heinz has as little understanding of Greek society as of the English Revolution or the shape of the universe. But this does not matter, since in the night all cats are grey. His point of view is that of vulgar abstract super-historical moralizing, which found its expression in the words of the old song: *"money is the root of all evil".*

Capitalism in the ancient world?

If Dieterich wants to find allies in his crusade against "Chrematistics" he can find plenty of people to quote, not only from Aristotle and other writers from slave society but from both earlier and later socio-economic formations. According to the Peters-Dieterich theory of history, all these formations for the last 6,000 years were based on the same thing: "chrematistics" and "unequal exchange".

In fact, most of the societies of antiquity were not based on trade and exchange. In fact, they were not money economies at all. Insofar as trade existed it was on the margins of ancient society, although there were, by way of exception, some trading nations like Phoenicia. But they were not the norm. Insofar as money and trade begin to develop in the ancient world they served to undermine it and paved the way for its dissolution. In the *Grundrisse* Marx writes:

"Among the ancients, we discover no single enquiry as to which form of landed property, etc., is the most productive, which creates maximum wealth. Wealth does not appear as the aim of production, although Cato may well investigate the most profitable cultivation of fields, or Brutus may even lend money at the most favourable rate of interest. The enquiry is always about what kind of property creates the best citizens." [9]

In the light of all this it should be no surprise to anybody except our friend Heinz that Aristotle speaks about trade and all economic activity carried on for a profit in negative terms. *Ancient economic thought was in general hostile to enrichment and the private accumulation of wealth.* This attitude was coherent with an economy mainly closed and static, based on agriculture and on slave labour. Usury (in the original sense of any interest) was denounced by a number of spiritual leaders and philosophers of ancient times, not only Aristotle but Plato, Cicero, Cato, Seneca,

9. Marx, *Grundrisse*, Notebook V. January 22, 1858, Penguin 1973, Chapter on capital. Continued. p.487.

Plutarch, Muhammad (interest of any kind is forbidden by Islam) Philo, Buddha and Moses. In Cato's *De Re Rustica* we read: "And what do you think of usury?" – "What do you think of murder?" We will find the same negative attitude towards trade and profit, not only throughout antiquity but also in the Middle Ages. Only with the dissolution of feudalism and the emergence of capitalist economic relations do we find the beginnings of a change.

The Ten Commandments condemn covetousness (Exodus 20:17). Solomon warned that wicked people are "greedy for gain" (Proverbs 1:10–19). The prophets railed against selfish material acquisition: "Woe to those who devise iniquity [...] they covet fields and take them by violence, also houses, and seize them [...] Behold, against this family I am *devising disaster*." (*Micah* 2:1–3.) The prophet Amos warned the Israelites that because of their rampant greed and exploitation of the poor: "I will destroy the winter house along with the summer house; the houses of ivory shall perish, and the great houses shall have an end." (*Amos* 2:6-7; 3:1, 14-15) Amos warned Israelite leaders, who lived in luxury: "Behold, the days shall come upon you when He [God] will take you away with fishhooks [...] and Israel shall surely be led away captive." (*Amos* 4:1-3; 5:27; 6:7; 7:11, 17.)

Egyptian capitalism?

There was no capitalist class in Egypt. There were small traders and moneylenders, but they did not constitute a separate economic class with influence based on commercial wealth. There was money but no money economy. Things were given a value in gold, silver and copper in fixed weights. In order to facilitate trade temple treasuries stamped silver ingots, but this did not lead to a monetary system worthy of the name. Trade was mostly conducted on the basis of barter. The economic life of the country was measured, not in money, but by the number of ships belonging to the state treasury. Artisans were paid, not in money, but *in kind* – in corn, barley, fish, beer, etc.

Under the Ramessides things were valued in sacks of barley. Even in Egyptian literature wealth was not expressed in terms of gold and silver but always in terms of full granaries, fine herds or marshes abounding in game. From all this it is clear that we cannot speak of an exchange economy in Egypt, but only an exchange of use values. Does this mean that there was no exploitation? Of course it does not. Exploitation did not need to be disguised in exchange. It took place openly, either as slavery or, more commonly, as obligatory labour-service (*corvée*) to the temple or the state.

What we are dealing with here is what Marx referred to as the ancient or Asiatic mode of production. The main factors were the national distribution of manpower (public works), the stockpiling of food to avoid the worse social consequences of years of poor inundation, providing for the gods (that is, Pharaoh and the pries caste) and, lastly, foreign trade. As the population of Egypt was relatively small and the flooding of the Nile created favourable conditions for agriculture, it usually produced a surplus above its immediate needs that could be exchanged. This was the prior condition for trade, but this was conducted with foreign merchants outside the frontiers of Egypt. Inside the frontiers the great majority of economic life was conducted on the basis of a subsistence economy and barter.

A good example of this foreign trade was the expedition that was sent as far as the land of Punt exclusively to obtain incense to burn at the temple. Trade was entirely monopolized by the state, which practiced a policy of strict protectionism. In the Bible we read that Joseph's brothers could not trade without informing the vizir in charge of granaries. Egypt's main imports were wood (from Lebanon), and spices, copper and bronze (from Asia). Trade was mainly conducted by barter, although gradually, in the New Kingdom, gold and silver were used as a standard of value.

There were, of course, classes in Egypt. The Egyptian language had a complex vocabulary to describe the difference between the son of a man of substance and one who had nothing. The Egyptian ruling class lived in conditions of great luxury on the basis of the exploitation of the peasantry. But when a pharaoh or a noble died his worldly wealth was buried with him, almost as if it formed part of his body. The difference with capitalism is most clearly revealed by this detail. The purpose of accumulation was extravagant personal display and finally to be buried in a tomb in preparation for the after-life. In this way huge amounts of wealth were effectively removed from the economy, and this seemed perfectly natural to the ancient Egyptians.

A similar situation existed, with certain peculiarities, in all the other early societies that functioned on the basis of the Asiatic mode of production. The village commune, the basic cell of these societies, was almost entirely self-sufficient. The few luxuries accessible to a population of subsistence farmers were obtained from the bazaar or from travelling peddlers who lived on the margins of society. Money was scarcely known. Taxes to the state were paid in kind. There was no connection between one village and another and internal trade was weak. The real cohesion came from the state.

People's mental horizons were extremely limited. The most powerful force in their lives was not the "nation" (which is really a product of capitalism) but the family or the clan, which educated them and taught them about their history, religion and traditions. About politics and the world at large they knew little or nothing. Their only contact with the state was the village headman who was responsible for collecting taxes. The tax system, and other methods of exploitation such as obligatory labour service for the state were oppressive but accepted as inevitable and the natural order of things sanctioned by tradition and religion.

In such a society, classes could not develop in the way they did in Western Europe, and capital accumulation remained on a primitive basis, as merchant capital and usury (hoarding). These societies were not based on money, which existed normally on the margins of society, as Marx points out in *Capital*. Wealthy merchants were constantly menaced by extortionate taxes, confiscation, imprisonment and torture. At best the merchants were tolerated and taxed, and worst they were stripped of everything. Even without this, there were problems due to the legal system. Laws on inheritance usually decreed that the property of the deceased be parcelled out among his heirs, producing a tendency to fragmentation of capital. Therefore, the Asiatic mode of production was an historical dead end.

Although internal trade was weak, external trade played an important role in these ancient empires. The rise and fall of ancient civilizations are very often connected with changes in the trade routes. The great empires of the East were connected to the West by trade (the Silk Road). This eventually led to their downfall as a result of the spread of capitalism in the 18th and 19th centuries. When European navigators sailed round the tip of Southern Africa to avoid the Turko-Mongol invaders, Asia was rapidly opened up. Tsarist Russia (itself half-Asiatic in character) pushed eastwards to the Pacific Ocean, conquering the Khanates of Central Asia, while the British moved steadily up through India. The Dutch, French, Portuguese and Spanish occupied the rest.

After a feeble resistance, China was reduced to the status of a semi-colony of the various imperialist powers. Empires need bureaucrats and bookkeepers. These had already existed for thousands of years. The imperialist merely took them over and used them for their own purposes, as the Mongols had done centuries earlier. But this time things were different. The capitalist system was on a higher level than the Asiatic mode of production, and therefore undermined and destroyed it.

Pre-Columbian America

Matters are no better for the "economy of equivalence" when we turn to the peoples of the American continent. If the comparison with ancient Rome with modern capitalism is misleading, the attempt to include the societies of ancient America in the equation gives a still more misleading impression. Before the arrival of Columbus in 1492, most of the peoples of this continent did not know what money was, and even private property existed only to a very limited extent.

The Incas were still in the Neolithic stage when the Spaniards invaded. They did not know what money was. These pre-Columbian societies resemble to some extent those based on the Asiatic mode of production. The supreme Inca was seen as the descendant of the Sun. His officials managed the storehouses and temples and organized the cultivation of the temple lands.

Although slavery existed (prisoners of war), these were not slave societies. In the Mexico of the Aztecs, prisoners of war were sacrificed to the gods, and the main purpose of war was the capture of prisoners for this purpose. Labour service was not free, but those who performed it were not slaves. There was certainly an element of coercion, but the main thing was habit, tradition and religion. The community served the god-king (or queen). It served the temple (as in ancient Israel). This was associated with the state, and was the state. The origins of the state are here mixed up with religion, and this religious aura is maintained to the present. People are taught to look up to the state with feelings of awe and reverence, as a force standing above society, above ordinary men and women, who must serve it blindly.

This is not to say that these people were backward. They had attained a very high level of economic and cultural development. Even before the Incas, the Peruvians constructed huge walls and fortresses. They were built by the state with incredibly large teams of labourers. Equally striking are other public works such as road building. Hernando Pizarro wrote that he had never seen roads like the roads built by the Incas in the high Andes in the entire Christian world. Communications were highly developed and the Incas were very well informed about even the most remote parts of their empire.

The Mexicans had their relay stations set two leagues apart (six miles) along their roads. In pre-Colombian Mexico, there were written codices that recorded forms of land holdings and the obligations attached to them. In Peru there seems to have been no such thing, however, the Incas kept records in the form of knots (quipus), which, according to some experts, may have been a form of writing.

Despite all these achievements, it is wrong to idealize these societies. The whole gigantic structure was supported by the exploitation of the peasantry at the bottom. Although not slaves, the peasants were subjected to a form of obligatory labour service (*corvée*), sanctioned by custom and if necessary upheld by force. Like all other societies based on classes, the ancient pre-Columbian societies of Central America and Peru depended on the exploitation of the labour of the peasants, who were obliged to give up part of their surplus labour to the state that was in the hands of a privileged priest caste, as in Egypt.

Thus, the pre-Columbian societies were also based on the exploitation of labour and the alienation of surplus labour. The results of this labour were often spectacular, and have left us some of the grandest monuments of antiquity. These monuments were intended for the aggrandisement and glorification of the rulers of society. In ancient Mexico, the king of Tezcoco, the second largest component of the Aztec federation, is said to have employed more than 200,000 workers in the construction of a magnificent palace and park. But the mode of appropriation was totally different to that which exists under capitalism. No more than Egypt were they based upon exchange, whether equal or unequal.

Greece

Hegel says that in the East, the ruling spirit was freedom for the One (i.e. for the ruler, the god-king), but in Greece it was freedom for the many, though he correctly qualified it to mean freedom for the citizens of Athens who did not happen to be slaves, foreigners or women. All the grandeur of Greek civilization was based ultimately on the labour of the slaves. Unlike Egypt, Greek mining was in the hands of licensed capitalists (slave owners).

A slave, as a châttel, could be bought and sold as an object of production, or a tool with a voice (*instrumentum vocale*) as the Romans put it. *Athenian democracy was based on slavery*. But for the free citizens it was a most advanced democracy. This new spirit, infused with humanity and individualism, affected Greek art, religion and philosophy, which are qualitatively different to that of Egypt and Mesopotamia. Not until October 1917 did the world see a more advanced form of participative democracy.

In Greece there was a sharp division between the classes, based on property. The main division was between free men and slaves. The free citizens did not usually pay taxes, which were regarded as degrading (as was manual labour). When Athens was mistress of all Greece, she had neither a treasury nor a regular system of taxation. This was completely different to the Asiatic system in Persia and other earlier civilizations. In the latter, as Hegel points out, all men were the slaves of one ruler, the god-king. Thus, class divisions were poorly developed in comparison to Greece.

The superiority of the Greek system was shown in the most decisive arena – that of war. They routed the Persians and then invaded and conquered the most powerful Empire of the East. The Greeks recognized the high quality of the Oriental elite warriors, but held in contempt the poorly trained mass of auxiliary soldiers who were obviously conscripted. Most of them therefore lacked the discipline and combativity that was the pride of the Greek citizen armies.

Ancient Greece had a different socio-economic structure, and consequently a different spirit and a different outlook, to the Asiatic mode of production. This was not the same as in Egypt, Mesopotamia, Peru or Mexico. Greek society was formed under different conditions. The small city-states of Greece lacked the vast expanses of cultivatable land, the great plains of the Indus Valley and Mesopotamia. Hemmed in by barren mountain ranges, they faced to the sea, and this fact determined their whole course of development. Ill suited to agriculture, they were pushed in the direction of the sea, becoming a trading nation and an intermediary, like Phoenicia earlier. This was the reason for the growth of trade and, to a certain extent, of industry (Athenian ceramics).

It seems that money was first developed by the Lydians of Asia Minor. At first precious metals were used as a means of calculating value, then personal seals, originally introduced to make documents, were used to stamp precious metals, producing coins. By around 600 BC coins had developed as a medium of exchange. Improved methods of engraving and manufacture made possible the creation of a mass coinage system, in place of the more cumbersome system of stamped ingots.

By the late 6th century BC new techniques permitted the separation of silver from lead ore. This led to a huge increase in the production of the Athenian silver mines in Laurion. The central Greek states were among the first to introduce silver coins. And yet every city had its own coinage. This means that exchange had not yet acquired a universal character at this stage. Athens developed as a manufacturing and trading centre, specializing in the production of pottery, especially the famous black figured vases, which reached a peak of refinement in about 600-530 BC.

There was a permanent shortage of good agricultural land and, with a growing population, constant land-hunger. This was partially solved through emigration and the establishment of Greek colonies in Sicily, Italy, France and Spain. But despite the rise of industry and trade, the Athenians still looked on wealth fundamentally in terms of land, which was worked by slave labour and dominated by a few wealthy families. This explains the contemptuous and distrustful attitude shown by Aristotle towards the pursuit of wealth.

Roman capitalism?

Terms such as the Roman proletariat and Roman capitalism are equally misleading. They are based on a superficial historical analogy. In the latter period of the Republic, the Roman victories, especially in the wars with Carthage, added new territories to its growing empire, including the prosperous Greek and Phoenician colonies on the coast of Spain. This gave a further impetus to the class of Roman capitalists, involved in trade in the Mediterranean. Spain opened up her valuable iron and silver mines – which were also worked by slave labour in terrible conditions.

Rome simply took over this business from Carthage. It also led to a further development of trade and exchange and therefore the rise of a money economy. In some respects, this calls to mind the rise of capitalism in Europe in the 18th century, and indeed the word "capitalism" is frequently used when speaking of this phase of Roman development. Yet, though there are certain analogies, the comparison is not exact. Modern capitalism depends on a free market for goods and labour. Large-scale slavery is incompatible with modern capitalism, which abolishes slavery as it develops. The American Civil War is sufficient proof of this assertion.

The basis of modern capitalism is the accumulation of capital for the purpose of re-investment. Such a conception would have been totally incomprehensible to a Roman capitalist. One of the most striking contradictions of the ancient world is that, having come so close to a capitalist economy, it always drew back on the edge and failed to develop, when it would seem that a potential existed. Take just one example: the Alexandrine Greeks invented a steam engine that worked. But they regarded it as a mere curiosity – a toy. Its productive potential never occurred to them.

Why should it? With a mass of cheap slave labour, there was no need to develop technology. Moreover, technology is incompatible with slave labour. Slaves working under compulsion will not treat delicate instruments with care – they will break them on purpose. The mule was developed in the slave states of the Southern USA because the slaves could not be trusted with a horse, which was too delicate to survive in their hands. Only the crudest, most resistant implements and tools could be entrusted to the slaves.

Thus, for the whole period of slavery, no great advances were made in technology and productivity remained on a low level. The slave owners, like the feudal lords who succeeded them, were not in the least interested in accumulating for investment. The purpose of accumulation was for their own personal enjoyment and consumption on a most lavish scale. The description of the extraordinary banquets, parties and orgies that have come down to us, the consumption of such things as stuffed lark's tongues and pearls dissolved in wine, are the end result of the labour of the slaves, along with extravagant games and festivals, silk dresses, colossal public buildings and – last but not least – the free handout of grain to the unemployed mob in Rome.

Just as the nomenclature of "capitalist" is not really adequate to describe the functions of the Roman slave owners, so the word "proletariat" is misleading when applied to the city-dwellers in the late Roman Republic and Empire, for reasons we have explained. There is a fundamental difference between the modern proletariat and that of the ancient world. The modern working class is the only really productive class (together with the peasantry, insofar as it still exists), but the Roman proletariat did not work – it had an entirely unproductive and parasitical character.

In the early days of Rome money played an unimportant role in the economic life of society. The early Republic was an agricultural economy based upon subsistence farming. Its backbone was the class of free peasants. But a long period of wars and foreign conquests had radically transformed it. Money then assumed an ever-greater role, first as silver, later as copper and gold. Money relations became more important with the rise of trade on an international scale. And together with trade and money economy, the Roman capitalists' power also increased.

With the rise of money economy the old equality was destroyed and in its place we see an increasing polarisation between rich and poor that no longer corresponds to the old tribal divisions between plebeians and patricians, noblemen and commoners. Very often the new men of money are commoners, and even freedmen – former slaves. In this way was born the class of Roman "capitalists" – the knights or *equites*, who were given political power by the Gracchi and became an important force in Roman society and politics.

To the extent that one can speak of capitalism in the later Roman Republic and Empire, it existed only in the margins of the Roman economy, which was based not on trade and exchange but on landed property and slavery. As for the Roman proletariat, this consisted of landless peasants who were ruined by the rise of slavery and the big latifundia after the Punic Wars (264-241, 218-201 and 149-146 BC). The human and economic cost of these wars was immense. In the first Punic war, in a five-year period, the census of Roman citizens fell by about 40,000 – one sixth of the total population. And these figures do not include the devastation suffered by Rome's allies, who suffered big losses at sea. It was a deadly, bloody slogging match, which lasted decades.

At this time the position of the Roman and Italian small farmer was inexorably eroded by a fatal combination of debt, slavery and the encroachment of the big estates. The free peasantry entered into a process of decay, being unable to compete with slave labour. Constant wars, debt and impoverishment ruined them. Attempts were made to force through legislation to protect the peasants. The Licinian laws stipulated that the landlords had to employ a certain proportion of free labourers alongside the slaves and that the burden of debt was to be reduced. But it was impossible to reverse the process. Slave labour on a large scale drove out free labour. All the laws designed to halt this process were in vain. Economic necessity tore up the laws before they could be enacted.

Over a long period of time, the dispossessed peasants flocked to Rome, where they could at least obtain handouts from the state. Although they were reduced to the status of *proletarii* – the lowest layer of propertyless citizens – they remained Roman citizens and had certain rights in the state. The presence of a large number of impoverished citizens gave a fresh impetus to the class struggle in Rome. There were violent insurrections against the burdens of debt. But despite the existence of a class struggle in the later Republic it is quite wrong to conclude that the Roman proletariat was the same as the modern working class. The term *lumpenproletariat* would be far more appropriate in this case. At one time, the emperor was importing grain to feed more than 100,000 people in Rome alone. Marx pointed this out long ago. In 1877 he wrote to the Editor of the *Otchecestvennive Zapisky*:

"In several parts of *Capital* I allude to the fate which overtook the plebeians of ancient Rome. They were originally free peasants, each cultivating his own piece of land on his own account. In the course of Roman history they were expropriated. The same movement which divorced them from their means of production and subsistence involved the formation not only of big landed property but also of big money capital. And so one fine morning there were to be found on the one hand free men, stripped of everything except their labour power, and on the other, in order to exploit this labour, those who held all the acquired wealth in possession. What happened? *The Roman proletarians became, not wage labourers but a mob of do-nothings more abject than the former 'poor whites' in the southern country of the United States, and alongside of them there developed a mode of production which was not capitalist but dependent upon slavery. Thus events strikingly analogous but taking place in different historic surroundings led to totally different results. By studying each of these forms of evolution separately and then comparing them one can eas-*

ily find the clue to this phenomenon, but one will never arrive there by the universal passport of a general historico-philosophical theory, the supreme virtue of which consists in being super-historical."[10]

The whole system depended upon a steady supply of slaves, and that depended on successful foreign wars. When the Empire reached its physical limits, the supply of slaves dried up, leading to what is known as the manpower crisis of the later Roman Empire. In this period, the bureaucratic-military state imposed a heavy burden on Roman society, which was crushed by the burden of taxation. Once the Romans stopped conquering new lands, the flow of gold into the Roman economy decreased. Yet huge quantities of gold were being spent by the wealthy parasites on luxury items. In the time of Nero, Seneca estimated that it cost Rome five million dollars a year to import its luxuries from the east (a colossal sum when translated into modern money). This meant that there was less gold to use in coins. As the amount of gold used in coins decreased, the value of the coins decreased.

The debasement of the currency led to inflation, which disrupted trade and led to increasing misery and economic chaos. After the reign of Marcus Aurelius the increase in prices became inexorable. To make up for this loss in value, merchants raised the prices on the goods they sold. No longer wanting to be paid with debased coinage, soldiers and wealthy citizens chose instead to be paid with actual objects of value. Many people stopped using coins and began to barter to get what they needed. Eventually, salaries had to be paid in food and clothing, and taxes were collected in fruits and vegetables.

It became difficult for the government to retain any money for itself, and it began to resort more and more to cheaper mercenaries to defend it. Since it was impossible for the government to keep track of its large grain supply, the landowners were legally required to collect taxes. The collapse of the slave economy was rooted in these conditions. In fact, the feudal system already existed in outline when the slave-owners converted their slaves into *coloni* (serfs). The *colonus* was formally free but was legally bound to his role of tenant farming to facilitate the collection of taxes. The Imperial government collected fixed grain taxes from tenant farmers. Gradually, the whole top-heavy system began to implode, creating the conditions for collapse. The barbarians merely gave the Empire a last push. But the structure was already rotten to its foundations, and ready to fall.

In *The Communist Manifesto* Marx explains that the class struggle can lead to a revolutionary reconstruction of society, or else to the common ruin of the contending classes. The fate of Rome is a graphic example of the second variant. It would be an interesting exercise to speculate on what could have happened if Spartacus and the slaves had succeeded in conquering Rome. But this did not occur because the only way the slaves could have succeeded was by uniting their forces with the

10. Marx and Engels, *Correspondence*, Progress Publishers, 2nd ed. 1965, p. 313, my emphasis, AW.

Roman proletariat. This did not happen and there are concrete reasons why it could not have happened.

Although the dispossessed masses in Rome were in constant conflict with the upper classes, and this class conflict assumed a particularly violent character in the latter stage of the Republic, preparing the way for Caesarism, the only productive class were the slaves. In the last analysis, the Roman proletariat almost always united with the slave-owning ruling class to suppress slave uprisings. From this fact alone we can see how incorrect it is to approach history from the standpoint of superficial analogies, or to try to impose upon the past categories and concepts derived from the present. But this is just what Dieterich does all the time.

'Chrematistics' under feudalism

The possessors of surplus value in the pre-capitalist epoch were not the merchants but the slave-owner, the feudal lord, and the state (for instance, the oriental despot). They were interested not in productive investment but in the consumption of wealth and luxury. But even in those societies the wealth was obtained in the last analysis through production, not exchange. With capitalism the conservation and accumulation of money becomes an end in itself. We see this even in the early days of capitalism when money was accumulated as the miser's hoard. Even in the ancient world these elements existed at certain periods, but only exceptionally, as Marx points out:

"The trading nations of ancient times existed like the gods of Epicurus in the intermediate worlds of the universe, or rather like the Jews in the pores of Polish society. The trade of the first independent flourishing merchant towns and trading nations rested as a pure carrying trade upon the barbarism of the producing nations, between whom they acted the middleman." [11]

Under feudalism, which was a hierarchal society based in the ownership of land and the exploitation of the labour of the serfs, money making was also regarded with distain. The Catholic Church, which was the ideological bulwark of feudalism prohibited usury (lending money at interest), which is considered a mortal sin. From 1179 the Catholic Church prohibited usury on pain of excommunication. It is not at all difficult to find quotations from churchmen and nobles of the Middle Ages denouncing money making and greed in similar terms to those used by Aristotle. Saint Anselm thought that charging interest was the same as theft.

Saint Thomas Aquinas maintained that charging of interest is wrong because it amounts to "double charging", charging for both the thing and the use of the thing. Aquinas said this would be morally wrong in the same way as if one sold a bottle of wine, charged for the bottle of wine, and then charged for the person using the

11. Marx, *Capital*, vol. 3, Chapter 20, Historical Considerations on Merchant Capital.

wine to actually drink it. Simply to invest the money and expect it to be returned regardless of the success of the venture was to make money simply by having money and not by taking any risk or by doing any work or by any effort or sacrifice at all. This is usury. St. Thomas quotes Aristotle as saying that "to live by usury is exceedingly unnatural".

All this did not prevent the same nobles and churchmen from borrowing large sums of money from the Jews (which they frequently did not repay). Neither does it make them the precursors of Socialism of the 21st Century, or any other kind of socialism. The reason that usury became associated with the Jews is that they were effectively excluded from the feudal system. Forbidden to own land and excluded from most professions, they were pushed into marginal occupations considered socially inferior, such as tax and rent collection and money lending. This was how the Jews got the reputation as greedy usurers. The tensions between creditors and debtors, added to religious strains, were the source of the anti-Semitism of medieval Europe, which was very useful to the kings, princes and aristocrats who used periodic pogroms as a convenient way of liquidating their debts.

In his great poem the *Inferno*, Dante places the usurers in the inner ring of the seventh circle of hell, below suicides, where the usurers had the pleasure of spending all eternity in the company of the blasphemers and sodomites. In Shakespeare's play, *The Merchant of Venice,* written in the 16th century, the Jew Shylock had to convert to Christianity and renounce usury before he could be redeemed. As late as the 18th century, the Catholic Church continued to condemn usury, although the development of capitalism, and banking forced it to modify its stance.

In 1745 Pope Benedict XIV in his encyclical *Vix Pervenit* strictly forbade charging interest on loans, but adds that "entirely just and legitimate reasons arise to demand something over and above the amount due on the contract" through separate, parallel contracts. All these people were opposed to "chrematistics". What does this tell us? Does it mean that the ideas of Heinz Dieterich are as old as Aristotle and Moses? No, it tells us that the moneymaking economy about which our Heinz complains so bitterly, is not so old after all. It developed in the course of the 17th century in England and Holland, and finally became dominant in the early 19th century as a result of the Industrial Revolution in Britain.

Commodities are all expressions of social labour. But they are not values of equal magnitude. At first the quantitative ratio in which products are exchanged is quite arbitrary. But with the expansion of trade and the consequent development of money this arbitrariness is reduced more and more. *It is capitalism that establishes equivalence*. In the third volume of *Capital* Marx deals with the question of the conversion of Commodity-Capital and Money-Capital into Commercial Capital (Merchant's Capital) from a historical perspective.

The merchant's profit is made from the circulation process, from buying and selling. The merchant's ideal is to buy cheap in order to sell dear. This is clearly not the exchange of equivalents! Before the real development of capitalism in the 18th century, trade was closely linked to plundering, piracy, kidnapping slaves, and colonial conquest; as in Carthage, Rome, and later the Venetians, Portuguese, Dutch. [12]

The rape of Latin America

The history of what we call civilization (that is, class society) is characterized on the one hand by the development of the productive potential of humankind, of art, science and technology. On the other hand, it is characterized by the material and cultural expropriation of the great majority of humankind. In *The Communist Manifesto* Marx explains the role of the "discovery" of America in the development of capitalism:

"The discovery of America, the rounding of the Cape, opened up fresh ground for the rising bourgeoisie. The East-Indian and Chinese markets, the colonisation of America, trade with the colonies, the increase in the means of exchange and in commodities generally, gave to commerce, to navigation, to industry, an impulse never before known, and thereby, to the revolutionary element in the tottering feudal society, a rapid development." [13]

But this development was achieved at the cost of the indigenous peoples of America. They suffered what can only be described as genocide. Precise pre-Columbian population figures are impossible to obtain, and estimates must be extrapolated from limited data. According to William Denevan about 54 million people perished, although some estimates put the real figure at more than 100 million. If we take an estimate of approximately 50 million people in 1492 (including 25 million in the Aztec Empire and 12 million in the Inca Empire), the lowest estimates give a death toll of 80 percent at the end of the 16th century. Latin America only recovered this level of population at the beginning of the 19th century, with 17 million in 1800; 30 million in 1850; 61 million in 1900; 105 million in 1930; 218 million in 1960; 361 million in 1980 and 563 million in 2005.

It was the misfortune of the Mexican people to come into contact with Europeans just at a time when the primitive accumulation of capital was in full swing. There is no need to repeat here the well-known story of the violence, treachery and deceit practiced by Cortez and his men. Montezuma received the Spaniards politely, believing them to be gods, but his hospitality was immediately violated. The vast and thriving lake-city of Tenochtitlan was burnt, plundered and destroyed without mercy.

The Native Americans also suffered the brutal destruction of their culture. In no country does the expression cultural expropriation hold a deeper or more tragic meaning than in Mexico. Before the arrival of the Spaniards, the Mexican people

12. See Marx, *Capital*, Vol. III, Part IV, Chapter 20. Historical Facts about Merchant's Capital.
13. Marx and Engels *The Manifesto of the Communist Party*, Selected Works, Vol. 1, p. 109.

had established one of the world's greatest and most remarkable civilizations. The cause of their ruin was not any Historical Project on the part of the Spanish conquistadores but *simple greed* – greed for gold – "the sweat of the sun", as the Aztecs called it. "We have a disease that only gold can cure" the invaders told them, by way of explanation, before seizing their land and wealth and enslaving them. The same disease afflicts the whole world today and causes the same terrible results.

The Aztecs, although they had reached a high level of social and cultural development, had no defence against the guns, steel and horses of the Spaniards, or the germs they brought with them. After a short, sharp war, they were reduced to slavery and their amazing civilization destroyed. The last Aztec chief, Cuauhtemoc, was tortured with fire to reveal where the gold was, and then hanged when the Spaniards did not find the quantities of gold they had expected. The results of the conquest were incalculable. When the Spaniards first came to Mexico, the country was a flourishing state with a population of 25 millions. 80 years later its culture was destroyed, its economy in ruins and its people enslaved. 90 percent of the population had lost their lives, either massacred by the Spaniards and their allies or from hunger or diseases like smallpox that decimated whole communities. In the last three decades of the 16th century, the Mexican population collapsed, falling to just one million people in 1600.

Crude, ignorant and contemptuous of the culture of the natives, the Spaniards crushed it underfoot without a second thought. Priceless works of art were melted down into gold ingots and lost forever to humanity. Part of the gold and silver was recast into huge Christian relics of little or no aesthetic value. I remember the indignation I felt some 25 years ago when I was shown the tasteless gold altarpieces, silver caskets and the like in the cathedral of Cadiz. Similar grandiose monuments to idiocy and fanaticism that decorate churches in other Spanish cities were likewise made from the melted down artefacts of a culture hundreds of years old.

The Mexicans, weakened and traumatized, were unable to prevent this spiritual enslavement, but resorted to a tactic of passive resistance, which in the last analysis saved important elements of the traditions and culture of their fathers. The Mexican sculptors, artisans and builders who were forced to toil on the construction of huge churches and cathedrals, triumphal monuments to celebrate their own servitude, took their revenge by injecting native elements into the art of the Christian invaders. In this way the spirit of Mexico was preserved, in spite of everything.

The primitive accumulation of capital

"The bourgeoisie, by the rapid improvement of all instruments of production, by the immensely facilitated means of communication, draws all, even the most barbarian, nations into civilisation. The cheap prices of commodities are the heavy artillery with which it batters down all Chinese walls, with which it forces the barbarians' intensely obstinate hatred of foreigners to capitulate. It compels all nations, on pain of extinction, to adopt the bourgeois mode of production; it compels them to introduce what it calls civilisation into their midst, i.e., to become bourgeois themselves. In one word, it creates a world after its own image." [14]

The barbaric destruction of a great culture was undoubtedly a terrible crime against humanity. But this is not an exception, but part of a general process, closely connected with the genesis of capitalism, which Marx described as the primitive accumulation of capital. In order to clear the path for the establishment of capitalism, it was necessary to ruthlessly destroy all hitherto existing socio-economic forms: slavery, feudalism and other pre-capitalist economic formations. This was accomplished with extreme brutality from the 16th to the 19th centuries, both in Europe and the Americas. In the first volume of *Capital* Marx wrote:

"The discovery of gold and silver in America, the extirpation, enslavement and entombment in mines of the aboriginal population, the beginning of the conquest and looting of the East Indies, the turning of Africa into a warren for the commercial hunting of black-skins, signalised the rosy dawn of the era of capitalist production. These idyllic proceedings are the chief momenta of primitive accumulation. [...] 'If money', according to Auger, 'comes into the world with a congenital bloodstain on one cheek,' capital comes dripping from head to foot, from every pore, with blood and dirt." [15]

The crimes of capitalism fill all normal human beings with a sense of horror and indignation. But horror and indignation do not help us to understand the phenomena we are dealing with, and it is unworthy of a man who describes himself as a "scientific economist" to approach history from a moralistic and sentimental point of view. If Heinz Dieterich goes to the dentist with a bad toothache, the latter may express all the horror and indignation in the world, but that will not help him extract the offending molar. Hegel once said "It was not so much *from* slavery as *through* slavery that humanity was emancipated." [16] Centuries of class oppression and exploitation have developed the means of production (science, technology, industry and agriculture) and by so doing have laid the material basis for the creation of a new and higher form of human society: socialism. As Marx wrote in a famous passage in *Capital*:

"Along with the constantly diminishing number of the magnates of capital, who usurp and monopolize all advantages of this process of transformation, grows the mass of misery, oppression, slavery, degradation, exploitation; but with this too grows the revolt of the working-class, a class always increasing in numbers, and disciplined, united, organized by the very mechanism of the process of capitalist production itself. The monopoly of capital becomes a fetter upon the mode of production, which has sprung up and flourished along with, and under it. Centralization of

14. Marx and Engels, *The Communist Manifesto* Ibid. p. 112

15. Marx, *Capital*, Volume One, Chapter 31: Genesis of the Industrial Capitalist.

16. Hegel, *Philosophy of History*, Part IV: The German World.

the means of production and socialization of labour at last reach a point where they become incompatible with their capitalist integument. Thus integument is burst asunder. The knell of capitalist private property sounds. The expropriators are expropriated."[17]

Dieterich against expropriation

It is well known that Marx stood for the expropriation of the capitalists. What does Heinz Dieterich think about this? In an article published in www.aporrea.org (19/02/07), Heinz Dieterich is perfectly explicit about his real intentions, which are very well conveyed by the title: *Mixed Economy is the road to Socialism of the 21st Century*. Here we read the following: "If state property were socialism, we would already have had socialism in Latin America at the time of (King) Charles V, because when the Spanish Monarchy arrived in America, all the property in and beneath the land was the patrimony of the king, but that was feudalism, not socialism. The only possible way is a mixed economy, which will have three subjects, the State, private enterprise and social property, like the cooperatives".

This is splendid! We now learn from our friend that – *socialism is not feudalism.* We had to wait for Heinz Dieterich to point this out, just as we had to wait for him to explain that caterpillars crawl and butterflies fly. But this butterfly cannot fly more than a few centimetres without making a mistake. With all due respect to our friend Heinz, *feudalism is not based on state property, but private property of land, including the private estates of the king.*

Actually, when the Spanish Monarchy arrived in America, all the land was held in common and private property was unknown. As soon as they landed, the conquistadors proclaimed all the lands in New Spain property of the Spanish Crown. Does that mean that Cortez carried out the nationalization of land in America? *Not at all! That was only the first step in expropriating the land, which was later divided up between different groups of feudal robbers, and this is the real origin of landed property in Latin America down to the present day.* What connection this has with socialism is a mystery that only a genius of Heinz Dieterich's stature can understand.

The first question that arises from this interesting historical analogy is: *what does Heinz Dieterich suggest we do with landed property in Venezuela, where big estates occupy the majority of productive land*? The Spanish Crown originally stole all this land from the native population. Moreover, the big latifundists have failed to develop agriculture. It is a disgrace that in such a fertile land as Venezuela most of the food has to be imported. The obvious answer is to expropriate the latifundists and nationalize the land. This is not even a socialist measure but part of the programme of the bourgeois democratic revolution. Is Dieterich in favour of this revo-

17. Marx, *Capital*, Volume One, Chapter 32: Historical Tendency of Capitalist Accumulation.

lutionary measure, yes or no? The old discredited Menshevik-Stalinist theory of revolution by stages postponed the socialist revolution to a remote future on the grounds that it is first necessary to carry out the bourgeois democratic revolution. What Dieterich advocates is even worse. He is not even in favour of fighting for the programme of the bourgeois democratic revolution!

The latifundists constitute the backbone of the counter-revolutionary oligarchy. The expropriation of the big landowners is therefore an absolutely necessary and urgent task of the Bolivarian revolution. Some steps have been made in this direction, but so far the agrarian policy has been timid, inconsistent and slow. Despite this it has met with ferocious resistance from the landowners. What does this prove? It proves that any attempt to improve the conditions of the masses under capitalism will be opposed and sabotaged by the rich and powerful. Any suggestion of touching of the land of the latifundists will be opposed by the capitalists and bankers because it challenges the "sacred right to private property".

The Venezuelan landowners, bankers and capitalists constitute a reactionary bloc that has opposed the Bolivarian Revolution right from the beginning, long before Chávez raised the question of socialism. In order to carry out a serious agrarian reform, which is the cornerstone of the bourgeois-democratic revolution, it is necessary to overcome the resistance of the oligarchy as a whole: that means the expropriation not only of the land but also of the banks and big businesses.

The reference to state property and Charles V is a deliberate attempt to confuse the issue of property. Dieterich is opposed to the expropriation of the land, just as he is opposed to nationalization in general (although he does not dare to criticize it when it has already been carried out) because he does not want the Revolution to challenge the "sacred right" of private property. He knows that the big landowners are closely linked to the bankers and capitalists, and that together they constitute a reactionary bloc that is bitterly opposed to the Bolivarian Revolution and is determined to overthrow it and reverse all its progressive measures. He is mortally afraid of the counter-revolution and sceptical of the prospects of success of the revolution, which he wishes to halt.

The essence of the matter is this: Heinz Dieterich is not opposed to capitalism *per se*, but *only to a particular "model" of capitalism – neo-liberalism* – which he finds disagreeable. This, he says, is unacceptable "because people will simple not accept it any more; the option is therefore whether I go for developmentalism ('desarrollismo') or try *to combine developmentalism with an attempt to arrive at a post-capitalist society*, and the President has declared that this is his intention, *but it is optional* and people will decide." [18]

This is a perfect example of how Dieterich tries to water down and distort the idea of socialism. Chávez has repeatedly said that capitalism is slavery, and that the

18. See *Aporrea*, 19/02/07.

aims of the Bolivarian Revolution are incompatible with capitalism and that the only way out is socialism, nationally and internationally. But what Dieterich says here is something completely different. In the first place, he does not oppose capitalism but only neo-liberalism. And he does not advocate socialism as an alternative but only some vague and ambiguous "post-capitalist society", which can mean just about anything you choose. In case anyone is tempted to assume that this "post-capitalist society" is the same as socialism, Dieterich is careful to water this new concept down even further. It is to be combined with "developmentalism", that is to say, with a capitalist model of development.

Moreover, even this "developmentalism" is not an immediate perspective but is *optional* (which means you can take it or leave it, like the mustard at the side of your plate). But all history has shown that a consistent struggle for the programme of revolutionary democracy inevitably leads to the question of private property and thus to socialism. That was the lesson of Russia in 1917, of Cuba in 1959-60 and it is the case in Venezuela today.

What Dieterich is proposing is even worse than the old theory of two stages. It is the perspective of *an infinite progression of stages* that Dieterich has erected before the question of socialism can be posed. The complicated "theoretical" justifications for this are of no real importance. The whole point is to convince the masses that on no account must they fight for socialism now! Although he prattles on about "Socialism for the 21st Century", Dieterich is not thinking about this at all, but socialism in the far distant future – so distant that it is completely out of sight. This reminds one of those memorable words from *Alice in Wonderland*: "the rule is: jam yesterday, jam tomorrow, but never jam today."

A philistine conception

To make things abundantly clear, Dieterich explains that his version of Socialism of the 21st Century will not lay a hand on the property of the oligarchy but will base itself on a mixed economy. *That is to say, it will be the same as capitalism!* The real model for Dieterichian socialism is – *Costa Rica*, "where the streets are safe"! We note in passing that even the language here is that of a frightened petty bourgeois philistine who identifies revolution with anarchy and "unsafe streets". But let us press on anyway... The citizens of 21st Socialism will experience a marked improvement in their material conditions, the quality of their lives, and also in "conditions of a psychological or spiritual type." (*Aporrea,* 19/02/07.) What more can anybody wish for?

In the Dieterichian socialist paradise, one will be able to walk the streets of Caracas without fear, experience the benefits of Costa Rican living standards and completely dispense with the services of the psychiatrist. Everybody will be happy – except maybe for the unfortunate psychiatrists who will find themselves out of work. But then, it is not possible to please everybody, even in 21st Socialism.

What a wonderful perspective! The only problem is that, once again, our Heinz has forgotten to explain one little detail, namely, *how to get from A to B.* The first question that occurs to us is: how is it possible to arrive at this postcapitalist paradise while leaving the economic power in the hands of the landlords, bankers and capitalists? As long as the latter continue to own and control the means of production (the land, banks and industries) all the most important decisions concerning employment, housing, health, schools, etc., will be subordinated to the interests of the rich. The government may have every good intention, but ultimately it will come up against a solid brick wall, since you cannot plan what you do not control and you cannot control what you do not own.

We thus return inevitably to the fundamental question: *the question of private property.* This is the fundamental line that separates reformists from revolutionaries. Our Heinz, pleasant chap that he is, does not want conflict. He wants to please the workers but he does not want to offend the landlords, bankers and capitalists. He therefore renounces socialist revolution in favour of reformism and social democracy:

"The project has a dual strategy of development, developmentalism, which is a Social Democratic way of development, where the State utilizes its economic and legal powers to foment, for example, reindustrialization, redistributes a big part of the wealth through PDVSA, etc. creates the welfare state alongside the rule of law ('state of right'), this leads to growth, to an improvement of the material situation, but the limit is that you do not go beyond the market economy (*no sales de la economía de mercado*), and that means that I always live with the fear of losing my job. One of the big gains of historical socialism was that there was no unemployment and that daily terror that you have to produce more and more because if not I will sack you disappears, it is an extraordinary liberation". [19]

We have already pointed out that the Stalinist regime in the USSR had nothing whatever to do with socialism whether historical or unhistorical. But, leaving this to one side, the question arises: why was there no unemployment in Russia? Dieterich does not ask the question much less answer it. *The reason was that the Russian Revolution nationalized the land, the banks and the industries and instituted a socialist planned economy.* The nationalization of the productive forces does not yet signify the existence of a classless society, but it undoubtedly constitutes the fundamental premise and the *conditio sine qua non* for advancing in that direction. The socialist planning of the economy represents a colossal advance over the anarchy of capitalist production.

Here our Heinz becomes entangled in contradictions. It is not possible to solve the problem of unemployment as long as key points of the economy remain in private hands. He says himself: "The mission of every enterprise is to generate profit

19. Ibid.
20. Ibid.

or at least cover a social need, and when people administer a good in an optimum way there will be no reason to change it". [20] This is yet another example of Dieterich's ducking and dodging. Capitalists only invest for profit and profit can only come from the unpaid labour of the working class. That is the ABC of Marxist economics. But Dieterich has to add: "*or at least cover a social need*". This is enough to make a cat laugh. Since when do capitalists invest to "*cover a social need*"? This is a complete nonsense that has been invented by Heinz Dieterich to cover his bare backside. For if a) capitalists are working for the common good, not for profit and b) are working efficiently, why change anything? To which we answer: *if pigs had wings they would fly.*

Heinz Dieterich presents us with a New Historical Project, which, he assures us, will enable us to build Socialism of the 21st Century. But before we can talk about a project for building, we first have to clear away all the rubbish from the building site. Before we have a have a Project for building Socialism we first require a programme for overthrowing capitalism. For this programme we will search in vain in all the books and articles of comrade Dieterich. This is no accident, because he believes it is possible to achieve socialism without expropriating the landlords and capitalists, in other words, without the class struggle and without revolution. On this point, yet again, he makes clear his complete abandonment of Marxism and his return to the antiquated and discredited ideas of pre-Marxian socialism, to the prehistory of the movement – *to utopian socialism.*

5. Socialism utopian and scientific

Socialism is not a new idea. The idea of a society in which all men and women are equal is very old and has constantly reappeared at different times and in different forms. It occurs in the New Testament, particularly in the Acts of the Apostles. Thomas More in the 16th century put it forward in his celebrated book Utopia (which means "no place" and has given us the word utopian). It was brilliantly expounded by the early socialists Saint Simon, Fourier and Mably in France and by the Welshman Robert Owen, who founded the co-operative movement in England in the early 19th century. These were great and original thinkers who were far ahead of their time, unlike Heinz Dieterich, who has never expressed a single original idea and is far behind the times. But despite all their brilliance and originality, Marx described them as utopian socialists, whereas he characterized his doctrine as scientific socialism.

Wherein lies the difference? For all the socialist and communist thinkers before Marx, socialism was seen in mainly moral and ethical terms. It was simply a good idea (a New Historical Project), which for some reason people had not thought of earlier. Had they done so, humanity could have been spared thousands of years of unnecessary suffering. The revolt of the oppressed against their oppressors is as old as class society. The earliest recorded strike was of the Egyptian pyramid builders. In Rome we had the revolt of the slaves under that marvellous revolutionary Spartacus. In the Middle Ages the peasants revolted against the *corvée* and other feudal impositions. In England the peasants rose up and seized London in 1381. In Germany the Peasant War was chronicled by Engels, who pointed to the communist tendencies in the teachings of Thomas Muentzer and the Anabaptists. Likewise, one of the leaders of the English Peasant Revolt, John Ball, expressed communist ideas in his famous verse:

When Adam delved and Eve span,
Who was then the gentleman?

The forerunners of modern socialism could never bring about the new and equal society that they dreamed of, because the material basis for a classless society did not exist. Thus, the early revolutionary movements of the masses directed against the old oppressors could only serve as the means whereby a new class of exploiters established itself in power. The English Peasants' Revolt at the end of the 14th century helped to overthrow the old feudal society but it did not lead to a world of social equality as envisaged by John Ball, but only to the development of capitalist relations in the English countryside.

In fact, very often those who spoke out against social inequality and in favour of equality had a reactionary element, harking back to the memory of an earlier society when men were freer and more equal. This is expressed in the myth the Golden Age that frequently recurs in the literature of antiquity. It is found in the writings of the Greek poet Hesiod, as early as the 7th century BC. More often than not it had a religious and messianic character, as with the early Christians, who looked forward anxiously to the Second Coming from one day to the next.

The slaves, serfs, craftsmen and journeymen were the ancestors of the modern proletariat. However, only under capitalism does the working class come into being, and with it the class basis for modern socialism. The ground for Marxism was prepared by the early utopian thinkers who arrived at conclusions and ideas that were brilliant and original for their day. The French utopian socialist Saint-Simon (1760-1825), was born an aristocrat (Count Claude de Saint-Simon). In essence, his socialist doctrine was directed against the aristocracy, the monarchy, clergy, bankers and rich entrepreneurs, rather than the new industrial bourgeoisie. This was natural, since the working class was still a nascent class in France.

When he spoke of the "workers," he included not only the proletarians but also the industrialists. Industry and labour were the twin motor forces of progress in Saint-Simon's view. His ideas received an echo not only among the workers but also among bourgeois liberals. The second great French utopian socialist was Charles Fourier (1772-1837). He launched a slashing attack against the basis of bourgeois society, private property. He subjected to a merciless criticism such things as the division of labour, in particular the division between agriculture and industry (and city and country), commodity production, the money economy, the bourgeois family and the oppression of women.

These were extremely advanced ideas, many of which were later to influence Marx and Engels. However, Fourier and his faithful lieutenant, Victor Considérant, believed the solution to these problems was to be found in the setting up of *phalansteries*. These were self-managed communities of 1,000 to 2,000 people who worked as farmers, craftspeople and artists. My great countryman, the Welsh utopian socialist Robert Owen (1771-1858) set out to find a remedy for the poverty of the workers of Britain. He founded a model workers' community in Scotland (New Lanark), based on principles far in advance of his time. But like Saint-Simon he appealed to the enlightened bourgeois to back his plans for social reforms. Disappointed in the results, he went to America, where he founded communist colonies. But this experiment only served to show that it is impossible to establish islands of socialism in a sea of capitalism. In every case, the egalitarian communities ended in failure.

Today in Latin America there are some people who imagine themselves to be very modern revolutionaries and far superior to Marx and Engels, who they regard as hopelessly old-fashioned. They argue that it is not necessary for the workers to take power, and instead recommend the masses to take power locally: to set up model communities that will by-pass the capitalist state and the bourgeois system altogether. They thus unwittingly repeat the utopian mistakes of Robert Owen – almost two centuries later!

For Robert Owen there was some excuse for committing this error. For the "modernists" of Socialism of the 21st Century there is no excuse whatever. They seek to drag the movement back to its prehistory. Marx and Engels approached the matter in an entirely different way. For the first time they explained that socialism was not just a good idea but the product of the development of society. For the first time they gave a scientific-materialist explanation of socialism, not an utopian-idealist one. Now Heinz Dieterich wants us to abandon the scientific standpoint of Marxism and regress to the old, discredited ideas of the utopian socialists. This is like advocating that an adult should forget everything he or she has learned in the course of his life and return to the embryonic stage of development. Children are charming precisely because of their naivety, but grown people who return to their infancy are not charming at all but only childish.

In the later part of his life Robert Owen tried to rectify his mistake. He abandoned the idea of communist colonies and instead returned to England, where he played a significant role in setting up a trade union. He advocated the formation of a single national confederation (the Grand National Consolidated Trade Union, 1834), and even pioneered the idea of a general strike, which he called the "grand national holiday". In all of this, Robert Owen showed himself to be far superior to those "clever" 21st Century utopians who imitate the *weak* side of Owen but are incapable of learning from his *strong* side.

Our modern day utopians vaguely recall that Robert Owen was responsible for the creation of the co-operative movement, and they are passionately fond of co-operatives, which they see as a convenient alternative to the workers taking power. But they are not aware that, in the first place, the British workers formed co-operatives as part of the strike movement – in order to provide the workers' families with cheap food during strikes. In the second place, Owen was especially interested in workers' production co-operatives, the first of which was established in Rochdale in 1844. Here, for the first time, it was demonstrated in practice that the workers can run industry without the bosses. That is a revolutionary message that was far ahead of its time. And even today co-operatives can play an important role in a planned economy, *once the workers have taken power*. But to put forward the idea of co-operatives as an alternative to workers' power and nationalization of the means of production is entirely reactionary.

Instead of a nationalized planned economy Dieterich advocates a mixed economy based on co-operatives. The movement towards factory occupations and workers' control in Latin America shows that the workers, through their own experience, are moving in the direction of socialism. The reformists are alarmed by this movement, which threatens to go beyond the limits of capitalism and calls into question the sacred rights of private property. Where they do not openly oppose workers' control, they try to water it down, empty it of its revolutionary content, and divert it into safe channels that do not threaten capitalism and the market economy. They use formulas like "co-management" (cogestión) and co-operation to confuse the workers and divert their attention away from workers' control and nationalization.

When Marx threw himself into the activities of the International Working Men's Association, he wrote to Engels that the movement had been set back so much by the defeat of the 1848 revolutions that he could no longer use the revolutionary language of *The Communist Manifesto*. "It will be necessary to be *fortiter in re, suaviter in modo*" – bold in content and mild in manner. [1] An excellent example of his approach is the Inaugural Address to the IWMA in 1864. He welcomes the growth of the co-operative movement as an advance for the workers' movement. But to secure the gains and win the benefits that co-operation aspires to, he skilfully shows how the working class must ultimately take power.

"But there was in store a still greater victory of the political economy of labour over the political economy of property. We speak of the co-operative movement, especially the co-operative factories raised by the unassisted efforts of a few bold 'hands'. The value of these great social experiments cannot be overrated. By deed, instead of by argument, they have shown that production on a large scale, and in accord with the behest of modern science, may be carried on without the existence of a class of masters employing a class of hands; that to bear fruit, the means of labour need not be monopolised as a means of dominion over, and of extortion against, the labouring man himself; and that, like slave labour, like serf labour, hired labour is but a transitory and inferior form, destined to disappear before associated labour plying its toil with a willing hand, a ready mind and a joyous heart. In England, the seeds of the co-operative system were sown by Robert Owen; the working men's experiments, tried on the Continent, were, in fact, the practical upshot of the theories, not invented, but loudly proclaimed, in 1848.

"At the same time, the experience of the period from 1848 to 1864 has proved beyond doubt (what the most intelligent leaders of the English working class

1. Marx and Engels, *Selected Correspondence*, Moscow, 1965, p. 149.

already maintained in 1851-52, regarding the co-operative movement) that however excellent in principle, and however useful in practice, co-operative labour, if kept within the narrow circle of the casual efforts of private workmen, will never be able to arrest the growth in geometrical proportion of monopoly, to free the masses, nor even to perceptibly lighten the burden of their miseries. *It is perhaps for this very reason that plausible noblemen, philanthropic middle-class spouters and even keen political economists, have all at once turned nauseously complimentary to the very co-operative labour system they had vainly tried to nip in the bud by deriding it as the utopia of the dreamer, or stigmatising it as the sacrilege of the socialist.* To save the industrious masses, co-operative labour ought to be developed to national dimensions and, consequently, to be fostered by national means. Yet the lords of the land and the lords of capital will always use their political privilege for the defence and perpetuation of their political monopolies. So far from promoting, they will continue to lay every possible impediment in the way of the emancipation of labour. Remember the sneer with which, last session, Lord Palmerston put down the advocates of the Irish Tenants' Rights Bill. The House of Commons, cried he, is a house of landed proprietors.

"*To conquer political power has therefore become the great duty of the working classes.*" [2]

These words could be applied with every justification to Dieterich and Peters. In Venezuela today the genuinely revolutionary idea of Robert Owen is summed up by the slogan launched by President Chávez: "Factory closed, factory occupied." The workers have occupied one factory after another and run them under workers' control. If the leaders of the trade unions had been worthy of the name they would have immediately drawn up a list of the factories named by the President and called on the workers to occupy them and demanded they be nationalized. Unfortunately, they did not do this. As a result, a golden opportunity was lost. Some of those factories that were taken over by the workers became co-operatives. The result was predictable. In many cases these co-operatives were run on capitalist lines, since they are forced to operate in market conditions. There has inevitably been a tendency of the leaders of such enterprises to rise above the workforce, acquire a privileged position and become corrupt, acting just like the former bosses or worse. This has happened many times in the history of the co-operative movement beginning with the co-operatives set up by Robert Owen in the 19th century. Yet this is the model that Heinz Dieterich holds up as a shining example of "Socialism of the 21st Century"!

These great pioneers of our movement, despite the limitations of their utopian views, anticipated the ideas of Marx and Engels. The main weakness of utopian socialism was that it did not set out from the objective contradictions of capitalism to explain the necessity of socialism. Marx and Engels, on the contrary, explained

2. Marx and Engels, *Collected Works*, Vol. 20, p.11, my emphasis, AW.

that the development of the productive forces and the socialization of labour under capitalism created the material conditions for the working class to transform society along socialist lines.

All the utopians saw a classless society as a desirable end that one must strive for. It could be brought about only when the human race accepted certain precepts and dogmas worked out by certain individuals. In this sense, Comrade Dieterich is a direct descendant of the utopian school, although only of its weakest, most outmoded and retrograde features. Marx and Engels, on the other hand, explained that socialism must have a material basis, and that this could only be created by the development of the productive forces under capitalism.

For the utopian socialists, the way to usher in the new society was education and propaganda, that is, by the educational work of individuals and institutions. The class struggle did not enter into it. That is also very much the point of view of Heinz Dieterich and his co-thinkers, as we shall see. Marx insisted that the emancipation of the working class is the task of the workers themselves. On the contrary, the utopians (including the 21st Century utopians) do not see the workers as the fundamental force for changing society (that is a role they have reserved for themselves), but as little children who must be "educated". And who shall do the educating? Why, the "educated" people, of course!

In Venezuela, these ladies and gentlemen never tire of telling us that the "conditions for socialism are absent because the level of consciousness of the masses is too low." I have on more than one occasion been obliged to listen to the pontificating of these sorry ex-communists lecturing to the workers and berating them for their "low level of consciousness" and their lack of understanding of socialism. These are the very same workers who at every decisive stage of the Revolution, when it was in mortal danger, saved it by their marvellous movement, when these sorry "teachers" were hiding under the bed with the blanket over their head.

For Marx and Engels, and above all for Lenin and Trotsky, the abolition of capitalism requires the active participation of the majority of the population – that is, the working class. *Socialism is democratic or it is nothing.* Of course, when Marxists speak of democracy we have in mind, not the caricature of bourgeois formal democracy but a genuine democracy where industry, society and the state are controlled by the working class.

Marx, Dieterich and the utopian socialists

The utopians (and Heinz Dieterich) treat socialism from the standpoint of distribution, whereas distribution and exchange cannot be considered apart from production. In the words of Marx: "the so-called relations of distribution are themselves relations of production". [3] Even in prehistoric times, before goods could be bartered

3. Marx, *Grundrisse*, p. 153.

they first had to be produced. But exchange in the form of barter has an accidental character, as we have seen. A particular tribe has a surplus of dried fish, skins or stone axes, and exchanges the surplus for the surplus of another tribe. What is exchanged in barter is not commodities (exchange values) but use values. They may be exchanged above or below their value, since exchange at this level is purely accidental. It is therefore incorrect to say that at this stage there was equal exchange. *On the contrary, in nine cases out of ten barter will produce unequal exchange.*

Whereas in the period of primitive tribal communism people produced use values – that is to say, objects for their own consumption – and exchange was an exceptional activity carried on at the margins of society, under capitalism all production has as its aim the realization of exchange value: goods are produced in order to be sold at a profit. *Only under capitalism does the production of commodities (exchange values) become the normal mode of production.*

In essence, Dieterich and Peters would like to have capitalism without its exploitative features. They would like prices to express true value. They would like capitalists to accept the wages of equivalence and renounce profits. They would like to replace the big monopolies with small associations of producers organized in co-operatives. They would like so many things! Alas! We cannot always have what we would like...Marx explains in his preparatory notebooks for *Capital* (the *Grundrisse*) that it is *impossible directly to express labour time as price*:

"*Thus, although money owes its existence only to the tendency of exchange value to separate itself from the substance of commodities and to take on a pure form, nevertheless commodities cannot be directly transformed into money*; i.e. the authentic certificate of the amount of labour time realized in the commodity cannot serve the commodity as its price in the world of exchange values." [4]

Marx was very well aware of information technology, which already in his day had taken great strides forward. Indeed some modern economists have pointed out that the invention of the telegraph, together with railways and steamships had a far greater effect in binding together the world market ("globalization") than computers and the internet. However, none of these inventions have removed the central contradictions of capitalism. On the contrary, they have only created the conditions for reproducing these contradictions on an ever vaster scale, preparing the way for even deeper and more catastrophic crises in the future.

Under capitalism the worker's product is alienated from him and becomes converted into Capital, in which the worker's labour confronts him as an alien force. As long as this remains the case, all the categories of political economy will continue to have a contradictory and mystified character. Only in a socialist planned economy will it be possible to arrive at a rational economic system in which the anarchy of the market will be replaced by the conscious decision-making of men and

4. Marx, *Grundrisse*, p 160, Penguin, 1973, my emphasis, AW.

women. Things will no longer control people but people will control their own lives and destinies. However, as long as capitalism continues to exist – that means, for the benefit of Dieterich and Peters, as long as there is private ownership of the means of production and exchange – it is impossible to have a rational economic system.

Under capitalism, for example, money is *not* a measure of exchange value but only a medium *of exchange*, which is histori cally evolved but which is ultimately expressed by gold. Prices are determined by supply and demand on the world market, which involves the constant interchange of a vast number of commodities, shares, etc. every second of the day. It is this spontaneous interconnection, "which is independent of the knowing and willing of individuals, and which presupposes their reciprocal independence and indifference" which constitutes the anarchy of capitalist production. The spontaneous development of the world market is one of the main achievements of capitalism, as Marx explains in *The Communist Manifesto*:

"The need of a constantly expanding market for its products chases the bourgeoisie over the entire surface of the globe. It must nestle everywhere, settle everywhere, establish connections everywhere.

"The bourgeoisie has through its exploitation of the world market given a cosmopolitan character to production and consumption in every country. To the great chagrin of Reactionists, it has drawn from under the feet of industry the national ground on which it stood. All old-established national industries have been destroyed or are daily being destroyed. They are dislodged by new industries, whose introduction becomes a life and death question for all civilized nations, by industries that no longer work up indigenous raw material, but raw material drawn from the remotest zones; industries whose products are consumed, not only at home, but in every quarter of the globe. In place of the old wants, satisfied by the production of the country, we find new wants, requiring for their satisfaction the products of distant lands and climes. In place of the old local and national seclusion and self-sufficiency, we have intercourse in every direction, universal inter-dependence of nations. And as in material, so also in intellectual production. The intellectual creations of individual nations become common property. National one-sidedness and narrow-mindedness become more and more impossible, and from the numerous national and local literatures, there arises a world literature."

It is quite true that capitalism achieved this through the most brutal methods and that the existence of the world market ("globalization") under capitalism is a means of enslavement and exploitation of millions of workers and peasants. Nevertheless, from a Marxist point of view it is a progressive development because it lays the basis for a qualitatively higher stage of human development – world socialism. What is needed is not a sentimental-moralistic "anti-globalization" but a conscious and scientific analysis and *a world-wide struggle against capitalism and imperialism for international socialism.* In reality the idea of Peters and Dieterich presupposes the return to a stage of history that has passed beyond recall. It expresses the yearning of the petty bourgeois for a return to small-scale production (the only kind of production the petty bourgeois can understand). Marx answers this petty bourgeois philistinism thus:

"The degree and the universality of the development of wealth where *this* individuality becomes possible supposes production on the basis of exchange values as a prior condition, whose universality produces not only the alienation of the individual from himself and from others, but also the universality and the comprehensiveness of his relations and capacities. In earlier stages of development the single individual seems to be developed more fully, because he has not yet worked out his relationships in their fullness, or erected them as independent social powers and relations opposite himself. It is as ridiculous to yearn for a return to that original fullness as it is to believe that with this complete emptiness history has come to a standstill. The bourgeois viewpoint has never advanced beyond this antithesis between itself and this romantic viewpoint, and therefore the latter will accompany it as legitimate antithesis up to its blessed end.)" [5]

These words might have been written with Heinz Dieterich specifically in mind.

Individualism

The class content of this utopian socialism is that of the middle class, which stands between the bourgeoisie and the proletariat. The petty bourgeois envies and hates the big capitalists who are crushing them through unequal competition, but they also fear the working class into which they are constantly being pushed. The standpoint of the proletariat is that of collective class struggle. The worker learns the virtues of organization and collectivism through the very conditions of factory life. A peasant can say "I grew that potato", but no individual worker in Ford can say "I made that car". The car was made by the collective efforts of many workers, both inside and outside the factory. That is why it is absurd to pose the question of commodity production in terms of the individual, as Arno Peters tries to do.

We see from this that the so-called theory of equivalence has absolutely nothing in common with the Marxist labour theory of value. In dealing with commodity production Marx did not approach it from the point of view of individual workers. He explains that what we are dealing with is not the concrete labour of a carpenter, a lathe operator or an electrician but labour in general, social labour in the abstract. What we have here is, in fact, only a regurgitation of the pre-Marxist ideas of Proudhon and the utopian socialists. This was the standpoint of petty bourgeois socialism, which attempted to abolish the contradictions of capitalism without abolishing capitalist relations of production. It ignored the class struggle and posed the question of the transformation of society by peaceful reform. Instead of basing itself

5. See Marx, *Grundrisse*, p. 162.

on the working class it talked in vague language about humanity and the individual – just like Peters and Dieterich.

Individualism is precisely the standpoint of the middle class, the class of small proprietors. The individual peasant cultivates his small plot of land. The individual shopkeeper runs his own business. The individual lawyer runs his own legal company. The individual student competes against all his classmates in exams, and so on. When Peters bases himself on the individual, he appears to be talking common sense, for what can be more concrete and familiar than the individual man and woman? He seems to be saying: let us leave behind all empty abstractions and concentrate instead on the Individual. All men and women have the same rights and must live together like brothers and sisters, receiving the wages of equivalence "independently of the type of activity he carries out."

In reality Peters' Individual is the emptiest of all empty abstractions. This moralistic-utopian rhetoric only serves as a fig leaf to hide the class contradictions in society and thereby banish the awful spectre of class struggle. Bill Gates and the rest of the billionaire owners of industry may all be Individuals, like you and me, but they nevertheless form part of a class that has interests directly opposed to those of the workers and peasants, and will fight with all the means at their disposal to prevent the latter from taking their wealth from them. This is a question that our 21st Century Socialists never deal with, and this is no accident, *since their central idea is to prevent revolution by peaceful reform.*

Peters claims that in the era of global economy, production is "rooted in the condition that every human being has the same category, the same value and the same rights – includes every individual, independently of the type of activity he carries out." [6] Where does he get this nonsense from? Certainly not from the realities of life in the first decade of the 21st century! It would rather be correct to say that under capitalism every individual worker is equally enslaved to the global market, equally deprived of rights, equally oppressed and exploited, equally stripped of value as an individual human being and equally reduced to a mere object, a "factor of production".

Is it correct, however, to refer in this context to "every individual, independently of the type of activity he carries out?" Bill Gates is also an individual, carrying out the activity of exploiting a very large number of other individuals. Does he really have the same rights as the workers he exploits? Some sentimental people never tire of repeating the platitude that money does not buy happiness and that rich people are never happy.

This reminds us of something Hegel wrote: "Thus in modern times it has been demonstrated ad nauseam that princes are generally unhappy on their thrones; in consideration of which the possession of a throne is tolerated, and men acquiesce in

6. Dieterich, *El Socialismo del Siglo XXI*, p. 100.

the fact that not themselves but the personages in question are its occupants."[7] It is possible to say that the capitalists are just as alienated as the workers. But there is a slight difference here: the capitalists are quite content with their alienated state, as long as they can enjoy the wealth and privileges it brings them. Indeed, they will fight every attempt to save them from this alienation, even when Peters and Dieterich explain the wonders of 21st Century Socialism to them so touchingly.

Where Dieterich's ideas come from

Dieterich's "revolutionary theory of the future" turns out to be as old as the hills. His socialism of the 21st Century turns out to be *no more than the idealized expression of capitalist economic relations* that were long ago described by Ricardo, never mind Marx. Unable to offer any real analysis or perspective for the new generation, Comrade Dieterich has rummaged around in the dustbin of history, where he has found *a few old ideas from the prehistory of the socialist movement*, which he has dusted down and now presents as the very last word in modernity. Dieterich writes:

"Eight years after the death of Ricardo, John Gray developed the *Doctrine of Wage-Money as the Realization of the right to the integral product of Labour*, created by Robert Owen, into a coherent system; after having assured the labour-time spent, a central bank issues certificates that refer to one hour's labour, one day's labour, one week's labour, and which are valid as payment for a product requiring the same amount of labour. This consistent comparison of the value of a product with the amount of labour-time contained in each product, deduces from the theory of labour the exact measure that Ricardo was looking for. And it is also in agreement with the theory of [Adam] Smith, who says in his main work: 'Of equal quantities of work it can be said that in all places and at all times, it is of equal value to the worker'."[8]

Dieterich quotes John Gray approvingly. But it appears that he did not read the works of Gray himself, but only learned of their existence second-hand, apparently following that other great modern genius Arno Peters. Since the punctuation marks are so confused here, it is impossible to see where Peters ends and Dieterich begins. But since one is as confused as the other, this really does not make much difference. Marx answered Gray's utopian theories even before he wrote *Capital*. He deals with them extensively in his preparatory manuscripts known as the *Grundrisse*, in the Chapter on Money. What does this theory consist of? It sets out from the following idea: under capitalism, the worker does not receive the full fruits of his or her labour, because the capitalist retains part of it in the form of surplus value. This is achieved by means of unequal exchange. The solution is therefore to alter the nature of exchange, abolishing its unequal character and providing every worker with the full value of his labour.

7. Hegel, *The Philosophy of History*, III. Philosophic History § 33.
8. Dieterich, *El Socialismo del Siglo XXI*, p.90, emphasis in original.

How are we to arrive at this system of equal exchange? Every worker will receive a receipt (chit) that represents the actual amount of labour-time he has used in the production of commodities. These labour-chits are issued by a special bank or labour exchange and will circulate instead of money, which will thus be abolished. Exchange will therefore be retained but it will lose its exploitative character and become transformed into *equal exchange*. This idea, which was already antiquated in the 19th century, is supposed to lay the basis for a non-exploitative and equal society – otherwise known as *Socialism of the 21st Century*.

Heinz Dieterich introduces the idea of equal exchange in an attempt to overcome the contradictions of capitalism without abolishing it. In the first place, the existence of exchange (even "equal exchange") presupposes the existence of capitalist market relations – of *exchange value and money*. The fact that the latter is given another name (labour chits or whatever) does not change this, since, contrary to the illusions of university socialists, one does not change the essence of a thing merely by changing its name. In common with the utopian socialists Owen and Gray, comrade Dieterich does not understand the nature of money. But that is another issue.

The theory of equal exchange was developed, not by Marx, but by John Bray, a follower of Owen (1809-1897), not to be confused with John Gray, who we have already mentioned. A printer by trade, Bray developed his theory of labour money following in the footsteps of Ricardo. Here we find the origin and genesis of the economic theories of the Socialism of the 21st Century – in 1839! Dieterich merely *copied* the idea of equal exchange and a labour bank from this 19th century English utopian and presented it as a wonderfully novel idea for the new millennium.

Comrade Dieterich does not emerge very well from a comparison between his convoluted prose and the simple, clear, precise language of John Bray. Nor was our Heinz the first one to plagiarize the utopian socialist Bray. Proudhon beat him to it over 150 years ago. He was answered by Marx in one of the pioneering works of scientific socialism, *The Poverty of Philosophy*. Here Marx pays tribute to the brilliant originality of Bray, particularly his remarkable pamphlet *Labour's Wrongs and Labour's Remedies*. But he also subjects the utopian idea of equal exchange and labour banks to a sharp criticism – exactly the same criticism that can be made against the Founder of 21st Century Socialism. Marx quotes extensively from Bray's remarkable work, *Labour's Wrongs and Labour's Remedy*, which was published in Leeds in 1839:

"It is labour alone which bestows value...

"Every man has an undoubted right to all that his honest labour can procure him. When he thus appropriates the fruits of his labour, he commits no injustice upon any other human being; for he interferes with no other man's right of doing the same with the produce of his labour..."

"From the very nature of labour and exchange, strict justice not only requires that all exchangers should be mutually, but that they should likewise be equally, benefited. Men have only two things which they can exchange with each other, namely, labour, and the produce of labour…

"If a just system of exchanges were acted upon, the value of articles would be determined by the entire cost of production; and equal values should always exchange for equal values. If, for instance, it takes a hatter one day to make a hat, and a shoemaker the same time to make a pair of shoes – supposing the material used by each to be of the same value – and they exchange these articles with each other, they are not only mutually but equally benefited: the advantage derived by either party cannot be a disadvantage to the other, as each has given the same amount of labour, and the materials made use of by each were of equal value. But if the hatter should obtain two pair of shoes for one hat – time and value of material being as before – the exchange would clearly be an unjust one. The hatter would defraud the shoemaker of one day's labour; and were the former to act thus in all his exchanges, he would receive, for the labour of half a year, the product of some other person's whole year. We have heretofore acted upon no other than this most unjust system of exchanges – the workmen have given the capitalist the labour of a whole year, in exchange for the value of only half a year – and from this, and not from the assumed inequality of bodily and mental powers in individuals, has arisen the inequality of wealth and power which at present exists around us. It is an inevitable condition inequality of exchanges – of buying at one price and selling at another – that capitalists shall continue to be capitalists, and working men to be working men – the one a class of tyrants and the other a class of slaves – to eternity…

"The whole transaction, therefore, plainly shows that the capitalists and proprietors do no more than give the working man, for his labour of one week, a part of the wealth which they obtained from him the week before! – which amounts to giving him nothing for something…

"The whole transaction, therefore, between the producer and the capitalist is a palpable deception, a mere farce: it is, in fact, in thousands of instances, no other than a barefaced though legalized robbery." [9]

"…The gain of the employer will never cease to be the loss of the unemployed – until the exchanges between the parties are equal; and exchanges never can be equal while society is divided into capitalists and producers – the last living upon their labour and the first bloating upon the profit of that labour.

"It is plain that, establish whatever form of government we will… we may talk of morality and brotherly love… no reciprocity can exist where there are unequal exchanges. Inequality of exchanges, as being the cause of inequality of possessions, is the secret enemy that devours us." [10]

"Where equal exchanges are maintained, the gain of one man cannot be the loss of another; for every exchange is then simply a *transfer*, and not a sacrifice of labour

9. Bray, *Labour's Wrongs and Labour's Remedy*, pp. 45, 48, 49 and 50.
10. Ibid. pp. 51 and 52.

and wealth. Thus, although under a social system based on equal exchanges, a parsimonious man may become rich, his wealth will be no more than the accumulated produce of his own labour. He may exchange his wealth, or he may give it to others... but a rich man cannot continue wealthy for any length of time after he has ceased to labour. Under equality of exchanges, wealth cannot have, as it now has, a procreative and apparently self-generating power, such as replenishes all waste from consumption; for, unless it be renewed by labour, wealth, when once consumed, is given up for ever. That which is now called *profit* and *interest* cannot exist as such in connection with equality of exchanges; for producer and distributor would be alike remunerated, and the sum total of their labour would determine the value of the article created and brought to the hands of the consumer...

"The principle of equal exchanges, therefore, must from its very nature ensure universal labour." [11]

From these quotes it is perfectly obvious from where our friends Peters and Dieterich have got the idea of equal exchange. While paying tribute to Bray's pioneering work, Marx already pointed out the utopian nature of his ideas:

"In principle, there is no exchange of products – but there is the exchange of the labour which co-operated in production. The mode of exchange of products depends upon the mode of exchange of the productive forces. In general, the form of exchange of products corresponds to the form of production. Change the latter, and the former will change in consequence. Thus in the history of society we see that the mode of exchanging products is regulated by the mode of producing them. Individual exchange corresponds also to a definite mode of production which itself corresponds to class antagonism. There is thus no individual exchange without the antagonism of classes.

"But the respectable conscience refuses to see this obvious fact. So long as one is a bourgeois, one cannot but see in this relation of antagonism a relation of harmony and eternal justice, which allows no one to gain at the expense of another. For the bourgeois, individual èxchange can exist without any antagonism of classes. For him, these are two quite unconnected things. Individual exchange, as the bourgeois conceives it, is far from resembling individual exchange as it actually exists in practice.

"Mr. Bray turns the illusion of the respectable bourgeois into an ideal he would like to attain. In a purified individual exchange, freed from all the elements of antagonism he finds in it, he sees an 'equalitarian' relation which he would like society to adopt generally.

"Mr. Bray does not see that this equalitarian relation, this corrective ideal that he would like to apply to the world, is itself nothing but the reflection of the actual world; and that therefore it is totally impossible to reconstitute society on the basis

11. Ibid., pp. 109-10.

of what is merely an embellished shadow of it. In proportion as this shadow takes on substance again, we perceive that this substance, far from being the transfiguration dreamt of, is the actual body of existing society." [12]

The idea of "equal exchange" is, to quote Marx, "*nothing but the reflection of the actual world*". In other words, the idea of equal exchange is not the recipe for a new socialist society, but only an attempt to modify the existing economic relations of capitalism, while retaining its essence (exchange of commodities). It is the eternal dream of the petty bourgeois: *the dream of constructing capitalism with a human face.* This utopian scheme was false in theory and disastrous in practice. We did not have to wait for the 21st century to find this out. Unlike comrade Dieterich, whose utopias, like all the productions of the university leftists, are confined to paper, the 19th century utopians had the courage of their convictions and actually attempted to put their theories into practice. Robert Owen bankrupted himself trying to establish ideal communist communities in the USA. Bray's supporters actually established equitable labour-exchange bazaars in London, Sheffield, Leeds and other towns in England. All ended in failure and the loss of considerable amounts of money.

Proudhon put the same idea forward. He argued that a certain quantity of labour is equivalent to the product created by this same quantity of labour. Each day's labour is worth as much as another day's labour. That is to say, if the quantities are equal, one man's labour is worth as much as another man's labour: there is no qualitative difference. Therefore, with the same quantity of work, one man's product can be given in exchange for another man's product. All men are wageworkers getting equal pay for an equal time of work. Perfect equality rules the exchanges and everyone is happy. In 1849 Proudhon set up a new Exchange bank in Paris, strictly on the lines advocated by Dieterich and Peters. What happened? It collapsed almost immediately and its founder found himself in court. The idea of "equal exchange" that is now being touted as the panacea for 21st Century Socialism thus revealed itself to be bankrupt a long time ago – in the most literal sense of the word. As the French say: "Plus ça change, plus c'est la même chose!" (The more things change, the more they stay the same.)

12. Quoted in Marx, *Poverty of philosophy*, International Publishers, New York 1963 pp. 70-72.

6. An outline of Marxist economics

Before we examine the economic theories of comrade Dieterich, we will attempt to provide the reader with a brief summary of the basic economic laws of capitalism, which Marx explained long ago. They are analysed in great detail in the three volumes of *Capital* and other works. He wrote less about the workings of a future communist society, but what he did write in works such as *The Critique of the Gotha Programme* is more than sufficient to establish the basic functioning of a socialist economy, which differs fundamentally from capitalism – and therefore also from Heinz Dieterich's conception of 21st Century Socialism. In his Introduction to *The Living Thoughts of Karl Marx*, Trotsky restates the basic propositions of Marx in a masterly way:

"In contemporary society man's cardinal tie is exchange. Any product of labour that enters into the process of exchange becomes a commodity. Marx began his investigation with the commodity and deduced from that fundamental cell of capitalist society those social relations that have objectively shaped themselves on the basis of exchange, independently of man's will. Only by pursuing this course is it possible to solve the fundamental puzzle – how in capitalist society, in which man thinks for himself and no one thinks for all, are created the relative proportions of the various branches of economy indispensable to life.

"The worker sells his labour power, the farmer takes his produce to the market, the money lender of banker grants loans, the storekeeper offers an assortment of merchandise, the industrialist builds a plant, the speculator buys and sells stocks and bonds – each having his own considerations, his own private plan, his own concern about wages or profit. Nevertheless, out of this chaos of individual strivings and actions emerges a certain economic whole, which, true, is not harmonious, but contradictory, yet does give society the possibility not merely to exist but even to develop. This means that, after all, chaos is not chaos at all, that in some way it is regulated automatically, if not consciously. To understand the mechanism whereby various aspects of economy are brought into a state of relative balance, is to discover the objective laws of capitalism.

"Clearly, the laws which govern the various spheres of capitalist economy – wages, price, land, rent, profit, interest, credit, the Stock Exchange – are numerous and complex. But in the final reckoning they come down to the single law that Marx discovered and explored to the end; that is, the law of labour value, which is indeed the basic regulator of capitalist economy. The essence of that law is simple. Society has at its disposal a certain reserve of living labour power. Applied to nature, that power produces products necessary for the satisfaction of human needs. In consequence of division of labour among independent producers, the products assume the form of commodities. Commodities are exchanged for each other in a given ratio, at first directly, and eventually through the medium of gold or money. The basic property of commodities, which in a certain relationship makes them equal to each other, is the human labour expended upon them – abstract labour, labour in general – the basis and the measure of value. Division of labour among millions of scattered producers does not lead to the disintegration of society, because commodities are exchanged according to the socially necessary labour time expended upon them. By accepting and rejecting commodities, the market, as the arena of exchange, decides whether they do or do not contain within themselves socially necessary labour, thereby determines the ratios of the various kinds of commodities necessary for society, and consequently also the distribution of labour power according to the various trades.

"The actual processes of the market are immeasurably more complex than has been here set forth in but a few lines. Thus, oscillating around the value of labour, prices fluctuate considerably above and below their value. The causes of these fluctuations are fully explained by Marx in the third volume of *Capital*, which describes 'the process of capitalist production considered as a whole'.

"Nevertheless, great as may be the divergences between the prices and the values of commodities in individual instances, the sum of all prices is equal to the sum of all values, for in the final reckoning only the values that have been created by human labour are at the disposal of society, and prices cannot break through this limitation, including even the monopoly prices of trusts; where labour has created no new value, there even Rockefeller can get nothing.

"But if commodities are exchanged for each other according to the quantity of labour invested in them, how does inequality come out of equality? Marx solved this puzzle by exposing the peculiar nature of one of the commodities, which lies at the basis of all other commodities: namely, labour power. The owner of means of production, the capitalist, buys labour power. Like all other commodities, it is evaluated according to the quantity of labour invested in it, i.e., of those means of subsistence which are necessary for the survival and the reproduction of the worker. But the consumption of that commodity – labour power – consists of work, i.e., the creation of new values. The quantity of these values is greater than those which the worker himself receives and which he expends for his upkeep. The capitalist buys labour power in order to exploit it. It is this exploitation which is the source of inequality.

"That part of the product which goes to cover the worker's own subsistence Marx calls necessary product; that part which the worker produces above this, is surplus product. Surplus product must have been produced by the slave, or the slave-owner would not have kept any slaves. Surplus product must have been produced by the serf, or serfdom would have been of no use to the landed gentry. Surplus product, only to a considerably greater extent, is likewise produced by the wage worker, or the capitalist would have no need to buy labour power. The class struggle is nothing else than the struggle for surplus product. He who owns surplus-product is master of the situation – owns wealth, owns the state, has the key to the church, to the courts, to the sciences and to the arts." [1]

Marx's great discovery

The basis of Marxist economics is the Labour Theory of Value: the basic regulator of capitalism. This marvellously profound law that Marx discovered determines prices and the allocation of capital to the various sectors of the economy. Thus, despite its anarchic nature, capitalism possesses a mechanism, which can make it work. And it has been working for about 200 years, with no plan, no Historical Project, and little or no conscious human intervention at all. Of course, the workings of the capitalist economy are very complicated. There are separate laws which govern the various spheres of capitalist economy – wages, prices, land, rent, profit, interest, credit, banking and the stock exchange, speculation, international trade, etc. But in the last analysis the basic regulator of capitalist economy is the law of labour value.

While the great classical economists, like David Ricardo, based themselves on the law of value, it was Marx who refined the theory and discovered the dual character of labour power and thus the real secret of capitalist economy. All surplus value arises from the labour of the working class. The working class however sells its labour power, which, while sold at its full value, is capable of creating new values greater than its own. Therefore, capitalism is to be understood not from its exchange of labour-time equivalents but from the capitalist's appropriation of surplus value. The class struggle is nothing more than a struggle over the surplus value. "An increase in wages", states Marx, "reduces the surplus value, while a lengthening of the working day and an increase in the intensity of labour add to it." [2]

1. L. Trotsky, *Introduction to The Living Thoughts of Karl Marx*, published as Marxism in our time, Pathfinder 1970, pp. 11-13.
2. Marx, *Capital*, Vol. 3, Progress Publishers, Moscow, 1966 p. 51.

The capitalist views this relation as a market-relation, in terms of *prices and costs of production*. Thus, it is the usual practice of bourgeois economics to seek the source of profits in *exchange*. But behind these market relations lie quantities of congealed labour-time that are incorporated into commodities in the process of *production*. The total labour time expended by capitalist society is divided between wages and profits. The means of production represent past expenditure of labour ("dead labour"). However, it is the continuous application of human labour is needed to make them worthwhile. In capitalist society, it is the owners of "dead labour" (means of production) who dominate "living labour" and subjugate it. "It is only the domination of accumulated, past, materialised labour over direct, living labour, which turns accumulated labour into capital." [3]

Like a body of which fresh and tissue must be continuously renewed if life is to be sustained, the physical substance of capital must constantly assume new forms. A factory or machine that remains idle deteriorates and becomes obsolete and brings no profit. But these in use give up their value to the commodities produced and once sold, the capitalists get back the values of this "dead labour" plus the new values added by living labour. Life for capital means making profit. Capital lives by being used. It must ceaselessly go through its cycle of transformations from money to raw materials, machines and wages of workers who use up these means of production in making new commodities, which are sold and transformed back into money. This is the cycle or turnover of capital. The quicker the turnover the greater the profit made. If stopped, profits are lost. The very existence of capital hinges on this unceasing turnover, which is underpinned by a series of limits imposed by the market.

Capital however is also divided amongst various capitals. Each sector yields different quantities of surplus value. Each employs different ratios of means of production (constant capital) to labour power (variable capital). As profit is surplus value measured against the total capital, on the surface, profits would appear to be higher where there was more variable capital employed than constant capital. Yet this is not the case because of the competition between different capitalists tends to result in the equalisation of the rate of profit, of an average rate of profit. Monopolies become a barrier to this process by ruthlessly keeping out competitors through all manner of means. Intel, for instance, the computer chip maker, controls 90 percent of all processors, and its market power is "magnified by its huge installed base, brand recognition and network effects", says the US Federal Trade Commission. But the magnitude of this average rate of profit is determined by the total mass of profit yielded by the total social capital.

Through the market, and its supply and demand fluctuations, capital tends to move from the more stagnant to the more developing/expanding industries, where

3. Marx, *Wage Labour and Capital*. Progress Publishers, Moscow, 1952 p.30.

there is a higher rate of profit. The latter is temporarily a higher rate than the average profit until the influx of capital has boosted production sufficiently to absorb the excess demand. This search for extra profit characterises capitalist competition. Again, the creation of monopolies cuts across this process, distorting the market, and maintaining monopoly prices. If the value or exchange value of commodities is made up from the amount of socially necessary labour involved in their production, increased investment leading to a rising productivity of labour, must result in every individual commodity containing less labour time than previously.

The amount of labour involved in production is spread over more and more commodities. This cheapening of commodities allows the capitalist who introduces new machinery/technology to undercut any rivals and increase his share of the market. The decrease in value of every single commodity is compensated by the increased number of commodities produced. Until the new technology is generalised, the new technologies will produce monopoly profits. The profitability of capital is increased, despite the lower prices. The commodity contains less newly added labour, but its unpaid portion grows in relation to its paid portion.

As Marx explained, the capitalist system has the potential to break down at a whole series of points. The separation of sale and purchase of commodities can be the starting point of crisis. "The *possibility* of crisis, which became apparent in the *simple metamorphosis* of the commodity, is once more demonstrated, and further developed, by the disjunction between the (direct) process of production and the process of circulation", states Marx. The process of capitalist production and circulation is summed up in the formula: C-M-C, or the metamorphosis of the commodity. The production of surplus value is only the first stage for the capitalist. So long as it remains surplus value it remains locked within the commodities. The next task is to sell these commodities on the market and *realise* the surplus value, i.e., turn it into money. At the point of sale, if the capitalist cannot find any buyers, the process breaks down. "The possibility of crisis..." states Marx, "lies therefore in the very separation between sale and purchase." [4] Here crisis appears in its simplest form.

Where does exploitation take place?

In every system based on the exploitation of one class by another, *exploitation takes place not in exchange but in production*. One would have thought that comrade Dieterich would be aware of this elementary proposition, but since he seems not to be acquainted with the ABCs of Marxist economics, we are obliged to restate them here. In the first volume of *Capital* Marx explains in great detail the historical development of the commodity form from accidental exchange in primitive tribal communism through all its manifold transitions, till we arrive at capitalist production – commodity production par excellence. The way in which workers are exploited

4. Marx, *Theories of surplus value*, volume II, pp. 502 and 510.

under capitalism differs from all previous forms of exploitation.

In slavery, to begin with, there is no question of exchange, unless we say that the slave exchanges his or her labour for the blows of the overseer. Slavery is forced labour. The slave is not free and is forced to work under compulsion. For that reason slave labour is based on an extremely low level of labour productivity. It can only function as an economic system on condition of a sufficiently large mass of slaves, who can be worked to death in the mines and plantations and replaced cheaply through wars.

As we have already explained, there is no incentive to invest in labour-saving machinery, partly because the slaves would break sensitive machinery and partly because the existence of large-scale cheap labour renders machinery unnecessary. That is why the Greeks and Romans, for all their ingenuity, never developed the steam engine for productive purposes. Although Heron of Alexandria invented a steam powered rotating ball about 100 AD – the first recorded steam power – it remained a mere toy with no productive application.

Under feudalism things are somewhat different. The serfs were not chattel slaves but were tied to the land and compelled to give up a part of their produce to their master. In both slavery and serfdom exploitation is open and clear for all to see. There is no mystery about it. As in slavery and capitalism, so in feudalism exploitation takes place not in exchange but in production: the serf works his plot of land and hands over a portion of his produce (the surplus) to the landowner. Neither slavery nor serfdom was dependent upon exchange, although trade and money existed and played an increasing role and was an important factor in the dissolution of both systems, as Marx points out. But money did not play the same role in feudalism as it does under capitalism.

The basis of feudalism was subsistence agriculture. The feudal lords had no more reason to accumulate capital and invest in boosting production, science and technique than the slave owners of Greece and Rome. They spent their fortunes on feasting, or donated to the Church to say prayers for their soul after death. The magnificent medieval cathedrals of Europe bear mute witness to the complete lack of interest of the feudal ruling class in productive investment.

Capitalism is an entirely different system to either slavery or feudalism and it works in an entirely different way. The prior condition for its existence is a class of free labourers who sell to the capitalists the only commodity they possess: their ability to work. Through robbery of common lands, the Enclosure Acts and other acts of plunder and oppression at the dawn of capitalism, the peasants were impoverished and driven off their ancestral lands. The ruination of the peasantry provided a pool of labour-power in the towns and cities. The class structure became more simplified. On the one hand were the capitalists and on the other the propertyless proletarians. All that these workers possessed was their ability to work. The only way they could remain alive was to sell their labour-power to the capitalists in return for wages. In the process of production, the proletarian produces more value than he receives in wages, the surplus value being expropriated by the capitalists.

The value of labour-power

The possibility of the capitalist purchasing labour-power on the market presupposes the existence of a class of free wage-labourers. "For the conversion of this money into capital ... the owner of money must meet in the market with the free labourer, free in the double sense that as a free man he can dispose of his labour-power as his own commodity, and that on the other hand he has no other commodity for sale, is short of everything necessary for the realization of his labour-power." [5] The creation of this class of free wage-labourers is an historical phenomenon, the product of a whole serious of social and economic revolutions.

The capitalist looks upon the labour market as just another branch of the general market for commodities. Labour power, for him, is just another commodity. In fact, although the capitalist does not understand, and is not concerned with, the theoretical explanation, he is quite correct in this assumption. Labour-power is a commodity, governed by the same laws as other commodities. Its value is determined by the labour-time necessary for its production. Labour-power is the ability of the worker to work. It is "consumed" by the capitalist in the actual labour-process. But this presupposes the existence and health and strength of the worker.

The production of labour-power therefore means the workers' self-maintenance and the reproduction his species. The labour-time necessary for the workers' maintenance is the labour-time necessary for the production of the means of subsistence: the food, clothing, heat, etc. necessary to his survival as an animal and his ability to work every day. This varies in different countries, different climates and different historical periods. As opposed to other commodities, there enters into the determination of the value of labour-power a historical and moral element. Nevertheless, in a given country, at a given period the average quantity of the means of subsistence necessary for the labourer is practically known.

Apart from this, the worker must have enough to reproduce his species, to provide fresh generations of labourers to replace the worn-out labour power. Secondly, as the complexity of labour increases, a certain amount has to be provided for the education of the workers, to raise their productivity. Unlike most commodities, labour-power is paid for only *after* it has been consumed. The workers actually extend credit to the capitalist! There is also all kinds of petty cheating, obliging workers to a "week-in hand", bankruptcy leading to loss of wages and so on. However, in advanced capitalism these aspects are entirely secondary elements in the extraction of surplus value.

Labour power, like every other commodity, is bought openly on the market but

5. Marx, *Capital*, Volume I, Penguin, p. 272.

used outside the sphere of the market, behind locked doors, in the sphere of production. The contract between Capital and Labour is freely arrived at, in the interest of both parties, on the basis of a fair exchange, and exchange of *equivalents* (from the standpoint of the market). The market price of labour power (wages) is determined, like any other commodity by supply and demand, although it can be influenced by trade union organization and the class struggle, which is ultimately a struggle between wage labour and Capital for the division of the surplus value produced by the working class.

Dieterich is therefore entirely wrong when he refers to "unequal exchange" under capitalism. It was Marx who first pointed out that what the worker actually sells to the capitalist is not his or her labour (as the vulgar economists suppose) but labour power. This is sold at its market value, and like any other commodity, the value of labour power (wages) is determined by the amount of socially necessary labour power expended in its production. This is not theft or unequal exchange, as comrade Dieterich imagines, but precisely the *exchange of equivalents*. To present it any other way is to abandon the scientific approach of Marx in favour of superficial impressionism and moralistic posturing.

Machinery and the working day

If we look at commodities as use-values (that is, from the standpoint of their utility), we see them as a "shoe", "watch", etc., and also as products of a particular kind of labour – the labour of the cobbler, watchmaker, etc. But in exchange, the special character of commodities is lost sight of and they appear as so many units of average labour. In exchange what is compared is quantities of human labour in general contained in the commodities: abstract human labour, not the labour of individual workers. In exchange, all labour is reduced to average simple units of labour.

Commodities produced by skilled labour contain more value than that produced by unskilled. Therefore in exchange, the units of skilled labour are reduced to so many units of unskilled, simple labour. For example, the ratio of 1 skilled unit = 3 unskilled units, or, to express the same idea in another way, skilled labour is worth three times as much as unskilled. Explained simply, the value of commodity is determined by the amount of average labour used in its production (or how long it takes to produce). But left like this, it would seem that a lazy worker or inefficient worker produces more values than the most efficient worker. A shoemaker who uses outdated methods to produce shoes would take a whole day to make a pair of shoes. But when he tries to sell them on the market, he will find that they will only fetch the same as shoes produced by the better equipped more modern factories.

If these factories produce a pair of shoes in, say half an hour, they will contain less labour (and therefore less value) and will be sold cheaper. This will drive the shoemaker using wasteful methods out of business. His labour producing a pair of shoes after half an hour is wasted labour, and unnecessary under modern conditions.

On pain of extinction he will be forced to introduce modern techniques and produce shoes at least equal to the necessary time developed by society. In other words, all commodities must be produced in a socially necessary time. At any given time, using the average labour, machines, methods, etc., all commodities take a particular time to make. This is governed by the level of technique in society. Any more labour-time spent over and above this will be useless labour, causing costs to rise and making the firm uncompetitive. Thus, the value of a commodity is determined by the amount of *socially necessary labour* contained in it. Naturally, this labour time is continually changing as new techniques and methods of work are introduced. Competition drives the inefficient to the wall.

The difference between skilled and unskilled labour is a difference of degree. "All labour of a higher or more complicated character than the average labour is expenditure of labour power of a more costly kind, labour-power whose production has cost more time and labour and which therefore has a higher value than unskilled or simple labour-power." [6] In the production of value it is inevitable to express skilled labour in terms of unskilled: one hour of skilled = three of unskilled, etc.

Heinz Dieterich seems to be fascinated by information technology, but the fact that modern capitalism has developed this technology does not at all signify a reduction of the working day, although logically, it ought to do so. What is the reason for this contradiction? Long ago Marx explained that under capitalism the introduction of new technology, far from leading to a reduction of the working day and a lessening of the burden of labour, signifies precisely the opposite: *the introduction of new technology under capitalism always leads to an increase in the hours worked.*

This general rule is confirmed by the whole history of capitalism and the advent of computer technology, far from refuting it, provides the most striking example of this. In the past the "experts" of the bourgeoisie promised us a glorious vista of the future when, on the basis of applied science and technology, the burden of work would be done away with, hours reduced and the central problem of society would be what to do with our leisure time. How ironic these arguments about technology leading to excess leisure sound today! While million of unemployed languish in conditions of enforced "leisure", other millions with the good luck to remain at work find themselves subjected to ever-increasing pressures to work longer hours with lower pay and worse conditions, forced to spend the maximum exertions of their nervous system and muscle-power in the cause of greater "productivity" (read: profitability).

Comrade Dieterich thinks that inventions like the computer, the Internet and cybernetics will solve all our problems and lead straight to socialism. This argument, like all the earlier predictions concerning the possibility for reducing the working day, is partially correct. But it is abstract because it leaves out of account

6. Marx, *Capital*, 1,7:2. Penguin ed. p. 305.

the small detail that under capitalism, as Marx explains, the introduction of new machinery and technology, which in principle should lay the basis for a reduction of the working day and the abolition of the slavery of wage labour, *actually leads to a lengthening of the working day.*

Dieterich repeatedly makes the same mistake – *confusing abstract potential for concrete reality.* The potential for a universal reduction in working hours – and thereby the abolition of unemployment – is implicit in the spectacular advance of technology in the past few decades. Moreover, this argument is not restricted to computer technology but applies to the advances of science and technology in general. Let us consider the implication of industrial robots.

Twenty years ago there were 500,000 of these machines in the world. Japan, with just 0.3 percent of the surface of the world, and 2.5 percent of its population, possessed more than 300,000 of the total – a number that had doubled in a five-year period. In the USA, the number of robots grew by 50 percent in the same period, according to figures published by the McKinsey Global Institute. Italy, France, Spain and other countries likewise increased their number of robots.

The introduction of these machines means that the number of workers in a factory can be drastically reduced, while the productivity of those who remain, vastly enhanced by machinery, registers a substantial increase. In France, for example, the two major car manufacturers have reduced their workforce by no fewer than 200,000 in a twelve-year period from the late 1980s, with an increased productivity of 12 percent in the same period. Similarly figures can be shown for Spain, Germany, the USA and other countries. Did the introduction of new technology lead to a fall in hours? *No, it led only to a reduction in the workforce, higher unemployment and even greater pressure on those who remained to produce more.*

The same technology of robot production can be applied to many other fields – the transformation of plastics, for example, or the textile industry. Even in the food industry, such operations as the packaging of cheese is done by robots, which can also be used to eliminate human participation in dangerous occupations. Robots mean greater quality, more flexibility in production, and speed. The universal application of such technology in the context of a rational and harmonious plan of production, with the democratic involvement of the workers at all levels, would signify a complete transformation of the life of society.

The working week could immediately be reduced to thirty hours without loss of pay, and at the same time production could be rapidly increased both in quantity and quality. Thereafter, the working day could be steadily reduced, thus providing the material conditions for such a flourishing of democracy, art, science and culture, as the world has never seen. This is precisely the material basis for socialism – a new and qualitatively higher form of human society. These are not utopian daydreams, but conclusions that flow logically and inevitably from the present state of knowledge and the actual demands of the productive forces.

And yet, at every step reality knocks its head against the potential of production and technique. Instead of a world of leisure and self-fulfilment, we have a social nightmare of mass "structural" unemployment on the one hand and relentless, inhuman squeezing of labour power on the other. This is especially true of computer technology. Such inventions as laptop computers, bleepers, pagers, mobile phones, etc. mean that the worker can be at the disposal of the employer 24 hours a day, seven days a week, and that, consequently, the working day can be prolonged indefinitely.

This also means that the white collar workers, who in the past had a relatively privileged position, and did not even see themselves as members of the working class, have been increasingly proletarianised and now suffer from an exploitation as severe as that which is found in many factories. Thus, the new technology, which in theory should lead to a lightening of the burden of labour, leads in practice to a further increase in exploitation and slavery for the working class. How can one explain such a crying contradiction?

Marx on machinery

In the first volume of *Capital*, Marx explains the reasons why the introduction of machinery under capitalism necessarily means a lengthening of the working day. The purpose of employing machinery is to cheapen the product by economizing on labour. However, there is a contradiction implicit in this. The profits of the capitalist are extracted from the unpaid labour of the working class. The increase in the productivity of labour made possible by the introduction of machinery is achieved by a heavy initial outlay on costly machinery, which in itself adds no new value to the end product, but merely imports to it, over a period, bit by bit, its own value:

"Machinery, like every other component of constant capital, creates no new value, but yields up its own value to the product that it serves to beget." [7] The only way to ensure a greater return on this outlay, is to make his machinery work non-stop, day and night, with no interruptions, while simultaneously squeezing every atom of surplus value from the worker, both by lengthening the working day through overtime, the abolition of tea-breaks, etc. (absolute surplus value), and by enormously increasing the intensity of labour by speed-ups, productivity deals and all kinds of pressure (relative surplus value).

Marx explains that "machinery, while augmenting the human material that forms the principal object of capital's exploiting power, at the same time raises the degree of exploitation." And again: "If machinery be the most powerful means for increasing the productiveness of labour – i.e. for shortening the working-time required in the production of a commodity, it becomes in the hands of capital the most power-

7. Marx, *Capital*, Vol. 1, Penguin ed. pp. 509 and 395.

ful means, in those countries first invaded by it, for lengthening the working-day beyond all bounds set by human nature."[8]

Competition, the constant revolutionizing of the productive forces and techniques, the desire to "corner the market" and get an advantage over others, were the factors which, in the past at least, compelled the capitalist constantly to re-invest in expensive machinery. However, once having introduced new machinery, it is in the capitalist's interest to use it to the maximum. It cannot be allowed to stand idle for an instant, partly because it deteriorates, and partly because it can quickly become obsolete. That is why, under capitalism, the introduction of machinery leads to greater exploitation and an increase in the working day.

The introduction of new technology to a given branch of production means that in that branch, for a time, huge super-profits can be earned. Later, however, the other capitalists catch up and the rate of profit is levelled out. Ultimately, the amount of surplus value obtained by the capitalist depends upon two things: a) the rate of surplus value and b) the number of workers employed. However, the introduction of machinery tends to reduce the number of workers and therefore change the ratio of variable to constant capital. Machinery (constant capital), as we have seen, does not add any new value to the final product above and beyond what is already present in it. "Hence, the application of machinery to the production of surplus value," Marx explains, "implies a contradiction which is immanent in it."[9]

From what we have already seen the question that should be asked is not why there are crises under capitalism, but why the capitalist system is not always in crisis. The explanation is to be found in the fact that under capitalism production is divided into two parts: production of commodities and production of the means of production (machinery, etc.). In *The Communist Manifesto*, Marx and Engels explain that: "The bourgeoisie cannot exist without constantly revolutionising the instruments of production, and thereby the relations of production, and with them the whole relations of society. Conservation of the old modes of production in unaltered form, was on the contrary, the first condition of existence for all earlier industrial classes."[10]

It is ABC for any Marxist that the capitalists must constantly find new and profitable avenues of investment. In every period of capitalist development there have been such fields of investments – steam power and textiles in the industrial revolution; the railways, steam ships and telegraphs in the last part of the 19th century; Fordism and automobiles in the 1920s and 1930s; then electricity, airplanes, the radio, telephone, television, chemicals, plastics, computers and so on.

More recently information technology has been a major field of investment. In the 1990s it displaced cars and steel as the main motor-force of the US economy.

8. Ibid. p. 526.
9. Ibid. p. 407.
10. Marx and Engels, *Selected Works*, Vo.1, p. 111

Nine million people now work in this sector – more than steel or automobiles. This is the classical model of capitalist accumulation. By investing in machinery, the capitalists in this sector have secured huge increases in productivity, allowing them to obtain simultaneously high profits (not for nothing did Bill Gates become the richest man in the world) at that time (although he has now been displaced by Carlos Slim – a Mexican).

In common with most bourgeois economists, Heinz Dieterich thinks that the advent of information technology has completely transformed the economy. In fact, the relative importance of information technique in fomenting globalisation and boosting the world economy is far less than the invention of railways, steam ships and the telegraph in the 19th century. In the USA from 1869 to 1893, the miles of rail track quadrupled, and rail shipping costs dropped dramatically, opening up large parts of the country for manufacturing and commercial agriculture. The railroads themselves consumed much of the US steel and coal production and accounted for almost 20 percent of all investment. Overall, the railroads' expansion fuelled an economy that grew an average of five percent a year.

This kind of thing has always happened throughout the history of capitalism, the capitalists invest in order to earn the maximum profits. Where a new and profitable field of investment opens up, the first to exploit it can obtain very large profits. But inevitably, as others pile in, the rate of profit tends to average out. Prices and profits begin to fall. The initial investment required to build a high-tech factory or to create a programme or a microprocessor is huge, although the cost of actually producing the chips or software for sale is relatively low.

Rising demand drives average costs down still further, making it possible to charge lower prices and boosting demand even further. This cheapening of the elements of production has been – alongside the systematic holding down of wages of the workers and the systematic plundering of the economies of the underdeveloped capitalist countries – one of the main reasons for the absence of inflationary pressures in the US economy during the recent cycles. But now this has reached its limits and the world economy is entering into a recession, the results of which are unforeseeable.

Crises of overproduction

In order to realise value in the act of exchange, a commodity has to satisfy a real want, and must also contain only that amount of labour that is average for its production at a given stage. Assuming that only the social necessary labour time has been expended, then the price (leaving out of consideration any accidental miscalculation, which will soon be rectified by the market) is merely an expression in money terms of the value of the commodity – the amount of socially necessary labour time embodied in it. However, the constant revolutionising of the means of production can mean that overnight socially necessary labour becomes socially unnecessary: reduced prices of goods produced by new methods undermines the market for others. Even without this, a glut in the market is possible:

"If the market cannot stomach the whole quantity at the normal price of two shillings a yard, this proves that too great a portion of the total labour of the community has been expanded in the form of weaving. The effect is the same as if each individual weaver had expanded more labour-time upon his particular product than is socially necessary." [11]

The market is limited in terms of social need and purchasing power: if the amount of a given product exceeds the limits of the market then a portion of that product is useless. It is impossible to realise the value and surplus value contained in it. These periodic crises bring out all the inherent contradictions of the system. "What is most strange in overproduction", comments Marx, "is that the actual producers of the very commodities which overfill the market – the workers – suffer from lack of them."

"The conditions of direct exploitation, and those of realising it, are not identical", states Marx. "They diverge not only in place and time but also logically. The first are only limited by the productive power of society, the latter by the proportional relation of the various branches of production and the consuming power of society." [12] This fall in demand has dire consequences for realising the surplus value contained in commodities. If unsold, the value contained in these commodities is useless, and the labour employed upon them also unproductive labour. Thus the element of crisis exists potentially at the very beginning of capitalist money making. It is the contradiction contained in the commodity between use-value and exchange value. Crises "can only be deduced from the real movement of capitalist production, competition, and credit," states Marx. [13]

While under capitalism, overproduction gives rise to crisis, from the point of view of society there is no overproduction; on the contrary there is a shortage of means of production capable of satisfying human needs. But capitalism works on the basis not of general demand or needs, but what bourgeois economists call "effective demand", i.e. *demand based on money*. So it is not a crisis of scarcity, like all previous crises of pre-capitalist societies, but crises of overproduction. People starve not as a result of scarcity, but because there is too much produced. This is a unique phenomenon that is only found in capitalism. If commodities cannot find buyers, their surplus value cannot be realised and the capitalists are forced to cut back production and throw workers out of work.

While the elements of crisis are contained in the production of commodities themselves through the production and appropriation of surplus value, it first

11. Marx, *Capital*, Vol. 1. 3:2.
12. Ibid., vol. 3, p. 244.
13. Marx, *Theories of Surplus Value*, vol 2, p. 512.

appears in the process of realisation, in circulation, or the reproduction of capital. "The circulation process as a whole or the reproduction process of capital as a whole is the unity of its production phase and its circulation phase, so that it comprises both these processes or phases. Therein lies a further developed possibility or abstract form of crisis... Crisis is the forcible establishment of unity between elements that have become independent and the enforced separation from one another of elements which are essentially one."[14]

Again, "Overproduction is specifically conditioned by the general law of production of capital: production is in accordance with the productive forces, that is with the possibility that the given quantity of labour, without regard to the actual limits of the market, the needs backed by the ability to pay. And this takes place through the constant expansion of reproduction and accumulation, and therefore the constant reconversion of revenue into capital; while on the other hand the mass of producers remain restricted to the average level of needs, and on the basis of capitalist production must remain so restricted."[15]

Unequal exchange?

The law of value states that the value of the product is determined by the average amount of socially necessary labour time expended on its production. This manifests itself through exchange. In exchange, however, commodities are sold above or below their value. Only accidentally is a commodity sold at its actual value. The "scientific economist" Dieterich has a position that resembles the vulgar notion that profits arise from *buying cheap and selling dear*. Marx answers this argument in *Value, Price and Profit*:

"What a man would certainly win as a seller he would lose as a purchaser. It would not do to say that there are men who are buyers without being sellers or consumers without being producers. What these people pay to the producers, they must first get from them for nothing. If a man first takes your money and afterwards returns that money in buying your commodities you will never enrich yourself by selling your commodities too dear to that same man. This sort of transaction might diminish a loss, but would not help in realizing a profit".

Following in the footsteps of Proudhon, Dieterich imagines that the profits of the capitalists are some kind of *swindle*, which he calls unequal exchange. This is merely an extension of the same vulgar idea, that the capitalists obtain their profits from exchange by buying cheap and selling dear (that is, through swindling the public). The whole idea of Dieterich and his genial mentor Arno Peters is that by establishing the "true price" of a commodity by calculating the amount of labour expended on its production, we can expose this swindle and thus create the necessary level of consciousness to introduce 21st Century Socialism.

14. Ibid., p. 513.
15. Ibid., 4d.

As a matter of fact, capitalism is not based on swindling. There can, of course, be swindling in particular cases and in the very early stages of capitalism, when the market economy was gradually emerging out of the age-old system of barter that Heinz and Arno find so attractive, there was quite a lot of swindling as merchants systematically cheated and sold underweight and shoddy goods. But the development of the market inevitably produced money, credit and the standardization of weights and measures. When individual capitalists engage in swindling, they cheat not only the consumers and shareholders but also other capitalists: what one gains the others lose. This is not in the interests of the capitalist class as a whole, and therefore the state intervenes and when such sharp practices are discovered, the perpetrators can find themselves behind bars.

Apart from the daily reproduction of his labour power, and the reproduction of the species, at a certain stage in the development of capitalist technique, a certain amount has to be provided for the education of the workers in order to fit them for the conditions of modern industry and raise their productivity. Unlike most commodities, labour power is paid for only after it has been consumed. The workers thus philanthropically extend credit to their employers! *Despite this, the worker has not been cheated.* He has arrived at an agreement of his own free will. As with all other commodities, equivalent values are exchanged: the worker's commodity, labour power, is sold to the boss at the "going rate". Everybody is satisfied. And if the worker is not, then he is free to leave and find work elsewhere – if he can.

Of course, there are cases where individual capitalists cheat the workers and use all kinds of miserable tricks to cut wages – petty cheating and bankruptcy, leading to loss of wages, etc. In the early days of capitalism there was the "truck" system where workers had to buy their food, tools and other necessities from the company shop, which systematically cheated the workers and overcharged them, leading to crippling debts that virtually enslaved the workers to their employers. There was also a system of factory fines, which the bosses levelled on the workers for all manner of trivial reasons.

Such practices have virtually disappeared in the advanced capitalist countries but still exist in Asia, Africa and Latin America. In general, the more backward the economy, the more such practices exist. And the immigrant workers in advanced capitalist countries (such as Mexican immigrants in the USA or Eastern European workers in Western Europe) are frequently robbed, cheated and underpaid by unscrupulous employers. But with the development of capitalism and the strengthening of the proletariat and its trade union organizations, the bosses are being compelled to abandon this kind of oppression, which, in any case, and contrary to the opinion of Dieterich and Peters, have never been the basis of capitalist exploitation.

The sale of labour power poses a problem. If nobody is cheated, if the worker receives the full value of his commodity, where does exploitation come from? Where does the capitalist make his profits? The answer is that the worker sells the capitalist not his labour (which is realised in the work process), but *his labour power* – his ability to work. Having purchased this as a commodity, the capitalist is free to use it as he pleases. As Marx explained: "From the instant he steps into the work shop, the use-value of his labour power, and therefore also its use, which is labour, belongs to the capitalist".[16]

The secret of the production of surplus value is that the worker continues to work longer after he has produced the value necessary to reproduce the value of his labour power (his wages). "The fact that half a day's labour is necessary to keep the labourer alive does not in any way prevent him from working a full day."[17] The worker has sold his commodity and cannot complain about the way he is used, any more than the tailor can sell a suit and then demand that his customer must not wear it as often as he likes. The working day is therefore so organised as to give the capitalist the maximum benefits from the labour power he has bought. Herein lies the secret of the transformation of money into capital.

A moralistic approach

Heinz Dieterich waxes indignant about injustice, and we may agree that there is plenty of injustice in the treatment of workers under capitalism. But if I go to the doctor with a problem I do not expect him to start weeping and wailing about it but to provide me with a scientific diagnosis of my complaint and a recipe that hopefully will cure me. To rage about injustice may be acceptable in revolutionary agitation, but it is surely out of place in what after all was advertised as the work of a "scientific economist" (and sociologist). This *sentimental and moralistic approach* really does not advance our understanding of the workings of capitalism by one millimetre.

As we have explained, the value of labour power (the level of wages) is determined in the same way as that of every other commodity – by the amount of socially necessary labour power contained in it. However, the price of labour power, like other commodities, is determined by the laws of supply and demand. When labour is in plentiful supply (for example, in periods of high unemployment), the level of wages will tend to fall, while in periods of intense economic activity, when the demand for labour exceeds supply, it will tend to fall. This may be affected by other factors, such as the strength of the unions or anti-labour laws, wage freezes, etc. But in general, the laws of supply and demand will prevail.

Marx explained that wages rise in certain conditions and fall in others. But even in the most prosperous periods of capitalism, the relative improvement of living standards can never abolish surplus value, and can never change the social position of the worker: "But just as little as better clothing, food and treatment, and a larger

16. Marx, *Capital*, vol. 1, chapter 7.
17. Ibid.

peculium [a slave's allowance], do away with the exploitation of the slave, so little do they set aside that of the wage-worker. A rise in the price of labour, as a consequence of accumulation of capital, only means, in fact, that the length and weight of the golden chain the wage-worker has already forged for himself, allow of a relaxation of the tension of it." [18]

As the productivity of labour grows, it is possible that the labourer may be able to purchase a greater quantity of use-values, owing to a fall in prices. Even with a fall in the money-value of labour-power, this may represent an increase in real wages, in the purchasing power of the workers. "In this way it is possible, with an increasing productiveness of labour, for the price of labour-power to keep on falling and yet this fall to be accompanied by a constant growth in the mass of the labourer's means of subsistence. But even in such case, the fall in the value of labour-power would cause a corresponding rise of surplus-value, and thus the abyss between the labourer's position and that of the capitalist would keep widening." [19]

When the capitalists are making super-profits from the labour of the working class, when demand is rising and order books are full, the workers feel strong enough to combine, through their trade unions to demand an increased share in the product of their labour-power. Under such circumstances, the capitalist can agree to part with some of the booty. At best, an increase in wages in a favourable period would signify a relative reduction in the amount on unpaid labour "given" by the worker to the capitalist. What it can never mean is the abolition of exploitation. On the contrary, a growth in wages is frequently accompanied by an increase in the rate of exploitation, and a relative worsening of the position of the worker in relation to the capitalist.

The value of wages is not reckoned in Marx on the basis of purchasing power, on the amount of commodities a worker can buy, but on the relation of his share of the total value of what he produces, i.e. the relation of wages to surplus value. The growth of productivity can lead to greater personal wealth at the same time as increased exploitation. "The position of the classes in relation to each other depends to a greater extent on the proportion which the wage forms than on the absolute amount of the wage."[20]

The needs of the working class are relative to society and in particular to those luxuries enjoyed by the capitalist class, which provide a tantalising picture of unattainable wealth, enjoyment and culture, and accentuates the dissatisfaction of the workers. As Marx put it: "Our wants and their satisfaction have their origin in society: we therefore measure them in their relation to society, and not in relation to the objects which satisfy them. Since their nature is social, it is therefore relative." [21]

18. K. Marx, *Capital*, Vol. 1, Lawrence & Wishart 1970, p. 618.
19. Ibid. Volume I, chapter 17, p. 659. Penguin ed.
20. Marx, *Theories of Surplus Value*, c.1, 3e.
21. Marx, *Wage, Labour and Capital*, Progress publishers, Moscow, 1952, p. 33.

It is true that many workers, in the last period, have been able to purchase things like televisions, videos, dishwashers, hi-fi equipment and the like which would have been unthinkable for an earlier generation. This creates a sensation of well being and "prosperity". However, on the one hand, this partly reflects the general cheapening of commodities, manifested in rapidly falling prices of what were previously considered luxury items (computers are a good example). On the other hand, the consumer boom of the USA has been achieved at the cost of a colossal increase in indebtedness through credit, which is one of the reasons why the present recession has been prolonged. But credit is only a way of carrying the market beyond its natural limits. It can avoid a recession today but only at the cost of preparing an even more serious recession tomorrow – a fact that the bourgeoisie of the USA is now beginning to realize.

Marx explains that *profits are the life-blood of capitalism and profits must come from surplus value – that is, from the unpaid labour of the workers*. Heinz Dieterich either does not understand this elementary proposition of Marxist economics or does not accept it. Like the bourgeois economists, he believes that exploitation does not occur in production but in *exchange* (through "unequal exchange") and moreover that it is possible to have socialism while leaving the means of production in the hands of the individual capitalists.

This is to be done simply by tinkering with the price mechanism while leaving the relations of production and property relations untouched. The bourgeois will voluntarily renounce profits and gratefully receive the "wages of equivalence". We will examine this idea in more detail later. But let us now examine the economics of 21st Century Socialism.

The 'equivalent economy'

Although we have here only presented a rough outline of the ideas that are developed with a wealth of detail in the three volumes of *Capital,* we see how rigorously Marx worked out his economic theories. What about the economic arguments of Heinz Dieterich? Let him speak for himself:

"Participatory democracy as 'the kingdom of the butterfly' will rest upon an economy of equivalences democratically organized in a State of majorities and a direct democracy in public affairs that are transcendental for the citizens. These three basic institutions, which will regulate the life of society and the state, will permit human beings to find their full rational-critical, ethical and aesthetic evolution." [22]

We will ignore the clumsy prose in which human beings "find" their evolution (when did they lose it?), as we are impatient to enter the kingdom of the butterfly and discover its marvellous laws, which are unlike anything ever seen in the world until now. Even a butterfly world, it seems, must be governed by *economics*. What

22. Dieterich, *Hugo Chávez y el Socialismo del Siglo XXI*, p. 21.

do these *butterfly economics* consist of? On page 107 of *Hugo Chávez and the Socialism of the 21st Century* we are treated to a lengthy quote by Arno Peters, where he sets forth his "theory of equivalence". We reproduce this passage in its entirety:

"The communist countries, like the capitalist ones [...] can only historically realize the return to the equivalent economy on a higher level if they *combine the labour theory of value with the principle of equivalence.* Then, wages would be equivalent to the labour time expended, independently of age, sex, civil state, colour of skin, nationality, physical exertion, level of education, wear and tear, skill, professional experience, personal dedication; independently also of the heaviness of the work and the dangers to health entailed in it. In short: wages will be the *direct and absolute equivalent* of the time worked." [23]

Arno Peters is in favour of a system in which the worker will receive the full fruits of his labour, plus or minus nothing. Everybody will receive in the form of wages "the *direct and absolute equivalent* of the time worked." This is the same idea that Marx subjected to a withering criticism in *The Critique of the Gotha Programme*. The economic theories of "21st Century Socialism" were comprehensively demolished by Marx long ago. He described them quite rightly as "as dogmas, ideas which in a certain period had some meaning but have now become obsolete verbal rubbish"[...]"ideological nonsense" and "trash".

We will express ourselves more politely so as not to offend anybody's sensibility. But one thing is abundantly clear: Under the guise of a "new" and "original" theory, Peters and Dieterich propose that we return to the old ideas of Lassalle and Proudhon. And we repeat the question asked by Marx: over one hundred years later, *why retrogress again to the infantile stage of the movement, to the obsolete ideas of pre-Marxist utopian socialism*?

According to Arno Peters, following in the footsteps of Lassalle, there will be *no exception* to his principle of equivalence, which will apply, without fear or favour to everybody. This is the Categorical Imperative of 21st Century Socialism, and, according to its author, it is as absolute and unassailable as any of the Categorical Imperatives of Kant. We shall see later just how absolute and unassailable it really is. But for the present let us attempt to follow Arno Peters' line of argument.

In the equivalent economy, he says: "*Prices are equivalent to values*, and do not contain anything that is not the absolute equivalent of the labour incorporated in commodities. In this way the circuit of the economy is closed in values, which take the place of prices. The exploitation of man by man, that is to say, the appropriation of the products of the labour of others above the value of labour itself, is ended. *Every human being receives the full value that he adds to goods or services.*" [24]

23. Ibid. p. 107, emphasis in original.
24. Dieterich, *Hugo Chávez y el socialismo del siglo XXI*, pp. 107-8, my emphasis, AW.

There is no possibility of error here, and no doubt about it: under 21st Century Socialism every worker will receive *the full fruits of his (or her) labour*. This will mean the end of exploitation and all will be for the best in the best of all 21st Century worlds. But here we meet with the first problem. Marx explained at great length in *Capital* that price and value are not at all the same thing. The value of a commodity is determined by the amount of socially necessary labour (not just "labour" as Arno Peters incorrectly says) expended on its production. Moreover, this labour is not limited to the labour of the individual worker, but includes the accumulated labour of many other workers embodied in other components (machinery, raw materials, electricity, etc.). The calculation of value in individual commodities is therefore a very complicated matter and not at all as simple as Arno Peters imagines it to be.

In the second place, prices are determined by supply and demand, which in the modern epoch means that the prices on the world market are determined by billions of individual transactions that take place every day on a global scale. It is true that, in the last analysis, the prices of all commodities are determined by value. But the price of an individual commodity almost never coincides with its real exchange value, and if this happens it is for completely accidental reasons. Prices fluctuate around exchange value and will eventually be brought into line with it. But in almost every case *a commodity will be sold either above or below its value*.

However, having sternly proclaimed *the absolute and unassailable nature of the equivalence principle*, Arno Peters immediately begins to backtrack: "This simple, easily understood, process (!), which transforms the basis of economics, is subject to a number of conditions. One will have to include all human activities that transcend the self-supply of individuals. It is above all a question of activities that are today included under the heading of 'services': the work that is carried out by doctors, judges, nurses, typists, postmen, lawyers, teachers, factory managers, lorry drivers, directors, road-sweepers, cooks, ministers, hairdressers, journalists and printers; in short, all the activities that do not enter directly into commodities."[25]

Immediately, what was supposed to be an *absolute and unassailable* principle turns out to be *conditional*. There are people like teachers, nurses, doctors and lorry drivers who do not produce commodities and surplus value, but are nevertheless of great importance to society. How do we calculate the value of their labour power? Apart from teachers, nurses, artists and ballet dancers, the equivalent economy, it seems, cannot do without the services of judges, lawyers, bureaucrats, policemen and factory managers.

How is the value of their wages to be calculated? However we answer this question, it is evident that their wages must come from the wealth produced by the working class, and therefore must be deducted from the surplus value. Since, even under

25. Ibid. p. 108.

the economy of equivalence people will still require some kind of education and health care, and will need to drink clean water and walk in streets sufficiently provided with illumination to see where they are going at night, *these things will have to be paid for*, and that can regrettably only be done by deducting a certain amount from the surplus value produced by the workers.

In the case of necessary social services like education and health, as well as roads, street lighting, street cleaning, sewers and waste disposal, water supply, etc., these are normally paid for out of taxes. Taxes are taken by the state either from the wages of the working class and middle class or from the profits of the capitalist. In either case, they are ultimately taken from the surplus value produced by the working class. Thus, the absolute and unassailable principle of equivalence falls to the ground at the first hurdle. Under Socialism of the 21st Century the worker will *not* receive the complete and undiminished value of the labour he has expended on production. This is only the first of many retreats made by the genial creator of the principle of equivalence. Let us not dismay but summon up the courage to follow step by step wherever genius may lead us:

"When we have analysed the time expended and, therefore, the value of each commodity, we can reduce it to a common denominator with the services through a calculation of the time expended [sic!]. This commensurability of services with productive work (which can only be achieved by deducting both from the medium of absolute, objective value [?]) places the entire economy under a uniform principle, and its circuit can be closed on an equivalent basis: a basis that *always begins with the individual and ends with him*: a basis that in the era of global economy – which is rooted in the condition that every human being has the same category, the same value and the same rights – includes every individual, independently of the type of activity he carries out." [26]

This is so beautifully simple and easily understood that nobody but a genius of the 21st Century can make head or tail of it. It is unclear whether Arno Peters ever considered himself a Marxist. If he did then both he and his admirer Heinz Dieterich have completely misunderstood Marx's procedure in *Capital*. He seems to think you can work out the amount of socially necessary labour time contained in *an individual commodity*. But how is this arrived at? Marx explains that socially necessary labour time is established by competition between producers. This process in effect takes place behind their backs. It is the unconscious effect of market forces ("the invisible hand of the market"). Moreover values are only established as a *norm* by prices, which, as we have pointed out, constantly deviate from value.

The 19th century British economist J.S. Mill used the analogy of sea level and waves. Marx does *not* calculate how much labour is embodied in individual commodities. He does *not* work out the labour time in 20 yards of linen and the labour

26. Ibid. p. 108, my emphasis, AW.

time needed to make a coat. He notes that the only thing they have in common apart from utility is that they are products of human labour – not concrete forms of labour but human labour in the abstract. He also points out that they are *equal in value.* Marx's use of value is ordinal, not cardinal.

César Augusto Sención, a Dominican economist resident in El Salvador, replying to Dieterich in *Rebelión* (13/8/07), in an article aptly entitled *La pretenciosa tarea de Heinz Dieterich* (The Pretentious Task of Heinz Dieterich) he writes:

"And how is socialism to be built? Dieterich says: by means of an economy of equivalences, where the prices of commodities are equal to their values. According to him, through computer science that is very easy to do. Let us see an example of what he proposes:

"'When we know its value and the price, the products of a socialist company are put on sale with the two units of measurement. The packaging of a litre of milk, for example, would take the following denomination: Price: 2,000 bolivars; Value: 10 minutes. When buying different products, the buyer will realize that the relation between value and price varies. For example, that in a given product 10 minutes of work is expressed as 2,000 bolivars and that in another product, 10,000 bolivars. The cognitive dissonance involved in both expressions inevitably generates a process of reflection and social discussion that generates socialist consciousness.' (See *Hugo Chávez requests a speed-up of Socialism of 21st Century*, in *Rebelión*, 22/06/2006.)

"The value of a commodity is determined by the socially necessary labour time used on its elaboration and the price is the expression of the value of this commodity. Nevertheless, that does not mean that if a product A is produced in 8 hours, it necessarily must have the same value as product B elaborated in the same time, because the value refers to a social average that is determined by the technology used in its production. In addition, if the parts which enter into the production of commodity A (transformed raw material and wear and tear of machinery) have accumulated value greater than those of product B, then product A will be worth more.

"Let us put it another way: a vehicle manufactured in 100 hours will not have the price of a computer produced in the same time, because the components of both commodities contain different amounts of labour time. The vehicle contains component parts for whose production more time was expended. According to the theory of the value, the vehicle is worth more than the computer.

"It is true that in capitalist society a non-equivalent interchange can occur, since there are commodities that have a greater price than their value, because they are monopolized or for other reasons. That is to say, in the exchange of commodities there are transfers of values in the interest of particular bourgeois. But that is not the essence of capitalism, but the exploitation (surplus value), that occurs in the production of commodities, not in exchange. When the proletarian transforms raw material into commodities he creates a new value that is divided in two parts: the one that belongs to him (necessary labour) and the one that belongs to the bourgeois (surplus labour). The difference is surplus value, that is exploitation itself. As the bourgeois takes possession of the commodities created by the proletarian, since this was created it already has a built-in surplus, it is sold or is not sold. In other words, surplus value is realised in production, not in exchange.

"What does this mean? That if one establishes an exact equivalence between the value and the price of commodities, surplus value does not disappear, because the bourgeois always retains that part of the wealth created by the proletarian. And where there is surplus value there is capitalism. The point, then, is not how commodities are exchanged in the market, but under what conditions they are produced. Exploitation is the essence of capitalism. And it does not disappear with the equivalent exchange of commodities, but through the abolition of the private property of the means of production which is enjoyed by a minority (bourgeoisie) and the establishment of a collective economy. It presupposes, of course, a change in production relations. If that does not occur, there will be surplus value, which, expressed in, money is called the mass of profit. That profit is exploitation. And where there is exploitation, there are social classes. And where there are classes there is no socialism, at least in the classic conception. Socialism means the abolition of classes. (Lenin, *Economics and politics in the era of the dictatorship of the proletariat,* 1919).

"From this, of course, we cannot conclude that it is enough to expropriate the bourgeoisie to achieve socialism. Only the Stalinists say that. Marx coined the phrase dictatorship of the proletariat (not socialism) to describe the transitional phase that is opened with this expropriation. Trotsky indicated that it was not enough to eliminate classes administratively (changes in the productive relations), that it is necessary to supersede them economically, that is, to create conditions of production that eliminate the human propensity to accumulate goods and to fight to each other to possess them. But that is another subject. I make no attempt here to evaluate how to build socialism, which in any case could not be achieved in an individual society, but necessarily on a world scale.

"Dieterich sets out from a basic idea that we did not share. For him it is not necessary first to attack private property, but to establish equivalent exchange that will do away with property and generate socialism. That is to say: The forms of property of the means of production do not have the slightest importance for the accomplishment of the principle of equivalence for the first stage in the transition towards the equivalent economy. Nevertheless, to the extent to which the equivalent economy overcomes the market economy, profits will disappear and private property of the means of production will lose its raison d'être, and will be eliminated by itself (See *Socialism of 21st Century. On the planned economy of equivalences*).

"Why will the equivalent economy defeat the market economy? We do not know. Market economy means an economy based on the production of commodities. It does not matter if these are sold at an equal price, superior or inferior to its value. If the exchange of commodities corresponds to equivalent values and capitalist private property stays, then surplus value also remains, even if this is distributed in a 'fair' way between the different sectors of the bourgeoisie. That is, we would still be in a market economy. We therefore believe that Dieterich is mistaken: profits will disappear if we change the relations of production, not the value-price relation of commodities.

"Dieterich sees injustice only in unequal exchange, not in capitalist private property, which is the foundation of profit and the accumulation of capital. According to him, Injustice exists, when product 'A' is exchanged for product 'B', and their values –the labour time necessary to produce each one of them – are not equal; that is to say, when they do not change equivalents (See *In Venezuela conditions have been created to build Socialism of 21st Century*, in *Rebelión*, 02/01/2007). Yet again he commits the error of not taking into account that value is a social average and that includes the working time expended on the production of the means production that is transformed into other commodities."

These remarks by César Augusto Sención are very much to the point. Is it really possible to calculate the amount of labour expended by an individual worker on the production of a commodity? Let us take a concrete example. I have a bar of chocolate and a pen on my desk. They both cost about one dollar, so they probably take about the same amount of labour time to produce. The pen is mainly plastic, which comes from oil. Is it possible to work out the depreciation on a oil platform in the North Sea (these things are twice the size of St. Paul's cathedral) that goes into the value of the pen? This would be necessary to work out the dead and living labour that went into the value of the pen.

Plainly the task is impossible. In any case, what would be the point? As Marx pointed out to the advocates of labour money, the point is to abolish commodity production. Some of the early utopian socialists did see the labour bank as a transitional stage to the abolition of commodity production. But Dieterich sees it as an alternative to socialist revolution. It is quite *illiterate* to contrast an economy of value (21st Century Socialism) to one of price (capitalism), as Arno Peters and Dieterich do. Marx explained many times that price is the monetary form of value. It is inevitable, as exchange is generalised, that the money (price) form will emerge with a universal equivalent.

From the relative and equivalent forms of value Marx moves to the universal equivalent – money. As he explains to Bray and co. commodities are not immediately social labour. In commodity production private labour turns into its opposite – *social labour* – in the process of exchange. Money itself is not some sort of swindle imposed on exchange, but something that naturally emerges to the degree that exchange becomes general, as opposed to the accidental exchange of individual products, as in barter.

The man who wanted to fly

Dieterich and Peters imagine they can eliminate the negative features of capitalism without touching private property – that is, they think they can square the circle. How is this miracle to be performed? *By simple accounting*. Using a most peculiar mode of reasoning, they conclude that there must be not one but two prices for every commodity: one, the regular market price, and another representing "true value".

Peters and Dieterich see the transformation of value into price as the central *swindle* by which workers are exploited and capitalists enriched. This, as we have seen, contradicts everything that Marx wrote. In the first volume of *Capital* he starts with an isolated exchange of products – 20 yards of linen for a coat. Here we have a relative and an equivalent form of value. The use value of one commodity serves as an equivalent of the exchange value of the other. The equivalent form is already the germ of *a universal equivalent* – money – which gradually develops as exchange becomes generalised. Dieterich proposes to move to 21st Socialism through substituting *price* (monetary calculation) with *value* (calculation in time).

Dieterich asserts that the market plays a dual role. On the one hand it plays a "cybernetic" role by disseminating information. This "original" insight actually comes from the right wing economist Austrian Friedrich Hayek, in particular his 1945 essay *The use of knowledge in society*. This bourgeois tract lay largely unread until the collapse of the Stalinist economies. It was then resurrected as a complete explanation of the alleged impossibility of socialism and planning. Apart from this benign cybernetic function, the price mechanism unfortunately serves to exploit the workers. The notion that workers are exploited in the process of exchange is entirely false and nothing to do with Marxism.

Is it possible to eliminate the law of value under capitalism? Let us consider the following little tale. Once upon a time there was a man who wanted to fly. Every morning he looked up to the sky and saw with envy the free-spirited little birds soaring up to the clouds and a deep sense of melancholy gripped his heart. "Why can't I be as free as a bird?" he asked himself again and again and he got more depressed every day by the thought of this terrible injustice. Then one day he had an idea: why not try to fly? After all, if birds can do this, why can't a man, since men are obviously far more intelligent than silly birds! So he climbed the stairs of his house, opened the window of his bedroom and jumped out. The next day he woke up in hospital with two broken legs and terrible pains all over. Now he was not just depressed. He was indignant. He now realized what the problem was: *it was the law of gravity*!

He became increasingly agitated as he thought of the monstrous injustice of it all. He now understood that all the ills of humanity were due to the law of gravity. This was the reason men found it so difficult to get out of bed in the morning. This is what made labour so hard. This is what made men and women prematurely old. And just think of all the people who have been killed or injured by falling over! If we add them all up it must amount to millions of people over the centuries! The more he thought about it the more unjust it seemed that people had had to suffer so much for thousands of years because of the law of gravity. He decided that enough was enough and something had to be done about this. He wrote agitational pamphlets which he distributed in the streets. He spoke at meetings and whenever he spoke the tears came into his eyes and his voice trembled with emotion as he recounted to his astonished audience all that they had to suffer because of the law of gravity.

On further reflection he concluded that this ridiculous and irrational the law was contrary to the Laws of Nature, and that, therefore, in the Beginning all men and women could fly, but then, by some eccentricity of Evolution, about 12,000 years ago, we were confined to the ground and subjected to the blind tyranny of the law of gravity. He did many calculations, helped by computers and the internet, through which he regularly consulted with people all over the world who shared his anti-gravitational concerns. He wrote many books on the subject and travelled the whole world over, trying to interest Kings and Presidents in his theories. He considered the law of gravity from every conceivable angle, discounting the effects of atmospheric pressure, wind resistance and so forth.

Finally one sunny morning he completed a very complicated equation that he had been working on for years. "Eureka!" he shouted as he jumped out of bed, defying the law of gravity. He ran to his garden shed where he had a small but well-equipped workshop that he operated with some neighbours as an anti-gravitational co-operative enterprise. He quickly manufactured a pair of wings made of the finest plywood. He then got on a bus and went to a high cliff that towered over the seashore. He approached the edge of the cliff very confidently, strapped on his wings and walked defiantly into space. This time he did not break his legs only but several other essential organs and members, and so he died – just another of the countless number of victims of the law of gravity.

Now like every good story, this has a moral at the end. Just as it is not possible to live on the planet earth and abolish the law of gravity, so it is impossible to retain the capitalist system and abolish the law of value. If you accept capitalism then you must accept the laws of capitalism. Therefore, irrespective of who wins an election, if they are not prepared to take serious measures of expropriation, if they allow the capitalists to continue to own the means of production, then it will be the latter who decide all the important questions, not the government. The laws of the market will continue to apply, just as much as the law of gravity, and it is useless to complain about it.

Simple and compound labour

Peters now begins to skate on very thin ice: "In order to ensure the right to a home and a room for all men [sic], the community which is organized in the State, must order the use of the soil and buildings according to the general needs. All public activities that do not produce values (like education, medical assistance, provision for retirement, jurisprudence, administration) could be paid for through taxation according to the time worked. The commensuration of productive work to services rendered, suggests the use of the same word for both activities: '*effort*' (*Leistung*). In this way, the entire course of the economy is reduced to the efforts of individuals to satisfy the general needs in the best possible manner. The principle of equivalence is realized at all levels through the equivalence between effort and compensation (Gegenleistung)." [27]

We like the phrase "the efforts of individuals to satisfy the general needs in the best possible manner", which powerfully calls to mind Voltaire's Doctor Pangloss in *Candide*, who was convinced that under all circumstances "everything is for the best in the best of all possible worlds". And what world could be better than the world of 21st Century Socialism a la Arno Peters and Heinz Dieterich? However, the deeper we immerse ourselves in this hypothetical world, the more problematical it becomes. We now enter into the Byzantine world of Taxation and Bureaucracy, which, naturally, will have a place of honour in the new Paradise of Equivalence. Arno Peters ties himself in knots over the problem of how to transform *unproductive* labour into the *productive* sort. How does one calculate the value of doctors, judges, nurses, typists, postmen, lawyers, teachers, factory managers, lorry drivers, directors, road-sweepers, cooks, ministers, hairdressers, journalists and printers?

Arno Peters and Dieterich have hit yet another problem here. Peters says: "The communist countries, like the capitalist ones [...] can only historically realise the return to the equivalent economy on a higher level if they combine the labour theory of value with the principle of equivalence. Then wages would be equivalent to the labour time expended independently of age, sex, civil state, colour of skin, nationality, physical exertion, level of education, wear and tear, skill, professional experience, personal dedication; independently also of the heaviness of the work and the dangers to health entailed in it. In short: wages will be the direct and absolute equivalent of the time worked." [28]

So Peters and Dieterich show a commendable commitment to the *principle of equality*. Why is equality a principle? Because the NHP declares it to be so. But there is no equality under capitalism, nor has there been for approximately 12,000 years. Why not? Because of unequal exchange! But why? Presumably the unexplained mechanism that turns equal values into unequal prices is at work! There are

27. Dieterich, *Hugo Chávez y el Socialismo del Siglo XXI*, p. 110.
28. Ibid. 107.

two separate issues involved here. Commodities are not sold at the price equivalent of the amount of labour time it takes to produce them individually or accidentally. They are sold at prices corresponding to the socially necessary labour time, at the existing level of productivity.

So if I lack skill, to use one concept in Peters' list, and it takes me two hours of my direct labour time to make a chair, when all the other carpenters can make a chair in one hour, what ought to happen? Under the law of value as it operates under capitalism I will have to sell my chair at the same price as everybody else. Is that wrong? Or should the other carpenters subsidise me? Or should the buyers of chairs pay extra to keep me in business? Neither of these solutions seems in accordance with the principle of equivalence. The actually existing law of value will indicate to me in a characteristically brutal fashion that perhaps I should find another way of making a living. That is, after all, how the division of labour is established under capitalism.

The second problem is this: if workers contribute unequal values in the same time, is it in accord with the principle of 'equivalence' that they should be paid the same wage? Marx is clear that skilled workers can add more value in the same time than unskilled workers. "More complex labour counts only as intensified, or rather multiplied simple labour, so that a smaller quantity of complex labour is considered equal to a larger quantity of simple labour. Experience shows that this reduction is constantly being made. A commodity may be the outcome of the most complicated labour, but through its value it is posited as equal to the product of simple labour, hence it represents only a specific quantity of simple labour. The various proportions in which different kinds of labour are reduced to simple labour as their unit of measurement are established by a social process that goes on behind the backs of the producers." [29]

There is a separate problem from different kinds of labour contributing different amounts of value in the same time. That is workers receiving different remuneration for their labour power on account of different levels of skill, etc. This is yet another sin against the Spirit of Equivalence. Like Peters and Dieterich, Marxists would also like to make wages more equal. But the first question that must be asked is: why are they unequal? This is not a moral question as Peters imagines when he talks about "injustice". It must be dealt with scientifically, as Engels did:

"In a society of private producers, private individuals or their families pay the costs of training the qualified worker; hence the higher price paid for qualified labour power accrues first of all to private individuals: the skilful slave is sold for a higher price and the skilful wage earner is paid higher wages. In a socialistically organised society these costs are borne by society and to it, therefore, belong the fruits, the greater 'values' produced by compound labour." [30]

29. Marx, *Capital*, Vol. I. p. 135. Penguin ed.
30. Engels, *Anti-Dühring*, pp. 277-8, Foreign language Publishing House, Moscow 1959.

How does a socialist society deal with the fact of differently qualified labour? Since the higher power of skilled labour does not arise from any mysterious property possessed by this labour itself, or by its human bearer, it is evident that this can only be based on the empirically given and empirically measurable difference in the training costs of skilled and unskilled workers themselves. Assume that 100 workers who work 10 days are necessary for the completion of a particular project, of which however 10 must be equipped with particular, above-average qualifications, especially for this project. In order to train these workers society must incur certain expenses, which let us say, amount to 200 working days. It is clear then that these 200 working days must also be accounted for by society if its economic plans are to have a sound basis. It would therefore allow not 1,000 working days but rather 1,200 for the carrying out of the project. Thus the distinction between skilled and unskilled labour will in the final analysis be reduced to the difference in the period of training of the various kinds of labour. [31]

The conclusion is always the same: *first socialise the economy; then we can proceed towards equalising wages*. But this is just what Peters and Dieterich do not want to accept. Unless we abolish private property of the means of production it is useless to talk about even a reduction of inequality, let alone its abolition. But how would we deal with the question of simple and compound labour in a workers' state? Firstly, it is not possible to leap straight from capitalism to socialism, whether in the 21st or the 31st century. In the transitional phase between capitalism and socialism, as Marx explained long ago, there would be elements of the old society alongside the new.

The huge profits and obscene wealth of the capitalists would immediately be removed through expropriation, as would the extreme poverty at the other end of the scale. But a certain differential would continue to exist for a time. It would not be possible immediately to introduce full equality of wages. A differential would remain between skilled and unskilled workers, although this capitalist differential would be far less than it is now and would tend to disappear as society moved towards socialism.

There is no doubt that a socialist society will need doctors, nurses and teachers and the more the merrier. Teachers may not directly produce commodities for consumption, but they help to train and educate the new generation of workers, who, above all in the new age of technology, require ever new and complex skills. It is this, and not any tender concern for culture and education per se, and still less any considerations about "justice" or "injustice", that makes the capitalists accept the need to build schools and pay teachers' wages, although they constantly grumble about the costs entailed and try to limit the scope of education to what is strictly needed for capitalist production.

31. See Rosdolsky, *The making of Marx's 'Capital'*, Pluto Press, 1977, p. 518.

So, in a sense, education is a form of productive labour that creates an educated and skilled workforce. It can be considered a productive investment for the future. Those capitalist nations, like Britain, who fall behind in education will find themselves outstripped in the future by nations who have developed education to the degree that is now demanded by modern production methods and technology.

The capitalists also need to maintain a fit and healthy workforce that is up to the demands of production, and therefore accept, in most developed nations at least, some kind of health service. Here again, they moan about the costs entailed and do their best to cut the provision of health to the bare minimum. But in the modern age, people are not prepared to see their health put at risk and rightly demand good health services. The struggles of the working class, especially (but not only) in Europe have forced the capitalists to concede what is known as the "social wage", involving a certain amount of expenditure on things like health, education and pensions. In many developed countries this now forms an important part of the worker's wage and is the subject of fierce struggles, as the capitalists try to cut welfare expenditure to increase the rate of profit at the workers' expense.

It is true that the nurses, teachers and doctors do not directly produce value in the form of commodities, but they indirectly make an important contribution to the maintenance and improvement of the labour power of both present and future generations. They also represent an advance from the barbarous conditions of the past, when disease and illiteracy were considered the normal conditions of life for the masses. They therefore represent the elements of a civilized life in the midst of capitalist barbarity, and must be defended at all costs by the rest of the working class. Only somebody with a completely narrow view could get themselves into contortions at the fact that these sections of the working class are paid out of the surplus value produced by the working class as a whole.

'Effort'

The question of unproductive labour gives Arno Peters a bad headache. Alexander the Great, as we know, also had a problem with a knot, which he solved very easily by slicing through it with his sword. If Alexander could do this, how could Arno Peters do any worse? Like the good professor he is, he cuts his self-made Gordian knot, not with a *sword* but a *word*: all workers make an *effort*, you see, and this is what makes them *commensurate*. In a flash all problems are resolved. All workers, whether they produce tin cans, transplant hearts, catch rats or write doctoral theses, *all make an effort*.

The policeman makes an effort to catch burglars and hit demonstrators on the head with truncheons and the high court judge makes an effort to send them to jail for the longest possible terms. Prison wardens make an effort to reform the prisoners by making their lives as miserable as possible. Army generals make an effort to kill as many of the enemy as possible. Stock exchange speculators make an effort to make easy fortunes at the public's expense. Bureaucrats make an effort to hasten the destruction of the Amazon rain forest by writing endless reams of useless memoranda. Bourgeois politicians make an effort to deceive the electorate. Heinz Dieterich makes an effort to write books. The list is endless, and all these worthy people, according to the theory of equivalence, must be remunerated out of the surplus value produced by the working class, *because they all make an effort.*

Now for any sensible person, the difference between these activities is fairly clear. Doctors, nurses and teachers are generally considered as a necessary part of a civilized society, but not everybody would think the same about all of the others, no matter how much effort they expend on their various activities. They are mostly the unproductive overheads of capitalism, *which would be either eliminated or reduced to a minimum in a genuinely socialist society*, though not in Arno Peters' socialist utopia. Since he has already admitted factory managers, judges, lawyers, capitalists (together with profits), the army, navy and air force, together with a hierarchical state, he is obliged of necessity to find a way to finance all these "efforts".

How would a workers' state work?

The Paris Commune showed us long ago how it would be possible to eliminate at a stroke the army of professional parasites that make up the bourgeois state: the thousands of over-paid bureaucrats, judges, lawyers, police chiefs and army generals. The first act of the socialist revolution will be to abolish the old state apparatus and replace it with a far simpler, more democratic state, the administration of which would be in the hands of the workers themselves. This is what Marx wrote in *The Civil War in France*:

"The Communal Constitution would have restored to the social body all the forces hitherto absorbed by the state parasite feeding upon, and clogging the free movement of, society. By this one act, it would have initiated the regeneration of France. [...]

"The Commune made that catchword of bourgeois revolutions – cheap government – a reality by destroying the two greatest sources of expenditure: the standing army and state functionarism. Its very existence presupposed the non-existence of monarchy, which, in Europe at least, is the normal encumbrance and indispensable cloak of class rule. It supplied the republic with the basis of really democratic institutions. But neither cheap government nor the 'true republic' was its ultimate aim; they were its mere concomitants."[32]

Once the workers take the running of society into their hands, they will assume control of all the functions of administration of industry (through workers' control and management), society and the state. "But the workers are ignorant! They cannot run industry and society without bosses and bureaucrats!" That is the usual reply

32. Marx, *The Civil War in France*, p. 71, Foreign Language Press, Peking, 1966.

of the middle class intellectual who has no knowledge of the working class or the realities of factory life except from textbooks.

In reality, the workers are the people most qualified to run the factories where they have worked for years and decades. The experience of the bosses' sabotage in Venezuela in 2002-03 showed that the workers are quite able to run industry without the "efforts" of the bureaucrats and capitalists. And if there are certain tasks that require the specialised knowledge of accountants and engineers, there are plenty of honest people graduating from the universities every year who are prepared to put themselves at the service of the working class and the Revolution, which must make use of their knowledge, but always under the democratic control of the workers themselves.

The experience not only of the Paris Commune but of every other revolution shows that the working class is more than prepared to take the administration of society into its hands. The Russian Revolution of 1917 and the Spanish Revolution in the 1930s are full of examples that show the colossal creativity and talent that lies dormant in the masses and is set free by a revolution. We see the same thing in Venezuela today. The masses are capable of running every aspect of social life far better than the thousands of corrupt and parasitical bureaucrats. They can keep order on the streets far better than the police. A workers' militia linked to the democratic committees in every suburb would swiftly eradicate crime and corruption by direct action.

By adopting the simple democratic programme of the Paris Commune and the October Revolution there would be a strict limit on the salaries of all elected officials, who would be subject to instant recall. From the very beginning, the bloated salaries of the officials would be abolished. The salaries of officials would be limited to the wage of a skilled worker. In big factories there is the need for overall planning of output and to that extent management is entitled to wages of superintendence as a reward for productive labour. On the day after the social revolution there will continue to be managers, but later, as the working class educates itself to run society, the tasks of management will be exercised collectively or by delegation to members of the workforce who will be held to account.

It is not possible to achieve complete equality at once, but to the degree that production increases thanks to the benefits of a nationalized planned economy, with a general increase in living standards and culture of the masses and a reduction of the working day, the differentials would be gradually reduced and finally eliminated. But none of this will be possible unless the working class takes power, overthrows the old oppressive state of the exploiters and expropriates the landlords, bankers and capitalists. This is the Marxist conception of the transitional semi-state between capitalism and socialism. Now let us see what Peters and Dieterich propose.

7. The economics of Socialism of the 21st Century

In an article called *Hugo Chávez asks to speed up XXI Century Socialism* that appeared in *Rebelión* in the summer of 2006, Dieterich is asked: What is a socialist economy? He answers as follows:

"The first step to implement a socialist economy is to know what distinguishes this economy from the capitalist market economy which we now have to suffer. The main differences, that is to say, the main characteristics of the socialist economy, are six: four that belong to economic democracy and two that belong to political economy and value.

"A. The four elements of economic democracy:

"1. The real participation of the citizens in the *macroeconomic* decisions for example, the national budget. 2. The real participation of the workers in the *microeconomic* decisions (the enterprise), particularly on the rate of surplus labour, which decides the rate of exploitation of labour, and the rate of investment. 3. The real participation of the citizens in the economic decisions of the community, for example, through the participative municipal budget. 4. The planning of the economy on the basis of this participation of the majorities.

"B. The two elements of the economy of value:

"1. The accountability and operation of the economy is realized through value (time expended), not on the basis of market prices. 2. The interchange of products is realized through equal values. This is the principle of equivalence that brings about social justice at the point of production, not capitalist (empresarial) distribution or state redistribution. Social justice is realized, in this way, from the first level of all economic activity: production.

"These are the six basic institutions of the socialist economy. Only when an economic system works on this basis, can we speak of a socialist economy. When they do not exist or are not operative, we have not emerged from the market economy, because the economic base has not entered into a post capitalist civilization.

Attempts to transcend the market economy that do not reach this socialist institutionality, will sooner or later revert to full capitalism, however much they declare themselves to be socialism or communism as the intention or reality on the part of the governments.

"The decisive step: the substitution of price by value

"The decisive step in the transformation of the market economy into a socialist economy consists in the substitution of price by value. To understand this decisive step it is necessary to understand the role played price in the market economy. This is a double role. Price fulfils two vital functions for the system: a) it is the cybernetic centre of the national, regional and global economy, which controls the flow of commodities (products), services, money and capitals; without prices, the market economy would not move, it would be a dead system; b) it is the principal mechanism for the appropriation of the surplus product or economic surplus (profit); that is, it is the principal instrument for the enrichment and the accumulation of capital by the bosses.

"And what is the relation between price and the ownership of the means of production? The form of ownership of the means of production – state, private, social or mixed – is the juridical base of the economy: it is the Magna Carta or Constitution of economic activity. But this general normativity does not serve to bring about the daily enrichment of the bosses. This enrichment requires a working instrument and this instrument is the market price.

"Price is the functional equivalent of the revolver in a bank robbery: whoever has the revolver (power) carries off the wealth. In this sense, the whole market economy is an unethical gangster economy, governed by the law of the strongest. Today, the strongest economic subjects are the transnational companies and the bourgeois States.

"Every socialist transformation therefore must take the revolver out of the hands of capital, that is to say, the power of price. In historical socialism this was done by taking over the means of production from the bosses and the State taking over the double function of price. In this way the accumulation of capital in the hands of private bosses, but it failed essentially in the cybernetic function, the optimization of the economic flows. In other words: the classical function of price was neutralized and its systemic function was distorted.

"A socialist transition in the present day world will only be successful if it manages to substitute the 'bourgeois' institution of price in such a way that its two fundamental functions, the cybernetic and the accumulative, can be resolved satisfactorily, by means of a qualitatively different institution: efficient in optimizing the economy and without any capacity for exploiting other human beings. This institution is value." [1]

1. Dieterich, *Hugo Chávez pide acelerar el Socialismo del Siglo XXI*, 22/6/06.

Why does the apparent equality of exchange (in contrast to Dieterich's view) prove to be an illusion? Why is the worker not really in an equal bargaining position against the capitalist? Because he has nothing to sell apart from his labour power. Because the capitalist class monopolises the ownership of the means of production. This is the most important point, and Dieterich does not want to admit it. He describes ownership of the means of production as the Magna Carta or constitution of capitalism. But the working instrument of exploitation, in his view, is market price. This is clearly not Marx's view.

One asks oneself whether Dieterich has ever seriously read the works Marx and Engels. Certainly his own theory of exploitation has nothing in common with that of Marx and is only a regurgitation of Dühring's "force theory". *It was Dühring, not Marx, who claimed that private property was the result of theft and violence, and that exploitation takes place in exchange, not production.* This extremely superficial and erroneous presentation of the nature of exploitation was answered long ago by Engels:

"1: Political economy, in the widest sense, is the science of the laws governing the production and exchange of the material means of subsistence in human society. Production and exchange are two different functions. *Production may occur without exchange, but exchange – being necessarily an exchange of products – cannot occur without production.*

"2: *Private property by no means makes its appearance in history as the result of robbery or force.* On the contrary. It already existed, though limited to certain objects, in the ancient primitive communities of all civilised peoples. It developed into the form of commodities within these communities...

"3: The question at issue is how we are to explain the origin of classes and relations based on domination, and if Herr Dühring's only answer is the one word 'force', we are left exactly where we were at the start." [2]

How does the "working instrument" work? Dieterich describes market price like a revolver in a bank robbery. This is a double error. Firstly, as we have already explained, the exploitation of the worker does not take place in the market through price, but in the workplace through the extraction of surplus value. Secondly, the compulsion upon the worker to work for the capitalist (that makes a mockery of his apparent freedom in the market place) is *the capitalist's ownership of the means of production.*

That, and not price, is their "revolver". And that revolver is in turn secured by other revolvers, real ones this time, in the hands of the state power. In order to remove the revolver from the hands of the capitalists it is necessary to overthrow the bourgeois state and nationalize the means of production. Despite his revolutionary-sounding rhetoric about revolvers, that is not what Dieterich proposes. His rhet-

2. Engels, *Anti-Dühring*, pp. 203, 233 and 246, my emphasis, AW.

oric is quite empty – as usual – and is intended to conceal the fact that he proposes to achieve "socialism" while retaining private property and the bourgeois state.

'Dual power'

Comrade Dieterich proposes what he himself describes as "dual power" within the factory as a stepping-stone towards the Socialism of the 21st Century. Again this sounds very revolutionary. It brings to mind the Russian Revolution, with workers storming the citadels of bourgeois power, arms in hand. But on closer inspection, the real aim of striving for "dual power" a la Dieterich turns out to be slightly more modest. What is the aim? The objective of this titanic struggle is – *to put an extra label on the bottles of milk.* But before turning to the important subject of labels on milk bottles, let us first ask what dual power is.

The phrase was first used by Lenin in an article published in April 1917 called *The Dual Power*. The first sentence in Lenin's article reads as follows: "The basic question of every revolution is that of state power. Unless this question is understood, there can be no intelligent participation in the revolution, not to speak of guidance of the revolution."

This is ABC for any Marxist. But comrade Dieterich does not deal with the question of state power here or anywhere else. At least, it is not dealt with in a Marxist sense – which is based on the idea of the working class overthrowing the old bourgeois state and taking power into its own hands. What did Lenin deal with in this article? In February 1917 the Russian workers and soldiers overthrew the tsarist regime. They accomplished this task although the tsarist state was one of the most powerful in the world, with a huge army, police and secret police.

The workers immediately set about establishing the soviets, which Lenin characterized as embryonic organs of workers' power. The workers and soldiers elected delegates to the soviets, which existed side by side with the old tsarist state, which, although severely shaken, was still in place. The counter-revolutionaries rallied around this state, under the cover of the reformists in the Provisional Government. They were waiting for a favourable moment to counterattack. Had they succeeded, the Revolution would have been liquidated, the soviets dispersed and a fascist regime would have come to power.

When he returned to Russia at the end of March, Lenin immediately began a campaign aimed at convincing the workers in the soviets of the need to take power under the slogan "all power to the soviets". This was opposed by the reformist leaders in the soviets and also by Stalin and Kamenev who led the opportunist wing of the Bolsheviks. In the aforementioned article, Lenin wrote:

"What is this dual power? Alongside the Provisional Government, the government of the *bourgeoisie, another government* has arisen, so far weak and incipient, but undoubtedly a government that actually exists and is growing – the Soviets of Workers' and Soldiers' Deputies.

"What is the class composition of this other government? It consists of the proletariat and the peasants (in soldiers' uniforms). What is the political nature of this government? It is a revolutionary dictatorship, i.e., a power directly based on revolutionary seizure, on the direct initiative of the people from below, and *not on a law* enacted by a centralized state power. It is an entirely different kind of power from the one that generally exists in the parliamentary bourgeois-democratic republics of the usual type still prevailing in the advanced countries of Europe and America. This circumstance often over looked, often not given enough thought, yet it is the crux of the matter. *This* power is of *the same type* as the Paris Commune of 1871.

"The fundamental characteristics of this type are: (1) the source of power is not a law previously discussed and enacted by parliament, but the direct initiative of the people from below, in their local areas – direct 'seizure', to use a current expression; (2) the replacement of the police and the army, which are institutions divorced from the people and set against the people, by the direct arming of the whole people; order in the state under such a power is maintained by the armed workers and peasants *themselves,* by the armed people *themselves*; (3) officialdom, the bureaucracy, are either similarly replaced by the direct rule of the people themselves or at least placed under special control; they not only become elected officials, but are also *subject to recall* at the people's first demand; they are reduced to the position of simple agents; from a privileged group holding '*jobs*' remunerated on a high, bourgeois scale, they become workers of a special 'arm of the service', whose remuneration *does not exceed* the ordinary pay of a competent worker." [3]

This is quite clear and is a classical restatement of the Marxist position on the state. In dealing with the question of dual power, Lenin did not use it as a mere phrase, as Dieterich does. He explains that the workers and soldiers could and should have taken power but failed to do so and this led to the abortion of dual power, which was only half a revolution. But a revolution cannot stop half way. Either the working class finishes the job by taking power into its hands, or else at a certain point the pendulum will swing the other way, creating the conditions for a counter-revolution. Whoever doubts this should study the experience of Chile and Nicaragua.

The situation today in Venezuela in many respects is similar to that faced by the Russian Revolution after February 1917. The Revolution has begun but has not been completed. The old state and the bureaucracy remain and the landlords and capitalists still own important sections of the economy. It is essential that the workers finish what was started. But reformists like Heinz Dieterich are doing everything possible to restrain them, arguing that it is not necessary to nationalize the property of the oligarchy. This is the opposite of the position that Lenin advocated.

It may be argued that comrade Dieterich is not talking about "dual power" in society but only in individual enterprises. In Venezuela in many factories the work-

3. Lenin, *Collected Works,* Volume 24, Progress Publishers, Moscow, 1964, p. 39.

ers are moving to take control into their hands. In factories like Inveval, they have introduced workers' control. In other factories, although they have not yet established workers' control, the workers are constantly encroaching on the "sacred rights of management". In a certain sense, therefore, one could therefore speak of dual power in the factories. This is a by-product of the revolution itself, which has stirred up the masses and awakened their limitless potential for creative activity. No longer are the workers prepared to leave the most important aspects of their lives to the bosses and bureaucrats. This is the secret of the movement for workers' control. It does not come from reading books but from the experience of life itself.

The Venezuelan Marxists are fully in favour of workers' control and are in the front line of those who are fighting for it. On the contrary, the reformists like Heinz Dieterich do not advocate workers' control but only co-operatives. This is what he understands by "dual power". But experience shows that co-operatives within a market economy always tend to degenerate into ordinary capitalist enterprises. They are forced to operate on market principles of profit and loss. The leaders acquire privileges and begin to act like bosses, pressurizing the workers to get maximum profits, sacking "superfluous labour" and so on.

Even workers' control is not an end in itself, only a means to an end. It is not possible to build islands of socialism in a sea of capitalism. Workers' control is only a transitional stage towards nationalization. Either the enterprise is nationalized or else workers' control will turn out to be a passing episode. It is therefore incorrect to juxtapose it to nationalization as if it was an alternative. What is necessary is to mobilize the workers to take over the factories, eject the bosses and demand nationalization. The only real perspective is the nationalization of the land, the banks and industries under democratic workers' control and management. Only this can lead to socialism.

The question of power

There is a famous British cookery book written over 100 years ago by a Mrs. Beeton. One of her recipes for hare begins with the immortal words "first catch and kill your hare". We laugh at Mrs. Beeton because it is excessively obvious we can't serve up hare on the dinner table without first catching a hare (even better, have it caught and killed by someone else). We face a similar difficulty with what comrade Dieterich is proposing. How is it possible to arrive at socialism unless we start with the seizure of power by the working class? The difference is that, whereas Mrs. Beeton could find a hare ready prepared in the shops, the working class cannot rely on anyone else to do its work for it.

But comrade Dieterich is not deterred by such small difficulties. He is preparing for "dual power" in the factories. And what does this consist of? The workers in the dairy (it could be any other workplace, of course) will establish dual power by the following procedure: in addition to the usual monetary price they will put a labour time calculation of the value of milk that they produce. But in the first place Dieterich has not shown that the process of exploitation takes place by labour time being turned into the "swindle" of money. Secondly why should workers engage in struggle to put extra labels on milk bottles? How will this help them carry home more food for their families? They might as well just labels on saying, "Help, we're being exploited".

But here we immediately hit a problem. Won't the boss mind? It is reasonable to suppose that he would mind very much indeed. It is equally reasonable to suppose that he would try to put an end to this dual power as soon as possible. And would the workers rally behind the defence of their right to put extra labels on milk bottles? If they did, they would very probably be shown the door and invited to play at dual power somewhere else. And since the capitalist remains the undisputed owner of his factory, there is not a lot that one could do about it.

But, Dieterich says, the dual labels would set up "cognitive dissonance". What is this supposed to mean? I think this means buyers of milk would be *puzzled*. They probably would be. The main question for the milk buyer is likely to be, 'how much do I actually pay for this?' Does this *puzzlement* generate socialist consciousness, as Dieterich goes on to suggest? Being puzzled doesn't necessarily lead to revolutionary conclusions. The Winter Palace wasn't stormed because the Petrograd working class all thought, "I wonder where my keys have got to?"

Dual power, as we have explained, is not a situation that is likely to last for very long. Dieterich suggests workers should participate in discussions in the workplace with the boss about the rate of surplus value and what to do with it. But isn't it obvious that this will involve conflicts of interest (or class struggle, as it used to be called)? The boss wants a yacht, the worker wants higher wages or more investment to create jobs. Who decides? This is the most important question. In fact, it is the only question. There are only two alternatives: *either the boss is going to move to eliminate dual power, or the workers, if they want to hold on to their gains, will have to move to take state power.* Even Lassalle (whose formulations in the Gotha Programme are criticised by Marx, and whose notion of 'the full fruits of their labour' is so similar to Dieterich's concept of "equivalence") was contemplating arrangements *after production had been socialised.*

In the past, experiments were carried out by utopian socialists who established communist communities in the USA and elsewhere based on "equal exchange". In every case they broke down and ended in disaster. In Mexico, the Zapatistas, who comrade Dieterich in the past greatly admired, have apparently introduced similar schemes in the areas they control. Subcomandante Marcos believes that this kind of thing is an alternative to taking power by revolutionary means. Actually, such utopian experiments do not disturb the ruling class in the slightest.

The Mexican ruling class was terrified by the movement of the masses when López Obrador was cheated of electoral victory. But they do not lose any sleep over

Marcos and the Zapatista leaders, who, when the question of power was posed by the movement of millions of workers and peasants, played a completely reactionary role and acted as *de facto* defenders of the existing bourgeois order. Nor do they lose any sleep over Professor Dieterich's utopian schemes, particularly when he also always acts "responsibly" in every key moment, like the constitutional referendum in Venezuela.

How is equal exchange to be achieved?

Let us ask how this equal exchange is achieved in practice. Presumably there will be some kind of labour bank that will issue certificates based on the hours worked, which can be exchanged for commodities containing the same amount of labour-time. The labour time needs to be authentically verified, which, despite the existence of computers, is not as easy as Dieterich imagines.

In effect, these certificates would be *a kind of money*. In reality they are only promissory notes, which at the end of the day must be exchanged for commodities in a definite ratio. But all history shows that in order to perform its function as a medium of exchange, money must be acceptable in society. People must accept that it actually is worth the amount that is printed on it – that it is "as good as gold". Otherwise the notes in circulation are merely printed bits of paper. How can this "labour money" circulate outside the bank? How does it become convertible?

In order to determine the value of a commodity it is necessary to determine the labour time in which commodities could be produced, with the average means of production available in a given industry, i.e. the time in which they would have to be produced. But that also would not be sufficient. One would have to determine the time in which a certain quantity of products had to be produced, and place the producers in conditions that made their labour equally productive, and also the amounts of labour time to be employed in the different branches of production.

It is not a question of an isolated individual calculating how many hours he or she has worked, since the value of a commodity is determined by the amount of socially necessary labour-time expended on its production. An economy based on exchange dissolves all individual relations of production and distribution and replaces them by universal dependence. In place of the local market we have the development first of the national market, then of the world market. The value of commodities in the modern era is determined by the sum total of production and distribution on a world scale.

Whether the labour time expended on production in a factory in Caracas is socially necessary or not is determined, not in that particular factory, but in hundreds of thousands of factories in China, India, etc. Each individual's production is dependent on the production and consumption of all others on a world scale. So what at first seemed like a very simple act of arithmetic now turns out to be an infinitely more complex calculation.

Adam Smith

Here we see the result of comrade Dieterich's error in lumping together different historical periods and establishing a false identity between qualitatively different socio-historical systems. Prices, money and exchange have a long history; determining the value of the articles exchanged by costs of production, but they only become dominant under the capitalist system. In earlier societies exchange has a more or less individual and accidental character.

Starting with Adam Smith the bourgeois economists imagine that every private individual pursues his private interest; and thereby unconsciously serves the general interest, through the "invisible hand of the market". This is an expression of the triumph of the market and exchange under capitalism. Like a good bourgeois Adam Smith assumed that the capitalist mode of exchange already existed in the prehistoric period. Dieterich does not go quite so far, limiting it to the past 5,000 years or so. In fact, only under capitalism does exchange develop to its full extent. In bourgeois society, the society of free competition production acquires absolute dominance over all relations of production.

This reciprocal dependence of producers and consumers is expressed in the constant necessity for exchange, and finds its all-sided mediation in exchange value. This universal interconnection has nothing to do with isolated individuals like Robinson Crusoe, as Marx explains:

"The reciprocal and all-sided dependence of individuals who are indifferent to one another forms their social connection. This social bond is expressed in *exchange value*, by means of which alone each individual's own activity or his product becomes an activity and a product for him; he must produce a general product – *exchange value*, or, the latter isolated for itself and individualized, *money*."

This is very different from previous societies, in which the individual or the individual member of a family or clan or community "directly and naturally reproduces himself, or in which his productive activity and his share in production are bound to a specific form of labour and of product, which determine his relation to others in just that specific way." [4] This kind of exchange was not possible in previous forms of society: the patriarchal relation, the community of antiquity, feudalism and the guild system. The latter had to be destroyed before capitalist economic relations could advance beyond the embryonic stage, as Marx explains:

"Patriarchal as well as ancient conditions (feudal, also) thus disintegrate with the development of commerce, of luxury, of *money*, of *exchange value*, while modern society arises and grows in the same measure." [5]

The central contradiction of capitalism is that between the social character of production and the private appropriation of wealth. In exchange value, the product of the worker's hand appears before him as something alien and objective, con-

4. Marx, *Grundrisse*, pp. 156-7.
5. Ibid., p. 158.

fronting the individual as an alien power over which he or she has no control. The way to abolish this contradiction is not to tinker with the market economy with utopian schemes for "equal exchange" but to expropriate the capitalists and thus create the conditions for a socialist planned economy, in which the workers can exercise conscious control over their productive and social activity.

"There can therefore be nothing more erroneous and absurd than to postulate the control by the united individuals of their total production, on the basis of *exchange value*, of *money*, as was done above in the case of the time-chit bank." [6]

Marx exposed the erroneous and absurd character of the idea of equal exchange as advocated by the utopian socialists and answered over a hundred years in advance the arguments of their lineal descendent Heinz Dieterich. It is an attempt to remove the contradictions of capitalism while retaining an economy based on exchange by individual producers. It is an attempt to create capitalism with a human face. That is to say, it is an attempt to square the circle.

The development of capitalism creates all kinds of contradictions: agglomeration, combination, cooperation, the antithesis of private interests, class interests, competition, concentration of capital, monopoly, stock companies and so on. From competition arises monopoly, and from the national market arises the world economy. The utopian socialists saw only the negative aspects of this: exploitation and injustice. But the development of capitalism also creates the conditions for its overthrow. The development of the means of production create the material base for a higher form of human society – socialism – and it also creates the class that is destined to act as its gravedigger – the working class.

Bourgeois society rests on exchange value, which is only an expression of existing socio-economic relations, including the relations of circulation and production. There are so many contradictions in this system that it is impossible to abolish them by isolating a single element (exchange). Utopian socialists like Gray (who is the real source of Dieterich's ideas on economics) believed that a *reform of the money market* could abolish the foundations of internal or external private trade. By means of peaceful reforms like the establishment of a labour bank and "equal exchange", the exploitative character of capitalism could be abolished, painlessly, without unpleasant conflicts.

Capitalism cannot be reformed

Marx explains that the "antithetical character [of capitalism] *can never be abolished through quiet metamorphosis*. On the other hand, if we did not find concealed in society as it is the material conditions of production and the corresponding relations of exchange prerequisite for a classless society, then all attempts to explode it would be quixotic." [7]

6. Ibid., p. 158-9.
7. Ibid., p. 159, my emphasis, AW.

Here we see the abysm that separates the thinking of Dieterich from Marxism. For Marx, the capitalist system had to be overthrown by the revolutionary movement of the working class. For the utopian socialists and Dieterich, it can metamorphose into a "new and just society" by abolishing "unequal exchange", while retaining the economic system based on exchange and money – that is, capitalism. What do these words mean? For Marx, socialism was not just a good idea, or, to quote Dieterich's favourite phrase "an historical project". It was the inevitable result of the development of capitalism itself. In its greed for personal gain, the bourgeoisie developed the productive forces to an unheard-of degree and therefore created the objective conditions for socialism.

Marx pointed out that "a bank which directly creates the mirror image of the commodity in the form of labour-money is a utopia". In reality, socialism takes its starting point from the development of capitalism. The development of gigantic monopolies in the present epoch is the logical result of free competition, which it negates. But the existence of huge monopolies, real industrial armies of workers spread out all over the terrestrial globe, abolishes any necessary role the individual capitalist may once have played in production.

The day when the entrepreneur personally ran the factory has long gone. Instead, today the owners of industry pay professional managers to administer their plants while they confine their activities to parasitism and speculation. The bourgeois, who have enriched themselves to an unprecedented extent at the expense of the working class, are as superfluous as the drones in a beehive. Therefore, the next step must be to eliminate this role altogether by expropriating the expropriators.

Today in all the main capitalist countries the big monopolies are closely linked to the state. Although they constantly complain about the state, taxes and government interference, the capitalists are paid lavish subsidies by the state, which relieves them of the need to pay for the education and health of the workers, pays for the police who defend their property and the armies that fight their wars for access to foreign markets, raw materials and spheres of influence, all while reducing taxation on the rich and passing the bill to the working class and the middle class. The next logical step is therefore the nationalization of the big banks and monopolies, under the democratic control and administration of the working class.

What is the point?

The principle of indeterminacy states that it is not possible to determine accurately the position and velocity of an individual subatomic particle, but quantum physics is capable of making very precise predictions about the movements of very large numbers of electrons and other particles. Similarly it is not possible to determine the exact position of a gas molecule, but it is possible to do so in relation to very large numbers of gas molecules. In the same way, it is neither possible nor necessary to work out the "true value" of a single commodity in order to understand the evolution of prices in the aggregate. This is absolutely necessary for a socialist planned economy, but fiddling and fussing about the exact value of individual commodities is a *ridiculous waste of time*.

Let us assume for the sake of argument that, with the aid, of one of Heinz Dieterich's computers, we are able to calculate the "true value" of commodities, what would the practical consequences be? The worker would then have the immense satisfaction of knowing that such-and-such an amount of his labour power has been used up on such-and-such a day in making such-and-such a product. What then? Will he able to demand that the boss raises his wages? No, because he has already agreed the amount of his wages with the employer before setting foot in the factory. As we have already seen, wages are not the price of labour but only of labour power, which, once he has purchased, the boss can use as he sees fit.

Moreover, if the worker wishes to receive his wages then the product of his labour must be sold. Otherwise its true value will be precisely zero. But here things begin to get complicated. At what price will the product be sold – at its "true value", or at the price dictated by the market? Why, at its market price, of course! One scratches one's head in bewilderment.

What was the point in spending so much time and effort working out the value of commodities, when in the end they are sold according to the laws of supply and demand? What difference does all this make to the worker, the capitalist, the consumer or anyone else, when the end result is exactly the same: the worker is paid exactly the same wages, the capitalist gets exactly the same profit (derived from the unpaid wages of the worker) and the consumer has to pay exactly the same price, determined by market forces. What was it all for?

Here we come to the essence of the whole business. Heinz Dieterich has caused the workers to spend a colossal amount of time and energy to work out a *purely symbolic* "price" which can be written on a ticket and displayed on the product in the shop window alongside the ordinary market price. We know that, in the real market place, nobody will pay any attention to this symbolic price, any more than smokers pay any attention to the health warnings printed on the side of cigarette packets.

"Ah," says Heinz, "but then the people will be able to compare the price and the 'true value"

So what? (We persist in our inquisition).

"After a while they will begin to notice that there is a difference between the two," Heinz replies.

So what? (We still persist).

"Then they will say: just a moment! This means that the capitalists are exploiting the workers! This is unjust! We demand the immediate introduction of Socialism of the 21st Century!"

Then everything will be all right.

Now it really requires a genius of the stature of Heinz Dieterich to think of something like this. He assumes a) that most people do not know that the bosses exploit the workers, b) that most people do not know that society is fundamentally unjust and c) they have had to wait until now for Heinz Dieterich to explain this to them. For our part, we have a somewhat higher opinion about the native intelligence of the masses than professor Dieterich.

Had he asked us (which, needless to say, he did not) we could have advised him that it is not necessary to have millions of workers armed with pocket calculators wasting their precious time computing "true value". The task is a lot simpler. All that is required is for Heinz to come out of his comfortable university study (not for long – a day should be enough) and just talk to ordinary men and women on the streets of Caracas or Mexico City. If he had taken the trouble to do this he would have a big surprise. He would soon discover that most workers are well aware that the bosses exploit them and that capitalist society is unjust.

The problem here is that professor Dieterich, like all the other reformists, treats the workers as if they were little children – and not very intelligent children, at that. He really imagines that without him and his wonderful theory of 21st Century Socialism the ignorant masses will never be capable of changing society. This is the exact opposite of the idea of Karl Marx, who said that *the emancipation of the workers is the task of the workers themselves*.

He thinks the masses are not capable of understanding socialism and that this is the real problem. If by this he means that they are not capable of understanding what he writes in his books, we can agree with him. But then, they are in very good company. The present writer can confirm that to plough through these writings is a painful task for which a great deal of time is needed, which the majority of suffering humanity does not possess. The masses have to suffer quite enough in the daily struggle for existence without having further tortures inflicted on them.

Heinz Dieterich complains that he is not understood, and he concludes that this reflects the low level of consciousness of the masses. If people do not understand what he writes he only has himself to blame. As a matter of fact, he is most fortunate that they do not understand what he writes, because if they did he would have even fewer supporters than he has now.

Why nationalization?

Having rejected nationalization and central planning, Dieterich's next step is to *reform the market* and move to the kingdom of equal exchange. How is this miracle to be accomplished? Why, through a network of computers, of course! This will, Heinz assures us, enable us to *calculate labour time* and thus ensure *equal exchange*. The project for 21st Century Socialism is thus based on *a network of PCs*.

This is approximately like making a brain that does not connect to any limbs. You cannot make the instruments of production do what you want them to do if you don't own them. Yet Heinz has rejected all suggestion of nationalizing the productive forces, so we must assume that in the 21st Century Socialist paradise, the land, the banks, the industries, and, yes, the computers will all remain safely in private hands.

Heinz is capable of stating the problem but not of providing a satisfactory solution. Once we have taken over the key points of the economy it will be possible to plan the productive forces in a rational way. It will be possible to mobilize the productive capacity of the nation to solve its most pressing problems. On this condition – *and only on this condition* – computers and other modern technology would be used to the full extent of their potential. Under such circumstances, Heinz Dieterich would be correct when he writes:

"There are millions of engineers, economists, mathematicians, activists and social fighters in India, Europe, the United States, Latin America and other latitudes who have computer capacity and unused time who, without doubt, would be disposed to collaborate in solidarity with the construction of the next phase of human evolution. It is simply a question of activating them with an ethical political project which will give them a sense of transcendence in life, which present capitalism lacks completely."[8]

It is certainly true that there are millions of engineers, economists, mathematicians, scientists and other qualified people all over the world whose talents and abilities are not being used for the benefit of humanity *because capitalism is unable to use them*. There are many graduates in all countries who are unemployed or working in supermarkets because an economic system entirely based on production for profit does not need their services.

Millions of people need trained doctors, teachers, nurses and so on. But capitalist production is not directed to the satisfaction of human needs but only the further accumulation of capital and the enrichment of the few at the expense of the many. The only way to put an end to this situation is to take the economic power out of the hands of the rich parasites and place it in the hands of the workers and peasants who make up the overwhelming majority of society.

Capitalists without profit?

Plato, as we know, banned poets from his ideal Republic. Arno Peters is far more broad-minded. In his ideal Socialist Republic of the 21st Century we will have *not just poets but judges, factory managers, directors and ministers*, but also *capitalists, army generals, policemen and a hierarchical state bureaucracy*:

"Also those activities that today still have as their objective personal enrichment must be included to the degree that the economy needs them. In this, trade is limited to the distribution of goods, their transportation and storage; these activities, as a necessary part of the division of labour, are converted into a part of value and must

8. Dieterich, *La revolución mundial pasa por Hugo Chávez*, in *Rebelión*. 6/3/2005.

be remunerated like any other work: according to the time worked. *Similar norms must be applied to the owners of enterprises that do not belong to trade but production.* After their profits have disappeared, their entrepreneurial activity – which, like any other work forms a proportional part of the commodities – must be paid in an equivalent manner, as long as society has *a hierarchical structure, and therefore continues to maintain a military organization* that requires its activity. At the present time, this is the situation in almost all countries."[9]

The reader might be forgiven for thinking that this 21st Century Socialism is beginning to look increasingly like good old-fashioned capitalism. But no, there is a difference! Under 21st Century Socialism there will be capitalists, who will continue to own the banks and industries, but they will be completely different to the capitalists that exist in "almost" all countries at the present time, or at any other time in the past. Arno Peters' capitalists will continue to own and run their businesses as before, but they will do so in a completely altruistic manner, renouncing all personal gain and cheerfully accepting the "wages of equivalence" for their pains.

Mr. Peters has here achieved a miracle, compared to which the transformation of lead into gold is mere child's play. He has achieved something that even the old alchemists never dreamed of: he has turned the capitalists into saints. Activities that today are carried out for the sake of personal enrichment, says Arno, "must be included to the degree that the economy needs them". But if we accept that private capitalists are necessary, then we must leave them to carry on their business – just as they do at present. And the whole purpose of the private capitalist is no other than the pursuit of profit. It is rather embarrassing to have to point out things that are obvious to any normal person. But since such things are by no means obvious to Arno and Heinz, we have no alternative but to do so.

The only locomotive of capitalist production is private profit. To imagine an economic system in which private individuals continue to own and administer the means of production without the profit motive is to imagine Hamlet without the Prince of Denmark or the Catholic Church without the Immaculate Conception. If private capitalists are still necessary, then it follows as night follows day that profits are still necessary, and therefore that the extraction of surplus value is still necessary and exploitation is still necessary, and the market is still necessary.

Arno Peters' capitalists are, of course, *individuals*, and, like everyone else in the equivalence economy, pursue their individual activity. But in the market they encounter many other capitalists who are doing just the same thing. The competition between these individual capitals is what gives rise to the anarchy of capitalist production, rendering planning utterly impossible and producing periodic crises of overproduction, unemployment and factory closures and all the other things that were supposed to be banned from Arno Peters' Socialist Paradise, but which now reappear as an integral and necessary part of the economy of equivalence. We now

9. Dieterich, *Hugo Chávez y el Socialismo del Siglo XXI*, pp. 108-9.

see very clearly that, under the pretext of abolishing capitalist economic relations, this theory (if we can grace it by this name) merely reproduces them in a different (and utterly fantastic) form.

The first question we need to ask is: *why are private capitalists necessary at all?* In Marx's day the factory owners played a direct role in production, as managers in their own factories. But that has long since disappeared. The modern owners of industry play no role at all in production, other than providing capital for investment, and this they do exclusively to obtain profit from the unpaid labour of the working class. The factories owned by Ford could not function for a single minute without workers, but the same factory could function very well if Henry Ford and all the other capitalists vanished from the face of the earth.

But maybe Peters is not referring to capitalists at all but only to managers? No, he is quite explicit on this point; he specifically refers to *the owners of industry*. In a socialist economy there would be a role for managers and engineers, who could play an important role, participating together with the workers in drawing up the plan of production and carrying it out in the most efficient way possible. In the words of Marx, they would be entitled to the "wages of superintendence". *But there would be no role whatsoever for private owners of industry*. From the very beginning the main means of production – the land, the banks, financial institutions and the big monopolies – would be in the hands of the state, and the state would be in the hands of the workers.

Peters quietly smuggles in the idea that under socialism the means of production could remain in private hands. This makes a mockery of the very idea of socialism. Why does he insist on this absurd idea of "capitalist socialism"? Because he does not like unpleasantness and he realizes that the capitalists will not remain with arms folded while the workers relieve them of their power and privileges. He wishes to soothe the nerves of the ruling class and at the same time sings lullabies to the workers about the beauties of class collaboration and a wonderful society in which capitalists voluntary surrender their profits and work for the common good on the "wages of equivalence".

The whole thing is reduced to a cheap conjuring trick, whereby all the basic economic relations of capitalism are retained but are alleged to have been transformed into something altogether less unpleasant. Thus, trade is "limited to the distribution of goods, their transportation and storage; these activities, as a necessary part of the division of labour, are converted into a part of value and must be remunerated like any other work: according to the time worked." This would be correct in a socialist planned economy, where the state would take over all the tasks of distribution, transportation, etc.

One of the first tasks would be to nationalize the railways, and all other forms of transport by land, sea and air. This would permit the introduction of an integrated transport system, operated for the benefit of society, not private profit. It would allow us to solve the problem of congested roads and city centres – something no capitalist government in the world has been able to do, despite all the talk about "green" politics. The introduction of free public transport in cities would make it possible to ban private cars from circulating in cities at all. The lunacy of heavy articulated lorries owned by private companies clogging the roads would be prevented by transporting most goods by rail and improving the railway system to take more passengers and relieve pressure on congested roads and motorways. But the prior condition for this is the abolition of private property. This is precisely what Peters and Dieterich do not want.

How to make profits disappear

Arno Peters is very clear on this: not only transport, but also industry will remain in private hands: "*Similar norms must be applied to the owners of enterprises that do not belong to trade but production.* After their profits have disappeared, their entrepreneurial activity – which, like any other work forms a proportional part of the commodities – must be paid in an equivalent manner [...]." [10] This is quite typical of the method of Peters-Dieterich. They first assume what has to be proved, and then express themselves in categorical terms that allow no contradiction. Here we have a classical example:

Step one: we are informed that socialism can be achieved while retaining private property of the means of production.

Step two: we are informed that "profits have disappeared", although precisely when and how this happened is not explained.

Step three: we are informed that from now on, the capitalists will be prepared to work for the wages of equivalence, just like everyone else in 21st Century Socialism. Why? *Because they must.* Why must they? Because Arno Peters says so.

Now the word "must" implies a degree of compulsion. I must do something because I am under compulsion to do it. Compulsion can either be physical or moral; it can either come from external constraints (the threat of imprisonment, fines, etc.) or the acceptance of a certain moral code, like, say, the Ten Commandments ("Thou shalt not steal", etc.).

It seems to us quite possible that when the advocates of 21st Century Socialism solemnly inform Bill Gates that profits have disappeared and that henceforth he must only receive the wages of equivalence, he might entertain some small doubts on the matter. He might say, for instance: "I have invested billions of dollars in my factories, machinery and scientific research, and now you ask me to receive in compensation a pittance that would hardly be enough to pay a tip in a decent restaurant. Why should I accept such a kind offer?" To which Arno and Heinz reply: *because you must.*

10. Dieterich, *Socialismo del Siglo XXI*, p. 101, my emphasis, AW.

Let us use a little imagination to recreate the whole of a conversation between Bill Gates and Heinz Dieterich:

Dieterich: Good morning, Mr. Gates; how kind of you to spare a moment of your valuable time to receive me.

BG: Not at all, Mr. Dieterich. What can I do for you?

Dieterich: I have come to inform you that your profits have disappeared.

BG: Really? I hadn't noticed. I'll ring my accountant and ask where they have gone to.

Dieterich: No, no, Mr. Gates, you don't understand. They have not exactly vanished, only you will not be seeing them any more.

BG: Is that so? How come?

Dieterich: Because we are building 21st Century Socialism and therefore you must only get an equivalent wage.

BG: And how much would that be?

Dieterich: It is the exact amount of labour you have expended on the production of commodities, no more, no less.

BG: I don't think I have produced any commodities lately, not myself anyway.

Dieterich: Don't worry, Mr. Gates, we theoreticians of the equivalent economy have already thought of that, and as long as your services are necessary to society, we will consider your labour as equivalent to that of any other individual.

BG: That is extremely decent of you. But I still would like to know exactly how much I get for my necessary services.

Dieterich: We shall have to do some tricky calculations here. You don't happen to have a calculator on you?

BG: No, I have no time for complicated technology.

Dieterich: Ah well, we shall manage without then. Now, how much time to you spend at work?

BG: That is hard to say. You see, I have an awful lot of clever people who do the work for me.

Dieterich: Maybe you do a bit of management?

BG: Nope, I got plenty of managers.

Dieterich: How about the science and technology angle?

BG: Got plenty of clever scientists and technicians, too.

Dieterich: But you do have overall control?

BG: Are you kidding? A firm like Microsoft is far too big for one man to control, even one as clever as me.

Dieterich: But you must do some work?

BG: Oh yes, I occasionally come into the office to see how things are going.

Dieterich: At last! How many labour hours is that?

BG: Pardon?

Dieterich (Irritated): How often do you go to the office?

BG: That's a hard one. You see I'm away half the year on important business.

Dieterich: What business is that?

BG: You know, horse-riding on my ranch, shooting and fishing in Scotland, scuba diving in the Caribbean, playing the casinos in Las Vegas, attending first nights at the opera at La Scala, Milan, that kind of thing. It's really a very exhausting schedule.

Dieterich: But that is not work. That is what we call living life. We don't pay you for that!

BG: A pity! Anyway, you must admit I take big risks. Surely I deserve to be rewarded for that?

Dieterich: What kind of risks, when Microsoft has a virtual monopoly on the global computer business?

BG: Well, I am taking a huge risk that one day I may lose my monopoly!

Dieterich: That seems most unlikely. But surely you must do some kind of work?

BG: I guess I go to the office a few hours a week when I am in town. And I suppose you could say I inspire the workforce with my presence. So how much is that worth?

Dieterich: About a hundred dollars a month.

BG: (after a pause) It's not very much, is it?

Dieterich: It's the going rate for the equivalent wage. Everybody gets it.

BG: Well, if you don't mind, Mr. Dieterich, I will pass on this one.

Dieterich: But you can't do that.

BG Why not?

Dieterich: Because it goes against all the principles of 21st Century Socialism.

BG: That's too bad.

Dieterich: Well, then, because the *majorities* say you must.

BG: And I say: "Get lost!" I am still the owner of Microsoft, am I not?

Dieterich: You certainly are, Mr. Gates. Nobody can touch your property. It is strictly against the principles of 21st Century Socialism.

BG: Very good! In that case, you can get out of my office right now.

Dieterich: You cannot go against the wishes of the majorities. The tide of history is against you…

BG (throwing him out): The majorities can do what they like, and I will do what I like. I will close my factories and throw every worker on the street before I surrender my sacred right to make a profit from honest labour, and you can go to hell."

This is probably a fairly accurate reconstruction of the likely content of an imaginary conversation, except that Bill Gates would undoubtedly have expressed himself in rather more forceful language. The class struggle is essentially the struggle for the division of the surplus created by the working class. This continues uninterruptedly, now open, now disguised. The interests of wage labour and capital are incompatible. Yet for all his moral indignation, Dieterich believes that it is possible to reconcile them. He believes that the lamb can lie down with the lion and the tiger can be taught to eat salads, and the capitalists can renounce profits and accept with a smile the "wages of equivalence": *in other words, he believes it is possible to square the circle.*

In Shakespeare's *Hamlet*, old Polonius says: "Though this be madness, yet there's method in it". And it is also the case here. If we accept that this is all a moral question, that the workers are being swindled by the bosses, then what is needed is to persuade the bosses to behave themselves and stop their thieving, and then all will be well. Sooner or later they will see the light and rush to embrace the joys of 21st Century Socialism. After all, Dieterich assures them constantly that they will not be expropriated, that the capitalists can keep the factories, the landlords can keep the land and the bankers can keep the banks, and the workers and peasants can keep – well, whatever they can.

It may, of course, take a little time to persuade the rich of the moral superiority of 21st Century Socialism, but after all, we still have almost another 92 years to go. And if we have not succeeded by then, doubtless some new Heinz Dieterich will arise to announce some new theory of 22nd Century Socialism that will transform the world – if there is still a world to transform.

How not to make a revolution

That the planet is in danger is evident to all but the most narrow-minded reactionary. The environment is being systematically destroyed by so-called market forces. Giant transnational companies ravage and loot the Third World, encouraging the destruction of the Amazon rain forest, polluting rivers and seas, depleting fish stocks, poisoning the Arctic. The future survival of humanity is under threat. But the only way to prevent disaster for future generations is to tackle the problem at its roots: by abolishing capitalism and instituting a world planned socialist economy. How would the founders of 21st Century Socialism solve the problem?

"The soil and the natural resources would become common property, as they were for the greater part of the epoch of the local equivalent economy. But not like that period, when they were freely available to all, like air and water, but as a valuable asset controlled by the State, whose conservation and use must have priority for all humanity, above any particular interest." [11]

Very cautiously, Arno Peters *hints* (only hints) at nationalization, a word he avoids as the devil avoids holy water. Instead, the land and natural resources mysteriously "*become common property*". But how do they do this? Presumably the owners of the big landed estates will have something to say on the subject, as will

11. Dieterich, *Hugo Chávez y el Socialismo del Siglo XXI*, p. 110.

the big mining companies that derive fat profits from exploiting the natural resources of the entire terrestrial globe. They will fight against this – as they are now doing in Venezuela. If we are to succeed, this resistance must be overcome. It cannot be done by preaching to the landowners and capitalists the virtues of equivalence. It can only be done by expropriating the oligarchy by revolutionary means. But this idea is firmly rejected by Peters, whose main obsession is precisely to *prevent revolution.* Peters is quite clear on this point, as we shall see shortly.

"It is more difficult to regulate materialized or accumulated labour. By socializing the means of production, this percentage of value that forms part of any new commodity, would favour the community represented by the State, which is also obliged to renew and modernize the means of production. If private property of the means of production is maintained, the percentage of value which comes from materialized labour and reappears in commodities, could continue to be part of the income of the entrepreneurs. Combined with the obligation to a complete reinvestment, here some structural elements of the non-equivalent economy could be retained in the transitional period to the equivalent economy." [12]

At this point, Arno is in full retreat. Having deducted from the "full value of labour" all the costs of schools, hospitals, judges and lawyers, and having further deducted the costs of the hierarchical state, army and police force, we now come full circle and deduct the *capitalists' profits* (which, as you recall, were supposed to have disappeared) – but only on strict condition that they are destined for "complete reinvestment". Thus, profit, which Arno Peters banished from the kingdom of 21st Century Socialism by the front door, rudely forces its way in via the tradesman's entrance.

In the transitional period that, we are assured, will eventually lead us to the Paradise of Equivalence, capitalists will be permitted to keep their profits (which, having mysteriously *disappeared*, have equally mysteriously *reappeared*) but only on condition that they are immediately reinvested. But just a moment! If the capitalists own the means of production, who can order them to reinvest? The decisions as to whether to invest or not, and how much and when to invest are entirely the competence of the owners of the business concerned. They will do so on the only grounds yet known for the functioning of the capitalist economy – and this is *profit.*

Capitalists like Bill Gates invest large sums, which may amount to billions of dollars. The state and the government have no real control over these activities, since you cannot control what you do not own. All attempts to regulate capitalism (for that is what Peters and Dieterich are really talking about) have led to failure. If the state accepts capitalist property relations and then acts in a way that the owners of industry do not like, the latter will stop investing, or move overseas. They will

12. Ibid., p. 101.

close their factories as if they were mere matchboxes, throwing thousands of workers onto the streets.

The whole of history shows this, including the recent history of Venezuela, where the capitalists have been organizing a strike of capital for years in order to destabilize the government of Hugo Chávez. To his credit, Chávez has stood up to the capitalist and responded by nationalizing parts of the Venezuelan economy. It is public knowledge that Heinz Dieterich is not enthusiastic about nationalizations and has done his best to dissuade President Chávez from "going too far" and "provoking the counter-revolution".

Maybe he is waiting for the Venezuelan bosses to read his books and convince themselves that it is a good idea to abstain from personal enrichment, accept the "wages of equivalence" and invest all their profits in the Bolivarian Revolution. The idea is so preposterous that it is enough to make even Pedro Carmona laugh. But the high priests of Socialism of the 21st Century take it very seriously indeed. They are the only people in the world who do.

A petty bourgeois utopia

We have already pointed out that the Marxist labour theory of value does not refer to the value of the labour of an individual worker but to the average socially necessary labour – to human labour in the abstract. It will never be possible to calculate the value of individual commodities produced by a particular worker, unless we refer to the medieval shoemaker or the individual small peasant proprietor on his cabbage patch. And this is really the kind of labour that Heinz and Arno are thinking about: not the kind of production we find in large-scale modern capitalist enterprises like Ford or IBM, but *small scale businesses* – the kind of productive units that were common in the early days of capitalism when it was still in the embryonic stages of development.

Here we see the essentially petty bourgeois mentality that underlies all this utopian thinking. The petty bourgeois idealises small business – the kind of business that is characteristic of the class of small proprietors. The petty bourgeois has a profound aversion to the big capitalist companies that are driving him out of business. He curses the big banks and monopolies, but at the same time he fears that he will lose his "privileged" position and be pushed down into the working class and desires at all costs to maintain what he regards as his superior status as an owner of property. This situation creates a contradictory psychology. The middle class constantly vacillates between the bourgeoisie and proletariat.

The confused, ambiguous and contradictory position of Dieterich and Peters is absolutely typical of this class. They hate and fear the monopoly capitalists and imperialists and rage against them. At the same time they are organically incapable of placing themselves in the camp of the proletariat, which they look down upon and which they distrust. They are constantly yearning for class peace and a "middle way". They preach humanity and democracy to the capitalists, appealing to them to be reasonable and give up their profits in exchange for the "wages of equivalence". At the same time they appeal to the workers not to go "too far", to be patient, to respect private property, and so on. In other words, despite their radical-sounding phrases, they act like vulgar reformists.

Although they consider themselves to be the greatest realists, they are in fact the worst kind of utopians. Their preaching to the bourgeoisie has absolutely no effect and insofar as they have any effect in the working class – or rather in sections of the leadership – it is to disorient and paralyse the movement. Though their subjective intentions may be of the very best, they play an entirely reactionary role.

Concentration of capital

The Communist Manifesto, written as long ago as 1848, is a remarkably modern document. It predicted long in advance the inevitable process of the concentration of capital, the inexorable concentration of obscene wealth on the one hand and extreme poverty on the other. The bourgeois economists have tried to argue that Marx was wrong when he predicted the concentration of capital and that the future is with small businesses. For decades bourgeois sociologists attempted to disprove these assertions and "prove" that society was becoming more equal and that, consequently, the class struggle was as antiquated as the handloom and the wooden plough. The working class had disappeared, they said, and we were all middle class.

Today only hopelessly naïve people can believe this nonsense. All the statistics confirm the fact that the concentration of capital has reached levels unimagined by Marx. In reality the march of capitalism has long ago cut the ground from under the feet of the petty bourgeoisie and its political representatives. It is ironic that, precisely in this epoch, when the entire world economy is dominated by huge multinationals, the apologists of capital try to show that the future lies with small enterprises. This wishful thinking is like the day-dreams of a decrepit old libertine who tries to forget his present ailments by recalling the vigour of youth. However, the youthful phase of capitalism is gone beyond recall.

Marx explains how free competition inevitably begets monopoly. In the struggle between big and small capital, the result is always the same: "It always ends in the ruin of many small capitalists, whose capitals partly pass into the hands of their conquerors, partly vanish." [13] Today, the vast power of the monopolies and multinationals exercises a total stranglehold on the world. With the access to staggering sums of money, their economies of scale, their ability to manipulate commodity prices and even their power to determine the policy of governments, they are the true masters of the planet.

13. K. Marx, *Capital*, Vol. 1, p. 626.

The brilliance of Marx's method is shown precisely from the fact that he was able to predict the inevitable tendency towards monopolization when free competition was still the norm. Nowadays, despite the demagogic twaddle of journals like *The Economist* about "small is beautiful", there can be no question of this general historical tendency being reversed. Quite the contrary. The last few decades have witnessed an unprecedented tendency towards the concentration of capital. The broad historical tendency towards the concentration of capital is absolutely incontrovertible. The situation as regards Germany, Britain, France and all the other countries of capitalism is no different.

In the period of capitalist ascent, the bourgeois played a progressive role in developing the productive forces, investing in industry, science and technology. In the epoch of capitalist decline, we see a very different picture emerging. Speculative activity and investment in the parasitic service sector is displacing investment in productive activity as a source of profit. When huge fortunes can be made by a single telephone call by a currency speculator, why bother to risk capital in costly machinery which may never make a profit? Gambling on the stock exchange has reached epidemic proportions. Hundreds of billions of dollars a year goes to finance speculative takeovers in the United States alone, while factories are being continuously closed.

The entire world economy is now dominated by no more than 200 giant companies, the great majority of which are based in the USA. The process of monopolization has reached unprecedented proportions. In the first quarter of 2006 mergers and acquisitions in the USA amounted to $10 billion dollars a day. This feverish activity does not signify a real development of the productive forces, but the opposite.

And the pace of monopolization does not diminish but increases. In November 2006 the value of mergers and acquisitions in the USA amounted to a record of $75 billion – in just 24 hours! Takeovers are a kind of corporate cannibalism that is inevitably followed by asset stripping, factory closures and sackings – that is, by the wholesale and wanton destruction of means of production and the sacrifice of thousands of jobs on the altar of Profit.

Alongside the most appalling misery and human suffering there is an orgy of obscene money-making and ostentatious wealth. Worldwide there are at present 945 billionaires with a total wealth of $3.5 trillion. Many are citizens of the USA. Bill Gates has a personal fortune estimated at around $56 billion. Warren Buffet is not far behind with $52 billion. Now they boast that this unseemly wealth is spreading to poorer nations. Among the super-rich there are 13 Chinese, 14 Indians – and 19 Russians. And let us not forget Latin America! The richest man in the world is a citizen of "our Great Fatherland" (Gran Patria). Carlos Slim, a Mexican, is now richer than Bill Gates. Yet millions of Mexicans live in conditions of dire poverty. The same story can be told of every other country in Latin America.

The oligarchies – the landowners, bankers and capitalists - have enriched themselves while the majority lives in poverty, and often on the border line of absolute misery. The polarization between rich and poor has never been as extreme as at the present. It is impossible to bridge the abysm that separates the classes. The only solution is to break the economic domination of the oligarchy, and this can only be achieved by the workers and peasants expropriating the landowners, bankers and capitalists by revolutionary means.

Anarchy of capitalism

In the third volume of *Capital* Marx explains the price of production of commodities. He points out that the capitalist only gets the cost of production of his commodity plus the average rate of profit. Some capitalists will be paid below the actual rate, others above, because of the different organic composition of different capitals, which is revealed through competition. Monopolies can extort a price above the value of the commodities, but only by other commodities being sold below their value. The total values produced by society would still amount to the same.

In the world market billions of commodities are exchanged every day. The prices of commodities rise and fall in a completely anarchic manner according to the blind play of market forces. The law of value ultimately regulates supply and demand, but not in an automatic manner. The market mechanism is a highly complex and contradictory phenomenon. Prices fluctuate constantly above or below the value of commodities, but sooner or later the labour theory of value will assert itself. The most striking manifestation of this is crises of overproduction.

This is the central contradiction of capitalism. Within a capitalist enterprise there is a plan. Ford and IBM do not leave their investment plans or the running of their factories to chance. They use the most up-to-date scientific methods to plan every aspect of their operations, down to the smallest details. Trained engineers and scientists measure every aspect of work in order to maximize the productivity of labour, precise inventories are kept and market trends carefully analysed. Armies of scientists, technicians and economists are mobilized.

The benefits of this plan of production are immediately evident in the constant improvements of technique and the raising of the productivity of labour. This is the basis of all human progress. Indeed, the main motor-force of the advance of civilization can ultimately be reduced to the struggle to increase labour productivity – to economize labour time. Never in the whole of history has such massive productive capacity been at our disposal. In a rational society this would be the used to bring about the well being of the whole of society, satisfying all human needs, reducing the hours of work and raising the cultural level of society.

However, under capitalism production is not intended to satisfy the needs of society but only to maximize profits through the extraction of surplus value. As long as the means of production remain in private hands, this situation will continue.

Instead of being a means of improving the human condition, every advance in production and technique is a step towards the further enslavement of the workers and the greater enrichment of the capitalists.

Moreover, the element of rational planning is restricted to the enterprise. Once the commodities leave the factory they enter into another world: a world of total anarchy – the world of market economics. This is wasteful and destructive in the extreme. The fate of millions of men and women are determined by the blind play of market forces, which decide whether they will have work or not, whether they will have bread to feed their children or a roof over their heads.

The apologists of capitalism argue that the free market is the most efficient way of distributing resources, capital and labour. They refer to the invisible hand of the market, which in the long run will correct all imbalances and solve all our problems. To this the English economist Keynes answered that in the long run we are all dead. More recently George Soros, the Hungarian-American investor compared market forces to a smashing ball. It was an apt comparison.

The only way to change this and bring the benefits of planning to the whole of society is to nationalize the means of production. Without taking this step, all talk of socialism is just so much empty demagogy and a deception of the people. Why do socialists insist on the nationalization of the economy? Because this is the only way of ending the anarchy of the market and introducing a socialist planned economy. Unless we take this step, all the levers of economic power will remain in the hands of the capitalists. It does not matter much which party is in government or which leader sits in the Presidential palace because all the most important decisions affecting the lives of the masses will be taken elsewhere – by small unelected groups of wealthy people, by the boards of directors of the banks and big companies.

We have pointed out that planning already exists inside the capitalist enterprise. By turning the instruments of production into the common property of the whole of society, we will arrive at a situation where the whole economy will be operated as a single enterprise with different departments, rather than a series of independent producers competing against one another.

The need for a socialist plan

The capitalist system, then, is an anarchic system. It cannot be planned. The financier George Soros a few years ago wrote a book in which he described in great detail the anarchic nature of financial markets, but then he advocated (a bit like Attac) measures to *regulate* them, which was a complete joke. Needless to say, this had not the slightest effect on international finance markets, or anything else.

In order to solve problems like unemployment or the lack of houses and schools it is necessary for the government to introduce economic planning – to draw up an economic plan based on the needs of the majority, not the profit of the minority. But you cannot plan what you do not control and you cannot control what you do not own. This can be seen in the housing problem. In all the big cities of the world there are many empty and under occupied dwellings, while the problem of homelessness has become a modern scourge even in the most advanced capitalist countries. Together with unemployment, homelessness and bad housing are linked to the epidemic of crime, drug abuse and alcoholism that threatens to demoralize a whole generation of young people. How do Peters and Dieterich propose to solve this?

"In order to ensure the right to a home and a room for all men, the community which is organized in the State, must order the use of the soil and buildings according to the general needs. All public activities that do not produce values (like education, medical assistance, provision for retirement, jurisprudence, administration) could be paid for through taxation according to the time worked." [14]

First of all let us note that this State of Arno Peters is not something for the faint-hearted. It has teeth. It does not request. It *orders*. But who is it ordering and for what purpose? It has just been stated that the soil has become common property and is under the control of the State. Does the State have to issue orders to itself? The sentence makes no logical sense, *unless the idea is to lease back the land to private owners*. In relation to buildings, matters are far clearer: since no mention is made of buildings becoming common property, we must assume that along with private capitalists (and their profits), the private landlord (and his rent) will also be alive and well in the economy of equivalence, hence the peremptory order that buildings be used "according to the general needs".

In the same way that it is impossible for the state to control the investment decisions of private companies, all experience shows that it is very difficult to get private landlords to act in a socially responsible manner. They often charge exorbitant rents and treat tenants badly. If the state acts to reduce rents, they evict their tenants and leave their properties unoccupied.

The Bible says: "The fox has his lair and the birds of the air have their nest, but the Son of Man has no place to lay his head." The right to a decent home ought to be a basic human right, along with the right to a job, a living wage, good education and health care. But today in no capitalist country are any of these things guaranteed. In a country like Britain the high cost of housing means that it is no longer for anybody except the very rich to contemplate buying a house. But the rents in the private sector are so high that they normally take up half a person's income or more.

The scandalous speculation of recent years has increased the price of housing to unheard-of levels, so that most young people can no longer contemplate owning a house of their own, while cheap public housing has become a dream of the past. Even the middle class who can afford to buy a home find themselves burdened with the repayment of large sums of money to the banks and other financial institutions. This modern form of usury often takes up over half of the earnings of a couple even when they are in well-paid jobs.

14. Dieterich, *Socialismo del Siglo XXI*, p. 102.

In all countries there is a severe housing problem, which is particularly acute in Venezuela. Millions of families are living in slums, shanty towns or dwellings unfit for human habitation. Others are at the tender mercy of private landlords, who shamelessly exploit the scarcity of available housing to charge exorbitant rents, increasing the poverty of the poorest and most vulnerable sections of society.

Serious problems demand serious remedies. After the October Revolution in Russia the Bolsheviks expropriated all empty and under-occupied dwellings, as well as the palaces of the rich and the property of the Church and used them to house the homeless and provide socially useful buildings, such as youth clubs, centres for the aged, clinics, art galleries and museums. The real solution for the housing question, however, is the nationalization of the land, the banks and finance houses and the big building companies. This would allow us to mobilize the unemployed building workers in a crash house-building programme, which, in the space of one or two five year plans, would build sufficient houses to solve this problem once and for all.

Arno Peters does not propose any such measures. In his socialist paradise, there will not only be judges, generals and capitalists but also *private landlords*. But the almighty State will *instruct* the latter to behave properly, while funding all the necessary social operations through taxations. Since the unfortunate capitalists have no profits to tax (they only receive the wages of equivalence), the Tax Collector of the 21st Century, in order to pay for this generosity, will have no alternative but to tax the workers. What now is left of the "full value of labour"? *Absolutely nothing*!

To cover his self-evident embarrassment, Peters resorts to subterfuge. "Some structural elements of the non-equivalent economy could be retained in the transitional period to the equivalent economy," he admits sheepishly. This sudden attack of timidity contrasts sharply with the earlier Categorical Imperatives and Absolutes of the Equivalence Principle. What are these "some elements" that will remain for a transition that will probably last for the rest of the 21st century, and several centuries more? *Only private ownership of the means of production, capitalists, landlords, rent and profit, taxes and the hierarchical state.* To describe these as only "some elements" is just as much of an understatement as the reply of a certain young lady who, when her father demanded to know if she had had an illegitimate baby, answered: "Yes, but it is only a little one."

Keynesianism and socialism

In his interview, *Weighty Alternatives for Latin America Discussion with Heinz Dieterich*, 7/1/2006, with *Junge Welt*, which also appeared in Number 21 of the *Marxistische Blätter Flugschriften*, Dieterich explains his position on the banking system and monetary policy thus:

"*Q*: In 2005, Venezuela introduced a new national bank. What's the plan there?

"*Dieterich*: The key idea involves the modernization of the role of the central bank, to get rid of an outdated monetarism that has blocked the economic and social development of Venezuela.

"There are basically two notions of what a central bank should do. One is the orthodox monetarist view, which restricts itself to the manipulation of liquidity in an effort to control inflation. That's a role abandoned by larger nations years ago. The prototype of the newer interpretation of the role of the central bank is that of Alan Greenspan, who on the one hand acts as a guardian of the value of currency and on the other gives equal weight to unemployment, all the while keeping an eye on the business cycle.

"The central bank in Venezuela was occupied by people opposed to the Bolivarian project. They refused to accept that the democratically elected government had the right to restructure the institution according to the new requirements. They blocked attempts to use surpluses for capital investment, and they blocked every kind of productive assistance of the sort that Greenspan or the European Central Bank would provide..." [15]

Let us first note that there is not one word here about the nationalization of the banks, without which there can be no question of a socialist planned economy in Venezuela. Dieterich assumes that Venezuela will continue to operate on the basis of *private ownership of the banks and financial system*, and that this is perfectly consistent with his version of Socialism of the 21st Century, that is to say, an economic system that functions on the basis of market economics.

He then goes on to point out, quite correctly, that "the central bank in Venezuela was occupied by people opposed to the Bolivarian project" and that these people used their position to sabotage the government and block its economic policies. What conclusions are we invited to draw from this? Logically, if the banks are owned and controlled by the enemies of the revolution, the revolution has the right to defend itself by expropriating the banks. But professor Dieterich does not like such radical measures. Instead, he speaks only of "modernization of the role of the central bank".

What does this modernization of the banking system consist of? It consists of abandoning "an *outdated monetarism* that has blocked the economic and social development of Venezuela." That is to say, he advocates, not the abolition of capitalism, but only the replacement of one capitalist economic model in favour of another capitalist model. He says that there are "basically two notions of what a central bank should do". What are these notions?

"One is the orthodox monetarist view, which restricts itself to the manipulation of liquidity in an effort to control inflation. That's a role abandoned by larger nations years ago." [16]

We do not know what economic textbooks they read in Mexican universities these days, but we have to say that it is professor Dieterich and nobody else who is

15. http://mrzine.monthlyreview.org/schiefer070206.html
16. Ibid.

outdated on economic questions. He informs us perfunctorily that "the orthodox monetarist view" has been abandoned by "larger nations" years ago. Which larger nations is he referring to? Certainly not the United States, the largest capitalist economy in the world: they have been operating on the basis of these policies for decades, and show no signs of abandoning them. Nor is it true of Britain, Japan, Germany, France or any other member of the Euro-zone.

The fact is that all the major capitalist nations are following similar economic policies, which can broadly be described as monetarist. The so-called neo-liberal economic model has been imposed everywhere, ever since the ignominious collapse of the Keynesian model, based on deficit financing, towards the end of the 1970s. Everywhere we see the ugly face of capitalism, with wage cuts, liquidation of reforms, abolition of the welfare state and attacks on living standards.

Our friend Heinz does not approve of this. On the other hand, he does not want to propose anything as radical as the abolition of the market economy, which is responsible for this sad state of affairs. He has a much more "realistic" proposal: why not return to the good old days of Keynesianism, deficit financing and managed capitalism? Heinz Dieterich wants to keep capitalism, but he does not want the present ugly model of capitalism. He wants the kind of capitalism in which humanistic sentiment and solidarity takes precedence over the sordid profit motive. He wants capitalism with a human face: that is, he demands pears from an elm-tree.

He complains that monetarism is outmoded. But the capitalists and bankers do not share his opinions. They tried his Keynesian model for a couple of decades after 1945 and for a while it seemed to work. The reformists were delighted. The state intervened to "manage" capitalism, using state funds to "straighten out" the business cycle and avoid recessions. This was a finished recipe for inflation. It is the explanation for the galloping inflation that existed at the end of the 1970s and caused enormous social and political instability both in Europe and Latin America.

Is Keynesianism the answer?

The capitalists have no answer to the problem of unemployment, which is the inevitable result of the fact that the capitalist system has now gone beyond its own limits. The growth of the productive forces has outstripped the narrow limits of private production and the nation state. That is the real reason for the phenomenon of organic (structural) unemployment. Does Dieterich have a solution for this problem, over which the best bourgeois economists have cracked their brains in vain? Of course!

The answer, as we are entitled to expect from the New Historical Project, is *new, modern and original.* If there is unemployment, the state must simply increase the budget deficit to subsidize the enterprises to provide employment. The problem is that this is neither new nor original. It is called *deficit financing* and was long ago invented by the English economist John Maynard Keynes.

Keynes was an intelligent bourgeois who understood the danger of a socialist revolution after the end of the First World War. He advocated what was then certainly a new, modern and original idea. This has been expressed in a popular manner thus: if there are unemployed workers, the state should pay one group of workers to dig a hole, and then pay another group to fill it in. The workers then pay taxes, the government gets its money back, demand is created, which creates more employment, and so on in an upward spiral.

This theory, apparently so logical and attractive, is based on an erroneous supposition, because the state itself has no money to pay anybody to do anything. It can only obtain finances from taxation. Here it has two options: tax the rich or tax the workers and the middle class. If it increases taxation for the capitalists it reduces the profit margins and creates a disincentive to invest, thus increasing unemployment. If it taxes the workers and the middle classes, it cuts into demand and thus increases unemployment. There is no way out of this vicious circle.

Is there a solution? Yes, there is. The state has a monopoly on the printing of promissory notes that we call money. In the past, this paper money was backed up by real values: gold and silver reserves. Every banknote contained a promise to pay the bearer a certain sum, based on the value of a precious metal, usually a certain amount of silver. Unlike paper money, which contains no intrinsic value, the value of gold and silver is determined by the amount of socially necessary labour expended on their production. In the good old days before the First World War, one could go to the bank and demand a silver coin in exchange for one's banknote. Money was "as good as gold". But all that has changed.

If a private individual prints banknotes in the cellar of his home, he runs the risk of being arrested for forgery. The law says, quite correctly, that these notes are worthless because there are no objective values to back them up. But if the state decides to increase the money supply, that is to say, to increase the amount of paper money in circulation, even when it is not backed up by either gold or other commodities, nobody can say anything about it. But by so doing, all that the state does is to change the relation between the amount of paper money in circulation and the commodities it can buy. The inevitable result is inflation.

The history of political economy knows many periods when the debasement of the currency led to a general rise in prices. A long time ago in England, Henry VIII needed money to pay for his fleet. One of his advisers came up with a brilliant plan (this was the NHP of the 16th century). He advised the king to call in all the gold coins in circulation, mix them with copper and distribute them to the population. They would have exactly the same appearance as before and nobody would notice the difference.

Henry was naturally delighted with the advice of this ancestor of J.M. Keynes and Heinz Dieterich. The plan was put into practice and gave excellent results. The king had twice as much money as before. But unfortunately after a few months, all the prices in the market had doubled. This 16th century Keynesian received the reward he deserved: he lost his head.

Keynesianism in action

The bourgeoisie adopted the so-called Keynesian model in the period after the Second World War, when it was again threatened by revolution and "Communism". For a period it appeared to give good results. The period after 1945 saw an astonishing fireworks display of the productive forces. In the industrialized capitalist countries there was full employment. This was ascribed by bourgeois economists, and particularly the reformists and Social Democrats to the miraculous results of Keynesian economics and "managed capitalism" (capitalism with a human face).

In reality the post-1945 economic upswing was not the result of Keynesianism, which played a subordinate role. The reasons for the post-war economic upswing have been explained by Marxists since the 1950s (see Ted Grant: *Will There Be a Slump?*). There were many different factors, such as post-war reconstruction, the discovery of new industries during the war, and to some extent the increased involvement of the state ("state capitalism") through arms expenditure, deficit financing, nationalization, and above all the expansion of world trade, which, for a temporary period partially mitigated the central contradiction of private ownership of the means of production.

The main factor which acted as a motor-force driving the world economy was the unprecedented expansion of world trade. In the period between 1950 and 1991, the volume of total world exports grew twelve times, while world output grew six times. More startlingly still, the volume of world exports of manufactures rose twenty three times, partly because this is where trade liberalisation was concentrated, while output grew eight times.

These figures clearly show how the rapid expansion of world trade in the post-war period acted as a powerful motor-force which drove the growth in output. This is the secret of the capitalist upswing from 1948-74. It means that, for a whole historical period, capitalism was able partially to overcome its other fundamental problem – the contradiction between the narrowness of the national market and the tendency of the means of production to develop on a global scale.

During the period of capitalist upswing from 1948-74, we saw a staggering increase in the productive forces, fuelled and stimulated by an unprecedented expansion of world trade. The capitalists, above all in Japan, the USA and Western Europe, were prepared to invest colossal sums in expanding the productive forces in pursuit of profit. The productivity of labour increased enormously as a result of a constant revolutionizing of the means of production. New branches of industry were established – plastics, atomic energy, computers, transistors, lasers, robots, etc.

From a Marxist point of view, this was a historically progressive development, which helped to create the material basis for a socialist society. The strengthening of the working class and the squeezing out of the peasantry in Western Europe, Japan and the United States also changed the class balance of forces within society to the advantage of the proletariat.

The theoreticians of reformism were really convinced that capitalism had solved its problems, and that unemployment, booms and slumps were a thing of the past. They spoke in ironic terms of "old fashioned Marxism", which belonged to the 19th century. However, all these dreams of the bourgeois and the Social Democracy were shattered by events. The long period of capitalist expansion came to an end with the recession of 1973-74. Already in that period we saw the re-emergence of mass unemployment, not seen since the 1930s.

Why the bourgeoisie abandoned Keynesianism

What was the reason for the abandonment of Keynesianism and the triumph of monetarism in the last period? Why is it that the bourgeoisie in every country has passed from reform to counter-reform? Was it the result of a caprice on the part of the bourgeois or the madness of Margaret Thatcher? Not at all, it had objective reasons, rooted in the whole of the previous period. The period of the 1970s was a period of high inflation everywhere. In Latin America it reached fantastic levels that created economic chaos. The same situation was beginning to threaten economic stability in Europe and the USA. The bourgeoisie paid a high price for the distortions caused by deficit financing.

In the period 1945-74 capitalism had gone beyond its natural limits. The application of deficit financing produced huge budget deficits and unmanageable rates of inflation everywhere. Trotsky once said that inflation is the syphilis of a planned economy, but this is also applicable to a capitalist market economy. The bourgeois were compelled to squeeze the poison of inflation out of its system. That was the real meaning of monetarism and the economic theories of people like Milton Freedman. There was really nothing new about the theories of Freedman. All they represented was an attempt to return to the old ideas and methods of the past, of capitalism in its raw state, "pure" market economics as they were in the good old days of the 19th century, before governments began to meddle in the workings of the market.

This was a purely reactionary theory, based on the notion of "trickle-down" economics. This has been wittily (but accurately) described by the American economist John Kenneth Galbraith as the theory that all our problems are caused by the fact that the poor have too much money and the rich not enough. It has led to a heavy increase in indirect taxation falling on the shoulders of the poor and a considerable reduction on taxation on the rich. It has also led to sharp cuts in the welfare state everywhere, as the bourgeois attempt to reduce the deficits they have accumulated over the past half century or more.

This is the reason for the "neo-liberal model" about which comrade Dieterich complains so bitterly. In common with all the other petty bourgeois reformists, Dieterich does not want to abolish capitalism, but only to change the *model.* That is why they all use capitalism and neo-liberalism as if they were one and the same thing. They are not. Neo-liberalism and Keynesianism are only the right boot and the left boot of capitalism. It is the choice between inflation and deflation. But for the worker, this is only the choice between death by hanging and death by slow roasting over a fire: that is to say, no choice at all.

From Keynesianism to 'neo-liberalism'

The abandonment of Keynesianism was followed by a return to the old model of "free market" capitalism ("neo-Liberalism"). The underdeveloped countries have been forced through the dictates of the IMF and the World Bank to open up their markets and privatise the nationalized industries. This is really a looting of the state. It will have far-reaching consequences in the next period.

Far from being an advance as they try to claim, it is an expression of the crisis of capitalism. They have created a whole new language ("downsizing", "liberalization", "opening up of the markets", "freeing the economy", etc.) to cover up for what is really a massive destruction of productive forces and jobs. This reminds one of the "Newspeak" of George Orwell's novel *1984*, where the Ministry of Plenty presides over shortages, the Ministry of Peace is the Ministry of War, and the Ministry of Love is the secret police.

The advocates of the free market conveniently forget that capitalism developed precisely on the basis of high tariff barriers and protectionism. In the early phase of capitalism British capitalism sheltered behind high trade barriers in order to defend its own nascent national industries. Only when its industry became strong did the British bourgeoisie become a fervent advocate of the principle of free trade. The same was true of France, Germany, America, Japan and all the others who now preach the virtues of free trade to the nations of Africa, Asia and Latin America. But this process creates new contradictions. Sections of the state apparatus and the national bourgeoisie see how this cuts their own share of the cake and also fear an explosion on the part of the masses.

In pursuit of short-term gains, the imperialists are provoking the masses in the ex-colonial world to the limits of their endurance. At a certain point, the whole process we have seen in the last twenty years will be thrown into reverse. Therefore we can conclude that in the next period, given the impasse of capitalism in the colonial countries, the backlash against privatisation and the pressing needs of the masses in these countries, we will witness new movements in the direction of revolution. This is shown by the Bolivarian Revolution in Venezuela, which itself was the result of the Caracazo, which was in turn the result of the application of free market economics by Carlos Andrés Pérez, following the dictates of the IMF.

The USA in the 1990s managed to achieve a relatively high rate of growth – partly at the expense of the working class and partly at the expense of its rivals. But this was on the basis of a consumer boom, which has now reached its limits. Bourgeois economists are now warning of the risk of recession and the next slump, when it comes, is likely to be severe. The long period of relative peace and prosperity in the advanced capitalist countries is drawing to a close. In the first decade of the 21st century the world is faced with a new period of wars, civil wars, revolution and counter-revolution. In the course of this period, the destiny of humanity will be settled, one way or another.

Over many decades, all the contradictions have been piling up. What way out can there be for capitalism? As Lenin used to say, the truth is always concrete. The bourgeois have tried Keynesianism and Monetarism. Both ultimately failed – the second far more quickly than the first. They can try a mix of both these witches' brews. That will bring them the worst of all worlds – a mixture of inflation and deflation, which will rapidly provoke new social and political convulsions. This means that the contradictions of capitalism must express themselves in an ever sharper conflict between the classes.

Dieterich's capitalist perspective

The recent boom was kept going by a massive expansion of credit and debt in the USA. As Marx explains, credit can temporarily take capitalism beyond its limits, before bouncing back like an elastic band stretched almost to breaking-point. There was a colossal increase in the public, private and corporate indebtedness in the USA, creating an artificial consumer boom which benefited the rest of the world for a while, but which has now collapsed.

The bourgeois economists manifest their total confusion and inability to understand the nature of the present crisis. They were forced to abandon the discredited ideas of Keynesianism and deficit financing, having burnt their fingers badly. But now the policies of neo-Liberalism have also led them into a blind alley. However, comrade Dieterich is undaunted by all this. Like the Bourbons in France he has learnt nothing and forgotten nothing. Now the *Junge Welt* interviewer comes to the point:

"*Q*: You state that, in middle range and in the long run, it is the economic elite who set the political course for a country. You are advocating a new kind of Keynesian development. But your Keynesianism proposes to stabilize capitalism rather than dispose of it. One could deduce from that that you want to strengthen the private economy rather than prepare the way for socialism, which seems paradoxical."

That is quite correct. The entire perspective of Heinz Dieterich is based on the continuation of capitalism for the foreseeable future, and his aim is precisely to stabilize capitalism rather than dispose of it. If the aim is really to move towards socialism, this would be indeed paradoxical. But since Heinz Dieterich long ago abandoned any idea of the socialist revolution, there is absolutely no paradox here, but only a systematic and consistent defence of capitalism.

However, aware that the masses in Venezuela and other countries are bitterly opposed to capitalism, our Heinz feels the need to cover his backside with the occasional reference to socialism. Answering the somewhat embarrassing question by the *Junge Welt* interviewer, he resorts to subterfuge and evasion:

"We'll have to see which sectors of the economy are strengthened. If the subsidies flow to large industry, transnational corporations, or wealthy landowners, that would of course strengthen international capital and the oligarchy. Some of these concerns of course have hung on to some subsidies; that is simply a question of their power."

Yes, my friend, it is precisely a question of power. And who can deny that, ten years after the start of the Bolivarian revolution, the oligarchy still has quite a lot of power, and that this power is based on their ownership and control of the land, the banks and key sections of industry? The President, following the wishes of the masses, is making inroads on private property, although still not sufficiently. You are doing your best to hold back the process, prevent further nationalizations and defend the power of the counter-revolutionary oligarchy. And no amount of subterfuge and evasion can conceal this fact.

Then Heinz continues: "For example, Chávez is not in a position to break from the large oil concerns. The great oil companies of the US and Russia are in place, and oil concessions are one method of applying the brakes to pressures from the US. But the bulk of the economic development must be organized around the small producers."

So there we are! Chávez is not in a position to break from the large oil concerns. And therefore, the professor concludes, he must meekly accept the dominance of the big US companies over the Venezuelan economy. Isn't this an absolute scandal? Doesn't this go against everything the Bolivarian revolution has ever stood for? And this man still has the nerve to pretend to stand for "Socialism of the 21st Century"! Come, come Heinz, let us at least be serious! You do not stand for socialism, either in the 21st or the 22nd century, but for the continuation of the rule of the big banks and monopolies for ever and ever, amen.

The bulk of the economic development must be organized around the small producers, professor Dieterich informs us – and he somehow manages to keep a straight face. This economics comes not from Marx but straight from the Chicago School, which for the past two decades has been assuring us that the future belongs to small businesses and that "small is beautiful". The purpose of this bourgeois propaganda is to draw our attention away from the fact that today, more than at any time in history, the economy is completely dominated by giant monopolies. Insofar as small producers play a role in the modern economy, it is an entirely subordinate one. The small peasants, shopkeepers, etc., are completely under the thumb of the banks and big monopolies.

Socialism on 'the horizon'

In an interview signed by Yásser Gómez in the magazine *Revista Mariátegui* dated 12/08/06 – that is, after President Chávez had said that socialism was the only answer – Dieterich is asked: "To accept that the only alternative to Neo-liberalism is Keynesianism, for many people may sound like scepticism or defeatism as opposed to more radical changes. What do you think of that?" To which he replies:

"The strategic alternative to Neo-liberalism is, of course, socialism, that is, a post-capitalist civilization, but in these moments *you do not have conditions to make socialism* (sic), because in the first place you do not have the historic project for the new socialism, massively divulged either by the leaders of the social movements, or the politicians, or by governments. This theory has scarcely reached its degree of maturity that permits it to be realized through the work of four scientific schools [?]. Furthermore, you do not have mass movements or vanguards integrated on a Latin American scale to carry it out, *it would be a chimera to speak of socialism as an alternative to neo-liberal capitalism.* The immediate alternative is Keynesianism, developmental State capitalism. Of course, this [will have] the strategic horizon of socialism, and will have to combine both elements, because the peasants, the unemployed want an immediate solution and *socialism cannot be the immediate answer.* We have to link the two historical projects: Keynesianism and Socialism of the 21st Century." [17]

The ancient Israelites had to wait a long time at the foot of Mount Sinai for Moses to come down with the tablets of stone containing the Ten Commandments. Now we will have to wait even longer for Heinz Dieterich and his friends to work out the details of the New Historical Project. Presumably the reason in this inordinate delay is the well-known unreliability of Internet connections, an irritating difficulty which Moses, with simple stone tablets and a direct line to the Almighty, did not have to struggle with.

The fact that nobody has the slightest idea what this theory consists of may go some way to explain its singular lack of support outside the mysterious "four scientific schools", about which nobody knows anything. It seems therefore a little unfair of Heinz to complain bitterly that, so far, his New Historical Project has met with no support, *either with leaders of the social movements, or politicians, or governments, or mass movements or vanguards.*

Because of this notable lack of success in "massively divulging" his theories, Heinz logically concludes that humanity is not yet ready for socialism and must therefore settle for *something less*. This "something" is called capitalism. But since

17. *Revista Mariátegui*, my emphasis, AW.

our Heinz – like so many other university professors – has a profound allergy to calling things by their real name, he prefers to use the expression Keynesianism. This he now baptises as yet another *historical project,* which is destined to co-exist happily with elements of socialism for the foreseeable future, until the whole of humanity finally grasps the NHP and immediately proceeds to "make socialism".

Since Dieterich is so fond of lists, let us lay out his arguments in a way he and everybody else can understand:

1) The neo-liberal model of capitalism has failed.

2) The "strategic solution" is socialism

3) In order to "make" socialism everybody needs to understand the New Historic Project of Heinz Dieterich.

4) Nobody understands the New Historic Project of Heinz Dieterich.

5) Therefore socialism is impossible.

6) Therefore we must accept capitalism.

7) But capitalism is unacceptable.

8) Therefore we must invent a New Historical Project for capitalism to make it acceptable.

9) We will call this Keynesianism, or "capitalism with a human face."

10) We will, of course, still have socialism on the horizon, but it will be so far off it will not worry anybody particularly.

11) The State will rule

12) The capitalists will be happy

13) The workers will be happy

14) Heinz Dieterich will he happy

15) Everyone will be happy

16) Forever and ever. Amen.

For decades the Social Democrats have tried to reform capitalism in order to give it a "human face". In order to do this, they proposed to use the state, which they envisaged as an instrument of social and economic policy above the interests of classes. The idea of a "democratic state" under capitalism is as old as the idea of the People's State (Volkstaat), which Marx and Engels subjected to a merciless criticism. This is entirely false from a theoretical point of view and entirely disastrous from a practical standpoint. Marx, Engels and Lenin explained that the state – any state – is the instrument of oppression of one class over another. As long as the working class does not take power, the state will remain a bourgeois state and will be used by the exploiters to oppress the working class.

It is true that after the Second World War, for entirely exceptional historical reasons, in a number of countries (mainly, but not entirely, the privileged nations of Western Europe), the capitalists used Keynesian methods to assist the economic upswing and were able to give certain concessions to the working class. However, this was an historic exception and by the 1970s had reached its limits. The Keynesian model showed its complete bankruptcy and the bourgeoisie threw it into the rubbish bin, from where it has been pulled out by Heinz Dieterich who presents it as the very latest thing in economic theory and the cornerstone of 21st Century Socialism.

The questioner from *Revista Mariátegui* was quite right to say that this advocacy of Keynesianism (that is, capitalism) is precisely an expression of complete scepticism and defeatism in relation to the possibility of carrying out the socialist transformation of society. In order to cover his backside, Dieterich is obliged to make all kinds of qualifications: "*of course*" socialism is the answer in the long run; *of course*, when we introduce state capitalism, socialism will still be "*on the horizon*", etc. But these are, as usual, only a smoke-screen calculated to deceive the workers, while in practice defending an anti-socialist, capitalist policy.

There is absolutely no ambiguity about Dieterich's position: the only possible solution is capitalism for the foreseeable future. But since this is a very bitter pill for the workers and peasants to swallow, Dr. Dieterich immediately gives it a generous coating of sugar: this is not the nasty, brutal old capitalism, he says, but *Keynesianism – capitalism with a human face*. And in the meantime we shall still, of course, have socialism as a "*horizon*". This reminds me of an old joke I heard many years ago while studying in the Soviet Union in the Brezhnev period. The economy was already practically stagnant, but the Stalinist bureaucracy was still talking about "building communism".

A Party Secretary comes to explain the results of the last Five Year Plan to the workers on a collective farm. He is asked in turn why there were no eggs, butter, shoes, and so on. In answer to each question the Party Secretary answers with a broad smile: "Yes, we do not have any of these things, but don't worry comrades. Remember: socialism is on the horizon". After the meeting one of the peasants who did not understand all these long words, looked up the word "horizon" in the dictionary and found the following definition: *an imaginary line which, as you approach it, gets further away*.

The answer is – deficits

In the same interview, the Founder of 21st Century Socialism is asked whether Bolivia can carry out the socialist transformation of society. On this point he is vehement: "*No, there is no way to socialism in Bolivia*, because you cannot fly if you do not have an aeroplane, the objective and theoretical conditions in our peoples for socialism are not given, you have to create them." [18]

This is exactly the same song that the Russian Mensheviks used to sing when they opposed the "utopian" ideas of Lenin and Trotsky: "How can we talk of social-

18. Ibid. my emphasis, AW.

ism in Russia when 'our people' lack 'the objective and theoretical conditions' for it? We must not attempt to introduce socialism but must fight for a democratic bourgeois republic, which is the best we can get. First we will build a strong democratic national capitalism. Then, maybe in fifty or a hundred years time, we can begin to talk about socialism in Russia."

The position of the Russian Mensheviks, which Lenin attacked mercilessly, was a mechanical caricature of Marxism. Like Dieterich, the Mensheviks presented Marxism in a castrated form, Marxism without the class struggle, without revolution, without dialectics: a lifeless caricature that had nothing in common with the real revolutionary ideas of Marx and Engels. Nevertheless, the ideas of the Mensheviks were infinitely more correct and logical than those of Heinz Dieterich. They did not chatter on about some ridiculous New Historical Project that they had invented to save suffering humanity. They produced very solid arguments, based on the material and cultural backwardness of Russia to show that the material basis for the construction of socialism was absent in their country.

That argument was correct as far as it went. Nobody, least of all Lenin, argued that socialism could be built in backward Russia. But Lenin and Trotsky also understood that it was impossible to carry out the programme of the bourgeois-democratic revolution in Russia without overthrowing and expropriating the landlords and capitalists. They were not afraid to take power in an economically underdeveloped country. But they did not regard the socialist revolution in Russia as a self-sufficient act but only the first act in the European and world revolution.

In his advice to the people of Bolivia Dieterich opposes the position of Lenin and the Bolsheviks and repeats almost word for word the arguments of the Mensheviks. The Bolivian workers and peasants must not take power because "our people" lack "the objective and theoretical conditions" for it. What the people of Bolivia and Venezuela need, according to Dieterich, is not socialism but a good dose of Keynesianism:

"What is happening is that Keynesian governments improve your conditions for working with the people and creating consciousness. That is what – correctly – Hugo Chávez is doing. Ninety five percent of the resources of labour [?] is being invested in defending the revolution against the oligarchy and the gringos and the construction of the Keynesian economy, and in generating conditions for socialism. In Bolivia there are strong movements with a socialist political consciousness from the past like the Central Obrera Boliviana (COB) and some elements of the conservative socialism of the past. So what you need in Bolivia is systematic work with the people, so that they can pass over to the vision of Socialism of the 21st. Because the historical socialism today is no longer viable. In the 21st century, you can only have the capitalism of the 21st Century or the Socialism of the 21st Century." [19]

19. Ibid.

We have already learned that socialism is not feudalism and that caterpillars crawl and butterflies fly. Now we learn that "one cannot fly if one does not have an aeroplane". Moreover, we are informed that in the 21st century, you can only have 21st century capitalism or 21st Century Socialism. One cannot, alas, aspire to capitalism or socialism of, say, the 15th century or the 23rd century, but must settle for whatever our own times permit us. This childishness is paraded as profound and original thought! What is really meant, however, is that the only real choice is not (as we foolishly thought) between capitalism and socialism but between capitalism and – *Heinz Dieterich's New Historical Project.* Since, as we have seen, that is the same as capitalism under another name (leaving socialism on the far distant horizon) we conclude that there is not much choice before us at all.

This is what Dieterich has to say about Venezuela: "In the case of Venezuela, it finds itself in the declaratory phase of Socialism of 21st Century [but] the systemic conditions for a socialist system have not been made. The first condition, for example, is to change the accountability of the firms over to value, based on the time employed, leaving behind price, which is the key element in the market economy, [and] this has not been done." [20]

Isn't this simply amazing? The two countries in Latin America where the masses have moved to take power on several occasions, showing enormous revolutionary energy and a high level of class consciousness are precisely Bolivia and Venezuela. That these countries are ripe for socialist revolution is beyond question. Yet this intellectual pedant assures us that socialism is out of the question in both cases. Why? Because the masses in these countries have not yet reached a sufficient level of maturity to read Heinz Dieterich's books and discover for themselves the deep secrets of 21st Socialism à la Dieterich!

We have already said enough on the subject of the Peters-Dieterich "theory" of equivalence to show that it is complete nonsense with no theoretical basis and absolutely no practical application. Yet Dieterich wants the workers of Venezuela (and everywhere else) to put aside all other tasks and occupy their time trying to work out the exact amount of labour-time expended on each and every commodity. And according to this man, until they accomplish this task (which is impossible) socialism is out of the question. It is like the tasks that were imposed upon Hercules, deliberately, in order that he should fail. Hercules was very determined and carried out all these impossible tasks. But the Venezuelan workers have better things to do than to waste their time on pettifogging nonsense that has absolutely nothing to do with socialism in this century or any other.

20. Ibid.

How Dieterich 'accelerates'

In an interview in *Rebelión, Hugo Chávez pide acelerar el socialismo del Siglo XXI*, 22/6/2006, Dieterich asks: "What is the first political step towards a socialist economy in Latin America?" And he replies: "The first step towards a socialist economy in Latin America is therefore *not the generalized statization of private property* – because it does not resolve the cybernetic problem – but the substitution of the system of market prices for calculation in values and the interchange of equal values (equivalence). The first step is neither spectacular nor glorious: *it is the prosaic task of establishing socialist accounting, based on value, alongside capitalist accounting, based on price*." (My emphasis.)

We agree with Heinz that what he proposes is "neither spectacular nor glorious": it is the usual petty fiddling and fussing of reformism combined with a large dose of utopianism. How is it possible to establish socialist accounting without a socialist planned economy? What Dieterich wants is to combine socialism with capitalism (that is what is meant by "establishing socialist accounting, based on value, alongside capitalist accounting, based on price"). In other words what he wants is a mixed economy, in which the landlords will own the land, the bankers will own the banks and financial institutions and the capitalists will own the factories, but there will be some nationalized enterprises and small-scale co-operatives. That means that the situation we had in Venezuela before Chávez must continue and nationalization must cease.

Heinz continues: "This first step consists in registering all the internal and external transactions of the enterprise in terms of *time inputs*, that is, values. This is easy to do, because every productive process is based on the factor (vector) time. In fact, the bosses calculate on the basis of the times of production, but they express these times in monetary units, that is, as cost/price, which permits them to appropriate the wealth of others.

"This relation value-price is owing to the fact that in modern digitalized enterprises values can be 'extracted' with extreme rapidity. In one of these Latin American firms where we are conducting a pilot study of a socialist economy, the systems engineers confirm what was by deductive inference an *a priori* truth: that in three weeks they could provide all the values (time expended) necessary for socialist accounting.

"The second step for the installation of a socialist economy consists in the formation of a group of specialists in software that will write programmes that permit us to work out all the flows of the business prices (money), values (time) and volumes (tons, litres, etc.). Through the three commensurable scales of measurement and expression of value of the product, the firm can continue trading in its economic environment of market economy, without violating the existing economic relations, that is, without loss of productivity, production or markets. Speaking with Lenin [sic], a dual power is established within the firm: the logic of socialism alongside the logic of capitalism." [21]

This is yet another superb example of Heinz's unconscious humour. It seems that comrade Dieterich, in addition to all his other remarkable gifts is also a *spiritualist* who is able to converse with the dead. He is "speaking with Lenin", so who are we to argue? Despite this spiritual dialogue with the leader of the October Revolution, we are not entirely convinced. We will not repeat what we have already said about his economy of equivalence, except that it is a completely unscientific amalgam of reformism and utopianism. But how do we arrive from this petty accountancy to Lenin and dual power?

Dual power is a concept first articulated in an article by Lenin, *The Dual Power*, which described a situation in the wake of the February Revolution in which two powers, the workers' councils (or Soviets) and the official state apparatus of the Provisional Government co-existed with each other and competed for power. Lenin argued that this essentially unstable situation constituted an opportunity for the Soviets to take power by overthrowing the Provisional Government and establishing themselves as the basis of a new form of state power. Lenin pointed out that if the leaders of the Soviets were prepared to act with decision to take power it could be done peacefully, without civil war. But the reformist leaders were not prepared to do this. Like comrade Dieterich they insisted that there were no conditions for taking power, the level of the masses was too low, etc.

What has Lenin's revolutionary idea got to do with the reformist tinkering of Dieterich? Instead of advocating the establishment of workers' control and action committees (soviets), which would really bring about a situation of dual power in Venezuela, Dieterich opposes workers' control and instead calls on the workers of Venezuela to waste their precious time calculating "true value" and sticking two labels on every commodity where previously there was only one. This does not threaten capitalism in the slightest, nor does it advance us one single step towards socialism. It is therefore "dual power" only inside comrade Dieterich's brain.

Undeterred, our Heinz continues with his glorious vision of the future: "Once we have made these *two great advances* the moment has arrived, to make the third step in the *implantation of a socialist economy in a market economy*." [22]

There is a poem by E.V. Rieu entitled *Night Thought of a Tortoise suffering from insomnia on a Lawn*, which goes like this:

"The world is very flat.
There is no doubt of that."

The tortoise concerned was a very profound philosopher and as he advanced slowly across the lawn he drew the most portentous conclusions. For some reason or other, this philosophical tortoise came into my mind when reading the above lines. Our Heinz can see two great advances, where we ordinary mortals can see

21. Ibid.
22. Ibid. My emphasis, AW.

none at all. But then the tortoise also imagined he was moving very fast... Let us confine ourselves to the observation that comrade Dieterich, like the philosophical tortoise, does not like sudden movements or violence of any sort. He crawls towards socialism with his heavy shell on his back, into which he can withdraw his head the moment there is any sign of danger.

One thing is clear: in this world of tortoise socialism there is no room for revolution. No! Gradually and imperceptibly we will have the "implantation of a socialist economy in a market economy". And what will the owners of the means of production be doing while this "implantation" is taking place? Presumably they will be quietly tucked up in their beds, just like the owners of the tortoise's lawn. But let the tortoise socialist continue on his way:

"Once we know the value and price, the products of a socialist enterprise are put on sale with the two units of measurement. The packaging of a litre of milk, for example, would carry the following denomination: Price: 2,000 bolívares; Value: 10 minutes. Upon buying different products, the purchaser will realise that the relation between value and price varies. For example, that in one product 10 minutes of work is expressed in 2,000 bolívares and that in another product they are worth 10,000 bolívares. The cognitive dissonance aroused by both expressions generates inevitably a process of reflection and social discussion, which generates socialist consciousness.

"That is, by expressing the value of the product with an objective and transparent medium, the socialist (time) and, at the same time, a dictatorial and exploitative medium, the capitalist (price), the duality of the socialist and capitalist economic logic is extended from the enterprise to the everyday life of the citizens: from the sphere of production of commodities to the sphere of circulation, the market, the heart of the capitalist system. There can be no more pedagogical and striking way of bringing home to the citizen the problem of socialist economy than this.

"Last week a group of young Venezuelans asked me to assess the possibility of constructing a nucleus of endogenous development, based on the economy of equivalence. I gave it to them in the sense of this essay. Together with the big company employing thousands of workers somewhere in the Patria Grande, these young people represent the first models of the implementation of a socialist economy that represents a civilizing model qualitatively different to the market economy.

"Advancing on the basis of the experience of these two models or prototypes of socialist enterprise, we can gradually extend the number of national enterprises that operate on the principle of the economy of equivalence, until finally they will be the dominant economic element of the national-regional system. It is through the multiplication of these experiences of political economy that we will lay solid bases for Socialism of the 21st Century in the Patria Grande."

And Heinz finishes with the following admonition: *"If the President is looking for the accelerator for his socialist project, here it is!"* [23]

In all our reading of Heinz's works we have found many things, but we have never found anything remotely resembling a sense of humour. Therefore we can only assume that this sentence is meant quite seriously. Heinz Dieterich is furiously slamming his foot on the brakes and at the same time shouting loudly: "this is how to accelerate!" We have already noted that in 21st Century Socialism anything is possible, so it is likely that under this system drivers will be required by law to accelerate – by braking. But since we have not yet arrived at the 21st Century Socialist Paradise, we strongly advise to those who wish to travel faster not to pay the slightest attention to our Heinz.

23. Heinz Dieterich, *Hugo Chávez pide acelerar el socialismo del Siglo XXI.*

8. Socialism or Stalinism?

Socialism and democracy

Since the fall of the USSR a whole new literary-historical genre has been born. More than a genre, it is a whole new industry, and moreover, it is an industry with a very satisfactory rate of profit. Every year a new pile of books and articles pours onto the market, each one with "new and startling revelations" about Lenin, Trotsky and the Bolsheviks. The purpose of this new and profitable line of production is quite clear. It is not at all to serve the interests of historical truth or to advance scientific research: it is to blacken the name of the leaders of the Russian Revolution and to cover them with dirt. Hugo Chávez has stated many times that his conception of socialism in the 21st century has nothing in common with the bureaucratic and totalitarian caricature of socialism that existed in the Soviet Union under Stalin and Brezhnev. But that also had nothing in common with the ideas of Marx and Lenin, which were profoundly democratic.

In his television programme *Aló Presidente* of 27th March, 2005, Hugo Chávez explained that he stood for socialism and a participatory democracy in accordance "with the original ideas of Karl Marx and Frederick Engels." The President's words are quite clear. How did Marx and Engels view the question of democracy? The founders of scientific socialism did not invent schemes for the new society, as Comrade Dieterich attempts to do. They based themselves on the real movement of the working class, in particular, the experience of the Paris Commune of 1871.

Marx explained that the workers cannot simply lay hold of the old state apparatus and use it to change society. He developed his theory of workers' power in *The Civil War in France: Address of the General Council of the International Working Men's Association, 1871*. What is the essence of this theory? Marx pointed out that the old state could not serve as an instrument to change society. It had to be destroyed and replaced with a new state power – a workers' state – that would be completely different to the old state machine, "the centralized state power, with its ubiquitous organs of standing army, police, bureaucracy, clergy, and judicature". It would be a semi-state, to use Marx's expression, dedicated to its own disappearance:

"The Commune was formed of the municipal councillors, chosen by universal suffrage in the various wards of the town, responsible and revocable at short terms. The majority of its members was naturally working men, or acknowledged representatives of the working class. The Commune was to be a working, not a parliamentary body, executive and legislative at the same time.

"Instead of continuing to be the agent of the Central Government, the police was at once stripped of its political attributes, and turned into the responsible, and at all times revocable, agent of the Commune. So were the officials of all other branches of the administration. From the members of the Commune downwards, the public service had to be done at *workman's wage*. The vested interests and the representation allowances of the high dignitaries of state disappeared along with the high dignitaries themselves. Public functions ceased to be the private property of the tools of the Central Government. Not only municipal administration, but the whole initiative hitherto exercised by the state was laid into the hands of the Commune.

"Having once got rid of the standing army and the police – the physical force elements of the old government – the Commune was anxious to break the spiritual force of repression, the 'parson-power', by the disestablishment and disendowment of all churches as proprietary bodies. The priests were sent back to the recesses of private life, there to feed upon the alms of the faithful in imitation of their predecessors, the apostles." [1]

This bears absolutely no relation to the bureaucratic totalitarian regime of Stalinist Russia where the state was a monstrous repressive power standing above society. Even the word "dictatorship" in Marx's day had an entirely different connotation to that which we attach to it today. After the experience of Stalin, Hitler, Mussolini, Franco and Pinochet the word dictatorship signifies concentration camps, the Gestapo and the KGB. But Marx actually had in mind the dictatorship of the Roman Republic, whereby in a state of emergency (usually war) the usual mechanisms of democracy were temporarily suspended and a dictator ruled for a temporary period with exceptional powers.

The Paris Commune was a very democratic form of popular government. Lenin and the Bolsheviks modelled the Soviet state on the same lines after the October Revolution. The workers took power through the soviets, which were the most democratic organs of popular representation ever invented. Despite the conditions of terrible backwardness in Russia the working class enjoyed democratic rights. The 1919 Party Programme specified that "all the working masses without exception must be induced to take part in the work of state administration". Direction of the

1. Marx, *The Civil War in France, The Third Address, May, 1871*. [The Paris Commune].

planned economy was to be mainly in the hands of the trade unions. This document was immediately translated into all the main languages of the world and widely distributed. However, by the time of the purges in 1936 it was already regarded as a dangerous document and all copies of it were quietly removed from all libraries and bookshops in the USSR.

The state and revolution

These Marxist principles were followed by Lenin in the Russian Revolution. In one of his most famous books, *State and Revolution*, written in the revolutionary days of 1917, Lenin laid down the four conditions for Soviet power – not for Socialism or Communism, but for the first days of workers' power. Using the Paris Commune as a prototype, Lenin argued for the abolition of parliamentarism by turning "representative institutions from mere 'talking shops' into working bodies". This would be done by removing the "division of labour between the legislative and the executive."

1) "All officials, without exception, to be elected and subject to *recall at any time*" and so "directly responsible to their constituents." "Democracy means equality." [2]

2) The "immediate introduction of control and superintendence by *all*, so that *all* shall become 'bureaucrats' for a time and so that, therefore, *no one* can become a 'bureaucrat'." Proletarian democracy would "take immediate steps to cut bureaucracy down to the roots [...] to the complete abolition of bureaucracy" since the "*essence* of bureaucracy" is officials becoming transformed "into privileged persons divorced from the masses and *superior* to the masses." [3]

3) There should be no special bodies of armed men standing apart from the people "since the majority of the people itself suppresses its oppressors, a 'special force' is no longer necessary." Using the example of the Paris Commune, Lenin suggested this meant "abolition of the standing army." Instead there would be the "armed masses."

4) The new workers' state would be "the organization of violence for the suppression of ... the exploiting class, i.e. the bourgeoisie. The toilers need a state only to overcome the resistance of the exploiters" who are "an insignificant minority", that is "the landlords and the capitalists". This would see "an immense expansion of democracy ... for the poor, democracy for the people" while, simultaneously, imposing "a series of restrictions on the freedom of the oppressors, the exploiters, the capitalists ... their resistance must be broken by force: it is clear that where is suppression there is also violence, there is no freedom, no democracy." [4]

2. Ibid.
3. Ibid.
4. Ibid., pp. 381-491.

For Lenin, as we see, the dictatorship of the proletariat signified the introduction of complete democracy for the people. The new workers' state would no longer be a state in the old sense but a *semi-state*, destined to gradually disappear as society advanced to socialism and a free association of producers. It is true that, under difficult conditions where the revolution was isolated amidst terrible backwardness, hunger and illiteracy, there were inevitable distortions. As early as 1920 Lenin said that "ours is *a workers' state with bureaucratic deformations*". But these were relatively small deformations, and nothing like the monstrous regime later established by Stalin.

The first condition for the establishment of a real workers' democracy is the active participation of the masses in the revolution from the very beginning. A revolution by its very essence is the work of the masses and can only succeed to the degree that it mobilizes and arms the masses. In November 1917 Lenin wrote an appeal in *Pravda*: "Comrades, working people! Remember that now you yourselves are at the helm of state. No one will help you if you yourselves do not unite and take into your hands all affairs of state. *Get on with the job yourselves; begin right at the bottom, do not wait for anyone.*" [5]

In December 1917 Lenin wrote: "One of the most important tasks of today, if not the most important, is *to develop [the] independent initiative of the workers, and of all the working and exploited people generally, develop it as widely as possible in creative organizational work.* At all costs we must break the old, absurd, savage, despicable and disgusting prejudice that only the so-called upper classes, only the rich, and those who have gone through the school of the rich, are capable of administering the state and directing the organizational development of socialist society." [6]

There are hundreds of similar passages in Lenin's writings that express the same idea: that socialism, from the very beginning, must be built up by the workers themselves, by the creative initiative of the masses. These lines show how anxious Lenin was for the masses to involve themselves in the running of industry and the state. It is true that in the end the workers lost control of the state, but not because of any inherent error in the ideas of Marx and Lenin, but as the result of adverse objective conditions.

The real cause of the problems faced by the Bolsheviks was the isolation of the revolution. Lenin and Trotsky formed the Communist International in 1919 as a means of breaking out of this isolation. This was the only way forward. The 1919 Party Programme was written in terms of uncompromising proletarian internationalism. It started from the premise that the era of the world-wide proletarian revolution had begun. It explained that "deprivation of political rights and any kind of limitation of freedom are necessary as temporary measures" due to war and that "the Party will aim to replace and completely abolish them". But this aim was postponed

5. Lenin, *Collected Works*, Vol. 26, p. 297, my emphasis, AW.
6. Ibid. p. 409, my emphasis, AW.

by the invasion of the Soviet state by 21 armies of foreign intervention that plunged the country into a bloodbath.

In the period of so-called War Communism the military defence of the Revolution was paramount. The millions who enrolled into the Red Army had to be fed and clothed. Requisitioning was vital if the workers and soldiers were to survive. The whole of Soviet society was put on a war footing. The so-called policy of War Communism represented a desperate and heroic attempt to defend the revolution against all the odds.

On the 7th March 1918, Lenin weighed up the situation: "Regarded from the world-historical point of view, there would doubtlessly be no hope of the ultimate victory of our revolution if it were to remain alone, if there were no revolutionary movements in other countries. When the Bolshevik Party tackled the job alone, it did so in the firm conviction that the revolution was maturing in all countries and that in the end – but not at the very beginning – no matter what difficulties we experienced, no matter what defeats were in store for us, the world socialist revolution would come – because it is coming; would mature – because it is maturing and will reach full maturity. I repeat, our salvation from all these difficulties is an all-European revolution." [7]

He then concluded: "At all events, under all conceivable circumstances, if the German Revolution does not come, we are doomed." [8] Weeks later he repeated the same position: "Our backwardness has put us in the front-line, and we shall perish unless we are capable of holding out until we shall receive powerful support from workers who have risen in revolt in other countries." [9]

The main task was to hold on to power for as long as possible. Lenin never envisaged the prolonged isolation of the Soviet state. Either the isolation would be broken or the Soviet regime would be doomed. Everything depended upon the world revolution. Its delay created enormous difficulties that were to have profound consequences. Instead of the withering away of the state, the opposite process took place. On the basis of destitution aggravated by the civil war and economic blockade, the struggle for individual existence, to use Marx's phrase, did not disappear or soften, but assumed in succeeding years an unheard of ferocity. Rather than building on the foundations of the most advanced capitalism, the Soviet regime was attempting to overcome pre-capitalist problems. The task became "catch up with Europe and America". This was very far from the lower stage of communism envisaged by Marx. The Bolsheviks were forced to tackle economic and cultural problems that had long ago been solved in the West. Lenin once declared that socialism was "Soviet power plus electrification" to illustrate the basic task at hand.

7. Lenin, *Collected Works*, vol. 27, p. 95.
8. Ibid. p. 98.
9. Ibid. p. 232.

The terrible backwardness of Russia, coupled with the isolation of the revolution, began to bear down on the Soviet working class. Civil war, famine and physical exhaustion forced them into political apathy and gave rise to increasing bureaucratic deformations in the state and party. International assistance was vital to ensure the survival of the young Soviet republic. All the Bolsheviks could do was to hold on to power – despite all the odds – for as long as possible until assistance came from the West. "History gives nothing free of cost," wrote Trotsky in 1923. "Having made a reduction on one point – in politics – it makes us pay the more on another – in culture. The more easily (comparatively, of course) did the Russian proletariat pass through the revolutionary crisis, the harder becomes now its socialist constructive work." [10]

From War Communism to the NEP

Lenin's uncompromising internationalism was not the product of sentimental utopianism, but on the contrary, of a realistic appraisal of the situation. Lenin was well aware that the material conditions for socialism did not exist in Russia, but they did exist on a world scale. The world socialist revolution would prevent the revival of those barbarous features of class society, which Marx referred to as "all the old crap" by guaranteeing at its inception a higher development than capitalist society. This was the reason why Lenin placed such strong emphasis on the perspective of international revolution, and why he devoted so much time and energy to the building of the Communist International.

Quite rapidly on the basis of a world wide plan of production and a new world division of labour, this would give rise to a mighty impulse to the productive forces. Science and modern technique would be used to harness nature and turn deserts into fertile plains. All the destruction of the planet and the appalling waste of capitalism would be brought to an end. Within a generation or so the material basis for socialism would be laid.

Over time, the tremendous growth of production would eliminate all material inequality and provide for a superabundance of things that would universally raise the quality of life to unheard-of levels. All the basic human needs would be satisfied by such a planned world economy. As a consequence, classes would dissolve into society, together with the last vestiges of class society – money and the state. This would give rise to genuine communism and the replacement of the domination of man by man with the administration of things, to use Engels' expression.

Yet the overthrow of capitalism did not follow this pattern. Rather than the working class coming to power in the advanced industrial countries, the capitalist system was to break, in Lenin's words, "at its weakest link". Weak Russian capital-

10. Trotsky, *Problems of Everyday Life*, p. 20.

ism paid the price for the bankruptcy of world capitalism. The Russian bourgeois had come on to the historic stage too late and was incapable of carrying through the tasks of the national-democratic revolution, which had been carried through long ago in the West.

However, through the law of uneven and combined development, foreign capital had established the largest and most modern industries in the cities of Russia, uprooting the peasantry and creating a proletariat virtually overnight. This new working class, on the basis of experience, was to look towards the most modern ideas of the workers' movement that reflected its needs – Marxism – and was the first proletariat to carry through the socialist revolution to a conclusion.

The fact that Russia was a backward country would not have been a problem if such a revolution had been a prelude to a successful world socialist revolution. That was the aim of the Bolshevik Party under Lenin and Trotsky. Internationalism was no sentimental gesture, but was rooted in the international character of capitalism and the class struggle. In the words of Trotsky: "Socialism is the organization of a planned and harmonious social production for the satisfaction of human wants. Collective ownership of the means of production is not yet socialism, but only its legal premise. The problem of a socialist society cannot be abstracted from the problem of the productive forces, which at the present stage of human development are worldwide in their very essence." [11]

Lenin and the Bolshevik Party never envisaged the Russian Revolution as a self-sufficient act, but as the beginning of the world socialist revolution. The Russian Revolution acted as a beacon to the workers of the world. In particular, it gave a mighty impetus to the German Revolution. But the cowardice of the Social Democratic leaders in Western Europe led to the defeat of the revolution in Germany, Italy and other countries, and the isolation of the Russian Revolution in conditions of appalling backwardness. Already by 1919 the number of industrial workers declined to 76 percent of the 1917 level, while that of building workers fell to 66 percent, railway workers to 63 percent. The figure for industrial workers generally fell to less than half from three million in 1917 to 1,240,000 in 1920. The population of Petrograd alone fell from 2,400,000 in 1917 to 574,000 in August 1920.

Under these circumstances, the Stalinist political counter-revolution became inevitable. The bureaucratic degeneration of the Russian Revolution did not emerge from some theoretical flaw in Bolshevism, but from crushing backwardness. The young Soviet Republic had been saved by international working class solidarity, but isolation was the cause of enormous cost and suffering. The Russian working class was stretched to breaking point. Physically exhausted and numerically weakened, it was faced with insurmountable cultural, economic and social obstacles. Herculean efforts were needed simply to hold out against imperialist encirclement.

11. Trotsky, *History of the Russian Revolution*, p. 1237.

Lenin had an honest and realistic attitude to the terrible problems that the Russian proletariat faced as a result of isolation and backwardness. In January 1919, he explained in a speech to the Russian trade unions: "The workers were never separated by a Great Wall of China from the old society. And they have preserved a good deal of the traditional mentality of capitalist society. The workers are building a new society without themselves having become new people, or cleansed of the filth of the old world; they are still standing up to their knees in that filth. We can only dream of clearing the filth away. It would be utterly utopian to think this could be done all at once. It would be so utopian that in practice it would only postpone socialism to kingdom come." [12]

Under the immensely difficult conditions that followed the Civil War, the Bolsheviks were compelled to make a tactical retreat, making concessions to the market and to the rich peasants (kulaks). This was the origin of the New Economic Policy. Within a short space of time industry began to revive. Production doubled in 1922 and 1923, although from a low base, and had managed to reach its pre-war level by 1926. Harvests were modestly increasing. The NEP had provided a breathing space, but the market had brought increasing social differentiation in its wake.

This retreat was completely justified, with increased production as a consequence, but it also gave rise to restorationist dangers with the enrichment of those hostile to socialism in town and country. The growth of the nascent bourgeois elements – the NEPmen and kulaks – was a by-product of this new policy. Alongside the re-emergence of class divisions, the rising bureaucracy in the state and party began to flex its muscles, hoping to consolidate and extend its position and influence. Under these conditions, the growth of these alien class and bureaucratic elements represented a mortal danger to the Revolution. Out of the continued isolation of the workers' state arose the threat of an internal bureaucratic degeneration.

Defending these concessions at the Tenth Congress, Lenin referred to the crushing pressure of the peasant masses on the working class as "a far greater danger than all the Denikins, Kolchaks, and Yudenichs [counter-revolutionary generals] put together. It would be fatal," he continued, "to be deluded on this score! The difficulties stemming from the petty-bourgeois element are enormous, and if they are to be overcome, we must have greater unity, and I don't just mean a resemblance of unity. We must all pull together with a single will, for in a peasant country only the will of the mass of the proletarians will enable the proletariat to accomplish the great task of its leadership and dictatorship. Assistance is on its way from the Western European countries but it is not coming quickly enough. Still it is coming and growing." [13]

Lenin, as always, put the matter clearly and honestly. The retreat of the NEP had been dictated by the enormous pressure of the peasantry on the workers' state, iso-

12. Lenin, *Collected Works*, vol. 25, pp. 424-5.
13. Ibid., vol. 32, p.179.

lated by the delay of the socialist revolution in the West. Lenin always referred to it as a temporary state of affairs, a breathing space, before the next dramatic developments of the international socialist revolution. But he was also acutely aware of the dangers that lay on that road, especially the dangers of a revival of the bourgeois and petty-bourgeois elements with the growth of the market economy:

"This peril – the development of small production and of the petty-bourgeois in the rural areas – is an extremely serious one," Lenin warned the Tenth Congress. In answer to those who were inclined to complacency, Lenin emphasised the point: "Do we have classes? Yes we do. Do we have a class struggle? Yes and a most furious one!" [14] These were the pressing considerations that induced Lenin to ban factions in the Party at the Tenth Congress. The reasons are given in the passage quoted from Lenin above, which clearly explains that this extraordinary measure was dictated by the dangers of alien class pressure expressing themselves through groups in the Party and was of a temporary character.

Dieterich and the Russian Revolution

We have grown accustomed to the slanders of the bourgeois and right wing reformists against the Russian Revolution, but over the past two decades there has been a new addition to the anti-communist chorus: the "theoretical" works of the ex-Stalinists who attempt to justify themselves by renouncing Marxist communism and all its works. These works fall into two broad categories: those who openly renounce Marxism and Leninism, and those who do so under false pretences. Heinz Dieterich belongs to the latter category. In an interview in the magazine *Revista Mariátegui* dated 2/2/2007, we read:

"Q. In your opinion, has there been any socialist country in the modern era?

"A. It depends on the criteria that are used for such judgment. As a scientific economist and sociologist, I prefer the parameters that Marx and Engels used: economy of value and participatory democracy. And under those criteria, there has been no socialist society since the French Revolution, although, yes, there have been many heroic and tragic attempts to achieve it."

We read with incredulity the statement that "there has been no socialist society since the French Revolution". Does that mean that the French Revolution was a *socialist* Revolution? Or that there was perhaps a socialist society *before* the French Revolution? We do not know, and comrade Dieterich, who specializes in imitating the Sphinx, has no desire to explain his mysterious utterances. In compensation for the lack of any explanation, he reminds us that he is not just an ordinary economist but a *scientific* economist and, if that were not enough, a sociologist as well. Well, that ought to be enough to silence even the most hardened sceptics!

14. Ibid. vol. 32, page 212.

The French Revolution was a bourgeois revolution. It was not and could not have been a socialist revolution because the means of production had not yet reached a sufficient level of development to achieve a classless society. Industry was as yet in its infancy and the working class was still in an embryonic state. The French Revolution of 1789-93 was carried out by the semi-proletarian and plebeian masses of Paris and the other big cities, with the support of the poor peasants. There were communist elements (as also in the English Revolution in the previous century). But these could not prevail. The masses did all the fighting but in the end the bourgeoisie enjoyed the fruits of the victory over the Ancien Régime.

The material conditions for socialism developed in Western Europe in the course of the 19th century. The rapid development of industry in England created the conditions for the growth of the working class, trade unions and political organizations. The Chartists were the first mass political movement of the working which fought for a programme of political democracy in the first half of the 19th century and were open to socialist and revolutionary ideas. The revolutions that swept the continent of Europe in 1848-49 for the first time showed the revolutionary potential of the working class and also revealed the complete bankruptcy of the bourgeois Liberals, who everywhere played a counter-revolutionary role.

The defeat of the revolutions in France, Germany, Austria and Hungary, paved the way for a further development of the productive forces under capitalism. This gave stability to the capitalist system, which was still in its phase of youthful vigour. The class struggle in England was in abeyance after the defeat of the Chartists. Engels later spoke of the "forty years' winter sleep of the English proletariat". The long delay of the socialist revolution had a material basis. Under these circumstances all the Historical Projects in the world would have made no difference.

The Paris Commune of 1871 was a proletarian revolution that led to the formation of the first workers' state in the world. This was not yet socialism. The Commune did not even nationalize the Bank of France – and this one of its main mistakes, as Marx pointed out. The Communards were crushed by the bourgeois counter-revolution and this prepared the way for a further development of capitalism.

There was a long period of capitalist expansion that lasted approximately from 1871 to the outbreak of the First World War in 1914. This was a period of "globalisation", with the invention of the telegraph and the steamship, and a massive expansion of the railways in the USA, Russia and other countries. It was also a period of imperialism, the enslavement of new colonies and increasing conflicts between the big imperialist powers.

In place of small workshops and "free enterprise" we had the concentration of capital, the formation of big cartels, the increasing domination of the banks and the export of capital. This gave rise to the phenomenon that Lenin described as combined and uneven development. The colonial and semi-colonial countries imported finished goods and capital and exported raw materials. Imperialism had at its disposal a vast army of colonial slaves producing surplus value at far higher rates than the workers at home and thus creating super-profits.

This was exploitation on a grand scale and was precisely based upon unequal exchange – the exchange of more labour for less. This unequal exchange on the world market exists to the present day and is the main mechanism whereby the imperialist countries continue to exploit and plunder the former colonies, even when the latter have long ago achieved formal independence.

In the past, comrade Dieterich had illusions in Stalinism. He still speaks of the former Stalinist economies as "real socialism" and "really existing socialism". Only now he has had second thoughts since 1989. The Soviet Union has collapsed, so it is no longer *really existing*. Therefore, he simply declares the whole "project" impossible. This is what the Germans call "throwing out the baby with the bath water". In one of his articles, comrade Dieterich gives us a brief lesson on the Russian Revolution. It is *very* brief. In fact he disposes of in *four lines*:

"At the fall of the bourgeois-tsarist power in (1917) revolutionary theory had to accomplish three tasks: a) explain the real events, b) conceptualise the necessary economic, military, cultural and political institutions of the future and, c) legitimate the policies of the vanguard (party) to the majority." [15]

Once more Heinz Dieterich poses the question in idealist terms. The task of the Bolsheviks after the overthrow of Tsarism was not to *conceptualize* "institutions of the future", but to actually carry out the socialist transformation of society under extremely difficult objective conditions. The institutions whereby the working class took power and administrated society did not have to be *conceptualized in theory* because they *already existed in practice.* The soviets, which were born as extended strike committees in 1905 and re-emerged in February 1917, were never "conceptualized in theory". They were not anticipated in the writings of Marx, Engels or Lenin, but improvised by the workers themselves. Nobody told them to set up the soviets, they just did it.

To people like Dieterich it is unthinkable that the working class should be capable of achieving its own emancipation. They regard the workers as little children who must be led by the hand to the paradise of Socialism of the 21st Century by kindly intellectual ladies and gentlemen who, out of the goodness of their hearts, condescend to place themselves at the head of suffering humanity and lead it to Salvation. This has nothing in common with Marxism, which bases itself on the self-movement of the revolutionary proletariat. Marx said: the task of the emancipation of the working class is the task of the workers themselves. The Russian Revolution is the best proof of this assertion.

Of course, leadership is necessary, the party is necessary and theory is necessary. These things are necessary because the working class is not entirely homogeneous.

15. Dieterich, *La disyuntiva de Cuba: Capitalismo o nuevo socialismo*, in *Rebelión*, 17/3/2006.

There are more advanced layers and more backward layers. Marx pointed out that the working class without organization is only raw material for exploitation. It is necessary to group the most advanced elements of the class (the vanguard) in a revolutionary party that fights to win the leadership of the class as a whole. There is no contradiction between this and the assertion that the working class must emancipate itself, and the October Revolution completely confirms the truth of this.

Without the leadership of Lenin and Trotsky the Russian Revolution would not have taken place in 1917. Either a workers' dictatorship or fascist reaction: that is the way in which Lenin posed the alternatives in 1917. Without the struggle waged, in particular by Lenin, with all his immense personal authority, the movement would undoubtedly have fallen beneath the mailed fist of reaction. The same choice stands before the people of Venezuela and Bolivia now: either finish the revolutionary task that has been started – that means, expropriate the landlords and capitalists – or sooner or later you will be confronted by a counter-revolutionary overthrow.

Achievements of the Russian Revolution

Nowadays, it is fashionable to belittle the results achieved, or even to deny them altogether. Yet the slightest consideration of the facts leads us to a very different conclusion. Despite all the problems, deficiencies and crimes (which, incidentally, the history of capitalism furnishes us in great abundance), the most astonishing advances were achieved by the nationalized planned economy in the Soviet Union in what was, historically speaking, a remarkably short space of time.

The nationalized planned economy in the USSR furnished proof of the most extraordinary vitality for decades. Such a transformation is unprecedented in the annals of human history. The Revolution radically abolished private ownership of the means of production. For the first time in history, the viability of a nationalized planned economy was demonstrated, not in theory but in practice. Over one-sixth of the earth's surface, in a gigantic, unprecedented experiment, it was proved that it was possible to run society without capitalists, landowners and moneylenders.

Russia in 1917 was considerably more backward than Pakistan today. Under frightful conditions of economic, social and cultural backwardness, the regime of workers' democracy established by Lenin and Trotsky was replaced by the bureaucratic dictatorship of Stalin. This was a terrible reverse, signifying the liquidation of the political power of the working class, but not of the fundamental socio-economic conquests of October, the new property relations, which had their clearest expression in the nationalized planned economy.

The viability of the new productive system was put to a severe test in 1941-45, when the Soviet Union was invaded by Nazi Germany with all the combined resources of Europe at its disposal. Despite the loss of 27 million lives, the USSR succeeded in defeating Hitler, and went on, after 1945, to reconstruct its shattered economy in a remarkably short space of time, transforming itself into the world's second power. From a backward, semi-feudal, mainly illiterate country in 1917, the USSR became a modern, developed economy, with a quarter of the world's scientists, a health and educational system equal or superior to anything found in the West, able to launch the first space satellite and put the first man into space.

Such astonishing advances, in a country that set out from a level more backward than Pakistan today, must give us pause for thought. One can sympathize with the ideals of the Bolshevik Revolution, or oppose them, but such a remarkable transformation in such a short space of time demands the attention of thinking people everywhere. In a period of 50 years, the USSR increased its gross domestic product nine times over.

Despite the terrible destruction of the Second World War, it increased its GDP five times over from 1945 to 1979. In 1950, the GDP of the USSR was only 33 percent that of the USA. By 1979, it was already 58 percent. By the late 1970s, the Soviet Union was a formidable industrial power, which in absolute terms had already overtaken the rest of the world in a whole series of key sectors. The USSR was the world's second biggest industrial producer after the USA and was the biggest producer of oil, steel, cement, asbestos, tractors, and many machine tools. The Soviet space programme was the envy of the world.

Nor is the full extent of the achievement expressed in these figures. All this was achieved without unemployment, which was virtually unknown in the Soviet Union. In fact, it was legally a crime. Moreover, for most of the post-war period, there was little or no inflation. The bureaucracy learned the truth of Trotsky's warning that "inflation is the syphilis of a planned economy". After the Second World War for most of the time the bureaucracy took care to ensure that inflation was kept under control. This was particularly the case with the prices of basic items of consumption. Before perestroika (reconstruction), the last time meat and dairy prices had been increased was in 1962 – twenty years earlier. The USSR had a balanced budget and even a small surplus every year. It is interesting to note that not a single Western government has succeeded in achieving this result (as the Maastricht conditions prove), just as they have not succeeded in achieving full employment and zero inflation, things which also existed in the Soviet Union. The Western critics of the Soviet Union kept very quiet about this, because it demonstrated the possibilities of even a transitional economy, never mind socialism.

Already in *The German Ideology*, written in 1845 to 1846, Marx and Engels explained that "...this development of productive forces (which itself implies the actual empirical existence of men in their world-historical, instead of local, being) is an absolutely necessary practical premise because without it want is merely made general, and with destitution the struggle for necessities and all the old crap would necessarily be reproduced..." [16]

16. Marx and Engels, *The German Ideology*, Feuerbach, part 5, in *Selected Works*, Vol. 1, p. 37.

By the phrase "all the old crap", Marx and Engels had in mind inequality, exploitation, oppression, corruption, bureaucracy, the state and all the other evils endemic in class society. Today, after the fall of Stalinism in Russia, the enemies of socialism try to show that the ideas of Marxism cannot be put into practice. They overlook the little detail that Russia before 1917 was an extremely backward country. Lenin and the Bolsheviks, who were quite well acquainted with the writings of Marx, were well aware that the material conditions for socialism were absent in Russia.

But Lenin and Trotsky never had the idea of a national revolution or "socialism in one country", and least of all in a backward country like Russia. The Bolsheviks took power in 1917 with the perspective of a world revolution. The October Revolution was a powerful impetus for the rest of Europe, beginning with Germany where the revolution could have succeeded had it not been for the cowardly betrayal of the social democratic leaders who saved capitalism. The world paid a terrible price for this crime, with the economic and social convulsions of the two decades between the wars, the triumph of Hitler in Germany, the civil war in Spain and finally the horrors of a new world war.

As Trotsky explains: "That socialization of the capitalist-created means of production is of tremendous economic benefit is today demonstrable not only in theory but also by the experiment of the USSR, not-withstanding the limitations of that experiment. True, capitalistic reactionaries, not without artifice, use Stalin's regime as a scarecrow against the ideas of socialism. As a matter of fact, Marx never said that socialism could be achieved in a single country, and moreover, a backward country. The continuing privations of the masses in the USSR, the omnipotence of the privileged caste, which has lifted itself above the nation and its misery, finally, the rampant club-law of the bureaucrats are not consequences of the socialist method of economy but of the isolation and backwardness of the USSR caught in the ring of capitalist encirclement. The wonder is that under such exceptionally unfavourable conditions planned economy has managed to demonstrate its insuperable benefits." [17]

Dieterich's 'explanation'

How does Heinz Dieterich explain the collapse of the USSR? He refers repeatedly to the implosion of the Soviet Union, but nowhere does he explain the reasons for it. This is not the place to deal in depth with the reasons for the collapse of Stalinism. That has been done elsewhere.[18] Dieterich offers no serious explanation for the collapse of the USSR, for the simple reason that he himself is incapable of understanding it. Yet without explaining this we cannot make a single step forward. The first question asked by workers and young people (and by all honest commu-

17. L. Trotsky, Introduction to *The Living Thoughts of Karl Marx*.
18. See Ted Grant, *Russia, from Revolution to Counter-revolution*.

nists who want to learn from the past in order not to repeat it) is: if socialism is really so good, why did it fail in Russia? This is what Dieterich says in an article in *Rebelión* (27/08/2005):

"5. The conditions for defeating capitalist civilization definitively have been explained with clarity by Lenin, possibly the greatest practical-theoretical revolutionary Socialist ever known in modern times. Those conditions are two: a) a productivity of labour superior to that of capitalism and, b) real participative democracy of the masses.

"6. Under Stalin, both criteria were drained of real content, undermining the viability of the original Historical Project in the medium term. The productivity of labour is, essentially, a function of two factors: the technological level of the productive forces and the rate of surplus value, that is to say, the relation between surplus labour and necessary labour that measures the degree of exploitation of the direct producer.

"Since the USSR did not have access to advanced technology, it was impossible to compete with capitalist labour productivity by this route. The increase of the rate of surplus labour by means of the militarization of labour was the answer of Stalin to the stated dilemma, with the consequence of work and the 'plan' of production became transformed into forces as coercive and alienating for the direct producer (worker) as they had been under capitalism and the market in the previous economy.

"The political absolutism of the Stalinist system, with total absorption and bureaucratic control of all the possible circuits of self-determination and democratic self-organization of the people and the State, by an omnipotent and omnipresent Party, destroyed the second criterion that Lenin had formulated as the precondition for the definitive triumph over capitalism: participative democracy. In this way, the evolutionary unviability of the system in the medium term was sealed and its implosion was only a question of time; unless it returned to the Leninist model of the socialist transition.

"7. Lenin had defined the mode of socialist production by a) a productivity of labour superior to that of capitalist production and, b) real democracy in economy, culture and State. The first criterion was born of the circumstances of extreme destruction and underdevelopment of Russia: it was an imperative necessity of the time. Nowadays it no longer necessary to postulate it in this way, because labour productivity has reached a sufficient level to provide the whole of humanity an adequate standard of life." [19]

It is very gratifying to see that Heinz Dieterich considers Lenin to be: "possibly the greatest practical-theoretical revolutionary Socialist ever known in modern times." (Presumably he has to include the word "possibly" in order to leave some space for Arno Peters and himself.) However, it would have been even better if he

19. Dieterich, *Venezuela: Ten Theses on the New Political Class*, in *Rebelión*, 27/8/2005.

had explained what Lenin had to say about real participative democracy of the masses and the precise nature of the Leninist model of the socialist transition. But since he has forgotten to do so, let us come to his assistance.

The regime established by the October Revolution was neither totalitarian nor bureaucratic, but the most democratic regime yet seen on earth – a regime in which, for the first time, millions of ordinary men and women overthrew their exploiters, took their destiny in their own hands, and at least began the task of transforming society. That this task, under specific conditions, was diverted along channels unforeseen by the leaders of the revolution does not invalidate the ideas of the October Revolution, nor does it lessen the significance of the colossal gains made by the USSR for the 70 years that followed.

After the Bolshevik Revolution the nationalized planned economy achieved unprecedented rates of growth: 20 percent every year under the first Five Year Plans, and ten percent after 1945. But in the period after 1965, the growth rate of the Soviet economy began to slow down. Between 1965 and 1970, the growth rate was 5.4 percent. Over the next seven-year period, between 1971 and 1978, the average rate of growth was only 3.7 percent. This compared to an average of 3.5 percent for the advanced capitalist economies of the OECD.

In other words, the growth rate of the Soviet Union was no longer much higher than that achieved under capitalism, a disastrous state of affairs. As a result, the USSR's share of total world production actually fell slightly, from 12.5 percent in 1960 to 12.3 percent in 1979. In the same period, Japan increased its share from 4.7 percent to 9.2 percent. All Khrushchev's talk about catching up with and overtaking America evaporated into thin air.

Subsequently the growth rate in the Soviet Union continued to fall. By the end of the Brezhnev period, (the "period of stagnation" as it was baptized by Gorbachov) it was reduced to zero. How do we explain this? As Trotsky explained, a nationalized planned economy needs democracy, as the human body requires oxygen. Without the democratic control and administration of the working class, a regime of nationalization and planning would inevitably seize up at a certain point, especially in a modern, sophisticated and complex economy. This fact is graphically reflected in the falling rate of growth of the Soviet economy since the early 1970s, after the unprecedented successes of the planned economy in the earlier period.

The regimes in the USSR and its Eastern European satellites in many ways were the opposite of socialism. They had nothing whatsoever to do with the regime of workers' democracy (soviet democracy) established by the Bolsheviks in 1917. This was completely destroyed by Stalin and the privileged bureaucracy he represented. Under Stalin, Khrushchev and Brezhnev, there was no workers' control or democratic participation. The top bureaucrats decided everything.

The command economy partially worked in the beginning, at the cost of great sacrifices by the masses, at a time when the Soviet Union was under-developed. But by the 1970s, due to the advantages given by the revolution and the abolition of landlordism and capitalism, Russia had developed a powerful developed economy, the second super-power. One million different commodities were being produced in Russia. With an advanced economy, bureaucratic command will not work. The whole economy seized up. From being a relative fetter, the bureaucracy became an absolute fetter on the development of society. And therefore the rule of the bureaucracy was doomed.

Once this stage had been reached, the bureaucracy ceased to play even the relatively progressive role it had played in the past. This is the reason why the Soviet regime entered into crisis. This is now common knowledge. But to be wise after the event is relatively easy. It is not so easy to predict historical processes in advance. But this was certainly the case with Ted Grant's remarkable writings on Russia, which accurately plotted the graph of the decline of Stalinism and predicted its outcome a quarter of a century before the fall of the Berlin Wall. Here alone we find a comprehensive analysis of the reasons for the crisis of the bureaucratic regime, which even today remains a book sealed with seven seals for all other commentators on events in the former USSR.

The isolation of the Russian Revolution in conditions of extreme economic and cultural backwardness was the soil in which the bureaucracy thrived, gradually pushing the workers out of the soviets and concentrating power into its own hands. Under Stalin, all the political gains of the October Revolution were eliminated. The bureaucracy constituted itself into a ruling caste that elevated itself above the working class and ruled in its name.

Like every other ruling class or caste in history, it used the state to defend its power and privileges. All elements of workers' democracy were ruthlessly suppressed and replaced with a repulsive totalitarian dictatorship. In the end, that voracious bureaucracy undermined and destroyed the nationalized planned economy, leading the land of October back to capitalism. Nowadays, the former leaders of the CPSU who used to talk about "socialism" and "communism" are singing the praises of market economics. They have every reason to, since they have plundered the state and converted themselves into the owners of big private monopolies.

Many of the present capitalists in Russia are themselves members of the old nomenklatura, people who not long ago carried a Communist Party card in their pocket and spoke in the name of "socialism". In fact, they had nothing to do with socialism, communism or the working class. They were part of a parasitic ruling caste, which lived a life of luxury on the backs of the Soviet workers. Now, with the same cynicism that always characterized these elements, they have openly gone over to capitalism. But this miraculous transformation cannot be consummated so easily. These people feel a compelling need to justify their apostasy by heaping curses on what they professed to believe in only yesterday. By these means they try to throw dust in the eyes of the masses, while salving their own consciences – always supposing that they possess such a thing, which is, in fact, highly improbable. But even the worst scoundrel likes to find some justification for his actions.

However, what the Western critics of Marxism do not want to publicise is that the movement in the direction of a capitalist market economy in the former Soviet Union and Eastern Europe, far from improving the situation, has caused an unmitigated social and economic disaster. It is true that the productive forces stagnated under Brezhnev, but when the economy was privatised it fell by at least 60 percent – a staggering collapse, far worse than the slump of 1929-32 in the USA. Under the planned economy, the people of the Soviet Union enjoyed a level of life expectancy, health care and education on a level with the most developed capitalist countries, or in advance of them.

What happened to living standards after the restoration of capitalism? *The Financial Times* of 14/2/94 carried a front-page article with the title *Russia faces population crisis as death rate soars*. The article points out that: "In the past year alone, the death rate jumped 20 percent, or 360,000 deaths more than in 1992. Researchers now believe that the average age for male mortality in Russia has sunk to 59 – far below the average in the industrialized world and the lowest in Russia since the early 1960s."

Dieterich's myths and Trotsky's prediction

How does comrade Dieterich explain the collapse of Stalinism? In the article *La disyuntiva de Cuba: Capitalismo o nuevo socialismo*, published in *Rebelión* (17/03/06) we read:

"The ideological 'necessity' to identify falsely (mystify) that which was State, as the social, was the original sin of the scientific social theory and philosophy of the socialist countries. It converted itself into a sterilizing founding myth of the nascent soviet civilization, which impeded the later evolution of revolutionary theory, especially when under the power of the Stalinist Party-State those whom Stalin considered the 'enemies of the people' were sanctioned even with death. 'Enemies of the people' was a reformulation of the Jacobin formula of the 'enemies of the revolution', which not only applied to the Trotskyists and the opposition of 'right' and 'left', but also served as a powerful preventive against any attempt to discover the historic truth of the new civilization."

Here we have a typical specimen of Dieterich's idealist and impressionistic method of analysis. He does not provide any real explanation for the Stalinist political counter-revolution in Russia. What was the reason for this "ideological necessity"? He cannot say because *he does not know*. From a Marxist point of view, if an idea (even an incorrect idea) is put forward and gets powerful support in society, it follows that this idea represents the interests of a class or caste in society. The question that must be asked (and which Dieterich never asks) is: what interests did Stalin represent? What drove him to order the imprisonment and murder of hundreds of thousands of dedicated Leninists ("Trotskyists")?

Comrade Dieterich refers us to Khrushchev's famous secret speech at the XX Congress of the CPSU in 1956. How did Khrushchev explain the crimes of Stalin? He explained them as the result of the cult of personality. This speech, which Dieterich regards as a "transcendental step to return to socialist constitutionality, accompanied by the rehabilitation of innumerable victims", explained *precisely nothing*. Khrushchev and Gorbachev blamed Stalin for the crimes of that epoch. Stalin was a monster. Dieterich agrees with them. But one man, however evil, could not be solely responsible for all these crimes. Stalin represented the counter-revolution of the privileged elite, the bureaucratic caste of millions of officials of the state, the party, the management of industry, the generals and so forth. That was where his power derived. He could not have carried out these crimes without the support of this bureaucracy.

The caste of privileged officials usurped power, taking it out of the hands of the working class. They abolished the movement towards equality and installed enormous privileges for themselves. These were increased over the decades. The top strata in Russian society lived like millionaires. Gorbachev's wife wore diamonds and imported dresses from the top fashion houses of Paris. What sort of socialism is that?

Heinz Dieterich is critical of Khrushchev, but not for the correct reasons. His criticism is that his measures did not lead to "*the deep revision of the founding myth of the nascent Soviet society*, which would have been able to return to Soviet science and art the great potential of emancipation inherent in dialectical materialism. The political destalinization was not followed by an epistemological destalinization of the dominant discourse, which was as essential and unpostponeable as the first." [20]

In his article *Venezuela: modo de producción socialista y fase de transición*, in *Rebelión*, 10/11/05, Dieterich says: "the evolutionary unviability of the system in the medium term was sealed and its implosion was only a question of time; unless it returned to the Leninist model of the socialist transition." This is what comrade Dieterich writes *today*. But if the collapse of the USSR and its return to capitalism were inevitable, Heinz Dieterich ought to have been able to predict it in advance.

Where are the predictions of Heinz Dieterich concerning the collapse of the USSR and its return to capitalism? One searches his writings in vain since these predictions were never made. On the contrary, our Heinz, a former Stalinist, was so hypnotised by the achievements of "real socialism" that he still uses this expression whenever he speaks about Stalinism. It is not very difficult to predict things that have already happened. But this is all that our scientific economist and sociologist is capable of.

Where can we find a Marxist analysis of Stalinism and a clear and unambiguous

20. Ibid. My emphasis, AW.

prediction of how it would end? We can find it only in one place: in a book written as long ago as 1936 by the man who was undoubtedly one of the two greatest practical-theoretical revolutionary Socialists ever known in modern times, the man who, alongside Lenin, led the Russian workers and peasants to power in October 1917: Leon Trotsky.

In *The Revolution Betrayed*, Trotsky not only predicted that the Stalinist bureaucracy could end by restoring capitalism in the USSR. He gave a precise description of what would happen afterwards: "*The fall of the present bureaucratic dictatorship, if it were not replaced by a new socialist power, would thus mean a return to capitalist relations with a catastrophic decline of industry and culture.*" [21] These words predict exactly what has happened in Russia since 1991.

Instead of dealing with the real material foundations of Stalinism as the political expression of the material interests of the bureaucracy, Dieterich attributes it to the *founding myth of the nascent Soviet society.* But Soviet society was not founded on a myth at all, but on real relations of production, real class relations and a real legal and state superstructure erected upon them. Without dealing with these questions we can never understand the evolution of the Soviet Union. But our Heinz does not deal with them. Instead he refers us to the rarefied world of *mythology*.

Instead of keeping our feet on the ground we are invited to float gently into the realms of fantasy. This is absolutely typical of the kind of bourgeois sociology that is taught in universities today, and which Heinz evidently feels more at home with than with Marxism. The founders of the Soviet Workers' Republic, Lenin, Trotsky and the Bolshevik Party that they led, were not guided by myths but by the scientific theories of Marx and Engels. The state they created, basing themselves on the movement of the working class, was modelled on the democratic model of the Paris Commune and was expressed through the rule of the soviets.

"The political destalinization," Dieterich complains, "was not followed by an epistemological destalinization of the dominant discourse." What does this mean? Only this: that Dieterich considers that Khrushchev really did carry out destalinization in practice, but failed to carry it out *epistemologically*. Epistemology is a branch of philosophy that investigates the origin, nature, methods, and limits of human knowledge.

So the only fault Dieterich finds with Khrushchev is that *he did not carry his destalinization into this particular branch of Soviet philosophy*. In *El Socialismo del Siglo XXI*, page 19, we read: "The fall of 'really existing' socialism clarified even more the logic of this process, making it evident than the so-called Cold War was not more than an episode in the long 'north-south' war, that is to say, part of the secular problem of western colonialism and imperialism, in which the USSR merely played the tragic role of Spartacus."

Dieterich compares the likes of Stalin, Brezhnev and Gorbachov with the great

21. Trotsky, *The Revolution Betrayed*, Is the Bureaucracy a ruling class? p. 251. My emphasis, AW.

revolutionary and leader of the slaves, Spartacus. It would be difficult to think of a more scandalous comparison. To liken the leader of the greatest slave rebellion in history to Stalin who organized the setting up of slave labour camps where he imprisoned hundreds of thousands of Russian revolutionaries is a disgrace. But then, we have already become accustomed to comrade Dieterich's absurdities and can expect nothing else from him.

Under Stalin, millions of Soviet citizens were sent to die of starvation in the labour camps. The democratic and internationalist traditions of Lenin were trampled underfoot. The most terrible crimes were committed against the working class. But all Heinz Dieterich can think about is epistemology! And Heinz would have us believe that the reason for the collapse of the Soviet Union was defects in Soviet epistemology! If only they had paid more attention to this branch of philosophy, all would have been for the best in the best of all "really existing socialist" worlds! Here we really do say good-bye to reality and ascend to the fantastic world, not of epistemology, but precisely of *mythology*.

Real Socialism?

On page 24 of the same book, Dieterich casually throws in the following phrase: "And nobody who claims to be a realist would dare to think that what used to be 'really existing' socialism could still serve as a world alternative, capable of overcoming capitalism through a mass movement".

In common with many other ex-admirers of the USSR Dieterich has thrown all his old ideas overboard, like a man throwing surplus ballast off a sinking ship. But at no time does he tell us why the ideas that he defended in the past must now be thrown overboard, and why the so-called really existing socialism is of no use. This shows an extremely light-minded attitude to theory and the socialist movement. It is true that Stalinism failed, and that the bureaucracy, having undermined the democratic socialist regime established by Lenin and Trotsky in 1917, ultimately destroyed the USSR.

Unless we are able to provide the working class with an explanation for this degeneration, we will be forever unable to convince the new generation that socialism and Marxism are the only viable alternative to senile capitalism. Yet, 16 years after the fall of the Soviet Union, Dieterich is not only incapable of providing such an explanation, but he still refers to the totalitarian caricature of Stalinism as "socialism". A greater service to the enemies of socialism and Marxism one cannot imagine.

Today, many honest Communists demand to know the truth about this "real socialism". They want to understand why the "socialist paradise" depicted by their leaders for so long, could collapse like a house of cards, without any attempt on the part of the Russian working class to defend it. They demand to know how it is possible that the great majority of the leaders of the CPSU, who sang the praises of socialism and communism in the past, have now become converted to capitalism and have transformed themselves into a capitalist oligarchy, which has enriched itself by plundering state-owned property. To these honest communists, Heinz Dieterich has nothing whatsoever to say, except the bare assertion that "real socialism" can no longer provide an alternative.

In the article *The Alternative of Cuba, Capitalism or New Socialism* (12/4/06), under the heading "Stalin and the Economic Theory of the New Order", we read: "The second difficulty of the constructors of socialism was not ideological but theoretical. The economy improvised under the conditions of the tyrannical Russian reality and the economic-political blockade of imperialism, was not the replica of a capitalist system, but neither did it represent the mode of socialist production, which the political economy and political ethics of Marx and Engels foresaw. Because it was not founded on value (time inputs) and the interchange of equal values (equivalences), nor in the self-determination of the direct producers."

We have already explained that Dieterich's idea of an economy based on the exchange of equal values (equivalences) is utopian nonsense that has nothing to do with Marxist economics, or with the real world in general. We have also explained that it is physically impossible to calculate the exact amount of value (time inputs) contained in individual commodities, since such a task, apart from being quite unnecessary, would exhaust all the computing power of all the computers in the world.

What about the "self-determination of the direct producers"? This formula is also wrong. It is an *anarchist notion*, not a Marxist one. The idea that the workers of a particular enterprise will directly own and control "their" factory, office, or mine would negate any possibility of socialist planning. It would tend to place one group of workers in contradiction with other groups of workers. And it would end up inevitably in a kind of market economy, with competition, money, profit and loss, in which the more productive enterprises would enrich themselves at the expense of the less productive ones. So much for Dieterich's utopia; but how does he analyse the character of the USSR?

"It was a reality *sui generis*, a hybrid, whose description and scientific explanation required its own theoretical paradigm, that is, an evolution of the paradigm of the classics which would be capable of apprehending scientifically the new economic reality." [22]

Something that is *sui generis* is unique, of its own kind, and therefore cannot be usefully compared to anything else. According to comrade Dieterich an analysis of the USSR "required its own theoretical paradigm, that is, an evolution of the paradigm of the classics". Paradigm is a word that some scientists tend to use when they do not know what to say. All that our Heinz is doing here is expressing his own bewilderment and his inability to say anything useful or even comprehensible about

22. Ibid.

an important question, which demands an answer.

He informs us that the USSR "required its own theoretical paradigm", but nowhere does he say what this theoretical paradigm is. He does not say what it is because he has absolutely no idea of what Stalinism was or why it arose. Nor does he say what ought to be said, namely that *Stalinism represents the absolute negation of socialism as understood by Marx and Lenin*. Moreover, to understand this phenomenon we do not require a "unique paradigm" but a thorough grounding in the Marxist method of analysis. But this is something comrade Dieterich certainly does not possess.

Is it true that the classical ideas of Marxism are incapable of shedding light on the phenomenon of Stalinism? Is it the case, as Dieterich argues, that an entirely new system of ideas and methodology ("paradigm") are necessary? No, it is not true at all. As a matter of fact, it is only possible to understand the bureaucratic degeneration of the Russian Revolution by using the Marxist method of dialectical and historical materialism. That is what enabled Leon Trotsky to analyse this phenomenon and to predict the fall of the USSR decades before it happened. Similarly, it is only possible to gain a rational understanding of the workings of the Soviet economy by going back to the economic writings of Marx. No matter how we look at the matter, it is clear that the prices of commodities even in a workers' state must be based on something: what else can this be but the value of the product, the socially necessary labour time contained in it? This question was dealt with by Marx in *Critique of the Gotha Programme*:

"Within the co-operative society based on common ownership of the means of production, the producers do not exchange their products; just as little does the labour employed on the products appear here as the *value* of these products, as a material quality possessed by them, since now, in contrast to capitalist society, individual labour no longer exists in an indirect fashion but directly as a component part of total labour. The phrase 'proceeds of labour', objectionable also today on account of its ambiguity, thus loses all meaning.

"What we have to deal with here is a communist society, not as it has *developed* on its own foundations, but, on the contrary, just as it *emerges* from capitalist society; which is thus in every respect, economically, morally, and intellectually, still stamped with the birthmarks of the old society from whose womb it emerges. Accordingly, the individual producer receives back from society – after the deductions have been made – exactly what he gives to it. What he has given to it is his individual quantum of labour. For example, the social working day consists of the sum of the individual hours of work; the individual labour time of the individual producer is the part of the social working day contributed by him, his share in it. He receives a certificate from society that he has furnished such-and-such an amount of labour (after deducting his labour for the common funds); and with this certificate, he draws from the social stock of means of consumption as much as the same amount of labour cost. The same amount of labour which he has given to society in one form, he receives back in another.

"Here, obviously, the same principle prevails as that which regulates the exchange of commodities, as far as this is exchange of equal values. Content and form are changed, because under the altered circumstances no one can give anything except his labour, and because, on the other hand, nothing can pass to the ownership of individuals, except individual means of consumption. But as far as the distribution of the latter among the individual producers is concerned, the same principle prevails as in the exchange of commodity equivalents: a given amount of labour in one form is exchanged for an equal amount of labour in another form.

"Hence, *equal right* here is still in principle – *bourgeois right*, although principle and practice are no longer at loggerheads, while the exchange of equivalents in commodity exchange exists only on the average and not in the individual case.

"In spite of this advance, this equal right is still constantly stigmatised by a bourgeois limitation. The right of the producers is *proportional* to the labour they supply; the equality consists in the fact that measurement is made with an *equal standard*, labour.

"But one man is superior to another physically, or mentally, and supplies more labour in the same time, or can labour for a longer time; and labour, to serve as a measure, must be defined by its duration or intensity, otherwise it ceases to be a standard of measurement. This *equal* right is an unequal right for unequal labour. It recognizes no class differences, because everyone is only a worker like everyone else; but it tacitly recognizes unequal individual endowment, and thus productive capacity, as a natural privilege. It is, therefore, a right of inequality, in its content, like every right. Right, by its very nature, can consist only in the application of an equal standard; but unequal individuals (and they would not be different individuals if they were not unequal) are measurable only by an equal standard insofar as they are brought under an equal point of view, are taken from one definite side only – for instance, in the present case, are regarded *only as workers* and nothing more is seen in them, everything else being ignored. Further, one worker is married, another is not; one has more children than another, and so on and so forth. Thus, with an equal performance of labour, and hence an equal in the social consumption fund, one will in fact receive more than another, one will be richer than another, and so on. To avoid all these defects, right, instead of being equal, would have to be unequal.

"But these defects are inevitable in the first phase of communist society as it is when it has just emerged after prolonged birth pangs from capitalist society. Right can never be higher than the economic structure of society and its cultural development conditioned thereby.

"In a higher phase of communist society, after the enslaving subordination of the individual to the division of labour, and therewith also the antithesis between mental and physical labour, has vanished; after labour has become not only a means of life but life's prime want; after the productive forces have also increased with the all-around development of the individual, and all the springs of co-operative wealth flow more abundantly – only then can the narrow horizon of bourgeois right be crossed in its entirety and society inscribe on its banners: From each according to his ability, to each according to his needs!" [23]

Lenin later wrote: "The great significance of Marx's explanation is, that here too, he consistently applies materialist dialectics, the theory of development, and regards communism as something which develops *out of* capitalism. Instead of scholastically invented, 'concocted' definitions and fruitless disputes over words (What is socialism? What is communism?), Marx gives analysis of what might be called the stages of the economic maturity of communism." [24]

We have quoted these works at length to show yet again how clearly Marx and Lenin always explained their ideas. It is a pity the same cannot be said for certain other writings we have had to read lately.

Did the law of value function in the USSR?

Heinz Dieterich writes: "In the discussion of mercantile relations, he [Stalin] took the following position. He observed that capital goods (means of production) were not freely sold, but were produced and assigned through the plan to their destinations, a fact for which they could not be considered merchandise. On the other hand, the means of consumption could be acquired freely, a fact, for which their mercantile character was undeniable.

"It is evident that Stalin was right so far as the mechanical application of capitalist terminology, and even classical political economics, to the Soviet economy was not justifiable, either politically or scientifically. But neither was it theoretically defendable to identify the new State with society in a system in which participative democracy did not exist, or to identify the economic model that it developed as 'socialist'.

"The new economy was not capitalist because there did not exist any class of private capitalists who controlled the three strategic variables of any modern economic system: the surplus, the prices and the rate of investment. For this reason it was a fallacy to qualify the hybrid Soviet system as State capitalism, as occurred in various debates of the seventies (see the Bettelheim-Sweezy polemics). But, on the other hand, yes it continued being essentially a market economy ruled by the price and lacking the decisive approaches of a socialist economic system: value and economic democracy. In rigor, I think an acceptable scientific definition of the new Soviet economy, would be the following: an economy primarily of the market, not

23. Marx and Engels, *Selected Works*, Vol. 3, pp. 16-19, *The Critique of the Gotha Programme.*
24. Lenin, *Collected Works*, Volume 25, p. 471.

chrematistic." [25]

Confusion is piled upon confusion. One minute Dieterich describes the USSR as "really existing socialism," and the next he says it "essentially a market economy ruled by the price and lacking the decisive approaches of a socialist economic system: value and economic democracy". If it was a market economy, then it must have had the law of motion of a market economy – that is, booms and slumps. But there were no booms and slumps in Stalin's Russia, which achieved unprecedented levels of economic growth. Thus, if we accept Heinz Dieterich's analysis we would have to explain an entirely new phenomenon, a socio-economic system completely unknown to Marxism: a market economy (that is, capitalism) without private capitalists, which has abolished booms and slumps. What is the nature of this strange beast, which is neither fish nor flesh nor fowl? Comrade Dieterich does not enlighten us. This is hardly surprising since he does not know himself. He merely repeats an endless string of contradictory statements and hopes nobody will notice.

Comrade Dieterich is incapable of thinking dialectically. He is only capable of thinking in terms of *capitalism* and *socialism* as fixed categories, and that is why he always ends in such a confused mess. Between capitalism and socialism there is a transitional period, in which the bourgeoisie is expropriated and a nationalised planned economy is installed. This represents a colossal conquest and a big step forward, as the history of the USSR demonstrated. *But it is not yet socialism.*

Even when we characterise the USSR as a transitional form of society, we do not exhaust the question. It is necessary to take into account the concrete conditions in which the October Revolution took place. The problem was that the Bolsheviks had taken power in Russia, an extremely backward country in which the material conditions for building socialism were absent. Lenin never claimed that socialism existed in Russia (let alone communism). What existed in Russia after the October Revolution was neither socialism nor communism but *a workers' state* or the dictatorship of the proletariat, as Marx called it. Moreover, as Lenin pointed out to Bukharin in 1920, given Russia's extreme backwardness, it was a workers' state *with bureaucratic deformations.*

In the transitional stage between capitalism and socialism it is inevitable that certain features left over from the old society (capitalism) will still exist, including the labour theory of value, money, prices, wages, etc. Of course, in a workers' state, the law of value will not function in the same way as under capitalism. In a nationalized planned economy the law of motion of a market economy (booms and slumps) is abolished. This is one of the most important advantages of a nationalized planned economy, permitting a colossal development of the productive forces. The history of the USSR, especially of the first Five Year Plans, completely confirms this. But the nationalization of the productive forces, although it is a necessary pre-

25. Dieterich, *The Alternative of Cuba: Capitalism or New Socialism*, April 12, 2006.

condition for socialism, in and of itself, does not signify that socialism has been achieved. It does not signify that manure can be transformed into gold, as Trotsky observed.

Marx explained that under socialism all that the managers would be entitled to would be the wages of superintendence. But the Soviet bureaucracy appropriated far more than this. Apart from their high salaries and legal privileges, cars, luxury flats, servants, dachas, holiday resorts, etc., they also had many illegal privileges and perks. This was not the same as the profits of a private capitalist, which in the end play a necessary role in the market economy. Every worker understands this. The workers may go on strike to increase their share of the surplus value and reduce that of the bosses, but it would never occur to them to demand that the bosses should not make any profit at all. By contrast, every rouble appropriated by the bureaucracy above the wages of superintendence was merely theft and parasitism.

Soviet Russia was not socialism but a transitional society in which capitalism had been abolished but in which capitalist laws continue to operate, albeit in a modified form, *alongside the laws of the future socialist society (elements of planning).* This is undoubtedly a dialectical contradiction, which flows from the contradictory nature of a society that has broken with the past but does not yet possess the necessary level of material, technological and cultural development that would permit it to pass immediately to what Engels described as the "realm of freedom". It is complete nonsense to refer to the USSR as a "market economy", which to any literate person signifies *capitalism.* In the Soviet Union the means of production were in the hands of the state, which took all the decisions concerning investment, distribution, consumption and so on. If everything is owned by the state and there are no private capitalists (as even comrade Dieterich can see) then the laws of capitalist market economy are annulled. You can call Stalin's Russia anything you like, but capitalism it was not.

The bureaucracy plundered the economy for its own interests. It enjoyed huge privileges that were completely unjustified from a socialist point of view. The wealth appropriated by the bureaucracy was taken from the surplus value produced by the Soviet workers. But this had nothing in common with the way in which the capitalists extract surplus value. The capitalists play a necessary role in a market economy, investing money for the sake of profit. But that was not the case with the Soviet Union, where the means of production were socially owned and investment decisions were not determined by private profit.

'Necessary and surplus work'

In the USSR, the state appropriated the surplus created by the labour of the working class. Part of that surplus was indeed spent on social security, health, education, etc. Part was spent on re-investment in industry, agriculture, science and technology, and part on defence. This would also be the case in a healthy workers' state, run on the lines of a workers' democracy. Under Lenin and Trotsky, the Soviet state did not spend the enormous sums that the Stalinist bureaucracy later dedicated to defence. This was because the Bolsheviks did not rely only on the Red Army to defend its frontiers. They relied on the solidarity of the international proletariat, which actually saved the young Workers' Republic from the threat of armed intervention. The ruling class of Britain and France, faced with the threat of civil war, were forced to abandon their plans for military intervention by pressure from the working class.

Lenin and Trotsky created the Communist International in 1919 as an instrument to spread the socialist revolution to Europe and the whole world – the only real way to save the Soviet state from the danger of war and foreign intervention. But Stalin, with his narrow national mentality, cynically used the foreign communist parties as an instrument of Russian foreign policy, and then disbanded the Communist International in 1943 as a gesture of good will to his British and American allies. For Stalin and the bureaucracy the defence of the USSR was reduced to a question of military power and diplomatic manoeuvring. This led to the arms race with the USA, which had ruinous results for the Soviet economy and played a significant part in undermining it. A disproportionate amount of the wealth produced by the workers of the USSR was diverted away from productive investment and raising living standards into wasteful military expenditure.

In addition to the huge military expenditure we must add the maintenance of an enormous apparatus of repression: the police, the secret police, a vast network of spies and informers, prisons and labour camps. This was necessary, not for the defence of the revolution against external enemies and internal counter-revolution, but to defend the privileges of the bureaucracy against the working class.

In a discussion with Soviet economists, in 1952, Stalin made the following statement: "The concepts of work *necessary work and surplus work* and *necessary product and surplus product* are not useful for our economy. Is not all that enters into social security and defence part of necessary work? Is not the worker interested in this? In a socialist economy we must make the following distinction *work for one's own necessities* and *work for society*." In the passage quoted here, Stalin attempts to conceal the parasitic role of the bureaucracy by means of a theoretical distortion. "The concepts of work *necessary work and surplus work* and *necessary product and surplus product* are not useful for our economy," he says. But from a Marxist point of view this is wrong. *Stalin denied the existence of necessary work and surplus work and necessary product and surplus product in the USSR because he wished to conceal the fact that the bureaucracy was exploiting the working class.*

This exploitation, however, was not the same as under capitalism, where private capitalists extract surplus value from the working class. Here the surplus product was appropriated by the state (which would also be the case in a healthy workers' state, as we have seen). "Is not all that enters into social security and defence part of necessary work? Is not the worker interested in this? In a socialist economy we must make the following distinction: *work for one's own necessities* and *work for society*." To this the Soviet worker would reply: "Yes, it is necessary to provide funds for social security and defence, and this is working for our own necessities. But working for society is not the same as working to pay for the unjustified privileges and luxurious life-style of a parasitic bureaucracy." Of course, the Soviet workers did not give this reply, *because nobody asked them*.

The bureaucracy was not interested in the opinions of the workers, only in giving orders. If they had had the computer technology that our Heinz regards as the magical key that will open all doors to the Socialism of the 21st century, they would have issued even more orders, but they would not have been anxious to enter into an Internet discussion with the workers. The first question the workers would ask is: in a society that is supposed to be socialist, how do you justify these huge wage differentials and all your privileges, big cars, dachas and servants?

The transitional society

In the transitional period between capitalism and socialism many of the features of the old system will remain in being, including money and price. The state cannot determine prices arbitrarily, nor can it determine the amount of money in circulation arbitrarily. Money is, after all, just a commodity, albeit a commodity of a special kind (the commodity of commodities). Engels already dealt with this problem in *Anti-Dühring*: "If the sword (i.e. the state) has the magic economic power ascribed to it by Herr Dühring, why is it that no government has been able to succeed in permanently compelling bad money to have the 'distribution value' of good money, or *assignats* to have the 'distribution value' of gold?" [26]

It is inevitable that some of the economic categories inherited from capitalism will still remain in the transitional society between capitalism and communism. Some of the laws of market economy will be abrogated but others will remain, although in a *modified form*. In *Revolution Betrayed,* Trotsky explains:

"The role of money in Soviet economy is not only unfinished but, as we have said, still has a long growth ahead. The transitional epoch between capitalism and socialism taken as a whole does not mean a cutting down of trade but, on the contrary, its extraordinary extension. All branches of industry transform themselves and grow. New ones continually arise, and all are compelled to define their relations to one another both quantitatively and qualitatively. The liquidation of the consummatory peasant economy, and at the same time of the shut-in family life, means a transfer to the sphere of social interchange, and *ipso facto* money circulation, of all the labour energy which was formerly expended within the limits of the peasant's yard, or within the walls of his private dwelling. All products and services begin for the

26. Engels, *Anti-Dühring*, p. 228.

first time in history to be exchanged for one another." [27]

The nationalization of the means of production and the introduction of a planned economy marks a big step forward as opposed to the anarchy of the market and private ownership. The state can now regulate and plan the economy, but only within the confines of the law of value. In the transitional period the law of value is not abolished, but is modified. Trotsky points out: "The nationalisation of the means of production and credit, the co-operativising or state-ising of internal trade, the monopoly of foreign trade, the collectivisation of agriculture, the law of inheritance – set strict limits upon the personal accumulation of money and hinder its conversion into private capital (usurious, commercial and industrial). These functions of money, however, bound up as they are with exploitation, are not liquidated at the beginning of a proletarian revolution, but in a modified form are transferred to the state, the universal merchant, creditor and industrialist. At the same time the more elementary functions of money as *measure of value, means of exchange* and *medium of payment,* are not only preserved, but acquire a broader field of action than they had under capitalism." [28]

By its very nature a transitional society will display some of the features of the old society, side by side with elements of the new, socialist, society. Thus, in the economic sphere some of the laws peculiar to socialism apply, side by side with some that have been inherited from capitalism. This is, of course, a contradiction that must be overcome by subsequent developments. With the further development of the productive forces, the reduction of the working day and the raising of productivity to undreamed-of heights, the raising of living standards and the cultural level of the whole population, the conditions will be prepared for a further development of the socialist element and the progressive elimination of the remnants left over from the past. The speed and the ease with which this transition is made depend above all upon the material conditions of society.

A nationalized planned economy, of course, gives us a huge advantage over capitalism. The workers' state can consciously regulate and plan production (though within limits determined by the general level of economic and social development). It can determine the rate of investment, the proportions between means of production and means of consumption, the price of articles of consumption, etc. Heinz Dieterich imagines that it is possible to eliminate completely all the exploitative elements of capitalism without abolishing capitalism itself. This, he assures us, can be achieved by simply abolishing prices and exchanging commodities on the basis of the "principle of equivalence". As a matter of fact, it will not be possible to abolish prices even in a workers' state, as we have just explained. Still less will it be possible to abolish prices on the basis of a capitalist market economy, as comrade

27. Trotsky, *Revolution Betrayed*, p. 67, NY, 1972.
28. Ibid., p. 66, emphasis in original.

Dieterich proposes.

Is it correct as Dieterich maintains that every worker will receive the exact amount that he or she has produced ("the wages of equivalence")? No it is not correct. Even if this were possible (and it is not), it would actually signify the continuation of inequality, not its abolition. Workers who are stronger, more skilled, etc. would receive more than their weaker and less skilled brothers and sisters. Certain groups of workers would find themselves in a privileged position vis a vis the rest of the class, and in a position to abuse that position. For example, in Venezuela the workers of PDVSA would be in a privileged position vis a vis, say, the agricultural labourers and so on.

In the transitional period there would still be commodity production, although it would be organized by the state instead of private capitalists. The state will still buy labour power and pay wages, though the differences between high and low incomes would be reduced considerably from the outset and the differentials would continue to be reduced as society proceeded in a socialist direction. The law of the circulation of commodities, including the circulation of money will be maintained in a transitional economy, together with the other elements of the old society within the new society: money, value, surplus value, etc. Trotsky explained that the only real money in Russia (or in any transitional economy – even an ideal workers' state) must be based on gold.

Even in a workers' state surplus value will still be produced by the working class, as in every other economic system for the last 10,000 years or so. The state will appropriate the surplus value produced by the workers in order to invest in production and provide necessary social services. In a workers' democracy, the way in which this is done – the precise proportions dedicated to production and consumption, investment and research, building and the arts – will be decided democratically. But in any case, surplus value will still exist.

The answer – cybernetics?

The idea put forward by Dieterich that the USSR collapsed because it lacked adequate cybernetic and computer science is equally false. If the bureaucracy had introduced computers without democratic workers' control and management of the economy, it would have led to even greater chaos. A single bureaucratic error (and there were millions of such errors every day) written into a computer programme and fed into a network linking all the computers in the USSR would have multiplied the error to the nth degree, causing total collapse faster than one could say "Heinz Dieterich".

One of the main reasons why central planning failed in the USSR was because there was no feedback. The bureaucratic planners gave orders and expected them to be carried out. Not for nothing were they described as "command economies". We know the reason for this. *There was no workers' democracy.* But for Heinz Dieterich the problem was quite different. It was the inability to process information, that is, it was not a political problem at all but a *technical* one – a *"cybernetic" problem.* This is completely false. The workers did not offer information (did not denounce the corruption, swindling, bungling and sabotage of the bureaucracy) not because the channels of communication had not been created, but because it was not in their interests to do so. Any worker who criticized the bureaucracy would have been sacked or imprisoned. The so-called trade unions were not unions at all but part of the bureaucratic state. The problem was therefore a political problem, not a technical one.

Incidentally, since we now have the computer power, the socialist "project" should now at last be viable for the 21st century. There should be no problem at all – except for the little detail that Dieterich has not noticed: that the capitalists and bankers still own the means of production, including the computers and the means of producing them, as well as the copyright to all the computer programmes, the computer technology, the scientists and the laboratories. For some strange reason, they insist that these things be used to produce profits for them, and not an "economy of equivalents" for the benefit of humankind. What are we going to do about this sad state of affairs? Dieterich does not say.

Having abandoned nationalization and central state planning as a means of getting to 21st Socialism, comrade Dieterich has no alternative but to retreat to – a market economy, which he hopes to transform by some miracle into a participatory democracy. Compared to this, the miracle of changing water into wine at the feast of Canaa pales into insignificance. Let us consider for a moment some of the problems involved in what Dieterich is proposing. Under capitalism markets are supposed to process information in a decentralised way without the need to assemble all the information centrally and then pass it down the chain of command. In fact, markets do no such thing. A most striking example of market misinformation is climate change. According to Nicolas Stern, a trained neoclassical economist says that this is the greatest example of market failure ever. We are in danger of making the planet uninhabitable, yet no market signal tells us this. The whole effect is not reflected on the profit and loss balance sheet. To accept the logic of the market is equivalent to unconditional surrender to the logic of capitalism.

The idea that markets process information comes from the reactionary bourgeois economist Friederich Hayek during the interwar debate on "socialist calculation". This dates from about 1920 when the Austrian economist Ludwig von Mises declared that economic calculation under socialism was impossible. The pro-capitalist economists received a sound thrashing over the next few years from socialists schooled in neoclassical economics and arguing within that tradition. Hayek then developed a second line of defence in this debate. He put forward the line that, though not impossible, rational economic calculation would be very complex under socialism. He claimed that the market made all these calculations without anyone having to think about the bigger picture. Hayek remained a minor figure for a long time after the Second World War. But the collapse of the Stalinist economies saw his ideas dusted off and widely publicised as an explanation of the events.

The Stalinist notion of planning as a top down process and its inevitable failure played into the hands of the likes of Hayek. Both Hayek and Dieterich equate Stalinism with socialism. First comrade Dieterich capitulates to the logic of the market. Then he conjures up an era of non-equivalent exchange, a concept that is entirely contrary to the letter and spirit of Marx. The idea that real planning is done just by issuing decrees from the centre was ridiculed by Trotsky in 1932. He wrote: "If there existed the universal mind that projected itself into the scientific fantasy of Laplace, a mind that would register simultaneously all the processes of nature and society, that could measure the dynamics of their motion, that could forecast the results of their inter-reactions, such a mind could of course a priori draw up an exhaustive economic plan, beginning with the number of hectares of wheat and down to the last button for a vest." [29]

Like all the other ex-Marxists, in abandoning Stalinism, Heinz has no desire to return to the genuine ideas of communism – the ideas and programme of the October Revolution, of Lenin and Trotsky and the Bolshevik Party. Instead, he is striving to revise Marxism, to strip it of all its revolutionary and class content, and to drag the movement into the swamp of reformism and social democracy. However, since Dieterich realises that social democracy has a bad name in Latin America, where the revolution is advancing in the direction of socialism everywhere, he is compelled to resort to subterfuge. He pretends to have invented an entirely new concept, which is far superior to capitalism or "real socialism", which will solve all our problems and lead us quite painlessly into the realm of a new civilisation.

He says this himself quite explicitly. On page 23 of *El Socialismo del Siglo XXI*, comrade Dieterich informs us that he is neither in favour of capitalism nor the so-called real socialism of the USSR. Instead, he has developed the idea of an entirely new kind of society, previously unknown to Marxism, which he calls the "participative democracy". This peculiar animal, neither fish nor fowl, is not to be found in any of the writings of Engels, Marx or Lenin. It is presented to us as an entirely new concept. On further examination, however, we find that there is nothing novel about it, and that it really expresses the utopian-democratic illusions of the petit bourgeoisie.

Socialism and consumerism

In the article in *Revista Mariátegui* (15/08/06) Dieterich is asked: "You state that consumerism is the opiate of the people. In 21st century Socialism will consumerism vanish?" Since 21st Century Socialism has already made profits disap-

29. *The Soviet economy in danger*, in Trotsky's *Writings, 1932*, p. 274.

pear and turned tigers into vegetarians, this particular question would seem superfluous, and the answer predictable:

"Yes, because a new economy is not only the accounting of value and participative democracy, but it also needs to change the entire profile of production and consumption, because, just from the point of view of ecology, the pattern of consumption we have is unsustainable. Any society of the future, including capitalism, would have to make substantial changes in this profile of consumption and I believe that a socialism (sic) will have a completely different face." [30]

It is quite true that the capitalist system is colossally wasteful and that the anarchy of capitalist production and the greed for profit is threatening the environment and putting the future of the planet in danger. The only answer to this is a socialist planned economy on a world scale. Mere tinkering with the system (Keynesianism) is useless. It is necessary to expropriate the banks and monopolies and institute a democratic plan of production that will put the interests of the human race first, not private profits.

One of the main arguments raised is the question of finite energy supplies and global warming. The use of fossil fuels is undoubtedly limited and causes many problems. But alternative supplies could have been developed decades ago, if the big oil monopolies had not sabotaged the research. The obvious alternative is nuclear fusion, which, unlike nuclear fission, is clean, cheap and virtually unlimited (hydrogen is present in vast quantities in water, with which our planet abounds). There are many more examples of how the present problems could be easily solved by the development of adequate technology and a rational plan of production.

The argument, so often repeated in petty bourgeois ecologist circles and so eagerly embraced by the right wing reformists, that we cannot afford to maintain present levels of consumption is both hypocritical and reactionary. The same middle class intellectuals who lecture the masses that they must restrict consumption do not exactly live in conditions of poverty themselves. On the other hand, the bourgeois are skilfully using the same arguments to justify raising taxes (on the poor) and cutting living standards. The notion that the planet "cannot sustain the present levels of production and consumption" is entirely false, superficial and in essence reactionary. *What is true is that the planet cannot stand indefinitely the monstrous plunder and rapine that is practiced by the big transnational companies in their lust for profits.*

A planned economy would enable humanity to exploit natural resources in a rational and scientific way, balancing the needs of human consumption with the need to preserve and cherish our beautiful world and pass on our natural heritage intact to future generations. Socialism in our time will not signify a regime of austerity. On the contrary, a genuine socialist society will begin at the highest point

30. Ibid.

achieved by capitalism. It will signify, not a reduction in living standards, but an all-round increase in the standard of living, together with a general reduction of working hours. This is the prior condition for a real participative democracy – that is, a workers' democracy. Without it, all talk of socialism will be mere empty demagogy.

It is clear from everything we have read that comrade Dieterich's approach to socialism has nothing in common with Marxism. Socialism, as understood by Marx and Lenin, presupposes that the development of the productive forces has reached a sufficient level that it would eliminate all material inequality. The abolition of classes cannot be established by decree. It must arise from a superabundance of things that would universally raise the quality of life to unheard-of levels.

All the basic human needs would be satisfied, and therefore the humiliating struggle for existence would cease. A general reduction in working hours would provide the conditions for an unparalleled development of culture. It would enable men and women to participate in the administration of industry, the state and society. From the very beginning the workers' state would be characterised by a level of democratic participation far superior to the most democratic bourgeois republic. As a consequence, classes would dissolve into society, together with the last vestiges of class society – money and the state. This would give rise to genuine communism and the replacement of the domination of man by man with the "administration of things", to use Engels' expression. This, and nothing else, is what Marxists call socialism. Ultimately, the success of socialism can only be guaranteed by world socialism and a socialist planned world economy.

The nationalization of the productive forces was a great step forward, but it by no means guaranteed the victory of socialism in Russia. As Trotsky put it: "Socialism is the organisation of a planned and harmonious social production for the satisfaction of human wants. Collective ownership of the means of production is not yet socialism, but only its legal premise. The problem of a socialist society cannot be abstracted from the problem of the productive forces, which at the present stage of human development are worldwide in their very essence." [31]

31. Trotsky, *History of the Russian Revolution*, p. 1237.

9. The future of the Cuban Revolution

The liquidation of the nationalized planned economy and the switch to market economics in Russia has signified, as Trotsky so brilliantly predicted, a sharp decline of culture. The capitalist counter-revolution has brought with it prostitution, drug addiction, AIDS, pornography, Great Russian chauvinism, the Black Hundreds, pogroms, anti-Semitism, astrology, superstition and the Russian Orthodox Church. These are the "blessings" capitalism has inflicted on the Russian people. The same fate will await the people of Cuba if the pro-capitalist elements succeed in their plans to restore capitalism.

In Cuba, as in the USSR, there are elements who want to go back to capitalism. It is not necessary to point out that a return to capitalism in Cuba would be a terrible disaster, not just for the people of Cuba but for the workers and peoples of the whole world. This must be prevented by all means! But it will not be prevented if we deny that the threat exists. The threat comes from Washington, but also from those layers in Cuba who would like to see a return to capitalism. Some of them are to be found amongst the new rich, others amongst corrupt layers of the state apparatus and administrators of companies. To deny this is to have learnt nothing from the fate of the USSR.

To his credit, Fidel Castro has remained implacably opposed to a return to capitalism. He firmly rejects the privatisation of the means of production and the dismantling of the planned economy. He has courageously stood up to the pressure and bullying of imperialism. This stand deserves support, though in itself it is insufficient to save the Cuban revolution. On the 17th of November 2005, Fidel warned at the University of La Havana that the Cuban Revolution was not irreversible and that it might end up like the Soviet Union. He referred to "our flaws, our mistakes, our inequalities, our injustice". He said: "As you know, we are presently waging a war against corruption, against the re-routing of resources, against thievery, and there is this force which we didn't have before we started with the battle of ideas, one designed to wage this battle." [1]

He appealed to revolutionary honour, but added that such appeals were insufficient: "The Revolution will establish the necessary controls". Control is precisely what is necessary. But the only really reliable control is the control from the bottom – control on the part of the working class. Without this, the bureaucrats and unscrupulous people can manipulate controls and regulations, which will remain just scraps of paper. Bureaucracy cannot be combated by the bureaucracy itself! Fidel wishes to defend the Cuban Revolution by attacking those distortions that threaten to undermine it from within. But many of those who applauded his speech in public will do nothing to put it into practice because to do so would undermine their privileges.

Fidel Castro stated correctly: "The first socialist revolution, the first real attempt at a just and egalitarian society, takes place in a huge semi-feudal, semi-under developed country." That is the root of the problem: "All these historical factors had a tremendous influence on revolutionary thinking, and of course there were abusive practices, at times even repugnant ones". Fidel does not specify what he is referring to but there can be no doubt at all from the context that he was talking about the crimes of Stalinism. For example, he mentioned the Hitler-Stalin Pact: "I think that the imperialist plans to throw Hitler against the USSR would never have justified the pact made between Hitler and Stalin, it was a very hard blow. The communist parties, well-known for their discipline, were obliged to defend the Molotov-Ribbentrop Pact and to politically bleed to death." And he went on to mention the role of the Cuban Stalinists who, following the dictates of Moscow, shamefully supported the dictator Batista against Castro and the revolutionary movement:

"Before this pact, the necessity for unification in the anti-fascist struggle led to the alliance in Cuba of the Cuban communists with Batista. By then, Batista had suppressed the famous strike of April 1934 that followed his coup against the provisional government in 1933 which was unquestionably revolutionary in nature and to a large degree, the result of the historical fight of the workers' movement and the Cuban communists. Before that anti-fascist alliance, Batista had assassinated countless numbers of people and robbed incredible sums of money, and had become a flunky of Yankee imperialism. The order came from Moscow: organize the anti-fascist front. It was a pact with the devil. Here the pact was with the fascist ABC and Batista, a fascist of a different colour, who was both a criminal and robber of the public coffer.

"[...] The members of the Cuban Communist Party were the most disciplined people, the most honourable and the most self-sacrificed for this country. The Party legislators handed over a portion of their salaries. They were the most honourable

1. See *Discurso pronunciado por Fidel Castro Ruz*, http://www.cuba.cu/gobierno/discursos/2005/esp/f171105e.html

people in the country notwithstanding the erroneous direction that was imposed by Stalin on the international movement."

Referring to Stalin's Russia he says: "We must have the courage to recognize our own errors exactly for that reason, for only in that manner will we reach the objective that we hope to attain. A tremendous vice was created, the abuse of power, the cruelty and, in particular, the habit of one country imposing its authority, that of one hegemonic party, over all other countries and parties." Castro condemned Stalin's purge of the Red Army: "Poland was invaded by the Nazis and the Soviet army had been purged of its best and most brilliant leaders due to scheming by the Nazis."

The menace of bureaucracy

The USSR used to buy Cuban sugar at 27 or 28 cents, and it paid in oil. The collapse of the USSR placed the Cuban economy in a very difficult situation. It produced the so-called Special Period, which imposed severe strains on the Cuban people and led to growing inequalities. The pressure of US imperialism intensified. The collapse of the USSR clearly had a powerful effect in Cuba. Many honest Cuban communists are asking how it was possible for a country that was supposed to be socialist to return so easily to capitalism. And is it not possible that a similar fate could await Cuba? Castro also raised this question in his speech:

"I believe that the experience of that first socialist State, a State that should have been fixed and not destroyed, was a bitter one. You may be sure that we have thought many times about that incredible phenomenon where one of the mightiest powers in the world disintegrated the way it did; for this was a power that had matched the strength of the other super-power and had paid with the lives of more than 20 million of her people in the battle against fascism.

"Is it that revolutions are doomed to fall apart, or that men cause revolutions to fall apart? Can either man or society prevent revolutions from collapsing? I could immediately add to this another question: Do you believe that this revolutionary socialist process can fall apart, or not? (*Exclamations of: 'No!!'*) Have you ever given that some thought? Have you ever deeply reflected about it?"

Fidel Castro showed greater awareness and realism than his audience. He pointed out correctly that the biggest danger to the Revolution was internal – in corruption, privileges and inequality:

"Were you aware of all these inequalities that I have been talking about? Were you aware of certain generalized habits? Did you know that there are people who earn forty or fifty times the amount one of those doctors over there in the mountains of Guatemala, part of the 'Henry Reeve' Contingent, earns in one month? It could be in other faraway reaches of Africa, or at an altitude of thousands of metres, in the Himalayas, saving lives and earning 5 percent or 10 percent of what one of those dirty little crooks earns, selling gasoline to the new rich, diverting resources from the ports in trucks and by the ton-load, stealing in the dollar shops, stealing in a five-star hotel by exchanging a bottle of rum for another of lesser quality and pocketing the dollars for which he sells the drinks".

The colossal personal authority of Fidel Castro is a very important element in the situation, and Washington is well aware of it. He is implacably opposed capitalist restoration, and this has played a most important role in keeping the pro-capitalist restoration tendencies in check. But nobody lives forever, and the question is being posed openly: what will happen when Castro is no longer present? He says at one point: "some thought that socialism could be constructed with capitalist methods. That is one of the great historical errors. I do not wish to speak of this, I don't want to theorize. But I have an infinite number of examples of many things that couldn't be resolved by those who called themselves theoreticians, blanketing themselves from head to toe in the books of Marx, Engels, Lenin and many others."

In so many words, he states that there are some people who wish to "construct socialism with capitalist methods." This is a clear reference to the pro-capitalist elements in the bureaucracy who are waiting impatiently for Fidel Castro to disappear from the scene in order to push their agenda. Since they cannot do this openly, they will use the fig-leaf of the so-called Chinese road to disguise their real intentions. It is necessary to wage an all-out struggle against these pro-capitalist elements, to defend the nationalized property relations established by the Revolution. But in order to do this effectively it is essential that the workers and youth of Cuba are actively involved in the running of society, industry and the state.

A military attack on Cuba would be unthinkable even for a man as stupid as George W. Bush. But the main danger to the Cuban Revolution is not military but economic and it comes from within, as Castro explained: "This country can self-destruct; this Revolution can destroy itself, but they can never destroy us; we can destroy ourselves, and it would be our fault." It is necessary to meditate on these words and to draw the logical conclusions.

Roque's speech

On the 23rd of December, 2005 Felipe Pérez Roque, Minister of Foreign Affairs of Cuba, delivered a speech at the 6th Session of the 6th Legislation of the Asamblea Nacional del Poder Popular (Cuban Parliament), with the title *Year of the Bolivarian Alternative for the Americas.* [2]

He said: "We must give all attention to this call launched by Fidel at the University, to this phrase never pronounced before publicly in the history of the revolution, that the revolution could be reversible, and not by the enemy which has done all in its power to do it, but by our errors".

He referred to the crisis of the Special Period and the problems caused by the blockade. He warned about the plans of US imperialism to lead a "transition" in

2. See http://cubaminrex.cu/Archivo/Canciller/2005/FPR_231205.htm

Cuba and turn it into a colony of the United States: "The enemy then bets on the idea that our Revolution will grow tired and be lost – as has happened before in history, because after the French Revolution there was a victorious counter-revolution and there were many other processes that were lost, they grew tired, they lost their course. But this has not been our case, and a long time has passed, more than four decades and this has not happened. Then that is the idea.

"Past successes in the struggle do not justify self-complacency or the idea that victory is won for eternity," he said. These words indicate that there are those in the leadership who are worried about the possibility of capitalist counter-revolution in Cuba and are aware that the danger lies within – in bureaucracy, corruption and inequality that undermine the revolutionary faith of the masses more than any propaganda from Miami or Washington:

"Therefore, there are lessons in ethics. Marti prepared the necessary war and refused to let his colleagues buy him a pair of shoes to replace his old worn ones." He went on: "Therefore, I think there are three basic premises: the first is that this Revolution cannot be defeated if those who lead it do so on the basis of the authority of their personal example, as is the case today, as has always been the case. The Revolution has come this far in the first place due to the moral authority of its leadership. You can have the power but no authority, and this is the case of Bush and his regime, because the authority does not stem from given attributes, it stems from the example of a person's acts. The way we understand such authority is like this, 'Well, I do not understand it very well, but if Fidel said so, I'm sure it is like that'."

There is no doubt that the colossal personal and moral authority of Fidel Castro plays a very important role in holding in check the pro-capitalist elements. But what will happen when Fidel is no longer present? Can the Cuban Revolution depend on the presence of one man to save it? Of course not! In the last analysis, the Revolution can only rely on one thing to defend it: the will of the masses. The working class and the people of Cuba have shown their determination to defend the Revolution for decades. They have been prepared to tolerate all kinds of hardships and privations. They will be prepared to do so in the future. But in order that the masses should defend the Revolution, it is necessary that they have a perspective that all their sacrifices will not have been in vain: that they will serve to bring about the final victory of socialism. This is only possible if the socialist revolution triumphs in other countries, beginning with Venezuela.

The extension of the revolution at least to Latin America is essential for the survival and strengthening of the Cuban Revolution. That was clearly understood by Che Guevara and it remains true today. Moreover, the conditions for the success of the revolution in Latin America today are infinitely better now than they were in 1967. That is the first point. Secondly, in order that the masses should make the necessary sacrifices, it is imperative that they should understand that the sacrifices are for everybody, without any distinction of rank or position. Che Guevara was an example in this respect. He refused to accept his minister's salary, drawing only his meagre wage as a comandante of the revolutionary army and was implacably opposed to any privileges.

This idea was expressed in the 1919 Party Programme of the Bolshevik Party. It was already expressed by Lenin in *State and Revolution*, which he derived from the experience of the Paris Commune. Marx described the abolition of privileges in the Commune in the following way: "From the members of the Commune downwards, the public service had to be done at *workmen's wages*. The privileges and the representation allowances of the high dignitaries of state disappeared along with the high dignitaries themselves..." [3] This was the basis of Soviet democracy established in 1917, which was abolished by Stalin after Lenin's death. Only by returning to the original ideas of October Revolution can the defence of the Cuban Revolution succeed. Those who will defend the Revolution with the greatest determination are not the bureaucrats with comfortable lifestyles and bourgeois aspirations who will desert to the camp of the counter-revolution as soon as conditions permit it. Those who will defend the Revolution to the end are the Cuban working class who have most to lose by the restoration of capitalism. As comrade Roque said:

"The second premise is that for as long as we have the support of the great majority of the people as we do today, not based on material consumption, but based on ideas and convictions – because I already referred to the peoples in the socialist countries that were disarmed and did not come out in the streets to fight when their future was being dismantled. On the other hand, we did see the poor people in Venezuela come out in the streets to fight for the return of Chávez when the Yankees orchestrated the oligarchic and military coup d'état. The destitute took to the streets, and most of those who joined the Rebel Army owned nothing, they were farmers and poor workers; in other words, support must be based on ideas and convictions; it is wrong to think that people will support us more because they have more."

The comparison with the events of April 2002 in Caracas is highly appropriate. This was the final answer to all the cowards and sceptics who doubted the ability of the working class to fight to change society. When Chávez was overthrown by the counter-revolutionaries and helpless in prison, awaiting certain death, who saved him? Who saved the Venezuelan Revolution in its moment of direst need? Only the Venezuelan workers and peasants, only the housewives and students, only the unemployed and destitute: only the men and women of no property. And the same is true in Cuba. Comrade Roque honestly deals with the facts of the situation. He does not attempt to hide the fact that a layer of the population has lost faith in the Revolution in recent years:

"The Revolution cannot survive without the support of the people; and this does not mean it couldn't be made all over again; but it would be hard to see the defeat of a Revolution that has been preserved, that has accomplished the historical deed

3. Marx, *The Civil War in France*.

of surviving here. This we all know, and today we have ratified to the Chief of the Revolution that we will defend it".

"*The Revolution cannot survive without the support of the people.*" That is the essence of the matter. Without that support the Cuban Revolution can never withstand the irresistible pressures of US imperialism. But the loyalty of the masses is being put under intolerable strain, not only by external but also by internal factors. The growth of inequality, privileges and corruption is undermining the Revolution from within. It is alienating sections of the population from the Revolution and breeding unhealthy moods of scepticism and cynicism among the youth.

It is not a question of "making the revolution all over again". Have there not been enough sacrifices made to achieve what has been achieved? A person who is not capable of defending what has already been won will never be capable of advancing to new conquests in the future. If capitalism is re-established in Cuba – and it is our fervent desire and conviction that this will not happen – it would be a terrible blow to the revolutionary movement in all Latin America and on a world scale. It would take a long time for the workers and youth of Cuba to recover from such a blow. We must do everything in our power to prevent it. The idea that Cuba would be a better place for the people if only the capitalists would return is false to the core. Roque says:

"In Cuba, there cannot be a national patriotic bourgeoisie as other countries had; in Cuba, the bourgeoisie always was, and would again be if we let it emerge, pro-Yankee, pro-transnational, and would need the rural guards, and the army of Batista, and the Yankee marines, to repress and subdue the people".

That is also correct. Nowhere in Latin America has the bourgeoisie been capable of playing a progressive role. Everywhere the so-called national bourgeoisie acts as the local office boys of imperialism. One of the most reactionary and harmful ideas that was put in circulation by the Stalinists was the myth of a progressive national bourgeois that the working class must form an alliance with and subordinate itself to. This monstrous counter-revolutionary theory, which is still supported by the Stalinists in Latin America, led the Cuban Stalinists to support Batista and oppose Castro. We must never forget this! If the capitalists ever returned, Cuba would become a municipality of Miami, to use Roque's phrase.

Heinz Dieterich comments on Fidel's speech

What does Heinz have to say about Fidel's speech? "It is an epistemological earthquake: The Comandante of certainty, of the security of final victory reintroduces the dialectic in the official Cuban discourse, without notice, without a preamble, without ambiguity. It is a matter of dialecticizing stagnation, Bertolt Brecht would say." [4]

4. Dieterich, *Cuba: Three premises to save the Revolution after the death of Fidel*, April 5, 2006. http://axisoflogic.com/cgi-bin/exec/view.pl?archive=144&num=21654

We do not know what Bertolt Brecht would say. But we know that Heinz Dieterich has a remarkable gift for *mystifying* everything he can get his hands on. And we admire the great German writer too much to make him responsible, even posthumously, for such twaddle (in good plain German *Quatsch*). Unlike Heinz Dieterich, Fidel Castro spoke with admirable clarity and honesty on the serious problems facing the Cuban Revolution. But for our friend Heinz it is all a question of *epistemology*, or, to mystify things a little bit more: "a matter of *dialecticizing stagnation*", a truly wonderful example of *Dieterichspeak.*

Later our Heinz turns his attention to Felipe Pérez Roque, whom he refers to as "the talented chancellor and former personal secretary of Fidel". This shameless flattery is the same tactic Dieterich habitually uses in relation to Chávez: to use flattering words that remind us of the tactics of the Byzantine eunuchs who were constantly involved in intrigues at the Palace in Constantinople. They would praise somebody to the skies in public and then quietly stab him in the back. In his usual arid and schematic manner, this is how comrade Dieterich, sums up the arguments of Felipe Pérez Roque:

"1. Maintain the moral authority of the leadership, through a leadership based on example and without privileges over the people. 2. Guarantee the support of the majority of the people, 'not on the basis of material consumption but on the basis of ideas and convictions'. 3. Prevent the emergence of a new bourgeoisie which "would be again, if we let it emerge, be pro-Yankee, pro transnational ....we must not fall into ingenuities....the decisive point is who gets the income (ingreso): if it is the majorities and the people or the oligarchic transnational and pro-Yankee minority; the point is, whose is the property? If of the people, the majority, or if it belongs to the corrupt and servile minority associated....with Yankee imperialism."

The Founder of 21st Century Socialism then proceeds to give the Cuban Secretary of State marks out of ten, as if he is marking an essay by one of his students: "The first proposal of the Chancellor is, obviously, correct and necessary. We will have to see if the future configuration of the Cuban political system will permit imposing it. As to the second imperative, which refers to the dialectic between the spiritual and the material, it is necessary to take into account the *dictum* of Lenin that the stability of a dominant class, in this case a leading class, can not free itself from its capacity to resolve 'the task of production'. Let us dedicate the following point to this problem."

What "the dialectic between the spiritual and the material" means is anybody's guess. We have no idea, and neither has Heinz, who, as we have seen, loves to repeat high-sounding phrases which mean nothing at all. But to continue:

"The central idea expressed by Fidel in November and now by Felipe is, that the loyalty to the leaders and their historic project must derive primarily from the ethics (values, ideas convictions) and not from consumerism. Defined thus, the dialectical unity of the contradictions of Cuban reality is not adequately reflected. The correc contradiction would be: ethics and consumption, not ethics and consumerism.

"For all epochs there are, as Marx already explained, a fund of consumption of the worker historically determined which is expressed, in terms of the valorisation of capital, in *variable capital*. This consumption fund determines, essentially in stratified form, the quality of material life of the people. At present, this standard of dominant consumption on the world level, is that of the middle class of the First World, and although it continues to be unreachable for the majorities, it exercises an irresistible attraction: to such an extent that many risk their lives to get to these First World countries." [5]

Comrade Dieterich refers to *Fidel* and *Felipe* to show to the reader that he is on first name terms with the leaders of the Cuban Revolution. (We wonder why he does not refer likewise to *Charlie* and *Freddy* when speaking of Marx and Engels). So he will forgive us if we continue to refer to him as *our friend Heinz*, which has just about as much validity. And since this *false familiarity* is just a way of preparing to make a fundamental criticism of the ideas of Fidel and Felipe, we are sure that our Heinz will not mind if we make one or two small criticisms of his arguments also.

Immediately, Heinz shows his extreme dissatisfaction with the ideas expressed by the two Cuban leaders: "the dialectical unity of the contradictions of Cuban reality is not adequately reflected," he complains. Worse still: "The correct contradiction would be: ethics and consumption, not ethics and consumerism." What is all this supposed to mean? It is known that in the years that followed the collapse of the Soviet Union, the Cuban masses suffered great material privation, which was deliberately intensified by the criminal blockade imposed by imperialism. Only gradually has Cuba succeeded in getting out of the worst and establishing some kind of equilibrium. But it is clear to everyone that this state of affairs is very fragile and cannot last. That was the real meaning of the speeches delivered by Castro and Roque.

What will happen when Fidel finally leaves the scene? We know that there are people in Cuba – as there were in Russia – who are waiting in the wings, ready to push through a capitalist programme and seize the privatised assets. And as in Russia, a large number of these elements call themselves "Communists". They hold privileged positions and will use these positions when the time comes to plunder the property of the state and turn themselves into private capitalists. The only hope, as Roque pointed out, is to trust in the Cuban workers and peasants and the revolutionary sections of the youth who have no interest in returning to capitalism.

The most pressing need is to strengthen the proletarian vanguard and reinforce that sector that wants to fight to defend the nationalized planned economy and remains loyal to the ideas of Marxism Leninism. It is necessary to open up a serious discussion about the perspectives for the Cuban and Venezuelan Revolutions and for the Marxist movement on a world scale. Such a discussion would be incom-

5. Ibid.

plete without the participation of the Trotskyists, who are the firmest defenders of the Cuban and Venezuelan Revolutions. In the last analysis, however, the only real guarantee for the Cuban revolution is the extension of the socialist revolution throughout Latin America, as Che Guevara maintained to the end.

Once again on 'real socialism'

Heinz Dieterich becomes indignant at the assertion that nobody knows how to build socialism: "For the overcoming of this theoretical stagnation it is not useful to say that no one knows about building the socialism of our century." Who possesses this knowledge? Why, our friend Heinz, of course! Having quickly disposed of the whole history of philosophy and the social sciences in Cuba and Latin America, comrade Dieterich now marches briskly on to deal with the "countries of historical socialism": "The academic discourse of 'really existing socialism' sustains itself on the bases of an idealistic philosophy of identity, such as we find in the philosophy of history of Hegel, which identifies human evolution with Christian teleology, and in the semi-illustrated romanticism of Rousseau, when it equips the 'general will' (the State) with the 'individual wills' (society).

"In the socialist ideology the proceedings have been similar, *identifying mistakenly State property with the social, State surplus with the social* and the policy of the Party with the will of the majority. That method liquidates the dialectic of reality, that is to say the contradictions which are the source of its movements, and make it canonical. 'Canonic' in the sense of structuring reality according to *sacred patterns* of the subject.

"This explains why in the last decades scientific-revolutionary paradigms of importance have not developed in the sociology, economy, theory of the State or the theory of Marx and Engels in the socialist countries. There is nothing of importance for science nor for the struggle of the peoples. There are no theoretical products in these fields which are comparable to liberation theology, to Cepalism, to the theory of dependence or to the Bolivarianism-developmentism of the Regional Latin American Power Bloc." [6]

We can agree with Heinz Dieterich about the lamentable state of philosophy and the social sciences in Stalinist Russia. One man, writing in the British Museum, was capable of producing *Capital*. Yet the Soviet Union, with the colossal resources of the state at its disposal, did not produce a single important work of Marxist philosophy or economics in over half a century after the death of Lenin. The question that should be asked is why this was the case? Were there not enough clever people in the USSR? No, there were many capable philosophers, just as there were many talented artists and brilliant scientists. The problem is that the USSR, despite all the formidable advantages of the nationalized planned economy, was not able to get the

6. Dieterich, *La disyuntiva de Cuba. Capitalismo o nuevo socialismo*, in *Rebelión*, 17/3/06. My emphasis, AW.

best out of this galaxy of human talent. The reason for this was the bureaucratic totalitarian regime that stifled all initiative and strangled artistic freedom.

In order to develop its potential to the fullest degree, human thought needs freedom: freedom to discuss and debate, freedom to make experiments and also to make mistakes. We know that not every scientific experiment is successful, in the sense that it does not get the desired results. But even an "unsuccessful" experiment is useful in the sense that it shows what avenues are *not* to be followed. What is true of science is even truer of art, literature and music. Art cannot flourish in a bureaucratic and totalitarian regime, where the artist is expected to produce works in accordance with the instructions of the state. The artistic norms of so-called socialist realism, were neither socialist nor realistic, but merely a reflection of the prejudices of the narrow minded caste of officials, which are similar to the prejudices of the petty bourgeois philistine everywhere. It is really a miracle that in spite of this petty tutelage the Soviet Union was capable of producing writers and composers of stature (the visual arts suffered most). Geniuses like Shostakovich wrote great masterpieces in spite of the Stalinist bureaucracy, not thanks to it.

When we come to philosophy the same observations apply. Philosophy demands the freedom to discuss and debate the big questions without petty rules and restrictions. In a healthy workers' state, this would be encouraged (always assuming that writers do not engage in counter-revolutionary propaganda). But in a Stalinist regime this is not the case. As a usurping caste that speaks in the name of socialism, the bureaucracy cannot allow freedom in any sphere of social or artistic life. It cannot allow anyone to question its leading role. Since political parties and tendencies were prohibited, the bureaucratic bloodhounds were always on the lookout for "deviations" in other spheres: art, literature, philosophy – even in music and genetics. The Party Line (that is to say, the will of Stalin and the bureaucracy) had to be obeyed unquestioningly in all things. Such a regime does not encourage original creative thought, but quite the opposite. It encourages mindless conformism, servility, routinism, careerism and toadyism.

The writer is always looking over his shoulder to see whether the "boss" is happy with what he writes, and he writes only what is pleasing to those in authority, because they determine whether his work will be published, how much he will earn and whether he will get a nice apartment in Moscow or be sent to languish in some god-forsaken province. It was these material conditions that led to the mediocrity of Soviet philosophy (although there were honourable exceptions). Bureaucratic thought is mediocre by definition. No great work was ever produced by a committee! But precisely this material side is not dealt with by comrade Dieterich, who approaches this question, as he does all others, from a purely idealistic and mystical point of view.

Dieterich's idealist approach

We leave aside such literary gems as "'Canonic' in the sense, of structuring reality according to sacred patterns of the subject" and "Cepalism [...] the theory of dependence or [...] the Bolivarianism-developmentism of the Regional Latin American Power Block." Let other, more subtle, minds than ours struggle to make sense of this ridiculous verbiage. Life is short and we must concentrate on more serious matters. Here we see immediately the *idealist* character of the presentation, which is only partially disguised by the confused and incoherent mode of writing that we have come to recognise as Heinz's principal distinguishing feature as an author. In the first place, what we should be discussing is not the "academic discourse of really existing socialism", but *what actually happened in the USSR*, not what the Moscow bureaucracy said about itself *but what it actually was and what it did*. Moreover, the Stalinist bureaucracy did not sustain itself "on the bases of an idealistic philosophy of identity", but on the basis of a *totalitarian state backed up with the police, the prisons, labour camps and the KGB*.

"In socialist ideology the proceedings have been similar, identifying mistakenly the State property with the social, the State surplus with the social and the policy of the Party with the will of the majority." [7] This is what comrade Dieterich writes. What does it mean? What socialist ideology is he referring to? If he means the monstrous Stalinist caricature of Marxism-Leninism that was taught for decades in Soviet schools and Party institutes, then he should say so. But no, he talks *of socialist ideology in general*. Heinz Dieterich argues as follows: 1) the reason for the degeneration and collapse of the Soviet Union must be looked for in ideological causes (that is, *ideas*). 2) If we accept this, we must also accept that there is some original defect in "socialist ideology" – *that is, some original defect in Marxism*. 3) "Socialist ideology" (Marxism) is the same as Stalinism 4) the collapse of the USSR is also the collapse of the "old ideas", i.e. Marxism. 5) Consequently, we must look for new ideas. 6) Consequently, we must embrace Heinz Dieterich's "socialism of the 21st century".

We shall now see how this applies to the case of Cuba. What is Dieterich's position on Cuba? In the article in *Revista Mariátegui* (15/08/06) he is asked:

"Faced with the illness of Comandante Fidel Castro, could the fate of the Cuban revolution be the same as that of the Russian revolution?

"I think that the possibility is real and, he Fidel himself indicated it in November 2005 in the University of Havana, raising the possible reversibility of the revolution through its own errors. It seems to me that the danger is real. I believe that if there are no significant reforms in the superstructure of historical socialism and the market economy that they have, if they do not make thorough reforms, in few years they are going to revert to capitalism."

7. Ibid.

Comrade Dieterich continues in another publication: "Once the genesis of the revolution has passed and the people have been formed under the educative system of the revolution, however, it would be normal that that function should be assimilated by the institutions, and only exceptionally by the leaders." [8]

What is this mysterious "educative system of the revolution"? Probably he wants to send the workers to school, where they can learn all about socialism of the 21st century, together with Historical Projects, institutions of the future, the exchange of equivalents, Regional Power Blocs, and other fascinating subjects. Once they have shown that they are proficient in all these important subjects, he will presumably issue them with a Certificate of 21st Century Socialist Proficiency, and they can start to think about changing society. Once again Dieterich stands reality on its head. The working class, whether in Russia in 1917 or in Venezuela in 2007, does not learn from books and "educative systems" but from life, from experience, and especially from great events. In a revolution, events move rapidly, the conditions of life of the masses change abruptly, and it is these abrupt changes that transform the consciousness of the masses. If a revolutionary party is present, like the Bolshevik Party in 1917, the masses, beginning with the most advanced layer, will learn much more quickly. That is all.

In normal conditions a man or woman can learn slowly through a process of trial and error. But in a revolution the changes take place so suddenly that there is no time for the class as a whole to learn in such a way. Every error is paid for very dearly. It is the task of the vanguard, organized in a party, to learn from the historical experience of the working class internationally and to apply the lessons to the concrete conditions of the class struggle in its own country. It must try by all means to win the rest of the class through patient work and explanation. This task is facilitated by the fact that in a revolution the masses learn ten times more quickly than in "normal" times. That is the only "educative system of the revolution": the experience of the masses themselves.

Once the workers are "educated", says Dieterich, they can be safely allowed to take decisions, or, more correctly, the taking of decisions can be safely left to "the institution" and the leaders should take decisions "only exceptionally". Behind the democratic verbiage we now see the *purely bureaucratic* mentality of Heinz Dieterich. At the Third All-Russian Congress of Soviets in January 1918, Lenin said: "Very often delegations of workers and peasants come to the government and ask, for example, what to do with such-and-such a piece of land. And frequently I have felt embarrassed when I saw that they had no very definite views. And I said to them: you are the power, do all you want to do, take all you want, we shall support you." [9] At the Seventh Party Congress, a few months later, he emphasized that

8. Ibid.

9. Lenin, *Collected Works*, vol. 26, p. 468.

"*socialism cannot be implemented by a minority, by the Party. It can be implemented only by tens of millions when they have learned to do it themselves*".[10]

These statements of Lenin, which can be duplicated at will, reflected his deep-rooted confidence in the ability of working people to decide their own future. It contrasts sharply to the lies of the bourgeois historians who have attempted to smear the democratic ideas of Leninism with the crimes of Stalinism. This "dictatorship of the proletariat" was in every sense a genuine workers' democracy, unlike the later totalitarian regime of Stalin. Political power was in the hands of the masses represented through the soviets. *Socialism means that the administration and control of industry, society and the state must be in the hands of the working class from the very beginning.* There is no question of anybody standing over the workers and taking decisions on their behalf even "occasionally". Such an idea would have been regarded as an abomination by Lenin, as the quotations above show very clearly.

Socialism and the market

Dieterich advises the Cubans that reform is necessary to prevent the restoration of capitalism. Most Cubans would agree with him. But there are reforms and reforms. Some reforms would undoubtedly help to avoid the restoration of capitalism. *But there are other reforms that would have precisely the opposite effect.* Like a drunken man staggering from one bar to another, our Heinz staggers from one theoretical confusion to the next:

"For the organization of the Soviet economy there were potentially three subjects: the State, the market and society. A particular form of property corresponded to each one: the State or public, private one and the social one. The revolution being of an anti-capitalist nature, the market, that is the business class, was excluded as an organizing option. Due to the scarce development of the productive forces, the destruction of the war and the low cultural level of the people (illiteracy), it was equally almost impossible that the population (society) would satisfactorily organize the economy in that gigantic country. There remained, then, the State as principal operator of the economy and, in consequence, the state or public property as dominant."[11]

To begin with, let us note that this paragraph constitutes *a veiled apology for Stalinism*. According to Heinz Russia was too backward and the workers too illiterate and ignorant for the proletariat to administer society. What period is comrade Dieterich talking about here? Unless this question is answered, it is not possible to make any sense of what he writes. As usual, he expresses himself in a most confused manner. What is meant by "For the organization of the Soviet economy there were potentially three subjects"? This does not make sense. *After the October Revolution the nationalized planed economy was run by the state with the democratic partici-*

10. Ibid, vol. 27, p. 135, my emphasis, AW.
11. Dieterich, *La disyuntiva de Cuba: capitalismo o nuevo socialismo*.

pation of the working class through the soviets. However, the revolution faced enormous difficulties. No sooner had the workers and peasants taken power, than they were faced with armed imperialist intervention to overthrow the Soviet power. Lenin and the Bolsheviks understood very well that if the revolution was not spread to the West, they would be doomed.

Dieterich refers to Lenin's NEP in Russia. But what was the NEP and how did it come into being? The first years of the Soviet power were characterized by acute economic difficulties, partly the result of war and civil war, partly as a result of shortages of both materials and skilled manpower, and partly of the opposition of the peasant small property owners to the socialist measures of the Bolsheviks. During the civil war nine million perished through famine, disease and freezing conditions. The economy was in ruins and on the verge of collapse. In order to put a stop to this catastrophic decline, drastic measures were introduced to get industry moving, to feed the hungry workers and to end the drift from town to country.

Dieterich is in favour of a mixed economy. Even in a workers' state with a nationalized economy, it would be correct to leave part of the economy in private hands: small shops and family businesses, small private farms, etc. These enterprises have no independent role in the economy. They are entirely dependent on the big banks and monopolies, supermarkets, big transport companies, etc. In a workers' state they would be entirely dependent on the state sector, which would treat them a lot better than they are now treated by the monopolies that ruthlessly exploit them and drive them out of business. We have no plans to imitate the Stalinists in Bulgaria who in 1945 even nationalized the shoe-shine boys.

However, when Dieterich speaks of a "mixed economy" he is talking about something entirely different. He is opposed to the expropriation of the banks and big industries in Venezuela (except PDVSA, which is nationalized already). That is to say, he is in favour of leaving intact the economic power of the oligarchy, confining the "socialist" element in the economy to the small businesses that are run as co-operatives. That is to say, by "mixed economy" he does not mean a socialist economy, where the bulk of the economy is in the hands of the state (and the state is in the hands of the workers) and there is a small private sector consisting mainly of small businesses. He means a capitalist economy, in which most of the key sectors of the economy are in the hands of the landowners, bankers and capitalists, and a minority, consisting mainly of small businesses are run as co-operatives. *That is, he advocates a system that is the precise opposite of Lenin's NEP.*

Comrade Dieterich says that "a big bourgeoisie in Cuba must not be permitted nor is it necessary to permit, because the State substitutes for its economic functions. The innovation-production-commercialization complex of biotechnology, for example, fills the functions of the transnational enterprises (competitivity, innovation, capital) together with economic contents more human than the capitalist." But then he immediately adds:

"There remains, then, the problem of the small bourgeoisie, that is, small mercantile production. We recall the advice of Lenin on this class, but we remember also, that at a certain historic moment he had to implement the NEP, with the certainty that the revolutionaries could control the bourgeois tendencies through the enormous monopolistic power of the Soviet State; b) that in no country in the world has the State been able to provide services of adequate quality, for example, in gastronomy; c) that no State has been able to give the cities the diversity of small enterprises, stores, subcultures, et cetera, which gives them life, which is particularly important in economies of tourism; d) that the political-economic control of this class could be achieved probably with the tax – and judicial system; e) that in the global economy of the FTAA the guarantees of economic reproduction of the small businessman can only be provided by the State through protectionism and subsidies, which is the fundamental reason why FEDEINDUSTRIA in Venezuela is with the Bolivarian process and why the small peasant and Latin American enterprise supports Hugo Chávez' ALBA initiative.

"In resume: the situation of the small bourgeoisie in the USSR under Lenin was fundamentally different from that of the Latin American small bourgeoisie today and will have to be analyzed concretely to know in what degree it may be tolerated or no." [12]

In a nationalized planned economy, where the state is in the hands of the working class, as was the case in Russia when Lenin and Trotsky stood at the helm of the Bolshevik Party, it is permissible to allow a certain amount of small businesses. But Lenin always warned of the dangers involved in this. Behind the small businesses stands the might of world capitalism and the tremendous pressure of the capitalist world market. Under certain conditions the private sector can become the transmission belt for the penetrations of these powerful pressures and they can threaten the very existence of the nationalized planned economy. Lenin honestly described NEP as a retreat. He warned of its consequences and insisted that the Soviet workers must have independent trade unions to defend themselves against the NEPmen and bureaucrats:

"The proletarian state may, without changing its own nature, permit freedom to trade and the development of capitalism only within certain bounds, and only on the condition that the state regulates (supervises, controls, determines the forms and methods of, etc.) private trade and private capitalism. The success of such regulation will depend not only on the state authorities but also, and to a larger extent, on the degree of maturity of the proletariat and of the masses of the working people generally, on their cultural level, etc. But even if this regulation is completely successful, the antagonism of class interests between labour and capital will certainly remain. Consequently, one of the main tasks that will henceforth confront the trade

12. Dieterich, *Cuba: Three premises to save the Revolution after the death of Fidel.*

unions is to protect in every way the class interests of the proletariat in its struggle against capital. This task should be openly put in the forefront, and the machinery of the trade unions must be reorganised, changed or supplemented accordingly (conflict commissions, strike funds, mutual aid funds, etc., should be formed, or rather, built up)." [13]

At the heart of NEP was the introduction of a tax-in-kind, which permitted peasants to dispose of their food surpluses on the open market. This concession to market forces soon resulted in the strengthening of the bourgeois elements in the towns and particularly in the countryside. It led to the denationalization of small-scale industry and services; the establishment of trusts for supplying, financing, and marketing the products of large-scale industry; the granting of concessions to foreign investors. It was only permissible as long as the state kept a firm grip on the commanding heights of the economy (large-scale industry, banking, and foreign trade).

The NEP permitted a revival of the Soviet economy and by 1926-27, most economic indices were at or near pre-war levels. But recovery via market forces was accompanied by the re-emergence of capitalist elements class in both the countryside (the kulaks) and the towns (nepmen). There was a growth of unemployment among workers and the loss of revolutionary dynamism. Lenin had repeatedly warned in his last writings and speeches of the danger of capitalist restoration. Behind the nepmen and kulaks stood the might of world imperialism. The NEP could be the transmission mechanism through which world imperialism could penetrate the Soviet Union. It could even express itself through the Communist Party itself.

At the end of his life Lenin was alarmed by the capitalist tendencies that had been unleashed by the NEP. He had always regarded the NEP in any case as a temporary measure taken in a moment of extreme danger. He intended to use the breathing space offered by the economic recovery to strengthen the socialist elements and gradually reverse the market policies of the NEP period, but he fell ill and died before he could do this.

It is frankly irresponsible to play with historical analogies without explaining the specific context in which they unfolded and their limits. The proposal of comrade Dieterich to make concessions to the small bourgeois elements carries an extreme danger of capitalist restoration in the given conditions of Cuba. The fact that Cuba is only a few miles from the most powerful and richest imperialist nation means that behind the small native bourgeois elements lie powerful forces: the big monopolies that dominate the world market and US imperialism, which is striving by every means at its disposal to restore capitalism in Cuba. It is completely false and unprincipled to cite "Lenin's NEP" as a policy for Cuba to follow without making a single reference to Lenin's warnings concerning the NEP and particularly his last

13. Lenin, *Role and Functions of the Trade Unions under the New Economic Policy, Decision of the CC, RCP(B)*, January 12, 1922.

speeches. At the Eleventh Congress of the Russian Communist Party – the last which Lenin attended – he emphasized repeatedly the dangers to the State and Party arising out of the pressures of backwardness and bureaucracy. Commenting on the direction of the State, Lenin warned:

"Well, we have lived through a year, the state is in our hands, but has it operated the New Economic Policy in the way we wanted in the past year? No. But we refuse to admit that it did not operate in the way we wanted. How did it operate? The machine refused to obey the hand that guided it. It was like a car that was going not in the direction the driver desired but in the direction someone else desired; as if it were being driven by some mysterious, lawless hand, God knows whose, perhaps of a profiteer, or of a private capitalist, or of both. *Be that as it may, the car is not going quite in the direction the man at the wheel imagines, and often it goes in an altogether different direction.*" [14]

At the same Congress Lenin explained, in a very clear and unambiguous language, the possibility of the degeneration of the revolution as a result of the pressure of alien classes. Already the most farsighted sections of the émigré bourgeoisie, the *Smena Vekh* group of Ustryalov, were openly placing their hopes upon the bureaucratic-bourgeois tendencies manifesting themselves in Soviet society, as a step in the direction of capitalist restoration. The same group was later to applaud and encourage the Stalinists in their struggle against "Trotskyism". At the 11th Congress Lenin quoted the words of Ustryalov:

"'...I am in favour of supporting the Soviet government,' says Ustryalov, although he was a Constitutional-Democrat, a bourgeois, and supported intervention. 'I am in favour of supporting Soviet power because it has taken the road that will lead it to the ordinary bourgeois state.' The *Smena Vekh* group, which Lenin gave credit for its class insight, correctly understood the struggle of Stalin against Trotsky, not in terms of personalities but as a *class question*, as a step away from the revolutionary traditions of October. Referring to the views of *Smena Vekh*, Lenin said:

"We must say frankly that the things Ustryalov speaks about are possible, history knows all sorts of metamorphoses. Relying on firmness of convictions, loyalty, and other splendid moral qualities is anything but a serious attitude in politics. A few people may be endowed with splendid moral qualities, but historical issues are decided by vast masses, which, if the few do not suit them, may at times treat them none too politely." [15]

After Lenin's death, Trotsky and the Left Opposition repeatedly demanded an end to the Right turn and a return to Lenin's policies. But the leading faction of Stalin-Bukharin ignored all the warnings. This placed the Revolution in extreme danger. By 1928 the dangers of capitalist restoration were clear even to Stalin. He

14. Lenin, *Collected Works*, vol. 33, p. 179, my emphasis, AW.
15. Ibid, vol. 33, page 287.

was compelled to abandon the NEP and launch the programme of collectivization and Five Year Plans that had been advocated by the Left Opposition. But Stalin carried out this policy in an ultra left, bureaucratic and hooligan manner that caused serious dislocation and an agricultural disaster that caused a famine and the deaths of millions.

"The machine no longer obeyed the driver" – the State was no longer under the control of the Communists, of the workers, but was increasingly raising itself above society. Lenin's warnings are very relevant for Cuba today. People who have no wish to return to capitalism may well become the agents of forces over which they have no control. If the Cuban Communists were so foolish as to follow the advice of Heinz Dieterich – the Ustryalov of the 21st century – they would very quickly find themselves on a slippery slope towards capitalism from which it would be difficult to turn back. Oh yes, history knows all kinds of peculiar transformations!

On 'heroic' and 'un-heroic' periods

The bureaucratic degeneration of the Russian Revolution was not the result of any defects in Marxist theory, or the fact that the human genome had not yet been discovered, or even the lack of computer skills, but the inevitable consequence of the isolation of the Revolution in conditions of the most frightful economic and cultural backwardness. From a Marxist point of view, there is nothing surprising about this. But it is not sufficient for our Heinz, who is always hankering after something new. How does Heinz Dieterich explain the Stalinist degeneration of the USSR? Let us see:

"That unavoidable practical necessity generated, however, two difficulties. In the first place, an insoluble ideological problem. With the heroic phase of the revolution passed, the people did not want to work mainly for the glory of a State. Once the revolution becomes mundane, the Stakhanovism, those 'Red Saturdays' and the martyrs become a minority, and the majorities expect from the socialist State that it would provide them with certain services, as are expected from whatever other type of State.

"They will be willing to work for their mystifications, such as the King, the Fatherland, God, or 'society'; but not for an apparatus of control and domination such as is the State. Confronted by this problem, a laic and socialist revolution like the Soviet one had few options available, in fact, only one: identify the State with Society, in that way the work on the land (kolkhozes or sovkhozes) or in state factories was work for society, that is, for one's self. The volonté générale of Rousseau and the Jacobins, the general will and the will of the individual could this way become identical." [16]

Even the language used by comrade Dieterich contains a reactionary idea: the working class, it seems, are prepared to "work for their mystifications, such as the

16. Dieterich, *La disyuntiva de Cuba: Capitalismo o nuevo socialismo.*

King, the Fatherland, God, or 'society', but not for an apparatus of control and domination such as is the State." This sneering sentence contains *a reactionary slander* against the working class. It shows the real attitude of the founder of "Socialism of the 21st century" towards working class people: the contemptuous attitude of an intellectual snob and a conservative reformist bureaucrat. It states that the workers are ignorant and prone to mystifications. They are prepared blindly to follow like sheep "the King, the Fatherland, God, or 'society' (?)" but they are not prepared to make sacrifices for a (workers') state.

If that were the case, how did the Russian workers take power in November 1917? That act entailed very serious sacrifices. Many people sacrificed their lives for the cause of the socialist revolution. Was this also a "mystification"? Did these backward Russian workers, ignorant and prone to monarchist and religious mystifications, suddenly decide to enlist in Dr. Dieterich's "academy of revolution" and receive an honorary degree in Socialism of the 21st century? Since our Heinz had not yet been born, this option was, regrettably, not available to them, as it is, fortunately, now available to us. So we are forced to seek alternative explanations as to how this miraculous transformation was achieved.

Naturally, our Heinz has a simple explanation. This was the "heroic phase of the revolution", you see. And in a "heroic phase", naturally, people behave *heroically*. On the other hand, in an un-heroic phase, people will always behave *un-heroically*. *Quod erat demonstrandum!* (which in the good old Latin tongue means: "*I have proved what I set out to prove!*"). The logic is *almost* impeccable, but unfortunately it answers nothing. What did the "heroic phase" of the revolution consist of? How did the un-heroic herd suddenly decide to become heroic, and why did they subsequently decide to become un-heroic again? On all of this our Heinz is as silent as the grave. As usual, he merely presupposes what was to be proven in the first place. But we have already become accustomed to this decidedly *un-heroic* method of argument.

In the summer of 1914 the workers, not only of Russia, but of Germany, France and Britain, were mobilized by the war machine in their respective countries to fight in an imperialist war. Mostly they went willingly, believing the propaganda of the ruling class, that they were fighting to defend their country, their families, etc., against a terrible external enemy (German militarism, Russian barbarians, etc.). Of course, it was all a lie, and they eventually realised that it was a lie. But the only way they could discover this for themselves was by experience, since that is the way the workers of all countries learn, not by attending our Heinz's classes on Socialism of the 21st century.

Was there nobody who could have explained this to them in 1914? Was there no force to counter the propaganda of the imperialists? Yes, such a force existed: the *Socialist International*, which represented millions of organized workers in Britain, Germany, Austria, Russia and all the other belligerent nations. Formally, the parties of the Second (Socialist) International stood for socialism and Marxism. In a series of international congresses before 1914 they voted for resolutions in which they pledged themselves to oppose imperialist war and, in the event of a war breaking out, to mobilize the masses for the overthrow of capitalism. But in the summer of 1914 the leader of every one of these parties (except the Russians and Serbs) supported the war.

It was this betrayal of the leaders of the international Social Democracy that destroyed any possibility of working class resistance to the imperialist war. Lenin, Trotsky, Rosa Luxemburg and Karl Liebknecht all denounced this as a monstrous betrayal of the International. Rosa Luxemburg described the Second International as a "stinking corpse". It was not the "false consciousness" of the workers that caused this situation, but the criminal betrayal of the reformist leaders, whom Lenin described as "social traitors". Yet on this subject Heinz Dieterich maintains a diplomatic silence. He prefers *to blame the working class.* And this is absolutely typical of his whole approach.

Since, according to Dieterich, the working class was to blame for the war (because of their firm attachment to the monarchy, religion, etc.) how does one explain the fact that the very same workers (there were no others) later overthrew the tsar and staged revolutions in Germany, Hungary and other countries? Dieterich has no explanation for this, except the nonsense about "heroic phases". But this is no explanation at all. How does comrade Dieterich explain that at one moment the workers are in a "reactionary phase" (1914) and then mysteriously enter a "heroic phase" (1917)? What is the reason for this?

The real reason is that the working class, having passed through the cruel school of imperialist war, began to draw revolutionary conclusions from their experience. Nobody taught them. The Bolshevik Party was weak and dispersed. Its leaders were in exile or in Siberia. In January 1917, Lenin, who was in exile in Switzerland and almost completely cut off from the workers in Russia, addressed a meeting of Swiss Young Socialists. In his speech, Lenin said: "We of the older generation may not live to see the decisive battles of this coming revolution." One month later, the tsar was overthrown. In less than a year, the Bolsheviks had come to power.

Beneath the surface, the mood of the masses had been slowly changing. Trotsky described this process as the molecular process of revolution. It is a process that proceeds so gradually that it is frequently imperceptible, even to revolutionaries, who sometimes draw the wrong conclusions from the appearance of apathy and the absence of surface manifestations of the accumulated frustration, rage and bitterness. It is very similar to the gradual building up of pressure beneath the earth's surface prior to an earthquake. This process is also invisible to the superficial observer who looks no further than the surface, without taking into account the seething processes that are unfolding in the bowels of the earth. When the eruption takes place, it produces general astonishment.

All kinds of "learned" people proffer explanations, which usually go no further than the immediate cause, which really explains nothing at all. Thus, the February revolution is said to be caused by the scarcity of bread. But in the years following the October revolution, the shortage of bread was far worse than before as a consequence of the civil war provoked by the counter-revolution and the invasion of 21 foreign armies of intervention. Why did this not produce a new revolution? This question is never asked, and cannot be answered if we persist in confusing the immediate incident that sparked off the movement with its deeper underlying causes, that is, to confuse accident with necessity, like the old school text-books that asserted that the First World War was caused by the assassination of the Archduke Ferdinand in Sarajevo, and not by the accumulation of contradictions between the main imperialist powers before 1914.

"They [the workers] will be willing to work for their mystifications, such as the King, the Fatherland, God, or society; *but not for an apparatus of control and domination such as is the State.*" This is how comrade Dieterich describes the attitude of the Russian working class. But wait a moment! From a Marxist point of view, the state is always an instrument of domination by one class over another. But there is a fundamental difference between the old capitalist state, which represents the *control and domination of a minority over the majority* and a workers' state (the dictatorship of the proletariat), which represents the *domination of the majority over a small minority of exploiters.* The kind of state envisaged by Marx and Lenin was a *semi-state*, in which the working class exercised control over industry, society and the state. It was a state designed to "wither away". This was the state established by the Bolsheviks in 1917 and enthusiastically supported by the overwhelming majority of society – the workers and poor peasants. This state had nothing in common with the monstrous bureaucratic totalitarian state that Stalin erected over the dead body of Lenin's Party.

What does Dieterich mean when he talks about the "heroic phase" of the Russian Revolution? In 1917 the workers exercised control of the Soviet state through their democratic organs of power. That was a genuine *participative democracy*! It was the most democratic state in history. But when the Russian Revolution was isolated in conditions of terrible backwardness, the situation changed. Revolution, as Trotsky explained, is a terrible devourer of human physical and nervous energy. By the time Lenin was obliged to sound the retreat with the introduction of the NEP, the working class was severely weakened.

After years of war, revolution and civil war, the masses were exhausted. Many of the most advanced elements were killed in the bloody Civil War that lasted until 1921. By the introduction of the NEP, the workers' control over the state was beginning to weaken. The Soviet bureaucracy began to flex its muscles and become conscious of its power. The officials began to elbow the workers to one side and take control of the state. This was a gradual process that took place over more than a decade. All this was rooted in *material conditions*. "Heroism" had nothing to do with it.

Bourgeois reformism

In *The Cuban Dilemma: Capitalism or New Socialism* (April 12, 2006), Heinz Dieterich writes: "Toward the middle of the seventies, the socialist ideology above described had exhausted its ability to hold the historic project of 1917 together and to provide strategic guidelines for the future. The revelations on Stalinism, the Soviet military repression in the GDR (1953), (1956), and Czechoslovakia (1968), and the schism with Chinese socialism, had stripped it of the historic world legitimacy which it enjoyed in the 20s. That crisis of the inherited ideological paradigm, sharpened by the crisis of the pattern of extensive accumulation of the post-war model, obliged the socialist leaders to choose between three options if they wanted to maintain themselves in power: a) return in a controlled manner to the market; b) advance toward socialism of the 21st century or, c) try to combine elements of both systems in a 'market socialism'."

Following his usual idealist, anti-Marxist method, Dieterich attributes the decline and fall of Stalinism to an *ideology*, which, moreover, he persists in calling "socialist". As usual, he explains nothing. He merely asserts that the "socialist ideology" (Stalinism) had "exhausted itself" by the mid-1970s. Why? Why did it exhaust itself? And why did this occur toward the middle of the seventies, and not ten or twenty years earlier? He does not say, because he does not know. He lists a series of crimes of Stalinism, such as the Soviet military repression in the GDR (1953), Hungary (1956), and Czechoslovakia (1968), and the schism with Chinese "socialism", and informs us that these things had stripped it of the "historic world legitimacy" which it enjoyed in the 1920s. This reminds us of the lines that George Gordon Byron wrote ridiculing another English poet, Ernest Hartely Coleridge:

Explaining Metaphysics to the nation,
I wish he would explain his explanation.

In the first place, let us remark that the things that, according to comrade Dieterich, stripped Stalinism of its "historic world legitimacy" were not at all ideological but very practical in character. The workers of East Berlin, Budapest and Prague were not repressed by ideological arguments or discourse but by tanks and bullets. And the Russian and Chinese comrades held their fraternal debates on the border not with dialectics but with rockets and machine guns. The crimes of Stalinism did not begin with the things Heinz Dieterich mentions. They have been known for decades. But they did not lead to the fall of the USSR. Why not? Once again, in order to understand this we must return to the method of Marxism, the materialist method, which explains historical development, not by mythologies and moralistic arguments, but ultimately in terms of the development of the productive forces.

It is quite useless to approach history from an abstract moralistic standpoint. Capitalism, in the words of Marx, came onto the scene of history dripping blood from every pore. Yet it successfully established itself as the dominant socio-economic system on a world scale in the 19th and 20th centuries. The reason is very simple: despite its monstrous exploitative and inhuman nature, capitalism led to an unheard-of development of the productive forces: industry, agriculture, science and technology. This, in turn created the material base for a new socialist civilization in the future.

It is true that the Stalinist bureaucracy acted as colossal brake on the development of culture, that it encouraged mediocrity and servile conformism. But these are only the secondary effects of the fundamental contradiction that undermined the nationalized planned economy and led to the collapse of the USSR. Yes, it is true that the Stalinist regime that comrade Dieterich used to praise, played a negative role in this field. But what does he choose to compare with the lack of development of social sciences in Stalinist Russia? Of all the things he could have chosen, he decides to cite Cepalism and the theory of dependency! What are these wonderful ideas that comrade Dieterich finds so appealing? They are nothing but vulgar Keynesianism, that is, *bourgeois reformism*, applied to the so-called Third World countries.

The CEPAL was created in 1948 as a body of the United Nations dealing with economic development in Latin America. In the 1950s, under the direction of Raul Presbich it developed the idea that the obstacle to economic growth in the continent was its dependency upon the advanced capitalist countries. What was their solution? It was state intervention in the economy, protectionism, import substitution, etc. This short-lived Keynesianism quickly led to hyper inflation and economic stagnation as soon as oil prices collapsed. Several of the proponents of *cepalismo* found themselves implementing structural adjustment plans and shock therapies (i.e. massive cuts in social spending and generalised attacks on workers' wages and conditions) in the 1980s and 1990s, showing the impossibility of reformist policies in Latin America.

Fernando Henrique Cardoso, who was closely linked to CEPAL and one of the main theoreticians of "dependency theory" in the 1960s, and then became the minister of Finances and eventually Prime Minister of Brazil, implementing a thoroughly anti-working class programme of cuts and "adjustment". This is what our Heinz chooses to praise! In the same way as he praises bourgeois democracy as the alternative to "real socialism", so he praises bourgeois reformism as the alternative to socialist revolution.

Dieterich's advocacy of *cepalismo* is even more scandalous in the case of Venezuela. These were precisely the ideas implemented by the first Carlos Andrés Pérez government in 1974-79, when, basing himself on high oil prices, he attempted to industrialise the country. These policies had the same disastrous results as elsewhere. They led to an inflationary crisis and a sharp reversal in 1989, when the "reformist" Carlos Andrés Pérez used the military to crush the Caracazo – a popular uprising against his package of cuts. The repetition of the old discredited formulas of Latin American Social Democracy and reformism is not only *mediocre* but completely *anti-socialist and anti-revolutionary.*

The 'Chinese road'?

"Significantly, none (!) of the socialist parties opted for the advance toward the socialism of the 21st century. The explanation of this incredible phenomenon is found in three reasons: 1) the lack of a scientific theory of transition to the new socialism, or, what is the same thing, the incapacity of the communist parties to understand socialism as a phenomenon in development, with which they had hardly shared an archaic stage and which they canonized as the only one; there is no clearer parameter than this one to indicate the loss of dialectics by these parties and leaders; 2) a party which administered the revolution, rather than direct it, due to its pragmatism and opportunism, and 3. a Party-State lacking cybernetic abilities.

"Before such a scenario the leaders hesitated. They oscillated between advances toward the capitalist market and returns toward socialist orthodoxy until the objective conditions, imperialism and or the population put an end to their governments by force. *Only the post-Mao Chinese leadership maintained itself stable, because it consciously chose (under Deng Xiao Ping) the road of autocratic capitalist modernization which the Asian tigers had travelled before with tremendous success.*"[17]

The last sentence makes us scratch our heads. What does this mean? If the road of autocratic capitalist modernization has been such a tremendous success then why not advocate it for Cuba and Venezuela? Our friend Heinz maintains a diplomatic silence, but he evidently does not think that "Chinese socialism" is such a bad thing. Moreover, we know that there are some people both in Cuba and Venezuela who think that this is indeed the road to travel. At least Heinz does not try to fool us on this question. He does not speak of Chinese *socialism* but directly says that China has entered on the road of autocratic *capitalist* modernization. That is correct, and it is also correct that China has achieved spectacular results, although a more careful analysis will show that these results were achieved by combining the tremendous gains made by the nationalized planned economy over the past half century with participation on the world market.

Those who advocate the "Chinese road" for Cuba and Venezuela are advocating capitalism. Let us be clear on that. To adopt the Chinese model in Venezuela means to halt the revolution, to keep private ownership of the means of production and to destroy the elements of workers' control and democracy that have been conquered and place all power in the hands of a privileged bureaucracy that is organi-

17. Ibid.

cally linked to big business. *This is a programme of outright counter-revolution.* It is a scandal that anyone associated with the Bolivarian Movement should defend it.

For Cuba it is even worse. It is the programme of privatization of the nationalized economy, the conversion of state industry into private monopolies. That is, it signifies the destruction of all the fundamental gains of the Cuban Revolution – and all this would be done under the banner of the Communist Party – as in China. The bureaucrats would rule but they would do so as private capitalists and billionaires, who could pass on their wealth to their children as private property. One can see how such a programme would be very attractive to the most corrupt and reactionary layer of state officials and administrators. But it would not be so appealing to millions of Cuban workers. The working class has no interest in the privatization of the industries and the creation of a new class of bureaucratic capitalists and billionaires to exploit and rob them as is now happening in China. The conditions of the Chinese workers and peasants have rapidly sunk to the levels described by Karl Marx in *Capital* or Charles Dickens in his descriptions of the conditions of the working class in Victorian England.

The workers, the revolutionary youth and the most advanced sectors of the Cuban intelligentsia will never accept the destruction of their revolutionary conquests without a struggle. Nor would it be so easy to make the Communist Party into an instrument of capitalist counter-revolution. Before that could happen there would be a fierce struggle between the traitors and pro-bourgeois elements and the genuine Communists who wish to defend the gains of the Cuban Revolution at all costs. In this struggle the Trotskyists will be unconditionally on the side of the latter. On whose side will Heinz Dieterich be?

Strategic crisis: tactical measures?

"The lessons for the island are clear. *The old socialist paradigm no longer sustains the Cuban Revolution, because it is not based on an effective historical truth, but on an ideology of the past.* Before such a situation, some economic improvements in the home, pressure cookers and saving electric bulbs, will not succeed in stabilizing the process. The dimension of the crisis is strategic: it is the end of a historical project. And before this dimension of the problem, tactical measures will not be sufficient to fill the double vacuum left by the exhaustion of the founding historical project and the disappearance of the heroic generation.

"If the Revolution does not comprehend or denies that the crisis is paradigmatic, if, in consequence, it does not try to take the step toward the Socialism of the 21st century and does not implement immediate economic-political measures which will make the population understand that a more democratic society and level of life awaits them, it will be difficult to save it. It would then follow the path of the Soviet Union and that would be a tragedy for mankind".

On one point at least we can agree with comrade Dieterich: the victory of the bourgeois counter-revolution in Cuba would not just be tragedy for mankind. It would be a heavy blow against the socialist revolution in Venezuela, in Latin America and on a world scale. It is the duty of every conscious worker to fight against it with all his strength and all the means at his disposal. But how does comrade Dieterich "fight" the bourgeois counter-revolution? He directs most of his fire, not against the bourgeois, but against "the old socialist paradigm [...], because it is not based on an effective historical truth, but on an ideology of the past". What is this old "paradigm"? It is the "old" idea that socialism must be based on a nationalized planned economy. And what is the "ideology of the past" that is "not based on an effective historical truth"? Why Marxism, of course!

Heinz is annoyed with the leaders of the Cuban Communist Party (and all the others) because they have not yet seen the light and embraced his theory of Socialism of the 21st Century. "Significantly, none of the socialist parties opted for the advance toward the socialism of the 21st century," he grumbles. And why not? Because of "the lack of a scientific theory of transition to the new socialism, or, what is the same thing, the incapacity of the communist parties to understand socialism as a phenomenon in development."

It is a very sad comment on the state of humanity when the Prophet of 21st Century Socialism appears with the Tablets of Stone in his hands (or rather, on the internet) and yet people pay not the slightest attention. Poor Heinz cannot conceal his frustration at this state of affairs, which he regards as incredible. Has he not written innumerable books and articles on this subject? Can Cuban communists not read? Of course they can! Cuba is well known for the high level of education of its population. Then it must be because they are incapable of understanding him – that is, because they are all stupid. Yes, it seems incredible, but what other explanation is possible from Heinz's point of view? Comrade Dieterich can console himself with the thought that he is not the first Prophet to experience such tribulations. Moses himself experienced the greatest difficulties getting the ancient Israelites to stop dancing around a certain gilded bovine, and in vain did Jesus cast his pearls before swine. The Founder of 21st Century Socialism is condemned to tread the weary path of John the Baptist: *vox clamans in deserto* (a voice crying in the wilderness). What a sad place this sinful world is for a poor Prophet who nobody understands!

Socialism in one country?

The socialist revolution cannot be a single, simultaneous act. The political and social conditions in every country have their own dynamic and its own dialectic. The October Revolution took place in a very backward country where the material conditions for socialism did not exist, but Lenin and the Bolsheviks never saw it as a self-sufficient act but as the first stage of the world revolution which would unavoidably extend over decades. The same could be said of the Cuban (and Venezuelan) Revolution.

The strength of the Cuban economy lies in the nationalization of the means of production and their planned direction. Its weakness lies in its isolation. As Trotsky explained: "The weakness of Soviet economy, in addition to the backwardness inherited from the past, lies in its isolation, that is, in its inability to gain access to the resources of world economy, in the shape of normal international credits and financing in general, which plays a decisive a role in the world economy." [18] In his speech at the Eleventh Party Congress March 27, 1922, Lenin spoke of the world market, "to which we are subordinated, with which we are bound up, and from which we cannot escape."

Cuba has managed partly to solve this problem by increasing the tourist sector, through the export of nickel and through the flow of remittances from Cubans working abroad. But this has created new contradictions. Some Cubans have access to foreign currency, while others do not. This creates a gap between "haves" and "have- nots" – in effect a two-tier economy. This is a most serious threat to the nationalized planned economy. It encourages corruption and all sorts of dishonest practices. It is not possible to eliminate these practices by exhortations and repression. Ordinary, honest Cuban citizens are compelled to some extent to participate in this "parallel economy" in order to survive.

Meanwhile, the contradictions inherited from Cuba's underdeveloped capitalist past have not disappeared despite the achievements of the planned economy, but have been encouraged by the recent recovery from the years of hardship; they can revive and be aggravated with the growth of the Cuban economy. In order to be overcome they demand that access to the resources of the world market be achieved.

The real danger to socialism is not imperialist intervention (they have abandoned that idea after they burned their fingers at the Bay of Pigs) but the penetration of cheap foreign goods that are of higher quality than the domestic products. If the US ruling class were more intelligent they would abandon the blockade of Cuba and encourage trade. This would undermine the nationalized economy far more effectively than any blockade. But the US imperialists are exceptionally stupid. They are too blinded by hate for "the Castro regime" to understand even what is in their own interest.

The isolation of Cuba creates all kinds of shortages and bottlenecks that find their expression in daily problems experienced by every worker and housewife. The conditions of the masses have improved in comparison with the past but do not keep step with expectations. There are particular difficulties with transport, housing and food. The situation is made much worse by the fact that some people have easier access to foreign currency and goods than others.

18. Trotsky, Introduction to the German edition of *The Permanent Revolution*.

Trotsky explained the kind of programme that would be necessary for a workers' state that found itself isolated for a time:

"A realistic program for an isolated workers' state cannot set itself the goal of achieving 'independence' from world economy, much less of constructing a national socialist society 'in the shortest time'. The task is not to attain the abstract maximum tempo, but the optimum tempo, that is, the best, that which follows from both internal and world economic conditions, strengthens the position of the proletariat, prepares the national elements of the future international socialist society, and at the same time, and above all, systematically improves the living standards of the proletariat and strengthens its alliance with the non-exploiting masses of the countryside. This prospect must remain in force for the whole preparatory period, that is, until the victorious revolution in the advanced countries liberates the Soviet Union from its present isolated position." [19]

If it was not possible to construct a self-sufficient socialist society in Russia and China, still less will it be possible in Cuba or Venezuela. There is an indivisible interdependence between the revolution in Cuba, Venezuela and the rest of the American continent. Success for the revolutionary movement in Venezuela presupposes a revolutionary movement in Bolivia, Ecuador and vice versa. Neither in Venezuela, nor in Bolivia, in Cuba or anywhere else is it possible to build an independent socialist society. They will have to enter as parts into a higher whole. This is the basis of Marxist internationalism.

The socialist order presupposes high levels of technology and culture and solidarity of population. In each of the countries of Latin America the material conditions for this are insufficient. However, the victory of socialism in Latin America would create a mighty bloc of power, mobilizing millions of people and with vast resources and reserves. What capitalist country, or coalition of countries, would dare think of intervention in these circumstances? Under such circumstances, the US imperialists would not be contemplating a military intervention in Latin America but revolutionary upheavals in the USA itself!

In the course of several Five-Year Plans, a socialist federation of Latin America would be able to construct a mighty socialist society with its own forces, with a standard of living higher than that of the USA and a democratic regime based on the active participation of the whole population in the administration of the economy, society and the state. This would mean a death blow to world capitalism, and would reduce to a minimum, if not to zero, the possibility of external intervention. This would create an irresistible movement in the direction of the world socialist revolution.

Platonic obscurantism

Dieterich is scathing about this proposal: "The idealistic ethic which follows Platonic obscurantism, daily reinforced by the moral hypocrisy of Catholicism,

19. Ibid.

denies this consumption – the material, sensual, carnal –as 'value'. For revolutionary socialism and science, which takes off from the constituent binomial of material-energy of the universe, all ethics have to be materialist-dialectical, which inevitably considers reproduction, enjoyment and sensuality of the material as an integral part of the human condition. And, in fact, the majority of humanity acts on this pattern. For it, to reach the historically determined quality of life is a value: as strong, or even stronger than certain moral values or 'spiritual virtues'. Dialectically, the material converts itself into its opposite, the spiritual." [20]

The above paragraph is a splendid example of Dieterichian obscurantism. What is the "constituent binomial of material-energy of the universe"? Only God and Heinz Dieterich know the answer. But let us once more take a sharp machete to Comrade Dieterich's jungle of twisted syntax and try to cut our way towards some semblance of meaning (a very exhausting task!). We are told that for revolutionary socialism and science "all ethics has to be materialist-dialectical, which inevitably considers reproduction, enjoyment and sensuality of the material as an integral part of the human condition."

Now in the first place historical materialism (which is only a particular application of dialectical materialism) teaches us that there have been many different systems of ethics in history, that all of them in the last analysis are only an idealised expression of the material interests of different classes or sub-classes. But have any of them ever been based on the principles of dialectical materialism? That certainly cannot be said either of Platonic, Catholic or Kantian ethics. Nor can it be said of the ethics of the modern revolutionary proletariat, of the Paris Commune or the October Revolution.

The proletariat has a class morality, which stands in opposition to the morality of the ruling class. It stands for the basic principles of equality and class solidarity as opposed to the selfish egoism and hypocrisy of bourgeois morality. Revolutionaries also have moral and ethical principles. The basic law of revolution is simply stated: the salvation of the revolution is the supreme law. That is moral which serves to raise the revolutionary consciousness of the proletariat; that is immoral which serves to lower it. From this revolutionary point of view, the reformists of all kinds retard the growth of revolutionary consciousness of the working class and this is immoral. And since comrade Dieterich is a reformist who is a little ashamed of his reformism and wants to disguise it with a pseudo-revolutionary ("dialectical-materialist") phraseology, we consider his activity to be in flagrant violation of the most elementary principles of proletarian revolutionary morality.

But let us return to comrade Dieterich's "materialist-dialectical ethics". What do they teach us? They teach us something really remarkable: *that reproduction, enjoyment and sensuality of the material [sic] are "an integral part of the human condition*. And, in fact, the majority of humanity acts on this pattern." Now this is really

20. Dieterich, *Cuba: Three premises to save the Revolution after the death of Fidel.*

something! Our Heinz informs us that human beings like to eat, drink and reproduce (we assume that this is what he means by "enjoyment and sensuality of the material", although the sentence does not make grammatical sense). These things are "*an integral part of the human condition*" and the *majority of* humanity acts on this pattern.

We were more or less aware that the *majority* of people eat, drink, make love and enjoy "the material" whenever they can of, although we are most grateful to comrade Dieterich for pointing it out to us. But who are the *minority* who do not do these things? Even Tibetan monks and Hindu ascetics have been known occasionally to eat and drink. So much are these activities part of the "human condition" that we cannot think of any exceptions (except maybe on the subject of reproduction). We can only conclude that our Heinz knows something we do not, and that in his Socialism of the 21st Century, men and women will no longer be obliged to eat, drink or reproduce, or otherwise "enjoy the material", which will undoubtedly save a lot of time and inconvenience. However, since humanity has not yet attained this state of Bliss, we are obliged to agree with comrade Dieterich that most people unfortunately still need to eat, drink and reproduce, and that society ought ideally to provide them with the necessary conditions for fulfilling these needs.

Equality of sacrifice

The pursuit of the construction of an isolated national socialist society outside the perspective of international socialism is entirely utopian. This has been abundantly demonstrated by Russia and China. These were, after all, subcontinents with huge populations and vast resources. Yet the pursuit of autarky led to disaster and paved the way for capitalist restoration. Does this mean that the future of a socialist Cuba is impossible? No, it does not mean anything of the sort. The task is to ensure the economic strengthening of the nationalized planned economy in Cuba until further victories of the socialist revolution in Latin America and on a world scale. In 1930, at a time when Stalin, in pursuit of the reactionary utopia of socialism in one country, was engaged in the crazy adventures of forced collectivisation and "five year plans in four years", Trotsky wrote the following:

"The collectivisation of peasant holdings is, of course, a most necessary and fundamental part of the socialist transformation of society. However, the scope and tempo of collectivisation are not determined by the government's will alone, but, in the last analysis, by the economic factors: by the height of the country's economic level, by the inter-relationship between industry and agriculture, and consequently by the technical resources of agriculture itself.

"Industrialization is the driving force of the whole of modern culture and by this token the only conceivable basis for socialism. In the conditions of the Soviet Union, industrialization means first of all the strengthening of the base of the proletariat as a ruling class. Simultaneously it creates the material and technical premises for the collectivisation of agriculture. The tempos of these two processes are interdependent. The proletariat is interested in the highest possible tempos for these processes to the extent that the new society in the making is thus best protected from external danger, and at the same time a source is created for systematically improving the material level of the toiling masses.

"However, the tempos that can be achieved are limited by the general material and cultural level of the country, by the relationship between the city and the village and by the most pressing needs of the masses, who are able to sacrifice their today for the sake of tomorrow *only up to a certain point.* The optimum tempos, i.e., the best and most advantageous ones, are those which not only promote the most rapid growth of industry and collectivisation at a given moment, but which also secure the necessary stability of the social regime, that is, first of all strengthen the alliance of the workers and peasants, thereby preparing the possibility for future successes." [21]

These lines express with admirable clarity the central dilemma facing the Cuban Revolution: how to maintain the nationalized planned economy and ensure economic growth while simultaneously guaranteeing a steady increase in the living standards of the masses. They are in complete contrast with the obscure mystifying and intellectual contortions of Dieterich. The question is really very simple: The problem of consumption is not a secondary one. The Cuban workers are loyal to the Revolution and its socialist ideals. They understand the importance of the gains made by the nationalized planned economy in terms of health, education, culture and other important spheres of life. The decisive layers of society are undoubtedly opposed to the restoration of capitalism and the privatization of the economy. What happened in Russia is a horrible warning of what this would mean.

Is it possible to combat corruption and bureaucratism by appeals to revolutionary morality? The question of morale is fundamental in all warfare and in effect the Cuban Revolution is in a state of war with the restorationist elements. This is an important element in the situation. The question is who will prevail? The Revolution can count on a large reserve of support among wide layers of the population. But imperialism has on its side enormous economic power. It possesses a vast propaganda machine that is constantly bombarding the Cuban population with the idea that life is better under capitalism. The question is: what effect is this having? Fidel Castro and Roque appeal to revolutionary consciousness and ethics. The masses in Cuba have repeatedly shown that they are prepared to make big sacrifices, ***but only on condition that there is equality of sacrifice.*** The existence of bureaucracy and corruption undermines the morale of the population and therefore places the whole of the Revolution in danger. This is not a secondary question. It is a question of the survival of the Revolution itself.

Dieterich continues: "As the pattern of popular consumption and culture today is a predominantly universal pattern, not a national variable, the shock in Cuba is

21. Leon Trotsky, Introduction to the German Edition of *The Permanent Revolution.*

produced between the universal pattern of consumption of the firstworldist middle class – which arrives annually to the Cuban population by way of two million tourists, and daily by the US films which television transmits – and the standard of life which the productive forces and the distributive system of the country permits.

"In such circumstances, a campaign of increasing conscientiousness can reduce certain superfluous consumptions, but the access to the internet, education, health, social and geographic mobility, adequate individual or collective transport, definite forms and places of entertainment, of sexual liberty, etcetera, together with definite formal liberties, are part of the historic pattern prevailing in present Latin America, and no educational campaign can neutralize this pattern." [22]

This is a fair comment, as far as it goes. But what is the solution proposed by comrade Dieterich?

"To appeal to the revolutionary discipline and ethical values in the present circumstances of Cuba, to have to be like Fidel or Che, will not change the general panorama of the situation because the objective conditions do not sustain this discourse. For the majority it would be more efficient to discuss democratically the alternatives of consumption, for example, if they prefer more hospitals, transport, or living allowances, private consumption, etc. and the paths to achieve that level within the possibilities of the country.

"Better education, knowledge and information are not an antidote to consumerism. The more inputs of this type are being produced, the more self-conscience, individuality and 'subjects' are being generated. And more 'subjects' mean, inevitably, more desire for democracy. Democracy in all senses – formal, social, participative– which converts itself, the same as historically 'just and necessary' consumption, into a fundamental value of human praxis: value, to which the government has to give answers if it is not to generate resistances which the system can not absorb." [23]

There can be no doubt that the influx of foreign goods and currency, together with the ceaseless pressure of the media are powerful weapons in the hands of imperialism. The impression is created that in the USA everyone enjoys a high standard of living, which is false but has an effect in certain layers of the population, especially the youth who have never had the experience of living under capitalism and are attracted by consumerism. These moods can partially be combated by revolutionary propaganda, education and explanation. But we agree with comrade Dieterich that there are limits to how far this can be successful. So what does he suggest instead?

"From cognitive and technological cybernetics we know that it is possible to try to repair detected system-problems (post festum) with proportional, integral or differential regulations. More efficient, certainly, is the normalizing preventative

22. Dieterich, *Cuba: Three premises to save the Revolution after the death of Fidel.*
23. Ibid.

which is possible in events statistically detectable. Both requisites are present in Cuba. The dramatic calls to attention of Fidel and Felipe refer to the preventive regulation, that is, the necessity to take measures before the death of Fidel: and the attitudes of the Cuban population towards the Revolution constitute 'events' statistically measurable." [24]

This is yet another piece of Dieterichian gobbledegook. Let us not waste any more time attempting to make sense of what is senseless but proceed, machete in hand, in the hope that eventually we will find at least one sentence that makes sense:

"The Chancellor defined with good reasons the economic surplus as the decisive variable in an economy. But it is necessary to amplify this determination: not only is it key who receives it but who decides about it and in what form. This is the issue of economic democracy which in the market economy ('crematística') is taboo, but which in the socialist economy is the key to success. As long as the majorities are de facto excluded from the decisions on the use of the surplus, (investment, consumption, national budget, payment on the foreign debt, etc.), it doesn't matter to them really if it is the State, the transnationals, or imperialisms who end up with it.

"As happens in the false dilemma of 'ethics versus consumerism', the affirmation that what is decisive is whether the people or the transnationals receive the income or have the productive property, distorts the real dialectics of the contradiction. The Cuban surplus product, in its greater part, is not received by the transnationals, nor the majorities: the State receives it. And this is the nodal point of the problems of the theft, corruption and the black market which Fidel has denounced.

"The productive property in Cuba belongs essentially to the State. It is not in the hands of the majorities. If it were, the majorities would protect it, because it is common sense that no one robs himself. The fact that it is robbed and mistreated has an irrefutable reading: state property is perceived by many as an alien or anonymous property, which can be privatized by stealing. While this is like that, it will be difficult to end the corruption and theft, as the example of China shows. In consequence, the idea of the socialist economy, to produce altruistically for all, makes itself nonviable.

"The perception of state productive property as something alienated, similar to capitalist property, which can be privatized, is reaffirmed daily by the fact that the people have no real influence on its use. Property, in the market economy means essentially, the right to alienate economic assets. For better or worse, this does not exist in Cuba. But neither does the worker determine the benefit of this property, its surplus product, made by him, and thus he neither is the possessor. On not being either proprietor nor real possessor of the individual or collective property, the direct producer does not identify with it and, in consequence, does not protect it adequately." [25]

24. Ibid.
25. Ibid.

Here, by accident, comrade Dieterich has made a serious point. In order that the workers should defend the Cuban state they must be convinced that the state belongs to them. In a nationalized planned economy the surplus created by the working class is in the hands of the state. But the issue of what should be done with the surplus – what part should be dedicated to investment and what part to consumption, for example, must be decided through a democratic debate in which everyone participates. Workers will accept certain limitations on consumption, as long as they have been involved directly in the process of economic decision-making.

The masses are prepared to make big sacrifices to defend the Revolution. Nevertheless, in the last analysis the question of the living standards and conditions of the masses is a decisive one. Moreover, this is not an absolute but a relative question. The presence of the richest and most powerful imperialist nation only a few kilometres away is a major factor, as is the role played by foreign remittances, tourism and the dual economy that expresses itself in two currencies. The presence of capitalist tendencies on the island cannot be denied. We ignore them at our peril. That is the basic message of the speeches of Fidel Castro and Felipe Pérez Roque.

However, as Trotsky explains, the masses are able to sacrifice their today for the sake of tomorrow *only up to a certain point*. The Cuban workers have demonstrated their willingness to make sacrifices to defend the Revolution for decades. They will continue to do so, but only when they are convinced of certain things and even then only up to a certain point. Beyond that, all appeals to revolutionary morality, ideals and so on become useless and even counterproductive. The constant appeals to sacrifice may breed sceptical and even cynical moods in the masses if they are not backed up with solid results. In the first place the workers must be convinced that there is equality of sacrifice for all. This does not mean that everyone must get the same wages or live in exactly the same conditions. But it does mean that excessive privileges are inadmissible. This principle was enshrined in the 1919 Bolshevik Party programme and was based on Lenin's *State and Revolution*, which in turn was based on the Paris Commune.

'Cognitive cybernetics'

"In June of 2002 Felipe had spoken on the same theme before the same Forum, concluding on that occasion that in the eventual absence of the Comandante, the defence of the Revolution would pass to the defence of the one party, the centralized economy, political unity and preservation of the armed forces. To maintain the one party is probably vital during the imperialist aggression, but equally vital is to give it a real cybernetic character, if it wants to avoid the project ending like the USSR and the GDR." [26]

It is true that the totalitarian and bureaucratic regime of the GDR undermined the nationalized planned economy and prepared the way for the return of capitalism.

26. Ibid.

But that is by no means the end of the story. The experience of almost 20 years of capitalism has made the people of the former GDR revise the impressions they had before. To the great annoyance of the bourgeois, many people in the eastern Länder now say that things were not all that bad in the old GDR. Of course, they do not want the return of a one-party totalitarian state, with a privileged caste of Party officials and the Stasi with its army of informers. But they remember that in the GDR there was no unemployment and everyone had the right to a decent education and health service. There was not the atmosphere of cut-throat competition, of dog-eat-dog, of selfishness and greed that characterizes capitalism.

What they want is what we also advocate, namely, a nationalized planned economy, but with democracy – a society in which the working people would rule, not only in name but in practice. In other words, what they want is what Lenin proposed in 1917, when he laid down the basic condition for a workers' democracy: What failed in Russia and the GDR was not socialism, but Stalinism. When the working people of Germany move to change society – as they will in the coming period – they will expropriate the banks and big concerns, but they will insist on a democratic regime, with workers' control and management of industry and the state. On the basis of the highly developed German industry, science and technology, they could then move quite quickly in the direction of socialism.

How do we "avoid the project ending like the USSR and the GDR"? We Marxists say by returning to the programme of Lenin. Heinz Dieterich says the answer is *cognitive cybernetics*: "Lenin, who conceived the party of democratic centralism knew, certainly, that any system of lasting political control has to guarantee three symmetrical currents of real information and debate: a) between the fractions of the vanguard or summit of real power, for example, of the Politburo and of the Central Committee; b) between these centres of decision and the political and information elite of the country, which, in theory would be the middle leadership and the members of the party; c) between the vanguard, the middle leadership and the masses. This cybernetic or feedback quality is fundamental for the optimisation of any cognitive cybernetic system, such as are the State, the party, and the human being." [27]

Lenin would be as astonished as we are to learn that the Bolshevik Party was – *a cognitive cybernetic system*. In fact the Bolshevik Party was the most democratic party that ever existed. It was not just a question of the transmission of information but of a genuine and constant debate and discussion at all levels of the Party. All this changed under Stalin. The democratic regime of Leninism was abolished and Lenin's Party was physically exterminated. How does comrade Dieterich deal with this question?

"In praxis, particularly under Stalin, the necessary equilibrium between real democracy and verticality, that is between the communication structures and sym-

27. Ibid.

metrical and asymmetrical power, were abandoned in favour of verticality. The Moscow Trials were the rite of passage (announcement of transition) of the new vertical party and the public notice of the disappearance of democracy in the USSR; they were the secular equivalent of the burnings at the stake of the Inquisition in America, whose ashes signalised the price of dissenting in the new order. Rituals of humiliation similar to the clerical confessional, like 'critique and self-critique', and the inquisition-like anonymous reports of the political police defined the quality and possibilities of life of the citizens.

"In this manner, the Stalin model generated an institutional environment and a political culture of conformism which liquidated the institutionality and culture of the public sphere of the pre-socialist societies, from the Greek Agora to the literary clubs of the French Revolution. In fact, the public sphere of strategic debate of the bourgeois system, which is constituent to it, disappeared from the superstructure of 'real existing socialism' with fatal consequences for socialist evolution, leaving the bourgeois political superstructure with a functional superiority in the optimisation of decisions. This does not mean that bourgeois governments don't make mistakes but the bourgeois superstructure evidently provides for a considerable capacity of perception and adaptability to structural changes, which has not been observed in the one-party system of historic socialism." [28]

Comrade Dieterich confines himself to mere description plus his usual moralistic judgements. Nowadays everybody knows about the crimes of Stalin. The question is, however, *why and how did all this come about*? How do we explain the totalitarian and bureaucratic degeneration of the Russian Revolution? To this question comrade Dieterich has no answer. But this is precisely what has to be explained.

"The real question is: 'How can we guarantee the vanguard or cybernetic character of the systems of leadership and coordination which we call State and Party?' The quality of whatever system of regulation depends essentially on two parameters: a) its sensibility, that is the time which passes between the discovery or recognition of a deviation of the system parameters, of its programmed values (Sollwert); b) the time that the system requires to correct the deviation (Istwert). Both parameters – which determine the dynamic behaviour of the system, in this case of the Party and the State – depend, in their turn, on the quantity and quality of the measurements of the state of the system (for example, polls of opinion, elections, etc.) and on the relative power of the diverse fractions of the leading class, for example, the revolutionary, the social democratic or the technocratic strata." [29]

Cybernetics for Heinz Dieterich is something like a combination of the Arc of the Covenant and the Philosopher's Stone. It is a magical key that opens all doors, a medicine that cures all illnesses. In fact, cybernetics is merely the study of infor-

28. Dieterich, *Cuba: Three premises to save the Revolution after the death of Fidel.*
29. Ibid.

mation flows. It can be used to analyse a living body or in relation to artificial intelligence. Our Heinz tries to use it to analyse society. That is perfectly legitimate as far as it goes, but to present cybernetics as a kind of panacea is a false method from start to finish. In the kind of university circles that comrade Dieterich inhabits it has become fashionable these days to look at the economy in terms of flows of information and even to assert that handling information is the central economic activity in society. But why do people need information? It is part of the process of transforming external nature, in other words, of *work*. Now there can be no harm in studying information flows as long as it is understood that it is connected to the world of human labour. But for our Heinz, it is far more than this.

As usual, the Prophet of 21st Century Socialism is using cybernetics as a *substitute* for looking at society as a body involved in labouring to make a living. He must have justified theorising society this way somewhere in the past, but in the piece we have just quoted he just takes it for granted. As always, *he assumes what has to be proven.* Also as always he is wilfully obscure. Only a German writing in Spanish could get away with defining "Wert" (Sollwert and Istwert) – in terms of *time*. He attempts to analyse Cuban society in terms of cybernetics and the circular flow of information. But the way he does it is completely idealist and formalistic. Messages are sent out, but the "head" doesn't immediately get feedback, such as: my fingers are burning because they're in the fire. This is his parameter (a) or *Sollwert*. Then there may be a delay in reacting to the message i.e. pulling the fingers out of the fire. This is parameter (b) or *Istwert*. Is this profundity? No, it is only pretentiousness carried to the nth degree – in fact, to the point of absurdity.

In reality, the problem is not one of cybernetics. It is one of *bureaucracy*. The reason the bureaucracy didn't get the message back is because they issued orders to the populace and had different material interests from the common people to whom they are issuing orders. Their "feedback" mechanism was switched off because they had no interest in listening. Both Fidel and Roque posed the central problem as a problem of bureaucracy, and this analysis is far more to the point than the complicated abstract meanderings of Dieterich. It is difficult to keep up with his constant mental acrobatics. But anyway, let us arm ourselves with courage and try to follow comrade Dieterich in his latest intellectual gyrations:

"When Fidel asked in his November speech, why the Cuban economists did not take account of the insensibility of maintaining the sugar sector after the fall of the USSR, the parameter 'a' was referred to. But the real answer is better found in parameter 'b'. If the Cuban economists did not detect he contradiction of maintaining the sugar sector, it means that they lacked professional skill and common sense. With all the reserves confronting my colleagues, it seems to me that this is an unreal supposition. It is much more probable that they did not speak out because the Cuban superstructure does not foresee the public sphere of debate which would have been the place to discuss the respective warnings.

"Another example of the parameter 'b' can be taken from the Bolivarian Revolution. During the Bolivarian Government the great landowners (latifundistas) have assassinated more than 130 peasant leaders, without a single one of the intellectual and material authors of these assassinations being in prison. How much time of correction of this counter-revolutionary 'deviation', and of the State of Rights, does the Revolution have, before it loses its credibility and power in its supposed 'war to the death against latifundism'?

"The questioning of Felipe is vital, provided it receives an answer which is not formal, but material: not tactics but strategy. If it is not achieved to return to the sole party the dialectic or cybernetic quality intended by Lenin and the restitution of public spheres of strategic and massive debate, together with the public transparency of their interactions, the Party will not be in conditions to defend the Revolution at the death of Fidel.

"The same Secretary of State understands in depth that the cybernetic of the Party is the key to the future. In explaining in his discourse why Cuba had not fallen like the USSR, he cited Gabriel García Márquez: 'The explanation for Cuba is that Fidel is at the same time the head of the government and the leader of the opposition'. Felipe added: 'He is the main non conformist with what is done, the principal critic of the work and this gives a particularity to our process'." [30]

"The political question of life or death for the Communist Party is, therefore: What will be the system of institutional dialectics which will substitute for the personalized dialectics of Fidel, after he no longer leads the Cuban Revolution?"

The conclusion he draws in relation to Cuba seems to be that Fidel Castro is the "brain" that can detect what is going on and make the necessary adjustments ("personalised dialectics"). After all, the original meaning of dialectics in Greek philosophy was a conversation. But there are some serious problems with this. In the first place, no single individual can have a detailed knowledge of every detail of the national economy. That is not just an idealist conception but simple mysticism. In the second place, even if comrade Fidel were endowed with such miraculous powers, what will happen when he's gone?

Cuba needs institutions of democracy ('institutional dialectics'), comrade Dieterich tells us. But the question is: what kind of democracy? Democracy is an abstraction, an empty shell that can be filled with different class contents. It seems that Dieterich has in mind some kind of bourgeois democracy ("public spheres of strategic and massive debate"). Heinz mentions opinion polls as a cybernetic mechanism. But everybody knows how opinion polls are scandalously manipulated in bourgeois democracies. Actually workers' democracy is a perfect cybernetic information flow, since the decision-makers collectively carry out the decisions and adjust them if things are not going according to plan. Socialism presupposes the active participation of the workers.

30. Ibid.

Dieterich and bourgeois democracy

Marxists oppose Stalinism from the standpoint of the working class and Leninist Soviet Democracy. Comrade Dieterich opposes Stalinism from the standpoint of the petty bourgeoisie and vulgar democracy. After attacking Stalinism, Dieterich sings the praises of *bourgeois democracy*, which "evidently provides for a considerable capacity of perception and adaptability to structural changes, which has not been observed in the one-party system of historic socialism." Admittedly, he speaks of its "mistakes" – but then, who does not make mistakes? There is not a shred of Marxist analysis here. It is not a question of mistakes but of class content. Evidently, comrade Dieterich is not aware that a bourgeois formal democracy is only another way of expressing *the dictatorship of big business*. He approaches the question of democracy, not from a class point of view, but from a purely technical standpoint ("functional superiority in the optimisation of decisions").

As a matter of fact, even this is not correct. Despite all the crimes of Stalinism, and despite all the bureaucratic distortions, the nationalized planned economy in the USSR was superior to the anarchy of capitalism and demonstrated this superiority on many occasions, particularly in the Second World War. Only a nationalized planned economy could achieve the miracle of transporting all of Russia's industries thousands of miles to a place of safety beyond the Urals. Thanks to the existence of a central plan, it was possible to make decisions that would be unthinkable for an economy based on market forces. It was not at all the supposed superiority of bourgeois formal democracy that brought about the collapse of the USSR, as Dieterich appears to imagine.

Hypnotised by the supposed superiority of bourgeois democracy, Dieterich goes from bad to worse: "This feedback quality of the public sphere can be exemplified with the war in Iraq. The great debates within the power elite and information elite on how to get out of the quagmire, in considerable measure take place within the public domain, for example, the US Congress, on television, in the most important dailies of the country like the *New York Times* and the *Washington Post* and in the universities." [31]

Our friend Heinz really could not have chosen a worse example of the supposed superiority of bourgeois democracy! The criminal invasion of Iraq was an irresponsible adventure, even from the standpoint of the real interests of imperialism. How was this decision arrived at? Was it the result of a free and democratic debate and "feedback" from the US public and its leaders? No, the decision was taken in secret, behind closed doors, even before the 11th September, by the White House clique around Bush and Rumsfeld. This was not a "mistake" but *the normal way in which all important decisions are taken in a bourgeois formal democracy*. In such a "democracy" anyone can say (almost) anything they like, as long as the boards of directors of the big banks and monopolies decide what happens.

31. Ibid.

It is true that in a formal democracy there are certain mechanisms through which different opinions can be expressed. There is a "free press" that is owned and controlled by a handful of super-rich press barons and which always defends the interests of the capitalist class as a whole. There are political parties like the Republicans and Democrats in the USA, which defend the same class but with slightly different methods (these methods are increasingly indistinguishable). There are parliaments and elections, which provide the masses with the illusion that there is democratic control and accountability. In reality this is a gigantic deception, although on certain occasions these democratic mechanisms can serve a useful purpose in defending the interests of the ruling class, as when they used them to get rid of Richard Nixon when he became an embarrassment for them.

Heinz Dieterich compares "real existing socialism" with bourgeois democracy – and comes down on favour of the latter: "In 'real existing socialism', that public sphere does not exist. The strategic debates take place behind the closed doors of the highest heads of the party. Afterward the official position is brought down and discussed in the lower levels of the party. Finally it is disclosed to the majorities through the press and roundtables on television.

"The constitutive majority is excluded and what it sees on television are tactical discussions or simple repetitions of the official vision, delivered generally by the same journalists. In contrast to what happens in the marvellous experience of the Cuban worker parliaments of the nineties, the citizen is converted into a spectator of the political-economic process, not its demiurge." [32]

We note in passing that the above lines could be applied exactly to the mechanism of bourgeois formal democracy that our Heinz finds so appealing. All the important decisions are taken behind closed doors in the boardrooms of the big banks and monopolies. Those that take these decisions are unelected and responsible to nobody. The so-called shareholders' democracy is another deception, since the bulk of the shares are invariably in the hands of a small number of powerful individuals and institutions. The big capitalists then inform our "elected representatives" in parliament what they have decided, and the latter act accordingly. They do this either directly or indirectly, through an army of professional lobbyers, corruption, donations to party funds and a thousand other well-developed mechanisms through which the bourgeoisie maintains control over politics and political institutions in "free" countries.

Parliament itself is increasingly irrelevant as all the important decisions are taken by small groups outside. In the case of Britain, which, despite everything, is probably still one of the most democratic capitalist countries, power has passed from parliament to the cabinet and from the cabinet to a clique of unelected advisers around the Prime Minister. In the USA this is even more the case. All power is in the hands of the White House clique around Bush. The only reason Congress is

32. Dieterich, *Cuba: Three premises to save the Revolution after the death of Fidel.*

now beginning to assert itself is that Bush – like Nixon – is beginning to tread on the toes of big business in the pursuit of his Middle East adventure and they want to clip his wings.

A bourgeois democracy is really the disguised dictatorship of the banks and monopolies. In the modern epoch, where the concentration of capital has assumed unheard of proportions, the power of the big monopolies has never been so absolute. Normally, the capitalist class prefers a democratic regime, which is the most economical form of government. They can permit the illusion of democracy, while, in practice, all the levers and controls remain firmly in their hands. They control the parliamentary representatives by a thousand invisible threads. They own the banks and monopolies and therefore can exert colossal pressure on any government. They own the mass media and can mould public opinion. Finally, they can rule by resting on the leaders of the labour movement who have no intention of going beyond the limits of the system.

Bourgeois democracy is a very fragile plant, which usually only exists when the ruling class does not feel directly threatened by revolution. Under conditions of economic upswing, the bourgeois can afford to give certain reforms and concessions in order to blunt class antagonisms. When the class struggle passes these limits the bourgeoisie casts away the smiling mask of democracy and begins to organize coups and dictatorships. As we saw once again in April 2002 in Venezuela, the bourgeois can shift from democracy to dictatorship with the ease of a man passing from a smoking to a non-smoking compartment of a train.

Dieterich's views exposed

After Fidel Castro announced that he was not standing again for any position in the Council of State in Cuba for reasons of health, the debate about the future of the Cuban revolution intensified. Our Heinz, naturally, could not remain silent. He lost no time in delivering a lecture to the Cubans telling them what they must do. Here Dieterich's ideas about the Cuban revolution suddenly become crystal clear – a most extraordinary feat for this most obscure of writers. This is what he has to say:

"I have defended on several occasions, in word and in writing, inside and outside of Cuba, that the only socialist way forward for Cuba lies in a combination of state developmentalism (on the model of Germany, Japan, the Asian tigers, China) with the participatory democracy and economy of Socialism of the XXI Century. In the light of history and economic science it seems obvious that the Cuban system has no other degree of evolutive freedom." [33]

What does this mean? It is quite clear that Dieterich is advising Cuba to follow the model of development of Germany, Japan, the Asian tigers and China. Now, as far as we know all these countries are capitalist (in relation to China, Dieterich himself has admitted that what we are witnessing there is a process of *capitalist* deve-

33. Dieterich, *El desmentido de Hans Modrow y el extraño papel de Prensa Latina*, 22/2/2008.

lopment). *This means that he is advocating a model of capitalist development for Cuba.* Of course, he tries to cover this up by "combining" it with "the participatory democracy and economy of Socialism of the XXI Century". But as we have already seen, the essence of this so-called Socialism of the XXI Century is to leave the means of production in private hands. In case there was any doubt, let us quote from another article by Dieterich in which he analyses the most recent measures taken by Raul Castro:

"1. It is fundamental to clarify the formulation that Cuba is adopting the 'Chinese model'. It would be more precise to say that Cuba is adopting a logic of developmental accumulation already started four centuries ago in Western Europe (Cromwell), which has proven to be the only one in the world system to be able to overcome neo-colonial misery." [34]

As usual Dieterich's historical references display his utter confusion. In Cromwell's time England was not at all a country living in "neo-colonial misery" but a prosperous and belligerent emergent colonialist power, enslaving the Irish, establishing colonies in the Caribbean and challenging the rival colonialist power of Holland for domination of the seas. However, more important than his excursions into the 17th century is what he is telling Cubans today. What is the "developmental accumulation already started four centuries ago in Western Europe"? This is only Dieterich's convoluted way of saying *capitalism*.

Dieterich is saying that Cuba will take the capitalist road, and that this is a very good thing because it is the only system in the world "which has proven to be the only one to be able to overcome neo-colonial misery." Really? Has capitalism solved the terrible problems of the masses in Africa, Asia and Latin America? To ask the question is to answer it. The history of the last hundred years shows precisely the impossibility of solving the problems of the peoples of the colonial and semi-colonial countries on the basis of capitalism. Even where the national bourgeoisie has achieved formal independence from foreign rule, it has, in the overwhelming majority of cases, been incapable of carrying society forward.

Let us consider the Indian Subcontinent. Since 1947 not one of the fundamental tasks of the bourgeois-democratic revolution has been solved. The land question, the national question, the modernization of society – none of these things has been achieved. The rotten Indian bourgeoisie has not even succeeded in abolishing the barbarous caste system. And the so-called national independence, for which the people fought so hard for, is a hollow sham. After more than half a century of formal independence, India, Pakistan and Bangladesh remain under the domination of world imperialism. The only difference is that instead of the direct military-bureaucratic rule of England they have fallen under domination of imperialism through the world market.

34. Dieterich, *La modernización de Cuba bajo el Comandante Raúl Castro y la preservación del socialismo*, April 6, 2008.

What is true for Asia is a thousand times truer for Africa. The Congo, with all its colossal mineral wealth, is in a state of chaos. Four million people were slaughtered in the recent civil war. Kenya, Uganda, Rwanda, Zimbabwe - are these examples of how to "overcome neo-colonial misery"? All have gone down the capitalist road, and with what results? Even as I write these lines there are food riots in West Africa, the Indian Subcontinent, Haiti and the Philippines.

Even more incredibly, Dieterich ignores the inconvenient detail that the bourgeoisie has failed to develop the colossal potential of Latin America for the last 200 years. Let us remind ourselves that Carlos Andres Perez was an enthusiastic advocate of market economics – precisely the model of "developmental accumulation already started four centuries ago in Western Europe". After 200 years to ask the Latin American bourgeoisie to start developing it now is to ask an elm tree to produce pears. This is yet another example of Dieterich's "realism", which always amounts to a complete surrender to capitalism and the market.

As a matter of fact, it was not capitalism but the nationalised planned economy that transformed backward tsarist Russia from conditions of semi-feudal misery into a mighty industrial power in only a few decades. Such a remarkable transformation has never been seen in the whole of history! It was a nationalised planned economy that transformed China from an oppressed semi-colonial nation into a powerful modern economy. And it was a nationalised planned economy that enabled Cuba to achieve the remarkable advances in education, health and culture that had no equal in all Latin America. Despite this, Dieterich insists that the only model of development possible for Cuba is a capitalist model. But under modern conditions, the return to capitalism could only mean the rapid penetration of the island by foreign capital and its transformation into a satellite of the United States. In other words, it would mean that Cuba would soon be reduced once again to a state of - *neo-colonial misery.*

In relation to Cuba, as in relation to every other subject, Dieterich's ideas are clearly reactionary and anti-socialist, and if they were to be adopted by the people of Cuba that would spell disaster for the future of the Cuban revolution. For those who stand on the basis of Marxism it is quite clear that the only way forward for Cuba is a return to Lenin's programme of workers democracy, of genuine participation of the population in the running of the economy and the state, and at the same time an internationalist policy that can break the isolation of the revolution through successful socialist revolutions in Venezuela, Bolivia, Ecuador and the Latin American continent as a whole. ***What is needed is not a return to capitalism but a socialist Cuba in a Socialist Federation of Latin America.***

10. Nationalism or internationalism?

Latin American integration

"This access to the intellectual resources of humanity is feasible, as much for the strategic phase of the struggle (postcapitalist institutionality) as for the transitional phase in Latin America, the Bolivarian integration of Latin America and the Caribbean. A single example for the transitional phase. With a hundred thousand dollars, the Venezuelan government could obtain in six months all the knowledge (the expertise), which is needed for the economic integration of Latin America."[1]

Thus far, Heinz Dieterich, but what does it mean? When we speak of the resources of humanity, we know what we mean: the sum total of the resources of the planet: its land, and all the mineral resources that is beneath the earth's surface, its seas and all that is in them, its industry, science and technology, its manpower and intellectual creativity: in short, the wealth of the world, whether in a physical or potential form. All this, Heinz informs us, is now at our disposal (at least "access to it is feasible"). This is news to us. As far as we are aware, the resources of humanity are not accessible at all *because they are in private hands*. As soon as we attempt to lay hands upon these resources, the owners will send a policeman, or set the dogs on us, or adopt other unpleasant methods to dissuade us from our aim. But in the very same sentence, Dieterich is already beating a retreat, even before he feels the policeman's hand on his collar. He apparently has in mind not the entire *resources of humanity*, but only the resources of Latin America.

Now we consider ourselves to be very moderate people with very modest appetites, and we can therefore readily agree to lower our expectations and settle for the resources of humanity – in Latin America. After all, these are considerable. The continent, together with the Caribbean, contains vast resources and a huge untapped potential. Here we have the oil of Venezuela and Ecuador, the gas and mineral wealth of Bolivia, the copper of Chile, the huge agricultural and industrial potential of Brazil and Argentina, and a huge and under exploited human potential in a con-

1. Dieterich, *La revolución mundial pasa por Hugo Chávez*, *Rebelión*, 5/3/05.

tinent surrounded by oceans teeming with fish and full of rivers and forests, with an astonishing range of scenery and climates. In short, we have all the potential for the creation of a paradise on earth.

The brilliant idea of Simon Bolivar, that great and visionary revolutionary, of uniting Latin America today retains its full validity. And yet 200 years later, what has become of this vision? After the death of the Liberator it was betrayed by the bourgeois of Latin America, who have Balkanized the continent, reducing it to a series of artificial nation states that divide the living body of the Patria Grande, separating peoples that speak the same language, have the same history, traditions, culture and interests. This is the real explanation why a huge continent could be dominated by Yankee imperialism for so long. Two hundred years is long enough for the bourgeoisie to show what it is capable of doing for Latin America. It has been weighed in the balance of history and found wanting. The weak and degenerate bourgeois of Latin America have turned what ought to be an earthly paradise into a hell for millions of men and women. Even the national independence that was won with so much sacrifice and blood turns out to be a fraud. The national bourgeoisie is only the local office boy of imperialism and the big transnational companies that have dominated and plundered the continent for so long.

The original idea of the Liberator was to unite Latin America by revolutionary means. Today we support this idea with every enthusiasm. But we need to add just one small amendment to it. After 200 years the bourgeoisie has revealed its reactionary character and its complete inability to carry out the progressive task of uniting the continent. Therefore, the only way in which this great historic mission can be achieved is through the revolutionary overthrow of the landlords and capitalists.

The unification of Latin America will be a reality only when the working class puts itself at the head of the nation and takes power into its hands. It will be achieved in the form of a Socialist Federation or it will not be achieved at all. Is this what Dieterich has in mind? No, it is not. We have already seen that he is opposed to the expropriation of the property of the oligarchy and that he is therefore against the socialist revolution. But if we leave intact the economic power of the oligarchies, what prospect can there be of uniting Latin America?

Dieterich wants to halt the revolution in Venezuela, and prevent any further nationalization. If he succeeds, it will mean not only the end of any prospect of socialism in Venezuela (whether of the 21st or any other century) but the eventual defeat of the Bolivarian revolution and the return to power of the counter-revolutionary Venezuelan bourgeoisie. We will return to this subject later, but for the present let us deal with our friend Heinz's recipe for Latin America: "This access to the intellectual resources of humanity is feasible," he says, "as much for the strategic phase of the struggle (postcapitalist institutionality) as for the transitional phase in Latin America, the Bolivarian integration of Latin America and the Caribbean." [2]

2. Ibid.

What is meant by "the strategic phase of the struggle" and in what way does it differ from "the transitional phase in Latin America"? Evidently comrade Dieterich likes to keep people guessing, since he offers no explanation. But in most dictionaries the word strategic signifies *pertaining to long term goals*. What are these goals? Again, your guess is good as mine. Probably the famous "economy of equivalence", a phrase that has the important merit that nobody really knows what it means. As for the "transitional phase", one has to ask; *transition from what to what*? Since yet again no answer is forthcoming, not for the first time or the last, we have no alternative to guess what he means.

The normal meaning of the transitional phase in Marxist parlance is the transitional phase between capitalism and socialism. Leon Trotsky wrote *The Revolution Betrayed* in 1936, which contains almost everything that needs to be said on this subject. No doubt Dieterich does not want to hear about the ideas of Trotsky (yet another point on which he disagrees with Hugo Chávez). That does not matter very much, because Trotsky based his programme almost entirely on the programme of the Bolshevik Party in 1917 and on the programmatic documents of the first four congresses of the Communist International. The question here is therefore not whether Trotsky was right, but whether the ideas of Marxism are right.

How does Dieterich pose the question? He rejects the Transitional Programme for the socialist revolution. He will not hear of nationalization or workers' control or a workers' and peasants' government. He cites only a single example for his "transitional phase": With a hundred thousand dollars, he says, the Venezuelan government could obtain in six months all the knowledge (the expertise), which is needed for the economic integration of Latin America. We have heard of government on the cheap. But this the first time we have heard of *revolution on the cheap*. This is really a very remarkable offer. For the trivial sum of a hundred thousand dollars, in just six months the Venezuelan government could have at its disposal all the knowledge needed for the economic integration of Latin America. What are we waiting for?

This is faulty logic. It assumes that what is preventing the unification of Latin America is *the lack of knowledge*. In the same way, it was the lack of knowledge (of computers) that was supposed to be the reason why Marx, Engels, Lenin and everyone else, until the Founder of 21st Century Socialism appeared on the scene, were unable to carry out the socialist transformation of society. But this is not the case. Even if we imagine that we know everything we need to know concerning Latin American economic integration, would that remove all obstacles to carrying it out in practice? No, it would not. *The main obstacles to carrying out the unification of Latin America is not ignorance but the vested interests of the oligarchies who hold economic power in their hands.*

Our Heinz approaches the question not as a revolutionary but as a reformist, not as a materialist but as an idealist, not as a realist but as a hopeless utopian. This emerges very clearly from the next few lines: "If it [the Venezuelan government] launched an international contest over Internet on, let us say, eight problems of economic integration – the monetary unit of reference, a Central Bank, high tech-development centres, comparative advantages in the global economy, etc. – and offered prizes of ten thousand dollars in each heading, it would have in six months an avalanche of proposals from the whole world which would dynamize extraordinarily the formation of the Regional Latin American Power Bloc (RLPB)." [3]

Isn't this absolutely priceless? The way to achieve the unification of Latin America is to launch *an international contest* over Internet with a prize of ten thousand dollars! When we have recovered our composure after an uncontrollable attack of laughter, it occurs to us to ask Heinz what has become of all those selfless individuals who, according to him, are queuing up to offer their services to humanity entirely free of charge? Now it turns out that they have to be offered *a bribe of 10,000 dollars* to serve the human race. This does not show much confidence in the future of the economy of equivalence when all capitalistic egotism will disappear.

Having held his competition and distributed his largesse (or rather, not his, but that of the Venezuelan government) to these selfless servants of humanity, all Heinz has to do is to sit back and wait for the inevitable result, which will be the immediate formation of the Regional Latin American Power Bloc (RLPB). Just how the mechanics of this operation would work remains something of a mystery. The selfless servants of humanity collect their winnings and deposit them in a bank where they will earn a good rate of interest, and all of a sudden, the movement towards the RLPB becomes irresistibly dynamized. Why? For what reason? Only Heinz knows the answer, but chooses not to let us in on his secret.

It is difficult to know whether the Founder of 21st Century Socialism is having a joke at our expense. But no, he is very serious about all this – which makes it even more amusing. However, let us try to find some solid content in all this nonsense. Let us ask yet another question that Dieterich prefers not to ask: namely, what does this Bloc consist of? Answer: it consists of a bloc between a number of existing governments in Latin America that Dieterich believes are progressive, such as Lula's government in Brazil. The purpose of this Bloc seems to be to prevent the aggression of US imperialism against Venezuela (presumably also Bolivia).

The 'Regional Power Bloc'

The present world situation is really unprecedented in history. Never before has such colossal power been concentrated in the hands of a single state. Not even the Roman Empire in its high point possessed such colossal supremacy as that which is now enjoyed by the United States of America. Never in the past 300 years has there been just one super power. There were always at least two or three great powers,

3. Ibid.

jostling for supremacy – Britain, Germany, France, Spain and so on. With colossal power comes colossal arrogance. Bush and the ruling clique in Washington now believe they can intervene anywhere in the world with no restrictions. It is a return to the old gunboat diplomacy pursued by British imperialism in the past.

The reformists and pacifists hypnotized by the supposedly absolute power of US imperialism. They conclude that, in the face of such overwhelming might, all resistance is futile. Instead of fighting against US imperialism, they say, it is better to seek a modus vivendi (way of living together), for any attempt to go beyond the bounds laid down by Washington will inevitably lead to disaster. This is the real message that Heinz Dieterich wishes to convey, although, as usual, he resorts to his "squid tactics" to conceal the fact.

Is it true, as the reformists imagine, that the power of US imperialism has no limits? No, it is not true. The fact is that the imperialists have over-reached themselves. We see the limits of the power of imperialism in Afghanistan and Iraq. With 160,000 troops the Americans cannot control Iraq. The occupation of Iraq is costing them at least one billion dollars a week, as well as the thousands of American soldiers killed and wounded. Not even the wealthiest nation on earth can sustain such a haemorrhage of blood and gold indefinitely. They will have to retreat with their tail between their legs.

Despite its huge power, US imperialism is really a colossus with feet of clay. Almost every day bush fires are breaking out everywhere. For years US imperialism has attempted to destroy the Cuban Revolution. Bush spoke of an "axis of evil" and named Iraq, Iran and North Korea. Later he added Venezuela to his list of "rogue states" that allegedly threaten peace and stability. However, Washington has not been able to impose its power in Latin America by military means as it has done previously. In the past, it would have sent the Marines to Venezuela long before. But now it is unable to do so.

We can increasingly see the limits of US imperialism in Latin America. The petty-bourgeois alarmists say: "the Americans are coming!" Like the character in the fairy story they are constantly crying wolf, trying to frighten people. But US imperialism is trapped in Iraq and Afghanistan and at the moment they cannot open another front directly. Any attempt to intervene militarily in Venezuela would be a tremendous reaction by the masses throughout Latin America. The effects would be felt inside the USA itself, where there are millions of Latinos living in poverty and a general mood of discontent reflected in the mass opposition to the Iraq adventure and the collapse in Bush's support.

Dieterich always uses the threat of imperialist intervention to argue against revolutionary measures. He says that the working class in Latin America must on no account take power. Instead they must support "progressive" bourgeois governments and the latter must come together to negotiate with imperialism to get a better deal for the Patria Grande. For example, in an article in *Revista Mariátegui* (15/08/06) he is asked:

Q: "How do you perceive to the new axis of evil in the Pacific: Alan Garcia, Michelle Bachelet and Alvaro Uribe?

A: "I feel that the potential of the axis of evil in the Pacific depends on the capacity of the axis of good in the Atlantic to extend the Mercosur, to deepen it and to democratize it. In itself, that axis of the Pacific has neither the territorial, economic nor demographic power to be an alternative to the Bolivarian bloc. But since the enemy knows this very well, they are going to try to prevent the integration of the Bolivarian bloc from advancing any further, and if it does not advance any further and it retreats, then it may be that that axis of evil in the Pacific, can make bilateral alliances with Paraguay or other countries and try to break up the Atlantic."

We note that this "scientific economist" here abandons all pretence at a scientific approach and uses the language of demonology (the axis of evil, as opposed to the axis of good). In place of a class policy we have the usual moralistic and sentimental approach to the Patria Grande. This comes as no surprise. After all, foreign policy is the continuation of domestic policy. Since Dieterich has embraced the policy of class collaboration at home, he must necessarily adopt the same policy in regard to other states. This is only an extension on the international plane of the reformist politics he advocates on the national scale. If the Venezuelan workers and peasants must reach a friendly agreement with the Venezuelan oligarchy, promising faithfully never to touch the private property of the landlords, bankers and capitalists, then it is logical that the Bolivarian Revolution must also strive for a friendly agreement with the oligarchs and bourgeois governments of the rest of Latin America. The only thing is that one must be careful to distinguish between the good capitalist who belong to the "axis of good" from the bad capitalists who belong to the "axis of evil".

Which countries does he include in this hypothetical Regional Power Bloc or "axis of good"? Argentina, Brazil, Bolivia, Cuba and Venezuela. This presupposes that all these countries have the same interests and the same foreign policy. But this is far from being the case. Cuba and Venezuela have taken a strong anti-imperialist stand. In Cuba the landlords and capitalists have been expropriated and in Venezuela we are moving in the same direction, although the process is far from complete and may still be reversed. But Brazil and Argentina, despite the leftish colouring of Lula and Cristina Fernández de Kirchner, are capitalist states that show no sign of moving in this direction. In domestic policy they attempt to pacify the masses by certain gestures (Keynesianism) and in foreign policy they strive to keep on good terms with imperialism, while not openly breaking with Venezuela. In order to break the diplomatic isolation that Washington seeks to impose on Venezuela, the Bolivarian government has developed relations with these countries, which is understandable. But in the last analysis, no trust can be placed on such diplomatic arrangements, which can change like the shifting sands of the desert, according to which way the wind blows.

Somebody once said: nations do not have friends, only interests. The governments of Brazil and Argentina can change at any time, leaving Venezuela in the lurch. Even now, Washington is constantly pressurising the governments of Lula y Cristina Fernández, who will not be able to resist such pressures. In addition, the policy of nationalizations in Venezuela is not at all to their liking. It gives dangerous ideas to the masses in Argentina and Brazil, who will say: if this can be done in Venezuela, why can't it be done here? The imperialists understand what we understand: there is a revolutionary process in Venezuela, and the masses are moving to change society. In the old days, all socialists were "communists" as far as Washington was concerned, but now US imperialism needs to deal with "good" socialists like Lula and Bachelet to isolate Chávez. They are trying to draw in Morales also. That is the meaning of Bush 's tour of Latin America in 2007 and the attempt to sign bilateral trade agreements with Brazil and other countries in the region.

In public, relations between Chávez and Lula and Cristina Fernández are cordial. The President of Brazil and Argentina cannot afford to come out against Chávez because that would cause a storm of protest at home. But in private their support for the Bolivarian Revolution, always lukewarm, is getting cooler all the time. As the revolution begins to take serious measures against private property, this attitude will harden. And all the time Washington is whispering in their ears: "Don't be a fool. Don't you see that Chávez is a danger to you as well as to us? This man is mad. He must be stopped. You must use your influence to put pressure on him to stop this revolutionary madness. He will destabilize the whole continent..." and so on and so forth.

The idea that countries with such different governments and economies could present an effective united front to world imperialism is just plain stupid. To begin with Brazil and Argentina – the two economic giants of Latin America – have serious economic contradictions and are traditional rivals for regional hegemony. On a capitalist basis, this rivalry will persist. In the event of a world recession, which is inevitable in the next period, the competition for markets in Latin America will become intense – especially between these two countries. It is even possible that Mercosur will break apart under the strain.

There are other contradictions. When Bolivia nationalized Brazilian-owned Petrobras, there were howls of protest from Brazil. It is true that an uneasy compromise was later patched up. But this incident shows how each national bourgeoisie jealously defends its own interests and has a reactionary attitude towards the revolutionary movement. On the contrary, the nationalizations in Bolivia were enthusiastically welcomed in Venezuela. This shows the real conflict of interest that exists behind the outward show of solidarity between these countries.

Later the Brazilian senate attacked the government of Venezuela for refusing to renew the license of the counter-revolutionary RCTV. Chávez correctly pointed out that this was an unwarranted interference in the internal affairs of Venezuela and threatened that Venezuela would withdraw from Mercosur if this kind of thing continued. This little incident tells us quite a lot about the real nature of Mercosur and the class interests that lie behind it. The idea that the members of Mercosur could establish a stable and powerful bloc capable of negotiating with imperialism and thus, presumably, extracting major concessions and arriving at a modus vivendi with imperialism is yet another of Dieterich's utopian schemes.

The inclusion of Cuba in this bloc serves to underline its utopian nature. The US imperialists have made it abundantly clear that they have no intention of negotiation with Cuba, for the same reason that they have no intention of negotiating with Venezuela. These countries represent a direct threat to the interests of US imperialism because of the example they give to the millions of exploited and oppressed people of Latin America. The imperialists are determined to destroy the Cuban and Venezuelan Revolutions. Whoever does not understand this is incapable of understanding anything.

It is clear that US imperialism is trying to isolate Venezuela internationally and in particular it has striven to incite the OAS against it. Under such circumstances, it is obviously necessary for the Bolivarian government to do everything in its power to break the isolation. This means that it is permissible to enter into negotiations with governments like that of Lula and attempt tó block the diplomatic intrigues of Washington aimed at inciting Brazil against Venezuela.

All this is self-evident and should not even have to be said. Revolutionaries must learn to master the art of diplomatic manoeuvring just as they must learn every other aspect of the art of war (diplomacy is really a subordinate aspect of warfare). But heaven help the revolutionary who allows himself to be deceived by diplomacy or tries to substitute diplomatic deals for a revolutionary policy. If we really believe that the Bolivarian revolution must become a socialist revolution or else fail, we must act accordingly. We must take steps to expropriate the oligarchy and make an appeal to the workers and peasants of Latin America to follow this example.

"But this will provoke the opposition and the Americans," Dieterich will protest. "It will place the Bolivarian Revolution in danger." To which we reply: the counter-revolutionary forces do not need to be provoked. They are already provoked and have been almost from the day Chávez was elected. What provokes them is not this or that speech by Chávez or this or that decree: what provokes them is the existence of the Bolivarian revolution itself. They have already tried to overthrow it on at least three occasions. If we do not destroy their economic power, they will try again and again until they succeed.

President Chávez attempted to reduce the threat from Colombia, partly by trying to build a rapprochement or understanding with Uribe. But this policy is now in ruins. Uribe, clearly prodded by Washington, brutally broke off connections with Chávez allegedly over his contacts with the FARC guerrillas and Colombian army officers during his attempt to mediate over hostages. This shows the limitation of bourgeois diplomacy in defending the Venezuelan Revolution. Diplomatic manoeuvres are necessary but can play only a subordinate role.

Foreign policy is only the continuation of domestic policy. A revolutionary government in Venezuela must pursue a revolutionary foreign policy, aimed at the extension of the revolution to the whole of America. The strategic goal is the revolutionary unification of Latin America. But this can only be achieved through the overthrow of the landlords and capitalists. This must be kept firmly in mind. In war, sometimes tactics can diverge from the overall strategic goal, but tactics must never be in open contradiction to the overall strategy. It is one thing to manoeuvre with the bourgeois governments of other countries to prevent the isolation of Venezuela and gain time. It is another thing to compromise the revolutionary socialist goals by unprincipled blocs with the enemies of socialism, which is what Heinz Dieterich proposes.

"But if we go too far we will alienate our allies in Latin America and destroy the RLPB!" he will howl. To which we will answer: the Venezuelan revolution needs allies, but it needs allies who are really ready to defend it and fight for it, not false friends who will abandon it in a decisive moment. The revolution has such allies: not the governments who can easily turn against us and go over to Washington, but the millions of workers and peasants, poor people, revolutionary youth and progressive intellectuals in Latin America and throughout the world. They are the only people we can rely upon.

Marx or List?

The Bible says: "*As a dog returns to his own vomit, so a fool repeats his folly*" (Proverbs 26:11). In plain language this means: *some people never learn from their mistakes*. This is clearly the problem with comrade Dieterich. In interview in *Junge Welt* (7/1/06) Carsten Schiefer asks him the following question:

"*Q*: How would you characterize the direction of the Bolivarian revolution in Latin America? How far has it come?

"*Dieterich*: I would say that one could characterize the process in terms of five macrodynamics. The first is the development of a *state capitalism* of the kind Friedrich List propagated in Germany 180 years ago and in Venezuela is designated as indigenous development. That's nothing new. The English invented it; the Germans and Japanese copied it. Today, China and the Asian tigers are following this path because *it's the only kind of development that is possible today within the context of world capitalism. One could speak of a kind of state capitalism of a Keynesian character that includes national dignity*." (our emphasis)

It is no accident that Dieterich quotes the ideas of Friedrich List, whom Marx and Engels regarded as *the archetype of a vulgar philistine and petty-bourgeois economist*. In fact, it would hardly be possible to find an economist whose views were more alien and repugnant to Marx than List, who Dieterich takes as his model. Here are a few examples of what Marx wrote about him in Draft of an Article on Friedrich List's book: *Das Nationale System der Politischen Oekonomie* (March 1845):

"Everywhere he allows the thing to remain in existence but idealises the expression of it. We shall trace this in detail. It is just this empty idealistic phraseology that enables him to ignore the *real* barriers standing in the way of his pious wishes and to indulge in the most absurd fantasies (what would have become of the English and French bourgeoisie if it had first to ask a high-ranking nobility, an esteemed bureaucracy and the ancient ruling dynastics for permission to give 'industry' the 'force of law'?)." [4]

"The German bourgeois is religious even when he is an industrialist. He shrinks from speaking about the nasty exchange values which he covets and speaks about productive forces [*von produktivkräften*]; he shrinks from speaking about competition and speaks of a national confederation of national productive forces; he shrinks from speaking of his private interest and speaks about the national interest. When one looks at the frank, classic cynicism with which the English and French bourgeoisie, as represented by its first – at least at the beginning of its domination – scientific spokesmen of political economy, elevated wealth into a god and ruthlessly sacrificed everything else to it, to this Moloch, in science as well, and when, on the other hand, one looks at the idealising, phrase-mongering, bombastic manner of Herr List, who in the midst of political economy despises the wealth of 'righteous men' and knows loftier aims, one is bound to find it 'also sad' that the present day is no longer a day for wealth."

"The German philistine here reveals his 'national' character in many ways.

"1) In the whole of political economy, he sees only systems concocted in academic study rooms. That the development of a science such as political economy is connected with the real movement of society, or is only its theoretical expression, Herr List, of course, does not suspect. A German theoretician."

Every word of this is applicable to Heinz Dieterich – the Friedrich List of the 21st Century. Even his comments on List's style of writing accurately describe the literary school of our Heinz: "He continually shows off in a clumsy and verbose rhetoric, the troubled waters of which always drive him in the end on to a sandbank, and the essence of which consists of constant repetitions about protective tariffs and true German [...] factories." [5] And if the style is similar, the content is exactly the same: empty, sentimental petty bourgeois moralising instead of a scientific analysis.

4. Marx, Draft of an Article on Friedrich List's book: *Das Nationale System der Politischen Oekonomie*, MECW Volume 4, p. 265.
5. Ibid, pp. 266-67.

What did List's economic wisdom consist of? *Protective tariffs*. This reflected the weakness of German capitalism at that time relative to its French and English rivals. "Let us protect 'our fatherland' with protective tariffs!" That was the position of List, who tried to push the German workers behind the German capitalists on a nationalist basis. What did Marx have to say about this? He writes:

"[8] What then does the German philistine want? He wants to be a *bourgeois*, an exploiter, inside the country, but he wants also not to be exploited outside the country. He puffs himself up into being the 'nation' in relation to foreign countries and says: I do not submit to the laws of competition; that is contrary to my national dignity; as the nation I am a being superior to huckstering.

"The nationality of the worker is neither French, nor English, nor German, it is *labour, free slavery, self-huckstering*. His government is neither French, nor English, nor German, it is capital. His native air is neither French, nor German, nor English, it is factory air. The land belonging to him is neither French, nor English, nor German, it lies a few feet *below the ground*. Within the country, money is the fatherland of the industrialist. Thus, the German philistine wants the laws of competition, of exchange value, of huckstering, to lose their power. at the frontier barriers of his country! He is willing to recognize the power of bourgeois society only in so far as it is in accord with *his interests*, the interests of his class! He does not want to fall victim to a power to which he wants to *sacrifice* others, and to which he sacrifices himself inside his own country! Outside the country he wants to show himself and be treated as a different being from what he is within the country and how he himself behaves within the country! He wants to leave the cause in existence and to abolish one of its *effects!* We shall prove to him that selling oneself out inside the country has as its necessary consequence selling out outside, that competition, which gives him his power inside the country, cannot prevent him from becoming powerless outside the country; that the state, which he subordinates to bourgeois society inside the country, cannot protect him from the action of bourgeois society outside the country.

"However much the individual bourgeois fights against the others, as a *class* the bourgeois have a common interest, and this community of interest, which is directed against the proletariat inside the country, is directed against the bourgeois of other nations outside the country. This the bourgeois calls his *nationality*." [6]

From the above lines we can see the abysm that separates the nationalist philistinism of the petty bourgeois List from the proletarian internationalism of Marx. We stand firmly in the tradition of Marx. Heinz Dieterich stands very clearly against Karl Marx and with Friedrich List. Here at least comrade Dieterich quite clear and unambiguous (and let us thank God for small mercies!). What he is advocating for Venezuela is not socialism at all, but state capitalism: "*a kind of state capitalism of a Keynesian character.*" That is to say, he advocates the same model invented by

6. Ibid., p. 280.

List that was embraced by the European Social Democracy in the period 1945-79, a model that collapsed in a welter of inflation at the end of the 1970s and which both the bourgeoisie and the Social Democrats have abandoned, *because it did not work.* Now our friend Heinz regards this as "*the only kind of development that is possible today within the context of world capitalism.*" That is perfectly clear, is it not? Yes, it is quite clear – and quite clearly in contradiction to the idea that has been expressed many times by Hugo Chávez, who says that the alternative before the human race is *capitalism or socialism.*

Here, moreover, Heinz gets entangled in a series of insoluble contradictions. On the one hand, he accepts the existence of capitalism on a world scale, and sees no possibility of overthrowing it (if he does, he keeps it very quiet). On the other hands, he thinks that it is possible for Venezuela to follow its own road on the basis of pursuing the kind of economic policies that were invented by the English and then copied by the Germans and Japanese. What are these policies that Heinz admires so much? They are the policies of protectionism that were adopted by the aforementioned countries in the nascent phase of capitalist development. Here our friend has a point. The argument of the liberal economists about the absolute necessity of free trade reflects the present state of development of capitalism in the USA, Japan, France, Britain and Germany. But in the past they sang a very different song. In the early days of capitalism, they were all protectionists. Their feeble nascent industries required protection against foreign competition, which would have destroyed it. Only when their industries were sufficiently strong to compete on world markets did they become converted to the virtues of free trade. That is why List, reflecting the interests of the weak German bourgeoisie of the mid-19th century called for protective tariffs.

Marx explained long ago that capitalism, beginning with the establishment of a national market, necessarily develops a world market. Today, the crushing domination of the world market has been established to an unheard-of degree. All nation states, even the biggest and most powerful, are compelled to participate on the world market and find themselves subordinate to it. In this context, the concept of national sovereignty has lost most of its meaning. Those states that succeeded in throwing off the shackles of direct imperialist domination now find themselves subjugated by imperialism through the mechanism of world trade and the stranglehold of giant transnational companies and foreign investors.

It is possible for weak colonial countries to achieve some respite on the basis of protectionism. The example of Malaysia in recent years is a case in point. However, such measures can only work *for a time and to some extent.* Ultimately, it will be impossible for Venezuela to free itself from the powerful pull of the world market, which is the most important manifestation of the present epoch. The idea that Venezuela can somehow cut itself off from the world economy is entirely false. If neither Russia nor China, with their gigantic internal markets and vast reserves could maintain a regime of autarky, how could this be achieved by Venezuela, a far smaller economy? The only real way to protect the national economy against the depredations of foreign capital is though a state monopoly of foreign trade, the cornerstone of a nationalized planned economy.

Here again, Heinz gets everything hopelessly mixed up. In the interview in *Junge Welt* already mentioned he says: "Neither a democratic socio-economic development nor a defence against US and European interests or even the separate development of socialism in Venezuela is possible. It's possible only in the context of a Latin American regional bloc. Venezuela surely will not be able to develop economically along social-democratic lines or make a transition to socialism without a regional bloc that includes Cuba, Brazil, Argentina, Uruguay, and Paraguay.

"The result of all is that the emphasis of the measures taken by the government is based on the development perspective of market economics. Venezuela is naturally a capitalist third world economy, completely distorted in its structure of production because everything depends upon oil; it is completely distorted as well in its lack of diversification in the global market, without a single technology for the future, and so forth.

"On the one hand, the government must concentrate its efforts on remedial action, while on the other improving the level of labour power and combating outright poverty. From the latter come measures such as the literacy campaign, the opening of new schools and universities and health clinics. That is at the centre of the political task. At the same time, one attempts to make some headway at the socialist project, first of all by beginning to think collectively."

What does all this mean? First of all, the perspective of socialism is conspicuous by its absence. Our professor considers that Venezuela is "naturally a capitalist third world economy", which is destined to "develop economically along social-democratic lines". What does this development social-democratic lines consist of? Firstly, *the maintenance of a capitalist market economy for the foreseeable future.* Secondly, remedial action (i.e., reforms) to alleviate poverty, tackle illiteracy, etc. In other words, to continue much as the Bolivarian government has done in the period since 1998. This means, in practice, the abandonment of the socialist transformation, or its postponement to a far-distant future.

Socialism and internationalism

Marx and Engels were not internationalists out of sentimentality but for scientific reasons. The tendency of capitalism to develop a world market, which was predicted in *The Communist Manifesto*, is a fact. Socialist internationalism is not an utopian dream but flows inevitably from the development of capitalism itself. The formation of the European Union was a tacit admission by the bourgeoisie that the old national states have outlived their usefulness and become transformed into reactionary barriers to the free development of the productive forces.

What is the alternative to capitalist globalisation – that is, to the domination of the entire world by a handful of gigantic corporations and imperialist states? Dieterich counterposes to globalization – bourgeois nationalism. We counterpose to it the class struggle and the fight for socialism nationally and internationally. The standpoint of Heinz Dieterich means the complete abandonment of Marxism and Leninism. *It signifies the abandonment of the proletarian standpoint in favour of bourgeois or petty bourgeois national philistinism.* One looks in vain in all the articles of Heinz Dieterich for even the slightest glimmerings of a class position. He refers in sentimental language to "our great Latin American fatherland", without explaining that this "fatherland" is composed of exploiters and exploited, masters and slaves.

Marxists do not gloss over the class contradictions, but on the contrary, bring them to the fore. As Lenin explains in *Critical Remarks on the National Question*: "On the boards of the joint-stock companies capitalists of different nations sit together, completely amalgamated with each other. In factories workers of different nations work side by side. *On all really serious and profound political issues sides are taken according to classes and not according to nations.*" What has the Argentinean worker got in common with the Argentinean factory owner? What has the Brazilian landless peasant got in common with the Brazilian latifundist? What has the Venezuelan proletarian got in common with the Venezuelan oligarch? In another work Lenin writes: "The interests of the working class and of its struggle against capitalism demand complete solidarity and the closest unity of the workers of all nations; they *demand resistance to the nationalist policy of the bourgeoisie of every nationality.*" [7]

Lenin always wrote in a clear and ambiguous way. There is no way his meaning can be misunderstood. And his meaning is this: that for Marxists, at all times and under all conditions, the class question comes first. *We stand for the sacred unity of the working class, irrespective of nationality, language, colour or religion. We are opposed to nationalism and in favour of internationalism.* In order to combat the pernicious illusions peddled by the bourgeois and petty bourgeois nationalists, Lenin warned that: "The proletariat cannot support any consolidation of nationalism, on the contrary, it supports everything that helps to obliterate national distinctions and remove national barriers, supports everything that makes the ties between nationalities closer and closer or leads to the amalgamation of nations. To act differently means taking the side of reactionary nationalist philistinism." [8]

The Communist Manifesto explains that the proletarian revolution, though national in form is international in content. The workers must first settle accounts with their own bourgeoisie and carry out the revolution in their own country. The Revolution has begun in Venezuela and it is moving in the direction of the socialist

7. Lenin, *The Right of Nations to Self-Determination.*
8. Ibid.

transformation of society, despite the strenuous efforts of reformists like Heinz Dieterich to prevent this. It is the duty of the workers and peasants of Venezuela to overthrow the power of the oligarchy and take the power into their own hands. The socialist revolution can succeed in Venezuela, but it cannot be consolidated unless it spreads at least to the rest of Latin America.

The anti-Marxist theory of "socialism in one country", first expounded by Stalin in the autumn of 1924, went against everything the Bolsheviks and the Communist International had preached. Such a notion could never have been countenanced by Marx or Lenin. Unless the Soviet state succeeded in breaking out of its isolation, Lenin thought that the October Revolution could not survive for any length of time. This idea is repeated time after time in his writings and speeches after the Revolution. In the end, the revolutionary movements in Germany, Hungary, Italy and other countries were defeated, but they were sufficient to halt the attempts of imperialism to overthrow the Bolsheviks by armed intervention. The Russian workers' state survived, but prolonged isolation in conditions of extreme backwardness produced a process of bureaucratic degeneration that was the basis for the Stalinist political counter-revolution.

The Cuban revolution from the beginning was inspired by revolutionary internationalism. This was personified by Che Guevara, that outstanding leader of the Cuban revolution. Che was born an Argentinian and fought in the front line of the Cuban revolution. But in reality he was a true internationalist and a citizen of the world. Like Bolivar he had the perspective of a Latin American revolution. After his tragic death there have been many attempts to turn Che Guevara into a harmless icon, a face on a tee shirt. He was presented by the bourgeois as a well-meaning romantic, an utopian idealist. This is unworthy of the memory of a great revolutionist! Che Guevara was not a hopeless dreamer but a revolutionary realist. It was not an accident that Che attempted to extend the revolution to other countries, not just in Latin America but also in Africa. He understood very well that, in the last analysis, the future of the Cuban revolution would be determined by this.

From the very beginning the destiny of the Cuban revolution has been tied to events on a world scale. How could it be otherwise when the revolution was threatened at birth by the most powerful imperialist state on earth? The Cuban revolution – like the Russian revolution – had a tremendous international impact, especially in Latin America and the Caribbean. That remains the case even today. Che tried to light a spark that would set the whole continent ablaze. Maybe he made a mistake in how he went about it, but nobody can question his intentions and his fundamental idea was correct: that the only way to save the Cuban revolution was to spread it to Latin America.

Unfortunately, some erroneous conclusions were drawn from the Cuban experience. The attempt to export the model of guerrilla war and "focos" led to one terrible defeat after another. There were several reasons for this. Firstly, the Cuban insurgency had taken US imperialism by surprise. But they soon learned the lessons and every time a "foco" appeared, they crushed it immediately before it could spread. A more important fact was that the majority of the population in Latin America now lives in towns and cities. Guerrilla war is a typical method of struggle of the peasantry. Therefore, while guerrilla war can play an important role as an auxiliary, it cannot play the main role in the socialist revolution. That is reserved for the working class in the towns. And tactics must be adapted accordingly. This is shown by the experience of Venezuela, where the attempt to organize a guerrilla war was a complete failure. The Venezuelan revolution is unfolding as an essentially urban revolution, based on the masses in the towns and cities and supported by the peasantry. The Bolivarian Movement of Hugo Chávez has used the parliamentary struggle very effectively to mobilize the masses. But it has been the movement of the masses that has defeated the counter-revolution on three occasions.

The destiny of the Cuban Revolution is now organically bound up with that of the Venezuelan Revolution. They will determine each other. If the Venezuelan Revolution is defeated, the Cuban Revolution will be in the greatest danger. Every effort must be made to prevent this. But here we must learn from history. The Venezuelan Revolution has accomplished miracles, but it is not yet finished. Like the Cuban Revolution, the Venezuelan Revolution began as a national-democratic revolution. In the early stages of the he programme advocated by Hugo Chávez was the programme of advanced bourgeois democracy. But experience has shown that the oligarchy and imperialism are the mortal enemies of democracy. They will stop at nothing to destroy the revolution. Therefore, to attempt to limit the Bolivarian Revolution to the bourgeois democratic tasks – that is, to halt the revolution – would be to prepare the way for the inevitable downfall of the revolution. Why is US imperialism so determined to destroy the Cuban and Venezuelan Revolutions? It is because of the effect they are having on a continental scale. The imperialists are terrified that Cuba and Venezuela will act as focal points. Therefore, they are determined to liquidate them.

The idea of Che was to open up twenty Vietnams in Latin America. That was not a bad idea, but it was not possible at that time, partly because the conditions had not ripened sufficiently, but mainly because of the false model of guerrilla war that was followed. But now things are different. The crisis of capitalism has had devastating effects in Latin America, and this has had revolutionary consequences. The conditions for revolution are maturing everywhere. In fact, at the present time there is not a single stable capitalist regime from Tierra del Fuego to the Rio Grande. With correct leadership, there is no reason why successful proletarian revolutions should not occur in one or several Latin American countries in the next period. *What is needed is not nationalism and blocs with the reactionary bourgeoisie, but a revolutionary socialist programme and revolutionary proletarian internationalism.*

For an internationalist policy!

Socialism is internationalist or it is nothing. Our policy must be a class policy, an anti-militarist and anti-imperialist policy. But such a policy can only succeed if it is firmly linked to an anti-capitalist policy and the perspective of socialism, nationally and internationally. Heinz Dieterich considers the socialist alternative utopian. But this should not surprise us, since he considers socialist revolution in general to be utopian. Instead he offers us yet another of his supposedly "realistic" alternatives, namely the Regional Bloc of Power This is a bourgeois reformist alternative to the Bolivarian idea of the revolutionary struggle for the unity of Latin America. The two ideas have absolutely nothing in common. The former is the idea of uniting the existing bourgeois regimes of Latin America without touching the existing property relations or expropriating the oligarchy. The latter is a revolutionary idea of uniting the workers and peasants of Latin America in a common struggle against imperialism and the oligarchies – the only way to establish a genuine and lasting union of the peoples of the continent in a socialist federation.

Like Simon Bolivar we stand firmly for the unification of Latin America, but we recognise that on the basis of capitalism, this will always be a utopia. As long as the oligarchies own the land, the banks and the industries, the only future possible for Latin America is one of unemployment, cuts and misery for millions. *The only alternative is the Socialist Federation of Latin America.* Does this seem so difficult? Yes, the struggle for socialism is difficult. Every great cause in history has always been difficult. But is it not far more difficult to accept the present situation of unemployment, cuts, wars, mass starvation and all the other horrors that capitalism has prepared for the peoples of the world? Despite the colossal potential, the bourgeoisie has failed to give the peoples of Latin America the future they deserved. For almost two centuries the bourgeoisie has ruled Latin America, and what has it achieved? The productive forces stagnate, while agriculture is ruined. Everywhere we see unemployment and poverty. The youth is faced with the choice: unemployment or emigration. And what remains of national independence when the entire continent is held fast in the embraces of the northern giant?

The victory of socialism in Venezuela would have profound and immediate repercussions in the rest of Latin America. How long would the oligarchy retain power in Bolivia, Ecuador and Peru? A revolutionary wave would sweep through Latin America and would have an effect north of the Rio Grande, where discontent is growing and the Latino population is now the biggest ethnic minority in the USA. A socialist planned economy would create the possibility of mobilizing the productive forces of Latin America – its fertile land, its industry, science and technology, and above all the enormous creative potential of its population – for the purpose of transforming society. The colossal talent of the peoples of Latin America, their artists, scientists, students, intellectuals, writers and architects, would flower as never before in the long history of this rich, beautiful and wonderfully diverse continent. It would transform the entire world, laying the basis for a socialist world federation. That is the only perspective worth fighting for in the first decade of the 21st century: the perspective of a socialist Latin America – the first gigantic step towards a socialist new world order.

11. The state and revolution

The state of 21st Century Socialism

The question of the state is the most fundamental question for all revolutions and has therefore occupied a central position in Marxist theory. The state is a special repressive force standing above society and increasingly alienating itself from it. This force has its origin in the remote past. The earliest forms of class society show the state as a monster, devouring huge amounts of labour and repressing the masses and depriving them of all rights. At the same time, by developing the division of labour, by organizing society and carrying co-operation to a far higher level than ever before, it enabled a huge amount of labour power to be mobilized, and thus raised human productive labour to undreamed-of heights. This in turn permitted a giant leap forward for culture and science.

"These actual relations [the economic structure of society] are in no way created by the State power, on the contrary they are the power creating it. The individuals who rule in these conditions, besides having to constitute their power in the form of the State, have to give their will, which is determined by these definite conditions, a universal expression as the will of the State, as law – an expression whose content is always determined by the relations of this class, as civil and criminal law demonstrate in the clearest possible way…" [1]

The state bureaucracy has powerful interests of its own. One can find similar features in every state, even the most democratic. The state, in the final analysis, consists of special armed bodies of men the purpose of which is precisely to regulate the class struggle, and to keep it within acceptable limits. The ruling class in normal periods exercises control over the state. But there are certain periods, when the class struggle reaches a pitch of intensity that goes beyond the "acceptable limits". In such revolutionary periods, the question of power is posed. Either the revolutionary class overthrows the old state and replaces it with a new power, or else the

1. Marx, *The German Ideology*, p. 184.

ruling class crushes the revolution and imposes a dictatorship – the state power in an open and undisguised form, as opposed to the state power in a "democratic" guise.

However, there is a further variant, which in different forms has been seen at different moments in history. Where the contending classes have fought themselves to a standstill with no clear result, and where the struggle between the classes reaches a kind of state of unstable equilibrium, the state itself can rise above society and acquire a large degree of independence. In modern times this phenomenon is known as Bonapartism, and in the ancient world it assumes the form of Caesarism.

Dieterich and Peters display utter confusion on the question of the state, and this is not accidental. On page 101 of *El Socialismo del Siglo XXI* we arrive at yet another contradiction in the theory of 21st Century Socialism. Marxism explains that the state is always an instrument for the oppression of one class by another. Yet Arno Peters informs us that "as long as society has *a hierarchical structure, and therefore continues to maintain a military organization* that requires its activity." What this means is that under 21st Century Socialism we will not only have *capitalists* but also *the capitalist state*. The state, as Lenin explained, in the last analysis is *groups of armed men in defence of property*. In Arno Peters' vision of 21st Century Socialism we have the state in all its glory: a standing army, a police force, judges, prisons organized on strictly hierarchical lines. Naturally, all this requires a sizeable bureaucracy, which will undoubtedly devour a considerable amount of the wealth produced by the working class, and not just the "wages of equivalence".

Although Arno does not go into detail, it is not difficult to see what this military organization will look like. It will be *hierarchical* he says. But if it is a *hierarchical organization,* in which the general staff can only receive *the wages of equivalence*, how can this hierarchy be identified? It is clear that under 21st Century Socialism, the generals, field marshals and brigadiers will be dressed in the most extravagant uniforms and covered with military insignia – just like now, in fact. In the same way that Dieterich wants to maintain a capitalist market economy but combine it with democracy and socialism, so he wishes to retain the state but also to render it harmless – like a bulldog with rubber teeth. We are informed on page 61 that the state is necessary, and will always be necessary in order to "attend to certain general necessities of society, such as health and public order but all its general functions pass through the filter of its class character and class". We are further informed on page 62: "The particular interest of the bosses of the system determines and distorts all the general functions of the State."

According to Dieterich, the state is necessary, and presumably will continue to exist in 21st Century socialism, not only to provide doctors and hospitals, but also 21st Century policemen equipped with truncheons to give a friendly lesson to 21st Century delinquents who disturb public order and cause distress to decent citizens – just like now. We are assured, however, that under 21st Century Socialism, the state will be completely different to the state as it exists at the present time: "This is the meaning of the class State, which historically substituted the proto-State about 6,000 years ago, and which will disappear with participative democracy. In its place there will be a new public authority which will prioritise the general interests and, having lost its class functions loses its repressive identity." [2] Confusion is piled upon confusion. Dieterich once again distorts history. What is this "proto-State" that was supposed to have been abolished 6,000 years ago? Only Arno Peters knows.

Dieterich and Engels on the state

Marx, Engels and Lenin explained many times that every state is an instrument of repression. How is it possible to retain the state, which by definition is an instrument of repression, and remove its repressive features? Only somebody completely ignorant of the ABCs of Marxism could suggest such a thing. It is about the same as "democratising" capitalism, introducing socialism without expropriating the capitalists, or teaching tigers to eat lettuce. At every step Dieterich contradicts himself on the question of the state. On page xvii of *Hugo Chávez y el socialismo del siglo XXI* the state is *overcome and consigned to the rubbish bin of history.* We are told that a certain Mr. Robert Kurz ("a masterly pen") has solved the question in the following way:

"Humanity's last adventure, therefore, consists of 'overcoming the market economy *beyond the old ideas of State socialism', which are no longer valid.*" But on page 21 the state is back again – this time as "*a State of majorities*". In capitalist society the *majority* is made up of workers, peasants, the urban and rural poor and the middle class. These are ruled over by a minority of exploiters: the landlords, bankers, capitalists and their families and hangers-on. In order to abolish capitalism and move towards socialism it is necessary for the majority to expropriate the minority.

How is this to be done? The working class must put itself at the head of society, rallying all the other oppressed and exploited layers to its side. A workers' government will nationalize the land, the banks and the key industries and begin to reorganize the economy on socialist lines. Having expropriated the capitalists, it will be possible to institute a socialist planned economy. Freed from the fetters of private ownership, the productive potential of industry and agriculture will be realized to the full. This is the prior condition for raising the living standards and cultural level of the masses, which is the prior condition for the participation of the working class in the running of industry, society and the state.

In the transitional period between capitalism and socialism the state will still exist, along with money, wage labour, certain inequalities and other remnants of the old society. But a workers' state is fundamentally different from other states. It is a

2. Dieterich, *Socialism of the 21st Century*, p. 62.

state that is dedicated to its own extinction, or, to use the phrase of Engels, a semi-state, like the Paris Commune. In his masterpiece *State and Revolution*, written in the heat of the 1917 Revolution, Lenin brilliantly summed up the Marxist theory of the state. Basing themselves on the experience of the Paris Commune, Marx and Engels pointed out:

"...One thing especially was proved by the Commune, viz., that 'the working class cannot simply lay hold of the ready-made state machinery, and wield it for its own purposes'..." [3]

Engels explained that the working class could not simply take over the existing state and use it to transform society:

"The proletariat seizes state power, and then transforms the means of production into state property. But in doing this, it puts an end to itself as the proletariat, it puts an end to all class differences and class antagonisms, it puts an end also to the state as the state. Former society, moving in class antagonisms, had need of the state, that is, an organization of the exploiting class at each period for the maintenance of its external conditions of production; therefore, in particular, for the forcible holding down of the exploited class in the conditions of oppression (slavery, bondage or serfdom, wage labour) determined by the existing mode of production. The state was the official representative of society as a whole, its embodiment in a visible corporate body; but it was this only in so far as it was the state of that class which itself in its epoch, represented society as a whole: in ancient times, the state of the slave owning citizens; in the Middle Ages, of the feudal nobility; in our epoch, of the bourgeoisie. When ultimately it becomes really representative of society as a whole, it makes itself superfluous. As soon as there is no longer any class of society to be held in subjection; as soon as, along with class domination and the struggle for individual existence based on the former anarchy of production, the collisions and excesses arising from these have also been abolished, there is nothing more to be repressed, and a special repressive force, a state, is no longer necessary. The first act in which the state really comes forward as the representative of society as a whole – the seizure of the means of production in the name of society – is at the same time its last independent act as a state. The interference of a state power in social relations becomes superfluous in one sphere after another, and then becomes dormant of itself Government over persons is replaced by the administration of things and the direction of the processes of production. The state is not 'abolished', it withers away. It is from this standpoint that we must appraise the phrase 'people's free state' – both its justification at times for agitational purposes, and its ultimate scientific inadequacy – and also the demand of the so-called Anarchists that the state should be abolished overnight." [4]

3. Preface to the 1872 German edition of *The Communist Manifesto* in Marx and Engels *Selected Works*, Vol. 1, pp. 98-9
4. Engels, *Anti-Dühring*, Laurence and Wishart, 1943, p. 308.

On the question of democracy, comrade Dieterich also shows a superficial and philistine point of view. By formal democracy he means bourgeois democracy, which is only another word for the dictatorship of the banks and big monopolies. By referring to the alleged gulf that separates modern bourgeois democracy from the original ideas of the "founding fathers" he makes a double mistake. Already in the pages of *The Communist Manifesto*, Marx explained the true nature of bourgeois democracy: "The executive of the modern state is but a committee for managing the common affairs of the whole bourgeoisie." [5] Incidentally, the "founding fathers" of bourgeois democracy of which Dieterich speaks in such reverent terms believed in a restricted franchise, excluding not only women and slaves but the majority of the working class. It took decades of struggle by the working class to conquer the right to vote and other democratic rights. As a result, in most countries there is more democracy than in the past, not less. However, the reality of bourgeois formal democracy is just the same now as what it was in Marx's day: a convenient fig leaf to conceal the crude reality of bourgeois class rule.

Democracy and dictatorship

Naturally, having conquered democratic rights, the working class will make full use of them to further its interests, develop the class struggle, and fight for the socialist transformation of society. We will make use of every democratic opportunity that is opened to us, not only the right to strike and demonstrate, but participation in elections. The Venezuelan revolution shows the importance of the parliamentary struggle. Under certain conditions, it would even be possible to carry out the socialist transformation of society through parliament. But only on one condition: that the revolutionary socialists, having won a majority in parliament, mobilised the workers and peasants outside parliament to expropriate the landlords, bankers and capitalists.

Marxists do not reject the parliamentary struggle in principle. The parliamentary struggle is one aspect of the class struggle, just like any other. However, we must always bear in mind the limitations of parliamentarism. It must never be forgotten that the fundamental issues can never be resolved by parliaments, laws and constitution. In the last analysis, the fundamental questions are always settled outside parliament: in the factories, on the streets, in the villages, and in the army barracks. If any proof is required for this assertion, we need only refer to the events in Venezuela in April 2002. Dieterich makes a passing reference to this:

"If in certain circumstances, the majorities manage to elect a truly popular and democratic government, the ruling class ignores its own constitutional rules and carries out a coup. This cynical mechanism is known in 'political science' as the paradox of democracy. The democratic institutions are only for the friends of democra-

5. Marx and Engels, *Communist Manifesto*, Chapter 1, *Bourgeois and Proletarians*.

cy, not for its enemies. Translated into good Spanish: formal democracy is only for the friends of the bourgeoisie, not for the people who want to change society structurally and peacefully. A lesson for which Salvador Allende paid a high price."

All history shows that no ruling class has ever surrendered its power and privileges without a fight. When the "democratic" ruling class sees that its power and privileges are being threatened by an elected government, it will result to extra-parliamentary action to undermine, subvert and overthrow the government. Under such circumstances, appeals to legality, constitutions, and so on are useless and counterproductive. This is all very true, but what conclusions does comrade Dieterich draw from it? He makes a brief reference to the fate of Salvador Allende, but does not tell us what Allende ought to have done to prevent the victory of the counter-revolution.

The conclusion that Dieterich wants us to draw is the following: that the mistake of Allende was to go too far, too fast, thereby provoking the anger of the ruling class and the powers that be, who responded with a coup d'état. That is why Heinz Dieterich is continuously advising President Chávez to moderate his policies, not to go "too far", not to nationalise the land, banks and industries, not to touch private property at all. for fear of provoking the anger of the oligarchy and imperialism. Dieterich reminds one of the little boy in the fairy tale who is always crying wolf. The point is how do we stop the wolf from coming? To this question our friend has no answer.

Anyone who knows anything about Chile, knows that it was perfectly possible for Allende to have defeated the counter-revolution. He had the support the millions of workers and peasants and a large part of the army, not just the common soldiers but also many officers, who warned him in advance of the coup and begged him to act. The mistake of Allende was to trust in the good faith of supposedly democratic army generals like Pinochet, in the force of law, the constitution, etc. Consequently he refused to arm the workers to defend their government, even when the masses were demanding arms in the period before 11th September.

The result was a bloody defeat and ferocious coup which cost tens of thousands of lives. The real lesson of Chile is this: that it is impossible to pacify the counter-revolution with beautiful speeches about democracy. It is necessary to disarm the counter-revolution and force it to submit to the will of the majority. It is not possible to make half a revolution. Ultimately, one class must win and another class must lose. In order to succeed the working class must take the power into its own hands. This means that it must expropriate the oligarchy. There is no other way.

"But this means civil war and bloodshed!" the reformists will protest. On the contrary, the only way to avoid bloodshed and civil war is to go onto the offensive. If the working class and its leadership show themselves to be firm and implacable, the reactionary forces will be weakened and thrown onto the defensive. But if the revolutionary forces show themselves to be weak, vacillating and indecisive, the counter-revolution will be strengthen and go onto the offensive. We see this lesson repeatedly in the course of the Bolivarian revolution.

Counterrevolutionary oligarchy

From the very beginning, the oligarchy and imperialism adopted a belligerent attitude towards the revolution. On at least three occasions they attempted to overthrow the democratically elected government of Hugo Chávez. But on each occasion they were defeated by the revolutionary movement of the masses. In April 2002, the Venezuelan landlords, bankers and capitalists, together with reactionary army officers, corrupt trade union leaders and the reactionary hierarchy of the Church, overthrew the legitimate government and seized power with the active support of American imperialism. President Chávez was arrested and would probably have been murdered, if it were not for the magnificent uprising of the people of Venezuela which defeated the coup in 48 hours.

There is no doubt whatever that if President Chávez had appealed to the masses to take power on the 13th April, they could have done so peacefully and without civil war. The counter-revolutionaries were shattered, split and demoralised. The streets, factories and army barracks were fully controlled by the revolutionary forces. Unfortunately, at that stage, the Bolivarian revolution still remained within the framework of capitalism and had no perspective. The President attempted to negotiate with the opposition. What was the result of this policy of moderation? Did the opposition adopt a more moderate stance? Did they abandon their counter-revolutionary plans? On the contrary, they saw only weakness on the part of the government and immediately began to prepare for another counter-revolutionary offensive.

The bosses' strike, which begun at the end of 2002 and lasted for two months, represented a serious threat to the Bolivarian revolution. Its aim was to create economic chaos and prepare the way for a second coup. They might have succeeded, except for the marvellous movement of the workers, who occupied the factories and oil installations, expelled the counter-revolutionary elements, and introduced workers' control. This is what saved the revolution. Unfortunately, the same mistake was repeated. President Chávez attempted to reach an agreement with the opposition. What was the result of this attempt to conciliate? Did it halt the counter-revolution? No, it enabled the opposition to regroup and reorganize. The counter-revolutionaries recovered their nerve and began to prepare a new counter-revolutionary offensive. They used the Bolivarian Constitution to campaign for a recall referendum of 2004. Only the marvellous revolutionary spirit of the masses defeated them once again.

What does all this prove? Only this: that the counter-revolutionary oligarchy and its imperialist backers will never be satisfied until Chávez is overthrown and the Bolivarian revolution destroyed. They cannot be won over by pleasant words and smiles, or by appeals to legality and constitutions. The opposition boycotted the legislative elections in December 2005 because they knew they would be overwhelmingly defeated. This indicated that the oligarchy was preparing to resort to extra-parliamentary measures. It is true that, after three consecutive defeats, the opposition leaders adopted a more moderate image. But that was only a tactic. They mobilized seriously for the Presidential elections and if Rosales had won, the smiling democratic mask would soon have been cast off. Encouraged by a victory, the counter-revolutionary forces would have gone on the offensive.

The masses once more ensured that this would not happen. The overwhelming victory of Hugo Chávez in the presidential elections in December 2006 created favourable conditions for a decisive advance of the Bolivarian revolution. The masses want change. They are demanding firm action against the oligarchy and the counter-revolutionaries. President Chávez has repeatedly indicated that he wants to make the revolution irreversible and advance to socialism. But not all the Bolivarian leaders are happy with this. There is a fifth column within the Bolivarian movement, especially at the top level, which wants to halt the revolution and reach a deal with the counter-revolutionary opposition. This would be a recipe for disaster. It would demoralise the masses and play into the hands of the counter-revolution. If it is to succeed, there is only one way for the revolution to go, and that is forward.

The conditions in which the revolution unfolds will differ from one country to another and from one period to another. That is obvious. And it is also obvious that the specific tactics of the revolutionary party will also differ according to these conditions. Such questions as the specific weight of the proletariat in the population, its relations to other classes, the strength of its organisations, its experience, cultural level, national traditions and temperament, all enter into the equation. The conditions for carrying out the socialist transformation of society in Venezuela at the present time are particularly favourable. Hugo Chávez has used elections to mobilize the broadest layers of society for socialism and has thereby raised their confidence and fighting spirit, while demoralizing and disorienting the forces of reaction. This is very important, *but it only poses the question of power; it does not solve it.*

The writing of a progressive Constitution creates a legal framework to regulate the class struggle, but it is by no means sufficient to guarantee a peaceful outcome. On the contrary, such an arrangement merely serves to delay the final conflict and to give it an even more violent and convulsive character in the end. The expectations of the masses are heightened and concentrated, and their aspirations are given ample scope to develop themselves. Thus, in modern times, the masses develop great illusions in their parliamentary representatives and the possibility of solving their most pressing problems by voting in elections. However, the most fundamental questions of society cannot be solved in this way. In reality the ruling class will only tolerate it to the degree that it does not threaten their power and privileges. The propertied classes are not interested in laws and constitutions and will not fail to prepare illegal conspiracies and coups behind the backs of the democratic institutions.

What is necessary to carry the revolution through to the end in Venezuela? An appeal should be made to the workers, peasants and soldiers to take over the land and factories, set up democratically elected committees, and arrest any counter-revolutionary elements. What is necessary is to pass an enabling act to expropriate the land, banks and key industries under democratic workers' control and management. This would suffice to eliminate the power of the landlords, bankers and capitalists and establish a nationalised planned economy. The President should use the television to appeal to the masses to support these measures and to take direct action to overcome the resistance of the counter-revolutionaries. A workers' and peasants' militia should be established to keep order and to prevent any provocations on the part of reactionaries. Immediate measures should be introduced to raise pensions and wages, lower the working day and improve the living standards of the small peasants and shopkeepers.

Such measures, resting on the revolutionary movement of the masses outside parliament would be more than enough to ensure a peaceful transition, with a minimum of conflict. To his credit, Chávez has already taken a number of steps in the direction of nationalization. But advisers like Dieterich are constantly urging him to halt the process, to desist from further nationalizations and so on. Reformists and bureaucrats surround him and exert pressure. If these elements prevail, the outcome will not be a peaceful transition but the opposite.

How Dieterich 'helps' Chávez

In 1999, Dieterich, according to his own account, predicted that that the military would conduct a coup against Chávez, a prediction the President at that time did not take seriously. Probably the reason why Chávez did not pay much attention is that Dieterich has been making the same predictions with tedious regularity. Every few months he predicts that the President will be overthrown or assassinated. Such predictions have the same scientific value as a man who continually repeats: "It is nine o'clock". He is certain to be proven correct at least twice every 24 hours. However, unlike the prediction concerning the time of day, predictions concerning counter-revolutionary plots require some kind of countervailing action to be taken. The question is *what action*?

As a matter of fact, it does not require any special prescience to predict that the counter-revolutionaries are plotting a coup or that the CIA would like to see Chávez dead. That there is a threat from the counter-revolutionary forces in Venezuela is self-evident and has been from the very first day. But how are we supposed to react to this threat? Do we take measures to disarm the counter-revolution and expropriate the oligarchy, or do we retreat, water down our programme to please the opposition – in other words, do the work of the counter-revolution ourselves? Here we will find a fundamental difference between what Heinz Dieterich wrote thirty years ago and what Heinz Dieterich writes now. It is the difference between somebody who is prepared to fight and defeat the enemy and a timid bourgeois reformer who is frightened of his own shadow and wishes to communicate his fear to everyone around him. This is living proof that the statement "older and wiser" is not always true.

On the 6th March 2005, Heinz Dieterich wrote an article in *Rebelión* entitled *The World Revolution advances through Hugo Chávez*. The title of the first section is thoroughly "Hegelian" in character: *Towards 21st Century Socialism with the Help of the World Spirit*. Dieterich begins:

"In an audacious commando operation, Hugo Chávez, on February 27, 2005, established his 'beachhead' of world vanguard in the ideological battlefield with the bourgeoisie, in proclaiming the necessity of 'inventing Socialism of the 21st Century' and 'to continue to distance ourselves from capitalism'. Following this, the Commander consolidated his position with two indestructible armoured divisions when he emphasized that Venezuela's socialism would be democratic and participative in character, 'in accord with the original ideas of Karl Marx and Friedrich Engels'."

Hugo Chávez was indeed audacious and courageous when he declared to the world that the Bolivarian revolution could only achieve its objectives by fighting for socialism in accord with the original ideas of Karl Marx and Friedrich Engels. For the first time since the fall of the USSR a leader of world stature had the courage to speak of socialism and Marxism. This was something that deserved the most enthusiastic applause of socialists everywhere, and the author of these lines greeted it with all possible enthusiasm. However, not everybody was equally enthusiastic about it.

I was present at the mass meeting in Caracas where the President publicly declared that he was a socialist. The thousands of working class *chavistas* present stood up and cheered. But I was sitting next to the Bolivarian ministers and I noticed that not all of them applauded, and others did so with little enthusiasm. Evidently the declarations took them by surprise. The next day the counter-revolutionaries ranted and raged. That was to be expected. But other circles on the "Left", although they applauded politely, were also not very pleased about Chávez's advocacy of revolutionary socialism. The ink was not even dry on the text of this speech when a host of reformists, Social Democrats and assorted revisionists came running to "correct" the President and modify his message, adding generous quantities of the purest tap water to it.

The above comments of Heinz Dieterich are a classical example of this kind of thing. In the first place, what we are dealing with here is not a "commando operation", but a *speech*. There was no "beachhead" and no "armoured divisions" were present. Yet again, comrade Dieterich makes use of *high-sounding rhetoric and r-r-*

r-revolutionary phrases to cover up the *timid reformist essence* of his own message. Whenever he refers to President Chávez he always resorts to a sort of sycophantic flattery, which is merely a device by which he hides the fact that he is actually contradicting what Chávez said.

This is not the straightforward and honest method of debate that we find in workers' meetings. It is the method of tortuous and indirect argument that has characterized university seminars ever since the medieval Schoolmen who used to argue about how many angels could dance on the head of a pin. More correctly, it is the method of a courtier, who flatters in order to deceive. We will later see what comrade Dieterich's real attitude is towards real revolutionary commando operation, armoured divisions and beachheads. For the present, let us remember Lenin's warning that *talk and flattery have destroyed more than one revolution*.

Let us hope that such things will not destroy the Bolivarian revolution. In order to prevent this it is absolutely necessary that the cadres of the Bolivarian Movement should turn their backs on those who wish to water down the ideas of socialism and halt the revolution. They should make a careful study of what Marx, Engels, Lenin and Trotsky really said and then make up their own minds on what socialism is, dispensing with the interpreting services of Dieterich and others like him. Since Heinz is inordinately fond of *lists*, let us make a brief list of his central argument. What is Dieterich's central message? Stripped of all rhetoric, it is basically this:

1) What we want is not socialism, as advocated by Marx and Lenin, but Socialism of the 21st Century as invented by Heinz Dieterich;

2) This "socialism" essentially is the same as "capitalism with a human face";

3) In order to bring about such socialism it is not necessary to expropriate the bourgeoisie; under Socialism of the 21st Century the landlords will own the land, the capitalists will own the factories and the bankers will own the banks – just like now;

4) Therefore, no revolution is necessary;

5) Therefore, the Bolivarian revolution has already gone far enough (rather it has gone too far) and must be halted before it provokes the bourgeoisie.

Thus, in only a few lines, the "beachhead" is dissolved, the "indestructible armoured divisions" have been destroyed, the "commandos" are in full flight and General Heinz Dieterich is demonstrating his revolutionary audacity by waving the white flag with every possible enthusiasm. What perspective does comrade Dieterich offer us? He does not put forward any concrete programme for achieving socialism, either in the 21st century or in the 31st. *He tries to frighten us with the spectre of counter-revolution and coups d'état, implying that we should not expropriate the capitalists for fear of provoking them.* On the other hand, he writes:

"Just as feudal political and economic absolutism was democratised through formal democratic rights, so the political and economic absolutism of big capital must be democratised through the extension of majority decisions to all social spheres.

Nevertheless, the democratisation of the bourgeois system is equivalent to its negation, because its predominantly plutocratic character is incompatible with real democracy in the military, cultural, economic, and political fields. Real democracy is the end of the civilisation of capital." [6]

What is this supposed to mean? In his usual unhistorical manner, Heinz Dieterich completely distorts the history of the bourgeois democratic revolution. How was feudal absolutism "democratised"? Dieterich implies that this was achieved by some kind of gradual and peaceful process. This is entirely false. The absolutist regimes in France and England were overthrown by revolutions. In both cases the absolutist monarchs were "democratised" by having their heads separated from their shoulders. If comrade Dieterich means that capitalism will be "democratised" in this way we could at least understand him. But he means no such thing.

What Dieterich means by "democratisation" is, to quote his own words, "the extension of majority decisions to all social spheres". What social spheres is he referring to? "Military, cultural, economic, and political fields". This sounds very fine, but what does it mean in practice? How is it possible to introduce democracy into the army, the schools and universities, the factories and the government on a local and national scale, while the ruling class continues to hold economic and state power? The answer is clear: it is not possible.

Let us begin with the clearest example: the army. How does Heinz Dieterich propose to democratise the army? Is he in favour of election of officers? Is he in favour of giving soldiers full civil and political rights, including the right to join trade unions and go on strike? Certainly not, since this would be "going too far and provoking reaction". How does he propose to "democratise" the economy? Is he in favour of workers' control of the factories, the abolition of business secrets and other measures to abolish the dictatorship of the bosses? Certainly not, for that would be to question the sacred rights of management – the 21st century equivalent of the Sacred Right of Kings.

What Heinz Dieterich wants is to maintain capitalism but remove from it all its negative and oppressive features. He wants a democratic capitalism, a pleasant capitalism or "capitalism with a human face". In other words, he wants to *square the circle*.

Counterrevolutionary role of the bourgeoisie

As we know, comrade Dieterich is very generous with his advice. Seated at his desk in Mexico City he meditates on all the problems facing the peoples of Latin America and then delivers his verdict with all the gravitas of a high court judge handing out sentences. In an article entitled *The Trap of Constituent Assemblies in the Latin American Revolution*, he writes:

6. Dieterich, *El Socialismo del Siglo XXI*, page 59.

"The theory of constitutional law is essentially the result of the bourgeois revolutions of France, Germany (?) and the United States. It was born under the spirit (Zeitgeist) of the Enlightenment, which propagated the illusion that power can be contained in Reason. This was an illusion against reality, soon to be converted into ideology. Thus, the Code Napoleon expressed the exploitative interests of the bourgeois ruling class, its Magna Carta that gave form to its domination.

"Applying the logic of military science, we may understand the Constitution as a final objective of war, but never as the theatre of operations of war nor as an instrument of war. The Constitution is always the result of the struggle for national macropower (macropoder nacional), and therefore it is not, nor can it be, a means of conquering power.

"The Constitution is the Palace of Versailles, where the First World War ends and the victors define the postwar order. But before signing the Magna Carta of the postwar order, it is first necessary to win victory on the battlefields of Verdun and the eastern front."

Comrade Dieterich works himself up into a paroxysm of rage against the original sin of "Latin American constitutionalism". He thunders:

"It is obvious that Latin American constitutionalism, as a product of the Atlantic bourgeoisie (burguesía atlántica), is Eurocentric, bourgeois-colonialist, racist and state-ist, and that, as such, must be changed root and branch. Theoretically, this task does not present a problem, because both the historical critique of the Left, for example, that of Karl Marx in *The18th Brumaire*, [and] the historical critique of the Right, e.g., that of the national socialist Carl Schmitt, have exposed the class character of bourgeois constitutionalism. To recognize constitutional change as a programmatic element of the struggle in the future is correct; to convert it into the political battlefield of the moment, however, may be a grave error." [7]

After all this revolutionary thunder and lightening the reader is left feeling dazed. With a stroke of the pen our Heinz has consigned every constitutional reform and every constituent assembly in Latin America to the dustbin of history. He denounces any idea that the Constituent Assembly can be the arena of the class struggle and insists that the battlefield of the class struggle is situated elsewhere. The precise location of this *battlefield*, however, is left unclear. This is very revolutionary stuff – at least it *sounds* very revolutionary, which is surely the same thing. In one of the plays of Richard Sheridan, the 18th century Irish satirist, a character who is addicted to gambling says: "I never lose at cards, or at least, I never feel I am losing – which is the same thing." Unfortunately for this character, it is not at all the same thing. And unfortunately for comrade Dieterich, to *sound* revolutionary is not the same as to *be* revolutionary.

7. Ibid.

Heinz refers to the constitutions established by bourgeois revolutions in France, Germany and the United States, and points out that these documents merely "expressed the exploitative interests of the bourgeois ruling class". That is quite true and was pointed out by Marx and Engels long before Comrade Dieterich ever thought of it. Nevertheless, the struggle for democratic constitutions in the past was an important part of the revolutionary struggle against the old autocratic regimes of Europe and played a most important role in the arousing the masses to fight against the old feudal order.

That was true in both France and United States, though it was not true of Germany, where the bourgeoisie betrayed the democratic revolution in 1848-49, as Marx and Engels explained. They pointed out that the German bourgeoisie played a counter-revolutionary role that led to the defeat of the revolution. They were particularly scathing in their criticism of the German bourgeois Liberals who played at constitutionalism in the Frankfurt Assembly. In fact, Germany only got a democratic constitution in 1918, but that was not the result of a victorious bourgeois democratic revolution but the defeat of a proletarian revolution as a result of the betrayal of the German Social Democracy.

The bourgeoisie has played a counter-revolutionary role ever since, and this has led to the betrayal of the bourgeois-democratic revolution in one country after another. The consequences of this have been particularly serious in Latin America. Almost two hundred years after the death of the Libertador, have the tasks of the bourgeois-democratic revolution been carried out in Latin America? In most cases they have not. What are the main tasks of the bourgeois-democratic revolution? Agrarian reform, national independence, modernization of the economy and society, the separation of church and state, and the introduction of a democratic constitution. Have these tasks been carried out?

In most cases they have not been carried out, or carried out only partially. *The very fact that we are still talking about constituent assemblies in Latin America in the first decade of the 21st century is itself a complete condemnation of the bourgeoisie, which has been unable to carry out the main tasks of its own revolution.* Everywhere the rotten and corrupt bourgeoisie of Latin America plays a counter-revolutionary role. The tasks of the bourgeois-democratic revolution (or, to use Lenin's more correct expression, the national-democratic revolution) can only be carried out by the working class together with its natural allies, the poor peasants and the urban poor and the revolutionary petty bourgeoisie.

If we say "a", we must also say "b", "c" and "d". The working class must include in its revolutionary programme the tasks that were left undone by the bourgeoisie. This includes not only a revolutionary solution to the land problem and national independence, but also a democratic constitution. The struggle for the Bolivarian Constitution in Venezuela played an important role in mobilizing the masses in the struggle against the oligarchy. It is an important weapon in the hands of the workers and peasants. Is this true or false, comrade Dieterich? On this question, the professor shuffles about uneasily. He issues an utterance that would be worthy of the Sybil, who answered the questions of the ancient Greeks in incomprehensible and ambiguous terms. He says: "To recognize constitutional change as a programmatic element of the struggle in the future is correct; to convert it into the political battlefield of the moment, however, may be a grave error."

What does this mean? That we should postpone the struggle for a democratic constitution to the future means that we should not fight for democracy today. That would be fine if the democratic demands had already been carried out, but that, as we know, is by no means the case in every country south of the Rio Grande. Comrade Dieterich does not say that parliamentarism in general is useless; but he argues against calling a Constituent Assembly in Bolivia. We agree with him. But we strongly disagree with the reasons he gives, namely that there is an alleged unfavourable balance of forces in Bolivia. Still less can we accept the "solutions" he suggests (deficit spending and calling of new elections).

There is something else he has said in writing about Bolivia. In an article called *Evo Morales, Communitarian Socialism, and the Regional Power Bloc*,[8] he mentions a conversation with García Linera (Evo Morales' vice-president), in which he explained his ideas about socialism based on "Andean capitalism". This is how Dieterich understood it: "If we translate the formulation to a more precise language, we have to say that we are treating with a model of third-worldist Keynesian developmentalism, that is, a market economy with a strong developmentalist and protectionist function of the State, within a bourgeois political superstructure and an envitronment of abysmal neocolonial socio-economic destruction."

To retranslate from Dieterich's "more precise language" into something understandable, García Linera's socialism is *not socialism at all but capitalism with reforms*. Dieterich then goes on to argue that this is very positive and that nothing else could be expected from Evo Morales and the MAS: "In such a situation it would be preposterous to hope or ask that the MAS convert itself into a socialist vanguard which would pull Latin America to post-capitalism."

What is the reason for this? That all of Latin America is capitalist (with the exception of Cuba), he tells us: "What doesn't exist is a socialist economy. Neither is there a socialist superstructure. Nor the 'socialist will' of Lula, Kirchner, Tabaré, and Duarte, nor mass movements, nor socialist structures." Comrade Dieterich's logic is clear for all to see: it would be foolish for the MAS in Bolivia to move towards socialism because there are no other countries in Latin America where there is socialism. If we follow this logic *then there will never be a situation in which it is right to move towards socialism*!

What if Bolivar, San Martin, Sucre and the other liberators had followed such a logic? They would have never even started the struggle for independence. We can

8. *Rebelión*, 27/12/2005

almost hear Dieterich saying in 1800: "There are no independent countries in the Patria Grande, in such a situation it would be preposterous to hope or ask that Bolivar converts himself into an independence vanguard which would pull Latin America to post-colonialism." So what is socialism in Latin America today, according to Dieterich? "The concept of Latin American socialism today, with the exceptional paths of Cuba and Venezuela, is an evolutionary idea which provides the strategic horizon of the mass struggles and of the progressive leaders of the Patria Grande." Ah, socialism is something in the horizon, to be achieved through evolution in the long and distant future!

The bourgeoisie and democracy

Dieterich assumes that the bourgeoisie always prefers dictatorship, but this is not the case. The forms with which the ruling class exercises its rule can change very easily according to circumstances. As a matter of fact, one of the features of the current situation in the colonial world is the shift of imperialism from supporting military rule to supporting "democratic rule" wherever that has been possible. In the last period Washington has withdrawn its support from puppets on whom Washington based itself in the past (Papa Doc, Mobutu, Noriega, Fujimori, Saddam Hussein, etc.)

The two main reasons for this change are on the one hand the fact that Stalinism is no longer a threat and therefore, under the pressure of the masses, the imperialists are able to concede formal democracy, as long as it does not threaten their economic and strategic interests. On the other hand dictatorial rule tends to acquire a dynamic of its own. Dictatorships create a massive and expensive bureaucratic apparatus, and the dictators themselves have a tendency to cronyism and to luxury which eats up part of the cake which the multinational companies are able to extract from these countries. Some of them even dare to challenge their masters and cause trouble for the Americans. This was the case with Noriega in Panama and with Saddam Hussein in Iraq, to name just a couple.

As long as the pressure of the mass movement does not threaten the very existence of the capitalist system, democracy is the most economical means of government from the capitalist point of view. In any case, the most important decisions will still be taken in Washington, Paris and London. The fact that, for the time being, imperialism prefers "democratic" rule does not mean that it is always able to achieve it, or that they cannot change back to supporting dictatorial regimes if it suits its interest to do so. If the coup of April 2002 in Venezuela had succeeded, does any one seriously doubt that the bourgeoisie would have soon introduced a ferocious dictatorship to "teach the masses a lesson" or that Washington would have supported such a regime?

The latest "love affair" of imperialism and democracy will only last for as long as formal democracy is able to guarantee their economic domination. In any case, what sort of "democracy" is this? At most, we can consider it as a semi-democracy, a fraud and a fig leaf to cover the domination of the banks, monopolies and imperialism. And as soon as the working class and the peasantry present any serious challenge to capitalist rule, they will resort again, without hesitation, to the same old methods of ruthless dictatorships.

In Latin America, most of the dictatorial regimes fell and we now have "normal" bourgeois democracy in almost the whole of the continent. But for the bourgeoisie and imperialism there is only one step from formal democracy (that is, a disguised dictatorship of Capital) to open dictatorship. As long as the ruling class in these countries does not oppose the interests of the big transnationals, they will get the full backing of US imperialism. They will not hesitate to take this step when conditions demand it. They will only resort to this when the movement of the workers fundamentally threatens the rule of capital, as is the case in Venezuela. But Venezuela also shows the problems they will face. At the moment, not only in Venezuela, but in all Latin America, the pendulum is swinging to the left. We have seen massive movements of the working class in the last period. Strikes, general strikes and virtual regional insurrections have taken place in Bolivia. In Ecuador and Peru the revolutionary movement is advancing and growing stronger by the day.

The only problem is the lack of a clear political alternative in the form of a revolutionary Marxist party able to give an organized expression to the revolutionary aspirations of the masses. Confused talk about a struggle for democracy and social justice cannot help the movement of the masses to raise itself to the level of the tasks posed by history. Only a revolutionary socialist programme can point the way forward to victory. Of course, the working class must fight for democratic demands, *but it must do so with its own methods, under its own independent class banner, and it will see them as part of the struggle to overthrow the oligarchy and take power into its own hands.*

But to pose the question as Dieterich does – to postpone the struggle for democratic demands to some vague programmatic demands "for the future" – is completely false and would (like all his other positions) tend to demobilize the mass movement and deliver it into the hands of the bourgeoisie. It goes without saying from a Marxist point of view that the struggle for democratic demands in general is always subordinate to the struggle for socialism. But from that correct statement to the argument that the working class must abstain from the fight for a democratic constitution, or must postpone it to a remote future, this has nothing in common with Marxism or revolution.

This is what Lenin had to say about the struggle for democratic demands and the relation between this struggle and the revolutionary struggle for socialism:

"We must *combine* the revolutionary struggle against capitalism with a revolutionary programme and tactics on all democratic demands: a republic, a militia, the popular election of officials, equal rights for women, the self-determination of nations, etc. While capitalism exists, these demands – all of them – can only be accomplished as an exception, and even then in an incomplete and distorted form. Basing ourselves on the democracy already achieved, and exposing its incompleteness under capitalism, we demand the overthrow of capitalism, the expropriation of the bourgeoisie, as a necessary basis both for the abolition of the poverty of the masses and for the *complete* and *all-round* institution of *all* democratic reforms. Some of these reforms will be started before the overthrow of the bourgeoisie, others *in the course* of that overthrow, and still others after it.

"The social revolution is not a single battle, but a period covering a series of battles over all sorts of problems of economic and democratic reform, which are consummated only by the expropriation of the bourgeoisie. It is for the sake of this final aim that we must formulate *every one* of our democratic demands in a consistently revolutionary way. It is quite conceivable that the workers of some particular country will overthrow the bourgeoisie *before* even a single fundamental democratic reform has been fully achieved. It is, however, quite inconceivable that the proletariat, as a historical class, will be able to defeat the bourgeoisie, unless it is prepared for that by being educated in the spirit of the most consistent and resolutely revolutionary democracy." [9]

'Local minipower'

Marxism is not anarchism. Marxists have never renounced the parliamentary struggle or the fight for democratic rights. But we understand very well the limits of bourgeois legality and parliamentarism. That is another matter. If what Dieterich means is that it is impossible to solve the fundamental problems of society by parliamentary means, then it would be correct. But that is not what Dieterich is saying. Let us look again at what he writes: "Applying the logic of military science, we may understand the Constitution as a final objective of war, but never as the theatre of operations of war nor as an instrument of war. The Constitution is always the result of the struggle for national macropower (macropoder nacional), and therefore it is not, nor can it be, a means of conquering power.

"The Constitution is the Palace of Versailles, where the First World War ends and the victors define the post-war order. But before signing the Magna Carta of the post-war order, it is first necessary to win victory on the battlefields of Verdun and the eastern front." [10]

Despite all the bluster and rhetoric about battlefields, war and the conquest of power, we see that the professor's real aims are far more limited. But before we deal with these aims, we cannot pass by two little details of a terminological nature. He refers here to the "struggle for national macropower (macropoder nacional)". The

9. Lenin, *The Revolutionary Proletariat and the Right of Nations to Self-Determination*, 1915.
10. Dieterich, *The Trap of Constituent Assemblies in the Latin American Revolution*, 3/12/06.

term macropower is not to be found in the Diccionario de la Academia Real. It has been invented especially by comrade Dieterich, who, not satisfied with revising Marxism is also determined to revise the language of Cervantes.

What is the "struggle for national macropower"? It must be something different from the struggle for "local minipower", a concept so beloved by all the army of semi-anarchist, semi-reformist ex-Marxists who have recently descended on Latin America like a swarm of hungry locusts. With all the fervour of recent converts, the missionaries of the New Left preach the gospel of non-state socialism to the unconverted. Following in the footsteps of Toni Negri and others, they try to dissuade the workers from taking state power, advocating instead all kinds of local initiatives, community politics and co-operatives.

This kind of politics has the extraordinary merit of suggesting that it is possible to build a new kind of society, abolishing forever the exploitation of man by man (not to mention woman by woman) without challenging the state or the rule of the big banks and monopolies. It can be achieved, they say, purely by ignoring the state and building up all kinds of things that bypass the market altogether. Thus, they say, socialism can be brought about without revolution, without even trimming the fingernails of the bourgeoisie, and everyone will live happily ever after. This is what the struggle for "local minipower" signifies.

Here we see that Dieterich's "new and original" formulae are only the warmed-up scraps borrowed from other, mainly pre-Marxian writers who expressed the same ideas far much more clearly than he does. There is absolutely nothing new in these threadbare ideas, which have been copied word for word from the old pre-Marxian texts of Proudhon, Saint-Simon and Robert Owen. The only difference is that when these great pioneers of socialism first wrote their utopian socialist works, they were original and imaginative, whereas our 21st Century utopians are mere plagiarists – and very clumsy ones at that.

In the early 19th century, when the proletariat had not yet developed as a powerful independent force, the utopian socialists played a most progressive role, despite the deficiencies of their views, the undeveloped and immature nature of which reflected the undeveloped and embryonic state of the proletariat. But to try to drag us back to that same undeveloped and embryonic stage now, after the colossal discoveries of Marx, Engels, Lenin and Trotsky, after the experience of the Russian Revolution and the titanic events of the past hundred years, that is entirely reactionary.

The intellectuals of the so-called New Left – the well-meaning and completely harmless people of *Le Monde Diplomatique*, Attac, the World Social Forum, etc. – imagine themselves to be radicals but in practice remain firmly rooted to capitalism. Maybe that is why capitalist institutions like the Ford Foundation pay the bills of the World Social Forum. It is quite a good investment since it pays to divert the attention of the masses into endless talking shops where nothing is ever decided.

This kind of thing is far worse than a bourgeois parliament, where occasionally some things are decided and even some laws are occasionally passed that benefit the working class. By contrast, the kind of "miniparliaments" represented by the World Social Forums, NGOs and the like, decide nothing at all, yet they give the impression that they are making very important decisions indeed. They are a substitute for revolutionary action "at the grassroots level"; they are "closer to the people" and so on and so forth.

This is just the kind of empty demagogy and gesturing that has been pursued by Marcos and the Zapatistas for years. They have attempted to establish "local minipower", complete with an "economy of equivalence". They demand autonomy for Chiapas. This is a substitute for the revolutionary struggle for power and a trap for the oppressed peasants of Chiapas. If the people of Chiapas got autonomy tomorrow, what would it solve? Would it solve the most pressing problems of the masse? Would it solve the problem of poverty, landlessness and unemployment? No it would not. The workers and peasants of Chiapas would be living in a ghetto, a kind of Bantustan, cut off from the real sources of wealth and power and completely dependent on the bourgeoisie of Mexico and the United States. They would be even worse off than they are today. The reactionary-utopian nature of the Zapatista's "local minipower" was glaringly revealed during the revolutionary crisis that shook the bourgeois state in Mexico during 2006.

In Mexico the bourgeois democratic revolution was carried out long ago. The Mexican bourgeoisie has had almost a century to show what it can do. The result has been a complete disaster for the Mexican people. The programme of the EZLN is not at all socialist but at best a bourgeois-democratic programme, but even their limited demands cannot be achieved within the limits of capitalism. This is a confirmation of the theory of the permanent revolution. The leaders of the EZLN do not have a programme which could appeal to the workers and their efforts to go beyond their basis of support amongst the peasants have been oriented mainly to the petty-bourgeois intellectuals and middle classes in the cities. We must remember that in Mexico today, 70 percent of the population live in urban areas. The key to the revolution in Mexico, and in the rest of Latin America lies, not in the peasantry, but in the multi-millioned ranks of the labour movement.

In theory there is a democratic regime in Mexico, but in practice the oligarchy denies the people their democratic rights. We saw this in the recent elections when López Obrador was cheated out of victory. Was it correct to struggle against electoral fraud in Mexico? Of course, it was. Not to have roused the masses to fight fraud – that is to say, to assert their democratic rights – would have been an abject surrender. Everybody in Mexico knows that López Obrador won the election and that Calderón has not been democratically elected. The workers and peasants wanted to get rid of the reactionary right wing government of Fox and the PAN. They rallied to López Obrador and the PRD. The reaction of the Mexican ruling class, obviously in agreement with Washington, was to try to prevent López Obrador from standing. The reason why Bush was determined to stop López Obrador from winning was that he feared another Chávez on his doorstep.

On the 31st July 2006, three million people were on the streets demanding the recognition of the PRD candidate López Obrador. In Oaxaca there was an insurrection that lasted for months, including the setting up of a soviet (the APPO – Asamblea Popular de los Pueblos de Oaxaca or Popular Assembly of the Peoples of Oaxaca), people's militia and the taking over of the television. The Oaxaca insurrection was crushed by brute force with hundreds of people arrested and an unknown number murdered by the security forces. There was, of course, not a word about this in our "free press", which only starts shouting about "dictatorship" when the interests of the rich are threatened. The limitations of the Zapatistas were clearly exposed in the course of this revolutionary movement that shook Mexico to its foundations. Heinz Dieterich is living in Mexico. And he is a great admirer of the Zapatistas (the EZLN and Subcomandante Marcos). However, lately he seems to have changed his mind. In the interview in *Revista Mariátegui* (15/08/06) we read the following interesting exchange:

"Why do you say that the Sub Commander Marcos works for the Mexican right?

"Because when Marcos left Chiapas and it made the call for the Other Campaign, protected by an escort of the Federal Police, he said that it was not necessary to vote, that the social movements should not vote for any of the three political parties in the election. Calling for non-participation obviously favoured the right, if he had called for a vote for López Obrador, who is the candidate of the people, perhaps we would have won. That is to say, he has done the work of the right."

For once we are in agreement with Heinz Dieterich. Marxists always set out from the real movement of the masses fighting for their most urgent and immediate demands. We participate in the mass movement, fighting in the front line, but at the same time we explain to the most advanced elements the need to go further, to transform the fight into an all-out assault on the capitalist system. In Mexico millions of workers and peasants came onto the streets to protest against electoral fraud. The masses wanted a change and voted for López Obrador. The Zapatistas and all the ultra left pseudo Marxist groups in Mexico refused to support the PRD. When the masses came out onto the streets, what was the position of the Zapatistas? They backed the so-called Other Campaign – that is, in practice, they acted in the interests of Fox and the PAN. This discredited them in the eyes of the mass of ordinary Mexican workers and peasants. This is a good example of how revolutionaries should not act.

Parliamentary struggle

To return for a moment to the "struggle for national macropower" (which is Dieterichese for the struggle for state power), we must now ask what this struggle consists of? Since the professor has denounced bourgeois constitutionalism in such contemptuous terms, we must assume that he advocates the struggle of the masses outside parliament, the class struggle in its purest form, the struggle to overthrow the bourgeois parliament and replace it with the rule of the proletariat. Surely his stern revolutionary message can mean nothing else but this? Well, not exactly... He goes on to explain: "Every Latin American party or movement that wins the elections on the basis of a developmentist and Bolivarian programme (un programa desarrollista y bolivariano) must choose the centre of gravity of its policy of transformation. The object of choosing this centrum gravitates is the consolidation and broadening of its own power, at the expense of the power of the imperial-oligarchic forces." [11]

Nobody understands what exactly is meant by "choosing the centre of gravity of its policy of transformation". Heinz tries to help us by translating the phrase into Latin, where it becomes *centrum gravitatis*. But this still gets us no further, since muddled ideas never improve, even if they are translated into Mandarin Chinese. Insofar as it is possible to translate the above mentioned passage into intelligible language of any sort, it means the following: *if you win an election, you must try to decide the best way to win the next election*. Now, this is a very sound piece of advice and one that every politician in the world would say *amen* to. It does not, however, appear to add a great deal to the sum total of human knowledge, even when expressed in Latin. Having once embarked on his course, comrade Dieterich sticks to it with grim determination:

"The determination of this political centre of gravity of the new government is a function of the centres of gravity of the enemy, that is to say, the points where the enemy concentrates his greatest mass. Having correctly understood the correlation of forces, their nature and situation in place and time [sic!], between the transforming government and the Right, the government must decide if it is obliged to adopt: a) a defensive strategy or if it can go over immediately to a strategic offensive, and b) if it decides to attack, which what forces and against which centres of gravity of the enemy. Let us remember that the relation between defensive and offensive is, of course, dialectical." [12]

This "of course" is really priceless! Having lost himself (and his readers) in this shapeless mass of prose, Comrade Dieterich is not really sure where he has come out, but he is sure (of course) that he has come out somewhere. What all these words mean, however, is anyone's guess. Let us again attempt a translation into the language of ordinary mortals: *once elected, the government must understand what it can and cannot do*. Such profundity! Such a grasp of politics and military strategy! What is the real correlation of forces and what are these points of gravity of the forces of reaction? Comrade Dieterich now enlightens us:

11. Dieterich, *The Trap of Constituent Assemblies in the Latin American Revolution*, 3/12/06.
12. Ibid.

"The points of greatest concentration of mass, and therefore, of greatest power and danger, of the bourgeoisie that has been electorally defeated, are: its Armed Forces; its national mass media, its big capitals; the church hierarchy; the judicial superstructure, particularly the corrupt and reactionary Supreme Courts; the legislative superstructure and sectors of the civil executive; the ideological control of certain social classes; the international mass media; the transnational corporations, and the interests of US and European imperialism."

At this point Comrade Dieterich has his readers shaking in their shoes. Against such a fearsome array of enemy forces, what is left for us to do but to raise the white flag and beg for mercy? Particularly as Comrade Dieterich insists that it is not the same "to win with 75 percent of the votes, with two thirds, with an absolute majority (51 percent) or with a relative majority; the centres of gravity of the enemy will still determine the battlefield and the form of the war that the newly elected government will have to chose, if they do not wish to be defeated in the medium term."

It is true that the class struggle can never be decided by the parliamentary arithmetic. Such things do not impress the ruling class. In general, the landlords and capitalists (and also the imperialists) prefer a formal bourgeois democracy because it is the most economical and effective way to express its class rule. But the bourgeoisie only abide by the rules of democracy insofar as it does not threaten their power and privileges. The moment it does, the smiling mask of democracy is cast to one side and they resort to conspiracies and coups designed to overthrow the democratically elected government.

Yes, all this is perfectly true and is confirmed by the recent experiences of both Venezuela and Bolivia. But is it true to say that the results of elections are a matter of indifference, that they tell us nothing about the real class balance of forces? No, it is not true at all. Lenin, who was very far from being a parliamentary cretin, paid a lot of attention to parliamentary statistics (and to every other kind of statistics that could shed light on the class correlation of forces). It is true that the results of an election only provide us with a snapshot of the mood of the masses at a particular time and that this can change and does not exhaust the question of the relations between the classes. But within these limits electoral statistics can tell us quite a lot about the state of the class struggle.

The electoral struggle can play an important role in the class struggle. In the case of Venezuela it served to mobilize, unite and galvanize the masses after the defeat of the Caracazo and the failure of the military uprising of 1992. The masses rallied to Chávez and inflicted one defeat after another on the oligarchy and imperialism. With each electoral defeat, the forces of reaction were weakened, disoriented and demoralized, while the masses were encouraged and strengthened. A decisive turning point was the defeat of the counter-revolution in the recall referendum in the summer of 2004. This demoralized the counter-revolutionary forces, who had suffered defeats on two previous occasions – in April 2002 and in the bosses' lockout.

In general, the petty bourgeois masses are unstable and easily discouraged. They lack the stamina of the proletariat. They need to go from success to success and are quickly discouraged by failure. The sight of a massive electoral victory for the chavistas utterly demoralized the opposition and convinced them that nothing was to be done, that Chávez was invincible. By contrast, the masses felt their own power and were strengthened as a result.

That was the situation up to December 2007, when the Bolivarian Movement suffered its first electoral setback with the defeat of the constitutional referendum. What was the reason for this defeat? Were the masses protesting that the revolution had gone too far, too fast? Or was it an expression of the "unfavourable balance of forces", as Dieterich maintains? No, it was none of these things. It was a warning to the Bolivarian leadership that the masses are becoming tired of endless speeches, parades and referendums that solve nothing. In December 2006 the masses voted overwhelmingly for a change, but no fundamental change has been forthcoming. This was a protest at the slow pace of the revolution. That is to say, it was a protest against the policies of reformists who are following the line of Heinz Dieterich. This is placing the Bolivarian Revolution in danger.

The Bolivian experience

In Bolivia, on at least two occasions in the last two years the objective conditions existed for the working class to have taken power. The workers of Bolivia displayed colossal energy, courage and initiative. On two occasions they overthrew the government – not through elections but through direct mass action. On the second occasion, in May-June 2005, I warned that, if the leaders of the COB did not take power, then the initiative would be lost and the whole movement would be derailed and would then have to pass through the school of bourgeois parliamentarism. This was subsequently shown to be correct. What has Comrade Dieterich got to say about the events in Bolivia? He criticizes the idea of a Constituent Assembly. The author of these lines also criticized it, but from a completely different point of view. In politics, what is important is not only what is said, but who says it and for what purpose. I criticized the idea of a Constituent Assembly because it did not go far enough, while Comrade Dieterich criticizes it for going too far.

I criticized the idea of a Constituent Assembly because the correlation of class forces at that time was sufficient for the workers to have taken power, while Comrade Dieterich thinks that the correlation of class forces is so unfavourable that it does not even permit the convening of a Constituent Assembly, and that such a "bold step" will only antagonize the reactionaries, leading to disaster. Is it true that the workers of Bolivia could have taken power? Yes, it is quite true and this fact was admitted by one of the leaders of the COB, Jaime Solares, who stated publicly "the reason we did not take power is because we did not have a revolutionary party." This fact is obvious to any thinking worker in Bolivia, but it is not obvious to Heinz

Dieterich, obsessed as he is with the power of the bourgeois state and imperialism and the alleged weakness of the working class. As a matter of fact, there is weakness, but it is not on the part of the workers and peasants of Bolivia, who have done everything in their power to transform society. *The weakness is on the part of the leadership.*

According to Dieterich, the working class of Bolivia is too weak even to achieve a Constituent Assembly, let alone take power. Besides, the imperialists would not like it! As a matter of fact, it was precisely the imperialists who supported the idea of a Constituent Assembly in Bolivia when they saw the danger of power slipping out of the impotent hands of the Bolivian bourgeoisie. The World Bank publicly came out in favour of a Constituent Assembly! Why did they do this? Was it out of charitable feelings for the people of Bolivia? In that case, why did they not advocate it before? No, it was not out of charity (which is not an emotion one normally associates with the World Bank) but out of fear.

It very often happens that the strategists of Capital come to the same conclusions as the Marxists. The serious defenders of imperialism have a far better understanding of the revolution than our academic friend in Mexico. Washington understood very well the real class balance of forces. They saw that the masses were moving towards the seizure of power and that the rotten and corrupt Bolivian bourgeoisie was powerless to control the situation. Under such circumstances the imperialists did what they always do: shift from the right boot to the left boot, and hand power over to the reformists.

The ruling class, when faced with the prospect of losing everything, will always be prepared to make concessions. They were compelled to call elections. Unfortunately, the leaders of the COB boycotted the elections, which were nevertheless won by Evo Morales by a landslide victory. This was a blow against the parties of the oligarchy. Naturally, the imperialist and the oligarchy had no intention of allowing this situation to continue. They rapidly passed over to the offensive, rallying the forces of counter-revolution under the banner of "autonomy", that is, of dividing the living body of Bolivia. The workers and peasants mobilized against the counter-revolution and the class struggle passed onto the streets. What conclusions does Dieterich draw from all this? He writes:

"The struggle for a new Constitution, begun with forces that do not have a clear superiority over those of the enemy, that is to say, with forces that do not guarantee his defeat, becomes a strategic political error." [13]

Dieterich once more puts on his military strategist's hat. He gravely warns us not to begin a battle unless we have "a clear superiority over those of the enemy, that is to say, with forces that do not *guarantee his defeat*" (my emphasis). In any war a serious commander will avoid a battle where he is likely to be defeated. That is a commonplace that is as profound as all the other commonplaces that are such a spe-

13. Ibid.

cialty of our learned professor. But wait a minute! It is one thing to avoid battle when the enemy enjoys a clear superiority. It is quite another thing to demand a guarantee of victory as a prior condition for entering a battle at all. If one buys a television set one can demand a guarantee and they will give you a very nice one, valid for twelve months, parts and labour included. Unfortunately, in war there can be no such guarantee, and the outcome of every battle is determined by the struggle itself. If one could possess such a guarantee, then comrade Dieterich would be a far greater general than Napoleon, Cromwell and Alexander the Great put together. But one cannot, and he is not.

A general who avoids battle because he thinks the conditions are unfavourable may, or may not, be a good general. A general who refuses to give battle on principle unless he has a written guarantee of success is a coward and a charlatan. Just imagine if in 1812, Dieterich would have been in charge of the revolutionary army instead of Simon Bolivar. What would he have said? "We have very small forces and the enemy has many more than us. In addition, he has the backing of a powerful empire, a lot of money and the support of the Roman Catholic Church. No! We cannot proceed unless we obtain a guarantee of victory." The revolutionary forces would have given up without firing a shot and the peoples of Latin America would still be living under the yoke of Spain. Fortunately the Liberator was made of sterner stuff than the man from Mexico.

Comrade Dieterich argues that "to have a new Constitution without having an overwhelming superiority of real forces (una abrumadora superioridad de fuerzas reales) does not have any importance [because] no ruling class in the world, whether feudal, bourgeois or real socialist (?), acts in accordance with the Constitution when this does not agree with its interests. To believe that the Constitution determines the realpolitik of a government or that this can be achieved in class society, is simply an illusion, although it is ethically desirable."

Here our friend reached hitherto unheard-of heights of Jesuitical casuistry. That the ruling class will only accept the rules of formal democracy as long as its power and privileges are guaranteed is well known to Marxists. But does it flow from this ABC proposition that we are indifferent to the forms of rule in class society? That is a stupid formulation that has nothing in common with Marxism, which states that the working class must always fight for the most advanced bourgeois democracy. This is elementary, but it does not exhaust the question. The fact that the workers must fight for the most advanced democratic demands is not dictated by illusions in formal bourgeois democracy, which is only camouflaged version of the dictatorship of the bourgeoisie. The working class is interested in democracy because it requires the broadest and freest camp of action upon which to develop the class struggle and fight for socialism. What is "ethically desirable" does not come into it. Whoever does not understand this elementary proposition has not understood the ABCs of Marxism and the class struggle.

The Constituent Assembly has turned out to be a trap for the masses in Bolivia. The oligarchy, backed by imperialism, has used it to construct a bulwark against the revolution. They are using the two-thirds voting rule of the new constitution to block progressive legislation and sabotage the Evo Morales government, while simultaneously mobilizing the counter-revolutionary forces on the streets. What else could one expect? It is foolish to imagine that even the most democratic constitutions and parliamentary institutions on earth can resolve the fundamental contradictions in society. The Bolivarian constitution is the most democratic constitution in the world, but that did not stop the Venezuelan oligarchy from organizing the coup of April 2002. The counter-revolution was not defeated by paper constitutions but only by the revolutionary movement of the masses. Bolivia is no different.

But from this elementary proposition very different conclusions can be drawn. The reformist Dieterich says: since the bourgeoisie holds power and does not accept democratic and progressive reforms, we must be careful and not do anything to upset the reactionaries. The Marxists say: since the landlords and capitalists form a reactionary bloc opposed to any democratic or progressive reforms we must fight for the most advanced demands and fight the reactionaries at every level: not only in parliament but on the streets, in the factories, on the land and in the army barracks, and we must not cease fighting until we have defeated and disarmed the enemy, and this can only be achieved through the revolutionary expropriation of the property of the landlords and capitalists. Heinz Dieterich once again tries to frighten the masses with the spectre of counter-revolution and an allegedly invincible bourgeoisie. He says:

"The reaction has on its side the absolute majority of the prefects (six out of nine); the Senate; the Church; big national and international Capital and the Supreme Court of Justice. In such a situation weapons decide. These are also on the side of reaction, because the majority of the generals are against the process of transformation. In these conditions the government cannot win (En estas condiciones, el triunfo del gobierno no es posible). The aim of the government in this conflict is therefore reduced to avoiding defeat and arriving at an acceptable compromise (evitar la derrota y alcanzar un compromiso acceptable)." [14]

So, according to Dieterich, the government of Evo Morales cannot win. What advice does our Heinz give to the Bolivian government? Only one conclusion is possible: if you cannot win, you must surrender to the enemy, wave the white flag and beg for some concessions from the enemy that can make the defeat look a little less shameful. The talk about an "acceptable compromise" is just a joke in bad taste. What acceptable compromise can there be between the Bolivian workers and peasants and the oligarchy that has oppressed them for generations? The only compromise that would be acceptable to the landlords and capitalists is the "compromise" between the donkey and the man sitting on its back. Why does Dieterich say the

14. Ibid.

government "cannot win". Because the reaction is too strong. Why is the reaction too strong? Because it has a majority of the prefects, senators, judges, bankers, capitalists and army generals. But just a moment, my friend! How many prefects, senators, judges, bankers, capitalists and army generals are there in Bolivia? A few hundreds or thousands. It is true that they can count on the support of a layer of the middle class and backward elements in the population. But how many are they? And how many of them are prepared to fight and die in defence of the oligarchy?

The election results showed the real balance of forces. That is why our friend Heinz is silent on the election statistics. Over fifty percent voted for Evo Morales and the old parties of the Bolivian bourgeoisie were shattered. It was an unprecedented result and it showed the burning desire of the masses for change. To ignore this fact, as Dieterich does, is to give an entirely false impression of the real balance of class forces in Bolivia. Ah but this is only a mater of votes, our friend will reply: elections, laws and constituent assemblies decide nothing. Yes, that is the case: in and of themselves, these things decide nothing. What is decisive is the class struggle outside parliament. But what the election results revealed was that the balance of class forces is enormously favourable for the revolution and unfavourable for the counter-revolutionary bourgeoisie – *on one condition, that the force of the workers is organized and mobilized to crush the counter-revolution.*

The question of violence

It may be that the government of Evo Morales will in the end be overthrown by the counter-revolutionary bourgeoisie. Certainly, the latter is doing everything in its power, in collaboration with US imperialism, to bring about this result. They are, of course, resorting to extra-parliamentary, methods in order to do this. Naturally! Who could expect anything else of the rotten and reactionary bourgeoisie, whether in Bolivia or in any other country? But if the bourgeoisie succeeds in its counter-revolutionary plans, it will not be, as comrade Dieterich imagines, because of the unfavourable balance of forces, but because of the weakness and vacillations of Evo Morales and the Bolivian reformists.

The fact that the counter-revolutionary bourgeoisie of Santa Cruz is threatening to split the country, that is, to destroy Bolivia as a nation, is itself a sign of weakness, not strength. Despite controlling a majority of the prefects, senators, judges, bankers, capitalists and army generals, the reactionary Bolivian bourgeoisie do not share Heinz Dieterich's confidence in the inevitability of victory. The demand for the division of Bolivia reflects desperation, not confidence, since it would not be accepted by the army, let alone the workers and peasants. What should be done? Heinz Dieterich says: we must surrender to the counter-revolutionary bourgeoisie because the balance of forces is not favourable. We must negotiate with the enemy and arrive at a "compromise" in order to avert disaster. Isn't this situation just monstrous? A tiny handful of wealthy parasites to hold an entire nation to ransom, impudently defying the will of the majority, and Dieterich advises the latter to "*reach an acceptable compromise*" with the blackmailers, because they are "too strong" for us to fight them!

This is what our friend Heinz calls "political realism". As a matter of fact, this is the very opposite of realism. Let us suppose for a moment that the Bolivian government followed Dieterich's advice. What would happen? The reactionaries would be emboldened and the masses would be bitterly disappointed. The very next day, the right wing would make new demands. What would comrade Dieterich say then? He would demand that the government *must retreat still further*, abandon all "unrealistic" reforms to improve the living standards of the masses, resist the impositions of the imperialists and carry through an agrarian reform. "We are not strong enough!" he will say. "The correlation of forces is unfavourable!" For every step back Evo Morales makes, the bourgeoisie demand ten more. With every step back the government makes, the workers and peasants who voted for it and who constitute its only reliable base, are further disenchanted and despondent, while the reactionaries will be ever more confident, aggressive and violent. In fact, this is already happening.

Encouraged by the weakness of the government, the counter-revolutionary bourgeoisie has passed onto the offensive. The sabotage of the right wing in the parliament is being supplemented by increasingly aggressive provocations of the fascists on the streets. They are trying to create disorder and chaos, in order to create the conditions for right wing conspiracies in the tops of the army, possibly leading to a military coup, once the masses have fallen into a state of apathy. *Thus, the methods advocated by comrade Dieterich have results that are diametrically opposed to what he intends*.

On paper Dieterich's arguments appear very sound and sensible. But in fact they can be reduced to just one idea: since, in the last analysis, fundamental questions are decided by force of arms, and since the ruling class has control of the state, including the army, we cannot succeed. Let us straight away point out that this is not about Venezuela or Bolivia: *it is an argument that denies the possibility of revolution in general.* It is self-evident that the ruling class in all normal periods controls the state, the judiciary, the bureaucracy, the prisons, the army, the police and the secret police. That was the case in Russia in 1917, and also in France in 1789. That fact did not prevent either the Russian or the French Revolution. In more recent times the Shah of Iran had a very large and powerful army and the most efficient and brutal secret police in the world, the Savak. Yet once the masses came out onto the streets, the whole edifice of repression came tumbling down like a pack of cards.

Yes, mumbles Comrade Dieterich, but there was a lot of bloodshed, and we wish to avoid bloodshed. As a matter of fact, the October Revolution in Russia was a relatively peaceful affair, at least in Petrograd. One bourgeois historian, Orlando Figes (by no means a friend of the Bolsheviks) described it as a "police operation". The reason for this is that the Bolsheviks had already won over the great majority of the workers and soldiers (even Stalin admitted that "comrade Trotsky was responsible for winning over the Petrograd garrison"). Nine-tenths of the work of the insurrection was accomplished in the nine months that preceded it.

Comrade Dieterich is so obsessed by the question of the army that he has not understood the fact that behind the bayonets are human beings, people who think and can be influenced by the general mood of society. Yes, the tsarist regime had the generals, but they did not have the ordinary soldiers. And what use are generals without an army? In the moment of truth, the generals and the entire tsarist state was suspended in mid air.

Like all the other reformist intellectuals, Dieterich has no confidence in the working class, and the mass movement does not enter his restricted field of vision. In reality, these intellectual "friends of the people" only see the tops of society. They are like a man who can only see the surface of the ocean, but is ignorant of the powerful currents moving below. Needless to say, this approach has nothing in common with Marxism. At the end of his article, Dieterich informs us that we "must win the real war, not a paper war:

"A new Constitution does not prevent counter-revolutionary coups, as we saw on 11 April 2002 in Venezuela and on 11 October 2006 in Bolivia."

Thus far, we are in complete agreement with comrade Dieterich. A democratic constitution does not prevent counter-revolutionary coups, although this is not an argument against democratic constitutions. It only expresses the limitations of bourgeois democracy in general. Lenin explained that the dialectic of parliamentary democracy inevitably leads to an intensification of the class struggle outside parliament and that that, in the last analysis, is decisive. The coup of 11 April 2002 in Venezuela proves just that. But what happened to the coup of 11 October 2006 in Bolivia? *There was no such coup.* It was confidently predicted by comrade Dieterich in articles that were distributed internationally, but it never arrived. This tells us a lot about comrade Dieterich's method. Heinz's prediction of a coup in Bolivia was shown to be wrong in 2006, but if Evo Morales continues to vacillate, it may prove right in the end. However, happens, it will not be for the reasons that comrade Dieterich gives, but for very different reasons.

How not to prevent a coup

So far, our friend Heinz has explained to us at great length what does *not* prevent counter-revolutionary coups. We wait with bated breath his opinion on what *does* prevent them. Here is what he says: "What does prevent them is real power, and, for this reason, the new governments in Latin America who do not recognize the Monroe Doctrine and the interests of the transnational companies (que desconoce la Doctrina Monroe y los intereses de las transnacionales) must concentrate their limited resources on the real war, not a paper war or concepts". [15]

15. Ibid.

By this time the reader will have become accustomed to Heinz's circumlocutions – a very indirect mode of expressing oneself that is based on the "economical" principle of writing, namely that one should never use one word where three will suffice. This style of writing and speaking is highly appreciated in university circles where one has all the time in the world in which to discuss fascinating theories that the rest of humanity has never heard of and is not remotely interested in. Having effortlessly disposed of detestable "paper wars or concepts" – the exact nature of which is never explained to us – Heinz now tells us what he means by "the real war". What is Heinz's magical solution for preventing counter-revolutionary coups, not just in Bolivia and Venezuela, but throughout Latin America. Let him speak for himself:

"The first necessity for these governments, for example, the Sandinistas in Nicaragua or the Alianza País in Ecuador, consists in broadening their power base through the few mechanisms at their disposal. Two ways are important in this sense: a) invest rapidly and generously on social spending, even if it is through the external debt, if there is not sufficient income from taxation, and, b) try to bring forward elections in order to generate a power base within the bourgeois superstructure [??], from which, in any case, one cannot escape, as long as the change is being carried out within the limits of bourgeois parliamentarism." [16]

Insofar as it is possible to extract some clear ideas from this muddle, it is only this: in order to avoid counter-revolutionary coups, the government must first of all *broaden their power base*. How is this to be done? By spending more money (a lot more money!) on social spending. How is this money to be obtained? By borrowing and increasing the public debt and by calling new elections. Heinz believes that we can persuade the landlords and capitalists that we are really harmless people by confining our programme to social spending. As a matter of fact, the oligarchy regards these reforms as part of a Communist plot and opposes them tooth and nail. It sees increases in taxes as part of the same plot. The capitalists are replying to this by a strike of capital (capitalists can strike as well as workers!) and closing factories like matchboxes. It was no accident that the first action of the counter-revolutionaries in April 2002 was to announce the abolition of all these reforms.

Heinz Dieterich does not want to confront the ruling class. He does not wish to appear too radical. Therefore, he does not want the "transforming governments" of Latin America to increase taxation on the rich – much less to expropriate them! Therefore, he cheerfully advocates Keynesian *deficit spending* as a means of avoiding such unpleasantness. However, governments cannot spend money they do not have, and if they attempt to do so, it will inevitably end in tears. One does not have to be a genius or even a scientific professor of sociology and political economy to understand that debts sooner or later have to be repaid with interest. The same is true of government deficits. All previous attempts to solve the problems of capitalism by

16. Ibid.

such means have led to colossal inflation that a later stage ends in a recession. That was precisely the experience of Argentina and most other governments in Latin America at the end of the 1970s.

The only realistic reply to the bosses' sabotage is the slogan launched by President Chávez: "Factory closed, factory occupied" (*fábrica cerrada, fábrica tomada*). The bosses' sabotage in 2002-03 was defeated by the marvellous movement of the workers, who, without a party, leadership or clear perspective, occupied the factories and installations of PDVSA, expelled the bosses and bureaucrats and took the running of industry into their own hands. But Heinz Dieterich cannot see any of this. For him the revolutionary movement of the masses is a book sealed with seven seals.

"The ideal executive instrument for carrying out such a policy is executive decrees. The implementation of neo-liberal policies was achieved to a great extent through executive decrees, foreseen in the political theory of John Locke as a legitimate means of government [!]. This instrument makes it difficult for the reaction to block reforms in parliament." [17]

The reference to the political theory of John Locke is an example of the sheer pedantry of Dieterich's thinking. *It matters little to the bourgeoisie whether political actions that go against their interests have been validated as "legitimate means of government" by John Locke, the Pope of Rome or Santa Claus.* The question of what is legitimate or not is decided not by political theory but by the class struggle. Here Dieterich is indulging precisely in *paper wars or concepts*. The *real war* – that is, *the class war* – does not appear anywhere in any of his pronouncements.

Heinz recommends *the carrying out of reforms by executive decrees*. But wait a moment, Heinz! Did you not just say that we were too weak to challenge the ruling class? Did you not further argue that the enemy was too strong for us to fight because they control all the key points of the state, including the army? And did you not state repeatedly that in any case, we cannot hope for anything from a bourgeois parliament? You see, we have quite good memories and have not entirely forgotten what was written only a few paragraphs ago.

Despite all these obvious objections, our Heinz is very pleased with himself and parades his arguments for everyone to see like a small boy with new shoes. In reality they are full of holes from start to finish. But he seems blissfully unaware of these contradictions. Instead of explaining and justifying his arguments, *he merely repeats them* at the end, as if by repeating an incorrect idea he will make it more correct: "Executive decrees, generous *deficit spending* [he uses the English phrase to demonstrate his skill at foreign languages] for the majorities, in order to broaden the social base of the government of transformation and neutralize the counter-revolutionary conspiracies: this would set the scene to gain time and rapidly arrive at

17. Ibid.

new elections, which can provide a solid superiority of political power in the face of the class enemy."

What is Dieterich's answer?

We have now received the recipe of the Father of 21st Century Socialism for saving the Revolution. This immediately brings to mind the words of the Roman poet Horace: *Parturient montes, nascetur ridiculus mus* ("The mountain has laboured and brought forth a mouse!"). Comrade Dieterich imagines that rule by decree will somehow prevent counter-revolutionary coups. That is to say, he believes that the class struggle can be resolved by legal rules and regulations. *He forgets that in Venezuela it was precisely the passing of the 49 Enabling Laws in December 2001 by Chávez (including agrarian reform and others) that convinced the ruling class they had to organise a coup and triggered the preparations for it.*

Whether progressive measures are passed by a vote in parliament or by an executive decree does not change anything of substance. The opposition of the reactionary bourgeoisie will not be reduced, but rather increased, if the measures are passed as a result of an executive decree. They will shout about dictatorship and step up their counter-revolutionary agitation, both inside and outside the parliament, as in Venezuela in 2002. They will use this to whip the middle class (of whom Heinz is very fond) into a frenzy. The international media will also be banging the drum about dictatorship yet again, intensifying their campaign to discredit the revolution and isolate it internationally.

The transforming government can avoid a coup and expand its power base by getting into a mountain of debt (deficit spending) and then calling new elections. In the meantime, one supposes, the class enemy will oblige us by remaining quietly in bed, politely refraining from any counter-revolutionary plots, since it has been informed that presidential decrees have been approved as "legitimate means of government" by an English philosopher of the 17th century. One rubs one's eyes in disbelief. This is supposed to be an example of the *supremely realistic thinking*! In Venezuela, President Chávez spent large sums of money on social reforms (the *misiones*). He has won many elections, local, national, the recall referendum… Did this abolish the risk of a coup? Not at all, and if we are to believe the writings of Heinz Dieterich (we are not entirely sure that he believes them himself), the risk is ever-present and, if the necessary measures are not taken to expropriate the oligarchy and carry through the revolution to the end, can end in a new coup and the victory of the counter-revolution in the future.

What is the central problem of 21st Century Socialism? Heinz now informs us of the problem and also the solution thereof:

"The secular solution of the 21st century is this: since we do not have access to the *supercomputers*, trademark Marx, Engels or Einstein, we have to substitute for them – until new ones appear – with *networks of personal computers*, whose joint capacity of data processing resembles that of the supercomputers, hoping, furthermore, that at some moment they will produce the transition of phase (qualitative leap) of the process toward the new paradigms of postcapitalist civilization." [18]

Marxists have always maintained that in order to change society, a revolutionary party and leadership is necessary. It is true that there have been cases where the revolution has been carried out – though not consolidated – without a revolutionary party, as in the Paris Commune. But it is clear that the task of carrying out the socialist revolution would be accomplished far more easily if an experienced and capable leadership existed. The Bolshevik Party under the leadership of Lenin and Trotsky was the decisive factor that allowed the Russian workers to take power with a minimum of violence in 1917. So far nobody has proposed any serious alternative to the revolutionary party. What does comrade Dieterich propose?

Heinz has a very serious alternative: his *laptop,* which is connected to a myriad of other laptops all over the world, connected at local, national and global levels and busy twenty four hours a day, seven days a week. Heinz is convinced that this 21st Century Supercomputer will in future render unnecessary things like revolutionary parties. It will render completely superfluous leaders and geniuses like Marx, Einstein or even Arno Peters. Dieterich's World Spirit turns out to be – *a computer network!* The solution is delightfully simple: by combining the thoughts of millions of ordinary minds, eventually a thought of genius will appear:

"This solution or method of stimulating the power of the individual through his/her work in coordinated networks is known in the information world as *internet-based Distributed Computing projects.* This concept means: that a complex task is resolved through the voluntary participation of owners of personal computers who for x-motive decide to allot computational time and work to the resolution of a task without asking for monetary retributions or material gratifications."

He further informs us: "The most successful program of this type is the SETI of the University of California at Berkeley, which, since its conception in 1999 has counted with the collaboration of more than five million participants, who in total have contributed more than two million years of aggregate computer time to the project. It constitutes the most powerful computer network of all time. [...] To put this 'World Spirit' at the service of humanity through its gratuitous contribution and solidarity in the New Historic Project (NHP) of the Socialism of the 21st Century will be relatively easy." [19]

There is a theory based on the law of probability that states that if you give a typewriter to a monkey and leave him alone for an infinite period of time, he will sooner or later produce the collected works of Shakespeare. But this is a typical

18. Dieterich, *La revolución mundial pasa por Hugo Chávez.*
19. Ibid.

mathematical abstraction. In practice, our monkey can bang away at his typewriter for as long as he likes, and he will not produce a single line of a Shakespearean sonnet, never mind the collected works. So what prospects have comrade Dieterich's computer network of the 21st Century? If someone talks *nonsense*, and this nonsense is spread all over the world over the internet, where it is added to by *other nonsense of the same kind*, the end result will not be an idea of genius but *only nonsense multiplied a million times over.*

Whether the authors of this nonsense charge money for their services to humanity is not really relevant. The purveyors of nonsense are very generous people. They are always happy to talk nonsense free of charge, for the sheer pleasure they derive from listening to the sound of their own stupidities. Anyone who has had the experience of being trapped by one of these at a party will know that such people have always existed. The Internet merely gives them a larger stage to engage in their chosen hobby.

Computers and the Internet will indeed have an enormous role to play in the democratically planned world socialist economy of the future. The tasks of accounting and control that are central to management of individual enterprises will be greatly facilitated by the use of powerful computers that can fit into one's pocket. Workers' control will be very simple to operate on this basis. On the other hand, a world socialist federation can be run on democratic lines with electronic voting and conferences held over the Internet. The technology already exists for this.

But here we come up against the first fatal flaw in Dieterich's central argument, which is that the existence of computer science means that socialism can be successful now, whereas it could not have been successful before. He also argues that this was one of the reasons for the failure of "really existing socialism" in Russia. Both arguments are false. It is correct to say that not only computers but the advances of modern technology in general provide the material basis for socialism. That is to say, the potential for socialism exists in the development of the productive forces: industry, agriculture, science and technology. The question must then be posed: *if the potential exists, why is it not realized?* Comrade Dieterich never asks this question because he has no answer for it.

The question that must be asked is this: is it possible to achieve socialism (whether of the 21st or any other century) as long as the land, the banks and the key industries remain in the hands of the landowners, bankers and capitalists? Comrade Dieterich says that it is. But he immediately contradicts himself. He has spent a lot of time explaining that the pursuit of profit ("chrematistics") is the source of all the problems of humanity. *But capitalists only invest to make a profit from the unpaid labour of the working class.* If they continue to own and control the means of production, it follows that the sole motor force of production will be private profit. So where does this leave the colossal potential of the computer economy? It leaves it precisely where it was before: *as a mere potential and nothing more than a mere potential.*

Setting out from a correct idea – that the achievements of modern science and technology provide the basis for socialism – he overlooks one small problem: namely, that these productive forces are in the hands of the bourgeoisie and constitute the basis of its wealth and power. In order that the productive forces that have been developed under capitalism should be used for the benefit of humanity and developed to their full extent, in other words, in order that the potential present in science and technology should cease to be merely a potential and become actual, it is necessary to remove them from private ownership.

The problem here is that our Heinz, who talks and talks about history and prehistory, the human genome and the theory of relativity, human evolution and religion, the past and the future, forgets to answer a very simple question: *how do we get from A to B*? It is impossible to get the desired results from computers (and everything else) as long as all the most important economic decisions are taken by a tiny handful of rich people whose only interest is personal gain. But this minority is unwilling to surrender their wealth and power without a fight. This is the central problem that comrade Dieterich wishes to ignore: *the problem of power*.

12. The Venezuelan Revolution

The Venezuelan Revolution at the crossroad

The Venezuelan revolution has been a source of inspiration for the workers, peasants and youth of all Latin America and on a world scale. The revolutionary masses have achieved miracles. But the Venezuelan revolution is not completed. It cannot be completed until it expropriates the oligarchy and nationalizes the land, the banks and the key industries that remain in private hands. After almost a decade this task has not been accomplished and this represents a threat to the future of the revolution.

In essence this is a problem of leadership. Hugo Chávez has shown himself to be a fearless anti-imperialist fighter and a consistent democrat. But this is not enough. The Venezuelan oligarchy is bitterly opposed to the Revolution. Behind it stands the might of US imperialism. Sooner or later the Venezuelan revolution will be faced with the alternative: either, or. And just as the Cuban revolution was capable of carrying through the expropriation of landlordism and capitalism, so the Venezuelan revolution must find the necessary resolve to follow the same road. That is really the only way.

A pernicious role in all this is being played by the reformists, Stalinists and bureaucrats who have occupied key posts in the Bolivarian Movement and are striving to put the brakes on the Revolution, to paralyse it from within and to eliminate all elements of genuine socialism. These people are constantly telling Chávez not to go too fast, to be more moderate and not to touch the private property of the oligarchy. Ever since Chávez first raised the question of socialism in Venezuela the reformists and Stalinists have been concentrating all their energies on reversing the socialist direction of the Revolution, alleging that the nationalization of the land, banks and industries would be a disaster, that the masses are not mature enough for socialism, that the expropriation of the oligarchy would alienate the middle class and so on. The most consistent advocate and "theoretician" of this line of capitulation is Heinz Dieterich.

The Bolivarian Revolution is now at the crossroads. It has reached the critical point at which decisions will have to be made that will have a determining influence on the fate of the Revolution. The role of the leadership is of great importance. But here we find the greatest weakness. In the absence of a firm proletarian revolutionary leadership armed with the scientific ideas of Marxism, the lead has been taken by the Bolivarian Movement. This includes in its ranks millions of workers, peasants and revolutionary youths who are striving for socialism, but it lacks a clear, worked out programme, policy and strategy to carry out the aspirations of the masses.

In the absence of these key elements, the Movement comes under pressure from contradictory class forces, which are reflected in its ranks and especially in the leadership. This produces an unstable situation, with constant vacillations and hesitations. These contradictions, which at bottom express class contradictions, are reflected in the political evolution of Chávez himself. No unprejudiced observer can deny that over the past decade Hugo Chávez has evolved in a striking way. Starting out from the programme of the most advanced revolutionary democracy, he has come into conflict repeatedly with the Venezuelan landlords, bankers and capitalists, with the hierarchy of the Church and with US imperialism. In all these conflicts he has based himself on the masses of workers, peasants and poor people, which represent the genuine motor force of the Bolivarian Revolution, its only real base of support.

Time and time again the masses, showing an unerring revolutionary instinct, have defeated the forces of the counter-revolution. This fact engendered a dangerous illusion in the leadership and in the masses themselves, that the Revolution was some kind of triumphal march that would automatically sweep aside all obstacles. Instead of a scientific ideology and a consistent revolutionary policy, a kind of revolutionary fatalism gripped the minds of the leaders: that all was for the best in the best of all Bolivarian worlds. No matter what mistakes were made by the leadership, the masses would always respond, the counter-revolutionaries would be defeated and the Revolution would triumph. The corollary of this revolutionary fatalism was the idea that the Bolivarian Revolution has all the time in the world, that socialism will come eventually, even if we have to wait fifty or a hundred years.

It is ironic that this idea (more correctly, this prejudice) is held up by Dieterich and others as "new and original". In reality, it comes straight from the dustbin of discredited 19th century Liberalism. The bourgeoisie, at a time when it was still capable of playing a progressive role in developing the productive forces, believed in the inevitability of progress – that today is better than yesterday and tomorrow will be better than today. This idea (now completely abandoned by the bourgeoisie and its "postmodern" philosophers) was later taken over by the reformist leaders of the international workers' movement in the period of capitalist upswing before 1914. The reformist Social Democrats argued that revolution was no longer necessary; that slowly, gradually, peacefully, the Social Democracy would change society until one day socialism would arrive before anyone even realized it. These reformist illusions were shattered by the outbreak of the First World War and the Russian Revolution that followed it. Yet they are now fished out of the dustbin of history, dusted down and presented as the very last word in 21st century socialist "realism".

A further corollary is that the Bolivarian Revolution must confine itself to the narrow limits of bourgeois laws and constitutions. This is ironical, when the Venezuelan bourgeoisie has shown a complete disregard for all laws and constitutions. It has engaged in economic sabotage and constant conspiracies, it has boycotted elections and taken to the streets in violent protests; it has carried out a coup d'état against the democratically elected government and, had it not been for the revolutionary initiative of the masses in the streets, would have not hesitated to murder the President and institute a vicious dictatorship on the lines of Pinochet's Chile. All this is well known and does not need to be explained. In the defence of its class interests the bourgeoisie has shown no respect whatsoever for laws and constitutions. Yet the masses are expected to follow every dot and comma of the existing legislation and obey the "rules of the game", as if it were a game of chess or baseball. Unfortunately, the class struggle is not a game and it has no rules and no referee. The only rule is that in the end one class must win and the other must lose. And as the Romans used to say: *Vae victis!* (Woe to the defeated).

At first these methods appeared to work. For almost ten years the masses have loyally turned out at every referendum and election and voted overwhelmingly for Chávez. In so doing they were voting for socialism, for a fundamental change in the conditions of their lives. In the Presidential elections of December 2006 they gave him the biggest vote in the history of Venezuela. This was a mandate for change. But although some progressive measures were taken, including nationalizations, the pace of change was too slow to satisfy the masses' demands and aspirations. It would have been quite possible for the President to have introduced an Enabling Act in the National Assembly to nationalize the land, the banks and the key industries under workers' control and management. This would have broken the power of the Venezuelan oligarchy. Moreover, this could have been done quite legally by the democratically elected parliament, since in a democracy the elected representatives of the people are supposed to be sovereign. Let the lawyers squabble over this or that point. The people expect the government they have elected to act in their interests, and to act decisively.

Instead of decisive action against the oligarchy, which would have enthused and mobilized the masses, the latter were presented with yet another constitutional referendum. But how many referenda and elections are necessary to carry out what the masses want? The people are tired of so many elections, so many votes, so many empty speeches about socialism that present them with a beautiful picture that does not correspond with what they see every day. What do the masses see? After nearly a decade of struggle they see that the same rich and powerful people still own the land, the banks, the factories, the newspapers, the television. They see corrupt people in positions of power – governors, mayors, functionaries of the state and the Bolivarian Movement – yes, and in Miraflores also – who wear red shirts and talk about Socialism of the 21st Century, but who are careerists and bureaucrats who have nothing in common with socialism or revolution.

The masses see that no action is taken against corrupt officials who are lining their pockets and undermining the revolution from within. They see that no action is taken against the capitalists who are sabotaging the economy by refusing to invest in production and increasing prices. They see that no action is taken against the conspirators who overthrew the President in April 2002. They see landowners who murder peasant activists with impunity. They see that essential foods are scarce and they see government spokesmen denying that there are any problems. They see all these things and they ask themselves: is this what we voted for?

The fundamental strength of Hugo Chávez is that he has expressed the deeply felt aspirations of the masses. Anyone who has been present at a mass rally in Caracas has witnessed the electrifying chemistry that exists between the President and the masses. They feed off each other. The masses see their aspirations reflected in the speeches of the President, and the President goes further to the left on the basis of the reaction of the masses and in turn gives a fresh impulse to these aspirations. This "revolutionary chemistry" has been understood by the bourgeoisie, who are striving to break the link between Chávez and the masses. They have planned to assassinate the President, calculating that his disappearance will cause the Bolivarian Movement to fragment and disintegrate. They have organized a conspiracy in the upper layers of the Bolivarian Movement to replace him with a candidate who would be more "moderate" – that is to say, more amenable to the pressures of the bourgeoisie.

The main purpose of defeating the constitutional referendum was not at all to "prevent dictatorship" (none of the provisions of the reform could be interpreted in this sense) but to stop Chávez from standing again for the Presidency. This would open the way for the success of the conspiracy that is known as "Chavism without Chávez". It is well known that the counter-revolutionary bureaucracy has taken measures to isolate Chávez from the masses by creating an iron ring around the Palace of Miraflores. The threat of assassination is real and justifies tight security. But this can also be used as a pretext for secretaries to filter and censure, ensuring that only certain people have access to the President's office while others are excluded on political grounds. By these means the pressure of the masses and the left wing is reduced, while that from the bourgeois and the reformists is increased.

The narrow defeat in the constitutional referendum is being presented as a swing towards the "centre" – that is, to the right, and as proof that it is necessary to conciliate the middle class (that is, to capitulate to the bourgeoisie). This is the line that is being assiduously peddled by Dieterich and the reformists. If Chávez listens to them – and there are certain indications that he does – the revolution will be placed in extreme danger. The arguments of the reformists are false to the core. The opposition did not win the constitutional referendum: the Bolivarians lost it. After superhuman efforts, the opposition only increased its vote by about 200,000, whereas the chavista vote went down by about two million. That does not prove that there is a swing towards the "centre" but on the contrary, that there is a huge and growing polarization between the classes. It also shows that there are elements of tiredness and disillusionment in the masses who are the base of the Bolivarian Movement.

The defeat of the constitutional referendum was a warning that the masses are becoming weary of a situation where the endless talk about socialism and revolution has not led to a fundamental change in the conditions of their lives. The masses have been very patient, but their patience is being exhausted. The idea that they will always follow the leaders – that false and dangerous idea of revolutionary fatalism – stands exposed as completely hollow. Dieterich argues that the constitutional referendum was lost because Chávez tried to go too far too fast. On the contrary! It is the slow pace of the Revolution that is causing disillusionment in a growing layer of the masses. For them, the problem is not that it has gone too far too fast, but that it has gone too slowly and not far enough.

If this disillusionment of the masses continues, it will lead to apathy and despair. The time has come to turn the words into action, to take decisive measures to disarm the counter-revolution and expropriate the oligarchy. Failure to do this will prepare a counter-offensive of the forces of reaction that can undermine the revolution and prepare for a serious defeat. Is defeat inevitable? No, of course it is not. The Revolution can be victorious, but only on condition that the reformist wing is exposed and defeated politically. The Movement must be purged of bureaucrats, careerists and bourgeois elements and stand firmly on a socialist programme. On that condition it can succeed, otherwise no.

A peculiar variant of Permanent Revolution

The theory of the Permanent Revolution was first developed by Trotsky as early as 1904. The Permanent Revolution, while accepting that the objective tasks facing the Russian workers were those of the bourgeois democratic revolution, nevertheless explained how, in a backward country in the epoch of imperialism, the national bourgeoisie was inseparably linked to the remains of feudalism on the one hand and to imperialist capital on the other and was therefore completely unable to carry through any of its historical tasks. The rottenness of the bourgeois liberals, and their counterrevolutionary role in the bourgeois-democratic revolution, was already observed by Marx and Engels in 1848 and has been repeatedly confirmed by the experience of the colonial revolution for the past 100 years.

The situation is clearer still today. The national bourgeoisie in the colonial countries entered into the scene of history too late, when the world had already been divided up between a few imperialist powers. It was not able to play any progressive role and was born completely subordinated to its former colonial masters. The weak and degenerate bourgeoisie in Asia, Latin America and Africa is too dependent on foreign capital and imperialism, to carry society forward. It is tied with a thousand threads, not only to foreign capital, but to the class of landowners, with which it forms a reactionary bloc that represents a bulwark against progress. Whatever differences may exist between these elements are insignificant in comparison with the fear that unites them against the masses. Only the proletariat, allied with the poor peasants and urban poor, can solve the problems of society by taking power into its own hands, expropriating the imperialists and the bourgeoisie, and beginning the task of transforming society on socialist lines.

By setting itself at the head of the nation, leading the oppressed layers of society (urban and rural petty-bourgeoisie), the proletariat could take power and then carry through the tasks of the bourgeois-democratic revolution (mainly the land reform and the unification and liberation of the country from foreign domination). However, once having come to power, the proletariat would not stop there but would start to implement socialist measures of expropriation of the capitalists. And as these tasks cannot be solved in one country alone, especially not in a backward country, this would be the beginning of the world revolution. Thus the revolution is "permanent" in two senses: because it starts with the bourgeois tasks and continues with the socialist ones, and because it starts in one country and continues at an international level.

In Venezuela Trotsky's theory of Permanent Revolution is being expressed in a peculiar way. Chávez first came to power on the programme of the bourgeois-democratic (or, more accurately, national-democratic) revolution. He did not propose to go beyond the limits of capitalism. But experience has demonstrated that it is impossible to carry out the tasks of the national democratic revolution on the basis of capitalism. Hugo Chávez has learnt many lessons from the living experience of the Bolivarian Revolution. Beginning as a revolutionary democrat, he has drawn the conclusion that in order to achieve its objectives the revolution must go beyond the bounds of capitalism. This means it is necessary to expropriate the bourgeoisie and move towards socialism. No other solution is possible.

The masses are the motor force of the process. All the attempts of the oligarchy and Washington to overthrow Chávez by a direct assault have failed. The reaction cannot overthrow Chávez – at this stage. But this situation cannot continue indefinitely. It is a struggle in which one side or another must win. The constitutional referendum of December 2007 was a serious warning. The Achilles' heel of the Revolution is the weakness of the leadership. The Bolivarian movement is a heterogeneous and confused movement, which reflects in its ranks the extreme polarization of class forces in society. Chávez, with the support of the masses, was moving to expropriate the landlords and capitalists. Imperialism is leaning on the right wing chavistas. At the top, there are lots of reactionary, counter-revolutionary elements. This means that there is a division along class lines of the Bolivarian movement.

The Revolution cannot stop halfway!

In order to achieve the objective of socialism what is needed is not a "Historical Project" as advocated by the utopian reformist Dieterich, but *a revolutionary programme that links the struggle for the immediate demands of the masses with the perspective of the socialist transformation of society: that is to say: a transitional programme*. In his weekly TV programme Aló Presidente, broadcast on Sunday April 22, 2007, President Chávez advised all Venezuelans to read and study the writings of León Trotsky, and commented favourably on *The Transitional Programme*, which was written by Trotsky for the founding congress of the Fourth International in 1938.

Responding to a call from a listener of the programme, Chávez explained that he had recently read the pamphlet, which he said was "worth its weight in gold" and added: "I cannot be classified as a Trotskyist, no, but I tend towards that, because I respect very much the thoughts of Leon Trotsky, and the more I respect him the more I understand him better. The Permanent Revolution for instance, is an extremely important thesis. We must read, we must study, all of us, nobody here can think he already knows", he stressed.

Chávez underlined Trotsky's idea about the conditions for socialism being ripe and said that this is certainly the case in Venezuela. President Chávez said he had been struck by Trotsky's statement that in Europe and other countries, the conditions for proletarian revolution were not only ripe but had started to rot. "This expression struck me in a powerful way, Maria Cristina [Minister of Popular Power for Light Industry and Commerce], because I had never read it before, what this means is that the conditions can be there, but if we do not see them, if we do not understand them, if we are not able to seize the moment they start to rot, like any other product of the Earth, a mango, etc."

That is absolutely correct. At present the objective conditions for socialist revolution in Venezuela are extremely favourable. But that will not last forever. Venezuela has not yet broken with capitalism but stands in an uneasy halfway position. There are great dangers in this. It is impossible to make half a revolution. The danger is that, by introducing some measures of nationalization and other progressive reforms, Chávez will make the operation of capitalism impossible, without having put in place the necessary mechanisms of planning and control that are the prior conditions for a socialist planned economy.

In the same speech Chávez referred also to the central thesis of Trotsky's Transitional Programme, when he explained that "the historical crisis of mankind is reduced to the crisis of the revolutionary leadership." "Then", Chávez continued, "Trotsky points out something which is extremely important, and he says that [the conditions for proletarian revolution] are starting to rot, not because of the workers, but because of the leadership which did not see, which did not know, which was cowardly, which subordinated itself to the mandates of capitalism, of the great bourgeois democracies, the trade unions. Well, they became adapted to the system, the big Communist parties, the Communist International became adapted to the system, and then no one was able to take advantage, because of the lack of a leadership, of an intelligent, audacious and timely leadership to orient the popular offensive in those conditions. And then the Second World War came and we know what happened, and after the Second World War, and then the century ended with the fall of the Soviet Union and the fall of the so-called real-existing socialism".

This is a world apart from those who argue that there cannot be socialism in Venezuela because the level of consciousness of the workers "is not high enough". And, surprising though this might be, there are people even in Venezuela who argue precisely this. One of them is Heinz Dieterich, whose opinions are by now well known to us. But Dieterich is not alone. Chávez's words are also an attack against the Stalinist leaders of the Communist Party of Venezuela (PCV) who have refused to join the new United Socialist Party. The PCV is a party that contains many honest and courageous working class militants, but the leadership has played a lamentable role during the Bolivarian revolution. Instead of being a vanguard party, arguing from the beginning that socialism was the only way forward, they did precisely the opposite. They spent the first years of the revolution arguing strenuously that the Venezuelan revolution was just in its "anti-imperialist democratic phase" and that socialism was not on the agenda. Only when Chávez spoke about socialism did the PCV dare mention the S word. And even now, they are still insisting that the current "stage" is that of "national liberation", one which demands a "many sided alliance of classes and social layers, including the non-monopolistic bourgeoisie"!!! [1]

Since Chávez started talking about socialism in January 2005, this has become a major subject of debate throughout Venezuela. Chávez's statement that under capitalism there was no solution for the problems of the masses and that the road forward was socialism represented a major step forward in his political development. He had started trying to reform the system and to give the masses of the Venezuelan poor decent health and education services and land, and he had realised through his own experience and reading that this was not possible under capitalism. But as soon as he mentioned socialism the reformists, bureaucrats and counter-revolutionary infiltrators within the Bolivarian movement panicked. They could not openly and publicly contradict the President because his words connected with the feelings and aspirations of the masses. Rather, they tried to water down the content of what he had said.

1. from the Theses of the XIII Congress, 2007.

Chief amongst these is Heinz Dieterich who has tried to develop a "theoretical" justification against socialism, but dressing it in the robes of "Socialism of the 21st Century". Basically, he argues, socialism does not mean the expropriation of the means of production, but rather a mixed economy. That is to say, socialism, for Dieterich, really means … capitalism. Like a magician, Dieterich thinks he can take Chávez's declaration in favour of socialism, put it in a hat, and pull out a capitalist rabbit.

Chávez in the first few months of 2007 expressed his increasingly impatience at the delaying tactics of the bureaucracy and the counter-revolution within the movement. In his comments about Trotsky he stressed: "Well, here the conditions are given, I think that this thought or reflection of Trotsky is useful for the moment we are living through, here the conditions are given, in Venezuela and Latin America, I am not going to comment on Europe now, nor on Asia, there the reality is another, another rhythm, another dynamic, but in Latin America conditions are given, and in Venezuela this is a matter of course, to carry out a genuine revolution". What a difference from the reformists and the Stalinists, who, even in present day Venezuela, still argue that the conditions are not ripe for revolution!

Dieterich and the Bolivarian Revolution

Now let us compare all this to the ideas put forward by comrade Dieterich. In the interview published in *Rebelión* (2/1/07) we read:

"Q. Do conditions for implementing Socialism of the 21st Century exist in Venezuela?

"A. Yes, now indeed they do. I mention only some. Two thirds of the population voted for the President with full knowledge of his banner of Socialism of the 21st Century. This is a substantial mandate of citizens. The advance of the educational and economic system and of the consciousness of the people has been remarkable. Latin American integration and the destruction of the Monroe Doctrine seem already unstoppable. The Armed Forces now are reliable, and three key sectors of the national economy are in the hands of the government: the state, PDVSA-CVG, and more than one hundred thousand cooperatives."

So far good, or so it seems. However, in an interview in Junge Welt, he says *precisely the opposite.* Evidently, when he says that conditions for implementing socialism exist in Venezuela, he means that they exist for his *reformist tinkering*, which does not threaten the rule of Capital in the slightest. And he delivers a stern warning: "Every other attempt to make steps toward socialism under today's conditions would lead rapidly to the collapse of the system *because there is no basis of power from which to execute it.*" [2]

2. Dieterich, *En Venezuela se han creado condiciones para construir el Socialismo del Siglo XXI*. My emphasis, AW

Dieterich now proceeds to list the factors that allegedly *render impossible the socialist transformation of society in Venezuela*: "The bourgeois state has not been destroyed, it has merely reorganized itself into a new way of governing. The church has not lost its influence. Eighty percent of the mass media are in the hands of large companies opposed to the government. Also, the kind of correlation of power that would allow for a repetition of what happened in Cuba or the Soviet Union is lacking."

If the bourgeois state is not yet destroyed, the task is to destroy it and rebuild it from the bottom up. And if eighty percent of the mass media are in the hands of large companies opposed to the government, then it is high time that this unacceptable situation was ended. The large companies should be expropriated, and the mass media should be taken out of their hand and placed in the hands of the people.

But that would be totalitarianism, our friend will exclaim. Not at all, we reply. Once the press is nationalized, we can guarantee access to the newspapers, radio and television to all parties and mass organizations, trade unions, co-operatives, etc., in proportion to their actual specific weight in society. On that basis, the different tendencies in the Bolivarian and workers' and peasants' movement would have several daily papers and television channels, and the present owners of the privately owned media can have the same right we now enjoy – to sell small duplicated newssheets and bulletins on the street corner advocating the joys of capitalism to anybody that wants to listen. Solon of Athens long ago answered the legalistic arguments of the reformists when he said: "The law is like a spider's web: the small are caught and the great tear it up." It is useless reading the oligarchy and imperialism lessons on morality and law.

The song that Dieterich sings all the time is very familiar to us. We have heard it many times before. We know the tune and we know the words too. The Mensheviks sang them long before 1917, only the Mensheviks sang far better than Dieterich does. They did their best to persuade the Russian workers and peasants that they could not take power. There were no conditions for it, you see! And in truth, the conditions in Russia in 1917 were a thousand times more difficult than in Venezuela at the present time. Nevertheless, the Russian workers and peasants, under the leadership of the party of Lenin and Trotsky, brushed the reformists to one side and took power in the October Revolution.

Once again the NEP

Heinz insists that the Venezuelan Revolution cannot go further than the NEP in Russia, which he completely misrepresents, as we have already explained. He says: "The new economic policy must be arranged in such a way that the social sectors that until now have been sidelined are strengthened: small farmers, industrial workers, small businesses. *Naturally, that does not lead automatically to socialism.* But a parallel development is made by devising structures for an economy of equivalence. That's the decisive difference."[3]

The whole point about it is that what our Professor advocates is *naturally* that *it will not, cannot and must not lead* (the word "automatically" is added to confuse the issue) *to socialism*. What will it lead to, then? To "*a parallel development* [...] *made by devising structures for an economy of equivalence*". What this means is anybody's guess! The words are plainly printed on the page, but nobody can say what they are saying.

What is an "*economy of equivalence*"? It is something that is quite unknown in all of Marxist literature (or, for that matter, non-Marxist literature). It is a strange creature that is neither capitalism not socialism, nor anything in between. In fact, it is a product of the ever-inventive brain of Comrade Dieterich, who has simply *sucked it out of his thumb* in order to confuse the issue. Dieterich says: "*It's not going to be a matter of making a democratic revolution first and following it sometime later with a socialist revolution*. It's a matter of doing both at the same time along parallel paths. That is the new, Latin American solution: safeguard against the Monroe Doctrine for survival while introducing socialist development.

"In other revolutions, how was the step toward socialism taken? Lenin defined different requirements for different times. First, there was electrification. That meant the insight that the objective conditions for socialism did not exist – they could be only created. That allowed for the collectivization of agriculture. The whole movement of farm collectives was a result of the political necessity, for the future of the revolution, of bringing under party control the potential within the population of making a decision for it. That was the deciding factor. And Lenin realized, of course, that the Soviet Union would remain bourgeois in the medium term if the peasants were not brought under the ideological direction of the party and the workers."[4]

This presentation is completely dishonest. First, Dieterich confuses Lenin's ideas about *building socialism* with his position on *socialist revolution*. The two things are entirely different. Elsewhere he writes: "In my view, one can only do today in Venezuela what Lenin did in the New Economic Policy. *Every other attempt to make steps toward socialism under today's conditions would lead rapidly to the collapse of the system because there is no basis of power from which to execute it*."[5]

There is a small difference between the NEP in Soviet Russia and the present situation in Venezuela. *In Russia the working class had already taken power. They had destroyed the old capitalist state and established workers' soviet power. The Bolsheviks stood at the helm of the workers' state and the land, the banks and the main industries were nationalized.* Under such conditions, the fundamental gains of

3. Interview to Dieterich by *Junge Welt, Weighty Alternatives for Latin America*, 7/1/2006.
4. Ibid.
5. Ibid. My emphasis, AW.

the October Revolution were in safe hands and it was possible to make certain concessions to foreign capitalists without endangering the soviet power. Lenin offered concessions to foreign investors in Russia.

This was both correct and necessary. The Bolsheviks did not have the economic or technological means of developing the vast mineral wealth of Siberia. It was correct to offer concessions to foreign companies to do this. On condition that they obeyed labour Soviet laws and paid taxes to the state, they could make big profits. But the state maintained a monopoly of foreign trade. Maybe Heinz has forgotten this "little detail", maybe he never knew, or maybe he chooses not to remember. Either way, his reference to the NEP in Russia is completely out of place and misleading.

If Dieterich is in favour of Lenin's NEP, we assume that he is also in favour of the working class taking power in Venezuela, expropriating the bourgeoisie and taking over the commanding heights of the economy? Under such circumstances *and only under such circumstances* would it be correct to talk about a NEP policy. However, when Dieterich speaks of a mixed economy he is talking about something entirely different. He is opposed to the expropriation of the banks and big industries in Venezuela (except PDVSA, which is nationalized already). That is to say, he is in favour of leaving intact the economic power of the oligarchy, confining the "socialist" element in the economy to the small businesses that are run as co-operatives.

By "mixed economy" he does not mean a socialist economy, where the bulk of the economy is in the hands of the state (and the state is in the hands of the workers) and there is a small private sector consisting mainly of small businesses. He means a capitalist economy, in which most of the key sectors of the economy are in the hands of the landowners, bankers and capitalists, and a minority, consisting mainly of small businesses are run as co-operatives. *That is, he advocates a system that is the precise opposite of Lenin's NEP.*

The role of the masses

The key to the success of the Bolivarian Revolution is the active participation of the masses. The Revolution will stand or fall depending whether the masses seize the initiative and the workers succeed in placing themselves at the head of the nation. The movement from below is gathering strength by the day, even by the hour. The workers are moving to take over the factories under the banner of Freteco. The peasants are moving to take over the land under the banner of the Ezequiel Zamora Peasants' Front. The idea of workers' control is gaining ground. The debate on socialism has penetrated every layer of society. There is a revolutionary ferment at every level.

Despite all this, comrade Dieterich does not want to see the real revolutionary movement of the masses and so he denies its existence. He behaves like Admiral Nelson, who looked through his telescope with his blind eye in order not to see a signal that was disagreeable to him. Dieterich has absolutely no confidence in the revolutionary potential of the masses. They do not figure as an independent creative force in his New Historical Project. This is the precise opposite of the view of Marx who said that the task of the emancipation of the workers is the task of the workers themselves. In the Preface to his masterpiece of historical materialism *The History of the Russian Revolution*, Leon Trotsky describes the fundamental mechanics of revolution in the following way:

"*The most indubitable feature of a revolution is the direct interference of the masses in historical events.* In ordinary times the state, be it monarchical or democratic, elevates itself above the nation, and history is made by specialists in that line of business – kings, ministers, bureaucrats, parliamentarians, journalists. But at those crucial moments when the old order becomes no longer endurable to the masses, they break over the barriers excluding them from the political arena, sweep aside their traditional representatives, and create by their own interference the initial groundwork for a new régime. Whether this is good or bad we leave to the judgement of moralists. We ourselves will take the facts as they are given by the objective course of development. *The history of a revolution is for us first of all a history of the forcible entrance of the masses into the realm of rulership over their own destiny.*" [6]

In normal periods the masses do not participate in politics. The conditions of life under capitalism place insurmountable barriers in their way: the long hours of labour, physical and mental tiredness, etc. Normally, people are content to leave the decisions affecting their lives to someone else: the local councillor, the professional politicians, the trade union official, etc. However, at certain critical moments, the masses burst onto the scene of history, take their lives and destinies into their hands and become transformed from passive agents into the protagonists of the historical process. One would have to be particularly blind or obtuse not to see that this is precisely the situation that now exists in Venezuela. In recent years, but especially since the attempted coup of April 2002, millions of workers and peasants have been on the move, fighting to change society. The masses, whether in Venezuela or any other country, can only learn from their experience. The working class has to go through the experience of the revolution in order to distinguish between the different tendencies, programmes and leaders. It learns by a method of successive approximations.

Trotsky explains: "The different stages of a revolutionary process, certified by a change of parties in which the more extreme always supersedes the less, express the growing pressure to the left of the masses – so long as the swing of the movement does not run into objective obstacles. When it does, there begins a reaction: disappointments of the different layers of the revolutionary class, growth of indifferentism, and therewith a strengthening of the position of the counter-revolutionary forces. Such, at least, is the general outline of the old revolutions. [...]"

6. Leon Trotsky, *The History of the Russian Revolution*, Preface, my emphasis.

"Only on the basis of a study of political processes in the masses themselves, can we understand the role of parties and leaders, whom we least of all are inclined to ignore. They constitute not an independent, but nevertheless a very important, element in the process. Without a guiding organisation, the energy of the masses would dissipate like steam not enclosed in a piston-box. But nevertheless what moves things is not the piston or the box, but the steam."[7]

These remarks exactly fit the situation in Venezuela. It is impossible to understand the process by confining oneself to an analysis of the leaders, their class origins, statements and programmes. This is really like the froth on the waves of the ocean, which are only a superficial reflection of the profound currents beneath the surface. The trouble with Dieterich is that he is completely incapable of understanding that the fundamental motor-force of the Venezuelan revolution is the masses. The self-movement of the masses, the masses as a creative force, as the motor-force of the revolution, this is something that our Heinz is also unable to accept. In common with all the other intellectual snobs who inhabit the stuffy world of university "Left" circles, he has a profound contempt for the masses, who he sees exclusively in terms of the "poor suffering people" who the "educated" ladies and gentlemen of the universities are destined to save from their own ignorance.

No serious person can deny that it was the millions of ordinary workers, peasants and urban poor, who at every decisive stage have saved the revolution and pushed it forward. The conduct of the Venezuelan workers and peasants over the last decade has been exemplary and has shown a very high level of revolutionary consciousness. It is true that if the masses had had the guidance of a genuine mass Marxist party, the process would have been far easier, and probably would have already ended in triumph. But what is really astonishing is how far the masses have gone even without the guiding hand of a Marxist party. The formation of the PSUV was a big step forward but in itself it is not enough. The Party must be armed with a scientific theory, a policy and a programme for changing society. The need for Marxist theory has never been more urgent. In a revolution there is no time to play games or indulge in utopian experiments of the Dieterich type. There is no time to learn by trial and error, because in a revolution an error can have the most serious consequences.

Those who deny the need for revolutionary theory argue that the masses can learn everything they need to know form their own experience, without the aid of parties or leaders. This idea is perfectly childish. If your bathroom needs fixing you call for the aid of a plumber. What would you think of a plumber who tells you that he has never fixed a tap and has never studied plumbing but is quite sure that he can solve the problem by trial and error? What would you think of a dentist who, when you arrive with toothache calmly informs you that he has never extracted a tooth or studied dentistry but is quite willing to experiment on you anyway? No sensible per-

7. Ibid.

son would allow such a dentist anywhere near his mouth. Yet it seems that revolutions, where there is much more at stake than a bad molar, can be approached in an utterly frivolous manner. This is a recipe for disaster.

Theory occupies a place in revolutions that military strategy occupies in war. A mistaken strategy in war will lead inevitably to mistakes in tactics and practical operations. It will undermine the morale of the troops and lead to all kinds of blunders, defeats and unnecessary loss of life. It is the same in a revolution. Mistakes in theory will sooner or later be reflected in mistakes in practice. A mistake in everyday life can often be rectified. Everyday mistakes are not usually matters of life and death. But revolutions are life and death struggles and mistakes can be paid for very dearly. Consequently, serious revolutionaries must pay serious attention to theory. They must make a careful study of past revolutions and draw the necessary lessons and conclusions from them. An arrogant attitude that says: "I have nothing to learn from revolutions of the past in other countries" is completely out of place. Likewise, the idea put forward by people like Heinz Dieterich that it is necessary to discard the "old" ideas of Marx and Lenin and look for an entirely new and original theory of "21st Century Socialism" is entirely false and harmful.

The fact is that under the influence of the "new and original ideas" of the reformists many mistakes have already been made in Venezuela. Many good opportunities have been lost. When the masses defeated the coup in April 2002, the counter-revolutionary forces were demoralized and in a state of disarray. It would have been possible at that time to carry through a peaceful socialist transformation of society. The oligarchy was powerless and there was no force that could have prevented it. But the opportunity was lost. The counter-revolutionaries were allowed to regroup for a new offensive – the bosses' economic sabotage – a few months later.

To this day, incredibly, there is not one of the conspirators in prison. In order to succeed the Bolivarian Revolution must be armed. But the first weapons that are needed are ideas – correct, scientific, revolutionary ideas that really correspond to the situation and the needs of the masses. Marx himself said that ideas become a material force when they grip the minds of the masses. And the only really consistent revolutionary ideas are the ideas of Marxism. It is absolutely imperative that the workers and youth of Venezuela, starting with the activists, the proletarian vanguard, should thoroughly acquaint themselves with these marvellous ideas. They are like a compass that points unerringly to the victory of the socialist revolution.

The role of the working class

Heinz Dieterich completely ignores the class composition of society and the class struggle, which he proposes to abolish altogether through the application of the economics of equivalence and other "new and original" ideas. Why does Dieterich refer only to "majorities" or the "the marginalized people of humanity" ("los marginados de la humanidad") in the context of the struggle against capitalism? It is well known that Marx and Lenin considered that the *working class* was the main force that would carry out the socialist revolution, in alliance with their natural allies, the poor peasants. Were they wrong? If so, why were they wrong? And who are these "marginalised people of humanity" to whom Dieterich refers? He does not say, so we are left looking for – an interpreter.

The Marxist point of view is entirely different to the sentimental and utopian concept of Dieterich. Why did Marx base himself on the proletariat and not the students, the intellectuals or the lumpenproletariat? It was not for any arbitrary reasons but *because of the special role of the proletariat in production and the consequent reflection of this in class consciousness.* Marxists analyze the different classes and layers in society and explain their relation towards the ruling class and towards each other. This is ultimately determined by their role in production. There is a minority of exploiters who own and control the means of production, and there is the working class, which creates the wealth of society through its labour. There are many sub-divisions but these are the two fundamental classes in society. If we ignore this fact, or try to blur the boundaries of classes by referring to unspecified "majorities", we immediately abandon scientific socialism and enter the realm of mystification and confusion. These are, in fact, the most characteristic feature of Dieterich's version of "21st Century Socialism".

The leading role of the proletariat in the revolution flows from the role of the workers in production, and the fact that participation in collective (social) production means that the working class develops a socialist (collectivist) consciousness. This is not the case with any other class. Through his or her life's experience, the proletarian learns to understand collective organization and discipline. This is the result of the hard school of capitalist production and exploitation, which prepares the worker for the class struggle. The working class and the bourgeoisie are two relatively homogeneous classes. They constitute two opposing poles, standing in a position of mutually exclusive antagonism. There may be periods of truce between them, but sooner or later the class struggle between wage labour and Capital breaks out anew, assuming a greater or lesser degree of intensity.

The normal weapons of the proletariat are the methods of mass struggle – the strike, the general strike, mass demonstrations, which act as a school that prepare it for the ultimate task of taking the running of society into its hands. The workers' movement everywhere is a school of democracy. Before the workers decide tc strike, there is a democratic discussion in which opinions for and against are heard. But once the vote is taken, the workers act as one. Those who attempt to defy the democratic decision of the workers and break the strike are treated as scabs ought to be treated. The picket line is the concrete expression of the will of the majority.

In the course of a strike, the workers participate, think and discuss. Every worker knows that you learn more during one day on strike than in years of "normal" activity. In effect, every strike contains elements of a revolution, and a revolution is like a strike on a vast scale. Many of the processes that occur in the class are analogous, although the two are qualitatively different of course. But in both cases the key element is the active and conscious participation of the working class, which begins to take its destiny into its own hands instead of leaving the important decisions in the hands of other people. This is the essence of socialism, or, more correctly, of workers' power.

The question that is never answered seriously by Dieterich is this: how does the capitalist class, which is a small minority, manage to maintain its domination over the "majorities"? He cannot answer this question because he has not understood the class nature of society. His unscientific definition of dividing society into two abstract categories with no concrete content makes it impossible to understand the real class dynamics of bourgeois society. It would be impossible for the bourgeoisie to stay in power for a day unless it had the support of other groups within society.

Between the proletariat and the bourgeoisie there are other classes and sub-classes that provide the bourgeoisie with the support it needs to keep in power. There are millions of sub-exploiters and sub-sub-exploiters, without whose support the bourgeois parties would never win an election. There are small proprietors, small businessmen, small shopkeepers, professional people, lawyers, judges, civil servants and university professors. Then there are the self-employed "autonomous" people. Lastly, at the bottom of the pile, there is the lumpenproletariat, the declassed elements, beggars, criminals and so on.

So we see that on closer inspection, Heinz Dieterich's "majorities" are a very mixed bunch indeed. Moreover, the class composition in a country like Venezuela is far more complicated and varied than, for example, France, the USA or Japan. In particular, the peasantry plays a very important role. As in Russia in 1917, it would be impossible for the workers to take power without allies, and the natural allies of the working class are the poor peasants. Formally, the peasantry is a class of small proprietors. In Russia the landless peasants, who fought on the side of the Bolsheviks in 1917, nevertheless lacked a socialist consciousness. They aspired to the possession of land, that is to say, they aspired to transform themselves into small landed proprietors. The slogan "land to the tiller", despite its tremendous revolutionary significance, had a bourgeois, not a socialist, content. That was expressed after the Bolsheviks came to power.

However, there is nothing to say that the peasants cannot adopt a socialist standpoint. In the Spanish revolution of the 1930s, the peasants of Catalonia, Aragon and Andalusia took over the big estates of the landlords and ran them as collectives under democratic control. In Venezuela today the peasantry is a minority and does not have the same specific gravity as the peasantry in tsarist Russia, which was the overwhelming majority of society. But the struggle of the Venezuelan peasants against the big landowners – a key part of the oligarchy – is a very important part of the revolution.

The landless peasants are really rural proletarians. In the struggle for socialism they will stand firmly on the side of the working class. They have displayed a similarly high revolutionary class-consciousness. Under the leadership of organizations like the Ezequiel Zamora National Peasant Front, the peasants are fighting for the expropriation of the big estates and their conversion into collective property, administered by the agricultural workers themselves. That is the only correct programme for the Venezuelan peasantry, which, together with the urban working class, will fight for the nationalization of the land, and the expropriation of the oligarchy.

However, in the last analysis the fate of the Venezuelan Revolution will be decided in the towns and cities, where between 85 and 90 percent of the population lives. The working class must place itself at the head of all the other oppressed classes: the peasants and the urban poor, the unemployed, street vendors and shanty-town dwellers, the natural allies of the proletariat, who have also shown a tremendous revolutionary spirit. These are the real living forces in Venezuelan society. A fighting alliance between these classes, which will draw behind them the lower layers of the middle class, the small shopkeepers, etc., will mobilize the vast majority of the population and wield them into an irresistible force that will sweep everything before it.

How not to win the middle class

An argument often used by Dieterich and other reformists is that it is necessary to win over the middle class and therefore we must not go too far in attacking capitalism. The first half of this statement is correct, but it directly contradicts the second half. It is both possible and necessary to win over a large section of the middle class, but we will never succeed in doing this if we accept the policies of the reformists, which can only alienate the mass of the petty bourgeoisie and push them into the arms of the counter-revolution.

Using their economic power and their control of the mass media, the exploiting classes have mobilized the mass of middle class Venezuelans to oppose the revolution. Under the false flag of democracy they have organized street riots and clashes. Their shock troops are the sons of the rich – the "*sifrinos*" – wealthy parasites, fanatically opposed to the masses. The enraged petty bourgeois resent the concessions made to the poor, which they see as a threat to their own privileges. They make a lot of noise when required, but they are really just human dust, easily scattered to the wind when confronted with the movement of the masses.

However, as we have explained, the petty bourgeoisie is not a homogeneous class. There are contradictions within the middle class that can be expressed in splits in the opposition. The upper layers of the middle class is composed of privileged elements – prosperous lawyers, university professors, bank managers and politicians – who stand close to the oligarchy and are its willing servants. The lower layers – the small shopkeepers, small peasants, bank clerks, etc. – stand closer to the working class and can be won over. However, the way to win over the lower ranks of the petty bourgeoisie is not to make concessions to their leaders (really their political exploiters) but to take the offensive against the big bankers and capitalists, to show an attitude of absolute firmness and decision.

A section of the opposition consists of people who have been deceived by the counter-revolutionaries. They can be won over to the side of the revolution. The way to win them over, however, is by carrying out measures to expropriate the big capitalists and adopting measures in the interests of the small shopkeepers and small businessmen. They must be convinced that the revolution is invincible and that their interests are best served by joining forces with the working class against the big banks and monopolies. In an interview published in *Rebelión* on 25 April 2004, entitled "Without the support of the middle class the process can be defeated", he was asked why the opposition in Venezuela was so violent. Dieterich replies:

"I believe that there is such virulence and we have lost a lot of the capital we had before, because we have not managed to convince the middle class and the petty bourgeoisie (sic) that the process is not their enemy. Lately the idea has been introduced that the workers are the subject of the transformation, which, in my opinion, means we are once again *repeating the mistake of exclusive language*." (My emphasis, AW.)

For this university professor, it is *all a question of language*. If only Chávez moderated his language and started to appear a bit more moderate, this would calm the nerves of the middle class and they would immediately leave the opposition and flock to the banner of Bolivarianism in droves. If only it were so simple! But let us begin by agreeing with Heinz on at least something. We agree that it is necessary to appeal to the middle class (which, by the way, is exactly the same as the petty bourgeoisie) and try to win at least part of them to the side of the revolution. The question is: how is this to be done? In an interview in *Junge Welt*, he says:

"The seizure of power to a large extent succeeded, though not as decisively as we wish. The question is whether we will be more successful in the formative stage than the Soviet Union and China, or whether we will also fail. We have one advantage over both of these historical examples: we are clear today about what a non-market economy is, and we have technical capacities that did not exist in the other two examples. For that reason I would say that today, for the first time, the objective conditions exist that can be used to convert this transition phase into a decision for socialism.

"*But in any case it must all be done democratically.* If at some point the people say, 'We have reached the level of development of Costa Rica and that's good enough for us, we don't want any socialist experiments in Venezuela,' then there is nothing to be done. Democracy means that the majority rules. *If the majority is satisfied with quasi-first world social conditions and does not wish to go any farther, socialism cannot be imposed.*" (My emphasis, AW.)

Comrade Dieterich says that socialism cannot be imposed but must be "done democratically". What is this supposed to mean? *The majority in Venezuela are the mass of workers, peasants and poor people who are the basis of the Bolivarian movement and have voted massively in favour of Chávez and socialism.* There is therefore no question of "imposing" socialism as far as the masses are concerned. Those who oppose socialism and loudly complain of impositions and dictatorship are a minority – the tiny minority of exploiters who have mobilised a section of the middle class to fight against the democratically elected government on the streets. In Venezuela it is only the middle class (and not all of them) who can enjoy "quasi-first world social conditions" and therefore does not wish to go any farther. In the same social category we must also include a large part of the Bolivarian bureaucracy, who enjoy a privileged position and secretly sympathise with the opposition.

The so-called bourgeois "democracy" is a gigantic fraud, behind which lurks the dictatorship of big capital. This dictatorship oppresses not only the workers but also the middle class. What is needed is not the hollow fraud of formal bourgeois democracy – in which real power is in the hands of the big banks and monopolies – but a real democracy – a democracy of the working people, based on the collective ownership of the land, the banks and industry.

It is logical that those sections of society with something to lose should oppose socialism and demand that the Bolivarian revolution be halted. But they are not the majority but only a minority. Democracy is the rule of the majority and the minority must accept the decision of the majority. Yet Héinz Dieterich has repeatedly stated that unless the middle class agrees, it is wrong to carry out the socialist transformation of society. In other words, he argues that the majority must accept the decision of the minority – that is, the opposite of democracy.

How to win the middle class

How do we win the middle class? We will certainly not do this showing by weakness and vacillation. Winston Churchill used to say that attack is the best form of defence. It is absolutely necessary to carry the revolution through to the end. It is necessary to put an end to the stranglehold that the landlords and capitalists exercise over the economy by nationalizing the banks, the land and the major industries under democratic workers' control and management.

The reformists are convinced that the socialist speeches of Chávez, the expropriations and the revolutionary *cogestión* (joint management) implemented after these expropriations are mistakes that drive away the middle class, provoke imperialism, and minimize support for the revolution. In reality, the contrary is the case. What provokes imperialism is each measure that does not serve them in subjugating the masses and does not allow them to continue exploiting the wealth of the country, as they have always done. Support for Chávez will decline if speeches are made about socialism but not translated quickly into action. The result of the constitutional referendum of December 2007 was a warning in this respect.

The masses of the workers and the middle class need to see that socialism is not a distant dream but an immediate solution to their problems. We do not want to nationalize every small shop and business. That is not necessary or desirable. We should try to win over the middle class by pointing out that our enemy is the big capitalists and imperialism. It must be made clear that these measures of nationalization are aimed only at the big capitalists, bankers and landowners. We have no intention of nationalizing small businesses, farms or shops. These play no independent role in the economy, since they are utterly dependent on the big banks, supermarkets, etc.

We will appeal to the small shopkeepers, etc., to support the programme of nationalization, which is in their interests. The nationalization of the banks will enable the government to grant small businesses cheap and easy credit. The nationalization of the big fertilizer plants will enable it to sell cheap fertilizer to the peasants. And by eliminating the middlemen and nationalizing the big supermarkets, distribution and transport companies, we can provide the peasants with a guaranteed market and a fair price for their products, while reducing prices to the consumer.

Without nationalizing the commanding heights of the economy, it will not be possible to take even half a step in the direction of socialism. By acting in this way, the President completely ignored the advice of his self-proclaimed advisers – including Heinz Dieterich. The latter was probably not very pleased, and was undoubtedly muttering (for the hundredth time) dark warnings about the danger of provoking the reaction and imperialism. But the workers of Venezuela and the rest of the world were delighted that the Revolution is striking blows against its enemies. They were quite right and Dieterich was quite wrong.

Immediately after taking office, the President announced a far-reaching nationalization programme: "Everything that was privatized will be nationalized," he stated. News of the nationalizations immediately provoked a wave of hysterical attacks from the defenders of capitalism. On Tuesday, 15 May 2007 James Ingham, the BBC News correspondent in Caracas, published an article entitled *Nationalization sweeps Venezuela*, which begins: "Private investors and the political opposition hate it; President Hugo Chávez's supporters love it. A whirlwind of nationalizations and threats to private companies is changing Venezuela's economic climate and threatens to widen a tense social divide. Mr Chávez is stepping up his campaign to turn Venezuela into a socialist state. He is taking more control of the country's assets and warning companies that do not agree with his vision that he will take them over."

This is precisely what comrade Dieterich has been warning us about! He has warned us that if we take action against private property we will earn the bitter enmity of the owners. The whole world will be against us. Public opinion will be against us. George Bush will be against us. Even the BBC will be against us.

Everybody will be against us! Everybody? Well, not quite everybody. President Chávez's announcement of sweeping measures of nationalization was greeted with enthusiasm by the workers of Venezuela and all countries. It represented a big step forward for the Venezuelan Revolution and a serious blow against capitalism and imperialism. What has Heinz Dieterich to say about this? We do not know. Probably he has just kept quiet about it, in order not to annoy the President.

For years the propagandists of Capital have been assiduously spreading the myth that capitalism works better than a planned economy and the fairy story that the wonders of the market in the long run will solve all problems. To this Keynes famously replied: "In the long run we are all dead." The application of market economics in Latin America has been an unmitigated disaster for the masses, who did not benefit from the economic growth of the past decade, which has only served to increase the huge profits of the bankers, capitalists and, above all, giant foreign monopolies like Exxon. The concern of these gentlemen is not that the Venezuelans lack expertise to exploit difficult oil fields, but that the owners of Exxon will be deprived of their fat profits.

The foreign monopolies have been plundering the oil wealth of Venezuela for generations. They have extracted a vast amount of loot at the expense of the people of Venezuela. For most of the time they did not even pay taxes. Yet now, when the people of Venezuela are taking back what is their own property, these fat, pampered vultures are demanding compensation. It is the Venezuelan people who should be demanding compensation from the transnationals for all the wealth they have robbed for decades. The nationalizations carried out were absolutely necessary, but in themselves are not sufficient to break the power of the oligarchy and create a socialist economy.

The nationalization of the banks is absolutely essential if Venezuela is to finally break with capitalism. The banks are an essential instrument of economic policy and a powerful lever. The control of credit is an essential element in a socialist planned economy and must be in the hands of the state. This will enable the state to allocate resources and investment according to the general needs of society, not the profits of a few wealthy parasites. *The question of nationalization lies at the heart of this critical stage, and upon the resolution of this issue the future of the revolution depends.*

In April 2008 Chávez announced the nationalization of large parts of the dairy and meat producing industries, as well as the nationalization of the cement industry and the re-nationalisation of SIDOR. These nationalizations are very important because they show the fundamental contradiction between private property and the interests of the majority of Venezuelans. Dairy plants were refusing to process milk because of the fixed prices that the government introduced. Three cement multinationals control the Venezuelan market, and while cement is much needed in the country to build houses, roads, hospitals and schools, they were exporting a large part of their production to the world market where they could get better prices and at the same time fixing artificially high prices for the internal market. SIDOR, privatised in 1997 and owned by an Argentinean multinational, was getting super-profits by using cheap state produced electricity and raw materials, over-exploiting the workers, and then selling steel to the world market which Venezuela had to buy in the form of manufactured products.

These nationalizations are a step in the right direction. But they are not enough. The banks, monopolies and most of the land remain in private hands, so that the whole of the Venezuelan economy cannot be integrated into a rational whole. Piecemeal nationalization and state intervention will create a situation where the normal functioning of a capitalist market economy is impossible. It will aggravate the flight of capital and encourage the resistance and sabotage of the capitalists, creating further shortages, unemployment and chaos. What is needed is a national plan of production, discussed and decided by the workers themselves, so that the urgent needs of the Venezuelan people can be fulfilled.

While we welcome wholeheartedly measures like the nationalization of SIDOR, we must also point out that the process remains unfinished. It is entirely false to argue, as the bureaucrats and reformists do, that we must proceed slowly and gradually in order not to upset the bourgeois and provoke imperialism. The bourgeois are already sufficiently upset and the imperialists are more than sufficiently provoked. There are worrying signs that all is not well with the economy. Inflation is rising, which is hitting the poorest sections hardest, and shortages are appearing at different levels. The capitalists are responding with a strike of capital and there is widespread sabotage, corruption and bureaucratic obstruction.

By delaying the inevitable showdown between the classes, we can only give time for the counter-revolutionary forces to regroup and organize new plots against the revolution. More seriously, by allowing the capitalists to continue their sabotage, creating artificial scarcities and disorganizing production, there is a danger that the masses will become tired of so many privations and fall into apathy and indifference. That is precisely what the reactionaries want. Once the balance of forces begins to move against the revolution, the counter-revolutionaries will strike again. And they have plenty of hidden allies in the leadership of the Bolivarian Movement who wish to halt the revolution and are waiting for the opportunity to turn against the President. The danger is still present. We therefore must act with urgency to tackle the problem at its roots.

The struggle for workers' control is an important element in the Revolution, but workers' control can only be an ephemeral phase if it does not lead to expropriation. This shows the unfinished nature of the Revolution and underlines the contradictions within it and the dangers facing it. At Inveval the workers occupied the factory and began producing under workers' control, while demanding the expropriation of the plant. They organized a factory committee to run the company and organize the struggle, which was successful. This is exactly the practical application of what

Trotsky talks about in *The Transitional Programme*, where Trotsky wrote:

"*Sit-down [occupation] strikes*, [...] go beyond the limits of 'normal' capitalist procedure. Independently of the demands of the strikers, the temporary seizure of factories deals a blow to the idol, capitalist property. Every sit-down strike poses in a practical manner the question of who is boss of the factory: the capitalist or the workers? If the sit-down strike raises this question episodically, the *factory committee* gives it organized expression. Elected by all the factory employees, the factory committee immediately creates a counterweight to the will of the administration."

In revolutionary times it is not enough to conduct the day-to-day struggle for immediate demands on wages and conditions, but rather to elevate the workers to the idea of taking power. As Trotsky explains in the Transitional Programme: "Trade unions are not ends in themselves; they are but means along the road to proletarian revolution.", and he adds "during a period of exceptional upsurges in the labour movement ... it is necessary to create organizations *ad hoc*, embracing the whole fighting mass: strike committees, factory committees, and finally, soviets."

The role of reformism

Chávez has shown that it is possible for revolutionaries to make use of the institutions of bourgeois formal democracy to mobilize the masses for the transformation. This policy has enabled him to win one election after another and served to rally and organize millions of workers and peasants to change society. However, the Revolution has still not passed the critical point where quantity becomes quality. Powerful forces are at work trying to halt the Revolution and weaken and sabotage it from within. The bourgeois counter-revolutionary forces are too weak to accomplish this task. It is being carried out by the Bolivarian bureaucracy – the right wing that represents a fifth column of the counter-revolution inside the movement, and consistently works to isolate the President and sabotage his decrees. The reformist wing is terrified of the masses and revolution and fearful of the bourgeoisie and counter-revolution. They are doing everything in their power to halt the revolution and prevent it moving in a socialist direction.

The Venezuelan Stalinists are the most consistent reformists. They repeat the same arguments of the Russian Mensheviks. They argue that the Bolivarian Revolution must limit itself to fighting for the bourgeois democratic tasks. They say that the Venezuelan Revolution is at the democratic stage and that the socialist tasks are not posed. They pay lip service to socialism – but only in the dim and distant future. They act like the Bourbons who "forgot nothing and learned nothing." They pose as the leaders of the proletariat but in reality they are defending a bourgeois policy. The PCV refuses to join the PSUV and has split over the question. But both the faction that joined the PSUV and those that remain outside defend the Stalinist-Menshevik theory of the two stages. They say that we must not touch private property, that we must remain within the bounds of capitalism – that is to say they defend a right wing position that, if it were accepted, would signify the inevitable defeat of the Venezuelan Revolution.

Heinz Dieterich has no party, no organization and no base in the working class or the "majorities" to which he constantly refers. He represents only himself. But he has powerful friends and backers: the right wing of the Bolivarian Movement, the bureaucracy and the reformists. They ensure that his books are published in large editions and his ideas are widely spread. This is quite natural because the current debate on socialism represents a serious threat to the reformists. They are doing everything in their power to erect barriers to prevent the workers, peasants and youth from arming themselves with the ideas of Marxism.

Contradictions in the Bolivarian Revolution

The December 2006 presidential elections marked yet another turn to the left in the Bolivarian revolution. The right wing of the Bolivarian movement was getting increasingly worried about the course events were taking, with Chávez talking of Trotskyism in the swearing in ceremony for the new Cabinet, and adopting an increasingly leftward course. The battle lines were drawn and the splits within the Bolivarian movement were become public, expressing themselves in the polemic about the founding of the new party. Chávez was acutely aware of this and in the first meeting of promoters of the new United Socialist Party, on March 24th 2007, he explained how "as the revolution deepens, as it expands, these contradictions will come out openly, even some that up until now had been covered up, they will intensify, because we are dealing here with economic issues, and there is nothing that hurts a capitalist more than his wallet".

In talking about the need for a revolutionary leadership Chávez quoted from Lenin: "Now, the leadership, this is why I insist so much in the need for a party, because we have not had a revolutionary leadership up to the tasks of the moment we are living in, united, orientated as a result of a strategy, united, as Vladimir Illich Lenin said, a machinery able to articulate millions of wills into one single will, this is indispensable to carry out a revolution, otherwise it is lost, like the rivers that overflow, like the Yaracuy that when it reaches the Caribbean loses its riverbed and becomes a swamp."

These words of Chávez were in tune and reflected the conclusions drawn by tens of thousands of revolutionary activists in Venezuela, in the factories, in the neighbourhoods, in the countryside. They are growing increasingly impatient and want to the revolution to be victorious once and for all. But there are other powerful pressures being exerted in the opposite direction. The destiny of the Revolution will be determined by the outcome of this struggle of opposed forces, which at bottom is a struggle between mutually exclusive class forces.

From the standpoint of the world working class the importance of these developments is self-evident. Ever since the fall of the Soviet Union, the bourgeois have been organizing a furious campaign against the ideas of socialism and Marxism. They solemnly pronounced the end of communism and socialism. They were so self-assured that they even pronounced the end of history. But history has not ended. It has scarcely begun. After a decade and a half, the workers of the world can see the crude reality of capitalist domination. They promised a world of peace, prosperity and democracy. Now all the illusions of the bourgeoisie are in ruins. More and more people are becoming aware that capitalism offers no future for humanity.

There are the beginnings of an awakening everywhere: workers, peasants, young people, are on the march. The idea that revolution and socialism are off the agenda has been disproved in practice. The revolution has begun in Venezuela, and is spreading throughout Latin America, as when a heavy rock is thrown into a pond. The waves from the revolution are beginning to be felt on a world scale. People are asking: what is happening in Venezuela and what does it mean?

It is not necessary to be one hundred percent in agreement with Hugo Chávez, or to idealize the Bolivarian Revolution to understand the colossal significance of these events. Here for the first time in decades, an important world leader has proclaimed the need for world socialism and condemned capitalism as slavery. He has spoken publicly before millions of people about the need to read Marx, Lenin, Rosa Luxemburg and Trotsky. Above all, Chávez has mobilized millions of workers, peasants and youth under the banner of socialist revolution. The significance of all this is not lost on the imperialists, who are doing all in their power to destroy the revolution in its cradle. They are mobilizing powerful forces to crush the Venezuelan Revolution. The workers of the world must mobilize the might of the international labour movement to stop them. But the most dangerous enemies of the Bolivarian Revolution are to be found within the movement itself.

Baduel's offensive

The declarations of General Raúl Isaías Baduel on 5 November 2007, when he came out against the constitutional reform referendum, were a key part of the counterrevolutionary offensive of the opposition against Chávez. Yet until his retirement in July 2007, Baduel was Defence Minister and apparently an ally of Hugo Chávez. Just a few months later, Baduel came out against the President. In a news conference, he described the President's proposed changes to the Constitution as "in effect a coup d'état" and a "non-democratic imposition that would put us into tragic retreat." This attack was clearly intended to cause a split in the ranks of the Bolivarian movement and promote a "No" vote in the referendum on the constitutional changes scheduled for December 2.

It is not a coincidence that General Baduel wrote the Preface to Heinz Dieterich's book *Hugo Chávez and Socialism of the XXI Century* and helped to launch it in Venezuela. One can say that Heinz Dieterich cannot be held responsible for the views and actions of Baduel. But what was his reaction to the General's statements? Was it to distance himself from Baduel? Did he repudiate what Baduel was saying? Not at all. On 8 November, Rebelión published an article by Heinz Dieterich entitled *The Chávez-Baduel Break: Stop the Collapse of the Popular Project.* In this article Heinz Dieterich tells us that "understanding the objective causes, consequences and possible solutions to this conflict is thus essential to avoid a triumph of the oligarchy and imperialism".

So what were these "objective causes"? Dieterich modestly informs us that he has "had a personal relationship of appreciation for both characters for many years". Heinz always likes to tell people that he is close to so-and-so and that he has met so-and-so. This is intended to give him a special authority and insight into affairs of state. He claims the right not only to tell us "what Chávez really means", but even to tell Chávez himself what he really means. Unfortunately, he now finds himself in difficulties, since Baduel and Chávez are in a head-on confrontation. How does Heinz get out of this little difficulty? Despite his friendship with both men, he "will not make a defence of either of the two protagonists, but a rational analysis, which seeks to contribute to a progressive solution of a grave situation."

Sybill in ancient Greece made mysterious utterances that nobody could understand. The priests then interpreted these utterances for the ignorant public. We would require the services of such a priest to answer a very simple question: in the conflict between Chávez and Baduel, where did Heinz Dieterich stand? He stood "in the middle". He tried to act as an arbiter between them, and in the process he placed himself above both – since the referee always decides in the case of a conflict and the referee's decision is final.

Dieterich defends Baduel

Pursuing his role as a Sybill-referee, Heinz informs us: "A key variable for understanding the conflict is the personality of both these military men, but this is not the time to introduce that variable in the analysis." This is classic Heinz Dieterich. It means: "I know these two men better than you. I know them better than anybody. In fact, I know them better than they know themselves. I also know that this is, at bottom, only a conflict of personalities. But I will not tell you how or why I know this, because then you would know as much as I do!"

Only a superficial mind seeks to interpret major political events in terms of personalities. This is a trivial approach to history and politics. It is on the level of sentimental novels and gossip journalism. It explains nothing at all. If Chávez and Baduel's personalities are different now, they were also different five or ten years ago. Why did the clash not occur then instead of now?

In reality, the conflict between Chávez and Baduel is at bottom a class question. Personal and psychological elements played at best a secondary role. These men do not act in a social vacuum. Baduel reflected the ideas, the interests and the psychology of the bourgeoisie, while Chávez was expressing the aspirations of the mass of poor and oppressed people. That is why immediately Baduel was received as a hero and saviour by the bourgeoisie and the media nationally and internationally, while Chávez received the support of the workers and peasants. Again, only a blind man cannot see this.

Now we come to the causes of the conflict. Heinz informs us: "The accusations that Baduel has sold out to the extreme right, that his anti-communism has got the better of him, or that he is a traitor, do not get to the heart of the problem." This is a very strange formulation indeed! Either Baduel has sold out to the right and is a traitor, or he has not and is not. What does comrade Dieterich think? We do not know. He does not say. All he says is that these accusations "do not get to the heart of the problem." What kind of statement is this? It is the kind of lawyer's circumlocution and sophistry that is not supposed to explain but only to distract ones' attention.

Dieterich is very anxious to present his friend in the most favourable light. We are informed: "He [Baduel] is a man who acts on conviction, not expediency." These words amount to a defence of the General who is attacking the Revolution and supporting the counterrevolutionary opposition. Even if we accept what Dieterich says, that Baduel only acted from conviction, that would be no justification. A counterrevolutionary who acts on conviction, not expediency is more dangerous than an enemy who is guided by short-term personal considerations.

He reminds us that he "confronted the coup of April 11 [2002]" and informs us that the fact that he did not participate in Chávez's attempted coup in 1992 "has an explanation, which the leaders involved know and one day will be made public". Yet again he puts on the cloak of Sybill and hints that he (Heinz Dieterich) knows many secret things about which we are ignorant and about which he cannot speak. This is a very interesting argument. It is like a man who is asked to pay the rent at the end of the month saying: "I know a secret formula that will enable me to win the lottery, but I cannot speak of it now". This may impress some people, but it will not convince the landlord or prevent him from throwing his insolvent lodger, together with his secret formulas, onto the street.

Why did Baduel oppose the reform on November 5? Baduel was unable to accept the government project because he was already excluded, Dieterich tells us: "He was marginalized, and the primary responsibility for this marginalization was that of the government". So there we have it! The fault for this situation is not Baduel's because the poor man was "already excluded". Whose fault was it, then? Why, the government and the President, of course! What does this signify? In the present conflict, which, as we have already explained, is a class conflict, a clash between the forces of revolution and counterrevolution, Dieterich stands with the latter against the former. And no amount of sophistry and ambiguity can conceal this fact.

The line of argument used by Dieterich here is absolutely typical: it is lawyer's sophistry. Let us draw an analogy that will make this clear. A man is accused of burning down his neighbour's house with everyone inside it. He goes to trial and his defence lawyer is a friend who has known him for many years. Does his friend plead not guilty? No, he cannot do this, because the house was burnt down in daylight and everybody saw who did it. The case being hopeless, the lawyer resorts to trickery to save his friend. What arguments does he use? He does not deny the accusation (because he cannot) but argues that the accusation "does not get to the heart of the problem."

Having thus begun to confuse the jury and draw its attention away from the central accusation, he then continues to create a smoke screen of irrelevant matters:

1) I have known the accused for many years and he is a very nice man.

2) The accused only acts out of conviction. He only burned the house out of conviction. In fact, he always burns down houses out of conviction.

3) The house was very ugly and deserved to be burnt anyway.

4) The neighbours stopped inviting him to dinner and this made him feel marginalized. Therefore, the neighbours were responsible for his actions and deserved to be burned.

When this lawyer's rhetoric is stripped of its embellishment, its dishonesty is clear to any normally intelligent person. The lawyer does not deny that his client is guilty as charged. But he defends him as a person and tries to present his criminal actions in the best possible light. He then proceeds to justify the crime itself and to make the victims of the crime appear the aggressors and the criminal look like the real victim. If the lawyer is sufficiently skilful, he can sometimes succeed in persuading a jury to release the criminal, who then immediately proceeds to burn down more houses.

A 'sincere' counterrevolutionary

Heinz Dieterich, as we have seen, did not deny that Baduel has gone over to the counterrevolutionary opposition. He could not deny this because everyone in Venezuela knew that it was true. He therefore attempted to justify his actions, presenting his counterrevolutionary speech as the action of a true democrat and patriot. He said he acted only out of conviction, not from bribery or other base motives.

Since we have not been present at the meetings between the General and the opposition and have no access to his bank account, we have no means of knowing whether this is true or false. However, let us note that Dieterich contradicts himself when he writes: "Part of the impact [of Baduel's statement] was due to the fact that some 18 days earlier he had publicly supported the constitutional reform." How did a "man of conviction" change his convictions about the Constitution in the space of 18 days? Evidently, the General's convictions resemble those of the politician who said: "All right, if you don't like my principles I'll change them!"

Even if we accept that he acted only out of conviction, this argument counts for nothing. Many of the greatest villains in history have acted out of conviction. The mad emperor Nero no doubt acted out of conviction when he burned Rome and blamed the Christians. Adolf Hitler always acted on the basis of very deep convictions – convictions of racial superiority and fascism. Both Tony Blair and George Bush are said to be motivated by deep convictions – imperialist convictions that they have a god-given right to rule the world. To justify his support for the criminal invasion of Iraq Blair told the British people: "I did what I did because I believed sincerely it was right". Does this make the crimes of these men any less atrocious because they were sincere and "acted from conviction"?

Many of the Venezuelan opposition are deeply convinced that Chávez is a dangerous revolutionary, a threat to the existing social order who must be overthrown and even killed to save the fatherland. Oh yes, they believe this quite sincerely. And from their class point of view they are correct. They are acting from conviction. The counterrevolutionary opposition sincerely defends the standpoint of the landlords, bankers and capitalists. Baduel sincerely defends the counterrevolutionary opposition. And Dieterich sincerely (we assume) defends Baduel. However, we are not interested in whether they are sincere or not, but what interests they defend.

The only way we can judge the actions of Baduel is not from the standpoint of personal sincerity but from a class point of view. For our part, we sincerely defend the standpoint of socialism and the working class. We defend President Chávez against the attacks of the counter-revolution. Not to do so in this situation would be a betrayal. And it is also the only way we can interpret the actions of those who use lawyer's sophistry to defend him.

If an arsonist is allowed to escape justice because of the arguments of clever lawyers, he will be free to burn houses. If a counter-revolutionary is tolerated, he will engage in counterrevolutionary conspiracies that threaten the lives of many more people than a single arsonist. In our opinion the Bolivarian Revolution has already been far too lenient with the counterrevolutionaries. How many of the golpistas of April 2002 are in prison? Until recently, not one, as far as we know. This is a serious mistake and the Revolution will pay a heavy price for such leniency.

Baduel and Dieterich

Baduel himself explained what his real concerns were at the time of his parting speech as Minister of Defence. While he dressed his speech in socialist phraseology, what he said was very clear. For instance, he declared that, "socialism is about distributing wealth, but before you can distribute wealth you have to create wealth" which is a typical argument of reformists everywhere against socialism and nationalization. He added that "a regime of socialist production is not incompatible with a political system which is profoundly democratic with counter-balances and divisions of power," adding that "*we must move away from Marxist orthodoxy* which says that democracy with division of powers is just an instrument of bourgeois domination". He said: "yes, we must go towards socialism, but this must be done *without chaos and disorganization*".

Using a very strange analogy with Lenin's New Economic Policy he said: "we cannot allow our system to become a type of State Capitalism, where the state is the only owner of the means of production". And added "war communism in the Soviet Union taught us that you cannot implement sharp changes in the economic system [...] the wholesale abolition of private property and the brutal socialisation of the means of production always have a negative effect on the production of goods and services and provoke general discontent amongst the population". It is quite clear what he was saying. These incorrect analogies with War Communism and the NEP in Russia are just a cover for what he was really saying: "we should not go towards nationalization of the economy".

Some people at the time argued that Baduel's speech was not a criticism of Chávez, but rather, that he was just putting forward his view of "democratic socialism" (that is, reforms within the limits of capitalism). These are by the way, exactly the same ideas that Heinz Dieterich has been putting forward under the name of Socialism of the XXI Century, socialism without nationalisation of the means of production, which is ... capitalism! It is for this reason that Baduel was so enthusiastic about Dieterich's ideas and wrote the prologue of the Venezuelan edition of his book *Hugo Chávez and Socialism of the 21st Century*.

In this prologue Baduel says very complimentary things about Dieterich's book: "I feel honoured, since I recognise in this work an immense contribution to the building of the theory of the new non-capitalist society". He adds that despite the appeal by the president to participate in the debate about socialism "after a while, Heinz Dieterich's contribution remains as an almost unique and compulsory point of reference, due to the clarity and simplicity of his ideas". Baduel was in fact, so impressed with Dieterich's ideas that he suggested that Chapter 7 of his book "should be published separately for massive distribution in schools, universities, trade unions, factories, hospitals, peasant communities, communal councils and in all those spaces where we need to generate a debate and a healthy discussion about the socialism that we want to build."

This has to be really embarrassing for Dieterich! The person who only a few months ago was praising his ideas so much has now broken with the Bolivarian project and joined the counterrevolution. Maybe this is the reason why Dieterich was so keen to argue that Baduel is not really a counterrevolutionary and that at the end of the day Chávez and Baduel should make an alliance. But one could argue that Baduel's ideas have changed and that therefore Dieterich is not really responsible for his latest ideological evolution. Nothing could be further from the truth. What attracted Baduel to Dieterich was Dieterich's idea that you can have "socialism" without nationalising the means of production. This was a kind of socialism that Baduel could live with. And this is what he explained in his parting speech on July

23. What did he say in his speech on November 5? Exactly the same thing. Let's quote him at length:

"The reasoning for the constitutional reform, as it has been presented, is to take the Venezuelan people towards a process of transition towards something which is generically called 'socialism', without clearly explaining what is meant by this term. As I already said on another occasion when I departed from the Ministry of Defence, the word socialism does not have a uniform meaning, and can include regimes like that of Pol Pot in Cambodia and the Stalinist Soviet Union, as well as Nordic Socialism or European Democratic Socialism. Which socialism are we being taken to? Why are the people not being told clearly where the nation is being led to? As a people we must demand that we are told clearly the destiny of our future and that we are not lied to with a so-called Venezuelan socialism".

Baduel admits himself that his ideas have not changed! And Dieterich himself described Baduel's parting speech as a "great step forward for Socialism of the 21st Century".[8] The reason why Baduel went over to the opposition is clear: he sees that all the talk about socialism might actually mean socialism and he does not agree with that. He was happy to accept socialism of the Dieterich variety (i.e. Social Democracy), but he is completely opposed to genuine socialism. Chávez explained this very well when he said: "It is not strange that when a submarine goes deeper the pressure is increased and can free a loose screw, the weak points are going to leave, and I believe it is good that they leave".

A candidate – for Bonapartism

Heinz Dieterich is a utopian reformist, an academic who lives in a world of dreams yet (for some reason) considers himself to be a supreme political realist. It would not be fair to describe him as a counter-revolutionary. No, the Professor detests the counter-revolution and wishes to avoid it. Nor would it be correct to describe him as a revolutionary, since he also fears that the Revolution, which is being propelled forward by the "untutored masses", will go too far (has already gone too far) and will provoke (has already provoked) the counterrevolution. For Heinz *all extremes are bad, and we must have moderation in all things*. Therefore, the answer is in the *Centre.*

Heinz Dieterich insists that the General has not gone to the right. Where has he gone, then? He is now *the candidate of the Centre*, Heinz tells us. But what is the Centre? In Venezuela there is no Centre, except in the fevered imagination of Heinz Dieterich. In Venezuela there is a sharp polarization between left and right - that is, a sharp polarization between the classes, which has now become an unbridgeable gap. Everybody knows this. The opposition knows it, the masses know it, Hugo Chávez knows it, Baduel knows it, the US State Department knows it, a child of six

8. See: *Hugo Chávez, Raúl Baduel, Raúl Castro and the Regional Block of Power advance the socialism of the future.* http://www.rebelion.org/noticia.php?id=54425

knows it, and even George W Bush knows it. But Heinz Dieterich does not know it. He intends to solve all the problems of the Revolution by uniting everybody in the Centre and forming an alliance between Chávez and Baduel.

This means *uniting revolution with counter-revolution*, which is only a little more difficult than uniting fire with water, turning lead into gold or squaring the circle. However, our friend Heinz is not a man to be deterred by such small details. Baduel, he tells us, is very intelligently positioning himself as candidate for leader of the Centre. But the General has a small problem. *The Centre does not exist.* Having broken with the Bolivarian Movement (where he was always on the right) he has no alternative but to go *even further to the right*.

Baduel has no alternative but to find common cause with the opposition, with whom he has no real differences. Some of the more stupid oppositionists do not want him. They see anybody remotely connected with *chavismo* as an enemy. But the more intelligent ones who lead the opposition will welcome him with open arms. More importantly, the US State Department, which pulls the strings of the opposition, will certainly welcome him with open arms. This has a logic of its own.

Baduel chose his moment to secure the maximum impact on public opinion nationally and internationally. Naturally, the mass media controlled by big business gave him a lot of publicity, praising him as a hero. He was the hero of the hour - for the counterrevolutionaries. He put himself forward as the future Saviour of the Nation, a nation that has left the path of "democracy" and is sliding towards chaos and anarchy. A firm hand was needed to save the Nation. That means the hand of a General, and that General is called Baduel.

For anyone with the slightest knowledge of history, *this is the language of Bonapartism*. The real historical analogy for Baduel is not Cincinnatus but Napoleon Bonaparte who rose to power over the dead body of the French Revolution. It was Bonaparte who came to power on the slogan of national Unity and Order. That meant the crushing of the revolutionary masses who under the Jacobins had "gone too far". It means the deposing and murder of Robespierre and the other revolutionary leaders and a White Terror against their followers. It meant the restoration of rank and privilege and the domination of France by the bankers and capitalists, in alliance with those who had made their fortunes out of the Revolution through corruption and careerism and who were convinced that the Revolution had gone too far.

If he succeeds, Baduel will not be the candidate of the non-existent Centre but the *candidate of the Reaction*. He will not be the candidate of the middle class but of the oligarchy that exploits the fears and prejudices of the middle class. He will not be the candidate of moderation and democracy, but of ferocious counterrevolution. Insofar as he speaks of unity, what he means is the Bonapartist notion of standing "above all classes" and speaking for the Nation. But there is no Nation apart from the classes that make up the Nation. The Bonapartist Leader who claims to speak for the Nation in reality speaks for the rich and powerful who own the wealth of the Nation and who jealously guard it.

The attempts of Dieterich to show that there are more than two sides in conflict in Venezuela, and that there is a so-called Centre with which Chávez should negotiate and make agreements, are all in vain. Former general Baduel, who as we have seen was so enthusiastic about Dieterich's ideas, has now been given a medal as a "Paladin of Freedom" by the Cuban National Democratic Party, a small extreme right wing party based in Miami which supports which supports people like the self-confessed reactionary terrorist Posada Carriles.

The state and the struggle against bureaucracy

In Venezuela the old state apparatus, though weakened, is still in place. There are counter-revolutionary governors disguised as Bolivarians, bureaucrats left over from the Fourth Republic, corrupt elements and careerists at every level. This serves to underline the point that the Marxists have always stressed: the workers cannot take the ready-made state machinery and use it for their own purposes. The question of the arming of the workers and peasants and setting up of *peoples' militias* (that the *Transitional Programme* talks about) is a crucial one, and one that could be carried out quite simply. If the workers were to join the reserve force and territorial guard, in an organized way factory by factory, this would go a long way in creating a peoples' militia under the control of the workers.

The counter-revolution is becoming increasingly alarmed at the leftward course of the revolution. They are sabotaging any experience of workers' control. In the recent months they have also tried again to sabotage the economy by creating scarcity of basic foodstuffs. The way forward is to expropriate the oligarchy and build a new revolutionary state based on factory and neighbourhood committees. In order to carry this out a revolutionary party and a revolutionary leadership are needed. This is why all revolutionaries should be part of the new United Socialist Party, accompanying the masses in their experience and raising in it the ideas of Trotsky, the ideas of Marxism, which provide the most accurate guide for the victorious completion of the revolution. This is exactly what the comrades of the Revolutionary Marxist Current are doing, and what people like Dieterich and all the other reformists and bureaucrats are striving to block.

In order to succeed, the Bolivarian Revolution must purge the movement of alien class elements and transform it into an instrument fit to change society. The launching of the unified socialist party (PSUV) provides the revolutionary workers, peasants and youth with a possibility to do this. They must strengthen the party and win over new layers of revolutionaries drawn from the masses and completely dedicated to the cause of socialism. They must expose and drive out the corrupt elements, careerists and bureaucrats who have joined the movement only to further their own interests and will betray it as soon as the opportunity presents itself. The new party can become a genuine revolutionary workers' party only if it is scrupulously democratic. The rank and file must decide all questions and the leadership must be elected, revocable and composed of elements of proven honesty and dedication to the cause of socialism and the working class.

The trade unions are the other key element in the equation. The Marxists fight for trade union unity, while at the same time fighting for a democratic and militant trade union movement. The unions must give support to the progressive measures of the government, especially nationalizations, and fight to extend all measures to improve the living standards of the masses and strike blows against the oligarchy. But the unions must retain total independence from the state. Only free and independent unions can defend the interests of the workers, while simultaneously defending the revolutionary government against its enemies.

The twin enemies are opportunism and sectarianism. The fight against opportunism consists on the one hand in the fight against corruption, careerism and bureaucratism, on the other hand, the fight against alien ideas that have penetrated the movement, and especially sections of the leadership, who have succumbed to the influence of reformism and abandoned the revolutionary line. The workers and peasants are struggling for bread and land. The counter-revolutionary bourgeoisie is fighting to defend its power and privileges and destroy the Revolution. And the Founder of 21st Century Socialism is delivering lectures on peace, class collaboration and the "economy of equivalence". In such a serious situation the reformist-utopian recipes of Dieterich stand exposed as completely empty. They would be merely laughable if it were not for the fact that they are being widely distributed and promoted for reasons that are self-evident.

The struggle for bread

"Reading Lenin, who made a call to the Russian people to struggle against the scarcity of meat and bread, we notice the same method; a hundred years have passed but they did the same with the Russian people; the old capitalist state is still alive… I'm not referring to the state but to the capitalist situation, the system, above all in the economic field and this is another part of the subject, socialism needs to enter in the economic arena, if it doesn't it will not be socialism that we are building, it will not be a revolution we are making." [9]

Regular shortages of basic foodstuffs both in public and private markets and supermarkets are part of the low intensity economic war going on against the Bolivarian revolution. The oligarchy, especially in the agro-business sector, is organising this open economic sabotage. This is not new, but since the beginning of

9. Extract from *Hugo Chávez's speech at the first meeting of the "Propulsores" of the Partido Socialista Unido – United Socialist Party*, 24/3/2007.

2007 the intensity and regularity of "organised scarcity" has clearly increased. There are shortages of basic products like eggs, milk and meat. The supply of some products to the markets is irregular and is at prices above the official price established by the government. Almost two thirds (64.3 percent) of the productive capacity of the milk industry is standing idle. Six plants, with a total daily capacity of 4.7 million litres of milk, are producing only 1.7 million litres or 35.7 percent of total capacity. It is a real tug-of-war between revolution and counter-revolution on the strategic terrain of food supplies.

This confrontation is undermining the efforts of the government to guarantee food supplies. It is also a field where the weaknesses of the revolution come to the fore. The mere fact that the main food processing plants, transport and distribution networks are still in private hands – that is, in *capitalist* hands – is a serious threat against the revolution. The capitalists in the other sectors of the food processing industry repeat in unison "keep away from our profit margins or we will starve you". On the part of the bosses this is a way of retaliating against the price controls, but it is also a political tool aimed at destabilising the country, trying to foment unrest and finally undermining confidence among the masses in the effectiveness of the social reforms of the revolution. It is part of more general strategy to sabotage the revolutionary process from within.

Those "organised shortages" also affect the famous public network of cheap food outlets, the Mercales, some of which have been complaining that the volume of goods delivered has been reduced by 80 percent. Corruption is a part of the problem when deliveries are channelled away from these supermarkets to be sold at high prices on the private markets. This situation highlights the limitations of developing a public network of supermarkets alongside a private network. This is precisely the model of 21st Century Socialism that Dieterich is advocating! What is the problem? The problem is that even the moderate reforms and partial measures of public ownership, co-operatives, etc. that have been introduced so far are too much for the bourgeoisie to accept. They are determined to sabotage them. What does this prove? Only this: that the contradiction between public and private ownership must be resolved. Either the socialist elements will liquidate the capitalist elements or the latter will liquidate the former. There is no middle way.

A law against hoarding and speculation was approved. Strategic food stocks are being established to guarantee food for three months in case of urgency and the intelligence services have been put to work to uncover secret stocks throughout the country. The problem is that in its struggle against hoarding, speculation and illegal price increases the government is still relying on the old capitalist state apparatus, which is notoriously inefficient, corrupt and linked to the oligarchy. Through this apparatus the bureaucrats are sabotaging the efforts of the government. This is the reformist way of dealing with the problem and is ineffective.

In order to succeed, a revolutionary Leninist content must be given to price controls. In order to achieve effective price controls and to be successful in combating the phenomenon of hoarding, the masses and their organisations must be put into action, through elected bodies of inspectors based on the communal councils and the factory councils for instance. They would have the task of controlling prices, uncovering secrets stocks, etc. These would guarantee that there is no impunity and that the law would be used against speculators.

However, price controls are only a halfway measure. In a capitalist economy such as that in Venezuela any attempt at imposing price controls is answered by economic sabotage by the bosses and furthers destabilise the economy. The government's answer in the ongoing crisis in the milk industry has been to establish new publicly owned milk-processing plants. This is a step in the right direction, but it is still not enough though to cover the existing national demand for milk or to compensate for the deficit in production of the private sector. To make up for this, increasing imports is being proposed as a solution by some sectors in the government.

To guarantee a sufficient level of milk production the private processing plants must be expropriated and nationalised under the control of the workers and the peasants. The same needs to happen with the other branches of the food industry. They then need to be integrated into an urgent plan of food production (including developing agriculture through expropriation of the big landowners) and distribution based not on meeting profit margins but on the social needs of the revolution.

The bourgeoisie is attempting to sabotage the revolution, using the levers it has in its hands, ownership of land and industry. The aim is to cause economic chaos and put the blame on the government, thus undermining confidence in the government and prepare for a reactionary backlash. Economic sabotage and how it is combated is an important question at this stage of the Venezuelan revolution. It is a litmus test for the different political currents within the Bolivarian movement.

Revolution and Parliament

Ultra lefts and anarchists imagine that it is not possible to use parliament for revolutionary ends. This has nothing in common with Marxism. We are obliged to use parliament as we are obliged to use any other platform or democratic institution to organize and mobilize the masses. However, it is necessary to understand the limits of parliamentarism. Hugo Chávez used parliament and elections very effectively to organize and mobilize the masses after the defeat of the Caracazo. This has been a very important element in the situation. The electoral victories of the Bolivarians have served to demoralize and disorient the opposition and weaken the counter-revolutionaries. But ultimately parliament cannot resolve the fundamental questions.

Big business will do everything in its power to sabotage and wreck the economy in order to bring down a government pledged to socialist policies. We have seen this many times in the past. When they do not like certain policies, they organise conspiracies, economic sabotage, speculation against the currency and so on. Therefore, it is necessary to mobilise the working class outside parliament to set up elected committees in every workplace, to establish workers' control and management of the nationalised industries, to prevent the sabotage of the bosses.

It is necessary to issue an appeal to the members of the police and the armed forces to support the democratically elected government (many of the officers and the overwhelming majority of the rank and file are Chávez supporters), immediately pass a law recognising the democratic right of soldiers to join parties and trade unions and legalising the right to strike for soldiers and police, and calling on them to arrest any officers who are plotting against the government. There must be measures to win over the middle class, the small businessmen and shopkeepers, who are being ruined by big business and the banks. Above all, a nationalised planned economy under the democratic control and management of the working class will enable us to eliminate unemployment and introduce the six hour day and four day week, while increasing production and raising wages.

By mobilising the working class on this basis, Chávez would rapidly cut the ground from under the feet of reaction. Any attempt to organise a counter-revolutionary conspiracy would be brushed aside. Under these conditions, a peaceful transformation of society would be entirely possible. The example of a democratic workers' state in Venezuela would have an even greater impact than Russia 1917. Given the enormous strength of the working class, and the impasse of capitalism everywhere, the bourgeois regimes in Latin America would fall rapidly, creating the basis for the Socialist Federation of Latin America and, finally world socialism. That is the perspective we offer.

In reality, what we propose is not so difficult. If the reformist leaders dedicated one tenth of the energies they spend in defending capitalism on mobilising the might of the working class to change society, the socialist transformation could be accomplished quickly and painlessly. But we warn that, if they fail to do this, the way will be prepared for a catastrophe for the working class. The failure to carry through a complete transformation of society in Venezuela will make the normal functioning of capitalism impossible, creating the conditions for conspiracies of the bourgeois with the tops of the armed forces for a coup, which this time could be successful.

Is a peaceful revolution possible?

The central argument of Dieterich and all the other reformists is that an assault on the private property of the oligarchy would mean terrible chaos, civil war, and the streets running with blood. In fact, this is not the case. It is possible to carry out the social revolution without civil war, on one condition: that the working class and its leadership acts with determination and energy to disarm the counter-revolutionaries and mobilize the masses for the revolutionary transformation of society. In the writings and speeches of Lenin from March 1917 right up to the eve of the October insurrection he constantly reiterated the theme that the reformist leaders should take power into their own hands, that this would guarantee a peaceful transformation of society. He insisted that the Bolsheviks were wholeheartedly in favour of this, and that, if *the reformist leaders were to take power, the Bolsheviks would limit themselves to the peaceful struggle for a majority inside the soviets.* Here are a couple of examples of how Lenin put the question (there are many more):

"Apparently, not all the supporters of the slogan 'All Power Must Be Transferred to the Soviets' have given adequate though to the fact that it was a slogan for peaceful progress of the revolution – peaceful not only in the sense that nobody, no class, no force of any importance, would then (between February 27 and July 4) have been able to resist and prevent the transfer of power to the Soviets. That is not all. Peaceful development would then have been possible, even in the sense that the struggle of classes and parties within the Soviets could have assumed a most peaceful and painless form, provided full state power had passed to the Soviets in good time." [10]

"No other condition would, I think, be advanced by the Bolsheviks, who would be confident that really full freedom of propaganda and the immediate realisation of a new democracy in the composition of the Soviets (new elections to them) and in their functioning would in themselves secure a peaceful forward movement of the revolution, a *peaceful outcome* of the party strife within the Soviets.

"Perhaps this is *already* impossible? Perhaps. But if there is even one chance in a hundred, the attempt at realising such a possibility would still be worthwhile." [11]

"Our business is to help do everything possible to secure the 'last' chance for a peaceful development of the revolution, to help this by presenting our programme, by making clear its general, national character, its absolute harmony with the interests and demands of an enormous majority of the population." [12]

"Having seized power, the Soviet could still at present – and that is probably their last chance – secure a peaceful development of the revolution, peaceful elections of the deputies by the people, a peaceful struggle of the parties inside the Soviets, a testing of the programmes of various parties in practice, a peaceful passing of power from one party to another." [13]

And here is how Trotsky sums up the position in *The History of the Russian Revolution*:

"The transfer of power to the Soviets meant, in its immediate sense, a transfer of power to the Compromisers. *That might have been accomplished peacefully, by way of a simple dismissal of the bourgeois government, which had survived only on the good will of the Compromisers and the relics of the confidence in them of the*

10. Lenin, *Collected Works*, Vol. 25, p. 184

11. Ibid., Vol. 21, pp. 153-4.

12. Ibid., p. 257.

13. Ibid., pp. 263-64.

masses. The dictatorship of the workers and soldiers had been a fact since the 27th of February. But the workers and soldiers were not to the point necessary aware of that fact. They had confided the power to the Compromisers, who in their turn had passed it over to the bourgeois. The calculations of the Bolsheviks on a peaceful development of the revolution rested, not on the hope that the bourgeois would voluntarily turn over the power to the workers and soldiers, but that the workers and soldiers would in good season prevent the Compromisers from surrendering the power to the bourgeois.

"The concentration of the power in the soviets under a regime of soviet democracy, would have opened before the Bolsheviks a complete opportunity to become a majority in the soviet, and consequently to create a government on the basis of their program. *For this end an armed insurrection would have been unnecessary. The interchange of power between the parties could have been accomplished peacefully. All the efforts of the party from April to July had been directed towards making possible a peaceful development of the revolution through the soviet. 'Patiently explain' – that had been the key to the Bolshevik policy.*" [14]

As a matter of fact, it would have been entirely possible to carry out a peaceful transfer of power, without civil war or bloodshed in Venezuela in April 2002. Unfortunately, the opportunity was lost and the counter-revolutionaries were allowed to regroup and prepare for a new offensive. The tactic of conciliation of the class enemy advocated by "realists" like Dieterich, far from guaranteeing a peaceful solution, will have precisely the opposite results to those intended.

Reformist blindness

There are none so blind as they who will not see. Despite everything, there are still those who continue to advocate slowing the pace of the revolution in order to placate the counter-revolution and imperialism. They may be sincere in their views, but they are giving false and dangerous advice. Either the revolution is carried through to the end, or else it must perish. Chávez himself has pointed out, the Venezuelan revolution resembles Sisyphus, the character in Greek mythology, who pushed a heavy boulder to the top of a steep mountain, only to see it roll back again. With a little effort, the boulder can be pushed over the top of the mountain, and the problem would be resolved. But if we stop, the boulder will slide back and crush many people in the process.

The reformists consider themselves to be great realists. In reality they are the blindest utopians. They want a "more humane" capitalism. To demand that capitalism should be humane is to ask pears from an elm tree. Not for nothing the Venezuelan capitalists are the bitterest enemies of the Bolivarian revolution. Not for nothing do they strive by all means to destroy it and overthrow Chávez. They can

14. Trotsky, *History of the Russian Revolution*, Vol. II, pp. 312-3, my emphasis.

never be reconciled to the revolution. Fine words will not convince them. They must be defeated and disarmed. Their economic power must be terminated. There is no other way.

After the 2002 coup Hugo Chávez tried to be conciliatory to the reactionaries. He tried to negotiate with them and even reinstated the old directors of the PVDSA. They rewarded him by organizing the bosses' lockout that inflicted serious damage on the Venezuelan economy. What was the result? Did this moderation and caution shown by the President after the collapse of the coup impress the counter-revolutionaries? Did it placate them? It did not. It encouraged them. The counter-revolutionaries regrouped and prepared a new offensive, the so-called strike that aimed to paralyze the economy. Everyone knows that this "strike" was organized and planned by the CIA with the help of the Venezuelan bosses and corrupt trade union bureaucrats of the CTV. Again, this attempt was defeated by the revolutionary movement of the Venezuelan workers.

What lessons can we draw from this? Do we conclude that that a conciliatory attitude is the only way to disarm the counter-revolution and imperialism? Only a fool would say so. The real conclusion that must be drawn is only this: *that weakness invites aggression*. Experience has shown that the only firm base of support the revolution has is the masses, and in the first ranks of the masses, the working class. The masses wish to defend Chávez. How do they do this? Only by stepping up the movement from below, setting up action committees, learning how to use arms. The way to help Chávez is to wage an implacable struggle against the enemies of the revolution, to drive them from the positions of power they hold and prepare the way for a radical reorganization of society.

In other words, the key to success consists in developing and strengthening the independent movement of the working class, and above all by building the revolutionary Marxist wing of the movement. Our advice to the workers of Venezuela is: trust only in your own strength and in your own forces! Trust only in the revolutionary movement of the masses! That is the only force that can sweep aside all obstacles, defeat the counter-revolution and begin to take power into its own hands. That is the only guarantee of success.

The only way to carry the revolution through to the end is to mobilize the masses for direct action. The most urgent task is the formation of action committees – committees for the defence of the revolution. But in the given situation, the committees must be armed. A people's militia is the slogan of the hour. The revolution can only defend itself against its enemies if it arms itself. Four years ago Chávez called for the arming of the people. He said: "Every fisherman, student, every member of the people, must learn how to use a rifle, because it is the concept of the armed people together with the National Armed Forces to defend the sovereignty of the sacred soil of Venezuela." This is a thousand times correct. A people that is not prepared to defend its freedom arms in hand does not deserve to be free. The general arming of the people is the *sine qua non*, not only for the defence of the revolution against internal and external enemies, but for carrying the revolution through to the end and defending the democratic rights of the people.

The words of President Chávez should immediately be translated into deeds. In view of the threat posed by the internal and external enemies of the Revolution, the government should set up special schools for the military training of the population. Competent officers loyal to the Revolution must provide the necessary training in the use of arms, tactics and strategy. The only way to answer the threat of aggression is by the formation of a mass people's militia. Every worker's district, every factory, every village, every school, must become a bulwark of the Revolution, prepared to fight.

Socialism – the only road!

Lenin once said that "capitalism is horror without end." It is sufficient to take a quick look at the state of our planet today to see the correctness of this assertion. The economic crises, wars, terrorism, political convulsions, hunger, disease and poverty, are not separate and unrelated phenomena. They are only the external symptoms of a global crisis of capitalism. The economic malaise that affects the entire continent of Latin America is part of this general crisis. Despite its almost unlimited resources, the continent is tormented by tremendous human suffering, hunger, malnutrition, illiteracy, disease. The gap that separates rich from poor has widened into an unbridgeable abyss. This produces an explosive mixture that undermines stability and causes frequent social and political convulsions.

To put things more clearly: the central problem is imperialism and capitalism. The giant corporations are trying to control the whole world and plunder it for profit. They are supported by the big imperialist bullies, in the first place the USA, which enjoys unprecedented power and uses it to make and unmake governments and subject whole countries and continents to its will. Not one of the problems facing the masses can be solved without an all-out struggle against capitalism and imperialism. Here we have the first point of disagreement with the reformists. They believe that it is possible to achieve our ends without a radical break with capitalism. They agree that things today are perhaps not quite as nice as we would like them to be, but that can change. All that is necessary is a little patience and moderation and all will be well.

Dieterich's whole approach is that of an abstract and lifeless schema that leaves out of account the class contradictions in society, and the determination of the oligarchy and imperialism to halt the revolution. Dieterich talks a lot about "the bourgeois counter-revolution advanced by the domestic oligarchy and the reactionary sectors of world capitalism." But he has not the slightest idea how to fight against this threat. In fact, his policies would guarantee the victory of the counter-revolution and the defeat of the revolution. He is like a man who meets a thug on the street corner and says to him: "Please don't bother to knock my teeth out. I will knock them out myself!" Like every reformist in history, Dieterich is anxious to prove just one thing: that *the workers cannot take power and must not take power.* That is the sum total of his wisdom and the reality of his message, once all the professorial verbiage has been stripped away. He constantly strives to frighten the working class with the spectre of counter-revolution: the gringos are coming! The oligarchy will overthrow us! They will assassinate the President! Remember what happened in Chile! And so the dreary litany goes on and on.

When Simon Bolivar first raised the banner of revolt against the might of the Spanish Empire, this seemed to many to be completely impossible. No doubt if Heinz Dieterich would have been alive at the time he would have poured scorn on the Libertador, as he now does with the Marxists. Yet Bolivar, starting with a small handful of supporters, eventually triumphed, just as Chávez, whose cause at first seemed hopeless, triumphed because he mobilized the masses for a struggle against the oligarchy. The battle is not yet over and victory is not guaranteed. It never is. But one thing is clear: the only way to succeed is to rouse the masses to revolutionary struggle.

Either the greatest of victories or the most terrible of defeats: these are the only two alternatives before the Bolivarian Revolution. Those who promise an easy path, the path of class compromise, are in reality playing a reactionary role, creating false hopes and illusions and disarming the masses in the face of the counter-revolutionary forces that have no such illusions and are preparing to overthrow Chávez as soon as the conditions permit it. They are continually acting to destroy the revolution. The idea that they will cease their counter-revolutionary acts if we "show moderation" and conciliate with the reactionaries is foolish and very dangerous. On the contrary, such behaviour will only serve to embolden them and encourage them.

Of course, in isolation, the Venezuelan revolution cannot ultimately succeed. But it would not be isolated for long. Revolutionary Venezuela must make an appeal to the workers and peasants of the rest of Latin America to follow its lead. Given the conditions that exist throughout the continent, such an appeal would not fall on deaf ears. The working day could be reduced immediately to 30 hours a week without loss of pay. As a reform to demonstrate the superiority of socialist methods, it would have immense consequences worldwide. But what is even more important, as Lenin explained, it would give the necessary time for the entire working class, to run industry and the state.

A socialist plan of production, controlled from top to bottom by the working class, would lead to immense increases in production, despite lowering the hours. Science and technique, liberated from the chains of private profiteering would develop to an unheard of extent. Democracy would no longer have its present restricted character but would be expressed in the democratic administration of society by the whole population. The basis would be laid for an enormous flowering of art, science and culture, drawing on all the rich cultural heritage of all the peoples of the whole continent. This is what Engels called humanity's leap from the realm of necessity to the realm of freedom. *That would be genuine Socialism of the 21st Century: the only way forward for the people of Venezuela, Latin America and the world.*

London, 7th May 2008

Bibliography

Aristotle. *Metaphysics*, Everyman's Library, 1961.

Bray, John. *Labour's Wrongs and Labour's Remedies.*

Carroll, Lewis. *Alice's Adventures in Wonderland.*

Castro, Fidel. *Discurso pronunciado por Fidel Castro Ruz*, http://www.cuba.cu/gobierno/discursos/2005/esp/f171105e.html

Cato the Elder. *De re rustica.*

Chávez, Hugo. *Hugo Chávez's speech at the first meeting of the "Propulsores" of the Partido Socialista Unido – United Socialist Party.* 24/3/2007.

— Speech in *Aló Presidente.* 27/ 3/ 2005.

— Speech in *Aló Presidente.* 22/ 4 /2007.

Dieterich, Heinz. *Cuba: Three premises to save the Revolution after the death of Fidel*, 5/4/2006 http://axisoflogic.com/cgi-bin/exec/view.pl?archive=144&num=21654

— *El desmentido de Hans Modrow y el extraño papel de Prensa Latina*, in *Aporrea*, 23/02/08.

— *El Socialismo del Siglo XXI*, Ediciones de Paradigmas y utopías, México, 2002.

— *Entre topos y gallinas. La bancarrota de la "izquierda" y sus intelectuales*, in *Rebelión*, 28/2/2004.

— *Evo Morales, el socialismo comunitario y el Bloque Regional del Poder*, in *Rebelión*, 25/12/05.

— *¿Existe una situación revolucionaria en América Latina?* (*Does a revolutionary situation exist in Latin America?*), in *Rebelión*, 18/04/2007.

— *Hugo Chávez pide acelerar el Socialismo del Siglo XXI*, (*Hugo

Chávez requests a speed-up of Socialism of 21st Century), in *Rebelión*, 22/06/2006.
— *Hugo Chávez, Raúl Baduel, Raúl Castro y el Bloque Regional de Poder Popular avanzan el Socialismo del futuro*, (*Hugo Chávez, Raúl Baduel, Raúl Castro and the Regional Block of Power advance the socialism of the future*) in *Rebelión*, 2/8/2007.
— *Hugo Chávez y el Socialismo del Siglo XXI.*
— *Identidad nacional y globalización. La tercera vía. Crisis en las cien cias sociales*. Editorial Nuestro Tiempo, México, 2000.
— *In Venezuela, Conditions for Building Socialism of the 21st Century Have Been Created*, interview by Cristina Marcano. http://mrzine.month lyreview.org/marcano030107.html.
— *La economía mixta es la vía al socialismo del siglo XXI.* (*Mixed Economy is the road to Socialism of the 21st Century*) www.aporrea.org (19/02/07).
— *La modernización de Cuba bajo el Comandante Raúl Castro y la pre servación del socialismo*, in Rebelión, 6/4/2008.
— *La revolución mundial pasa por Hugo Chávez*, (*The World Revolution advances through Hugo Chávez*) 5/3/2005.
— *La ruptura Chávez-Baduel: impedir el colapso del proyecto popular*, (*The Chavez-Baduel Break: Stop the Collapse of the Popular Project*), in http://www.rebelion.org/noticia.php?id=58708
— *La trampa de las Asambleas Constituyentes en América Latina* (*The Trap of Constituent Assemblies in the Latin American Revolution*), in *Rebelión*, 4/12/2006.
— *Sin apoyo de la clase media el proceso se puede perder*, interview by Alejandro Botia in *Rebelión* el 25 de abril de 2004.
— *The Alternative of Cuba: Capitalism or New Socialism*, in http://axisoflogic.com/cgi-bin/exec/view.pl?archive=144&num=21734, 12/4/2006.
— *Weighty Alternatives for Latin America. Discussion with Heinz Dieterich*, (7/1/2006) in *Junge Welt*, http://mrzine.monthlyreview.org/schiefer070206.html)
— *Venezuela: Diez tesis sobre la nueva clase política* (*Venezuela: Ten Theses on the New Political Class*), in *Rebelión*, 27/08/2005.
— *Venezuela: Modo de producción socialista y fase de transición*, en *Rebelión*, 10/11/2005.

Engels, Frederick. *Anti-Dühring*, Foreign language Publishing House, Moscow, 1959.
— *Anti-Dühring*, Laurence and Wishart, 1943.

— Letter to Bloch, September 21st 1890, Marx and Engels, *Selected Works*, Vol.3.

— Letter to Marx, June 6, 1853, Marx-Engels, *Selected Correspondence*.

— *The Dialectics of Nature*, Natural Science and Philosophy, in Marx and Engels, *Collected Works*, Vol. 25.

— *The Origin of the Family, Private Property and the State*, *Selected Works*, Vol.3. Engels, Frederick. *The Part Played by Labour in the Transition from Ape to Man*,

— *Socialism, Utopian and Scientific*, in Marx and Engels, *Selected Works*, Vol.3.

— *Ludwig Feuerbach and the end of German classical philosophy*, Marx and Engels, *Selected Works*, Vol.3, chapter IV.

Gibbon, Edward. *The Decline and Fall of the Roman Empire*.

Gould, Stephen Jay. *Ever since Darwin*. New York, 1977.

Grant, Ted. *Russia, from Revolution to Counter-revolution*. London, Wellred Books, 1997.

— *Will There be a Slump?* (In *The Unbroken Thread*)

Hegel, Georg Wilhelm Friedrich. *The Phenomenology of Mind*.

— *Philosophy of History*.

— *Logic*.

Kautsky, Karl. *Foundations of Christianity*.

Kuhn, Thomas Samuel. *The Structure of Scientific Revolutions*.

Lenin, Vladimir Ilich. *Economics and politics in the era of the dictatorship of the proletariat*, 1919.

— *On the Significance of Militant Materialism* (1922), *Collected Works*, vol. 33.

— *Role and Functions of the Trade Unions under the New Economic Policy, Decision of the CC, RCP(B)*, January 12, 1922.

— *The Revolutionary Proletariat and the Right of Nations to Self-Determination*, 1915

— *The Right of Nations to Self-Determination*.

— *The State and Revolution*. *Collected Works*. Vol. 25.

— *Collected Works*, Progress Publishers Moscow, 1964, volumes 24, 25, 26, 27, 32, 33.

Lukács, György. *History and Class Consciousness*.

Marcuse, Herbert. *One-Dimensional Man*.

Marx, Karl and Engels, Frederick. *The Manifesto of the Communist Party*,

— *The German Ideology. Selected Works*, Vol.1.
— Preface to *A Critique of Political Economy, Selected Works*, Vol.1.
— Selected Works, Vo.1.
— *Collected Works*, Vol. 20.

Marx, Karl. *A contribution to the Critique of Political Economy.*
— *Capital.* Penguin, 1976.
— *Capital*, Vol. 3, Progress Publishers, Moscow, 1966.
— *Capital*, Vol. 1, Lawrence & Wishart 1970.
— *Critique of Political Economy.*
— *Critique of the Gotha Programme, Selected Works*, Vol. 3, p. 17.
— Draft of an Article on Friedrich List's book: *Das Nationale System der Politischen Oekonomie*, in MECW, Laurence and Wishart, Volume 4, p. 265.
— *Grundrisse*, Penguin, 1973.
— *Poverty of philosophy*, International Publishers, New York 1963.
— *The Civil War in France, Selected Works*, vol.3. and Marx, *The Civil War in France*, Foreign Language Press, Peking, 1966.
— *The Eighteenth Brumaire of Louis Bonaparte, Selected Works*, Vol.1.
— *Theories of surplus value*, volume 2.
— *Value, Price and Profit.*
— *Wage Labour and Capital.* Progress Publishers, Moscow, 1952.

Pérez Roque, Felipe. Discurso en la Asamblea Nacional del Poder Popular: *Year of the Bolivarian Alternative for the Americas.* http://www.cubaminrex.cu/Archivo/Canciller/2005/FPR_231205.htm

Rosdolsky, Roman. *The making of Marx's 'Capital'*, Pluto Press, 1977.

Sención, César Augusto. *La pretenciosa tarea de Heinz Dieterich* (The Pretentious Task of Heinz Dieterich) in *Rebelión* (13/8/07).

Shakespeare, William. *Henry IV Part One.*
— *Hamlet.*

Trotsky, Leon. *History of the Russian Revolution.* London, Wellred Books, 2008.
— *Problems of Everyday Life.* Monad Press, 1973.
— *The Living Thoughts of Karl Marx,* published as a pamphlet, *Marxism in our Time*, Pathfinder 1970.
— *The Revolution Betrayed.* NY, 1972.
— *The Permanent Revolution.* New Park Publications, 1962.
— *The Soviet economy in danger*, in Trotsky's Writings, 1932, Pathfinder, 1973.

Urton, Gary. *Inca Myths (The Legendary Past).*

Watson, Peter. *Ideas: A History of Thought and Invention from Fire to Freud.*

Woods, Alan and Grant, Ted. *Reason in Revolt. Marxist Philosophy and modern science*. London, Wellred books, 1995.

Magazines and newspapers:

Junge Welt
The Economist
Revista Mariátegui
Le Monde Diplomatic
Time magazine